MOON

NEW MEXICO

ZORA O'NEILL

Contents

Discover New Mexico **6**
Planning Your Trip 10
• If You Have 11
New Mexico Road Trip............. 14
A Week in the Wild West 16
• Best Drives 17
• Not Just Hot Tamales 18
Black Stone, White Sands........... 20
• Retro Route 66 and Beyond 21
Native New Mexico, Ancient and
    Modern...................... 22
• Weird and Wonderful........... 23

Albuquerque................... **25**
Sights 31
Entertainment and Events......... 43
Shopping 46
Sports and Recreation............ 47
Food 51
Accommodations 55
Outside Albuquerque 57
Information and Services 71
Getting There and Around 72

Santa Fe........................ **74**
Sights 79
Entertainment and Events......... 91

Shopping 95
Sports and Recreation............. 96
Food 100
Accommodations 105
Outside Santa Fe................. 108
Information and Services 129
Getting There and Around 130

**Taos and North Central
    New Mexico**.................. **131**
Sights 137
Entertainment and Events.......... 150
Shopping 153
Sports and Recreation............. 154
Food 157
Accommodations 161
West on U.S. 64 164
The Enchanted Circle 170
Information and Services 177
Getting There and Around 177

Las Vegas and the Northeast.. **179**
Pecos and Villanueva.............. 184
Las Vegas........................ 186
Mora Valley...................... 194
The Northern Plains............... 195
The Rockies...................... 204

**Navajo Nation and
the Northwest** **213**
  Route 66: Albuquerque
    Toward Gallup 218
  Zuni Pueblo 227
  Gallup 229
  Navajo Nation 237
  Farmington 240
  Aztec 247
  Bloomfield 250
  Chaco Culture National
    Historical Park 252
  U.S. 550 South to Bernalillo 259

**Las Cruces and
the Southwest** **261**
  South from Albuquerque 266
  Socorro and the Plains of San Agustín . . 267
  El Camino Real 272
  Truth or Consequences 274
  The Geronimo Trail 281
  Mesilla Valley 285
  Las Cruces 287
  West to the Bootheel 298
  Silver City 307
  Trail of the Mountain Spirits 312
  Gila National Forest 316

**Carlsbad Caverns and
the Southeast** **320**
  East on the Interstate and Route 66 . . 324
  The Llano 331

Roswell 338
Carlsbad 346
Carlsbad Caverns National Park 352
Cloudcroft 355
Alamogordo 358
White Sands National Monument 362
Ruidoso 364
Billy the Kid Trail 370
Northern Tularosa Basin 372

Background **375**
  The Landscape 376
  Plants and Animals 378
  History 382
  Government and Economy 386
  Local Culture 388
  The Arts 391

Essentials **395**
  Transportation 396
  Food 400
  Accommodations 403
  Travel Tips 404
  Health and Safety 408

Resources **410**
  Glossary 410
  Suggested Reading 411
  Internet Resources 416

Index **418**

List of Maps **428**

DISCOVER
New Mexico

There's a reason it's called the Land of Enchantment. The smells alone would be entrancing enough: lilacs in spring, ozone after summer thunderstorms, green chiles roasting in supermarket parking lots in fall, and fragrant piñon crackling in woodstoves and corner fireplaces. Listen, too, and you'll hear what makes the state special: Western tanagers warble in the trees, coyotes yelp in the night, and the deep boom of drums and jingle of bells resound at pueblo ceremonies. And that green chile adds a distinct taste to everything—it finds its way onto hamburgers and pizzas and even into ice cream and beer.

But none of that matches the majesty of the view: across austere mesas, down narrow sandstone canyons, or up to snowcapped mountain peaks. Straight above is a cloudless dome the precise hue of the turquoise in the locally crafted jewelry. At night, stars clot the velvety sky, so close you can almost touch them. Many visitors to New Mexico feel disoriented by all this new sensory input—and perhaps by the dizzying altitude, which soars over 13,000 feet at its highest point. And on top of everything, they feel like Alice in Wonderland, ever shrinking, when compared with the vast landscape.

Clockwise from top left: blooming prickly pear; the Classical Gas Museum in Embudo; Santuario de Guadalupe; turquoise necklace in Santa Fe; cow skull in Española; Taos Pueblo.

New Mexico is a sort of alternate world, one that lives by different rules. Santa Fe is an adobe-looking utopia where the economy seems to thrive magically on nothing but art and politics. Los Alamos is a hidden city on a hill with a secret that changed the world, and half of Roswell, it seems, is still obsessed with an alleged UFO crash there in 1947. There are settlements named Truth or Consequences and Pie Town.

Visitors might need time to adjust—to the altitude, certainly, and maybe also to the laid-back attitude. But there's a point of entry for everyone. Outdoor adventurers can hike for an hour or a week, along mountainsides thick with yellow-leafed aspens, and camp on the surreal dunes of White Sands National Monument. Culture mavens thrive in Santa Fe, with its world-class art scene and an eclectic calendar of international film and music. History buffs can explore the ruined civilization at Chaco Canyon, spy ruts dug by thousands of passing wagon wheels on the Santa Fe Trail, or bunk down under a buzzing neon motel sign along Route 66.

At the end of the day, you can always pull yourself back into the present with a cold margarita and cuisine with a hot-chile kick—but that's no guarantee you'll shake off New Mexico's spell.

Clockwise from top left: bench in Rodeo; New Mexico Farm & Ranch Heritage Museum; inside Old Town's Capilla de Nuestra Señora de Guadalupe; International UFO Museum & Research Center in Roswell.

Planning Your Trip

Where to Go

Albuquerque

A modern Western city, Albuquerque sprawls over 189 square miles at the base of the **Sandia Mountains**. It's proud of its **Route 66** style, and it's also preserving **farmland** along the **Rio Grande** and redesigning itself as a green city. Head north to Santa Fe via the ghost towns of the **Turquoise Trail**, the hot springs in the

Jemez Mountains, or the solitary wilderness of the **Valles Caldera**.

Santa Fe

New Mexico's picturesque capital has a human scale and a golden glow (partly from the loads of money spent here). **Museums** are a major draw—for state history, folk art, and more—as

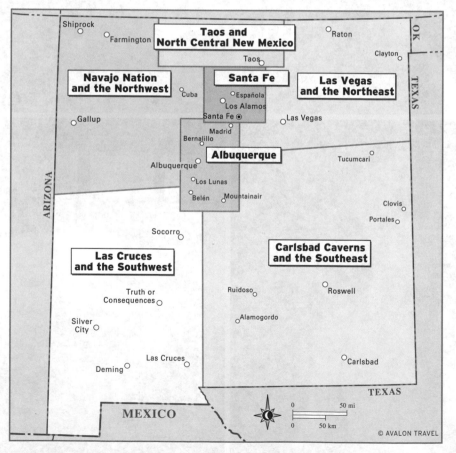

If You Have . . .

- **FIVE DAYS:** Visit Santa Fe, with an overnight trip to Taos.

- **ONE WEEK:** See one city and a quadrant of the state: Albuquerque plus the Navajo Nation in the northwest, for instance.

- **TWO WEEKS:** Follow the New Mexico Road Trip itinerary, or cover most of the southwest and southeast.

- **THREE WEEKS:** Go crazy: You have time for backpacking, rafting trips, or other wilderness excursions.

Visit Santuario de Chimayó on your New Mexico road trip.

are the scores of **galleries.** Outside of town are the cliff dwellings at **Bandelier National Monument;** the scenery of **Abiquiu,** which inspired painter Georgia O'Keeffe; and **Los Alamos,** birthplace of the A-bomb.

Taos and North-Central New Mexico

Taos melds artists, spiritual seekers, and ski bums—plus centuries-old Spanish and American Indian families. Make time to enjoy the **atmosphere,** cultivated in coffee shops and creative restaurants. A good day drive is the **Enchanted Circle,** a loop of two-lane roads with **Wheeler Peak,** the highest in New Mexico, at the center. Or head over the mountains to **Chama,** home to a historic steam train that forges the pass to Colorado.

Las Vegas and the Northeast

Past the Pecos Mountains, **Las Vegas,** aka Meadow City, is a well-preserved historic town, often used as a Western film set. From there the terrain, where the **Santa Fe Trail** once ran, is all short-grass prairie, once the western edge of the Dust Bowl. To get a view, drive the spiral road up **Capulin Volcano,** then soar across gorgeous **Johnson Mesa** to the mountain burgs of **Raton** and **Cimarron.**

Navajo Nation and the Northwest

Stark volcanic landscapes, lonesome roads, and tall mesas—this is some of the most dramatic desert terrain in the state, along with its oldest cultures. This quadrant is in the Four Corners area, which includes parts of Arizona, Utah, and Colorado. This is where the Ancestral Puebloans lived in **Chaco Canyon** and where **Gallup** is the self-proclaimed American Indian capital. The city is surrounded by hiking and mountain biking trails.

Las Cruces and the Southwest

This corner of the state has both the rugged **Gila Wilderness** and the mesmerizing **Chihuahuan Desert.** It's a long drive between the river-fed farmland around **Las Cruces** and colorful, artsy **Silver City,** tucked in the mountains, but worth it—especially for the food-focused, who will find a number of excellent restaurants. **Truth or Consequences** reels in the curious, delivering hot springs and quirkiness.

Carlsbad Caverns and the Southeast

Parts of this area feel more like neighboring Texas: Many flatland towns are dominated by the oil industry, and ski spots like **Ruidoso** are beloved by Texans. Most visitors make a beeline to the amazing natural wonders of **White Sands National Monument** and **Carlsbad Caverns National Park.** On the way, you can track outlaw Billy the Kid, who dueled in the mountain town of **Lincoln,** now an excellent outdoor museum.

Know Before You Go

High and Low Seasons

Summer, June-September, is high season in northern New Mexico, though it's prettiest late in the season, when the so-called monsoon rains, which usually start in late June, have revived the landscape. Summer is the only time to hike at higher elevations, as snow finally melts, but lower elevations are baking and sleepy. Be prepared for a temperature drop from the 90s to as low as the 60s after sunset, especially outside of cities, and bring an umbrella.

Fall is the most beautiful time across the state, with crisp temperatures, clear skies, and brilliant leaves in the mountains. For New Mexico's most temperate season, pack a sweater and a windbreaker to keep out the nighttime chill.

Winter is busy (and pricier) in ski towns like Taos, but traditional celebrations preceding Christmas are wonderful. Many sights are closed or have limited hours, however. Towns at lower elevations, such as Truth or Consequences and Carlsbad, remain balmy, and prices in these places hold steady year-round. Be prepared for temps below freezing, even in southern desert

Yes, it snows in New Mexico!

summer flowers in Santa Fe

visiting churches and pueblos, women should cover their shoulders.

Advance Reservations

New Mexico is mostly a just-show-up kind of place, but a few attractions require some forethought.

Attending a **ceremonial dance** is worth planning a trip around. Dances are held at New Mexico pueblos year-round. Check the schedules for those near Albuquerque (page 45) and Santa Fe (page 112), as well as for Taos (page 146) and Zuni, Laguna, and Acoma Pueblos (page 220) in advance.

The **Georgia O'Keeffe Home** in Abiquiu is open to guided tours mid-March through November. Book at least a month in advance (page 120).

Online ticket sales for the **Santa Fe Opera** start in October for the July and August summer season. Book in the winter for the best seat selection (page 93).

Book **Santa Fe hotels** 6-8 months ahead if you plan to visit during the **Santa Fe Indian Market** (August), **Spanish Market** (July), and **Christmas.**

Visiting the extraordinary land art *The Lightning Field* requires advance overnight reservations (May-Oct., $150-250 pp). Booking for the season starts in March; if your preferred dates are full, ask to be put on a waiting list (page 272).

Museum Pass

A **New Mexico Museum Pass** ($25) is good for 12 months and grants onetime access to 15 state-run museums and historic sites. This includes four Santa Fe institutions—the New Mexico Museum of Art, the New Mexico History Museum, the Museum of Indian Arts & Culture, and the Museum of International Folk Art—as well as two in Albuquerque (the National Hispanic Cultural Center and the natural history museum), and the Coronado and Jemez historic sites. It also covers attractions farther afield, in Las Cruces, Alamogordo, and more.

areas. If you think you'll attend winter pueblo dances, pack mittens, long underwear, double-thick wool socks, and a hat with earflaps—there's a lot of standing around outside.

The cheaper **shoulder seasons** are March, April, and May, and, to a lesser extent, November, before ski season starts. Spring is perhaps the harshest time in the state. Weather can be extreme, switching from snowfall and mud to dry, hot winds (pack boots for rural or muddy areas, and a clean pair of shoes for around town). But it is a good season for river rafting. Book a hotel at least six months in advance for the week between Christmas and New Year's, Santa Fe's summer art markets, or the Albuquerque balloon fest in October.

Be prepared for a **wide range of temperatures** whenever you go, and always pack sunglasses, sunscreen, and a brimmed hat. Local "formal" wear is only clean jeans and boots; when

New Mexico Road Trip

You could conceivably explore New Mexico for a month or so, seeking out ever more obscure towns, but a two-week road trip gives enough time to appreciate the distinct character of the cities and enjoy a few bumpy back roads. This itinerary involves a lot of driving to cover the state's most scenic routes, but you'll still have opportunities for leisurely lunches and other out-of-car activities.

Day 1
Albuquerque

Arrive at Albuquerque's Sunport airport; transfer to a hotel in the city or one of the rural-feeling bed-and-breakfasts in the North Valley. Have drinks and dinner in **Nob Hill.**

Day 2
Albuquerque to Gallup
150 MILES; 3 HOURS

Visit the **Indian Pueblo Cultural Center,** then head west to **Acoma Pueblo.** Lunch in Grants and stay the night in **Gallup.**

Day 3
Gallup to Abiquiu
220 MILES; 4.5 HOURS

Get an early start for the long, bumpy ride along the back road to **Chaco Culture National Historical Park.** When you're done exploring, grab a late lunch at **El Bruno's** in Cuba, then take Highway 96 over the mountains to **Abiquiu,** where you'll spend the night.

Day 4
Abiquiu to Santa Fe
95 MILES; 2.5 HOURS

If you like hiking, explore Abiquiu's red rocks at **Ghost Ranch** or drive down the road to **Bandelier National Monument.** If you prefer the city, head straight in to **Santa Fe** and the excellent museums around the plaza. In either case, stay the night there, at classic **La Fonda** or more modern **Hacienda Nicholas.**

Day 5
Santa Fe

Take in Santa Fe's contemporary culture, with shopping, gallery-hopping, or a visit to the description-defying **House of Eternal Return.** Round out a colorful day with dinner at **Café Pasqual's.**

Day 6
Santa Fe to Taos
75 MILES; 2 HOURS

Head to **Taos** via the high road, with stops at the **Santuario de Chimayó,** where you can also pick up some delicious tamales, and in the villages of **Truchas** and **Las Trampas.** Settle into your hotel in **Taos** after a de rigueur margarita at the **Adobe Bar.**

Day 7
Taos

Start with an early visit to **San Francisco de Asis Church,** followed by breakfast at **Ranchos Plaza Grill.** Then head to the **Taos Art Museum** for background on the town's art scene. Spend the afternoon at **Taos Pueblo,** followed by a local-produce dinner at **The Love Apple.**

Day 8
Taos to Las Vegas
150 MILES; 3 HOURS

Drive the first leg of the **Enchanted Circle,** turning east at Eagle Nest to reach **Cimarron.** Lunch at **The Porch,** then head down to **Las Vegas** via I-25. Check in at the **Plaza Hotel,** and walk down Bridge Street and over to **El Fidel Restaurant** for dinner.

Day 9
Las Vegas to Carlsbad
270 MILES; 4.5 HOURS

Today is a long day of driving, but you'll pass through pretty old villages like **Villanueva** and the plains around **Vaughn.** Have a late the iconic San Francisco de Asis Church in Taos

lunch in **Roswell**, and visit the **International UFO Museum & Research Center** or the **Anderson Museum of Contemporary Art.** You're bunking down at Carlsbad's **Trinity Hotel & Suites.**

Day 10
Carlsbad
42 MILES; 1 HOUR
Head out early to **Carlsbad Caverns National Park.** Back in town, have dinner at **Danny's Place BBQ** and take in a movie at the **Fiesta Drive-In,** then head back to the Trinity for bed.

Day 11
Carlsbad to Las Cruces
215 MILES; 4 HOURS
Head west to Alamogordo and **White Sands National Monument,** winding up in **Las Cruces** that evening. Have dinner in historic **Mesilla.**

Day 12
Las Cruces to Albuquerque
225 MILES; 3.5 HOURS
Drive up I-25 to return to Albuquerque, stopping in **Truth or Consequences** for coffee and a snack and a dip in the hot springs. Plan on lunch at the **Owl Bar & Café** in San Antonio. You should be in Albuquerque by nightfall—check out the scene downtown.

Day 13
Albuquerque
Take it easy today, and take one last look at the Southwestern scenery, either with a dawn **hot-air balloon ride** or a sunset tram ride to **Sandia Peak.**

Day 14
Albuquerque
Fuel up for your flight with breakfast at **The Frontier,** where you can also grab some house-made tortillas to take home.

A Week in the Wild West

Gunslingers, cattle rustlers, and Apache warriors made New Mexico a colorful, if violent, place in the 19th century, and relics of that frontier lifestyle are still visible everywhere. History buffs can visit old forts, count bullet holes in saloon ceilings, and trace the fortunes of prospectors in ghost-town graveyards. Though the major cities have their share of history, this route takes you away from the modern centers and into emptier quarters. It can be expanded with a stop in Santa Fe or a more leisurely pace up to Las Vegas (Highway 3, which connects I-40 to I-25, for instance, is exceptionally pretty, if a bit out of the way).

Day 1

Arrive in Albuquerque. Take in the western sunset at the base of the **Sandia Peak Tramway,** in the foothills, then come back to the center of the city for dinner at the appropriately named and Western-themed restaurant **The Frontier.** Bed

Spend the night in Lincoln's Wortley Hotel.

down at the **Los Poblanos Historic Inn,** amid horse farms in the North Valley.

Day 2

Head southeast to **Mountainair** and the rustic-bizarre **Shaffer Hotel;** you'll also pass the **Salinas Pueblo Missions.** By mid-afternoon, you should be in **Lincoln,** where Billy the Kid earned his greatest notoriety. Tour the buildings here, then settle in for the evening at the **Wortley Hotel.**

Day 3

After breakfast, you're headed north to **Fort Sumner** to see Billy the Kid's grave and a memorial to Navajo internment in the 1860s. Take an afternoon dip in the **Blue Hole** in Santa Rosa to fortify yourself for the last leg of the drive, to **Las Vegas,** where you'll stay and dine at the wonderfully restored **Plaza Hotel.**

Motor west through New Mexico on Route 66.

There's hardly a bad road in New Mexico, but these drives are outstanding.

- **Turquoise Trail:** (55 miles, 1.5 hours) From Albuquerque to Santa Fe, **Highway 14** offers great vistas around every curve and ghost towns to break up the drive (page 61).

- **Jemez Mountain Trail:** (32 miles, 1 hour) **Highway 4** through Jemez Springs to Valles Caldera is especially good in fall, with yellow aspens highlighted against red rock (page 65).

- **U.S. 84:** (93 miles, 1 hour 45 minutes) North of Santa Fe, ascend through the red rocks of **Abiquiu** (page 119), then past the Brazos Cliffs near **Tierra Amarilla** (page 164).

- **La Frontera del Llano Scenic Byway:** (26 miles, 30 minutes) Highway 39 zigzags across the northeastern plains, from Roy to Abbott, with pronghorns and ruined homesteads along the way (page 197).

- **Highway 72:** (37 miles, 1 hour) This tiny road between Raton and Folsom soars over the bucolic **Johnson Mesa** (page 203).

- **U.S. 180:** (98 miles, 2 hours) From Silver City to Reserve, this highway passes largely through the **Gila National Forest** (page 316).

- **Sunspot Highway:** (17 miles, 30 minutes) Highway 6563 winds south from Cloudcroft to Sunspot National Solar Observatory, with White Sands visible below (page 355).

- **Historic Route 66:** (350 miles, 7 hours) Pieces of I-40 frontage road and more remote detours make up the decommissioned Mother Road, passing vintage Americana motels, diners, and more along the way (pages 218 and 324).

Day 4

Tour the Meadow City's historic buildings in the morning, with lunch at **Abraham's Tiendita**, then head for sprawling **Fort Union National Monument** in the afternoon—the slanting sun should highlight the ruts of the **Santa Fe Trail** off to one side. Return to Las Vegas for the evening.

Day 5

I-25 north takes you to **Raton**, where you turn east to **Capulin Volcano National Monument**, which affords a grand view over the plains. Loop back via **Folsom** (site of numerous train robberies) and the awesome, empty expanse of **Johnson Mesa**. Have a late lunch in

BEST TRADITIONAL NEW MEXICAN

"Red or green?" is the official state question, referring to the dilemma diners face when they order enchiladas, huevos rancheros, or anything else that can be drowned in an earthy red-chile sauce or a chunky, vegetal green one.

- **Mary & Tito's Café:** An Albuquerque institution, this family restaurant was named a James Beard American Classic in 2009. Red chile is the star here (page 53).

- **San Felipe Restaurant:** In the category of restaurants in a gas station, this one's a winner: big enchilada platters, as well as pueblo favorites like blue-corn mush (page 70).

- **Tia Sophia's:** The alleged inventors of the breakfast burrito, in Santa Fe (page 100).

- **Zuly's:** A dreamy rich, deep red sauce bathes enchiladas and burritos at this café in the bucolic village of Dixon (page 124).

- **El Bruno's:** The restaurant in Cuba processes all its green chile by hand (page 259).

BEST GREEN-CHILE CHEESEBURGER

- **Santa Fe Bite:** Ten-ounce burgers, from meat that's hand-ground every day. Legendary (page 100).

- **Joseph's:** A rare case of fine dining improving upon road food: pasture-raised lamb with local feta and chile, on a housemade English muffin (page: 102).

- **Laguna Burger:** Devotees regularly drive to Laguna Pueblo for these GCCBs made from fresh, never frozen meat (page 219).

- **Owl Bar & Café:** A twofer in the village of San Antonio: not only the old-school Owl, but rival Buckhorn Burgers is right across the street (page 273).

- **Big D's Downtown Dive:** An outpost of gourmet fast food in Roswell, this place does a succulent burger, with garlic fries on the side (page 344).

BEST LOCAL AND ORGANIC

- **Vinaigrette:** This "salad bistro" in Santa Fe and Albuquerque grows its own greens on a Tesuque farm and can vouch for every ingredient on its menu (page 51).

- **La Merienda:** The restaurant at historic farm inn Los Poblanos serves a few perfect dishes each evening; overnight for the full farm-life experience in Albuquerque (page 54).

- **Café Pasqual's:** A Santa Fe institution, serving New Mexican and international dishes with organic ingredients since the late 1970s (page 101).

- **The Love Apple:** At this candlelit New Mexican bistro, a chalkboard displays the sourced ingredients: Tucumcari cheese, Pecos beef, and more (page 158).

- **Gallup Flea Market:** As local as it gets: grilled lamb from sheep raised here, with a roasted green chile, on fry bread made with flour from Colorado (page 234).

grilled lamb sandwich at the Gallup Flea Market

Traces of the movie set for *Young Guns* still show in Cerrillos.

Raton at **Enchanted Grounds,** or farther down the road at the ultimate Western roadhouse, **Colfax Tavern.** Then cruise on to **Cimarron,** where you'll spend the night in the spooky **St. James Hotel.**

Day 6

Depending on your interests, hang out in Cimarron in the morning until the **Old Aztec Mill Museum** opens, or make a beeline through dramatic Cimarron Canyon to **Eagle Nest** and on to **Taos.** The long way around the **Enchanted Circle** yields the best views and takes you past abandoned **Elizabethtown,** site of the state's first gold rush. In **Red River,** the scene is livelier: Bars play both kinds of music (country *and* western). Spend the night in Taos at the **Historic Taos Inn** or **Hotel La Fonda de Taos.** Both wear their years well.

Day 7

Drive south back to Albuquerque via the **low road** and, if you have the time, the **Turquoise Trail**—you can have lunch at **San Marcos Café,** then stop in **Cerrillos,** which has been used as a Western film set. If you don't have to meet a flight out, plan on stopping in **Madrid** too, for a burger or a beer at the **Mine Shaft Tavern.**

the Old Aztec Mill Museum in Cimarron

Black Stone, White Sands

Temperate climates, plain old "pretty" landscapes—who needs 'em? New Mexico's extreme terrain, from stark lava beds to gleaming fields of gypsum, is much more exciting. Snowcapped peaks are just a short drive from arid deserts, and you can spot hardy animals, odd birds, and stunning rock formations everywhere in between. Whether remote wilderness areas or lesser-known routes in popular parks, these otherworldly spots are almost always empty.

Every corner of the state holds some enticing natural adventure, but due to long driving distances, you're better off limiting your exploration to one quadrant at a time. This way, you'll spend less time in the car and more time on the land. Which ones you visit depends on what time of year it is and, equally important, what altitude you can handle. When you arrive, it's tempting to put on your boots and head straight out, but

marmots on Wheeler Peak

unless you're coming from a comparable elevation, stick to clambering in foothills and scenic drives for the first couple of days. Drink plenty of liquids, and head to bed early.

Wheeler Peak

From Red River, a hike up the **state's highest mountain** typically requires a few days. Or you can take the short, steep route from Taos Ski Valley, doable in a long afternoon. Either way, don't go any time other than June, July, or August.

Bisti/De-Na-Zin Wilderness

Top-heavy **hoodoos**—precarious, windswept sandstone towers—are the hallmark of this barren landscape south of Farmington. There are **no trails** and **no services,** and virtually no other hikers, so come prepared with plenty of water, a compass, and an appreciation for solitude. Prefer a driving tour? Head to nearby **Angel Peak Scenic Area** instead, for fine views.

Valles Caldera National Preserve

The lush alpine meadows that line this **ancient volcanic basin** are some of the state's most pristine. Every season here is beautiful, whether the trout streams are high with spring runoff or the knee-deep snow is prime for **snowshoeing.** But if you plan just to **hike** on your own, without a larger group tour, plan to come between June and September, before the cold snap.

Kiowa and Rita Blanca National Grasslands

Once the edge of the brutal Dust Bowl, this **protected prairie** now looks a bit more hospitable, brushy and green. The real surprise comes when you drive down to **Mills Canyon,** a red-striped chasm with a lush bottom. **Camping** in this hidden spot, with hawks wheeling overhead, is like being hidden away from the world.

Retro Route 66 and Beyond

great pie in Pie Town

"Get your kicks," advises Nat King Cole's classic anthem of the Mother Road. Though officially decommissioned, Route 66 (now traced by I-40) is still alive in New Mexico in the form of neon signs and cruising culture. And even off that iconic highway, many parts of the state foster nostalgia for the mid-20th century.

DRIVE-IN MOVIE MAGIC

Hit the road, preferably in a convertible, to enjoy good old-fashioned fun like drive-in movie theaters in Las Vegas (summers only) and Carlsbad. The car is still king in Clovis, where you'll find original drive-ins, such as Foxy, complete with carhops—this is the way burgers and fries were meant to be eaten.

ROCKIN' HISTORY

Clovis is also where 1950s crooner Buddy Holly recorded his early hits—check out the Norman & Vi Petty Rock & Roll Museum, or plan a trip for the September Clovis Music Festival. Hot-rod fans can see one of Elvis's Caddies at B-Square Ranch in Farmington (the taxidermy museum here also seems like a relic of another age).

DESSERT DETOURS

Capture the real spirit of a road trip by heading out U.S. 60 to remote Pie Town, so named because it served intrepid motorists sweets in the 1930s. Several cafés keep this slice (pun intended) of Americana alive with mixed berry, chocolate cream, and more at the ready. In Portales, Pat's Twin Cronnie burger stand is famous for its peanut butter milkshake.

MOTOR LODGES

The best legacy of the Route 66 era is the motels. Tuck yourself into 1939 at the Blue Swallow Motel or the slightly newer Motel Safari in Tucumcari, or at El Rancho Hotel & Motel in Gallup, which hosted Ronald Reagan and other Western movie stars. Farther afield, in Raton, the Maverick Motel is meticulously preserved, and the Budget Host Melody Lane Motel has vintage saunas in the rooms. In Truth or Consequences (a town named for a 1950s radio show), the owners of Blackstone Hotsprings have decorated rooms as homages to The Twilight Zone and Lucille Ball. Sleep tight, and dream of the charm of yesteryear.

yucca at White Sands National Monument

Sky Islands

The mountains that spike out of the flat, hot **Chihuahuan Desert** are little-visited crags, each fostering its own flora and fauna. The most accessible are the **Organ Mountains** in Las Cruces; the **Florida Mountains** near Deming, which harbor bighorn sheep and vivid wildflowers; and

Cave Creek Canyon (technically in Arizona) near Rodeo, teeming with birds.

Valley of Fires National Recreation Area

The **volcano** that produced these **badlands** exploded just yesterday, relatively speaking—the blackened landscape hardened about 1,500 years ago, setting in wedges, whorls, and fantastically odd lumps. Come at the end of the summer rain season to see them at their surprising greenest.

White Sands National Monument

After you've slid down the **gypsum dunes,** really get to know this amazing place on a ranger-led car tour to the sands' source, **Lake Lucero,** or a hike on **Alkali Flats Trail.** Better still, **camp** here overnight after taking a hike or **mountain biking tour** under the full moon. Try to avoid the boiling peak of summer and midwinter, when periods of heavy rain can close off parts of the park.

Carlsbad Caverns National Park

Go deeper—literally—than the average day-tripper by signing up for the hardcore **Spider Cave** tour, on which you'll wiggle through tiny tunnels into lofty halls. The park supplies helmets and headlamps, but it's BYOB: bring your own batteries. Handily, the temperature underground holds steady year-round; just book ahead during peak summer months.

Native New Mexico, Ancient and Modern

The culture that developed before the arrival of the Spanish in the 16th century is visible in both ruined and inhabited pueblos and in excellent museums that hold some of the state's finest treasures. Even if you're visiting only a small area on your trip, there's a lot of American Indian history to see in and around each place. Definitely try to schedule around a dance ceremony at a pueblo, as you'll see the living culture. If you're serious about purchasing art and jewelry, you may want to time your visit with the **Santa Fe Indian Market,** which takes place every August and showcases more than 1,200 artisans. But you'll also have a chance to buy directly from craftspeople in Zuni, Acoma, Crownpoint, and Santa Fe. If you have plenty of time to explore, you could also head south of Albuquerque to the Salinas Pueblo

Weird and Wonderful

Sometimes New Mexico feels like an entirely different planet. Here's where to see the state at its most eccentric.

TRUTH OR CONSEQUENCES

From its attention-grabbing name (a 1950 publicity stunt) to its downtown of hot baths, odd shops, and the labyrinthine Geronimo Springs Museum, this is a small town with more than its share of character.

MADRID

It's pronounced MAD-rid, which gives you an idea about this ghost-town-turned-galleryville's wacky residents, who have brought the place back from the dead since the 1970s. South of here is Tinkertown Museum, a miniature wonderland whittled from wood, cobbled together from bottle caps and bits of string.

SANTA FE AND TAOS

Poll your fellow hot-tubbers at Ten Thousand Waves about their past lives, or ask your neighbor at the World Cup coffee shop if he can hear the "Taos hum." Take a trip to another dimension at the House of Eternal Return, or check out the Greater World Earthship Development, an off-the-grid suburb of Taos where the buildings

crafted from beer cans and tires look straight off a *Star Wars* set.

LOS ALAMOS

This mesa-top town is where the atomic bomb was devised and scientists still toil in secrecy; one museum here touts the joys of nuclear science. Round out your visit to "the Hill" with a jaunt south to Trinity Site, where the bomb was first tested in July 1945; it's open to visitors only two days a year.

ROSWELL

Ever have cryptic dreams about green creatures with big heads and long, skinny arms? You'll feel right at home at the International UFO Museum & Research Center, where alien visitations are treated as a matter of course. The work at the outstanding Anderson Museum of Contemporary Art depicts all manner of alternate realities.

PLAINS OF SAN AGUSTÍN

If Roswell gets you in the mood to peer into the solar system, cruise out to this installation of radio telescopes that make up the The Very Large Array. They don't actually receive messages from across the galaxy, but the images they take of deep space are nearly as illuminating.

Evidence of alien landings is everywhere in Roswell.

Zuni dance finery

mission church, with its resplendent kachina murals, and check out the **A:shíwi A:wan Museum.** The dance ritual **Shalako,** in late November or early December, is amazing, but you must book at the inn many months ahead.

Gallup

Hosting a huge annual powwow, **Gallup** has the largest native population in the state, as well as the small **WWII Navajo Code Talkers Museum.** Visit on a Saturday, for the funky and diverse **flea market.** About an hour's drive away is **Crownpoint,** which hosts a monthly rug auction—a must-visit even if you don't buy anything.

Shiprock and Farmington

Head into the Navajo Nation via U.S. 491, passing the **Toadlena Trading Post,** which displays beautiful rugs. **Shiprock** offers another chance at a flea market, or traditional mutton stew at the fast-food joints—or hold out till Farmington and **Ash-Kii's Navajo Grill.** Farmington is usually the base for visiting **Chaco Culture National Historical Park,** a little over two hours south—though you can also camp at the site, under starry skies.

Missions, the Gila Cliff Dwellings, and the Bosque Redondo Memorial at Fort Sumner.

Albuquerque

The **Indian Pueblo Cultural Center** should be your first stop, for its good museum and information on all the American Indian settlements. Also pay a quick visit to **Petroglyph National Monument,** to see ancient rock carvings, and **Coronado Historic Site,** to see inside a painted kiva. The **Hyatt Regency Tamaya** resort nearby is owned by Santa Ana Pueblo.

Acoma Pueblo

West of Albuquerque, this weathered **fortress village** atop a mesa is accessible only by **guided tour.** At the base is an excellent **cultural museum,** which displays the pueblo's specialty, delicate white pottery painted with fine black lines. You can grab lunch here, or down the road in Grants.

Zuni Pueblo

This is the only pueblo where you can stay overnight, at the **Inn at Halona.** It's also the source of beautiful jewelry. Take a walking tour of the

Taos

Taos Pueblo is as much a relic as Acoma but still regularly used. If your visit doesn't coincide with a **ceremonial dance** there, stop by the Kachina Lodge in the early evening to see a demonstration performance (summer only)—but better to stay the night across the road at **El Pueblo Lodge,** a well-tended motel.

Santa Fe

Check out the modern arts scene at the Museum of Indian Arts & Culture and the Museum of Contemporary Native Arts, as well as several galleries representing pueblo artists. And don't miss the jewelry vendors under the portal at the Palace of the Governors. A short drive away are the ruins at Bandelier National Monument and the Puyé Cliff Dwellings, where Santa Clara residents lead the tours.

Albuquerque

Sights 31

Entertainment and Events 43

Shopping...................... 46

Sports and Recreation 47

Food 51

Accommodations.............. 55

Outside Albuquerque.......... 57

Information and Services 71

Getting There and Around...... 72

Look for ★ to find recommended
sights, activities, dining, and lodging.

Highlights

★ **ABQ Trolley Co.:** The best tour in the state, aboard an open-sided, faux-adobe tram-on-wheels, with the lively, knowledgeable owners sharing Albuquerque lore (page 31).

★ **KiMo Theatre:** A fantasia of Southwestern decorative styles, this former cinema is one of the few examples of Pueblo Deco style. Restored and run with city money, it's the showpiece of downtown (page 35).

★ **Sandia Peak Tramway:** Zip up the world's longest single-cable tram to the crest of the mountain that looms over the east side of Albuquerque. At the top, you'll get a vertigo-inducing view across the whole metro area and out to the hazy western horizon (page 41).

★ **Ballooning:** In the American capital for hot-air balloons, enjoy the silent city on a dawn flight. You'll get a true bird's-eye view, and dip down to skim the Rio Grande (page 48).

★ **Tinkertown Museum:** An enthralling collection of one man's lifetime of whittling projects, this folk-art exhibit is inspiring for adults and a delight for kids (page 62).

★ **Valles Caldera National Preserve:** In the crater formed by a collapsed volcano, some 89,000 acres of grassy valleys are set aside for very controlled public access. You must make reservations to hike here, but it's worth planning ahead (page 68).

★ **Kasha-Katuwe Tent Rocks National Monument:** A great attraction off the otherwise unremarkable freeway to Santa Fe—drive a few miles west to hike in this eerie canyon landscape (page 69).

A s a tourist destination, Albuquerque has long labored in the shadow of the jet-set arts colonies to the north, but that has slowly started to change as visitors discover a city that's fun, down-to-earth, and affordable.

If Santa Fe is the "City Different" (a moniker *Burqueños* razz for its pretentiousness), then New Mexico's largest city, with a population of 900,000 in the greater metro area, is proudly the "City Indifferent," unconcerned with fads and flawless facades.

The city does have its pockets of historic charm—they're just not visible from the arteries of I-40 and I-25, which intersect in the center in a graceful tangle of turquoise-trimmed bridges. The Duke City was founded three centuries ago, its cumbersome name that of a Spanish nobleman but its character the product of later eras: the post-1880 downtown district; the University of New Mexico campus, built in the early 20th century by John Gaw Meem, the architect who defined Pueblo Revival style; and Route 66, the highway that joined Albuquerque to Chicago and Los Angeles in 1926.

Spread out on either side of the Rio Grande, from volcanic mesas on the west to the foothills of the Sandia Mountains along the east, Albuquerque has accessible hiking and biking trails that run through diverse environments. In the morning, you can stroll under centuries-old cottonwood trees near the wide, muddy river; in the afternoon, you can hike along the edge of a windswept mountain range with views across the vast empty land beyond the city grid. And at the end of the day, you'll see Albuquerque's most remarkable feature, the dramatic light show on the Sandia Mountains—Spanish for "watermelon," for the bright pink hue they turn at sundown.

The city is also an excellent base for exploring the many interesting pueblos and natural attractions nearby, and it's just an hour's drive to Santa Fe, with easy day trips or scenic drives through the mountains in between. In the Manzano Mountains southeast of town, for instance, lie a series of ruined pueblos, last inhabited during the early years of the Conquest. The road that links them

---

Previous: colorful mailboxes in Madrid; the Sandia Peak Tramway. **Above:** A hot-air balloon drifts over Albuquerque's West Mesa.

Albuquerque

© AVALON TRAVEL

also winds past a canyon known for its fall colors and a historic hotel in a distinctly New Mexican style.

Additionally, there are several ways to head north to Santa Fe (or simply make a loop). The most direct is I-25, which cuts through dramatic rolling hills; take a short detour to Kasha-Katuwe Tent Rocks National Monument, where pointed white rocks tower above a narrow canyon. Beginning east of Albuquerque, the historic Turquoise Trail winds along the back side of the Sandias, then through the former mining town of Madrid, resettled as an arts colony, with galleries occupying the cabins built against the black, coal-rich hills.

The most roundabout route north is along the Jemez Mountain Trail, a scenic byway northwest of Albuquerque through the brick-red rocks surrounding Jemez Pueblo, then past natural hot springs. The road runs along the edge of Valles Caldera National Preserve, a pristine valley where the daily number of visitors is carefully limited, so you can enjoy the vistas in solitude.

PLANNING YOUR TIME

Precisely because it's not so full of must-see historic attractions, Albuquerque fares best as the primary focus of a trip, so you have time to enjoy the natural setting, the food, and the people. A possible incentive: Your money will go farther here than it will farther north, especially when it comes to hotels, which offer great value and don't dramatically hike rates for **summer** high season, as is standard in Taos and Santa Fe. Ideally, you would spend a leisurely **four days** here, soaking up a little Route 66 neon, enjoying the downtown entertainment, hiking in the Sandias, taking scenic drives, and bicycling along the Rio Grande.

But if you're also planning to visit other parts of the state, it is difficult to recommend more than a **couple of days** in Albuquerque—preferably on the way out, as the city's modern, get-real attitude is best appreciated after you've been in the adobe dreamland of Santa Fe for a bit. Spend a day

cruising the neighborhoods along Central Avenue, and for a last dose of open sky, take the tramway up to Sandia Peak and hike along the Crest Trail. At the end of your trip, you'll be able to handle the elevation with no problem.

In the city proper, most of the year is enjoyable. **Winters** are mild in the low basin around the river, though the Sandias often get heavy snow. As elsewhere in the state, the heat of July and August is usually broken by heavy afternoon rainstorms (though May and June are typically hot and dry). And because Albuquerque is seldom at the top of tourists' lists, there's never a time when it's unpleasantly mobbed.

ORIENTATION

Albuquerque's greater metro area covers more than 100 square miles, but visitors will likely see only a handful of neighborhoods, all linked by Central Avenue (historic Route 66), the main east-west thoroughfare across town. Visitors typically start in **Old Town:** The best museums are clustered here, a few blocks from the Rio Grande, which runs north-south through the city. East from Old Town lies **downtown,** with most of the city's bars and clubs, along with the bus and train depots. Central continues under I-25 and past the **University of New Mexico** campus, followed by the **Nob Hill** shopping district, which occupies about 10 blocks of Central. After this, the rest of Albuquerque blurs into the broad area known as the Northeast Heights; the main attractions up this way are hiking trails in the foothills and the Sandia Peak Tramway. The other notable parts of town—technically, separate villages—are **Los Ranchos de Albuquerque** and **Corrales.** These are two districts in the North Valley— the stretch of the river north of Central—that contain a few of the city's better lodging options; from Old Town, head north on Rio Grande Boulevard to reach Los Ranchos, then jog west over the river and north again to Corrales.

To keep your bearings, remember that the

Albuquerque Weekend Getaway

- **Day 1:** Arrive at **Albuquerque airport** and transfer to your hotel: try **Los Poblanos Historic Inn** for rural quiet, or the **Hotel Andaluz** downtown if you want to be in the middle of the action. Stroll around downtown and peek in the **KiMo Theatre,** then have sunset drinks at the **Apothecary Lounge,** followed by dinner down the street at **Farina Pizzeria.**

- **Day 2:** Stroll around Old Town and take the **ABQ Trolley Co.** tour. Have lunch at **Duran Central Pharmacy,** then check out the **Indian Pueblo Cultural Center.** Spend the evening in **Nob Hill.**

- **Day 3:** Get up early (again) for a **hot-air balloon ride,** overlooking the city from the mesas to the mountains. Head to **Barelas Coffee House** or **The Grove** for a late breakfast, then cruise Route 66 and up to the East Mountains to see the **Tinkertown Museum** and Madrid. Optional: Cut west on dirt roads to **Kasha-Katuwe Tent Rocks National Monument** and get a last dose of chile at **San Felipe Restaurant.**

Tinkertown Museum

mountains run along the east side of the city. Street addresses are followed by the city quadrant (NE, NW, SE, SW); the axes are Central and 1st Street. When locals talk about "the Big I," they mean the relatively central point where I-40 and I-25 intersect.

HISTORY

Albuquerque was established in 1706 as a small farming outpost on the banks of the Rio Grande, where Pueblo Indians had been cultivating crops since 1100, and named after a Spanish duke. Decades later, the Villa de San Felipe de Alburquerque (the first "r" was lost over the years) flourished as a waypoint on the Camino Real trade route.

The city began to transform in 1880, when the railroad arrived, two miles from the main plaza—this sparked the growth of "New Town" (now the downtown business district) and drew tuberculosis patients, who saw the city's crisp air as beneficial. By 1912, these patients made up nearly a quarter of the state's population.

More modernization and growth came from Route 66, which was laid down Central Avenue in the 1930s, and the establishment of Sandia National Labs in 1949, in response to the escalating Cold War. Tourism boomed (and neon signs buzzed on), and new streets were carved into the northeast foothills for lab workers' tract homes. In the 1940s, the population exploded from 35,000 to 100,000; by 1959, 207,000 people lived in Albuquerque.

Growth has been steady ever since, and recent development has been spurred by a growing film industry and other technical innovations. Subdivisions have spread across the West Mesa, and small outlying communities have become suburbs—though portions along the river retain a village feel that's not too far from the city's roots as a farming community three centuries back.

Sights

Most sightseeing destinations are somewhere along Central Avenue (historic Route 66), with a few destinations elsewhere in the greater metro area.

OLD TOWN

Until the railroad arrived in 1880, this wasn't just the old town—it was the *only* town. The labyrinthine old adobes have been repurposed as souvenir emporiums and galleries; the city's major museums are nearby on Mountain Road. Despite the chile-pepper magnets and cheap cowboy hats, the residential areas surrounding the shady plaza retain a strong Hispano flavor, and the historic Old Town buildings have a certain endearing scruffiness—they're lived-in, not polished.

★ ABQ Trolley Co.

To cruise the major attractions in town and get oriented, put yourself in the hands of the excellent locally owned and operated **ABQ Trolley Co.** (800 Rio Grande Blvd. NW, 505/240-8000, www.abqtrolley.com)—even if you're not normally the bus tour type. The difference here is first of all in the bus itself: in summer, a goofy faux-adobe open-sided trolley-bus; in winter, a stealthy black van. But much more important are the enthusiastic owners, who give the tours themselves,

Old Town

© AVALON TRAVEL

Breaking Bad

Walter White and Jesse Pinkman may be gone from television, but their legacy lives on in Albuquerque. The AMC show about a high school chemistry teacher turned meth cook, *Breaking Bad* was originally written for a California setting, but production moved to Albuquerque following tax incentives. It was a happy accident, and unlike other productions shot here anonymously, *Breaking Bad* was explicitly down with the 505.

Dedicated fans can book the twice-monthly "BaD Tour" with the **ABQ Trolley Co.** (800 Rio Grande Blvd. NW, 505/240-8000, www.abqtrolley.com, 3.5 hours, $65)—though its standard route passes a few filming locations as well. The bike rental company **Routes** (404 San Felipe St. NW, 505/933-5667, www.routesrentals.com, $60) offers "Biking Bad" tours every other Saturday. A few other sights around town include:

- The **Dog House** hot-dog stand, with its exceptionally fine neon sign, is at 1216 Central Avenue Southwest, near Old Town.

- **Los Pollos Hermanos** is actually Twisters, at 4257 Isleta Boulevard Southwest, but the PH logo is painted on the wall outside.

- Walt and Skyler's **A1A Car Wash** is at Menaul and Eubank (9516 Snow Heights Circle NE, for your GPS).

- **The Grove** (600 Central Ave. SE), where Lydia loved her Stevia too well, is a popular café downtown.

As souvenirs of your Albuquerque visit, **Great Face & Body** (123 Broadway SE, 505/404-6670) sells "Bathing Bad" blue bath salts. **The Candy Lady** (424 San Felipe St. NW, 505/243-6239), which cooked the prop "meth" for a few episodes, sells its blue hard candy in zip-top baggies.

and their love of the city is clear as they wave at pedestrians and tell stories about onetime Albuquerque resident Bill Gates.

All tours depart from the Hotel Albuquerque at Old Town. The 85-minute standard tour (11am and 1pm Tues.-Sat., 1pm Sun., $25) runs through downtown and some off-the-beaten-track old neighborhoods, passing many TV and movie locations. There's also a periodic *Breaking Bad* tour (3.5 hours, $65) that's hugely popular—book well in advance for this. Or join one of the monthly nighttime theme tours—such as The Hopper, a brew-pub crawl—which draws locals as well. Buy tickets online to guarantee a spot; the tickets also get you discounts around town, so it's good to do this early in your visit.

ABQ BioPark

The kid-friendly **ABQ BioPark** (505/768-2000, www.cabq.gov/biopark, 9am-5pm daily, till 6pm Sat.-Sun. June-Aug.) is made up of several components, linked by parkland along the river. On the riverbank just west of Old Town (2601 Central Ave. NW) are an **aquarium** and **botanic gardens**. The aquarium is small but well stocked, with a giant shark tank and displays on underwater life from the Gulf of Mexico and up the Rio Grande. In the adjoining gardens are a desert hothouse, a butterfly habitat, a garden railroad, and a "bugarium" full of insects that will make you squirm. The gardens also include the 10-acre **Rio Grande Heritage Farm,** a re-creation of a 1930s operation with heirloom apple orchards and rare types of livestock, such as Percheron horses and Churro sheep, in an idyllic setting near the river. The whole facility is of course very kid-friendly, but in the desert rose garden, there's a pleasant mini-café where you can enjoy a glass of wine too.

A few blocks away is the **zoo** (903 10th St. SW), which you can reach from the aquarium via a miniature train. The zoo is not particularly groundbreaking, but there's plenty of space for kids to run around among trumpeting elephants and screeching peacocks. The window into the gorilla nursery is probably the most fascinating exhibit. Tickets for each section (zoo or aquarium/gardens) are $12.50, and a combo ticket for entry at all three, which includes the mini-train ride, is $20. Ticket booths close 30 minutes before the posted closing times.

The land between the zoo and aquarium, on the east bank of the river, south of Central, is so-called **Tingley Beach** (1800 Tingley Dr. SW, sunrise-sunset, free), 18 acres of paths and ponds for fishing; you can also rent pedal boats and bicycles here.

Albuquerque Museum of Art and History

The **Albuquerque Museum of Art and History** (2000 Mountain Rd. NW, 505/243-7255, www.cabq.gov/museum, 9am-5pm Tues.-Sun., $4) has a permanent collection ranging from a few choice Taos Society of Artists members to contemporary work by the likes of Nick Abdalla, whose sensual imagery makes Georgia O'Keeffe's flower paintings look positively literal. The history wing covers four centuries,

with emphasis on Spanish military trappings, Mexican cowboys, and Albuquerque's early railroad years. Free guided tours run daily around the sculpture garden, or you can join the informative **Old Town walking tour** (11am Tues.-Sun. mid-Mar.-mid-Dec.). The museum has free admission Saturday afternoon (after 2pm) and Sunday morning (9am-1pm), as well as the third Thursday night of the month, when it's open till 8:30pm.

American International Rattlesnake Museum

You'd never guess that a small storefront just off the plaza houses the largest collection of live rattlesnakes in the world. At its entrance, the **American International Rattlesnake Museum** (202 San Felipe St. NW, 505/242-6569, www.rattlesnakes.com, 10am-6pm Mon.-Sat., 1pm-5pm Sun. June-Aug., $5) is an enormous gift shop. Press past the snake swag to see the live critters in the back. You'll also see some fuzzy tarantulas and big desert lizards, and the reptile-mad staff are usually showing off some animals outside to help educate the phobic. In the off-season, September-May, weekday hours are 11:30am-5:30pm (weekends are the same).

The ABQ BioPark's Rio Grande Heritage Farm shows off New Mexico's Churro sheep.

Capilla de Nuestra Señora de Guadalupe

One of the nifty secrets of Old Town, the tiny adobe **Capilla de Nuestra Señora de Guadalupe** (404 San Felipe St. NW) is tucked off a small side alley. It's dedicated to the first saint of Mexico; her image dominates the wall facing the entrance. The dimly lit room, furnished only with heavy carved seats against the walls, is still in regular use (although, unfortunately, a fire put an end to lit votive candles, and the image of the Virgin was repainted in a more modern style). Despite the building's small scale, it follows the scheme of many traditional New Mexican churches, with a clerestory that allows sunlight to shine down on the altar.

Museum of Natural History and Science

The **Museum of Natural History and Science** (1801 Mountain Rd. NW, 505/841-2800, www.nmnaturalhistory.org, 9am-5pm daily) is a large exhibit space containing three core attractions: a **planetarium** and observatory, a wide-format **theater** screening the latest vertigo-inducing nature documentaries, and an **exhibit** of Earth's geological history. Admission is $7 to the main exhibit space

or the planetarium and $10 for the theater, though there are discounts if you buy tickets to more than one.

The museum section devotes plenty of space to the crowd-pleasers: dinosaurs. New Mexico has been particularly rich soil for paleontologists, and several of the most interesting finds are on display, such as *Coelophysis* and *Pentaceratops*. In addition, the *Startup* exhibit details the early history of the personal computer in Albuquerque and elsewhere. The show was funded by Paul Allen, who founded Microsoft here with Bill Gates, *then* moved to Seattle.

San Felipe de Neri Church

Established in 1706 along with the city itself, **San Felipe de Neri Church** (2005 N. Plaza St. NW) was originally built on what would become the west side of the plaza—but it dissolved in a puddle of mud after a rainy season in 1792. The replacement structure, on the north side, has fared much better, perhaps because its walls, made of adobe-like *terrones* (sun-dried bricks cut out of sod) are more than five feet thick. As they have for two centuries, local parishioners attend Mass here, which is conducted three times a day, once in Spanish.

inside Old Town's Capilla de Nuestra Señora de Guadalupe

Like many religious structures in the area, this church received a late-19th-century makeover from Eurocentric Bishop Jean-Baptiste Lamy of Santa Fe. Under his direction, the place got its wooden folk Gothic spires, as well as new Jesuit priests from Naples, who added such non-Spanish details as the gabled entrance and the widow's walk. The small yet grand interior has brick floors, a baroque gilt altar, and an elaborate pressed-tin ceiling with Moorish geometric patterns. A tiny **museum** (9:30am-5pm Mon.-Sat., free), accessible through the gift shop, contains some historic church furnishings.

Turquoise Museum

The **Turquoise Museum** (2107 Central Ave. NW, 505/247-8650, tours 11am and 1pm Mon.-Sat., $10) is much more substantial than it looks from its strip-mall facade. Exhibits present the geology and history of turquoise, along with legendary trader J. C. Zachary's beautiful specimens from all over the world. But most folks can't help but think how this relates to all the jewelry they plan to buy. So come here to learn the distinction between "natural" and "real" turquoise and otherwise arm yourself for the shopping ahead. Admission is by **guided tour** only (1.5 hours).

DOWNTOWN

Albuquerque's downtown district, along Central Avenue between the train tracks and Marquette Avenue, was once known as bustling New Town, crowded with mule-drawn streetcars, bargain hunters, and wheeler-dealers from the East Coast. At Central Avenue and 4th Street, two versions of Route 66 intersect. When the original highway was commissioned in 1926, the road from Chicago to the West Coast ran along 4th Street; after 1937, the route was smoothed so that it ran east-west along Central. The route brought more business, but spread it through the city: In the 1950s and 1960s, shopping plazas farther east in Nob Hill and the Northeast Heights drew business away from downtown. By the 1970s,

the neighborhood was a wasteland of government office buildings. Thanks to an aggressive urban-renewal scheme initiated in 2000, downtown has regained some of its old vigor, and Central is now a thoroughfare best known for its bars.

By day, you won't see too many specific attractions, but you can join a walking tour with **Albuquerque Tourism & Sightseeing Factory** (219 Central Ave. NW, 505/200-2642, www.atsfworks.com), the friendly, informed crew that also runs the city trolley tours. Walks include Albu-Quirky (1.5 hours, $18), a daytime stroll pointing out architectural details and the odd stories behind them, and Albucreepy (1.5 hours, $20), a nighttime ghost tour.

★ KiMo Theatre

Albuquerque's most distinctive building is the **KiMo Theatre** (423 Central Ave. NW, 505/768-3522 or 505/768-3544, www.cabq.gov/kimo). In 1927, local businessman and

The splendid KiMo Theatre is preserved and managed by the city.

Downtown Albuquerque

To Rio Grande Pool
12TH ST
11TH ST
10TH ST
9TH ST
8TH ST
7TH ST
6TH ST
5TH ST
4TH ST
3RD ST
2ND ST
1ST ST

To Old Town
14TH ST
13TH ST
12TH ST
11TH ST
9TH ST

ABQ BioPark Zoo
Tingley Park
Barelas Coffee House and National Hispanic Cultural Center To

STOVER AVE
COAL AVE
9TH ST
8TH ST
7TH ST
IRON AVE
HAZELDINE
6TH ST
5TH ST
4TH ST
STOVER AVE
3RD ST
2ND ST
1ST ST
HIGH ST
ELM ST

PARK AVE
12TH ST
11TH ST
SILVER AVE
LEAD AVE
COAL AVE

ROUTE 66 HOSTEL
Robinson Park
FARMERS MARKET
CENTRAL AVE (ROUTE 66)
COPPER AVE
THE HOTEL BLUE
LAUNCHPAD
BOESE BROTHERS
CECILIA'S CAFÉ
POST OFFICE
GOLD AVE
SKIP MAISEL
ANODYNE/ SISTER
SOPHIA'S PLACE
CHAMA RIVER MICROBAR
GREYHOUND/ AMTRAK
BURT'S TIKI LOUNGE
PUBLIC LIBRARY
KIMO THEATRE
AT&SF
HOTEL ANDALUZ
ALVARADO TRANSPORTATION CENTER
RAIL RUNNER

CENTRAL AVE (ROUTE 66)
KENT AVE
TIJERAS AVE
PARK AVE

KELEHER ST
8TH ST
7TH ST
MARQUETTE AVE
ROMA AVE
4TH ST
CIVIC Plaza
CONVENTION CENTER
1ST ST
LOMAS BLVD
COMMERCIAL ST
JOHN ST
ROMA AVE
MARTIN LUTHER KING JR AVE
ARNO ST
FRUIT AVE

FRUIT AVE

Tractor-Brewing To
To Marble Brewery & Pub

To Rail Yards Market and Wheels Museum

0 0
0.25 km 0.25 mi

BROADWAY BLVD
ARNO ST
EDITH BLVD
WALTER ST
HIGH ST
ELM ST
IRON AVE
SILVER AVE
GOLD AVE
CENTRAL AVE (ROUTE 66)
COPPER AVE
25
AVALON TRAVEL

GATOS Y GALLETAS
FARINA PIZZERIA
THE GROVE
PARQ CENTRAL/ APOTHECARY LOUNGE
DOWNTOWN HISTORIC B&Bs

KING AVE
ROMA AVE
LOCUST ST
HIGH ST
25

To University of New Mexico and Nob Hill

Italian immigrant Carlo Bachechi hired Carl Boller, an architect specializing in movie palaces, to design this marvelously ornate building. Boller was inspired by the local adobe and native culture to create a unique style dubbed Pueblo Deco—a flamboyant treatment of Southwestern motifs, in the same vein as Moorish- and Chinese-look cinemas of the same era. The tripartite stucco facade is encrusted with ceramic tiles and Native American iconography (including a traditional Navajo symbol that had not yet been completely appropriated by the Nazi Party when the KiMo was built).

To get the full effect, take a **self-guided tour** (11am-8pm Wed.-Sat., 11am-3pm Sun.) of the interior to see the cow-skull sconces and murals of pueblo life; enter through the business office just west of the ticket booth.

THE UNIVERSITY AND NOB HILL

When it was established in 1889, what's now the state's largest university was only a tiny outpost on the far side of the railroad tracks. Surrounding the campus, which sprawls for blocks, is the typical student-friendly scrum of cheap pizza places and dilapidated bungalow rentals. The next neighborhood east along Central is Nob Hill, developed around a shopping plaza in the late 1940s and still showing that decade's distinctive style in marquees and shop facades.

The University of New Mexico

More than 25,000 students use the **University of New Mexico** campus, the core of which is bounded by Central Avenue and University Boulevard. The school's oldest buildings are a distinct pueblo-inspired style, commissioned in the early 1900s by college president William George Tight. Trustees later fired Tight in part for his non-Ivy League aesthetics, but the style was in motion. Pueblo Revival pioneer John Gaw Meem carried on the vision through the 1940s, and even with contemporary structures now set among the original halls, it's still a remarkably harmonious vision, uniting the

pastoral sanctuary feel of the great East Coast campuses with a minimalist interpretation of native New Mexican forms.

Visitors can park in a complex just inside the UNM campus across from Cornell Street. The info center, where you can pick up a detailed map, is in the southwest corner of the structure. Just across the way, the **University Art Museum** (203 Cornell Dr. NE, 505/277-4001, www.unmartmuseum.org, 10am-4pm Tues.-Fri., 10am-8pm Sat., $5 donation) displays treasures from the permanent fine art collection of more than 30,000 pieces from all over the globe.

Elsewhere on the grounds, you'll see such classic Meem buildings as **Mesa Vista Hall** and **Zimmerman Library.** Rest up at the bucolic duck pond, then head for the **Maxwell Museum of Anthropology** (off University Blvd., north of M. L. K. Jr. Blvd., 505/277-4405, 10am-4pm Tues.-Sat., free), a Meem building designed as the student union. The museum has a particularly good overview of

Architect John Gaw Meem designed the University of New Mexico's first major buildings.

The University Area

LOMAS BLVD

LAS LOMAS RD

CAMPUS BLVD

ROMA AVE

ROMA AVE

MAXWELL MUSEUM
OF ANTHROPOLOGY

ASH ST

MLK JR AVE

UNIVERSITY BLVD

PINE ST

ZIMMERMAN
LIBRARY

Duck
Pond

UNIVERSITY OF

NEW MEXICO

MESA VISTA
HALL

UNIVERSITY
ART MUSEUM

POPEJOY
HALL

VISITORS
CENTER

REDONDO DR S

REDONDO DR E

To
Tia B's
La Waffleria

UNM BOOKSTORE/
LA MONTAÑITA TAKEOUT

CENTRAL AVE (ROUTE 66)

To
Downtown
and Old Town

GOLD AVE

THE
FRONTIER

POST
OFFICE

EL PATIO

To
Geckos and Nob Hill

DR

VISTA

SILVER AVE

SILVER AVE

MESA ST

TERRACE ST

BUENA

YALE BLVD

HARVARD DR

CORNELL DR

STANFORD DR

COLUMBIA DR

PRINCETON DR

VASSAR DR

GIRARD BLVD

LEAD AVE

LEAD AVE

To
Airport

© AVALON TRAVEL

0   200 yds
0   200 m

Southwestern Indian culture and a collection of Native American artifacts from university-sponsored digs all over the state.

Nob Hill

At Girard Street, a neon-trimmed gate marks the start of the **Nob Hill** district, which extends east along Central Avenue about 10 blocks to Washington Boulevard. The area began to grow after 1937, when Route 66 was rejiggered to run along Central. The Nob Hill shopping plaza, at Central and Carlisle, signaled the neighborhood's success when it opened as the glitziest shopping district in town a decade later. It's still a lively district, with more refined bars and restaurants than downtown, and good quirky shops.

NORTH VALLEY

The stretch of the river north of Central is one of Albuquerque's prettier areas, shaded with cottonwoods and spotted with patches of farmland. The scenic route is Rio Grande Boulevard; the commercial strip is 4th Street.

Indian Pueblo Cultural Center

Just north of I-40 from Old Town, the **Indian Pueblo Cultural Center** (2401 12th St. NW, 505/843-7270, www.indianpueblo.org, 9am-5pm daily, $8) is a must-visit before heading to any of the nearby Indian communities. The horseshoe-shaped building (modeled after the Pueblo Bonito ruins in Chaco Canyon in northwestern New Mexico) houses a large museum that traces the history of the first settlers along the Rio Grande. Renovated in 2016, it is illustrated with some beautiful artifacts and showcases the best craftwork from each pueblo.

The central plaza hosts **dance performances** (11am and 2pm Sat. and Sun. Apr.-Oct., noon Sat. and Sun. Nov.-Mar.), one of the only places to see them outside of the pueblos themselves. The extensively stocked gift shop is a very good place to buy pottery and jewelry; you can also have a lunch of posole and fry bread at the Pueblo Harvest Café. Don't miss the south wing, which contains a gallery for contemporary art. At the information desk, check on ceremony schedules and get directions to the various pueblos.

Rio Grande Nature Center State Park

Familiarize yourself with river ecology at the **Rio Grande Nature Center State Park** (2901 Candelaria St. NW, 505/344-7240, www.rgnc.org, 8am-5pm daily, $3/car). You enter the sleek, concrete **visitors center** (10am-5pm daily) through a drainage culvert. Beyond an exhibit on water conservation

Rio Grande Nature Center State Park

and river ecology is a comfortable glassed-in "living room," where you can watch birds on the pond from the comfort of a lounge chair, with the outdoor sounds piped in through speakers.

Outside, several **paved trails** run across irrigation channels and along the river, shaded by towering cottonwoods. In the spring and fall, the area draws all manner of migrating birdlife. Borrow binoculars from the staff if you want to scout on your own, or join one of the frequent **nature walks** (including full-moon tours) that take place year-round.

Los Ranchos and Corrales Scenic Byway

For a pretty drive (or bike ride) through these villages that have been all but consumed by greater Albuquerque, head north from Old Town on Rio Grande Boulevard; you first reach **Los Ranchos,** then cross the river at Alameda to Corrales Road and continue up the west bank. These districts remain pockets of pastoral calm, a practical melding of old agricultural heritage with modern suburban bliss.

The only real sights are in central Corrales, two blocks west of the main road. The folk Gothic **Old San Ysidro Church** (505/897-1513, 1pm-4pm Sat.-Sun. June-Oct.) stands where the center of the village was in 1868, when its bulging adobe piers were first constructed. Every spring, the church gets a fresh coat of mud from the community. Across the road, **Casa San Ysidro** (973 Old Church Rd., 505/898-3915, www.cabq.gov/museum, $4) was the home of obsessive collectors Alan and Shirley Minge. While they lived in the place, from 1952 to 1997, they heated with firewood and squirreled away New Mexican antiques and craftwork. It is a lovingly preserved monument to a distinct way of life. The Albuquerque Museum gives **tours** (10:30am, noon, and 1:30pm Tues.-Sat. June-Aug.) of the interior with its beautiful brickwork and wood carving; tours are less frequent September-November and February-May (9:30am and 1:30pm Tues.-Fri., 10:30am, noon, and 1:30pm

Sat.). You can just turn up, but it's a good idea to call to confirm the times.

ALBUQUERQUE METRO AREA

Beyond Central Avenue, Albuquerque is a haze of houses and shopping centers built during the 1960s and later—decades one local journalist dubbed the city's "Asphalt Period." A few sights are well worth seeking out, however.

National Hispanic Cultural Center

Just south of downtown (but not quite walking distance), the modern **National Hispanic Cultural Center** (1701 4th St. SW, 505/246-2261, www.nhccnm.org) lauds the cultural contributions of Spanish speakers the world over. It has had a positive influence in the down-at-the-heels district of Barelas (even the McDonald's across the street mimics its architecture), but numerous houses—occupied by Hispanics, no less—were demolished for its construction. One woman refused the buyout, and her two small houses still sit in the parking lot, a kind of exhibit of their own.

The central attraction is the **museum** (10am-5pm Tues.-Sun., $3, free on Sun.), which shows work ranging from the traditional *bultos* and *retablos* by New Mexican craftspeople to contemporary painting, photography, and even furniture by artists from Chile, Cuba, Argentina, and more. If you can, visit on Saturday or Sunday, when the *torreón* (tower) is open (noon-5pm) to show Frederico Vigil's amazing fresco *Mundos de mestizaje*, a decadelong project depicting the many strands—Arab, Celtic, African—that have contributed to Hispanic culture today.

Adjacent to the museum is the largest Hispanic genealogy library in existence, as well as the giant Roy E. Disney Center for Performing Arts.

National Museum of Nuclear Science & History

The spiffy **National Museum of Nuclear Science & History** (601 Eubank Blvd. SE, 505/245-2137, www.nuclearmuseum.org, 9am-5pm daily, $12) covers everything you wanted to know about the nuclear era, from the development of the weapon on through current energy issues. Exhibits cover the ghastly elements of the atomic bomb, but also wonky tech details (check out the display of decoders, set in suitcases for emergency deployment) and pop-culture artifacts, such as

Learn the history of the atom bomb at the National Museum of Nuclear Science & History.

"duck and cover" films from the Cold War. Don't miss the beautiful posters by Swiss American artist Erik Nitsche.

margarita (one of which, the Doogie, honors Albuquerque actor Neil Patrick Harris, who attended a nearby high school).

★ Sandia Peak Tramway

The longest tramway of its type in the world, the **Sandia Peak Tramway** (505/856-7325, www.sandiapeak.com, $1 parking, $25 round-trip, $15 one-way) whisks passengers 2.7 miles and 4,000 feet up, along a continuous line of Swiss-made cables. The ride from Albuquerque's northeast foothills to the crest takes about 15 minutes. It's a convenient way to get to the ski area in winter, and in summer and fall, you can hike along the ridgeline a few miles to the visitors center. There's a so-so restaurant at the top and a small exhibit about local flora and fauna. The service runs frequently year-round (9am-9pm daily June-Aug., 9am-8pm Wed.-Mon., 5pm-8pm Tues. Sept.-May)—but check the website for periodic maintenance closures in fall and spring.

At the base of the tram, there's a small, free museum about skiing in New Mexico, and even from this point, the view across the city is very good. The casual Mexican restaurant here, **Sandiago's** (38 Tramway Rd. NE, 505/856-6692, 11am-8pm daily, $13), is a bit cheesy, but it's still a nice spot for a sunset

Petroglyph National Monument

Albuquerque's west side is bordered by **Petroglyph National Monument,** 7,500 acres of black boulders that crawl with some 20,000 carved lizards, birds, and assorted other beasts. Most of the images, which were created by chipping away the blackish surface "varnish" of the volcanic rock to reach the paler stone beneath, are between 400 and 700 years old, while others may date back three millennia. A few more recent examples of rock art include Maltese crosses made by Spanish settlers and initials left by explorers (not to mention a few by idle 20th-century teenagers).

Stop in first at the **visitors center** (Unser Blvd. at Western Tr., 505/899-0205, www.nps.gov/petr, 8am-5pm daily) for park maps, flyers on flora and fauna, and general orientation. From here, you will have to drive to the major trails: **Boca Negra Canyon,** a short paved loop and the only fee area ($1/car on weekdays, $2 on weekends); **Piedras Marcadas Canyon,** a 1.5-mile unpaved loop; and **Rinconada Canyon,** an out-and-back

Critters and odd creatures adorn the rocks at Petroglyph National Monument.

hike (2.2 miles round-trip) that can be tedious going in some spots because the ground is sandy. The clearest, most impressive images can be found here, in the canyon at the end of the trail. Everywhere in the park area, keep an eye out for millipedes, which thrive in this environment; dead, their curled-up shells resemble the spirals carved on the rocks—coincidence?

For the best overview (literally) of this area's geology, head for the back (west) side of the parkland, the **Volcanoes Day Use Area** (9am-5pm daily), where three cinder cones mark Albuquerque's western horizon. Access is via Atrisco Vista Boulevard (exit 149) off I-40; turn right (east) 4.3 miles north of the highway at a dirt road to the parking area.

From this vantage point, you can look down on the lava "fingers" that stretch east to form the crumbled edges of the escarpment where the petroglyphs are found. The fingers were formed when molten rock flowed between sandstone bluffs, which later crumbled away. The volcanoes were last reported emitting steam in 1881, though a group of practical jokers set smoky fires in them in the 1950s, briefly convincing city dwellers of an impending eruption. But the peaks are not entirely dead: Patches of green plants flourish around the steam vents that stud the hillocks, particularly visible on the middle of the three volcanoes.

Anderson Abruzzo Albuquerque International Balloon Museum

Boosters of Albuquerque's hot-air balloon scene—which has been flourishing since the first rally in 1972—include locals Ben Abruzzo, Larry Newman, and Maxie Anderson, who in 1978 made the first Atlantic crossing by balloon in the *Double Eagle II* helium craft. Abruzzo and Anderson also crossed the Pacific and set a long-distance record (5,678 miles) in the *Double Eagle V.*

These pioneers are honored at the so-called **BaMu** (9201 Balloon Museum Dr. NE, 505/768-6020, www.balloonmuseum.com, 9am-5pm Tues.-Sun., $4), in Balloon Fiesta Park just off Alameda Boulevard. The displays are a great mix of historical background, interactive physics lessons, and inspiring footage of record-setting balloon ventures. As long as you don't dwell too long on the zeppelin exhibit, complete with china and tableware from the *Hindenburg,* you may come away inspired by the grace of balloons and wanting to take a ride in one yourself.

Coronado Historic Site

Though named for Spanish explorer Francisco Vásquez de Coronado, who camped on this lush riverside spot during his 1540 search for gold, the **Coronado Historic Site** (485 Kuaua Rd., Bernalillo, 505/867-5351, 8:30am-5pm Wed.-Mon., $3) is actually a Native American relic, the partially restored pueblo of Kuaua (Tiwa for "evergreen"), inhabited between 1300 and the early 1600s. The centerpiece is one of the partially sunken kivas, inside which murals of life-size human figures and animals were discovered in the 1930s. The images were carefully salvaged, then reproduced in the kiva

Coronado Historic Site is a rare chance to see inside a painted kiva.

by Velino Herrera (Ma Pe Wi), a member of a key group of early American Indian figurative painters that also painted murals in the U.S. Department of the Interior in Washington DC.

With Herrera's reproductions in place (themselves freshly restored), this is the only opportunity to see the usually protected, sacred space of a kiva close to how its original users would have. And once you've seen the complete images, it's easier to pick out the images on the original frescoes mounted in the visitors center—some of the oldest examples of indigenous art on display anywhere in the United States.

Join a tour of the kiva, if possible—the guides add a lot to the story. On occasional weekends, there are traditional craft demonstrations as well. And even if none of that is going on, it's a beautiful spot for a picnic. Facing the river and the mountains, with the city hidden from view behind a dense screen of cottonwoods, you get a sense of the lush, calm life along the Rio Grande in the centuries before the Spanish arrived. To reach the monument, exit I-25 in Bernalillo and head west on Highway 550; Kuaua Road is on your right, before the Santa Ana Star casino.

Entertainment and Events

NIGHTLIFE

Because Albuquerque doesn't have enough members of any one particular subculture to pack a whole bar, the city's drinking dens can host a remarkable cross section, and even the most chic-appearing places might see an absentminded professor and a veteran Earth Firster propping up the bar next to well-groomed professionals.

That said, the city's main bar and club scene, in a few square blocks of downtown, can feel a bit generic, with free-flowing beer specials for non-choosy students. It ends in a rowdy scene after closing time on weekends, when crowds spill out onto several blocks of Central that are closed to car traffic. So although this area does have a few good bars, you'll find more interesting entertainment elsewhere.

Downtown

The **Hotel Andaluz lobby** (125 2nd St. NW, 505/242-9090) touts itself as "Albuquerque's living room"—Conrad Hilton's original vision for the place—and it's a comfy spot to sip cocktails and nibble Spain-inspired snacks, especially if you reserve one of the private booths ("casbahs") on the weekend.

A great spot to watch the Sandia Mountains turn pink at sunset, the **Apothecary Lounge**

(806 Central Ave. SE, 505/242-0040, 3pm-10:30pm Mon.-Thurs., 3pm-1am Fri.-Sun.) is the rooftop bar at the Parq Central hotel in East Downtown. Fitting with the historic atmosphere of the hotel, the bar is good at vintage cocktails (if sometimes a bit slow).

The best all-purpose casual bars downtown are at the same address. Upstairs, **Anodyne** (409 Central Ave. NW, 505/244-1820, 4pm-1:30am Mon.-Fri., 7pm-1:30am Sat., 7pm-11:30pm Sun.) is a long, wood-floor room filled with pool tables and thrift-store sofas. Choose from more than a hundred beers, and get some quarters to plug in to the good collection of pinball machines. Happy hour is 4pm-8pm Monday-Thursday, and till 9pm on Friday. Downstairs, the more cavernous **Sister** (505/242-4900, www.sisterthebar.com, 4pm-2am Mon.-Thurs., 11am-2am Fri.-Sat., 11am-midnight Sun.) has tacos, live bands, and more pinball.

To catch touring indie rockers or the local crew about to hit it big, head to the very professional **Launchpad** (618 Central Ave. SW, 505/764-8887, www.launchpadrocks.com). With free live music and a pool table, **Burt's Tiki Lounge** (515 Central Ave. NW, 505/247-2878, www.burtstikilounge.com, 8:30pm-2am Wed.-Sat.) has a funky feel and an eclectic bill, from British psychedelia to reggae.

Albuquerque Beer Culture

Burque's beer scene is so lively that the *Journal* has a dedicated "Brews News" beat. These are some of the best spots in town; for more, see the **New Mexico Brewers Guild** (www.nmbeer. org). For car-free sampling, check out **The Hopper trolley tour** (www.abqtrolley.com).

- **Il Vicino** (3403 Central Ave. NE, 505/266-7855, 11am-11pm Sun.-Thurs., 11am-midnight Fri.-Sat.): This Nob Hill pizza parlor has been brewing its own beer since 1994 and now has a large brewing facility, the **Canteen Brewhouse,** at 2381 Aztec Road Northeast (noon-10pm Sun.-Thurs., noon-midnight Fri.-Sat.).

- **Kellys Brew Pub** (3222 Central Ave. SE, 505/262-2739, 8am-10:30pm Sun.-Thurs., 8am-midnight Fri.-Sat.): Another long-established Nob Hill brewery, set in an old car showroom. Great outdoor seating.

- **Matanza** (3225 Central Ave. NE, 505/312-7305, 4pm-9pm Mon., 11:30am-10pm Tues.-Thurs., 11:30am-11pm Fri.-Sat., 11:30am-9pm Sun.): The newest on the Nob Hill scene, with 100 craft beers on tap and tasty "sangwiches" and other bar food with New Mexican flair.

- **Marble Pub** (111 Marble Ave. NW, 505/243-2739, noon-midnight Mon.-Sat., noon-10:30pm Sun.): The drinking space for one of the best newer breweries. Pleasantly out of the downtown fray, with a dog-friendly outdoor area with eclectic bands.

- **Boese Brothers** (601 Gold Ave. SW, 505/382-7060, 3pm-midnight Mon.-Thurs., 3pm-1am Fri., 1pm-2am Sat., 1pm-10pm Sun.): This downtown brewery, opened in 2015, is big and lively, usually with six house brews on tap.

- **Tractor Brewing:** This popular place has two locations: its brewery, in the industrial area north of downtown (1800 4th St. NW, 505/243-6752, 3pm-late Mon.-Thurs, 1pm-late Fri.-Sun.), and a bar in Nob Hill (118 Tulane St. SE, 505/433-5654, 3pm-midnight Mon.-Wed., 3pm-2am Thurs., 1pm-2am Fri.-Sat., 1pm-midnight Sun.). Both have low-fi live music.

- **La Cumbre Brewing** (3313 Girard Blvd. NE, 505/872-0225, noon-late daily): La Cumbre is in a fairly isolated industrial area, with only the occasional food truck for sustenance, but locals love this beer.

- **Chama River Microbar** (106 2nd St. SW, 505/842-8329, 4pm-midnight daily): A small outpost (no food) downtown, handy for tastings. If you like it, head to the brewery itself (4939 Pan American Fwy. NE, 505/342-1800, 11am-10pm Sun.-Thurs., 11am-11pm Fri.-Sat.), a slick place with a full steakhouse menu.

some of New Mexico's many craft beers

The University and Nob Hill

In the Nob Hill shopping plaza, **Gecko's** (3500 Central Ave. SE, 505/262-1848, 11:30am-late Mon.-Fri., noon-late Sat.-Sun.) is a good place for a snack (anything from Thai curry shrimp to chipotle hot wings) and a drink in the sidewalk seats. Sporting its own breezy patio, **O'Niell's** (4310 Central Ave. SE, 505/255-6782, 11am-midnight daily) is a great Irish pub that draws a varied crowd, whether for quiz night or weekend folk bands; the kitchen is open until 11pm.

FESTIVALS AND EVENTS

The city's biggest annual event is the **Albuquerque International Balloon Fiesta** (505/821-1000, www.balloonfiesta. com), nine days in October dedicated to New Mexico's official state aircraft, with more than 700 hot-air balloons of all colors, shapes, and sizes gathering at a dedicated park on the north side of town, west of I-25. During the fiesta, the city is packed with "airheads," who claim this is the best gathering of its kind in

Ceremonial Dances

This is an approximate schedule for dances at Albuquerque-area pueblos. Pueblo feast days are always on the same date and generally open to all, but seasonal dances (especially Easter and other spring rituals) can vary, and are sometimes closed to visitors. Confirm details and start times with the **Indian Pueblo Cultural Center** (505/843-7270, www.indianpueblo.org) before setting out.

- **January 1** - Jemez: Los Matachines; Kewa (Santo Domingo): corn dance
- **January 6** - Most pueblos: various dances to honor new tribal officials
- **Easter** - Most pueblos: various dances
- **May 1** - San Felipe: Feast of San Felipe
- **Memorial Day weekend** - Jemez craft show and powwow
- **June 13** - Sandia: Feast of San Antonio
- **June 29** - Santa Ana and Kewa (Santo Domingo): Feast of San Pedro
- **July 14** - Cochiti: Feast of San Bonaventura
- **July 26** - Santa Ana: Feast of Santa Ana
- **August 2** - Jemez: Feast of Santa Persingula
- **August 4** - Kewa (Santo Domingo): Feast of Santo Domingo
- **August 10** - Jemez: Pueblo Independence Day and Fair
- **August 15** - Zia: Feast of the Assumption of Our Blessed Mother
- **August 28** - Isleta: Feast of San Agustín (ends September 4)
- **Labor Day** - Kewa (Santo Domingo): craft market
- **November 12** - Jemez: Feast of San Diego
- **December 12** - Jemez: Los Matachines
- **December 25** - Santa Ana, Kewa (Santo Domingo), and Zia: various dances
- **December 26-28** - Kewa (Santo Domingo): corn dance; also dances at most other pueblos

the world. If you go, don't miss an early-morning mass ascension, when the balloons glow against the dark sky, then lift silently into the air in a great wave. Parking can be a nightmare—take the park-and-ride bus, or ride a bike (valet parking available!).

In April is the equally colorful **Gathering of Nations Powwow** (505/836-2810, www.gatheringofnations.com), the largest tribal get-together in the United States, with more than 3,000 dancers and singers in full regalia from over 500 tribes crowding the floor of the University Arena. Miss Indian World earns her crown by showing off traditional talents such as spearfishing or storytelling.

Just after Labor Day, the state's agricultural roots get their due at the **New Mexico State Fair** (www.exponm.com), two weeks of fried foods, prizewinning livestock, midway rides,

and really excellent rodeos, which often end with shows by country music legends.

Around November 2, don't miss the **Marigold Parade** (505/363-1326, www.muertosymarigolds.org), celebrating the Mexican Day of the Dead and general South Valley pride. The parade is a procession of skeletons, cars bedecked in flowers, and a little civil-rights activism.

For the **winter holidays,** the city is trimmed with luminarias (paper-bag lanterns), especially in Old Town and the Country Club neighborhood just to the south. The Albuquerque Botanic Garden (www.abq.gov/biopark) is decked out with holiday lights and model trains for much of December, and ABQ Ride, the city bus service, offers a bus tour around the prettiest neighborhoods on Christmas Eve.

Shopping

Old Town and its environs are where you can pick up traditional American Indian jewelry and pottery for very reasonable prices, while Nob Hill is the commercial center of Albuquerque's counterculture, with body-piercing studios adjacent to comic book shops next to herbal apothecaries.

OLD TOWN

The galleries and gift shops around the plaza can blur together after just a little bit of browsing, but the **Blue Portal Gallery** (2107 Church St. NW, 505/243-6005, 10am-4:30pm Mon.-Sat.) is a nice change, with well-priced and often very refined arts and crafts, from quilts to woodwork, by Albuquerque's senior citizens. And the **street vendors** set up on the east side of the plaza are all artisans selling their own work, at fair prices.

For a great selection of interesting New Mexico gifts and books, as well as local herbal treatments, visit **Duran Central Pharmacy** (1815 Central Ave. NW, 505/247-4141,

8:30am-7pm Mon.-Fri., 8:30am-3pm Sat., 9am-3pm Sun.), just outside Old Town.

DOWNTOWN

An emporium of American Indian goods, **Skip Maisel's Indian Jewelry & Crafts** (510 Central Ave. SW, 505/242-6526, 9am-5:30pm Mon.-Sat.) feels like a relic from downtown's heyday. Whether you want a warbonnet, a turquoise-studded watch, or deerskin moccasins, it's all here in a vast, overstocked shop with kindly salespeople. Don't miss the beautiful murals above the display windows and in the foyer; they were painted in the 1930s by local Indian artists such as Awa Tsireh, whose work hangs in the New Mexico Museum of Art in Santa Fe.

Set in the old Santa Fe workshops south of downtown, **Rail Yards Market** (777 1st St. SW, www.railyardsmarket.org, 10am-2pm Sun. May-Oct.) is a festive gathering of arts and crafts, produce, snacks, and live music. It's a good place to shop for offbeat souvenirs—and it's a great chance to see inside the majestic

Rail Yards Market runs every Sunday in summer, combining a farmers market, crafts, and live music.

old buildings where locomotives for the Santa Fe line were built from the ground up.

THE UNIVERSITY AND NOB HILL

Among the various quirky boutiques in this area, of note is **Absolutely Neon** (3903 Central Ave. NE, 505/265-6366, 11am-6pm Mon.-Sat.), a gallery of new and vintage signs. And on the east edge of Nob Hill is a slew of **antiques marts**.

NORTH VALLEY

For excellent crafts, head to **Shumakolowa Native Arts** (2401 12th St. NW, 505/843-7270, www.indianpueblo.org, 9am-5:30pm daily), the shop at the Indian Pueblo Cultural Center. Not only are prices reasonable, but the staff is happy to explain the work that goes into various pieces.

Los Poblanos Farm Shop (4803 Rio Grande Blvd. NW, 505/938-2192, 9am-5pm daily) sells soaps, bath salts, and lotions scented with the organic lavender grown in the adjacent field. It also stocks an excellently curated selection of garden gear, books, kitchen supplies, and locally made snacks.

Sports and Recreation

From the river basin up to mountain peaks, Albuquerque gives outdoorsy types plenty to do. Late summer (after rains have started and fire danger is past) and fall are the best times to head to the higher elevations on the Sandia Mountains. Once the cooler weather sets in, the scrub-covered foothills and the bare, rocky West Mesa are more hospitable. The valley along the Rio Grande, running through the center of the city, is remarkably pleasant year-round: mild in winter and cool and shady in summer. As everywhere in the desert, always pack extra layers of clothing and plenty of water before you set out, and don't go charging up Sandia Peak (10,678 feet above sea level) your first day off the plane.

★ BALLOONING

You don't have to be in town for the Balloon Fiesta to go up, up, and away. Take advantage of Albuquerque's near-flawless weather to take a hot-air balloon ride almost any morning of the year. A trip is admittedly an investment (and you have to wake up before dawn), but the sensation is unlike any other sort of ride, as it's slow and almost completely silent. One of the best established operations is **Rainbow Ryders** (505/823-1111, www.rainbowryders.com, $169 pp). Typically, you're up in the balloon for an hour or so, depending on wind conditions, and you get a champagne toast when you're back on solid ground.

HIKING

Between the West Mesa and the East Mountains, Albuquerque offers a range of day hikes. The least strenuous is the *bosque* (the wooded area along the Rio Grande), where level paths lead through groves of cottonwoods, willows, and olive trees. The **Rio Grande Nature Center State Park** (2901 Candelaria St. NW, 505/344-7240, www.rgnc.

org, 8am-5pm daily, $3/car) is the best starting point for any walk around the area.

On the east side, the easiest approach to the mountains is to take the tram to **Sandia Peak** or drive up the east face of the mountain via scenic byway Highway 536, aka the Crest Road, to the **Sandia Crest Visitor Center** ($3/car). The 1.6-mile **Crest Trail** links the two points (tram and visitors center), with possible smaller loops in between. The views are fantastic, and the river-stone Kiwanis Cabin, a Civilian Conservation Corps project on a cliff edge, makes a nice picnic destination about halfway along.

In the fall, a hike in **Fourth of July Canyon,** in the Manzano Mountains east of the city, is a wonderful place to see the leaves changing color.

For a little elevation gain, head to the Sandia foothills, ideal in the winter but a little hot in the summertime. The best access is at **Elena Gallegos Picnic Area** (7am-9pm daily Apr.-Oct., 7am-7pm daily Nov.-Mar., $1 weekdays, $2 weekends), east of Tramway Boulevard and north of Academy, at the end of Simms Park Road.

The foothills are also the starting point for the popular but tough **La Luz Trail,** a 7.5-mile ascent to the Sandia Crest Visitor Center. The

Hot-air balloon rides typically drift down the Rio Grande and across the West Mesa.

From Sandia Peak, you can see the whole city of Albuquerque.

trail has a 12 percent grade at certain points, and passes through four climate zones (pack lots of layers) as you climb 3,200 vertical feet. Near the top, you can take a spur that leads north to the Sandia Crest observation point or continue on the main trail south to the ski area and the Sandia Peak Tramway, which you can take back down the mountain. Ideally you'd have someone pick you up at the bottom, because the 2.5-mile trail from the tram back to the trailhead has no shade. (You might be tempted to take the tram up and hike down, but the steep descent can be deadly to toes and knees.) The La Luz trailhead ($3/car) is at the far north end of Tramway Boulevard just before the road turns west.

BIKING

Albuquerque maintains a great network of paved trails in the city, and the mountains and foothills have challenging dirt tracks. The most visitor-friendly bike store in town is **Routes** (404 San Felipe St. NW, 505/933-5667, www.routesrentals.com, 8am-7pm Mon.-Fri., 7am-7pm Sat.-Sun. Mar.-Oct., 9am-6pm Mon.-Fri., 8am-6pm Sat.-Sun. Nov.-Feb., $15/hour, $35/day), which rents city cruisers, mountain bikes, and more at its handy location in Old Town; pickup and drop-off from hotels is free. It also runs fun daylong **bike tours,** and rents snowshoes in the winter.

City Cycling

Recreational cyclists need head no farther than the river, where the **Paseo del**

Routes rents bikes in Old Town and runs city cycling tours.

Birding on the Peak

In the dead of winter, **Sandia Peak** does not seem hospitable to life in any form, much less flocks of delicate-looking birds the size of your fist, fluffing around cheerfully in the frigid air. But that's precisely what you'll see if you visit right after a big snowfall. These are rosy finches, a contrary, cold-loving variety (sometimes called "refrigerator birds") that migrate from as far north as the Arctic tundra to the higher elevations of New Mexico, which must seem relatively tropical by comparison.

What's special about Sandia is that it draws all three species of **rosy finch,** which in turn draws dedicated birders looking to add the finches to their life lists, and it's one of the few places to see them that's close to a city and accessible by car. So if you see the finches—they're midsize brown or black birds with pink bellies, rumps, and wings—you'll probably also spy some human finch fans. But they might not have time to talk, as it's not unheard-of for the most obsessive birders— those on their "big year," out to spot as many species as possible in precisely 365 days—to fly in to Albuquerque, drive to the crest, eyeball the finches, and drive right back to the airport again.

Bosque, a 16-mile-long, completely flat biking and jogging path, runs through the Rio Grande Valley State Park. The northern starting point is at **Alameda/Rio Grande Open Space** (7am-9pm daily Apr.-Oct., 7am-7pm daily Nov.-Mar.) on Alameda Boulevard. You can also reach the trail through the **Rio Grande Nature Center** (www.rgnc.org, 8am-5pm daily, $3/car), at the end of Candelaria, and at several other major intersections along the way. For details on this and other bike trails in Albuquerque, download a map from the city's bike info page (www.cabq.gov/bike), or pick up a free copy at bike shops around town.

Corrales, in the far North Valley, is also good for an afternoon bike ride: The speed limit on the main street is low, and you can dip into smaller side streets and bike along the acequias. The excellent **Stevie's Happy Bikes** (4685 Corrales Rd., 505/897-7900, 10am-6pm Tues.-Sat.) rents comfy cruisers ($25/day) and even tandems ($35/day), and can advise on the best routes on and around the river.

Mountain Biking

Mountain bikers can take the Sandia Peak Tramway to the **ski area,** then rent wheels to explore the 30 miles of wooded trails. Bikes aren't allowed on the tram, though, so if you have your own ride, you can drive around the east side of the mountain.

Also on the east side of the mountains, a whole network of trails lead off Highway 337 (south of I-25), through **Otero Canyon** and other routes through the juniper-studded Manzanos. Or stay in the city and explore the foothills. Locals built a small but fun BMX terrain park at **Embudo Canyon;** park at the end of Indian School Road. For a longer cruise, head for the **foothills trails,** a web of dirt tracks all along the edge of the Northeast Heights.

Road Biking

A popular tour is up to **Sandia Peak** via the Crest Road on the east side—you can park and ride from any point, but cyclists typically start somewhere along Highway 14 north of I-40, then ride up Highway 536, which winds 13.5 miles along increasingly steep switchbacks to the crest. The **New Mexico Touring Society** (www.nmts.org) lists descriptions of other routes and organizes group rides.

WINTER SPORTS

Sandia Peak Ski Area (505/242-9052, www. sandiapeak.com, $55 full-day lift ticket) is open mid-December-mid-March, though it often takes till about February for a good base to build up. The 10 main trails, serviced by four lifts, are not dramatic, but they are good and long. The area is open daily in the holiday season, then Wednesday-Sunday for the rest of the winter.

Sandia Peak also has plenty of opportunities for cross-country skiing. Groomed trails start from **Capulin Springs Snow Play Area** (9:30am-3:30pm Fri.-Sun. in winter, $3/car), where there are also big hills for tubing and sledding. Look for the parking nine miles up Highway 536 to the crest. Farther up on the mountain, **10K Trail** is usually groomed for skiers, as is a service road heading south to the upper tramway terminal; the latter is wide and relatively level, good for beginners. For trail conditions, call or visit the Sandia **ranger station** (505/281-3304) on Highway 337 in Tijeras.

Food

Albuquerque has a few dress-up establishments, but the real spirit of the city's cuisine is in its lower-rent spots where dedicated owners follow their individual visions. A lot of the most traditional New Mexican places are open only for breakfast and lunch, so plan accordingly. Prices given are those of the average entrée.

OLD TOWN

Aside from the few recommended here, the restaurants in the blocks immediately adjacent to the Old Town plaza are expensive and only so-so; better to walk another block or two for real New Mexican flavor, or drive a short way west on Central.

New Mexican

Look behind the magazine rack at ★ **Duran Central Pharmacy** (1815 Central Ave. NW, 505/247-4141, 9am-6:30pm Mon.-Fri., 9am-2pm Sat.-Sun., $9, cash only), and you'll find an old-fashioned lunch counter. Regulars pack this place at lunch for all the New Mexican staples: huevos rancheros, green-chile stew, and big enchilada plates.

Steak

Don't be put off by the brown, windowless cinderblock facade, with a package-liquor store in the front. **Monte Carlo Steakhouse** (3916 Central Ave. SW, 505/831-2444, 11am-10pm Mon.-Thurs, 11am-11pm Fri.-Sat., $18) is a wondrous time machine, lined with vintage Naugahyde booths and serving good, hearty food: the prime-rib special Thursday-Saturday, a softball-size green-chile cheeseburger, or marinated pork kebab—all with delicious hand-cut fries. Greek ownership means you get a tangy feta dressing on your salad and baklava for dessert. And even though there's a full bar, you're still welcome to buy wine from the package store up front and have it with your dinner, for a nominal markup.

Cafés

Inside the Albuquerque Museum, **Slate Street Café** (2000 Mountain Rd. NW, 505/243-2220, 10am-2:30pm Tues.-Fri. and Sun., 10am-4pm Sat., $8) is great for coffee and cupcakes, as well as more substantial breakfast and lunch, like a chipotle-spiked meat-loaf sandwich. (Its larger, original location is at 515 Slate Ave. NW.)

A 10-minute walk from Old Town, **Golden Crown Panaderia** (1103 Mountain Rd. NW, 505/243-2424, 7am-8pm Tues.-Sat., 10am-8pm Sun., $4-9) is a real neighborhood hangout that's so much more than a bakery. Famous for its green-chile bread and *bizcochitos* (the anise-laced state cookie), it also does pizza with blue-corn or green-chile crust, to take away or to eat at the picnic tables out back. Wash it down with a coffee milk shake.

Fresh and Local

Founded in Santa Fe, **Vinaigrette** (1828

Central Ave. SW, 505/842-5507, 11am-10pm daily, $13) is an excellent "salad bistro" that's more substantial than it sounds—and it's a welcome spot of healthy eating around Old Town.

Diner

Built on the bones of an old fast-food joint, **Central Grill** (2056 Central Ave. SW, 505/554-1424, 6:30am-4pm Mon.-Thurs., 6:30am-8pm Fri., 8am-8pm Sat., $7) still does quick food, but with a fresher, more homemade feel. Like a good diner should, it serves breakfast all day, and real maple syrup is an option. Its daily special plate is usually a solid deal, with a main like barbecue chicken plus sides and a drink for $9 or so.

DOWNTOWN

With so many bars in this area, there's little room left for food.

New Mexican

Even though it's in the middle of Albuquerque's main business district, ★ **Cecilia's Café** (230 6th St. SW, 505/243-7070, 7am-2pm daily, $8) feels more like a living room than a restaurant. Maybe it's the woodstove in the corner—as well as the personal attention from Cecilia and her daughters and the food that's clearly made with care. The rich, dark red chile really shines here.

Cafés

Past the railroad tracks in EDo (East Downtown), **The Grove** (600 Central Ave. SE, 505/248-9800, 7am-4pm Tues.-Sat., 8am-3pm Sun., $12) complements its local-organic menu with big front windows facing Central and a screened-in patio. The chalkboard menu features creative salads (spinach, orange slices, and dates is one combo) as well as sandwiches and cupcakes; breakfast, with farm-fresh eggs and homemade English muffins, is served all day.

Albuquerque's own cat café, **Gatos y Galletas** (412 Central Ave. SE, 505/289-0775, 10am-8pm Mon. and Wed.-Thurs., 10am-9pm Fri.-Sat., 10am-6pm Sun., $4) is filled with friendly felines from the local Humane

Society that are all up for adoption. All the food is vegetarian, and there's yoga classes, comedy, and more.

Fresh and Local

There are a number of **farmers markets** throughout the city; one of the largest is downtown at Robinson Park on Central Avenue at 8th Street (7am-noon Sat. May-Aug., 8am-1pm Sept.-Nov.). For other markets around the city, visit www.farmersmarketsnm.org.

Also look for a new restaurant in the freshly renovated Imperial Building, perhaps called **Sophia's Place** (205 Silver Ave. SW), or something else entirely. It's a venture by the Apodaca family, owners of wildly popular, funky farm café **Eli's Place** (also known as Sophia's) in the North Valley (6313 4th St. NW, 505/345-3935).

Italian

A popular hangout for urban pioneers in the EDo neighborhood, ★ **Farina Pizzeria** (510 Central Ave. SE, 505/908-9490, 11am-9pm Mon., 11am-10pm Tues.-Fri., noon-10pm Sat., 5pm-9pm Sun., $17) has exposed brick walls and a casual vibe. The pies come out of the wood-fired oven suitably crisp-chewy and topped with seasonal veggies. Make sure you get a cup of the Gorgonzola-crème fraîche-chive dip for your crusts—it's the upscale version of the ranch dressing that's more commonly offered. There's usually a pasta special as well.

THE UNIVERSITY AND NOB HILL

Thanks to the large student population, this area has some great and varied spots to grab a cheap bite, but Nob Hill has some upscale options too.

New Mexican

You haven't been to Albuquerque unless you've been to ★ **The Frontier** (2400 Central Ave. SE, 505/266-0550, 5am-1am daily, $6), across from UNM. Everyone in the city passes through its doors at some point in their lives, so all you have to do is pick a seat in one of the five Western-themed rooms (Hmm, under the big portrait of John Wayne? Or maybe one of the smaller ones?) and watch the characters file in. You'll want some food, of course: a green-chile-smothered breakfast burrito filled with crispy hash browns, or a hamburger, or one of the signature cinnamon rolls, a deadly amalgam of flour, sugar, and some addictive drug that compels you to eat them despite all common sense. If you feel a little unhealthy, you can always get some fresh orange juice and restore your balance by vegging out in front of the mesmerizing tortilla machine.

Near the university, **El Patio** (142 Harvard Dr. SE, 505/268-4245, 11am-9pm Sun.-Thurs., 11am-9:30pm Fri.-Sat., $9) is the kind of old-reliable place that ex-locals get misty-eyed about after they've moved away. The green-chile-and-chicken enchiladas are high on many citywide favorite lists. It doesn't hurt that the setting, in an old bungalow with a shady outdoor space, feels like an extension of someone's home kitchen. The menu is more vegetarian-friendly than most New Mexican joints.

Cafés

Step in to **Flying Star Café** (3416 Central Ave. SE, 505/255-6633, 7am-9:30pm Sun.-Thurs., 7am-10:30pm Fri.-Sat., $11), and you'll likely be mesmerized by the pastry case, packed with triple-ginger cookies, lemon-blueberry cheesecake, and fat éclairs. But try to look up to appreciate the range on the menu boards: Asian noodles, hot and cold sandwiches, mac-and-cheese, and enchiladas. The food isn't always quite as great as it looks, but with speedy service and locations all over town, it's a handy place to zip in or to lounge around (wireless Internet access is free).

Pick up goods for a picnic at **La Montañita Co-op** (3500 Central Ave. SE, 505/265-4631, 7am-10pm Mon.-Sat., 8am-10pm Sun.), where quinoa salads and stuffed grape leaves are all the rage; look in the dairy section for "sampler" pieces of locally made cheese.

There's a snacks-only operation in the **UNM Bookstore** (2301 Central Ave. NE, 505/277-9586, 7am-6pm Mon.-Fri., 10am-4pm Sat.), across from the Frontier.

Waffles sweet or savory are the thing at **Tia B's La Waffleria** (3710 Campus Blvd. NE, 505/492-2007, 8am-2pm daily, $8), set in a funky old house with front and back patios. Of course you can get a blue-corn waffle with eggs and good hot chile.

NORTH VALLEY

New Mexican

For New Mexican food with a heavier American Indian influence, hit the **Pueblo Harvest Café** (2401 12th St. NW, 505/724-3510, 8am-8:30pm Mon.-Thurs., 8am-9pm Fri.-Sat., 8am-4pm Sun., $10), at the Indian Pueblo Cultural Center. The menu has standard burgers and fries, but specialties such as mutton stew with a side of *horno* bread and a green-chile-and-lamb sandwich are rich and earthy and hard to find elsewhere. Breakfast is also good, with blue-corn mush topped with *carne adovada*, and apple-raisin "Indian toast." The "Rez Breakfast," with Spam on the side, may be a treat for some. There's live music Friday and Saturday evenings, as well as Sunday around noon.

Experts agree: **Mary & Tito's Café** (2711 4th St. NW, 505/344-6266, 9am-6pm Mon.-Thurs., 9am-8pm Fri.-Sat., $7) is the place to go for *carne adovada*, the dish of tender pork braised in red chile, particularly good in what they call a Mexican turnover (a stuffed sopaipilla). The meat is flavorful enough to stand alone, but the fruity, bright red-chile sauce, flecked with seeds, is so good you'll want to put it on everything. This place is such a local icon, seemingly untouched since the 1980s (ah, lovely dusty-rose vinyl!), it won a James Beard America's Classics award. Sadly, both Mary and Tito have passed on now, leaving the place ripe for a decline in standards; so far, though, it seems to be holding strong.

Out in Corrales, **Perea's Restaurant & Tijuana Bar** (4590 Corrales Rd., 505/898-2442, 11am-2pm Mon.-Sat., $7) is open only for lunch, but it's worth scheduling around if you know you'll be out this way. Everything's home-cooked, from Frito pie to *carne adovada*.

Cafés

There are two branches of **Flying Star** up this way: one in Los Ranchos (4026 Rio Grande Blvd. NW, 505/344-6714, 6:30am-9pm Mon.-Sat., 7am-9pm Sun., $11) and another in Corrales (10700 Corrales Rd., 505/938-4717, 6:30am-9:30pm Sun.-Thurs., 6:30am-10pm Fri.-Sat., $11).

La Montañita Co-op (2400 Rio Grande Blvd. NW, 505/242-8800, 7am-10pm daily) also has a branch here, good for picnic goodies.

Fresh and Local

The restaurant at Los Poblanos Historic Inn, ★ **La Merienda** (4803 Rio Grande Blvd. NW, 505/344-9297, 6pm-9pm Wed.-Sat., $26), serves flawless food, a bit Mediterranean in style, but undeniably New Mexican in ingredients like heirloom beans. The short menu

changes each night, based on produce. Book well ahead—hotel guests get priority, so tables fill up fast.

You wouldn't know it from the former-gas-station vibe of the place, but ★ **Eli's Place** (6313 4th St. NW, 505/345-3935, 7am-9pm Mon.-Fri., 9am-9pm Sat., 9am-2pm Sun., $10) is dedicated to farm-freshness—just doesn't bother bragging about it. Order at the counter—a breakfast sandwich with eggs, plus a side of highly addictive red chile-dusted home fries, or perhaps duck enchiladas with tomatillo sauce for lunch or dinner. A note on Eli's: Despite an official name change, regulars know the café as Sophia's Place, and will likely always call it that—even after a new branch with that name opens downtown.

ALBUQUERQUE METRO AREA

Great places to eat are scattered all over the city, often in unlikely looking strip malls. These places are worth making a trip for, or will provide a pick-me-up when you're far afield.

The Green Jeans Farmery is a hub that shows off local food.

New Mexican

Cruise down by the rail yards south of downtown to find **El Modelo** (1715 2nd St. SW, 505/242-1843, 7am-7pm daily, $7), a local go-to for a hangover-curing *chicharrón* burrito, chile-smothered spareribs, or tamales for the whole family—you can order a single tamale or a whole platter of food. Because it's really a front for a tortilla factory, the flour tortillas are also particularly tender. If the weather's nice, grab a seat at a picnic table outside and watch the freight trains go by.

Just two blocks from the National Hispanic Cultural Center, popular **Barelas Coffee House** (1502 4th St. SW, 505/843-7577, 7:30am-3pm Mon.-Fri., 7:30am-2:30pm Sat., $7) is potentially confusing to the first-timer: The attraction is not coffee, but chile—especially the red, which infuses hearty, timeless New Mexican standards like posole, *chicharrones*, and *menudo*. The restaurant occupies several storefronts, and even then there's often a line out the door at lunch. But it's worth the wait—this is timeless food.

Fresh and Local

One-stop noshing can be done at **Green Jeans Farmery** (3600 Cutler Ave. NE, www.greenjeansfarmery.com), a kind of outdoor food court and general hangout spot built from shipping containers. Pick from tacos, big sandwiches, artisanal pizza, espresso, and an outpost of Santa Fe Brewing. It draws a nice cross-section of Albuquerqueans.

Accommodations

Because Albuquerque isn't quite a tourist mecca, you can find some great value hotels. Whether on the low or high end, you'll pay substantially less here than you would in Santa Fe for similar amenities. The only time you'll need to book in advance is early October, during Balloon Fiesta (when prices are usually a bit higher).

UNDER $100

Funky and affordable, the **Route 66 Hostel** (1012 Central Ave. SW, 505/247-1813, www.route66hostel.com) is in a century-old house midway between downtown and Old Town and has been offering bargain accommodations since 1978. It's hardly modern and minimalist, but it's clean enough. Upstairs, along creaky wood hallways, are private rooms ($25-35) with various configurations. Downstairs and in the basement area are single-sex dorms ($25 pp). Guests have run of the kitchen, and there's a laundry and room to lounge. The most useful city bus lines run right out front. There have been complaints of staff not being on hand for early or late check-ins—be sure to call and confirm before you arrive.

The Hotel Blue (717 Central Ave. NW, 877/878-4868, www.thehotelblue.com, $69 s, $79 d) offers decent value downtown. The rooms in this 1960s block are a slightly odd mix of cheesy motel decor (gold quilted bedspreads) and bachelor-pad flair (a gas "fireplace"), and the windows don't open. But the Tempur-Pedic beds are undeniably comfortable, and the low rates include breakfast, parking, and a shuttle to the airport. There's also a decent-size outdoor pool, open in summer. Request a room on the northeast side for a mountain view.

Central Avenue is dotted with motels, many built in Route 66's heyday. Almost all of them are unsavory, except for ★ **Monterey Non-Smokers Motel** (2402 Central Ave. SW, 505/243-3554, www.nonsmokersmotel.com, $77 s, $82 d), which is as practical as its name implies. The place doesn't really capitalize on 1950s kitsch—it just offers meticulously clean, good-value rooms with no extra frills or flair. One large family suite has two beds and a foldout sofa. The outdoor pool is a treat, the laundry facilities are a bonus, and the location near Old Town is very convenient.

A fully renovated motel on the west side, just over the river from Old Town, ★ **Sandia Peak Inn** (4614 Central Ave. SW, 505/831-5036, www.sandiapeakinnmotel.com, $62 s, $82 d) is named not for its proximity to the mountain, but its view of it. It's certainly the best value in this category, offering large, spotless rooms, all with bathtubs, fridges, microwaves, and huge TVs. Breakfast is included in the rate, and the proprietors are positively sunny. There's a small indoor pool and free wireless Internet throughout.

$100-150

On the north side of town, **Nativo Lodge** (6000 Pan American Fwy. NE, 505/798-4300, www.nativolodge.com, $101 d) is convenient for the Balloon Fiesta, an early start to Santa Fe, or a cheap off-airport rental-car pickup, as a Hertz office is in walking distance. The price is great for this level of comfort and style, with some rooms designed by local American Indian artists. Request a room in the back so you're not overlooking I-25.

The heart of **Cinnamon Morning** (2700 Rio Grande Blvd. NW, 505/345-3541, www.cinnamonmorning.com, $125 s), in the North Valley about a mile north of Old Town, is its lavish outdoor kitchen, with a huge round dining table and a fireplace to encourage lounging on nippier nights. Rooms are simply furnished, with minimalist Southwestern detail—choose from three smaller rooms in the main house, each with a private bath, or, across the garden, a two-bedroom guesthouse and a casita with a private patio and a kitchenette.

The exceptionally tasteful ★ **Downtown Historic Bed & Breakfasts of Albuquerque** (207 High St. NE, 505/842-0223, www.albuquerquebedandbreakfasts.com, $139 s) occupies two neighboring old houses on the east side of downtown, walking distance to good restaurants on Central in the EDo (East Downtown) stretch. Heritage House has more of a Victorian feel, while Spy House has a sparer, 1940s look—but both are nicely clutter-free. Two outbuildings are more private suites.

Set in the original AT&SF railroad hospital and sporting a storied past, the stylishly renovated **Parq Central** (806 Central Ave. SE, 505/242-0040, www.hotelparqcentral.com, $145 d), opened in late 2010. The rooms are a bit small but feel light and airy thanks to big windows and gray and white furnishings, with retro chrome fixtures and honeycomb tiles in the bath. The hospital vibe is largely eradicated, though whimsical vitrines in the halls conjure old-time medical treatments, and the rooftop bar sports a gurney. Perks include free parking, a decent continental breakfast, and an airport shuttle.

A beautiful relic of early 20th-century travel, ★ **Hotel Andaluz** (125 2nd St. NW, 505/242-9090, www.hotelandaluz.com, $147 d) was first opened in 1939 by New Mexico-raised hotelier Conrad Hilton. It received a massive overhaul in 2009, keeping all the old wood and murals but updating the core to be fully environmentally friendly, from solar hot-water heaters to a composting program. The neutral-palette rooms are soothing and well designed, with a little Moorish flair in the curvy door outlines. The place is worth a visit for the lobby alone; check out the exhibits from local museums on the 2nd-floor mezzanine.

$150-250

At Albuquerque's nicest place to stay, you don't actually feel like you're anywhere near the city. ★ **Los Poblanos Historic Inn** (4803 Rio Grande Blvd. NW, 505/344-9297, www.lospoblanos.com, $235 d) sits on 25 acres, the largest remaining plot of land in the city, and the rooms are tucked in various corners of a sprawling rancho built in the 1930s by John Gaw Meem and beautifully maintained and preserved—even the huge old kitchen ranges are still in place, as are murals by Taos artist Gustave Baumann and frescoes by Peter Hurd. In the main house, the guest rooms are set around a central patio and retain their old wood floors and heavy viga ceilings. Newer, larger rooms have been added and fit in flawlessly—deluxe rooms have a

Los Poblanos Historic Inn gives guests a taste of farm life in the North Valley.

very light Southwest touch, while the farm suites have a whitewashed rustic aesthetic, accented by prints and fabrics by modernist designer Alexander Girard, of the folk-art museum in Santa Fe. (A new block of rooms was being added as this book was going to press.) There's also a saltwater pool and a gym, as well as extensive gardens. The included breakfast is exceptional, as is dinner at the restaurant, La Merienda.

North of the city, on Santa Ana Pueblo land, **Hyatt Regency Tamaya** (1300 Tuyuna Tr., Santa Ana Pueblo, 505/867-1234, www. hyattregencytamaya.com, $209 d) is a pretty resort. Rooms aren't always maintained as well as they could be, but even the standard ones are quite large, with either terraces or balconies. Three swimming pools and a full spa offer relaxation; the more active can play golf or tennis, take an archery class, or attend an evening storytelling program with a pueblo member.

Outside Albuquerque

Within 45 minutes of the city are some great natural attractions. Southeast of town, a winding road through the mountains brings you past the ruined Salinas Pueblo Missions, an intriguing bit of early Conquest history. To the east is the start of one of three routes to Santa Fe, the Turquoise Trail, which leads through some vestiges of New Mexico's mining past. An equally scenic route north is the more circuitous Jemez Mountain Trail, winding past red rocks and hot springs. Or you can zip directly up the interstate, where you'll pass the windswept region known as Tent Rocks.

SALINAS PUEBLO MISSIONS NATIONAL MONUMENT

The **Salinas Pueblo Missions** are a trio of ruined pueblos (Quarai, Gran Quivira, and Abó) southeast of Albuquerque, on the plains on the far side of the Manzano Mountains. The ruined mission churches, built by the pueblo residents under pressure from Franciscan brothers in the early years of the Conquest, stand up stark and beautiful amid the other ruined buildings. The drive here also passes one of the area's most beautiful fall hiking spots, a few very old Hispano villages, and the little town of Mountainair.

Allow the better part of a day for a leisurely drive. The whole loop route, starting and ending in Albuquerque, is about 200 miles, and straight driving time is about four hours. From Albuquerque, take I-40 east to exit 179, to the village of Tijeras (Scissors, for the way the canyons meet here), established in the 1850s. Turn south on Highway 337.

Tijeras

Fuel your drive with breakfast at **Roots Farm Café** (11784 Hwy. 337, 505/900-4118, 7am-4pm Mon.-Fri., 8am-4pm Sat.-Sun., $6),

Outside Albuquerque

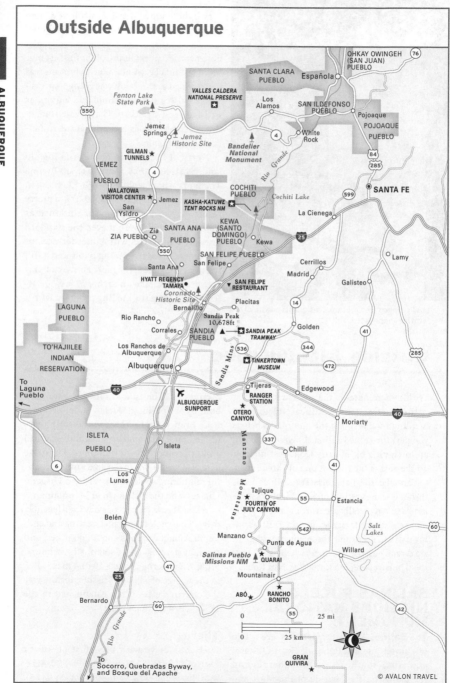

© AVALON TRAVEL

a cozy cabin space run by a couple who also own a farm up the road. In high season, some of that produce goes into the daily quiche and soup and in the pressed sandwiches. The coffee is exceptionally good.

Fourth of July Canyon

After you pass through the Spanish land grant of Chililí, Highway 337 runs into Highway 55—make a right and head to Tajique, then turn onto Forest Road 55 to reach **Fourth of July Canyon.** The area in the foothills of the Manzanos, seven miles down the dirt road, is a destination in late September and early October, when the red maples and oak trees turn every shade of pink, crimson, and orange imaginable. (Surprisingly, the place got its name not for this fireworks-like show of colors, but for the date an Anglo explorer happened across it in 1906.) The canyon is also pretty in late summer, when the rains bring wildflowers. You can explore on the short **Spring Loop Trail** or **Crimson Maple Trail,** or really get into the woods on **Fourth of July Trail** (no. 173), which wanders into the canyon 1.8 miles and connects with **Albuquerque Trail** (no. 78) to form a loop.

Technically, Forest Road 55 continues on to rejoin Highway 55 farther south, but after the Fourth of July campground, the road is not always maintained and can be very rough going. It's wiser to backtrack rather than carry on, especially if you're in a rental car.

Quarai

The first ruins you reach are those at **Quarai** (505/847-2290, www.nps.gov/sapu, 9am-6pm daily June-Aug., 9am-5pm daily Sept.-May, free), a pueblo inhabited from the 14th-17th century. Like the other two Salinas pueblos, Quarai was a hardscrabble place with no natural source of water and very little food, though it did act as a trading outpost for salt, brought from small salt lakes (*salinas*) farther east. When the Franciscans arrived, they put more than the usual strain on this community. The 400 or so Tiwa speakers nonetheless were pressed to build a grand sandstone-and-adobe mission, the most impressive of the ones at these pueblos.

The priests also found themselves at odds with the Spanish governors, who helped protect them but undermined their conversion work by encouraging ceremonial dances. At the same time, raids by Apaches increased because any crop surplus no longer went to them in trade, but to the Spanish. *And* there were terrible famines between 1663 and 1670. No wonder, then, the place was abandoned even before the Pueblo Revolt of 1680. Only the mission has been excavated; the surrounding hillocks are all pueblo structures.

Mountainair

Highway 55 meets U.S. 60 in the village of **Mountainair,** once known as the Pinto Bean Capital of the World. It's less booming now, but you can still pick up a pound of local beans at the grocery store on the main road.

You'll find the **Salinas Pueblo Missions Visitors Center** (505/847-2585, www.nps.gov/sapu, 8am-5pm daily) on U.S. 60 west of the intersection—though it offers not much more information than what's available at the small but detailed museums at each site. The **Mountainair ranger station** (505/847-2990, 8am-noon and 12:30pm-4:30pm Mon.-Fri.) is here as well; coming from the north, follow signs west off Highway 55 before you reach the U.S. 60 intersection.

Mountainair is also home to the weird architectural treasure that is the **Shaffer Hotel** (103 Main St.), a 1923 Pueblo Deco confection with a folk-art twist, built by one Clem "Pop" Shaffer, who had a way with cast concrete—look for his name in the wall enclosing the little garden. (Similar stonework of his can also be spotted in the garden at Los Poblanos in Albuquerque.) At last pass, the place was closed, but if it reopens, peek in the hotel dining room to admire the ceiling, Shaffer's masterpiece of carved and painted turtles, snakes, and other critters.

For food, stop at bustling **Alpine Alley** (210 N. Summit Ave., 505/847-2478, 6am-2pm Mon.-Fri., 8am-2pm Sat., $8), just north of the main intersection on Highway 55. This café is the town living room, serving good baked treats, soups, and creative sandwiches and drinks to a crew of regulars, many of whom have inspired the menu's concoctions.

Gran Quivira

South from Mountainair 26 miles lies Gran Quivira—a bit of a drive, and you'll have to backtrack. On the way, about one mile south of town, you'll pass another Pop Shaffer creation, **Rancho Bonito,** his actual home. As it's private property, you can't go poking around, but from the road you can see a bit of the little log cabin painted in black, red, white, and blue. (If you happen to be in Mountainair in May for its art tour, the house is open then.)

Where Highway 55 makes a sharp turn east, **Gran Quivira** (505/847-2770, www. nps.gov/sapu, 9am-6pm daily June-Aug., 9am-5pm daily Sept.-May, free) looks different from the other two Salinas pueblos because it is built of gray San Andres limestone slab and finished with plaster that was painted with symbols. It's the largest of the three, with an estimated population between 1,500 and 2,000. The array of feathers and pottery styles found here indicate the community was devoted to trade. Like the people of Abó, the

Gran Quivira, one of the Salinas Pueblo Missions

residents spoke Tompiro, and the Spanish dubbed them Los Rayados, for the striped decorations they wore on their faces. They appear to have outwardly accepted the Franciscan mission after the first sermon was preached here in 1627. But they took their own religion literally underground, building hidden kivas underneath the residential structures even as

the excavated kiva at Abó

they toiled on two successive missions ordered by the Catholics. Nonetheless, the place was deserted by 1671, after more than a third of the population had starved to death.

Abó

From Gran Quivira, drive back the way you came and turn west on U.S. 60 in Mountainair to reach **Abó** (505/847-2400, www.nps.gov/sapu, 9am-6pm daily June-Aug., 9am-5pm daily Sept.-May, free), nine miles on. This was the first pueblo the Franciscans visited, in 1622; the mission here, constructed over more than 60 years, shows details such as old wood stairs leading to the choir loft. (The Franciscans were so dedicated to re-creating the Catholic church experience here in the desert that they brought in portable pipe organs and trained their converts to sing.)

Abó is also notable for the placement of its kiva, right in the center of the *convento* (the compound adjoining the mission) and apparently dating from the same period. This suggests that the local populace came to some agreement with the priests, though no archaeologist or historian has been able to find proof of this. The excellent condition of all of these ruins is due in part to the efforts of the family that owned the land from the mid-19th century. One member, Federico Sisneros, is buried near the mission, at his request.

From Abó, continue west through the mountain pass, then down into the long, flat Rio Grande Valley on U.S. 60. It runs straight into I-25 at Bernardo, but if you're heading back to Albuquerque, you can take Highway 47 northwest to Belén, about 25 miles closer to the city.

THE TURQUOISE TRAIL

This scenic back route to Santa Fe, along the east side of the Sandias and up across high plateaus, revisits New Mexico's mining history as it passes through a series of ghost towns. From Albuquerque, it's about 70 miles and can be driven straight through in just an hour and a half.

Take I-40 east from Albuquerque to exit 175. For hiking maps of the area, bear right

Turquoise Trail

© AVALON TRAVEL

to go into the village of Tijeras and the Sandia ranger station (11776 Hwy. 337, 505/281-3304), and to gas up if you need it—it's one of the last stops until close to Santa Fe. Go left to continue directly to the junction with Highway 14, the beginning of the Turquoise Trail.

East Mountains

The four-lane road heads north through alternating communities of old Spanish land grants and modern subdivisions collectively referred to as the East Mountains. Despite a few strip malls, the area still has a distinct identity from the city; one hub of mountain culture is **Burger Boy** (12023 Hwy. 14, 505/281-3949, 8am-7pm Mon. and Wed.-Sat., 8am-4pm Sun., $8), which does a mean green-chile cheeseburger, plus a range of breakfast and lunch specials. Don't miss the paintings, inside and out, of founding owner Green Chili Bill, by Ross Ward.

In Sandia Park is a large triangle intersection—to the left is Highway 536, the so-called **Crest Road** up to Sandia Peak, a beautiful winding drive through steadily thinning forests until you reach the exposed top of the mountain, more than 10,000 feet above sea level and more than 5,500 feet above the

center of Albuquerque. At the peak is the Sandia Crest Visitor Center ($3/car), and the 1.6-mile Crest Trail along the rim.

★ Tinkertown Museum

Just 1.5 miles up the Crest Road is **Tinkertown Museum** (121 Sandia Crest Rd., 505/281-5233, www.tinkertown.com, 9am-6pm daily Apr.-Oct., $3.50), a temple to efficient use of downtime. Ross Ward, an artist, a certified circus-model builder, and a sign painter who learned his trade doing banners for carnivals, was also a master whittler and creative engineer who built, over 40 years, thousands of miniature figures and dioramas out of wood, clay, and found objects. Some of the scenes are even animated with tiny pulleys and levers: A man with a cleaver chases chickens in a circle; circus performers soar; the blacksmith's bellows huff and puff.

Much of the building is Ward's creation as well—undulating walls made of bottles and studded with odd collectibles, for instance. The museum, like an amoeba, even seems to have taken over a neighbor's 35-foot wooden boat. Ward died in 2002; his family keeps up the museum, and even though it's no longer growing as it used to, it remains a remarkable piece of pure American folk art.

Folk artist Ross Ward built the Tinkertown Museum from wood scraps and bottles.

Golden

Back on Highway 14, continue north through rolling hills and ever-broader sky. After 15 miles, you reach the all-but-gone town of **Golden,** site of the first gold strike west of the Mississippi, in 1825. All that's left now is a handful of homes, an attractive adobe church, and **Henderson Store** (10am-3:30pm Tues.-Sat.), open since 1918. It's largely given over to Indian jewelry and pottery, and antique trinkets line the upper shelves. One other small attraction: the house across the road, bedecked with thousands of colored bottles.

Madrid

Thirteen miles beyond Golden, and about midway along the drive, **Madrid** (pronounced MAD-rid) is a ghost town back from the dead. Built by the Albuquerque & Cerrillos Coal Co. in 1906, it once housed 4,000 people, but by the end of World War II, when natural gas became the norm, it was deserted. By the late 1970s, a few of the swaybacked wood houses were squatted by hippies willing to live where indoor plumbing was barely available.

Over the decades, Madrid slowly revived. Portable toilets are still more common than flush models, but the arts scene has flourished, and a real sense of community pervades the main street, which is lined with galleries and pretty painted bungalows. In 2006, the village was the setting for the John Travolta film *Wild Hogs,* and the set-piece café built for the production (now a souvenir shop) has become a minor pilgrimage site for bikers. While you're in the area, tune in to local radio station KMRD, 96.9 FM.

You can learn more about Madrid's history at the **Old Coal Town Museum** (2846 Hwy. 14, 505/473-0743, www.themineshafttavern. com, 11am-4:30pm Sat.-Sun., $5), where you can wander among sinister-looking machine parts and old locomotives. You'll feel the "ghost" in "ghost town" here.

FOOD AND ACCOMMODATIONS

The **Mine Shaft Tavern** (2846 Hwy. 14, 505/473-0743, www.themineshafttavern. com, 11:30am-7:30pm Sun.-Thurs., 11:30am-9pm Fri.-Sat.) is a vibrant remnant of Madrid's company-town days, where you can belly up to a 40-foot-long pine-pole bar. Above it are murals by local artist Ross Ward, who built the Tinkertown Museum in Sandia Park. "It is better to drink than to work," reads the Latin inscription interwoven among the mural panels, and certainly everyone in the bar, from long-distance bikers to gallery-hoppers, is living by

Shops and galleries in Madrid bring creativity and new life to an old coal-mining town.

those encouraging words. It serves solidly satisfying "New Mexico roadhouse cuisine."

For morning coffee and local gossip, hit **Java Junction** (2855 Hwy. 14, 505/438-2772, www.java-junction.com, 7:30am-close daily), which also rents a **guest room** ($129 d).

For more substance, head straight to ★ **Mama Lisa's Ghost Town Kitchen** (Hwy. 14, 505/471-5769, $10). When it's open (seemingly not on a regular basis, but chances are better in the summer, 10am-3pm or so), it's a true treat, a cozy place with an all-over-the-map menu: bison enchiladas, gluten-free pizza, lemon butter cake, and hibiscus mint tea, which you can enjoy out on the tree-shaded front patio. At the very least, get a cookie. When it's closed, all you can do is press your face against the window and dream.

The Hollar (Hwy. 14, 505/471-4821, 11am-9pm daily May-Sept., 11am-7pm Mon.-Wed., 11am-9pm Thurs.-Sun. Oct.-Apr., $9) does Southern standards like po'boys and fried okra. The green tomatoes and goat cheese are both local—and there's a special menu for dogs.

Cerrillos

The source of turquoise that has been traced to Chaco Canyon, Spain, and Chichén Itzá in Mexico's Yucatán Peninsula, **Cerrillos** hasn't been gallerified the way Madrid, its neighbor down the road, has, though many residents are wealthy escapees from Santa Fe. Representing old-time Cerrillos is a combo **petting zoo-trading post** with some llamas and goats, plus turquoise nuggets and taxidermied jackalopes, and the barest ghost of a bar, **Mary's**, filled with cats and serving primarily as the package liquor store. New-look Cerrillos is next door at **Cerrillos Station** (15-B First St., 505/474-9326), a rather swank shop, gallery, dance studio, and spa. At research time, a café was set to open in town as well.

If you want to do something besides wave to the Amtrak train in the afternoon, you can go horseback riding with the **Broken Saddle Riding Co.** (505/424-7774, www.brokensaddle.com, $85 for two hours) or hiking in **Cerrillos Hills State Park** (head north across the railroad tracks, www.nmparks.com, $5/car), which has more than 1,000 acres of rolling hills and narrow canyons that are also good for mountain biking. **Cerrillos e-Bike** (505/473-8560, www.cerrillosebike.com) rents fat-tire electric-assist bikes ($20/hour) and runs guided tours ($55/two hours). A visitors center is in the village, but is open only 2pm-4pm daily.

Mama Lisa's Ghost Town Kitchen in Madrid does fresh, colorful food.

The Home Stretch

After ascending from the canyons around Cerrillos onto a high plateau (look out for pronghorn), you're on the home stretch to Santa Fe—but you'll pass one more dining option, the **San Marcos Café** (3877 Hwy. 14, 505/471-9298, 8am-2pm daily, $10), which shares space with a working feed store where chickens and the occasional peacock scratch in the yard. Hearty meals are served in a country-style dining room (complete with potbellied stove); for breakfast, there are great cinnamon buns, homemade chicken sausage, and a variety of egg dishes.

Five miles farther, off the west side of the road, is the **"Old Main" State Penitentiary** (4337 Hwy. 14, www.corrections.state.nm.us), site of a vicious riot in 1980 that is still counted as one of the worst in American history. The state corrections department offers surprisingly detailed and thought-provoking **tours** ($15) of the old facility on Saturday in summer and early fall.

If you're heading into central Santa Fe, look for the on-ramp to I-25 (signs point to Las Vegas), then go north to the Old Santa Fe Trail exit. This is faster and prettier than continuing straight in on Highway 14, which turns into Cerrillos Road, a particularly slow and unscenic route to the plaza.

THE JEMEZ MOUNTAIN TRAIL

Beginning just northwest of Albuquerque, the **Jemez** (HAY-mez) **Mountain Trail** is a beautiful drive through Jemez Indian Reservation, the Santa Fe National Forest, and the Valles Caldera National Preserve. It's the least direct way of getting to Santa Fe—from Albuquerque, it covers about 140 miles, and you wind up near Los Alamos and must backtrack a bit south to reach the city. But anyone in search of natural beauty will want to set aside a full day for the trip, or plan an overnight in Jemez Springs, especially in the fall, when the aspen leaves turn gold against the red rocks.

The drive begins on U.S. 550, northwest out of the satellite town of Bernalillo, just west of I-25. (Stop here for gas, if necessary—stations are few on this route.) At the village of San Ysidro, bear right onto Highway 4, which forms the major part of the route north.

Jemez Pueblo

This community of some 1,800 tribal members was settled in the late 13th century, and Highway 4 runs through the middle of the 89,000 acres it still maintains. Before the Spanish arrived, the Hemish (literally, "the

red rocks at Jemez Pueblo

people," and which the Spanish spelled *Jemez*) had established more than 10 large villages in the area. **Jemez Pueblo** is quite conservative and closed to outsiders except for holidays. Because Jemez absorbed members of Pecos Pueblo in 1838, it celebrates two feast days, San Diego (November 12) and San Persingula (August 2), as well as Pueblo Independence Day (August 10), commemorating the Pueblo Revolt of 1680. It's also the only remaining pueblo where residents speak the Towa language, the rarest of the related New Mexico languages (Tewa and Tiwa are the other two).

The pueblo operates the **Walatowa Visitor Center** (575/834-7235, www.jemezpueblo.com, 8am-5pm daily Apr.-Dec., 10am-4pm Wed.-Sun. Jan.-Mar.), about five miles north of San Ysidro. You might miss it if you're gawking off the east side of the road at the vivid red sandstone cliffs at the mouth of the **San Diego Canyon.** From April till October, another, tastier distraction is the Indian fry bread and enchiladas sold by roadside vendors. The center has exhibits about the local geology and the people of Jemez and doubles as a ranger station, dispensing maps and advice on outdoor recreation farther up the road. You can take a one-mile guided hike ($5) up into the red rocks; it's a good idea to call ahead and arrange a time.

Gilman Tunnels

Blasted in the 1920s for a spur of a logging railroad, the two narrow **Gilman Tunnels** over scenic Highway 485 make a good excuse to drive up this narrow road and through a dramatic canyon. Look for the turn left (west) off Highway 4, a couple of miles after the Walatowa Visitor Center, after mile marker 9; the tunnels are about five miles along. After the tunnels, the road turns to dirt and heads into the national forest. (Sturdy vehicles can make a big loop around via Fenton Lake, rejoining Highway 4 north of Jemez Springs.)

Jemez Springs

A funky old resort town where hippies and Jemez Pueblo residents meet, **Jemez Springs**

Gilman Tunnels, off the Jemez Mountain Trail

is a handful of little clapboard buildings tucked in the narrow valley along the road. As the most convenient place to indulge in the area's springs, which have inspired tales of miraculous healing since the 1870s, the town makes for a nice afternoon pause or an overnight getaway. **Giggling Springs** (Hwy. 4, 575/829-9175, www.gigglingsprings.com, 11am-sunset Wed.-Sun., $18/one hour, 30/ two hours, $60/day) has a spring-fed pool enclosed in an attractively landscaped flagstone area right near the Jemez River; reserve ahead, as occupancy is capped at 10. The **Jemez Springs Bath House** (Hwy. 4, 575/829-3303, www.jemezspringsbathhouse.com, 10am-6pm Mon.-Tues. and Thurs.-Sat., 10am-5pm Sun., $18/hour), in one of the original historic buildings, is operated by the village. (The source is in a gazebo next door—check out the mineral buildup!) Here, the springs have been diverted into eight concrete soaking tubs—a bit austere, but with a cool historic vibe. Reserve ahead here too; massages and other spa treatments are available. The most natural springs (expect some algae) are on the riverside at the **Bodhi Manda Zen Center** (Hwy. 4, 575/829-3854, www.bmzc. org, $10 donation); payment is cash only, on the honor system.

If you're planning to explore the wilderness and missed the Walatowa Visitor Center at Jemez Pueblo, you can stop at the **Jemez Ranger District office** (Hwy. 4, 575/829-3535, 8am-4:30pm Mon.-Fri.) for info; it's on the north edge of town.

FOOD AND ACCOMMODATIONS

The **Bodhi Manda Zen Center** (Hwy. 4, 575/829-3854, www.bmzc.org), which has its own hot pools, rents bare-bones rooms ($50 pp) and offers vegetarian meals to guests. Another bargain place to stay, with a few more amenities, is the **Laughing Lizard Inn** (Hwy. 4, 575/829-3108, www.thelaughinglizard.com, $70 d); its four simple but pretty rooms, plus one suite, open onto a long porch. Just across the street, **Jemez Mountain Inn** (Hwy. 4, 575/829-3926, www.jemezmtninn.com, $95 d) is slightly plusher, and its rooms a bit quieter, as they're back from the road. Hot springs are within easy walking distance.

Next door to the Laughing Lizard, **Highway 4 Coffee** (17478 Hwy. 4, 575/829-4655, 8am-3pm Mon., Tues., and Thurs., 8am-11am Wed., 8am-4pm Fri. and Sun., 8am-7pm Sat., $6) has pastries and hearty homemade lunches. For dinner, the only place open all the time is **Los Ojos Restaurant & Saloon** (17596 Hwy. 4, 575/829-3547, 11am-midnight Mon.-Fri., 8am-midnight Sat.-Sun., $10), where horseshoes double as window grills, tree trunks act as bar stools, and the atmosphere hasn't changed in decades. Burgers are the way to go. The kitchen shuts around 9pm, and bar closing time can come earlier if business is slow, so call ahead in the evenings.

Jemez Historic Site

Just north of Jemez Springs, you pass the **Jemez Historic Site** (Hwy. 4, 575/829-3530, 8:30am-5pm Wed.-Sun., $3), a set of ruins where ancestors of the present Jemez people settled more than 700 years ago and apparently lived until 1694 or so, when De Vargas returned after the Pueblo Revolt. The old pueblo, named Giusewa, has almost entirely dissolved; as at the Salinas Pueblo Missions south of Albuquerque, the attraction is the Franciscan convent and church. Built starting around 1620, it has been partially reconstructed, enough to show how the architecture—a floor that sloped up to the altar, a unique octagonal bell tower—created maximum awe in the local populace. If you pay $5 admission, you can also visit Coronado State Monument, on the north edge of Albuquerque, on the same or next day.

A couple of curves in the highway past the monument, you reach the rocks of **Soda Dam** off the right side of the road. The pale, bulbous mineral accretions that have developed around this spring resemble nothing so much as the top of a root beer float, with a waterfall crashing through the middle. You can't really get in the water here, but it's a good photo op.

Hot Springs

Outside Jemez Springs, you pass two other opportunities to take a hot bath. Five miles north, where the red rocks of the canyon have given way to steely-gray stone and Battleship Rock looms above the road, is the start of the East Fork Trail (no. 137)—there's a dedicated parking lot just north of the picnic area. From here, the hike up the trail to **McCauley Warm Springs** is a bit more than two miles, mostly uphill; follow the trail until it meets a small stream flowing down from your left (north), then walk up the creek about a quarter mile to the spring, which has been diverted so it flows into a series of pools, only 85°F at most points. (You can also reach the springs from the other direction along East Fork Trail, parking at Jemez Falls, farther north on Highway 4; from here, the hike is downhill—but of course a slog back up.)

More accessible are **Spence Hot Springs,** about two miles north of Battleship Rock, between mile markers 24 and 25. Look for a loop parking area on the east side of the road (if it's full, there is another lot a short way north along the highway). The half-mile trail down to the river is wide and well tended, but then it's a bit more strenuous heading up the steep hillside to two sets of 100°F pools with milky-blue mineral water.

Hiking

Several trails run through the Jemez, but damage from the 2011 Las Conchas Fire has made some less scenic. Portions of **East Fork Trail** (no. 137) are still quite nice, however. The route runs between Battleship Rock (on the southwest end) and Las Conchas (on the northeast), crossing Highway 4 at a convenient midpoint. If you head south from the highway parking area (about 3 miles after a hairpin turn southeast), you reach Jemez Falls after 1 mile, then gradually descend to Battleship Rock in about 6 miles, passing McCauley Springs on the way. Heading north from the highway is fine too, following a stream through a pine forest, though near the end of 4.5 miles, you approach the burned area.

★ Valles Caldera National Preserve

Spreading out for 89,000 acres to the north of Highway 4, **Valles Caldera National Preserve** (575/829-4100, www.nps.gov/vall, $20/car) is a series of vast green valleys, rimmed by the edges of a volcano that collapsed into a huge bowl millennia ago. At the center is rounded Redondo Peak (11,254 feet), and the grasslands around it are home to herds of elk. The land has been very carefully managed since it was converted from a ranch in 2000, and it is not heavily visited—it's easy to get out into the wilderness and feel utterly alone under the dome of the sky. The entrance fee is good for seven days.

To get oriented, drive in two miles to the **visitors center** (8am-8pm daily mid-May-Sept., 9am-5pm daily Oct.-mid-May), where you can get details on the best day hikes. A full roster of guided activities is available too, in winter and summer: group day hikes, for instance, and full-moon snowshoeing in winter.

Past Valles Caldera, Highway 4 leads to Bandelier National Monument in about 20 miles. If you're carrying on to Santa Fe, it's another hour's drive (about 40 miles). Continue on Highway 4 through the town of White Rock and join Highway 502. This leads to U.S. 285, which then goes south to the capital.

Valles Caldera National Preserve

THE INTERSTATE TO SANTA FE

The most direct route north from Albuquerque to Santa Fe is along I-25, a drive of about 60 miles and just one hour without stops. The road, which passes through the broad valley between the Sandia and Jemez mountain ranges, is not as scenic as the more meandering routes, but it does cross wide swaths of the undeveloped pueblo lands of Sandia, San Felipe, and Kewa (formerly Santo Domingo).

Kewa (Santo Domingo)

The pueblo of **Kewa** (505/465-2214, www.santodomingotribe.org) is a short drive from exit 259, via Highway 22. Formerly known as Santo Domingo, this Keresan-speaking community of 2,500 people has been here since the 1200s. If you're going to Tent Rocks anyway, you'll pass a freshly repainted old-time curio stand, the **Santo Domingo Trading Post** (by the Rail Runner station stop), just reopening in fall 2016. Then it's worth a short detour west on Indian Service Route 88, to the center of the pueblo, to see the whitewashed village church, its facade adorned with two large horses. Set against the red earth here, it's a vivid image—but remember, no photography is allowed on pueblo land.

To continue to Tent Rocks, backtrack to Highway 22. The Indian service route to Cochiti does not go through.

★ Kasha-Katuwe Tent Rocks National Monument

A bit west of I-25 is **Kasha-Katuwe Tent Rocks National Monument** (Forest Rd. 266, 505/331-6259, 7am-7pm daily mid-Mar.-Oct., 8am-5pm daily Nov.-mid-Mar., $5/car), one of the region's most striking natural phenomena. The wind-whittled clusters of volcanic pumice and tuff do indeed resemble enormous tepees, some up to 90 feet tall. To reach the area, continue past Kewa Pueblo and head northwest toward Cochiti Pueblo on Highway 22. After about 15 miles, turn south in front of Cochiti Dam. In less than

Interstate 25 to Santa Fe

© AVALON TRAVEL

two miles, in the middle of the pueblo, turn right on Indian Service Route 92.

From the monument parking area, you have the choice of two short trails: An easy, relatively flat loop runs up to the base of the rocks, passing a small cave, while a longer option runs 1.5 miles into a narrow canyon where the rock towers loom up dramatically on either side. The latter trail is level at first, but the last stretch is steep and requires a little clambering. Even if you just want to take a quick peek and don't intend to hike, don't come too late in the day: The gates (close to the junction with Highway 22) are shut one hour before official closing time.

To get back to the freeway without backtracking, continue northeast on Highway 22, which makes a sharp turn at the base of Cochiti Dam (turn left, or north, and you'll reach **Cochiti Lake,** a popular summer destination for boaters). Follow Highway 22 back southeast, then take Highway 16 to rejoin the interstate at exit 264.

Kasha-Katuwe Tent Rocks National Monument

Food

At exit 252, hop off for a meal at the ★ **San Felipe Restaurant** (26 Hagen Rd., 505/867-4706, 6am-9pm daily, $8), alongside a gas station and past a short hall of dinging slot machines. Its broad diner-ish menu offers spaghetti and meatballs as well as New Mexican favorites. The pueblo dishes, such as posole with extra-thick tortillas, are excellent. Dig in alongside pueblo residents, day-trippers, and long-haul truckers.

posole at the San Felipe Restaurant

Information and Services

TOURIST INFORMATION

The **Albuquerque Convention and Visitors Bureau** (800/284-2282, www.visitalbuquerque.org) offers the most detailed information on the city, maintaining a kiosk on the Old Town plaza in the summer and a desk at the airport near the baggage claim (9:30am-8pm daily). The **City of Albuquerque** website (www.cabq.gov) is very well organized, with all the essentials about city-run attractions and services.

Books and Maps

In the North Valley, **Bookworks** (4022 Rio Grande Blvd. NW, 505/344-8139, 9am-8pm Mon.-Sat., 9am-7pm Sun.) has a large stock of New Mexico-related work as well as plenty of other titles, all recommended with the personal care of the staff.

The **University of New Mexico Bookstore** (2301 Central Ave. NE, 505/277-5451, 8am-6pm Mon.-Fri., 11am-4pm Sat.) maintains a good stock of travel titles and maps, along with state history tomes and the like. In summer, it closes an hour earlier on weekdays.

Local Media

The *Albuquerque Journal* (www.abqjournal.com) publishes cultural-events listings in the Friday entertainment supplement. On Wednesday, pick up the new issue of the free weekly *Alibi* (www.alibi.com), which will give you a hipper, more critical outlook on city goings-on, from art openings to city council debates. The free *Local Flavor* (www.localflavormagazine.com) covers food topics.

Radio

KUNM (89.9 FM) is the university's radio station, delivering eclectic music, news from NPR and PRI, and local-interest shows, such as *Singing Wire*, where you'll hear traditional Native American music as well as pop anthems like Keith Secola's oft-requested "NDN Kars" and the Black Lodge Singers chanting the Mighty Mouse theme song.

KANW (89.1 FM) is a project of Albuquerque Public Schools, with an emphasis on New Mexican music, particularly mariachi and other music in Spanish. It also hosts a Saturday-night old-time country show, and the most popular NPR programs.

SERVICES

Banks

Banks are plentiful, and grocery stores and pharmacies increasingly have ATMs inside. Downtown, look for **New Mexico Bank & Trust** (320 Gold Ave. SW, 505/830-8100, 9am-4pm Mon.-Thurs., 9am-5pm Fri.). In Nob Hill, **Wells Fargo** (3022 Central Ave. SE, 505/255-4372, 9am-5pm Mon.-Thurs., 9am-6pm Fri., 9am-1pm Sat.) is on Central at Dartmouth. Both have 24-hour ATMs.

Post Offices

Most convenient for visitors are the **Old Town Plaza Station** (303 Romero St. NW, 505/242-5927, 11am-4pm Mon.-Fri., noon-3pm Sat.), **Downtown Station** (201 5th St. SW, 505/346-1256, 9am-4:30pm Mon.-Fri.), and an office near **UNM** (115 Cornell Dr. SE, 505/346-0923, 8am-5pm Mon.-Fri.).

Internet

City-maintained **wireless hotspots** are listed at www.cabq.gov/wifi; many businesses around town also provide service.

Getting There and Around

AIR

Albuquerque International Sunport (ABQ, 505/244-7700, www.cabq.gov/airport) is a pleasant single-terminal airport served by all major U.S. airlines. It's on the south side of the city, just east of I-25, about four miles from downtown. It has free wireless Internet access. Near baggage claim is an info desk maintained by the convention and visitors bureau.

Transit from the airport includes **bus Route 50** ($1), which runs to the Alvarado Transportation Center downtown every half hour 7am-8pm, and on Saturday every hour and 10 minutes 9:45am-6:50pm; there is no Sunday service. The ride takes about 25 minutes.

Less frequent, but free, the **Airport Connection shuttle** (aka city bus Route 250) runs weekdays only (9:10am, 4:01pm, 5:09pm, and 6:10pm) to the downtown Alvarado Transportation Center (Central and 1st St.). The schedule is timed to meet the Rail Runner train to Santa Fe, departing about 30 minutes later. Another free weekday bus (Route 222) runs to the Bernalillo Rail Runner stop, though this is less convenient for visitors. Verify online at www.riometro. org, as the train schedule can change.

TRAIN

Amtrak (800/872-7245, www.amtrak. com) runs the *Southwest Chief* through Albuquerque. It arrives daily in the afternoon from Chicago and Los Angeles. The depot shares space with the Greyhound terminal, downtown on 1st Street, south of Central Avenue and the Alvarado Transportation Center.

The **Rail Runner** (866/795-7245, www. riometro.org) connects downtown Santa Fe with Albuquerque and continues as far south as Belén. The main stop in Albuquerque is downtown, at the Alvarado Transportation Center, at Central and 1st Street. If the not-so-frequent schedule fits yours, it's fantastic service to or from Santa Fe, but within Albuquerque, the system doesn't go anywhere visitors typically go. If you ride, keep your ticket—you get a free transfer from the train to any city bus.

The Rail Runner connects Albuquerque and Santa Fe.

BUS

Greyhound (800/231-2222, www.greyhound.com) runs buses from all major points east, west, north, and south, though departures are not frequent. The bus station (320 1st St. SW, 505/243-4435) is downtown, just south of Central Avenue. Cheaper *and* nicer are the bus services that cater to Mexicans traveling across the Southwest and into Mexico, though they offer service only to Las Cruces and Denver; **El Paso-Los Angeles Limousine Express** (2901 Pan American Fwy. NE, 505/247-8036, www.eplalimo.com) is the biggest operator, running since 1966.

With the city bus system, **ABQ Ride** (505/243-7433, www.cabq.gov/transit), it's possible to reach all the major sights along Central Avenue, but you can't get to the Sandia Peak Tramway or anywhere in the East Mountains. The most tourist-friendly bus line is Route 66 (of course), along Central Avenue, linking Old Town, downtown, and Nob Hill; service runs until a bit past 1am on summer weekends. The double-length red **Rapid Ride** buses (Route 766) follow the same route but stop at only the most popular stops. The fare for all buses, regardless of trip length, is $1 (coins or bills, no change given); passes are available for one ($2), two ($4), and three ($6) days and can be purchased on the bus. The D-Ride bus is a free loop-route bus around downtown that runs weekdays 6:30am-5:30pm.

CAR

From Santa Fe, Albuquerque is 60 miles (one hour) south on I-25; from Las Cruces, it is 225 miles (a little more than three hours) north on I-25. From Denver, the drive takes about 6.5 hours (445 miles); Phoenix is about the same distance west on I-40.

All the major car-rental companies are in a single complex adjacent to the airport, connected by shuttle bus. **Hertz** and **Enterprise** offer service at the Amtrak depot (really just a refund for the cab ride to the airport offices). Hertz's two other city locations are usually less expensive because you bypass the airport service fee; if you're renting for more than a week, the savings can offset the cab fare.

BIKE

Albuquerque's **bike-route system** (www.cabq.gov/bike) is reasonably well developed, the terrain is flat, and the sun is usually shining. Rent bikes from **Routes** (404 San Felipe St. NW, 505/933-5667, www.routesrentals.com, 8am-7pm Mon.-Fri., 7am-7pm Sat.-Sun. Mar.-Oct., 9am-6pm Mon.-Fri., 8am-6pm Sat.-Sun. Nov.-Feb., $15/hour, $35/day). You can also try the **bikeshare program** (www zagster.com/abq, $3/1.5 hours) that covers downtown and Old Town. If you think you might use the bikes more than one day, applying for the monthly pass ($15) may be a better deal.

Santa Fe

Sights 79
Entertainment and Events 91
Shopping. 95
Sports and Recreation 96
Food 100

Accommodations. 105
Outside Santa Fe 108
Information and Services 129
Getting There and Around 130

One of Santa Fe's several monikers is "Fanta Se," a play on the name that suggests the city's disconnection from reality.

And indeed, this small cluster of mud-colored buildings in the mountains of northern New Mexico does seem to subsist on dreams alone, as this city of 70,000 has a larger proportion of writers, artists, and performers than any other community in the United States. In the local Yellow Pages, "Art galleries" take up five pages, and "Artists" have their own heading. In all, nearly half the city is employed in the larger arts industry. (Cynics would lump the state legislature, which convenes in the capitol here, into this category as well.)

The city fabric itself is a by-product of this creativity—many of the "adobe" buildings in the distinctive downtown area are in fact plaster and stucco, built in the early 20th century to satisfy an official vision of what Santa Fe ought to look like to appeal to tourists. And the mix of old-guard Spanish, Pueblo Indians, groovy Anglos, and international jet-setters of all stripes has even developed a soft but distinct accent—a vaguely continental intonation, with a vocabulary drawn from the 1960s counterculture and alternative healing.

What keeps Santa Fe grounded, to use the local lingo, is its location, tucked in the foothills of the Sangre de Cristos. The wilderness is never far, even if you're just admiring the forest view from your massage table at a Japanese-style spa or dining at an elegant restaurant on lamb that grazed in high meadows. You can be out of town at a trailhead in 15 minutes, skiing down a precipitous slope in 30, or wandering among the hills you've seen in Georgia O'Keeffe's paintings of Abiquiu in 60. East of the city is the Pecos Wilderness Area, a couple of hundred thousand acres studded with summits such as Santa Fe Baldy and Truchas Peak.

Santa Fe's history, too, gives it strong roots. It's the second-oldest city in the United States (after St. Augustine, Florida), and it's surrounded by pueblos that have been inhabited since well before the Spanish arrived, alongside remnants of older settlements, such as the cliff dwellings in Bandelier National Monument. As the capital of the Spanish territory of Nuevo México, Santa Fe was a

Previous: Santuario de Chimayó; Georgia O'Keeffe's favorite mountain, Pedernal, as seen from Ghost Ranch. **Above:** a corn-and-chile wreath on a Santa Fe door.

Look for ★ to find recommended
sights, activities, dining, and lodging.

Highlights

★ **New Mexico Museum of Art:** See the state's long history of creative output, all in one place (page 83).

★ **Canyon Road Galleries:** This winding street is the heart of Santa Fe's art scene—and its social life—when it's packed with potential collectors and party hoppers on summer Friday nights (page 86).

★ **Museum of International Folk Art:** In the main exhibition hall, all the world's crafts, from Appalachian quilts to Zulu masks, are jumbled together in an inspiring display of human creativity (page 89).

★ **House of Eternal Return:** Meow Wolf's immersive installation expands the mind—and the definition of art in Santa Fe. Appropriate for anyone ages 6-106, it's also a lot of fun (page 90).

★ **Bandelier National Monument:** The hidden valley of Frijoles Canyon was home to the ancestors of today's Pueblo people, in an elaborate city complex with cliff-side cave apartments (page 115).

★ **Ghost Ranch:** The spread where Georgia O'Keeffe kept a house has dramatic cliffs and windblown pinnacles. Check out the dinosaur museum and hike to Chimney Rock for a view across Abiquiu (page 121).

★ **Santuario de Chimayó:** Faith is palpable in this village church north of Santa Fe, known as "the Lourdes of America," thanks to the healing powers attributed to the holy dirt found here (page 125).

Santa Fe

0 — 0.5 mi
0 — 0.5 km

To
Santa Fe Airport,
and La Tierra Trails

▼ PLAZA CAFE SOUTHSIDE

AIRPORT RD

To
Rancho de las Golondrinas

▼ HORSEMAN'S HAVEN

To
Public Lands Information Center,
Hwy 14, and Albuquerque

To
Café Fina and Lamy

HARRY'S
ROADHOUSE ★

© AVALON TRAVEL

RUFINA ST

ZAFARANO DR

14

RUFINA
CIRCLE

HOUSE OF
ETERNAL RETURN ✦

SILER RD

SILER LN

JACKALOPE •

SILVER SADDLE
MOTEL •

SF UNIVERSITY
OF ART & DESIGN

CERRILLOS RD

2A RD

LLANO ST

SIRINGO RD

ST. MICHAEL'S DR

285
84

RODEO RD

25

285

ST. FRANCIS DR

W ALAMEDA ST

AGUA FRIA ST

OSAGE AVE

Santa Fe River

SECOND STREET
BREWERY ●

THE
PANTRY ■
EL REY
INN

2ND ST

LENA ST

BACA ST

ST. FRANCIS DR

SANTA FE
INTERNATIONAL HOSTEL

COUNTER
CULTURE ▼

EL CHILE
TOREADO ▼

WHOO'S DONUTS/
CHOCOLATESMITH ▼

OHORI'S ●

MARIA'S ▼

DON DIEGO AVE

CORDOVA

DON GASPAR ST

BODY OF
SANTA FE

ST. VINCENT
HOSPITAL ■

CORDOVA
RD

OLD PECOS TRAIL

CAMINO LEJO

OLD PECOS TRAIL

OLD SANTA FE TRAIL

WHEELWRIGHT
MUSEUM OF THE
AMERICAN INDIAN

MUSEUM OF THE
INTERNATIONAL FOLK ART ✦

MUSEUM OF
INTERNATIONAL FOLK ART

MUSEUM OF INDIAN
ARTS & CULTURE ★

MUSEUM OF SPANISH
COLONIAL ART

CAMINO DEL MONTE SOL

ST. JOHN'S
COLLEGE ★

Santa Fe
Canyon Preserve

To
Santa Fe
Canyon

TUNE-UP
CAFE ■

HICKOX ST

ALTO RD

Santa Fe Opera and
Highway 599

To

285

84

"DOWNTOWN SANTA FE"
SEE MAP

Railyard
Park

NEW MEXICO
MUSEUM OF ART ✦

QUAKER
MEETING
HOUSE ●

PASEO DE PERALTA

PALACE AVE

CANYON RD

NOART
GALLERY ●

EL FAROL ▼

DEVARGAS
CENTER ■

CANYON ROAD
GALLERIES ✦

GONZALES RD

HYDE PARK RD

475

UPPER CANYON RD.

To
Tesuque

To
Ten Thousand
Waves and Dale
Ball Trails

Ft. Marcy
Park

Santa Fe Weekend Getaway

- **Day 1:** Fly in to Albuquerque. Head to Santa Fe via the scenic **Turquoise Trail** and check in to your hotel: **La Fonda** for a touch of history, or **Inn of the Governors.** If it's summertime, head to **Canyon Road** for the gallery crawl, which gets started around 5pm. In winter, have a cocktail at **Secreto Lounge,** then walk over to dinner at **Joseph's.**

- **Day 2:** Pick up breakfast at the **French Pastry Shop.** Traditionalists can spend the morning at the **New Mexico Museum of Art** and **Georgia O'Keeffe Museum.** Quirkier taste? Head for the **House of Eternal Return** and **Museum of International Folk Art.** In the afternoon, soak in a private hot tub at **Ten Thousand Waves,** followed by a massage then dinner at the spa's restaurant, **Izanami.** Hit the late-night movie at the **Jean Cocteau Cinema.**

- **Day 3:** Take an early-morning hike on the **Dale Ball Trails** or a less strenuous stroll around the **Santa Fe Canyon Preserve.** Treat yourself to brunch at **Harry's Roadhouse** or **Café Fina,** a little south of town, for high-end diner-style goodies and one last great view. Then drive back down I-25 to catch your flight out.

far-flung outpost, a gateway to the wilder, emptier lands to the north. And it still is, with two scenic routes running north to Taos: The high road winds along mountain ridges, while the low road follows the Rio Grande.

PLANNING YOUR TIME

Santa Fe is an ideal destination for a **three-day weekend.** Add another day or two to take a hike outside of town or make the drive to Taos, Los Alamos, or Abiquiu. **Summer** is ultra-high season, especially for Spanish Market and Indian Market, in July and August, respectively. This is also when the gallery scene is in full swing; plan to be in the city on a Friday night, when the Canyon Road galleries have their convivial openings.

In **fall,** the city is much calmer and offers beautiful hiking because the hills are greener, and in October, dense groves of aspen trees on the Sangre de Cristo Mountains turn bright yellow. As in the rest of New Mexico, **spring** and early summer can be hot and windy, but the city is still pleasant, as lilacs bloom in May, tumbling over adobe walls and filling the air with scent. **Winter** is cold and occasionally snowy, but clear. Late December in Santa Fe is a special time, as houses are decked with paper-bag lanterns (*farolitos*), and bonfires light Canyon Road on Christmas Eve. After this, in January and February, hotel prices can drop dramatically, as the few tourists in town are here only to ski.

ORIENTATION

Santa Fe is a small town. Most of the major sights are within walking distance from the central plaza. Generally, you'll find yourself within the oval formed by **Paseo de Peralta,** a main road that almost completely circles the central district. On its southwest side it connects with **Cerrillos Road,** a main avenue lined with motel courts, shopping plazas, and chain restaurants. Compared with the central historic district, it's unsightly, but there are some great local places to eat here, as well as the few inexpensive hotels in town.

HISTORY

Around 1609, La Villa Real de la Santa Fé (The Royal City of the Holy Faith) was established as the capital of Spain's northernmost territory in the New World. The Camino Real, the route that connected the outpost with Mexico, ended in the newly built plaza. Mexico's independence from Spain in 1821 marked a shift in the city's fortunes, as the new government opened up its northernmost territory to outside trade, via the Santa Fe Trail, from Missouri.

When the railroad arrived in nearby Lamy in 1880, it spurred what's still Santa Fe's life-blood: tourism. Loads of curious Easterners flocked in. In 1912, a council of city planners decided to promote Santa Fe as a tourist destination and preserve its distinctive architecture. By 1917, the Museum of Fine Arts (now the New Mexico Museum of Art) had opened, and the first Indian Market was held in 1922, in response to the trend of Anglos collecting local craft work.

A new element was added to Santa Fe's mix in 1943, when the building at 109 East Palace Avenue became the "front office" and only known address for Los Alamos, where the country's greatest scientists were developing the atomic bomb under a cloud of confidentiality. But the rational scientists left little mark. Right-brain thinking has continued to flourish, and the city is a modern, creative version of its old self, a meeting place where international art dealers swap goods and ideas.

Sights

DOWNTOWN
Santa Fe Plaza

When Santa Fe was established in 1610, its layout was based on Spanish laws governing town planning in the colonies—hence the central plaza fronted by the Casas Reales (Palace of the Governors) on its north side. The **Santa Fe Plaza** is still the city's social hub, and the blocks surrounding it are rich with history. In the center of the plaza is the **Soldiers' Monument,** now also a monument to how history gets rewritten. On the original panel, dedicated in 1867 to those who died in "battles with [. . .] Indians in the territory of New Mexico," the word "savage" was excised in the 1970s, following a debate about the word. One activist took it upon himself to chisel out the word himself, even as some Pueblo leaders thought the word should stand, on the logic that it could accurately describe the way in which Native people fought the Spanish at the time. Another, later panel has been modified too, as "rebel," referring to Southern forces in the Civil War, has been cut away. And then next to it all is yet another plaque, apologizing for the whole mess.

relaxing on Santa Fe Plaza

Downtown Santa Fe

© AVALON TRAVEL

Along the north side, under the portal of the **Palace of the Governors,** is one of the more iconic sights of Santa Fe: American Indians from all over New Mexico selling their craft work as they've been doing since the 1930s. More than 500 vendors are licensed to sell here after going through a strict application process that evaluates their technical skills. Every morning the 69 spots, each 12 bricks wide, are doled out by lottery. Expect anything from silver bracelets to pottery to *heishi* (shell bead) necklaces to freshly harvested piñon nuts. It's a great opportunity to buy direct from a skilled artisan and learn about the work that went into a piece.

New Mexico History Museum and Palace of the Governors

Opened in 2009, the **New Mexico History Museum** (113 Lincoln Ave., 505/476-5200, www.nmhistorymuseum.org, 10am-5pm daily May-Oct., 10am-5pm Tues.-Sun. Nov.-Apr., $9) was intended to give a little breathing room for a collection that had been in storage for decades. Oddly, though, it feels like very few actual objects are on display. The permanent exhibits give a good overview, though if you're already familiar with the state's storied past, you might not find much new here.

Your ticket also admits you to the adjacent **Palace of the Governors,** the former seat of Santa Fe's government, and a generally more interesting display. Built 1610-1612, it's one of the oldest government buildings in the United States, giving it plenty of time to accumulate stories. De Vargas fought the Indian rebels here room by room when he retook the city in 1693; ill-fated Mexican governor Albino Pérez was beheaded in his office in 1837; and Governor Lew Wallace penned *Ben Hur* here in the late 1870s. The exhibits here showcase some of the most beautiful items in the state's collection: trinkets and photos from the 19th century, as well as the beautiful 18th-century Segesser hide paintings, two wall-size panels of buffalo skin. These works, along with the room they're in (trimmed with 1909 murals of the Puyé cliffs) are worth the price of admission. In a couple of the restored furnished rooms, you can compare the living conditions of the Mexican leadership circa 1845 to the relative comfort the U.S. governor enjoyed in 1893.

The museum has **free admission** every Friday (5pm-8pm) May-October, and the

the Palace of the Governors

New Mexico Museum of Art

first Friday of the month in winter. **Walking tours** depart from the blue gate on the Lincoln Avenue side of the New Mexico History Museum at 10:15am (Mon.-Sat. mid-Apr.-mid-Oct., $10), covering all the plaza-area highlights in about two hours.

★ New Mexico Museum of Art

Famed as much for its building as for what it contains, the **New Mexico Museum of Art** (107 W. Palace Ave., 505/476-5072, www.nmartmuseum.org, 10am-5pm daily May-Oct., 10am-5pm Tues.-Sun. Nov.-Apr., $9) is dedicated to work by New Mexican artists. Built in 1917, it is a beautiful example of Pueblo Revival architecture, originally designed as the New Mexico pavilion for a world expo in San Diego two years prior. The curvaceous stucco-clad building combines elements from the most iconic pueblo mission churches—the bell towers, for instance, mimic those found at San Felipe. Inside, the collection starts with Gerald Cassidy's oil painting *Cui Bono?*, on display since the museum's

opening in 1917 and still relevant, as it questions the benefits of pueblo tourism. Look out for an excellent collection of Awa Tsireh's meticulous watercolors of ceremonial dances at San Ildefonso Pueblo, alongside works by other local American Indian artists.

On your way out, don't miss the adjacent St. Francis Auditorium, where three artists adorned the walls with art nouveau murals depicting the life of Santa Fe's patron saint. It's rare to see a secular style—usually reserved for languorous ladies in flowing togas—used to render such scenes as the apotheosis of Saint Francis and Santa Clara's renunciation, and the effect is beautiful.

As at the history museum, Friday evenings (5pm-8pm) are **free admission** in summer; November-April, only the first Friday of the month is free. Free docent-led **tours** around the museum run daily at 10:30am and 2pm. The museum also runs art-themed **walking tours** ($10) around the city center at 10am Monday; June-August, they also run at 10am Friday.

Cathedral Basilica of St. Francis of Assisi

Santa Fe's showpiece **Cathedral Basilica of St. Francis of Assisi** (131 Cathedral Pl., 505/982-5619, www.cbsfa.org, 9:30am-4:30pm Mon.-Sat., free), visible from the plaza at the end of East San Francisco Street, was built over some 15 years in the late 19th century, by domineering Bishop Jean-Baptiste Lamy. For more than three decades, the Frenchman struggled to "elevate" the city to European standards, and his folly is exemplified in this grandiose cathedral.

Lamy looked down on the locals' religious practices, as the cult of the Virgin of Guadalupe was already well established, and the Penitente brotherhood was performing public self-flagellation. He also disliked their aesthetics. How could a person possibly reach heaven while praying on a dirt floor inside a building made of mud? Lamy assessed the tiny adobe church dedicated to St. Francis of Assisi, which had stood for 170 years, and decided he could do better. Construction on his Romanesque revival St. Francis Cathedral began in 1869, under the direction of architects and craftsmen from Europe. They used the old church as a frame for the new stone structure, then demolished all of the adobe, save for a small side chapel. Lamy ran short of cash, however—hence the stumpy aspect of the cathedral's facade, which should be topped with domed towers.

Inside is all Gothic-inspired light and space and glowing stained-glass windows, with a gilt altar screen installed in 1987, for the centennial of the building's dedication. It features primarily New World saints, such as Kateri Tekakwitha, a 17th-century Mohawk woman beatified in 1980 and canonized in 2012 (her statue also stands outside the cathedral). She is depicted with a turtle, representing her membership in the Turtle Clan.

The salvaged adobe chapel is to the left of the altar. It is dedicated to the figure of La Conquistadora, a statue brought to Santa Fe from Mexico in 1625, carried away by the retreating Spanish during the Pueblo Revolt, then proudly reinstated in 1693 and honored ever since. She glows in her shimmering robes, under a heavy viga ceiling. Lamy, who died in 1888, probably shudders in his crypt in front of the main altar.

On your way out, check the great cast-bronze doors—they're usually propped open, so you'll have to peer behind to see the images depicting the history of Catholicism in New Mexico. One plaque shows the Italian stoneworkers constructing the cathedral, and another shows families fleeing from attack in 1680—a rare depiction of the Pueblo Revolt that's sympathetic to the Spanish.

Museum of Contemporary Native Arts

Set in the city's former post office, the **Museum of Contemporary Native Arts** (108 Cathedral Pl., 505/983-8900, www.iaia. edu, 10am-5pm Mon. and Wed.-Sat., noon-5pm Sun., $10) is the showcase for students, professors, and alumni of the prestigious

Cathedral Basilica of St. Francis of Assisi

Institute of American Indian Arts. The space is relatively small, and the shows can be hit or miss. If your time is limited, the Museum of Indian Arts & Culture is a better bet. The gift shop stocks items with a good blend of modern and traditional styles.

Loretto Chapel

Initiated by Bishop Lamy in 1873, the **Loretto Chapel** (207 Old Santa Fe Tr., 505/982-0092, 9:30am-4:30pm Mon.-Sat., 10:30am-4:30pm Sun., $3) was the first Gothic structure built west of the Mississippi. It's a beautiful interior with a great story to match, although the recording broadcast inside (the place was de-sanctified in 1971) explaining all this is slightly maddening, on endless loop.

The chapel's decorative elements reflect Lamy's fondness for all things European: the stations of the cross rendered by Italian masons, the harmonium and stained-glass windows imported from France. Even the stone from which it was built was hauled at great expense from quarries 200 miles south.

What draws the eye is the elegant spiral staircase leading to the choir loft. Made entirely of wood, it makes two complete turns without a central support pole. It was built in 1878 by a mysterious carpenter who appeared seemingly at the spiritual behest of the resident Sisters of Loretto. The carpenter toiled in silence for six months, the story goes, then disappeared, without taking any payment. He was never heard from again—though some historians claim to have tracked him down to Las Cruces, where he met his end in a bar fight.

San Miguel Mission

The **San Miguel Mission** (401 Old Santa Fe Tr., 505/983-3974, 10am-4pm Mon.-Sat., $1, free silent worship 5pm-7pm Thurs.) is a sturdy adobe building where Mass is still said in Latin at noon on Sunday. It is the oldest church structure in the United States, and it's set in Barrio de Analco, the city's oldest residential neighborhood, at the head of De Vargas, the oldest street. The church was built starting in 1610, then partially reconstructed a century later, after it was set aflame in the Pueblo Revolt. Its stone buttresses are the product of a desperate attempt to shore up the sagging walls in the late 19th century.

The interior is snug and whitewashed, with a restored altar screen that had been covered over in house paint for decades. The late 18th-century work is attributed to the anonymous Laguna Santero, a Mexican artist who earned his name from the intricately carved and painted screen at the Laguna Pueblo church, near Albuquerque. The screen functions as an enormous picture frame, with both oil paintings and *bultos* (painted wood statues of saints) inserted in the openings. In front of the altar, cutouts in the floor reveal the building's original foundations.

The old church bell, set at the back of the church, is said to have been cast in Spain in 1356. It was brought to the New World and installed at San Miguel in the early 19th century, and it hums beautifully even when tapped.

New Mexico State Capitol

A round building with an entrance at each of the cardinal points, the 1966 **New Mexico State Capitol** (491 Old Santa Fe Tr.) mimics the zia sun symbol used on the state flag. In the center of the rotunda is a mosaic rendition of the state seal: the Mexican brown eagle, grasping a snake and shielded by the American bald eagle. And don't forget to look up at the stained-glass skylight, with its intricate Indian basket-weave pattern.

San Miguel Mission

The New Mexico State Capitol holds an excellent art collection that's free to browse.

But the real attraction of the Roundhouse, as the building is commonly known, is its excellent but often overlooked **art collection** (505/986-4589, www.nmcapitolart.org, 8am-5:30pm Mon.-Fri., also Sat. June-Aug., free), with works by the state's best-known creatives. You'll find paintings and photographs in the halls on every floor, in the upstairs balcony area of the senate, and in the 4th-floor Governor's Gallery.

Oh, and the building is used for legislating—though not particularly often (beginning on the third Tuesday in January, for 30 days in even-numbered years, and 60 days in odd). When house and senate meetings are in session, visitors are welcome to sit in the galleries and watch the proceedings.

Georgia O'Keeffe Museum

Opened in 1997, the **Georgia O'Keeffe Museum** (217 Johnson St., 505/946-1000, www.okeeffemuseum.org, 10am-5pm Sat.-Thurs., 10am-7pm Fri., $12), northwest of the plaza, honors the artist whose name is inextricably bound with New Mexico. The contrarian member of the New York avant-garde ("Nothing is less real than realism," she famously said) started making regular visits to the state in the 1920s, then moved to Abiquiu full-time in 1949, a few years after the death of her husband, photographer Alfred Stieglitz.

Many of O'Keeffe's finest works—her signature sensuous, near-abstract flower blossoms, for instance—have already been ensconced in other famous museums, so the collection here can seem a little thin. Exhibits draw on the work that she kept, plus ephemera and other work her foundation has amassed since her death in 1986. Often the space is given over to exhibitions on her contemporaries or those whose work she influenced or admired.

CANYON ROAD

This narrow one-way street southeast of the plaza epitomizes "Santa Fe style," or at least the ritzy side of it. The galleries are the primary draw, but it's worth heading a bit off the main drag too. There's a city **parking** lot at the east (upper) end of the road. Public **restrooms** (9:30am-5:30pm daily) are near the west end, in the complex at 225 Canyon Road, behind Expressions gallery.

★ Canyon Road Galleries

The intersection of Paseo de Peralta and Canyon Road is ground zero for the city's **art market.** This is the beginning of a half-mile strip that contains more than 80 galleries. In his fortune in 1881. Its **garden** (9am-5pm Mon.-Sat.), laid out in the late 19th century, is a lovely place to rest in the summer.

GUADALUPE AND THE RAILYARD

This neighborhood southwest of the plaza developed around the depot for the rail spur from the main line at Lamy. Now it's the terminus for the Rail Runner from Albuquerque. The clutch of cafés and shops here are more casual and local, and generally lighter on the adobe look, as **Guadalupe Street** is just outside the most stringently policed historic zone.

South of the train depot is **The Railyard** (www.railyardsantafe.com), a mixed-use district where former warehouses and workshops have been adapted to new business, including a permanent indoor home for the city's farmers market. The south side of this area is the green space of **Railyard Park,** nicely landscaped with local grasses and fruit trees.

Santuario de Guadalupe

Built 1776-1796, the **Santuario de Guadalupe** (417 Agua Fria St., 505/983-8868, 9am-noon and 1pm-4pm Mon.-Sat., free) is the oldest shrine to the Virgin of Guadalupe in the United States. The interior is spare, in front of a Mexican baroque oil-on-canvas altar painting from 1783. Mass is still said regularly, and a museum in the small anteroom displays relics from earlier incarnations of the building, such as Greek-style columns carved in wood. In winter, the church is closed on Saturday.

SITE Santa Fe

The boxy, modern exhibition space of **SITE Santa Fe** (1606 Paseo de Peralta, 505/989-1199, www.sitesantafe.org, 10am-5pm Thurs. and Sat., 10am-7pm Fri., noon-5pm Sun., $10) was started in 1995 to bring a biennial contemporary art show to the city. In the years since, the organization has expanded to show edgy art year-round, often installations that take over the whole interior (and sometimes exterior). In July and August, it's also open on Wednesday, and entrance is free on Friday and Saturday till

Canyon Road's galleries range from formal to funky.

the summer, Canyon Road is a solid mass of strolling art lovers—pro collectors and amateurs alike. It's especially thronged on summer Fridays, when most galleries have an open house or an exhibition opening, from around 5pm until 7pm or 8pm.

Hard to believe, but the street wasn't always chockablock with thousand-dollar canvases. Long ago, it was farmland, irrigated by the "Mother Ditch," Acequia Madre, which still runs parallel one block to the south. Starting in the 1920s, transplant artists settled on this muddy dirt road, and the area gradually came to be associated with creative exploits. Eventually the art market really boomed in the 1980s.

In addition to the galleries, you'll also pass the mid-19th-century house **El Zaguán,** which contains the offices of the **Historic Santa Fe Foundation** (545 Canyon Rd., 505/983-2567, www.historicsantafe.org, 9am-noon and 1:30pm-3pm Mon.-Fri., free). Named for its long internal hallway (*zaguán*), the building was the home of a local merchant, James L. Johnson, from 1854, and then occupied by several other city bigwigs after he lost

It's Not *All* Adobe

Catron Building on the plaza

Santa Fe's distinctive look is the product of stringent building codes that define and maintain "old Santa Fe style," from the thickness of walls (at least eight inches) to the shade of stucco finish, in only "brown, tan, or local earth tones." But look closely, and you'll see some variations. **Colonial** is the term applied to adobe (or adobe-look) buildings, usually one story, with their typical rounded edges and flat roofs supported by vigas, the long crossbeams made of single tree trunks. The style mimics one developed by the Spanish colonists in the 16th, 17th, and 18th centuries, based on their previous experience with adobe architecture and forms they saw in the pueblos.

In the 19th century, when New Mexico became a U.S. territory and the railroad could carry new building materials, timber-frame houses came into fashion. These so-called **territorial** buildings were often two stories tall, with balconies, and trimmed with brick cornices and Greek revival details, such as fluted wood columns and pediments above windows. The Catron Building, on the northeast corner of the plaza, is a fine example of the style developed in this period.

In the early part of the 20th century, the **Pueblo Revival** style was the product of architects like John Gaw Meem and Isaac Rapp, who admired the pueblo mission churches and Spanish colonial adobes for their clean-lined minimalism. Because they used frame construction, Pueblo Revival buildings could be taller: Rapp's New Mexico Museum of Art towers on the northwest corner of the plaza, and Meem's additions to La Fonda hotel make it five stories. The trend coincided with an aggressive tourism campaign and the development of a comprehensive look for the city, and in the process many territorial houses were simply covered over in a thick layer of faux-adobe plaster. The result is not really true to history, but the city planners achieved their goal: Santa Fe looks like no other city in the United States.

noon, when the farmers market is on, kitty-corner across the train tracks. The building will be expanding substantially in late 2017.

MUSEUM HILL

These museums on the southeast side merit the trip from the plaza area. It's a short drive, or you can take the "M" route bus or the free Santa Fe Pick-Up shuttle, optionally strolling back downhill to the center, about a 30-minute walk.

Museum of Spanish Colonial Art

The museum of the **Spanish Colonial Arts Society** (750 Camino Lejo, 505/982-2226, www.spanishcolonial.org, 10am-5pm daily June-Aug., 10am-5pm Tues.-Sun. Sept.-May, $8) exhibits a strong collection of folk art and historical objects dating from the earliest Spanish contact. One-of-a-kind treasures—such as the only signed *retablo* by the 19th-century *santero* Rafael Aragón—are shown alongside more utilitarian items from the colonial past, such as silk mantas, wool rugs, and decorative tin. New work by contemporary artisans is also on display—don't miss Luis Tapia's meta-*bulto*, *The Folk-Art Collectors.*

Museum of Indian Arts & Culture

The excellent **Museum of Indian Arts & Culture** (710 Camino Lejo, 505/476-1250, www.miaclab.org, 10am-5pm daily May-Oct., 10am-5pm Tues.-Sun. Nov.-Apr., $9) is devoted to Native American culture from across the country. Cornerstone exhibit *Here, Now and Always* traces the New Mexican Indians from their ancestors on the mesas and plains up to their present-day efforts at preserving their culture. It displays inventive spaces (looking into a HUD-house kitchen on the rez, or sitting at desks in a public schoolroom), sound clips, and stories. Another wing is devoted to contemporary art, while the halls of craft work display gorgeous beaded moccasins, elaborate headdresses, and more. The gift shop has beautiful jewelry and other tidbits from local artisans.

★ Museum of International Folk Art

A marvelous hodgepodge, the **Museum of International Folk Art** (708 Camino Lejo, 505/476-1200, www.internationalfolkart.org, 10am-5pm daily May-Oct., 10am-5pm Tues.-Sun. Nov.-Apr., $9) is one of Santa Fe's biggest treats—if you can handle visual overload. In

the Museum of Indian Arts & Culture on Museum Hill

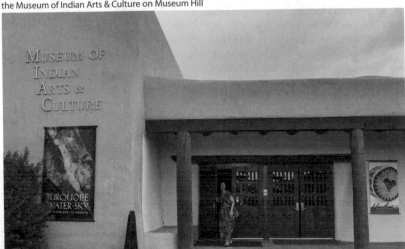

the main exhibition space, some 10,000 folk-art pieces from more than 100 countries are on permanent display, hung on walls, set in cases, even dangling from the ceiling, juxtaposed to show off similar themes, colors, and materials. The approach initially seems jumbled but in fact underscores the universality of certain concepts and preoccupations. Join a guided **tour** (10:30am, 11:30am, and 2pm) to learn all the details.

A separate wing is dedicated to northern New Mexican Hispano crafts (a good complement to the Museum of Spanish Colonial Art) and a lab area where you can see how pieces are preserved. Temporary exhibits take up the rest of the space, usually with colorful interactive shows. Don't skip the gift shop, which stocks some smaller versions of the items in the galleries.

Wheelwright Museum of the American Indian

In the early 1920s, Mary Cabot Wheelwright, an adventurous East Coast heiress, made her way to New Mexico, where she met a Navajo medicine man named Hastiin Klah. Together they devised the **Wheelwright Museum of the American Indian** (704 Camino Lejo, 505/982-4636, www.wheelwright.org, 10am-5pm daily, $5), which opened in 1937 as the House of Navajo Religion. The mission has since incorporated all Native American cultures, with exhibits of new work by individual artists rotating every few months. The building is modeled after a traditional Navajo hogan, with huge timbers supporting the eight-sided structure, and a new wing (added in 2015) is dedicated to Southwestern jewelry. The basement gift shop is a re-creation of a 19th-century trading post, which would feel like a tourist trap if it weren't for the authentically creaky wood floors and the beautiful antique crafts on display.

SANTA FE METRO AREA
★ House of Eternal Return

The work of young Santa Fe art collective Meow Wolf, which specializes in elaborate installations, is hard to explain. Its most elaborate work yet is **House of Eternal Return** (1352 Rufina Circle, 505/780-4458, www.meowwolf.com, 10am-8pm Wed.-Mon., $18), a permanent project installed in a 30,000-square-foot former bowling alley. Exploring the space is a bit like being inside a very, very psychedelic video game, as everything moves, glows, or emits music. Hidden throughout the "house" are cryptic pieces of a story about a family ripped apart by a mysterious space-time anomaly—you can hunt for these, or just wander around in awe. It's no coincidence that local arts patron and fantasy-fiction specialist George R. R. Martin invested a lot to help Meow Wolf build this mind-blowing playground.

It's great for both kids and adults, and you'll want to block out at least two hours, if not four. There are snacks available on the premises (and a full café was on the drawing board at research time).

Meow Wolf's art installation occupies a former bowling alley at the House of Eternal Return.

Rancho de las Golondrinas

Rancho de las Golondrinas

About a 15-minute drive southeast, **Rancho de las Golondrinas** (334 Los Pinos Rd., 505/471-2261, www.golondrinas.org, 10am-4pm Wed.-Sun. June-Sept., $6), the "Ranch of the Swallows," is Santa Fe's equivalent of Colonial Williamsburg, a 200-acre museum where staff members in period costumes demonstrate crafts and other aspects of early New Mexican history. The core of it is a restored Spanish colonial *paraje*, a way station on the Camino Real, and outbuildings contain a blacksmith shop, a schoolhouse, mills, and even a rebuilt Penitente *morada* (the docent who works here is a Penitente himself and may sing some of the group's hymns).

The ranch hosts big to-dos—a sheep-shearing fair in early June and a frontier-themed horse show in August, among other things. It's a good idea to pack your own picnic; there's a basic café at the ranch, but it's open only on weekends. Allow a few hours to see the whole place. In April, May, and October, the museum is open on weekdays for guided tours by appointment; call 505/473-4169 to make arrangements. In these shoulder months, the ranch is also occasionally open for special theme weekends.

Entertainment and Events

NIGHTLIFE

With balmy summer evenings and a populace that always seems to be able to knock off work a little early, Santa Fe typically favors happy hour over late-night carousing.

Bars and Clubs

Longtime city haunt the **Dragon Room Lounge** (406 Old Santa Fe Tr., 505/983-7712, 4pm-midnight Tues.-Sun.) is so dim you might not notice at first the huge tree growing up from the left side of the bar. Guys in cowboy hats chat with mountain bikers and dressed-up cocktail drinkers. There's live music Tuesday, Thursday, and Saturday.

Stalwart **Maria's** (555 W. Cordova Rd., 505/983-7929, 11am-10pm daily) is worth the trip out from the center for its impeccably balanced margaritas, with fresh lime and nearly any brand of tequila you can imagine.

If you're hankering for the grungier side of Santa Fe, head to **Evangelo's** (200 W.

San Francisco St., 505/982-9014, 11am-1am daily), where soul and blues bands take the small stage at the back; when there's no band, there's room at the pool tables, plus a crew of crusty characters. Its basement space, **The Underground,** hosts all kinds of bands. On the opposite corner, those who descend the stairs to the basement-level **Matador** (116 W. San Francisco St., entrance on Galisteo St., no phone) will find a good cross section of Santa Fe's younger artists, among other renowned drinkers. If there's not a live band, there's punk rock on the stereo to match the concert posters on the walls.

Breweries

Local operation **Second Street Brewery** has two locations: its original place that gave it its name (1814 2nd St., 505/982-3030, 11am-10pm Mon.-Thurs., 11am-11pm Fri.-Sat., noon-9pm Sun.) and a newer, more central branch in The Railyard (1607 Paseo de Peralta, 505/989-3278), with the same hours. Either way, they usually have half a dozen varieties of their own beer on tap, in a chummy, semi-industrial atmosphere, sometimes backed up by a band. Happy hour is 4pm-6:30pm daily.

Cocktails

While most Santa Fe bars stick to margaritas, **Secreto Lounge** (210 Don Gaspar Ave., 505/983-5700, 4pm-midnight Mon.-Thurs., noon-midnight Fri.-Sat., noon-10pm Sun.) is up on the cutting edge of cocktail culture. Its "garden to glass" menu uses only fresh herbs and other seasonal ingredients (plus bitters from local crafters The Bitter End) in such drinks as the Local Beet, a gin-and-tonic turned vivid pink with earthy beet syrup. Of course, it still does a margarita or two: Its Agave Way is a pseudo-margarita that's spicy and sweet with red grapes. Happy hour (4pm-7pm weekdays) is worth planning around, as it knocks the price down to $7 or so, and you can sit out in the loggia of the Hotel St. Francis and watch the passing parade.

Boozehounds will also want to drop by the tasting room of **Santa Fe Spirits** (308 Read St., 505/780-5906, 3pm-9pm Mon.-Thurs., 3pm-10pm Fri.-Sat.), a relaxed place to sample all the local distiller's products. Order a full flight, or enjoy a showcase drink like the Whiskeyrita, which features the distiller's un-aged Silver Coyote whiskey, or a simple gin and tonic with its aromatic, sage-infused gin.

Open-Air Bars

For a sunset drink, get to the **Bell Tower Bar** (100 E. San Francisco St., 505/982-5511, 11am-sunset daily May-Oct.) early if you can, as this spot on the rooftop at La Fonda fills up fast. It's usually packed with tourists, but the view—from the 5th floor, the highest in the center of town—is inspiring.

If there's no room at La Fonda, the next best spot is **Thunderbird** (50 Lincoln Ave., 505/490-6550, 11:30am-10pm daily), which has a 2nd-floor porch with views onto the plaza. At happy hour (4pm-6pm), margaritas are $6.

Hidden away inside a block near the plaza, **Taberna** (125 Lincoln Ave., 505/988-7102, 5pm-11pm Wed.-Sun.) has a nice patio with a chummy scene starting at happy hour (5pm-6pm). At that time, wine or sherry can be had from $3 a glass.

The mellow patio scene at **Cowgirl BBQ** (319 S. Guadalupe St., 505/982-2565, 11:30am-midnight Mon.-Thurs., 11am-1am Fri.-Sat., 11am-11:30pm Sun.) gets started early, with happy hour kicking off at 3pm and lasting till 6pm, with two-for-one apps and $4 margaritas. It's good later too, with live music many nights.

On Canyon Road, stalwart **El Farol** (808 Canyon Rd., 505/983-9912, 11am-10pm Sun.-Thurs., 11am-11pm Fri.-Sat.) is the gallerists' after-work hangout, with seats outside on a creaky wooden portal and a back patio.

Live Music

El Mesón (213 Washington St., 505/983-6756, 5pm-11pm Tues.-Sat.) has live music five nights a week, with a particularly devoted crew of regulars for tango on Tuesdays. You can order traditional tapas, or bigger dishes from El Mesón's excellent dinner menu, or just join in the dancing on the small wood floor.

The only larger event space downtown, **Skylight** (139 W. San Francisco St., 505/982-0775, www.skylightsantafe.com, 4pm-2am Mon.-Sat., 4pm-midnight Sun.) is run by well-known local DJs. It has music every night, including touring bands, and a kitchen to provide munchies for those up past the city's usual bedtime.

THE ARTS
Performing Arts

Set in a 1931 Moorish curlicue palace, the **Lensic Performing Arts Center** (211 W. San Francisco St., 505/988-1234, www.lensic.com) is Santa Fe's best stage downtown, with 820 seats and an eclectic schedule. The six-week-long summer **Santa Fe Chamber Music Festival** (www.sfcmf.org) holds events here, with performances nearly every day in July and August. The chamber orchestra **Santa Fe Pro Musica** (505/988-4640, www.santafepromusica.com) also performs at the Lensic, fall through spring, as well as in Loretto Chapel and other intimate venues.

If you think opera is all about tuxes, plush seats, and too-long arias, give the **Santa Fe Opera** (U.S. 84/285, 505/986-5900, www.santafeopera.org) a chance. Half the fun is arriving early to "tailgate" in the parking lot, which involves gourmet goodies, lots of champagne, and time to mill around and check out other attendees' bolo ties. And then there's the show itself, featuring the country's best singers, who treat this as their "summer camp" in July and August. The elegant 2,000-plus-seat open amphitheater is beautiful at sunset; pack blankets to ward off the chill later. If you have kids to entertain, time your visit for bargain-priced "family nights" or a special dress rehearsal with extra info to introduce young ones to the art form.

Cinema

The delightful little **Jean Cocteau Cinema** (418 Montezuma Ave., 505/466-5528, www.jeancocteaucinema.com, $10) gets press for being owned by resident author George R. R. Martin (the man behind *Game of Thrones*), but it's a treat on its own, a 120-seat theater that shows eclectic art-house offerings to an enthusiastic local audience. Nearby in the Railyard complex, **Violet Crown** (1606 Alcaldesa St., 505/216-5678, www.violetcrownsantafe.com) is a multiplex with an artsy bent and a restaurant-bar.

FESTIVALS AND EVENTS

Santa Fe's summer is packed. In mid-July, the **International Folk Art Market** (505/992-7600, www.folkartalliance.org) showcases traditional crafts from all over the globe, often from the artists in person. It's set up on

The International Folk Art Market takes over Museum Hill in July.

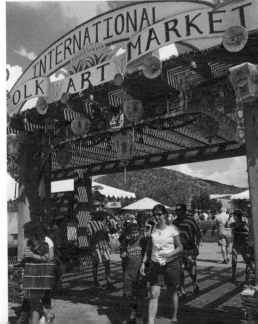

The Burning of Zozobra

Every fall a raucous chant fills the air in Santa Fe's Fort Marcy Park: "Burn him! Burn him! Burn him!" It's the ritual torching of Zozobra, a 50-foot-tall marionette with long, grasping arms, glowering eyes, and a moaning voice. In the weeks before the event, Old Man Gloom, as he's also known, is stuffed with divorce papers, pictures of ex-girlfriends, hospital gowns, and other anxiety-inducing scraps. Setting this aflame purges these troubles and allows for a fresh start.

O.M.G., aka Zozobra, waits to be torched.

This Santa Fe tradition sounds like a medieval rite, but it dates only from the 1920s, when artist Will Shuster—a bit of a local legend who's also credited with inventing piñon-juniper incense and starting the tradition of city-wide bonfires on Christmas Eve—wanted to lighten up the heavily Catholic Fiesta de Santa Fe. Shuster, who had moved to Santa Fe in 1920 to treat his tuberculosis, was inspired by the Mummers Parade from his native Philadelphia, as well as the Yaqui Indians in Tucson, Arizona, who burn Judas in effigy in the week before Easter. A 1926 *Santa Fe New Mexican* article describes the spectacle Shuster developed, with the help of the Kiwanis Club:

Zozobra . . . stood in ghastly silence illuminated by weird green fires. While the band played a funeral march, a group of Kiwanians in black robes and hoods stole around the figure. . . . [Then] red fires blazed at the foot . . . and leaped into a column of many colored flames. . . . And throwing off their black robes the spectators emerged in gala costume, joining an invading army of bright-hued harlequins with torches in a dance around the fires as the band struck up "La Cucaracha."

Shuster oversaw Zozobra nearly every year until 1964. In the late 1930s, Errol Flynn, in town with Olivia de Havilland and Ronald Reagan to film *The Santa Fe Trail,* set Zozobra aflame. A few years later, during World War II, the puppet was dubbed Hirohitlomus. In 1950, Zozobra appeared on the New Mexico state float in the Rose Bowl parade and won the national trophy.

Although Zozobra (aka O.M.G.) now has a Twitter account and accepts worries-to-burn online, the spectacle is roughly unchanged, with dozens of white-clad children playing "glooms," followed by a "fire dancer" who taunts Zozo until he bursts into flame; fireworks cap it off. It's a fine sight, and a great cross section of Santa Feans attend. But anyone leery of crowds may prefer to watch from outside the perimeter of the ball field.

Museum Hill, so the center of the city is not disrupted. On Sunday, tickets are cheaper and vendors are ready to make deals.

In late July, **Spanish Market** (505/982-2226, www.spanishcolonial.org) takes over the plaza with traditional New Mexican woodwork (especially santos), weaving, and furniture.

Finally, the city's biggest annual event is in late August, when 100,000 visitors come for **Santa Fe Indian Market** (505/983-5220, www.swaia.org). Like Spanish Market, it's centered on the plaza, with some 1,200 Native American artisans selling jewelry, pottery, weaving, and more. Alongside, the upstart **Indigenous Fine Art Market** (www.indigefam.org), based at Railyard Park, emphasizes more contemporary work. It's all a bit of a frenzy, but festive, due to free music and dance performances in the week leading up to the market itself.

After all the frenzy of summer tourism, locals celebrate the arrival of fall with the weeklong **Fiesta de Santa Fe** (505/204-1598, www.santafefiesta.org), which has been celebrated in some form since 1712. It begins with a reenactment of De Vargas's *entrada* into the city, then a whole slew of balls and parades, including the Historical/Hysterical Parade and a children's pet parade—eccentric

Santa Fe at its finest. The kickoff event is usually the **Burning of Zozobra** (855/969-6272, www.burnzozobra.com), a neo-pagan bonfire; the schedule has fluctuated a bit, but most recently, it was on the Friday before Labor Day. Some downtown businesses close for some fiestas, particularly on Zozobra day.

In late September, foodies flock to the city for the **Santa Fe Wine and Chile Festival** (505/438-8060, www.santafewineandchile. org), five days of tastings and special dinners at various venues around town.

Shopping

Even people who clutch their purse strings tight may be a little undone by the treasures for sale in Santa Fe. The rational approach would be to consider the most expensive shops more as free museums. (The cheapest, on the other hand, are stocked with made-in-China junk and eternally on the brink of "going out of business" and should be avoided.) Downtown around the plaza are souvenir shops and a few influential galleries. On Canyon Road cluster art dealers of all stripes. South Guadalupe Street and surrounding blocks have more funky and fun boutiques. If you buy too much to carry, **Pak Mail** (369 Montezuma Ave., 505/989-7380) can ship your treasures home safely; it even offers free pickup from hotels.

ART GALLERIES

The densest concentration of artwork is on Canyon Road, though it can seem a bit crowded with Southwestern kitsch. Summer hours are given here; in the winter, most galleries are closed at least Monday and Tuesday.

Local Artists

At the top end of Canyon Road, **Red Dot Gallery** (826 Canyon Rd., 505/820-7338, 10am-5pm Thurs.-Sun.) is the exhibition space for Santa Fe Community College students and alumni, a nice antidote to the

high-toned vibe on the rest of the street. In the convention center, the **Community Gallery** (201 W. Marcy St., 505/955-6705, 10am-5pm Tues.-Fri., 9:30am-4pm Sat.) is run by the Santa Fe Arts Commission and always has a wide mix of work on display.

Contemporary

Santa Fe's contemporary scene has cooled a bit since its boom in the 2000s. But granddaddy **LewAllen** (1613 Paseo de Peralta, 505/988-3250, 10am-6pm Mon.-Fri., 10am-5pm Sat.) has survived and is one of the anchors in The Railyard, with a vast industrial space, fittingly across the street from the SITE Santa Fe museum. Just up the road, **Eight Modern** (1601 Paseo de Peralta, 505/984-1387, 9:30am-5:30pm Mon.-Sat., 11am-4pm Sun.) focuses on colorful, abstract, and pop art.

A rare spot for abstraction on Canyon Road, **Nüart Gallery** (670 Canyon Rd., 505/988-3888, 10am-5pm daily) also showcases Latin American magical realism.

Native American and Southwestern

Near Canyon Road, **Gerald Peters Gallery** (1005 Paseo de Peralta, 505/954-5700, 10am-5pm Mon.-Sat.) and **Nedra Matteucci Galleries** (1075 Paseo de Peralta, 505/982-4631, 9am-5pm Mon.-Sat.) are the biggies when it comes to Taos Society of Artists and other Western art, though both have contemporary artists too. Even if nothing inside hits the spot, the one-acre sculpture garden and ponds in back of Nedra Matteucci are a treat. Smaller **Robert Nichols Gallery** (419 Canyon Rd., 505/982-2145, 10am-5pm Mon.-Sat., 11am-5pm Sun.) specializes in Native American pottery, including some with often funny, boundary-pushing sensibilities.

Near the plaza, **Blue Rain Gallery** (130 Lincoln Ave., 505/954-9902, 10am-6pm Mon.-Sat.) showcases work from many pueblo residents, such as Tammy Garcia's modern takes on traditional Santa Clara pottery forms—she sometimes renders bowls in blown glass or applies the geometric decoration to jewelry. Across the street, **Allan Houser Gallery** (125 Lincoln Ave., 505/982-4705, 10am-5pm Mon.-Sat.) showcases the work of the Southwest's best-known Native sculptor; it also maintains a sculpture garden outside the city, with visits by appointment.

CLOTHING AND JEWELRY

¡Mira! (101 W. Marcy St., 505/988-3585, 10:30am-5:30pm Mon.-Sat., noon-5pm Sun.) has a hip mix of clothes and housewares, with T-shirts by local designers ("Fanta Se" in the old Santa Fe Railroad logo, say) as well as cool imports from places like Ghana. Just down the block, **Glorianna's** (55 W. Marcy St., 505/982-0353, 10am-4:30pm Mon.-Tues.)

and Thurs.-Sat., often closed for lunch 1pm-2pm) is a treasure trove of beads, packed to bursting with veritable eggs of raw turquoise, trays of glittering Czech glass, and ropes of African trade beads.

The city's best consignment shop is **Double Take** (321 S. Guadalupe St., 505/989-8886, 10am-6pm Mon.-Sat.), a sprawling two-story space with an excellent selection of boots, as well as cool clothing, rodeo-themed 1950s sofas, Fiestaware, and plenty more.

GIFT AND HOME

Santa Fe icon **Seret & Sons** (224 Galisteo St., 505/988-9151, 9am-5:30pm Mon.-Fri., 9am-6pm Sat., 9:30am-5pm Sun.) deals in finely woven rugs, antique doors, and life-size wooden elephants from his cavernous warehouse just south of the plaza.

For funky folk art that won't break the bank, head for the equally gigantic **Jackalope** (2820 Cerrillos Rd., 505/471-8539, 9am-6pm Mon.-Sat., 10am-6pm Sun.), crammed with mosaic-topped tables, wooden chickens, Mexican pottery vases, and inexpensive souvenirs. Sharing the space is a community of prairie dogs—good distraction for children while adults cruise the breakables.

Open since 1995, **Doodlet's** (120 Don Gaspar St., 505/983-3771, 10am-5:30pm Mon.-Sat., 10am-5pm Sun.) is a totally absorbing corner shop filled with bits and bobs for kids and adults, from toy accordions to kitchen tchotchkes.

Sports and Recreation

It's no accident *Outside* magazine has its offices here. After work and on weekends, Santa Feans leave the town to the tourists and scatter into the surrounding mountains on foot or bike. You'll find something to do all four seasons, though hikes above the foothills shouldn't be attempted till mid-May at least (and not until you're acclimated to the altitude). If you're in town in the fall, don't miss

the aspen leaves turning, usually in mid-October. The access route for activities in the Sangre de Cristos is Highway 475—it starts out from the north side of Santa Fe as Artists Road, then the name changes to Hyde Park Road, and farther north it's Ski Basin Road.

Information and Guides

Just off Highway 14, immediately south of

I-25, the **Public Lands Information Center** (301 Dinosaur Tr., 505/954-2002, www.publiclands.org, 8am-4:30pm Mon.-Fri.) is the best starting point for any planning. The staff will also know the latest status on areas affected by wildfires or floods. **Outspire!** (505/660-0394, www.outspire.com) runs guided full- and half-day outings—hiking in summer, snowshoeing in winter. For gear, visit **REI** (500 Market St., 505/982-3557, 10am-8pm Mon.-Fri., 10am-7pm Sat., 11am-6pm Sun.) in the Railyard district.

HIKING

In addition to the multiuse trails for cyclists, hikers can enjoy the following dedicated trails.

Santa Fe Canyon Preserve

For an easy saunter in town, head for this 190-acre patch of the foothills managed by **The Nature Conservancy** (505/988-3867). The area is open only to people on foot—no mountain bikes and no pets. The preserve covers the canyon formed by the now-diverted Santa Fe River. An easy interpretive loop trail leads around the area for 1.5 miles, passing the remnants of the dam and winding through dense stands of cottonwoods and willows. The trailhead is on Cerro Gordo Road, just north of its intersection with Upper Canyon Road.

Atalaya Mountain

One of the easiest-to-reach trails in the Santa Fe area (you can take the M city bus to the trailhead on the campus of St. John's College) is also one of the more challenging. The hike heads up to a **9,121-foot peak,** starting out as a gentle stroll along the city's edge, then becoming increasingly steep, for a round-trip of approximately seven miles. Allow about four hours for the full up-and-back.

Aspen Vista

The most popular trail in the Sangre de Cristos is probably **Aspen Vista.** It is well traveled in fall, as the promised views of golden aspen groves are spectacular. In

the densest spots, when the sun is shining through the leaves, the air itself feels yellow. Even though it's at a high elevation, it's an easy hike, on a service road with a gradual slope. The full length is 11.5 miles, but it's the first 2.5 miles that are the most aspen-intense. A little under 4 miles in, you get a great view of Santa Fe below; this makes a good turn-around point for a two-hour hike. Look for the parking area on the right of Ski Basin Road (Hwy. 475), just under 13 miles up the road from town.

BIKING

Mountain bikers have fantastic outlets very close to Santa Fe, while those who prefer the open road will love the challenges in the winding highways through the mountains north of the city. **Rob & Charlie's** (1632 St. Michaels Dr., 505/471-9119, 9:30am-6pm Mon.-Sat., noon-5pm Sun. in summer) is a reliable shop.

For **bike rentals,** see **Mellow Velo** (132 E. Marcy St., 505/995-8356, 9am-6pm Mon.-Fri., 9am-5pm Sat., 9am-3pm Sun., from

Central Santa Fe is easy to cruise on two wheels.

$20/day), just off the plaza. It stocks cruisers for around town as well as deluxe mountain and road bikes.

Mountain Biking

The **Dale Ball Trails** are 22 miles of single-track routes for both hikers and mountain bikers, winding through stands of piñon and juniper in the foothills. Two trailheads give access to the North, Central, and South Sections of the trail. From the northern trailhead, on Sierra del Norte (immediately off Highway 475 after mile marker 3), the North Section trails vary a bit in elevation, but the Central Section (south from the parking area) is more fun because it's a longer chunk of trails. The southern trailhead, on Cerro Gordo just north of its intersection with Canyon Road, gives access to the Central Section and the South Section, which is for advanced riders only. Note that the trail that starts at the southern trailhead lot, part of the Santa Fe Canyon Preserve, is for foot traffic only—ride your bike one-tenth of a mile down Cerro Gordo to the start of the Dale Ball system.

A local classic, the **Santa Fe Rail Trail** starts as a paved path in Railyard Park, then turns to dirt outside the city limits, following a relatively easy route along the railroad tracks to Lamy. The trail is about 12.5 miles one-way; except for a grade near I-25, it's fairly level.

In the rolling hills west of the city, **La Tierra Trails** are for biking, hiking, and horseback riding—though it's the two-wheel crew who makes the most use of them, especially after work, when the day is cooler (there's not much shade out here). There are three trailheads, all interconnected by various loops. Look for the turn west (not at a light) off Highway 599, the bypass road around the city.

The most popular mountain trail is **Winsor Trail** (no. 254), covering a great range of scenery and terrain. Heading up, there are few deadly steep ascents, so it's tiring but not impossible, and you'll rarely have to hike-a-bike; you're rewarded with a long, joyful downhill run. The trailhead is in Tesuque: Take Washington Avenue north out of the

center of Santa Fe, continuing as it becomes Bishops Lodge Road (Highway 590). After not quite four miles, turn right onto County Road 72-A, also signed as Big Tesuque Canyon. There are two small pullout areas for parallel parking, and the trail starts about one-tenth of a mile up the road from the second parking area—the first half mile is through private land.

Road Biking

Make sure you're acclimated to the altitude before you set out on any lengthy trip—the best tour, along the high road to Taos, will take you through some of the area's highest elevations. Starting in Chimayó shaves some not-so-scenic miles off the ride and gives you a reasonable 45-mile jaunt to Taos. The annual **Santa Fe Century** (www.santafecentury.com) takes place every May, running a 104-mile loop south down the Turquoise Trail and back north via the old farm towns in the Galisteo Basin, southeast of Santa Fe.

SPAS

★**Ten Thousand Waves** (3451 Hyde Park Rd., 505/982-9304, www.tenthousandwaves.com, 9am-10:30pm Wed.-Mon., noon-10:30pm Tues. July-Oct.) is such a Santa Fe institution that it could just as well be listed under the city's major attractions. This traditional Japanese-style bathhouse just outside of town has two big communal pools and seven smaller private ones tucked among the trees; many have adjoining cold plunges and saunas. The place also offers full day-spa services, with intense massages and luxe facials and body scrubs. Prices are relatively reasonable, starting at $24 for unlimited time in the public baths and $115 for one-hour massages. In the winter (Nov.-June), the baths open at 10:30am (at 2pm Tues.) and close earlier on weeknights.

In town, **Absolute Nirvana Spa** (106 Faithway St., 505/983-7942, www.absolutenirvana.com, 10am-6pm Sun.-Thurs., 10am-8pm Fri.-Sat.) runs a "green" operation with a Balinese inspiration for many of its treatments

The hot tubs at Ten Thousand Waves are a great place to warm up in winter.

and massages (from $115). Afterward, you can relax in the gardens with a cup of tea and some organic sweets from the adjacent tearoom.

Very highly rated by locals, **Body of Santa Fe** (333 W. Cordova Rd., 505/986-0362, www. bodyofsantafe.com, 9am-9pm Mon.-Sat., 9am-3pm Sun.) is praised for its affordable treatments (massages from $80/hour) and relaxed atmosphere. There's a nice café on-site too.

WINTER SPORTS

Sixteen miles northeast of town in the Santa Fe National Forest, **Ski Santa Fe** (Hwy. 475, 505/982-4429, www.skisantafe.com, $72 full-day lift ticket) is a well-used day area with 79 fairly challenging trails. A major selling point: virtually no lift lines.

Exclusively for cross-country skiers, the groomed **Norski Trail** starts about a quarter of a mile before the Ski Santa Fe parking lot, off the west side of the road. The standard route is about 2.5 miles, winding through the trees and along a ridgeline, and you can shorten or lengthen the tour by taking various loops and shortcuts, as long as you follow the directional arrows counterclockwise.

Just seven miles out of town along the road to the ski area, **Hyde Memorial State Park** (Hwy. 475, 505/983-7175, www.nmparks.com) has an ice rink, a couple of nicely maintained sledding runs, and some shorter cross-country ski routes.

For gear, **Cottam's Ski Shop** (740 Hwy. 475, 505/982-0495, from 7:30am daily in ski season) is the biggest rental operation in the area, handily located on the way to Aspen Vista.

Food

Dining is one of Santa Fe's great pleasures. For a relatively tiny population, the city supports a dazzling range of restaurants. Sure, you can get a cheese-smothered, crazy-hot plate of green-chile-and-chicken enchiladas, but most locals eat more globally than that. "Santa Fe cuisine" cheerfully incorporates Asian, Southwestern, and Mediterranean flavors, with an emphasis on organic and holistic.

DOWNTOWN

The ring formed by Alameda Street and Paseo de Peralta contains some classic Santa Fe spots, plus a few hidden treats. On the plaza itself, the carnitas cart and the fajitas cart are classics too—and the Chicago hot dog stand, when it's set up, gets strong votes for authenticity.

New Mexican

The Shed (113½ E. Palace Ave., 505/982-9030, 11am-2:30pm and 5pm-9pm daily, $17) has been serving up platters of enchiladas since 1953—bizarrely, with a side of garlic bread. But that's just part of the tradition at this colorful, comfortable, marginally fancy place that's as popular with tourists as it is with die-hard residents. There are perfectly decent distractions like lemon-garlic shrimp and fish tacos on the menu, but it's the red chile you should focus on.

Cafés

Ecco (128 E. Marcy St., 505/986-9778, 7am-9pm Mon.-Thurs., 7am-10pm Fri., 8am-10pm Sat., 8am-7pm Sun.) is packed with coffee junkies and Wi-Fi fanatics in the mornings, giving way to gelato lovers later in the day.

Longtime burger connoisseurs may remember Bobcat Bite, just outside the city. It closed in 2013, and ★ **Santa Fe Bite** (311 Old Santa Fe Tr., 505/982-0544, 11am-8pm Tues.-Thurs., 11am-9pm Fri., 8am-9pm Sat.,

8am-8pm Sun., $12) is the new and even better incarnation, close to the plaza, in much more comfortable digs. The same 10-ounce burgers, from beef ground fresh every day, on a home-baked bun, are the stars. But there's plenty more, including tacos, big salads, and, on Friday, fish-and-chips. Wash it down with a cold Mexican Coke.

The **French Pastry Shop** (100 E. San Francisco St., 505/983-6697, 6:30am-5pm daily, $7) has been doling out sweet crepes, buttery pastries, croques monsieurs, and chewy baguette sandwiches for more than 40 years. Early mornings attract a fascinating crew of Santa Fe regulars.

★ **Tia Sophia's** (210 W. San Francisco St., 505/983-9880, 7am-2pm Mon.-Sat., 8am-1pm Sun., $9) is one of the last places in the plaza area that feels untouched by time and tourists, serving old-time New Mexican plates to a slew of regulars without a touch of fusion—so authentic, in fact, the kitchen claims to have invented the breakfast burrito decades back.

Plaza Café (54 Lincoln Ave., 505/982-1664, 7am-9pm daily, $11) may look shiny and new, but it's a city institution where residents roll in to read the paper and load up on coffee and great renditions of New Mexican and American diner favorites. This is no greasy spoon, though—the granola is house-made, the posole is perfectly toothsome, and the piñon blue-corn pancakes are fluffy and fresh. There's another outpost on the **southside** (3466 Zafarano Dr., 505/424-0755, 8am-9pm Sun.-Thurs., 8am-10pm Fri.-Sat.), very popular with locals.

For a very casual lunch, stop in at the **Five & Dime General Store** (58 E. San Francisco St., 505/992-1800, 8:30am-10pm Mon.-Sat., 9am-9pm Sun., $5), on the plaza. In this former Woolworth's where, allegedly, the Frito pie was invented (Frito-Lay historians beg to differ), the knickknack shop has maintained

Santa Fe's Finest Dining

In Santa Fe, there is a certain category of restaurant that one reader of this guide dubbed "Vegas-style"—that is, a place where the blingier your bolo tie and boots, the better. They're not totally superficial—in fact, **Coyote Café** (132 W. Water St., 505/983-1615, 5:30pm-9pm Sun.-Thurs., 5:30pm-10pm Fri.-Sat., $42) at least deserves a spot in the history books for having pioneered haute Southwestern cuisine in the late 1980s, under Chef Mark Miller. Today that restaurant is owned by the same team as **Geronimo** (724 Canyon Rd., 505/982-1500, 5:45pm-9pm daily, $42), and both have opted for more generic fine dining with the occasional local nod—chile-rubbed pork chops, haute green-chile mac-and-cheese, etc. **La Casa Sena** (125 E. Palace Ave., 505/988-9232, 11am-9pm Mon.-Wed., 11am-10pm Thurs.-Sat., $36) and **The Compound** (653 Canyon Rd., 505/982-4353, 11:30am-2:30pm and 5pm-9pm Mon.-Sat., 5:30pm-9pm Sun., $38) run in the same vein, though both have notably beautiful settings.

They're all acceptable in terms of food, but certainly not great value, and you'll be dining, for the most part, alongside other visitors, not locals. The best way to see the scene without empty-ing your wallet is at their bars. The Coyote Café has its lively **Rooftop Cantina** (505/983-1615, 11:30am-11pm daily, Apr.-Oct.), and the snug bar at Geronimo is a good place to put your feet up after a Canyon Road cruise. La Casa Sena is set in a truly dreamy garden courtyard; order a cocktail and an appetizer, or perhaps lunch, and enjoy the eye candy.

its lunch counter and still serves the deadly combo of corn chips, homemade red chile, onions, and shredded cheese, all composed directly in the Fritos bag. Eat in, or, better, lounge on the plaza grass—and don't forget the napkins.

Fresh and Local

Open since the late 1970s, ★ **Café Pasqual's** (121 Don Gaspar St., 505/983-9340, 8am-3pm and 5:30pm-9:30pm daily, $33) has defined its own culinary category, relying almost entirely on organic ingredients. Its breakfasts are legendary, but the food is delicious any time of day. Just brace yourself for the inevitable line, as the brightly painted dining room seats only 50 people, and loyal fans number in the thousands. Expect nearly anything on the menu: smoked-trout hash or Yucatán-style *huevos motuleños* for breakfast; for dinner, mole enchiladas or Vietnamese squid salad.

Spanish

Cozy creative-tapas joint **La Boca** (72 W. Marcy St., 505/982-3433, 11:30am-10pm daily, little plates $7-16) starts from Spain, then pulls in other Mediterranean influences: a salad spiked with apricots and figs, Moroccan

merguez, and more. The little plates can add up fast, unless you're there 3pm-5pm week-days, when there's a selection for half price. Reserve, ideally, and go early if you're sensitive to noise.

Italian

Off the plaza, next to Mission San Miguel, **Upper Crust Pizza** (329 Old Santa Fe Tr., 505/982-0000, 11am-10pm daily, $12) is a slice of old-school Santa Fe, with a nice creaky front porch, often with a live country crooner. It does regular, whole-wheat, or gluten-free crust. Hot deli sandwiches and big super-fresh salads round out the menu.

Locals head to amber-lit **Il Piatto** (95 W. Marcy St., 505/984-1091, 4:30pm-10:30pm Sun.-Tues., 11:30am-10:30pm Wed.-Sat., $28) for casual Italian and a neighborly welcome from the staff, who seem to be on a first-name basis with everyone in the place. Hearty pastas like pappardelle with duck are served in generous portions—a half order will more than satisfy lighter eaters. This is a great place to take a breather from enchiladas and burritos, without breaking the bank. Its bar offers a pleasant later happy hour, 9pm-10:30pm every night.

GUADALUPE AND THE RAILYARD

An easy walk from the plaza, these few square blocks hold some of the better, quirkier dining options in town.

New Mexican

The cousin of The Shed, **La Choza** (905 Alarid St., 505/982-0909, 11am-2:30pm and 5pm-9pm Mon.-Sat., $16) has a similar creative New Mexican menu but can be more of a local hangout—though it has become better known now that The Railyard has been developed around it. This also makes it a handy destination if you're coming to Santa Fe on the train—just walk back down the tracks a few minutes.

Fine Dining

Whether you want hearty bar food or an ethereal creation that will take your taste buds in new directions, Chef Joseph Wrede delivers. His lovely, candlelit space, ★ **Joseph's** (428 Agua Fria St., 505/982-1272, www.josephsofsantafe.com, 5:30pm-10pm Sun.-Thurs., 5:30pm-11pm Fri.-Sat., $28), is this author's favorite restaurant in Santa Fe. Wrede's best dishes are vegetable-centric, though not necessarily vegetarian. But he's also into local meats, so carnivores will find hearty elk steaks and a seemingly simple lamb patty that may be the state's best green-chile cheeseburger. Book ahead if you can, or try for a seat at the bar. And whatever happens, don't miss the duck-fat ice cream.

Burgers and Barbecue

All things Texan are the specialty at **Cowgirl BBQ** (319 S. Guadalupe St., 505/982-2565, 11:30am-10:30pm Sun.-Wed., 11:30am-4pm Thurs., 11:30am-11pm Fri., 11am-11pm Sat., $15). But the place has been a Santa Fe fixture for so long that it doesn't seem like "foreign" food. It's a kitsch-filled spot that's as friendly to kids as it is to margarita-guzzling, barbecue-rib-gnawing adults. Non-meat-eaters won't feel left out: An ooey-gooey butternut squash casserole comes with a salad on the side. Both carnivores and veggies can agree on the pineapple upside-down cake and the ice-cream "baked potato."

Take it even more casual at **Shake Foundation** (631 Cerrillos Rd., 505/988-8992, 11am-6pm daily, $6), an outdoor burger joint that's so good people flock to it even in winter. The dainty burgers (you might want a double) are good, vouched-for beef or lamb, served on lavishly buttered buns, and piñon nuts are an optional topping for the Taos Cow ice cream. Even the Caesar salad is ingenious: a veritable bouquet of whole romaine leaves, to dip and dunk in a creamy dressing.

Cafés

Make room in your morning for an almond croissant from ★ **Sage Bakehouse** (535 Cerrillos Rd., 505/820-7243, 7:30am-2:30pm Mon.-Sat., $4). Washed down with a mug of coffee, these butter-soaked pastries will have you set for hours. Before you leave, pick up some sandwiches for later—classic combos like smoked turkey and cheddar on the bakery's excellent crust. And maybe a pecan-raisin wreath. And a cookie too.

A few steps away is **Ohori's Coffee, Tea & Chocolate** (505 Cerrillos Rd., 505/988-9692, 7am-6pm Mon.-Fri., 8am-6pm Sat., 9am-2pm Sun.), Santa Fe's small-batch coffee epicures. Its dark-as-night brew makes Starbucks seem weak. There's a second shop just out of the center at 1098 South St. Francis Drive.

One of the most dangerous addresses in Santa Fe, **Whoo's Donuts** (851-B Cerrillos Rd., 505/629-1678, 7am-3pm daily, $2) is in a duplex with **ChocolateSmith** (851-A Cerrillos Rd., 505/473-2111, 10am-5:30pm Mon.-Sat., noon-5pm Sun.). Bear right for organic blue-corn-and-raspberry cake donuts; bear left for intense hand-dipped truffles.

Fresh and Local

If you're on green-chile-and-cheese overload, head to ★ **Vinaigrette** (709 Don Cubero Alley, 505/820-9205, 11am-9pm Mon.-Sat., $14) and dig into a big pile of fresh greens. The so-called salad bistro uses largely organic

The Santa Fe Farmers Market runs year-round.

santafefarmersmarket.com, 7am-1pm Tues. and Sat. May-Nov., 8am-1pm Sat. Dec.-Apr.) is a buzzing social scene and a great place to pick up fresh treats as well as souvenir chile *ristras*. It's in a market hall in the Railyard complex, off Paseo de Peralta near Guadalupe Street.

CANYON ROAD

Gallery hopping can make you hungry—but there are only a handful of places to eat on Canyon Road, and most are more dedicated to getting caffeine into your system.

Cafés

For morning brew, jog off the strip to **Downtown Subscription** (376 Garcia St., 505/983-3085, 7am-6pm daily), an airy coffee shop that stocks perhaps a million magazines.

Chocolate freaks should go a little farther to ★ **Kakawa Chocolate House** (1050 E. Paseo de Peralta, 505/982-0388, 10am-6pm Mon.-Sat., noon-6pm Sun., $4). It specializes in historically accurate hot chocolate, based on Mesoamerican and medieval European recipes, and you can also get regular coffee drinks, truffles, and pastries here. It's in a tiny adobe house—after one drink, you'll be bouncing off the walls.

For a mellower high, head to the top end of Canyon Road and **The Teahouse** (821 Canyon Rd., 505/992-0972, 9am-9pm daily, $12), where some 13 pages of the menu are devoted to teas, plus organic vittles such as kale salad with sunflower-seed dressing, and a deliciously hearty bowl of oats, rice, and wheat berries for breakfast. The service could be euphemistically described as "very Santa Fe" (i.e., spacey), but the food is good, and it's a great place to put your feet up after a long art crawl.

CERRILLOS ROAD

This commercial strip isn't Santa Fe's most scenic zone, but you'll find some great culinary gems out this way.

New Mexican

Green chile has been getting milder over the years—but not at ★ **Horseman's Haven**

ingredients from its farm in Nambé, in imaginative combos, like a highbrow taco salad with chorizo and honey-lime dressing. The setting is pure homey Santa Fe, with tea towels for napkins, iced tea served in canning jars, and local art on the whitewashed walls. There's a pretty patio too. Heading north on Cerrillos Road, turn off just after La Unica Cleaners. You'll first see the same owner's newer faux farm shop and café, **Modern General** (637 Cerrillos Rd., 505/930-5462, 8am-5pm Mon.-Sat., 10am-5pm Sun., $7), which is also good, with its simple menu of juices, avocado toast, and a few other breakfasts all day. Vinaigrette is in the building behind that.

Just outside the Paseo de Peralta loop, the **Tune-Up Café** (1115 Hickox St., 505/983-7060, 7am-10pm Mon.-Fri., 8am-10pm Sat.-Sun., $9) is a homey one-room joint that locals love, whether for fish tacos or a suitably Santa Fe ish brown-rice-and-nut burger. The Salvadoran *pupusas* are tasty.

The popular **Santa Fe Farmers Market** (1607 Paseo de Peralta, 505/983-4098, www.

(4354 Cerrillos Rd., 505/471-5420, 8am-8:30pm Mon.-Sat., 8:30am-2pm Sun., $8), which claims to serve the hottest green chile in Santa Fe. It picks and mixes chile varieties to offer a couple of consistent grades. Like all good chile purveyors, it's in an unassuming box of a building next to a gas station, and it takes cash only.

Long notorious for its dazzling list of margaritas, ★ Maria's (555 W. Cordova Rd., 505/983-7929, 11am-10pm daily, $10) is well worth settling into for a meal of hearty New Mexican classics, starting with a genuinely hot table salsa and chips. Both red and green are solid here, and the tamales are exceptionally rich and creamy (even the vegetarian ones!).

A nice no-frills family diner, The Pantry (1820 Cerrillos Rd., 505/986-0022, 6:30am-8:30pm Mon.-Sat., 7am-8:30pm Sun., $9) has been slinging eggs, pancakes, and chile since 1948. There's a lunch counter up front, but regulars request the back room.

Mexican

Great things come out of the modest hut called El Chile Toreado (950 W. Cordova Rd., 505/800-0033, 8:15am-3pm Mon.-Fri., 8:15am-2pm Sat., $7), in a parking lot on Cordova Road, just east of Cerrillos. Its green salsa is a near-mystical cilantro experience, and its carnitas may be the best in town. It also serves excellent breakfast burritos—get one with Mexican chorizo.

Cafés

Counter Culture (930 Baca St., 505/995-1105, 8am-3pm Sun.-Mon., 8am-9pm Tues.-Sat., $12) is generally a locals-only scene, well liked for its range of food (green chile, Vietnamese sandwiches, cinnamon buns), its casual-industrial vibe, and its outdoor space where kids can run around.

SANTA FE METRO AREA

Out on Old Las Vegas Highway, the frontage road for I-25, Harry's Roadhouse (96 Old Las Vegas Hwy., 505/989-4629, 7am-9:30pm daily, $13) is an easy place to pop off the freeway (at the Old Santa Fe Trail exit). The patio has a great view across the flatlands, there's a full bar, and the diner-style menu includes everything from cold meat-loaf sandwiches to coconut cream pie.

For a calmer, more wholesome vibe, keep driving down the road to Café Fina (624 Old Las Vegas Hwy., 505/466-3886, 7am-3pm Mon.-Wed., 7am-3pm and 5:30pm-8:30pm Thurs.-Fri., 8am-3pm and 5:30pm-8:30pm Sat., 8am-3pm Sun., $10), also easily accessible at exit 290 off I-25. This is a casual order-at-the-counter place, with a short but flavor-packed menu (ricotta pancakes, Reuben sandwiches) from mostly organic ingredients. The view from the hill here is lovely.

The restaurant at Ten Thousand Waves, Izanami (3451 Hyde Park Rd., 505/428-6390, noon-10pm Wed.-Mon., 5pm-10pm Tues., small plates $5-14), melds old Japan and new, without feeling like a theme restaurant. On the menu, there's pickled burdock root and sticky sweet potatoes, as well as wagyu-beef burgers and tempura-fried artichokes, served in small plates to share. The dining room has a rustic mountain-lodge feel, with an optional shoes-off tatami-mat seating area. Throw in a vast sake menu and surprisingly reasonable prices, and it's one of Santa Fe's cooler places to eat, whether you make the drive up for dinner or just wander over after your bath.

Accommodations

Santa Fe offers some great places to stay, but few are particularly cheap. Prices quoted for the bigger hotels are standard rack rates; chances are, you'll find substantially lower ones by calling or booking online, at least at the higher-end properties. Prices spike in July and August, often up to holiday rates. If you're coming for Indian Market or Christmas, try to book at least eight months in advance. On the other hand, despite ski season, rates are often quite low in early December, January, and February.

UNDER $100

As hostels go, **Santa Fe International Hostel** (1412 Cerrillos Rd., 505/988-1153, www.hostelsantafe.com) is best appreciated with rose-colored glasses firmly in place, viewed as an old-school hippie project (it *is* run as a nonprofit). The dorms ($20 pp) and private rooms ($25 s, $35 d) are dim, and cleanliness can be spotty, as you're relying on the previous guests' efforts, as part of the required daily chores. The kitchen has free food, but you have to pay for Internet access ($2/day), and everything is cash only.

For camping, the closest tent sites to the center are at **Hyde Memorial State Park** (Hwy. 475, 505/983-7175, www.nmparks.com), about four miles northwest of the city, with both primitive ($8) and developed sites with electricity ($14).

Possibly the best lodging deal in Santa Fe, the **Quaker Meeting House** (630 Canyon Rd., 505/983-7241, www.santa-fe.quaker.org, $45 s, $55 d) rents a guest casita with a kitchenette. It's a small space, and it has a three-night minimum, but the location on Canyon Road can't be beat. Payment is cash only.

Wedged in among the chain hotels on Cerrillos, the self-described "kitschy" ★ **Silver Saddle Motel** (2810 Cerrillos Rd., 505/471-7663, www.santafesilversaddlemotel.com, $60 s, $65 d) plays up the retro charm.

Cozy rooms may be pretty basic and have cinder-block walls, but they're decked out with Western accoutrements and kept clean—and the price, which includes breakfast, can't be beat. A handful of later-built rooms have some extra square footage.

$100-150

The bones of ★ **Santa Fe Sage Inn** (725 Cerrillos Rd., 505/982-5952, www.santafesageinn.com, $115 d) are a standard highway motel, but the superclean rooms are done in sharp, modern red and black, with Southwestern rugs hung on the walls. Little touches such as free Wi-Fi, plush beds, and an above-average breakfast (fresh bagels, fruit, yogurt, and more) make this an excellent deal. The place even has a swimming pool. It's still walking distance to the center, and it's right across the street from the Railyard Park and the farmers market.

Despite its location on uncharming Cerrillos Road, ★ **El Rey Inn** (1862 Cerrillos Rd., 505/982-1931, www.elreyinnsantafe.com, $115 s, $145 d) counts as one of the more charming motels in Santa Fe. Built around a 1935 motor court, it has been expanded and meticulously kept up and adjusted for modern standards of comfort, with beautiful gardens, a big swimming pool, a hot tub, and a sauna. The 86 rooms, spread over 4.5 acres, vary considerably in style (and in price), from the oldest section with snug adobe walls and heavy viga ceilings to airier rooms with balconies. Guests get a voucher for breakfast at the Pantry, a nice old-time restaurant next door. The only drawback is that the plaza is too far to walk, but a city bus stops right outside, if you prefer to avoid the parking challenge.

$150-200

Santa Fe Motel & Inn (510 Cerrillos Rd., 505/982-1039, www.santafemotel.com, $159

d) is a good budget option close to the center, with rooms done up in simple, bright decor that avoids motel sameness despite the generic motel layout. A few kitchenettes are available, along with some more-private casitas with fireplaces. Lots of nice touches—such as bread from the Sage Bakehouse across the street along with the full breakfast—give the place a homey feel without the tight quarters of a typical bed-and-breakfast.

Hotel Chimayó (125 Washington Ave., 505/988-4900, www.hotelchimayo.com, $159 d), offers good value very close to the plaza, though not everyone will like its folksy style, done up with wooden crosses and striped rugs from its namesake village. Upstairs rooms have private balconies, and some suites have fireplaces.

East of the plaza, twin bed-and-breakfasts under the same ownership offer two kinds of style: The rooms at **Hacienda Nicholas** (320 E. Marcy St., 505/986-1431, www.haciendanicholas.com, $165 d) have a tasteful Southwest flavor, decorated with a few cowboy trappings and Gustave Baumann prints; most rooms have fireplaces. Across the street, **The Madeleine** (106 Faithway St., 505/982-3465, www.madeleineinn.com, $160 d) is set in a wood Victorian, and antique furniture is offset with rich Balinese fabrics. At both spots, breakfasts show the same attention to sumptuous detail, with items like blue-corn waffles or poblano-quinoa casserole.

$200-250

The 100-room **Inn of the Governors** (101 W. Alameda St., 505/982-4333, www.innofthegovernors.com, $219 d) isn't very flashy on the outside, but inside it has a personable only-in-Santa-Fe feel, starting with the afternoon "tea and sherry hour," when guests are plied with free drinks and *bizcochitos*. Its unique profit-sharing system may account for the exceptionally nice staff. Other perks: Breakfast is generous, parking is free (unheard-of elsewhere downtown), and there's even a tiny pool. Rooms in the Governors Wing are quietest.

Inn on the Alameda (303 E. Alameda St., 505/984-2121, www.innonthealameda.com, $229 d) is a good option for people who

Hotel Chimayó is conveniently located near the plaza.

want adobe style *and* space, and its location near Canyon Road is handy for gallery-hoppers. The big rooms have triple-sheeted beds, wireless Internet access, and overstuffed armchairs that are only lightly dusted with Southwestern flair; most also have a patio or balcony. Gas fireplaces are usually an additional $20. The continental breakfast spread is generous, and there's a wine-and-cheese hour every afternoon.

Opened in 2014, **Drury Plaza Santa Fe** (828 Paseo de Peralta, 505/424-2175, www.druryplazasantafe.com, $240 d) has a somewhat corporate feel, but it occupies a big historic hospital complex behind the St. Francis Cathedral—a very convenient location at a pretty good price for amenities like a rooftop pool, full breakfast, and free drinks in the afternoon. Rooms are a little small but very comfortably furnished.

A rental condo is a great option if you have a family or group, and those at **Campanilla Compound** (334 Otero St., 800/828-9700, www.campanillacompound.com, $247) are especially nice, with whitewashed walls, fireplaces, and Mexican-tiled kitchens. Each unit has plenty of space inside and out, with a private patio or porch, and, thanks to the location on a hill, some have excellent views of the city and the sunset. There's a three-night minimum in summer, and two nights the rest of the year.

A wonderfully restful spot is ★ **Houses of the Moon** (3451 Hyde Park Rd., 505/992-5003, www.tenthousandwaves.com, $249 d), the guest cottages at Ten Thousand Waves spa. Some have more of a local feel, with viga ceilings and kiva fireplaces, while others are straight from Japan, both samurai era and contemporary anime. Some larger suites have kitchens. Rates include a suitably organic granola breakfast as well as free access to the communal and women's tubs.

OVER $250

The iconic, family-owned **La Fonda** (100 E. San Francisco St., 505/982-5511, www.lafondasantafe.com, $269 d), which has been offering respite to travelers in some form or another since 1607, has been undergoing renovation since 2013. This has lightened up its guest rooms considerably but also spoiled the impeccable historic feeling in the public areas. The whole place feels more generic and modern as a result, though many rooms do have original folk art, and a few have *latilla* ceilings and kiva fireplaces—along with all the necessary luxuries, such as pillow-top beds. You can soak up most of the place's atmosphere in the public areas, of course, but the location couldn't be better. It helps to have flexible dates—in periods of high demand, the rates can spike to exorbitant levels. Even if you don't stay here, do at least take a spin through the lobby and the mezzanine—there are still traces of the 1920 designs by Mary Colter (best known for the hotels at the Grand Canyon), and some great paintings.

Special occasion? The Relais & Chateaux property **The Inn of the Five Graces** (150 E. De Vargas St., 505/992-0957, www.fivegraces.com, $550 suite) can transport you to exotic lands—for at least slightly less than a plane ticket. Outside, it looks like a typical historic Southwestern lodge, a collection of interconnected adobe casitas on Santa Fe's oldest street. But inside, the 24 sumptuous suites are done in the style of an opium dream: antique Turkish kilims, heavy wood doors, and mosaics—all courtesy of the boho-style dealers Seret & Sons. Rates include full breakfast, delivered to your room if you like.

Outside Santa Fe

Less than an hour's drive from Santa Fe are six-century-old ruins of Ancestral Puebloan culture at Bandelier, and the 20th-century atomic developments in Los Alamos, home of the Manhattan Project. Abiquiu, best known as Georgia O'Keeffe country, is a landscape of rich red rocks along the tree-lined Rio Chama. The most popular outing from Santa Fe is to Taos, but even that presents several possibilities. The main options are the low road along the Rio Grande or the high road that passes through tiny mountain villages. You can also take a more roundabout route through Ojo Caliente, a village built around hot springs.

THE PUEBLOS

Between Santa Fe and Taos lie seven pueblos, each on a separate patch of reservation land. Unlike scenic Taos Pueblo, these are not notable for their ancient architecture and, with a few small exceptions, do not have any tourist attractions. Some pueblos are closed to visitors all or part of the year, but do make the trip on feast days or for other ceremonial dances if you can.

Tesuque and Pojoaque

Just north of Santa Fe, the highway overpasses are decorated with the original Tewa names of the pueblos. Tesuque (Te Tesugeh Owingeh, "village of the cottonwood trees") is marked by **Camel Rock,** a piece of sandstone on the west side of the highway that has eroded to resemble a creature that looks right at home in this rocky desert.

Farther north, Pojoaque manages the **Poeh Museum** (78 Cities of Gold Rd., 505/455-5041, www.poehcenter.org, 10am-4pm Mon.-Sat., free), in a striking old-style adobe building just off the highway. It shows (and sells) local artwork, as well as a permanent installation relating the Pojoaque people's path (*poeh*) through history.

Just north of the Cities of Gold Casino is a tasting room for New Mexico's largest craft distillery, **Don Quixote Distillery** (18057-A

the Poeh Museum

Outside Santa Fe

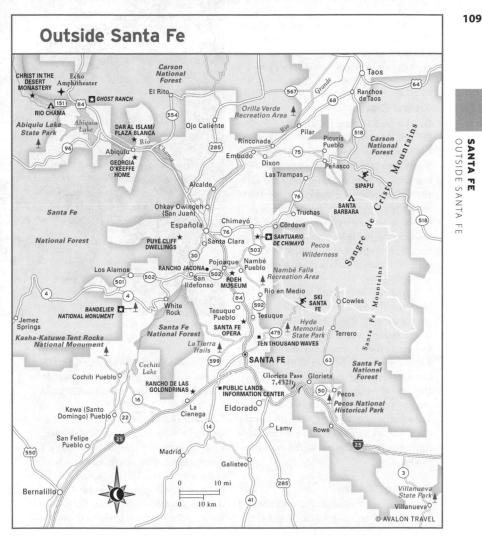

U.S. 84/285, www.dqdistillery.com, noon-6pm daily). You can sample the husband-and-wife team's blue-corn-based vodka and gin flavored with locally foraged juniper berries and other botanicals. They also make intense vanilla extract, bitters, and port wine based on New Mexican monks' 16th-century recipe.

San Ildefonso

Best known for its black-on-black pottery (first by María Martinez and her husband,

Julian, and now from a number of skilled potters), the pueblo of San Ildefonso is off Highway 502, on the way to Los Alamos. Of all the pueblos just north of Santa Fe, it's probably the most scenic, with even its newer houses done in faux-adobe style, and the main plaza shaded by giant old cottonwoods. You must first register at the **visitors center** (off Hwy. 502, 505/455-3549, 8am-5pm Mon.-Fri., $10/car), then proceed on foot. There is a very small **museum** (8am-4:30pm daily), which is really just an excuse to walk across the village. The only other attractions are pottery shops—which are interesting even if you're not in the market, as it's a chance to peek inside people's homes and chat a bit.

Santa Clara

On the land of Santa Clara (Kha P'o, or Shining Water), on Highway 30 south of Española, are the beautiful **Puyé Cliff Dwellings** (888/320-5008, www.puyecliffs. com), which were occupied until the early 1600s. They're accessible only by guided tour, and a slightly expensive one at that: $20 for a one-hour walk either along the cliff side or the mesa top, or $35 for both. But tour leaders come from the pueblo and connect the ancient ruins with current culture in an intimate and fascinating way.

At the base of the cliffs is a stone building from the Fred Harvey Indian Detour days of the early 1900s, when carloads of intrepid visitors would trundle off the train and out to these exotic sights; it now houses a small museum. The Puyé Cliffs Welcome Center—better recognized as a gas station on Highway 30—marks the turn to the cliffs; you can buy your tickets here (preferred, so they know you're coming) or up the road at the site. **Tours** run on the hour 9am-5pm daily April-September; the rest of the year, tours run 9am-2pm.

Getting There

From downtown Santa Fe, northbound Guadalupe Street turns into U.S. 84/285, which runs north through Tesuque in 5 miles and Pojoaque in 15 miles. Though this stretch of casinos and tax-free cigarette shops isn't particularly scenic, don't be tempted to race through it—the area is a major speed trap.

To reach San Ildefonso, turn off U.S. 84/285 in Pojoaque at the exit for Highway 502 to Los Alamos; the turn for the pueblo is about 6 miles ahead on the right. From San Ildefonso, you can continue to Santa Clara by turning north on Highway 30; the cliff dwellings are 7 miles ahead on the left. The slightly more

Puyé Cliff Dwellings at Santa Clara

direct route to Santa Clara is via Española, following signs for Highway 30; the total drive from the edge of Santa Fe is about 23 miles.

LOS ALAMOS

Unlike so many other sights in New Mexico, which are rooted in centuries of history, Los Alamos, home of the atomic bomb, is a product of the modern age. You may spend only a few hours here, visiting the museum and admiring the view from this high plateau, but you'll still sense a different atmosphere from anywhere else in New Mexico. If you can, visit on a weekday, as more businesses are open; weekends are quite sleepy in this town that draws specialized commuters from around the state.

During World War II, the army requisitioned an elite, rugged boys' school on a New Mexico mesa in order to build a top-secret base for development of the nuclear bomb. It was home for a time to J. Robert Oppenheimer, Richard Feynman, Niels Bohr, and other science luminaries. The Manhattan Project and its aftermath, the Cold War arms

Los Alamos

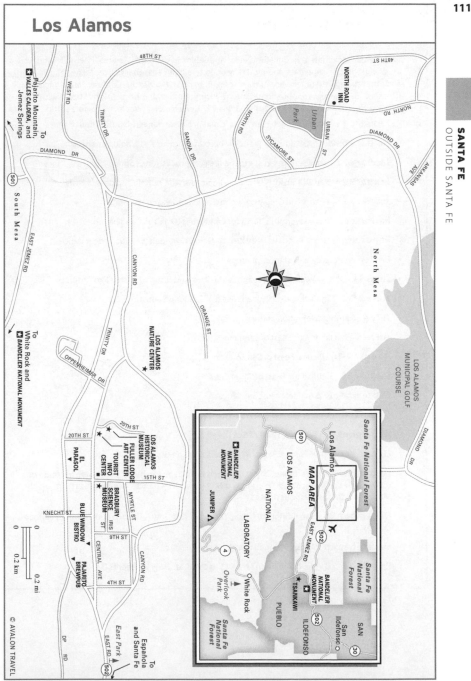

© AVALON TRAVEL

Ceremonial Dances

This is an approximate schedule for dances at pueblos in the Santa Fe area. Pueblo feast days are always on the same date and generally open to all, but seasonal dances (especially Easter and other spring rituals) can vary, and are sometimes closed to visitors. Confirm details and start times—usually afternoon, but sometimes following an evening or midnight Mass—with the **Indian Pueblo Cultural Center** (505/843-7270, www.indianpueblo.org) before setting out.

- **January 1** - Ohkay Owingeh (San Juan): cloud or basket dance; Picurís: various dances

- **January 6** - Picurís: various dances; Nambé: buffalo, deer, and antelope dances

- **January 22** - San Ildefonso: vespers and firelight procession at 6pm

- **January 23** - San Ildefonso: Feast of San Ildefonso, with buffalo and deer dances

- **January 25** - Picurís and Ohkay Owingeh (San Juan): Feast of San Pablo

- **February 2** - Picurís: various dances for Candlemas (Día de la Candelaria)

- **February, first or second weekend** - Ohkay Owingeh (San Juan): deer dance

- **Easter** - various dances at most pueblos

- **June 13** - Ohkay Owingeh (San Juan), Santa Clara, and Picurís: Feast of San Antonio

- **June 24** - Ohkay Owingeh (San Juan): Feast of San Juan Bautista

- **July 4** - Nambé: celebration at the waterfall

- **July 25** - San Ildefonso: Feast of Santiago

- **August 9-10** - Picurís: Feast of San Lorenzo

- **August 12** - Santa Clara: Feast of Santa Clara

- **September 8** - San Ildefonso: corn dance

- **October 4** - Nambé: Feast of San Francisco de Asís

- **November 12** - Tesuque: Feast of San Diego

- **December 12** - Pojoaque: Feast of Nuestra Señora de Guadalupe

- **December 24** - Picurís and Ohkay Owingeh (San Juan): torchlight procession at sundown, followed by Los Matachines; Tesuque and Nambé: various dances, beginning after midnight Mass; San Ildefonso: various dances

- **December 25** - San Ildefonso, Ohkay Owingeh (San Juan), Picurís, and Tesuque: various dances

- **December 26** - Ohkay Owingeh (San Juan): turtle dance

- **December 28** - Picurís: children's dances to celebrate Holy Innocents Day race, led to the establishment of Los Alamos National Lab (LANL). Only in 1957 did the onetime military base become an actual public town; it's now home to about 18,000 people (if you count the "suburb" of White Rock, just down the hill on Highway 4). The highway up the mountainside is wider than it used to be, but the winding ascent to the mesa of "Lost Almost"—as the first scientists dubbed their officially nonexistent camp—still carries an air of the clandestine. The town has a jarring newness about it, with street names like Bikini Atoll Road, and it's only emphasized by the dramatic landscape surrounding it.

The town is spread over three long mesas that extend like fingers from the mountain behind. Highway 502 arrives in the middle mesa, depositing you on Central Avenue and the main downtown area. The north mesa is mostly residential, while the south mesa is occupied by the labs and two routes running back down the mountain and connecting with Highway 4.

Sights
LOS ALAMOS HISTORICAL MUSEUM

Even a manufactured town like Los Alamos has a history. See what the area was like

pre-Manhattan Project at the fascinating **Los Alamos Historical Museum** (1050 Bathtub Row, 505/662-4493, www.losalamoshistory. org, 9:30am-4:30pm Mon.-Fri., 11am-4pm Sat.-Sun., free), set in an old building of the Los Alamos Ranch School, the boys' camp that got the boot when the army moved in. The exhibits cover everything from relics of the early Tewa-speaking people up to juicy details on the social intrigue during the development of "the gadget," as the A-bomb was known. Volunteer docents lead two-hour **walking tours** (11am Mon., Fri., and Sat., $10) from the museum late May-early October; if you miss this, pick up a brochure for a self-guided walk.

In front of the museum is **Fuller Lodge Art Center** (2132 Central Ave., 505/662-1635, 10am-4pm Mon.-Sat., free), originally the ranch school's dining room and kitchen. It usually has a community art exhibit downstairs, plus a room upstairs restored to the era when schoolteachers bunked here. The architect John Gaw Meem built the structure in 1928, handpicking more than 700 pine poles to form the walls, and designing the cowboy-silhouette light fixtures in the main hall.

The museum is just west of the main street, Central Avenue—you'll see Fuller Lodge on

a replica of Los Alamos's "main gate" (now a rest area)

Central, with the museum set back behind it. At research time, the museum was undergoing major renovation, scheduled to be finished by late 2016, but check the website to confirm.

BRADBURY SCIENCE MUSEUM

Set up by Los Alamos National Lab, the **Bradbury Science Museum** (1350 Central Ave., 505/667-4444, www.lanl.gov/museum, 10am-5pm Tues.-Sat., 1pm-5pm Sun.-Mon., free) on the miracles of atomic energy has the feel of a very high-grade science fair, with plenty of buttons to push and gadgets to play with. There's also an air of a convention sales booth—the museum's mission is definitely to sell the public on LANL's work and nuclear technology in general, though a public forum corner gives space to opposing views. More interesting are the relics of the early nuclear age: Fat Man and Little Boy casings, gadgetry from the Nevada Test Site, and the like.

Atomic City Van Tours (505/662-3965, www.buffalotoursla.com, 1:30pm daily Mar.-Oct., $15) leave from the parking lot in front of the museum. The 1.5-hour tour is a good way to see more of the town, which is otherwise a bit difficult to navigate, and learn some of the history. Call ahead to reserve. If you can't make the set tour time, you can download a short self-guided tour from the website; this route takes the free city bus to the main part of LANL, pointing out town landmarks along the way.

Recreation

The mountain behind Los Alamos is recovering from the 2011 Las Conchas Fire, but the canyons below Los Alamos were untouched, and offer good hiking. They are crisscrossed with a network of county-maintained hiking trails, easily accessible from the town's main roads. Pick up a map and get recommendations from the visitors center or **Los Alamos Nature Center** (2600 Canyon Rd., 505/662-0460, www.pajaritoeec.org, 10am-8pm Tues., 10am-4pm Wed. and Fri.-Mon., free), which also is a good place to get to know the plants and animals in the area.

The most dramatic views in the area are in White Rock, where the **White Rock Rim Trail** runs three miles along the cliff edge—you'll have suburban tract homes to your back and a dizzying canyon out in front of you. Even if you don't much feel like a hike, stop

Los Alamos Nature Center has details on local hikes.

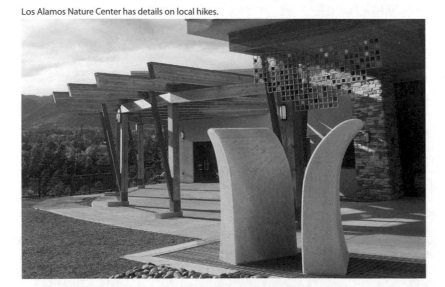

by where the walk starts in Overlook Park, just for the view; follow signs from Highway 4 at the first stoplight in town. You can also take a strenuous hike into the gorge along the **Red Dot Trail,** which passes a few petroglyphs on its way down to the Rio Grande; follow signs from Highway 4 for Overlook Park, at the back end of a subdivision.

A bit of a locals' secret, **Pajarito Mountain** (505/662-5725, www.skipajarito. com, 9am-4pm Fri.-Sun. and holidays) offers good skiing and snowboarding for relatively cheap ($49/full day), with five lifts giving access to bunny slopes as well as double-black-diamond trails. The area is just a few miles northeast of Los Alamos, off Highway 501.

Food

Los Alamos is not exactly bursting with restaurants, and many are open weekdays only. For lunch, the branch of the Española taco specialists **El Parasol** (1903 Central Ave., 505/661-0303, 7am-7pm Mon.-Fri., 8am-7pm Sat., 8am-3pm Sun., $6) is reliable and well priced.

Blue Window Bistro (813 Central Ave., 505/662-6305, 11am-2:30pm and 5pm-8:30pm Mon.-Fri., 5pm-9pm Sat., $18) is the fanciest restaurant in town, which in Los Alamos still doesn't mean too fancy. It's a colorful, bustling place with a bit of outdoor seating. Food is typical fresh American: huge salads and hot sandwiches for lunch, creative pasta and steaks in the evening. If you're headed back down the hill for the night, it's not worth staying for dinner, but if you're here overnight, it's your best option.

Kitty-corner across the parking lot, **Pajarito Brewpub** (614 Trinity Dr., 505/662-8877, 4pm-10pm Mon., 11am-11pm Tues., 11am-10pm Wed., 11am-midnight Thurs.-Sat., 11am-10pm Sun.) is the liveliest (er, maybe only) bar in town, but the food is pricey.

Starbucks on Central Avenue is notable just for the deeply scientific conversations on which you can eavesdrop.

Accommodations

The few hotels in Los Alamos cater primarily to visiting engineers, though it's a handy place to bunk if you want to get an early start at Bandelier. The chain hotels are functional, and **North Road Inn** (2127 North Rd., 505/662-3678, www.northroadinn.com, $86 d), a converted apartment complex in a quiet residential area, has large rooms (some are suites with kitchenettes). Those on the upper level are a bit more private.

Information

Stop at the **tourist info center** (109 Central Park Sq., 505/662-8105, www.visitlosalamos.org, 9am-5pm Mon.-Fri., 9am-4pm Sat., 10am-3pm Sun.) for maps and advice on hikes. There's a bigger office in **White Rock** (115 Hwy 4, 505/672-3183, 8am-6pm daily, 10am-2pm daily in winter), en route to Bandelier. Check the events calendar at www.fyilosalamos.com.

Getting There

Los Alamos is 36 miles (45 minutes by car) from downtown Santa Fe via U.S. 84/285 north to Highway 502 west. From Española, it's 20 miles (30 minutes) west on Highway 30 to Highway 502. There is an airport (LAM, www.flylosalamos.com), but at research time, the city had no commercial service.

★ BANDELIER NATIONAL MONUMENT

One of New Mexico's most atmospheric ancient sites, **Bandelier National Monument** (www.nps.gov/band, $20/car) comprises 23,000 acres of wilderness, including the remarkable Frijoles Canyon, lined on either side with cave "apartments," while the remnants of a massive settlement from the 16th century occupy the valley floor.

The place gets so busy in summer that mid-May-mid-October, the park is accessible only by shuttle bus from the visitors center in White Rock. The best way to avoid crowds is to arrive early on a weekday, if possible. Another approach is to join a torch-lit, silent **night walk** ($6) into Frijoles Canyon; they're

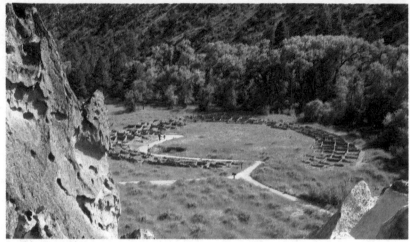

Bandelier National Monument

typically on Friday nights, but call the visitors center or check online for the schedule.

In the park, another **visitors center** (505/672-3861, 9am-6pm daily mid-May-mid-Oct., 9am-4:30pm mid-Oct.-mid-May) has a museum and the usual array of maps and guides. If you're interested in wildflowers, pick up a Falls Trail guide, as it has good illustrations of what grows in the area. Rangers run free **guided walks** around the main loop a few times a day, or you can pick up the trail guide for $1.

Main Loop Trail and Alcove House Trail

A paved walkway leads out the back of the visitors center into Frijoles Canyon, passing the ruins of the major settlements—or at least the ones that have been thoroughly excavated. You first reach **Tyuonyi** (chew-ON-yee), a circle of buildings that was settled for about 200 years, beginning in the 1300s. Built of bricks cut from tuff (the volcanic rock that makes up most of the area) and adobe plaster, some of the 250 rooms at one time stood several stories tall.

The trail then goes up next to the cliffs, dotted with small caves dug out of the soft stone, and to **Long House,** the remnants of

a strip of condo-style buildings tucked into the rock wall. Paintings and carvings decorate the cliff face above. If you're here near sunset, keep an eye on the **bat cave** near the end of the strip, home to thousands of the animals.

Continue another half mile to the **Alcove House,** accessible by 140 feet of ladders. It's well worth the climb up, if you can handle heights.

Frey Trail

The 1.5-mile **Frey Trail** used to be the main access route to Frijoles Canyon, before the access road was built by the Civilian Conservation Corps in the 1930s. Descending from **Juniper Campground** (just off Highway 4 northwest of the park access road), it's a nice approach to the area, with great views over Tyuonyi and a general sense of what it must have been like to "discover" the canyon. The trail has no shade, however, so it's best hiked early in the day. The shuttle bus can drop you at the trailhead, so you can hike down, then ride back to the depot.

Tsankawi

Well before you reach the main entrance to Bandelier, you pass **Tsankawi** on the east side of Highway 4. (This area is accessible by car year-round.) Unique pottery excavated in this separate section, disconnected from the main park, suggests that it was inhabited by a different people from those who settled in Frijoles Canyon, and some sort of natural border seems to have formed here, despite a shared cliff-dwelling culture: Today the pueblos immediately north of the Bandelier area speak Tewa, while those to the south speak Keresan. A 1.5-mile loop, with ladders to climb along the way, leads past unexcavated ruins, cave houses, and even a few petroglyphs.

Española

Camping

Juniper Campground ($12), just inside the park's northern border, is usually open year-round, with 94 sites. There are no hookups or showers. No reservations are taken, but it's usually not full. The scenery up on the plateau is a bit bleak, due to the 2011 fire, but you will get an early start on the day if you overnight here.

Getting There

Bandelier is 45 miles (one hour) from downtown Santa Fe via U.S. 84/285 north to Highway 502 and Highway 4 west. From Jemez Springs, it's 41 miles (one hour) via Highway 4 east.

From mid-May to mid-October, access to the park is via free **shuttle bus** only. The service departs from the **White Rock visitors center** (Hwy. 4) every 20 or 30 minutes between 9am and 3pm; before or after that time, you can enter the park by car.

White Rock is a 40-minute drive from Santa Fe via U.S. 84/285 north to Highway 502 and Highway 4 west. From Jemez Springs, it's about an hour drive via Highway 4 north and east (but you'll have to drive past the Bandelier entrance, and double back in the shuttle bus). The bus also stops at the Frey Trail trailhead en route to the main park.

ESPAÑOLA

Midway between Santa Fe and Taos, Española lacks the glamour or scenery of its neighbors. The town of 10,000 is fairly rough around the

edges, but if you're driving through at mealtime, it's a great place to stop for some local food. And although it doesn't have much in the way of its own sights (except for the occasional excellent lowrider), it is at a convenient crossroads and has a couple of good-value hotels.

Plaza de Española

Clustered around this public space are the town's museums. The tiny **Bond House** (706 Bond St., 505/747-8535, 1pm-3:30pm Mon.-Wed., noon-4pm Thurs.-Fri., free) devotes half its space to artwork and the other small room to various historic artifacts. Down the hill, past the replica Alhambra fountain, is the **Misión Museum,** another replica, of the town's original mission church, furnished with traditional craft work from around the valley. It is open sporadically—ask at the Bond House if no one is around.

Food

Thirsty? Look out for **Saints & Sinners** (503 S. Riverside Dr., 505/753-2757, 1pm-10pm Mon.-Thurs., 1pm-midnight Fri. and Sat.), a long-established package liquor store where you can also crack open a beer. It stocks an excellent selection of tequilas, and the neon sign should get landmark status (yes, they sell souvenir T-shirts). Cash only.

For a quick bite, stop at **El Parasol** (603 Santa Cruz Rd., 505/753-8852, 7am-9pm Mon.-Sat., 8am-8pm Sun., $5), a take-out stand with picnic tables under cotton-wood trees and a Spanglish menu ("pollo with guacamole taco"). Another option: the big Mexican-style sandwiches at **Tortas Rainbow** (745 N. Riverside Dr., 505/747-1791, 9am-8pm daily, $6). It's in a strip mall and can be easy to miss—look for (ironically) the Subway.

For a sit-down breakfast or lunch, diner-style **JoAnn's Ranch O Casados** (938 N. Riverside Dr., 505/753-1334, 7am-9pm Mon.-Sat., 7am-4pm Sun., $10) does all-day breakfast, plus very good and inexpensive enchiladas, fajitas, and more. The red chile is rich and mellow, and you can get half orders of many dishes.

A slightly more formal option, **La Cocina** (415 S. Santa Clara Bridge Rd., 505/753-3016, 7am-8pm Mon.-Sat., 8am-3pm Sun., $13) does all the New Mexican classics, including bur-ritos made with local lamb.

Accommodations

Española is not a common overnight stop, but it has some hotels that are so nice, you might rethink your itinerary. They can be especially handy after a night at the Santa Fe Opera, when all the traffic toward Santa Fe is backed up—but the road north is wide open. The ★ **Inn at the Delta** (243 Paseo de Oñate, 505/753-9466, www.innatthedelta.biz, $110 s, $140 d) is a beautiful rambling adobe complex built by a longtime Española family. The positively palatial rooms are decorated with locally made furniture, and each has a fireplace, a porch, and a jetted tub. Rates in-clude breakfast.

A project of the local pueblo, the **Santa Claran** (460 N. Riverside Dr., 877/505-4949, www.santaclaran.com, $85 d) also has spa-cious rooms, tastefully done in subdued grays

and browns. Perks include fridges and laun-dry machines, but Internet is wired-only in rooms; there's wireless access in the lobby.

South of town, on the road to Los Alamos, ★ **Rancho Jacona** (277 County Rd. 84, 505/455-7948, www.ranchojacona.com, $170 d) is a working farm dotted with 11 casitas, each with a kitchen and space for 3-8 people. You'll likely get some fresh chicken eggs for breakfast, and kids can frolic in the pool. There's a three-night minimum.

Getting There

Española is about a 45-minute drive from cen-tral Santa Fe via U.S. 84/285 north. Leaving Española, take Highway 68 (also called Riverside Drive) north from here to Taos (45 miles), or cross over the Rio Grande and con-tinue on U.S. 84 to Abiquiu (22 miles) or U.S. 285 to Ojo Caliente (25 miles). From an inter-section in the middle of Española, Highway 76 leads east to Chimayó (8 miles), then to Truchas and the other high-road towns on the way to Taos. From the old main plaza on the west side of the Rio Grande, Highway 30 is the back road to Los Alamos (20 miles).

OJO CALIENTE

Twenty-six miles north of Española on U.S. 285, **Ojo Caliente Mineral Springs** (505/583-2233, www.ojospa.com, 8am-10pm daily) is effectively the center of a tiny settle-ment that built up around the hot springs here. Established in 1916, it's now a some-what posh resort. The various paved pools ($20 Mon.-Thurs., $32 Fri.-Sun., $16/$28 after 6pm) have different mineral contents, and there's a mud area with rich local clay, as well as private soaking tubs and a full spa. It's a pretty little place, set up against sandstone bluffs, but not necessarily worth the drive spe-cifically from Santa Fe, unless you've tired of Ten Thousand Waves or you prefer mineral waters; in any case, try to go on a weekday, as it gets busy on weekends.

The hotel rooms at the resort ($149 d, no shower; $189 d, full bath) are no great value (although rates do include access to the springs). But camping ($20) is an option, and the bathroom facilities were upgraded in 2014. If you do want to stay overnight, **The Inn at Ojo** (505/583-9131, www.ojocaliente.com, $130 d), just down the road, is a better value.

Just behind the springs, **Posi Trail** leads into public land; the area is especially popular with mountain bikers. The resort office has trail maps.

Getting There

Ojo Caliente is 50 miles from downtown Santa Fe, about an hour's drive north on U.S. 84/285, then U.S. 285 east where it splits, north of Española. From Española, allow 30 minutes' driving time. From Abiquiu, avoid backtracking by going through El Rito; take Highway 554 north to Highway 111 north, coming out on U.S. 285 a few miles north of Ojo Caliente. This route takes about 45 minutes.

From Ojo Caliente, you can continue 41 miles to Taos (about a one-hour drive). Follow U.S. 285 north for 10 miles, then turn right (east) on Highway 567. In nine miles, Highway 567 ends at a T junction; turn left (north) on Taos County Road and continue about eight miles. You will meet U.S. 64 about one mile west of the Rio Grande Gorge; Taos is to the right (east).

ABIQUIU

Northwest of Española, along U.S. 84, the valley formed by the Rio Chama is one of the most striking landscapes in northern New Mexico. Lush greenery on the riverbanks clashes with bright red mud; roaming sheep and cattle graze by the roadside. The striated hills represent dramatic geological shifts, from purple stone formed in the dinosaur era 200 million years ago to red clay formed by forests, then gypsum from sand dunes, then a layer of lava only eight million years old. Far more recently, Abiquiu became inextricably linked with the artist Georgia O'Keeffe, who made the place her home for more than 40 years, entranced by the glowing light and dramatic skyline.

Although Abiquiu often refers to the whole river valley, the unofficial town center is **Bode's** (21196 U.S. 84, 505/685-4422, 6:30am-7pm Mon.-Thurs., 6:30am-8pm Fri., 7am-8pm Sat., 7am-7pm Sun.), pronounced BO-deez. This long-established general store also has gas, pastries and green-chile cheeseburgers (11:30am-3pm daily), fishing licenses and tackle, and local crafts. In winter, it closes earlier on weekends.

Up the hill opposite Bode's is the actual **village of Abiquiu,** established in 1754 by

the hot springs at Ojo Caliente

genízaros (Hispanicized Indians) through a land grant from the Spanish Crown. O'Keeffe's house forms one side of the old plaza; on the other is the Santo Tomás de Abiquiu Church, built in the 1930s after the community opted for the legal status of village rather than pueblo. Past O'Keeffe's house is the village *morada,* dramatically set on a hilltop. You're not really welcome to poke around, however—the village maintains a privacy policy similar to those of the pueblos. So it's best to visit on a guided tour of the house, or come on the village's feast day, for Santa Rosa de Lima, on the weekend closest to August 25.

Georgia O'Keeffe Home

The artist's main residence, where she lived 1949-1984, fronts the small plaza in the village center of Abiquiu. The **Georgia O'Keeffe Home** (505/685-4539, www.okeeffemuseum. org) is open for hour-long guided tours mid-March-November. The price, even for the basic tour, can seem a bit steep, but for fans of modernism of any kind, it's a beautiful place to see. The rambling adobe, parts of which were built in the 18th century, is a great reflection of O'Keeffe's aesthetic, which fused the starkness of modernism with an organic sensuality. If you're on a budget, console yourself with the fact that in many ways the surrounding landscape reflects O'Keeffe's work as much as her home does—and be sure to stop at Ghost Ranch, for more (and cheaper) info on the painter.

The schedule varies by month, but there are five **tours** ($35) daily on Tuesday, Thursday, and Friday. June-October, tours are also on Wednesday and Saturday, when the price goes up to $45. Longer, special tours with Judy Lopez ($65), who worked with O'Keeffe for more than a decade, run Thursday June-November. A Wednesday-night "behind-the-scenes" tour ($65) includes a visit to O'Keeffe's fallout shelter, among other things. Tours depart from the Abiquiu Inn on U.S. 84; you must make reservations at least a month in advance.

Egyptian architect Hassan Fathy's Dar al Islam

Dar al Islam and Plaza Blanca

In another chapter of New Mexico's long utopian history, a few American converts established **Dar al Islam** (505/685-4515 ext. 21, www.daralislam.org, 10am-4pm Mon.-Fri., free), an intentional religious community, in 1980. It was meant to be a place in which Muslims—some 30 families to start with—could practice their religion in every aspect of life, from education to food. The group set up a ranch and built the Abiquiu Inn and a few other local businesses, but the village concept eventually foundered. More recently, Dar al Islam has been reinvented as a retreat center that's open to visitors.

Anyone interested in architecture will want to visit to see the adobe mosque by Egyptian architect Hassan Fathy, all organic, sinuous lines, and in general, the view from the hilltop across the Chama River valley is a beautiful one. The head of the center requests that visitors dress modestly (arms, legs, and cleavage covered) and be quiet, so as not to disturb classes or workshops in session. Stop at the office first (back a bit and to the right of the parking area) to introduce yourself.

The community's land, some 8,500 acres, also includes the towering gypsum formations of **Plaza Blanca** (White Place). The eerie space, bleached as bones, was recorded in a series of Georgia O'Keeffe paintings, and it has also been used for numerous movie shoots. Two main trails lead out from the parking area.

Coming from the south, the community is accessible via Highway 554, which runs east from U.S. 84, just south of Abiquiu (follow signs for El Rito). Immediately after crossing the Chama River, turn left on County Road 0155. Continue 3.2 miles and turn right through a wooden gate made of telephone poles. Coming from the north on U.S. 84, look for County Road 0155, which is unpaved here, just north of Bode's; the wooden gate will be on the left, 2.3 miles on, shortly after the paving starts. Once through the gate, the road forks after less than a mile: To the left is the entrance to Dar al Islam; to the right, Plaza Blanca.

Abiquiu Lake

An Army Corps of Engineers dam project created the 4,000-acre **Abiquiu Lake** with fingers running into the canyons all around. The view coming in is marred by the power station, but past that the water glimmers at the base of the flat-topped mountain Pedernal ("Flint") Peak, the distinctive silhouette that found its way into so many of O'Keeffe's paintings. ("It's my private mountain," she often said. "God told me if I painted it often enough, I could have it.") The overly paved **campground** (505/685-4433, www.nmparks.com) at the lake is open year-round, but water and electric hookups ($14) are available only in the summer.

★ Ghost Ranch

Ghost Ranch (U.S. 84, 505/685-1000, www.ghostranch.org), a 21,000-acre retreat owned by the Presbyterian Church, is best known because Georgia O'Keeffe owned a small parcel of the land and maintained a studio here. In the science world, it's also known as the place where, in 1947, paleontologists combing the red hills discovered about a thousand skeletons of the dinosaur *Coelophysis* ("hollow form," for its hollow, birdlike bones), the largest group discovered in the world.

The grounds are open to day visitors ($5 suggested donation), for **hiking.** The best trek, which takes about two hours round-trip, is to **Chimney Rock,** a towering landmark with panoramic views of the entire area. Don't

a cabin at Ghost Ranch

be daunted—the steepest part of the trail is at the start—but do slather on the sunscreen, as there's no shade on this route. **Box Canyon** is an easier, shadier, all-level walk that's about four miles round-trip. **Kitchen Mesa Trail,** which starts at the same point, is much more difficult, requiring some climbing to get up the cliffs at the end (though you could hike the easy first two-thirds, then turn around).

Visitors can also see the **Florence Hawley Ellis Museum of Anthropology** and the **Ruth Hall Museum of Paleontology** (both 9am-5pm Mon.-Sat., 1pm-5pm Sun., $4), which display the local finds, including remnants of the prehistoric Gallina culture from the ridge above the valley and an eight-ton chunk of *Coelophysis*-filled siltstone in the process of being excavated. In summer, both museums are also open 1pm-5pm on Sunday.

Guided **tours** (various times, $25-35) of the ranch grounds run mid-March-November, on various topics, from local archaeology to movie settings. One walking tour visits O'Keeffe's painting spot in the red Chinle hills behind the ranch. **Horseback rides** ($85) are another option, visiting various spots key to O'Keeffe's painting life.

Christ in the Desert Monastery

Thirteen miles up a dirt road, the Benedictine **Christ in the Desert Monastery** (Forest Rd. 151, 575/613-4233, www.christdesert.org, 8am-6pm Sun.-Fri.) is said to be the remotest monastery in the Western Hemisphere. The drive follows the Chama River through a lush valley, ending at a striking modern church designed in 1972 by the woodworker and architect George Nakashima to blend in with the dramatic cliffs behind. Most of the outbuildings are straw-bale construction, running on solar power, and the monks grow much of their food and brew their own Belgian-style beer, Monks Ale (look for it at Bode's in Abiquiu). A gift shop next to the modern church sells various monastery products. The annual hop harvest, in late August, is a convivial event that draws volunteers from all

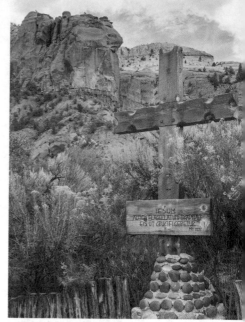

Christ in the Desert Monastery

over. Look for Forest Road 151 off the west side of U.S. 84, north of Ghost Ranch.

For a hike with a view across the valley and the red rocks, **Rim Vista trail** (no. 15) is a good route, climbing up to a mesa in about 2.3 miles one-way. Look for the trailhead less than one mile in on Forest Road 151, off the north side of the road; turn right, then bear right at the fork and park after a quarter mile. The trail is best in spring and fall, as there is not much shade here.

Echo Amphitheater

A bandshell-shaped rock formation, **Echo Amphitheater** is a natural wonder of acoustics and a great place to let kids run around and yell to their hearts' content. It's four miles north of Ghost Ranch on U.S. 84. There are pleasant picnic areas ($2/car) tucked in the brush.

Food and Accommodations

The **Abiquiu Inn** (21120 U.S. 84, 505/685-4378, www.abiquiuinn.com) functions as the area's visitors center. Lodging ($170 d) consists of some pretty casitas ($220) at the back of the property near the river, and a cluster of motel rooms closer to the front (request one facing away from the road). Two economy rooms ($130) are well kept but best for early risers, as they have skylights over the beds. The inn's restaurant, **Café Abiquiu** (7am-9pm daily, $14) serves a nice mix of traditional New Mexican and more creative food, with especially good breakfasts.

You can also stay at **Ghost Ranch** (U.S. 84, 505/685-4333, www.ghostranch.org) when it's not full for retreats, in various room options. The cheapest are cabins with shared bath ($69 s, $89 d, with breakfast), which are an especially good deal for solo travelers. Private-bath rooms ($119 s, $139 d) have fine views over the valley. You can also camp (from $25). Rates for rooms (but not campsites) include breakfast, and day visitors can take simple **meals** (noon-1pm and 5pm-6pm) at the dining hall.

Christ in the Desert Monastery (Forest Rd. 151, 801/545-8567, www.christdesert. org, $90 d) offers wonderful accommodations (two-night minimum) for a suggested donation, which includes all meals. At the 11.5-mile mark on the same road, **Rio Chama Campground** is preferable to Abiquiu Lake if you really want to get away from it all.

Getting There

Abiquiu is about 50 miles (one hour) from downtown Santa Fe. From Santa Fe, take U.S. 84/285 north for 26 miles to Española. From Española, continue on U.S. 84 north for 23 miles to Abiquiu. From Abiquiu to Taos, it's about 70 miles, or an hour and a half, via El Rito or Ojo Caliente. Continuing north on U.S. 84, you'll reach the Rio Chama in another 60 miles (one hour).

LOW ROAD TO TAOS

Following the winding Rio Grande up into the mountains is the highlight of this drive north. The route begins past the modern town of Española, passing into a narrowing canyon and finally emerging at the point where the high plains meet the mountains. This dramatic arrival makes it the better route for heading north to Taos; you can then loop back south via the high road.

Embudo and Dixon

The village of Embudo is really just a bend in the river where the Chili Line railroad from Denver used to stop (the old station is across the river). But it offers a random roadside attraction in the **Classical Gas Museum** (1819 Hwy. 68, 505/852-2995, free), a front yard filled

the Classical Gas Museum in Embudo

with old service station accoutrements. If the gate is open, the owner is probably home, and you can peek inside to see a beautiful collection of neon signs and restored gas pumps. There's also a good eating option: **Sugar's** (1799 Hwy. 68, 505/852-0604, 11am-6pm Thurs.-Sun., $6), a small roadside trailer that doles out seriously big food, such as barbecue brisket burritos. It's takeout only, but there are a few plastic picnic tables where you can sit down.

If you're into wine, keep an eye out for the various wineries just north of here: **Vivác** (2075 Hwy. 68, 505/579-4441, 10am-6pm Mon.-Sat., 11am-6pm Sun.) is on the main highway, and **La Chiripada** (505/579-4437, 11am-5pm Mon.-Sat., noon-5pm Sun.) is down Highway 75 a few miles in the pleasant little town of Dixon, known for its dense concentration of artists, organic farmers, and vintners. The convivial **farmers market** runs on summer and fall Wednesdays (4:30pm-7pm), and in early November, look for the long-running **Dixon Studio Tour** (www.dixonarts.org). A good year-round reason to make the turn is ★ **Zuly's** (234 Hwy. 275, 505/579-4001, 8:30am-3pm Tues.-Thurs., 8:30am-7pm Fri., 9am-7pm Sat., $8), serving strong coffee and classic New Mexican food with a bit of hippie flair; hours cut back slightly in winter.

Pilar

Beginning just south of the village of Pilar and stretching several miles north, **Orilla Verde Recreation Area** ($3/car) is public land along either side of the Rio Grande, used primarily as a put-in or haul-out for rafting, but you can camp on the riverbanks as well. Petaca and Taos Junction have the best sites ($7/night).

Running about 1.2 miles one-way along the west edge of the river, the **Vista Verde Trail** is an easy walk with great views and a few petroglyphs to spot in a small arroyo about a third of the way out. The trailhead is located on the other side of the river, half a mile up the hill from the Taos Junction Bridge off the dirt road Highway 567 (turn left off the highway in Pilar, then follow signs into Orilla Verde). Stop first on the main highway at the **Rio Grande Gorge Visitors Center** (Hwy. 68, 575/751-4899, 8:30am-4:30pm daily June-Aug., 10am-2pm daily Sept.-May) for maps and other information.

Across the road, **Pilar Yacht Club** (Hwy. 68, 575/758-9072, 8am-6pm daily mid-May-Aug., 9am-2pm daily Apr.-mid-May and Sept.-Oct.) is the center of the action, selling tubes for lazy floats, serving food to hungry river rats, and functioning as an office for a couple of outfitters.

rafting on the Rio Grande near Pilar

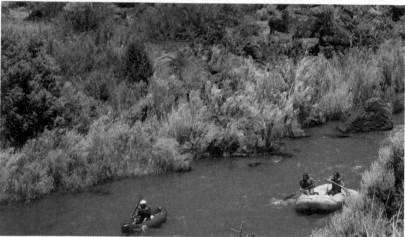

Getting There

This low-road route is more direct than the high road to Taos, and has fewer potential diversions. Driving the 70 miles from downtown Santa Fe to Taos (on U.S. 84/285 and Hwy. 68), with no stops, takes about an hour and a half. There are no gas stations between Española and Taos.

HIGH ROAD TO TAOS

Chimayó, Córdova, Truchas, Las Trampas, Peñasco—these are the tiny villages strung, like beads on a necklace, along the winding highway through the mountains to Taos. This is probably the area of New Mexico where Spanish heritage has been least diluted—or at any rate relatively untouched by Anglo influence, for there has been a long history of exchange between the Spanish towns and the adjacent pueblos. The local dialect is distinctive, and residents can claim ancestors who settled the towns in the 18th century. The first families learned to survive in the harsh climate with a 90-day growing season, and much of the technology that worked then continues to work now; electricity was still scarce even in the 1970s, and adobe construction is common.

To casual visitors, these communities, closed off by geography, can seem a little insular, but pop in at the galleries that have sprung up in a couple of the towns, and you'll get a warm welcome. And during the **High Road Art Tour** (www.highroadnewmexico. com), over two weekends in September, modern artists and more traditional craftspeople, famed particularly for their wood-carving skills, open their home studios.

The route starts on Highway 503, heading east off U.S. 84/285 just north of Pojoaque.

Chimayó

From Nambé Pueblo, Highway 503 continues to a T junction; make a hard left onto Highway 98 to descend into the valley of Chimayó, site of the largest mass pilgrimage in the United States. During Holy Week, some 50,000 people arrive on foot, often bearing large crosses. The destination is a remarkable church.

★ SANTUARIO DE CHIMAYÓ

The pilgrimage tradition began in 1945, as a commemoration of the Bataan Death March, but the **Santuario de Chimayó** (Hwy. 98, 505/351-9961, www.holychimayo.us, 9am-6pm daily May-Sept., 9am-5pm daily Oct.-Apr.) had a reputation as a miraculous spot from its start, in 1814. It began as a small chapel, built at the place where a local farmer,

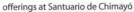
offerings at Santuario de Chimayó

Bernardo Abeyta, is said to have dug up a glowing crucifix; the carved wood figure was placed on the altar. The building later fell into disrepair, but in 1929, the architect John Gaw Meem bought it, restored it, and added its sturdy metal roof; Meem then granted it back to the archdiocese in Santa Fe.

Unlike many of the older churches farther north, which are now open very seldom, Chimayó is an active place of prayer, always busy with tourists as well as visitors seeking solace, with many side chapels and a busy gift shop. (Mass is said weekdays at 11am and on Sunday at 10:30am and noon year-round.) The approach from the parking area passes chain-link fencing into which visitors have woven twigs to form crosses, each set of sticks representing a prayer. Outdoor pews made of split tree trunks accommodate overflow crowds, and a wheelchair ramp gives easy access to the church.

But the original adobe *santuario* seems untouched by modernity. The front wall of the dim main chapel is filled with an elaborately painted altar screen from the first half of the 19th century, the work of Molleno (nicknamed "the Chile Painter" because forms, especially robes, in his paintings often resemble red and green chiles). The vibrant colors seem to shimmer in the gloom, forming a sort of stage set for Abeyta's crucifix, Nuestro Señor de las Esquípulas, as the centerpiece. Painted on the screen above the crucifix is the symbol of the Franciscans: a cross over which the arms of Christ and Saint Francis meet.

Most pilgrims make their way directly to the small, low-ceiling antechamber that holds *el pocito*, the little hole where the glowing crucifix was allegedly first dug up. From this pit they scoop up a small portion of the exposed red earth, to apply to withered limbs and arthritic joints, or to eat in hopes of curing internal ailments. (The parish refreshes the well each year with new dirt, after it has been blessed by the priests.) The adjacent sacristy displays handwritten testimonials, prayers, and abandoned crutches; the figurine of Santo Niño de Atocha is also said to have been dug

out of the holy ground here as well. (Santo Niño de Atocha has a dedicated chapel just down the road—the artwork here is modern, bordering on cutesy, but the back room, filled with baby shoes, is poignant.)

CHIMAYÓ MUSEUM

The only other official sight in the village is the tiny **Chimayó Museum** (Plaza del Cerro, 505/351-0945, www.chimayomuseum.com, 11am-3pm Wed.-Sat. May-Aug., free), set on the old fortified plaza. It functions as a local archive and displays a neat collection of vintage photographs. Look for it behind Ortega's weaving shop.

FOOD AND ACCOMMODATIONS

For lunch, head across the parking lot from the Santuario de Chimayó to **Leona's** (505/351-4569, 10am-5pm Fri.-Mon., $3), where you can pick up bulk chiles and pistachios as well as delicious tamales and crumbly *bizcochitos*. For a more leisurely sit-down meal, the family-owned ★ **Rancho de Chimayó** (County Rd. 98, 505/351-4444, www.ranchodechimayo.com, 11:30am-9pm daily May-Oct., 11:30am-9pm Tues.-Sun. Nov.-Apr., $12) has earned a James Beard America's Classics award for its great local food: posole or rice, whole pintos or refried beans, smooth red sauce (from Chimayó chiles) or chunkier *chile caribe*. Enjoy it on a beautiful terrace—or inside the old adobe home by the fireplace in wintertime. The place is also open for breakfast on weekends, 8:30am-10:30am, and it rents seven **rooms** (from $79 d) in an old farmhouse across the road.

If you want to spend the night in the area, or use it as a base for exploring, you have a few good options. Not far from the church, off County Road 98, **Rancho Manzana** (26 Camino de Mision, 505/351-2227, www.ranchomanzana.com, $95 d) has a rustic-chic feel, with excellent breakfasts. En route to Española, **Casa Escondida** (64 County Rd. 100, 505/351-4805, www.casaescondida.com, $105 s, $145 d) is a polished country hideaway with nine modern-Southwest-style rooms and a big backyard with lots of birdlife.

Córdova

From Chimayó, turn right (east) on Highway 76 (west takes you to Española) to begin the climb up the Sangre de Cristo Mountains. Near the crest of the hill, about three miles along, a small sign points to Córdova, a village best known for its austere unpainted santos and *bultos* done by masters such as George López and José Dolores López. Another family member, **Sabinita López Ortiz** (9 County Rd. 1317, 505/351-4572, variable hours), sells her work and that of five other generations of woodcarvers. **Castillo Gallery** (County Rd. 1317, 505/351-4067, variable hours) mixes traditional woodwork with more contemporary sculpture.

Truchas

Highway 76 winds along to the little village of Truchas (Trout), founded in 1754 and still not much more than a long row of buildings set into the ridgeline. On the corner where the highway makes a hard left north is the village *morada*, the meeting place of the local Penitente brotherhood.

Head straight down the smaller road to reach **Nuestra Señora del Rosario de las Truchas Church,** tucked into a small plaza off to the right of the main street. It's open to visitors only June-August—if you do have a chance to look inside the dim, thick-walled mission, you'll see precious examples of local wood carving. Though many of the more delicate ones have been moved to a museum for preservation, those remaining display an essential New Mexican style—the sort of "primitive" thing that Bishop Lamy of Santa Fe hated. They're preserved today because Truchas residents hid them at home during the late 19th century. Santa Lucia, with her eyeballs in her hand, graces the altar, and a finely wrought crucifix hangs to the right, clad in a skirt because the legs have broken off.

Just up the road is **The Cordovas Handweaving Workshop** (32 County Rd. 75, 505/689-1124, 8am-5pm Mon.-Sat.), an unassuming wooden house that echoes with the soft click-clack of a broadloom, as this Hispano family turns out subtly striped rugs in flawless traditional style, as it has done for generations. Prices are quite reasonable.

Las Trampas

Farther north on Highway 76, the village of Las Trampas was settled in 1751, and its showpiece, **San José de Gracia Church** (10am-4pm Sat.-Sun. June-Aug.), was built nine years later. It remains one of the finest examples of New Mexican village church architecture. Its thick adobe walls are balanced by vertical bell towers; inside, the clerestory at the front of the church—a very typical design—lets light in to shine down on the altar, which was carved and painted in the late 1700s. Other paradigmatic elements include the *atrio,* or small plaza, between the low adobe boundary wall and the church itself, utilized as a cemetery, and the dark narthex where you enter, confined by the choir loft above, but serving only to emphasize the sense of light and space created in the rest

Las Trampas's weatherbeaten San José de Gracia Church

of the church by the clerestory and the small windows near the viga ceiling.

As you leave the town heading north, look to the right—you'll see a centuries-old acequia that has been channeled through a log flume to cross a small arroyo.

Picurís Pueblo

The smallest pueblo in New Mexico, Picurís has only about 300 members. It is also one of the few Rio Grande pueblos that has not built a casino. Instead, it capitalizes on its beautiful natural setting, a lush valley where bison roam and aspen leaves rustle. You can picnic here and fish in small but well-stocked Tu-Tah Lake. The **San Lorenzo de Picurís Church** looks old, but it was in fact rebuilt by hand in 1989, following the original 1776 design, a process that took eight years. As at Nambé, local traditions have melded with those of the surrounding villages, and the Hispano-Indian Matachines dances are well attended on Christmas Eve. Start at the **visitors center** (575/587-1099 or 575/587-1071, 9am-5pm Mon.-Sat.) to pick up maps. The pueblo is a short detour from the high road proper: At the junction with Highway 75, turn west, then follow signs off the main road.

Peñasco

Peñasco is best known to tourists as the home of ★ **Sugar Nymphs Bistro** (15046 Hwy. 75, 575/587-0311, 11:30am-2:30pm Mon.-Wed., 11:30am-3pm and 5:30pm-8pm Thurs.-Sat., 11am-2:30pm Sun., $12), a place with "country atmosphere and city cuisine," where you can get treats like grilled lamb, fresh-pressed cider, piñon couscous, and staggering wedges of layer cake. An adjoining **Peñasco Theatre** (www.penascotheatre.org) hosts quirky music and theatrical performances June-September. In winter, restaurant hours are more limited, so call ahead.

This is also the northern gateway to the **Pecos Wilderness Area**—turn on Forest

Sugar Nymphs Bistro is a sweet spot in Peñasco.

Road 116 to reach Santa Barbara Campground and the Santa Barbara Trail to Truchas Peak, a 23-mile round-trip that requires advance planning. Contact the **Española ranger district office** (1710 N. Riverside Dr., 505/753-7331, 8am-4:30pm Mon.-Fri.) or the one in the town of Pecos for conditions before you hike.

Getting There

From downtown Santa Fe, the high road to Taos is about 90 miles. Follow U.S. 84/285 north for 17 miles to Pojoaque. Turn right (east) on Highway 503, following signs for Nambé Pueblo; turn left where signed, onto County Road 98, to Chimayó, then left again on Highway 76. In about 30 miles, make a hard left onto Highway 518, and in 16 miles, you'll arrive in Ranchos de Taos, just north of the church and about 3 miles south of the main Taos plaza. The drive straight through takes a little more than two hours; leave time to dawdle at churches and galleries, take a hike, or have lunch along the way.

Information and Services

TOURIST INFORMATION

The **Santa Fe Convention and Visitors Bureau** (800/777-2489, www.santafe.org) hands out its visitors guide and other brochures from offices at the **convention center** (201 W. Marcy St., 8am-5pm Mon.-Fri.) and at the **Rail Runner depot** (401 S. Guadalupe St., 9am-5pm Mon.-Sat.); the depot office is also open Sunday May-October. The New Mexico Tourism Department runs a **visitors center** (491 Old Santa Fe Tr., 505/827-7336, www.newmexico.org, 8am-5pm Mon.-Fri.) near San Miguel Mission.

For info on the outdoors, head to the Bureau of Land Management's comprehensive **Public Lands Information Center** (301 Dinosaur Tr., 505/954-2000, www.publiclands.org, 8am-4:30pm Mon.-Fri.), just off Highway 14 (follow Cerrillos Road until it passes under I-25). You can pick up detailed route descriptions for area day hikes, as well as guidebooks, topo maps, and hunting and fishing licenses.

Books and Maps

Santa Fe has several particularly good bookshops in the center of town. **Travel Bug** (839 Paseo de Peralta, 505/992-0418, 7:30am-5:30pm Mon.-Sat., 11am-4pm Sun.) specializes in maps, travel guides, gear, and free advice. For more general books, **Collected Works** (202 Galisteo St., 505/988-4226, 8am-8pm Mon.-Sat., 8am-6pm Sun.) is the place to go for a trove of local-interest titles.

Local Media

The *Santa Fe New Mexican* is Santa Fe's daily paper. On Friday, it publishes events listings and gallery news in its *Pasatiempo* insert. For left-of-center news and commentary, the *Santa Fe Reporter* is the free weekly rag, available in most coffee shops and cafés.

Radio

KBAC (98.1 FM), better known as Radio Free Santa Fe, is a dynamic community station with eclectic music and talk. Tune in Friday afternoons for news on the gallery scene. Another public station is **KSFR** (101.1 FM), run by Santa Fe Community College.

SERVICES

Banks

First National Santa Fe (62 Lincoln Ave., 505/992-2000, 8am-5pm Mon.-Fri.) is on the west side of the plaza.

Post Office

Santa Fe's **main post office** (120 S. Federal Pl., 505/988-2239, 8am-5:30pm Mon.-Fri., 9am-4pm Sat.) is conveniently just north of the plaza, near the district courthouse.

Laundry

Most self-service laundries are on or near Cerrillos Road. Nearer to the center is **Solana Laundry** (949 W. Alameda, 505/982-9877, 7am-8pm daily). It also has drop-off service.

Getting There and Around

AIR

Santa Fe Municipal Airport (SAF, 121 Aviation Dr., 505/955-2900), west of the city, receives direct flights from Dallas and Los Angeles (seasonal) with American Eagle, and from Denver with United. Typically, fares are better to the Albuquerque airport (ABQ), an hour's drive away.

Sandia Shuttle Express (888/775-5696, www.sandiashuttle.com) does hourly pick-ups from the Albuquerque airport 8:45am-11:45pm and will deliver to any hotel or B&B ($30 one-way).

TRAIN

The **Rail Runner** (866/795-7245, www.riometro.org) goes from Albuquerque to downtown Santa Fe—the final stop is at the rail yard in the Guadalupe district (410 S. Guadalupe St.). The ride takes a little over 90 minutes and costs $9, or $10 for a day pass (only $9 if you buy it online), and the last train back to Albuquerque leaves at 9pm weekdays, 10:07pm Saturday, and 8:12pm Sunday.

Amtrak (800/872-7245, www.amtrak.com) runs the *Southwest Chief* once a day through Lamy, 18 miles south of Santa Fe. It's a dramatic place to step off the train—you'll feel very Wild West, as there's little visible civilization for miles around. Trains arrive from Chicago and Los Angeles in the afternoon, and Amtrak provides a shuttle van to the city.

BUS AND SHUTTLE

Santa Fe Pick-Up (505/231-2573, www.santafenm.gov, every 10 minutes 6:30am-5:30pm Mon.-Fri., 8:30am-5:30pm Sat., 10am-5:30pm Sun., free) is a service for tourists, with two routes covering all the main sights. It's free and runs more frequently than the regular city bus. The main circuit starts and ends in front of Jean Cocteau Cinema, on Montezuma Avenue just north of the Rail Runner depot, and it stops at the capitol, the St. Francis Cathedral, four points on Canyon Road, Museum Hill, and a few other tourist-friendly spots around town. From the capitol, the second route runs a loop up Canyon Road and out to Museum Hill.

For Cerrillos Road, you can use Route 2 on the city bus system, **Santa Fe Trails** (505/955-2001, www.santafenm.gov), from the handy central depot on Sheridan Street northwest of the plaza. Buses on all routes are not terribly frequent, every 20 minutes at the most. Fare is $1, or you can buy a day pass for $2, payable on board with exact change.

CAR

Ideally, you would not have a car while in Santa Fe itself, as parking is limited and expensive. **Hertz, Budget, Avis,** and **Thrifty** all have branches on Cerrillos Road.

From Albuquerque to Santa Fe, it's a straight shot north on I-25 for 65 miles; you'll reach Santa Fe in about an hour.

Coming from Taos, allow 1.5-2.5 hours, depending on whether you come on the low road (on Hwy. 68 and U.S. 84/285, via Española), via Ojo Caliente (mostly on U.S. 285), or on the high road (mostly on Hwy. 76, via Truchas).

Taos and North Central New Mexico

Sights 137

Entertainment and Events 150

Shopping. 153

Sports and Recreation 154

Food 157

Accommodations. 161

West on U.S. 64 164

The Enchanted Circle 170

Information and Services 177

Getting There and Around. 177

Look for ★ to find recommended
sights, activities, dining, and lodging.

Highlights

★ **Taos Art Museum at Fechin House:**
In the early 1930s, Russian artist Nicolai Fechin
designed his home in a fusion of Tartar, Spanish,
and American Indian styles. His and other artists'
paintings hang inside (page 141).

★ **San Francisco de Asis Church:** With its
massive adobe buttresses and rich earthy glow,
this 350-year-old Franciscan mission is one of the
most recognizable in the world, thanks to its frequent depiction in paintings and photographs
(page 145).

★ **Taos Pueblo:** The stepped adobe buildings at New Mexico's most remarkable pueblo
seem to rise organically from the earth. Don't
miss the ceremonial dances performed here,
about eight times a year (page 146).

★ **Rio Grande Gorge:** Think how dismayed
the first homesteaders must have been when
they reached "New Mexico's Grand Canyon," an
800-foot-deep channel cut through the rock to
the west of Taos. Think how overjoyed today's
white-water rafters are in the spring, when
mountain runoff surges through the rift (page
147).

★ **Hiking:** The mountains and mesas around
Taos are some of the most stunning places in
northern New Mexico to get some fresh air—you
can even climb the state's highest peak (page
154).

★ **Cumbres & Toltec Scenic Railroad:**
Ascending the pass through the Rockies into
Colorado on this rumbling old steam train, soot
and wind in your hair, you'll feel like you've
climbed to the very top of the world (page 167).

A dobe buildings cluster around a plaza. Steep mountains beckon. Art galleries, organic bakeries, and yoga studios proliferate. But the town of Taos is not just a miniature Santa Fe.

It's more isolated, reached by two-lane roads along either the winding mountain-ridge route or the fertile Rio Grande Valley, and it has a rougher, muddier feel. The glory of the landscape, from looming Taos Mountain to the blue mesas dissolving into the flat western horizon, can be breathtaking. The mysticism surrounding Taos Pueblo is intense, as is the often wild creativity of the artists who have lived here. No wonder people flock here on pilgrimages: to the ranch where D. H. Lawrence lived, to the hip-deep powder at Taos Ski Valley, to the San Francisco de Asis Church that Georgia O'Keeffe painted. Then they wind up staying. The person pouring your coffee at the café probably has a variation on this story.

Taos has long been associated with artists and writers, and even some more recent Hollywood types, but this doesn't translate to wealth and exclusivity. Hispano farmers in Valle Valdez scrape by on acequia-fed farm plots as they have for centuries. The same goes for residents of old Taos Pueblo, the living World Heritage Site that still uses no electricity or running water. Add to that a strong subculture of ski bums, artists, off-the-grid eco-homesteaders, and spiritual seekers, and you have a community that, while not typically prosperous, is more loyal and dedicated to preserving its unique way of life than perhaps any other small town in the western United States.

Jump the Taos Gorge on U.S. 64 west out of town for a beautiful drive over the mountains to Tierra Amarilla, where sheepherding continues as it has for centuries. North from here, you're nearly at the Colorado state line in Chama, best known as the depot for a scenic steam train.

North and east from Taos, the so-called Enchanted Circle byway loops around Wheeler Peak, the highest mountain in New Mexico at 13,161 feet. Unlike the rest of

Taos and North Central New Mexico

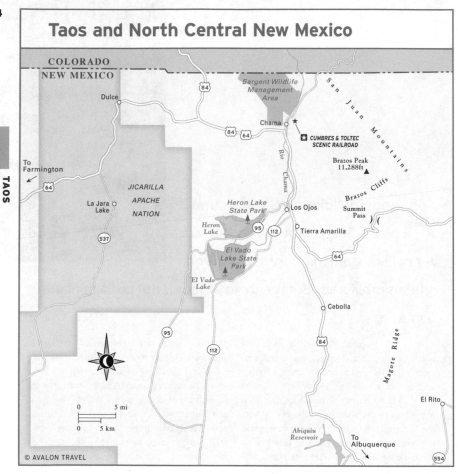

© AVALON TRAVEL

northern New Mexico, the area was settled primarily by miners and ranchers in the late 19th century. Along the way, you can stop at a mining ghost town, a moving Vietnam veterans' memorial, or a couple of less extreme ski resorts.

PLANNING YOUR TIME

Taos's busiest tourist season is **summer,** when a day's entertainment can consist of some strolling and museum-going, then settling in to watch the afternoon thunderheads gather and churn, followed by the sun setting under lurid red streaks across the broad western mesas. **Wintertime** also gets busy

with skiers between November and April, but as they're all up on the mountain during the day, museums scale back their hours, and residents reclaim the town center, curling up with books at the many coffee shops. **Taos Pueblo closes to visitors** for up to 10 weeks in February and March. By May, the peaks are relatively clear of snow, and you can hike to high meadows filled with wildflowers. **Fall** is dominated by the smell of wood smoke and the beat of drums, as the pueblo and the rest of the town turn out for the Feast of San Geronimo at the end of September.

From Santa Fe, it's possible to visit Taos as a **day trip**—as plenty of people do in the

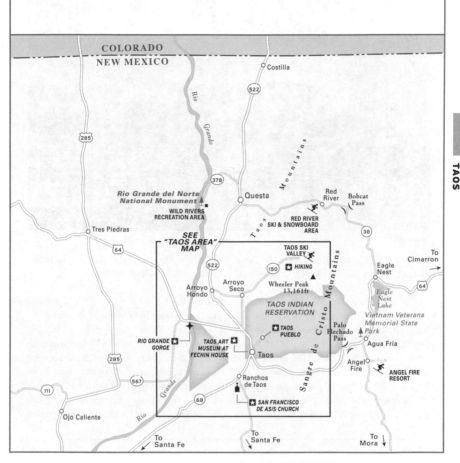

COLORADO
NEW MEXICO

Costilla

522

Rio Grande

285

378

Rio Grande del Norte
National Monument
WILD RIVERS
RECREATION AREA

Questa

Red
River

Bobcat
Pass

Mountains

RED RIVER
SKI & SNOWBOARD
AREA

38

Tres Piedras

SEE
"TAOS AREA"
MAP

TAOS SKI
VALLEY

To
Cimarron

64

522

150

HIKING

Eagle
Nest

Arroyo
Hondo

Arroyo
Seco

Wheeler Peak
13,161ft

Mountains

Eagle
Nest
Lake

64

TAOS INDIAN
RESERVATION

Vietnam Veterans
Memorial State
Park

RIO GRANDE
GORGE

TAOS ART
MUSEUM AT
FECHIN HOUSE

TAOS
PUEBLO

Palo
Flechado
Pass

Agua Fria

de Cristo Mountains

285

Taos

Angel
Fire

ANGEL FIRE
RESORT

567

Ranchos
de Taos

Sangre

68

SAN FRANCISCO
DE ASIS CHURCH

Ojo Caliente

Rio

To
Santa Fe

To
Santa Fe

To
Mora

summertime—but you'll get a better sense of the place if you stay overnight. A three- or four-night visit gives you time for an afternoon at Taos Pueblo, a couple of mornings at galleries and museums, a hike or skiing, and a day tour of the Enchanted Circle.

For Chama, you can easily make the drive from Taos and back in a day, though if you plan to ride the train, you'll have to get an early start or book a hotel there. As for the **Enchanted Circle,** the 84-mile loop is typically done as a day trip. By no means attempt to visit Taos *and* do the Enchanted Circle loop in a single day—you'd be terribly rushed, and this is hardly the spirit of Taos.

ORIENTATION

The area referred to as Taos encompasses a few nearby communities as well. Arriving via the low road, on Highway 68, you pass first through **Ranchos de Taos;** it's connected to Taos Plaza by Paseo del Pueblo Sur, a stretch of chain stores and cheap motels. The intersection with Kit Carson Road (U.S. 64) is the center of town proper (**Taos Plaza** is just west); for **parking,** there's a pay lot at the light, or a free lot a few blocks farther east on Kit Carson.

Heading north past Kit Carson, the road becomes Paseo del Pueblo Norte. It curves west after half a mile, and a smaller road

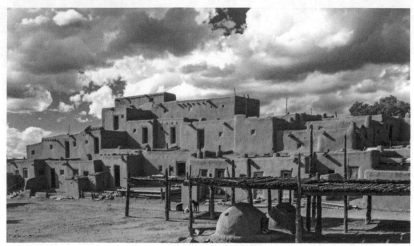

Taos Pueblo

continues north about two miles to **Taos Pueblo.** Paseo del Pueblo Norte carries on through what is technically the separate village of El Prado, then to a four-way intersection that will forever be called "the old blinking light," even though the flashing yellow signal was replaced with a newfangled three-color traffic light in the 1990s. Here U.S. 64 shoots **west to the Rio Grande,** and Highway 522 leads northwest to the outlying village of **Arroyo Hondo,** then to Questa and the Enchanted Circle. Highway 150 goes north to **Arroyo Seco,** and eventually to **Taos Ski Valley,** at the base of the slopes.

HISTORY

The first human inhabitants of the area at the base of Taos Mountain were Tiwa-speaking descendants of the Ancestral Puebloans (also called Anasazi) who migrated from the Four Corners area around AD 1000. Taos (how Spaniards heard the Tiwa word for "village") was a thriving village when Spanish explorers, part of Francisco de Coronado's crew, passed

Taos Weekend Getaway

- **Day 1:** Fly in to Albuquerque. Head to Taos via I-25 and the **low road.** Pick a prime plaza-view room at **Hotel La Fonda de Taos** or luxuriate in a suite at **Palacio de Marquesa.** Stroll the **plaza** and visit the **E. L. Blumenschein Home** and the galleries on Ledoux Street. Have a gourmet burger for dinner at **The Burger Stand,** then check out **The Alley Cantina.**

- **Day 2:** Visit **Taos Pueblo** in the morning. In the afternoon, tour the **Taos Art Museum** and **Millicent Rogers Museum.** If you'd rather hike, head for the **West Rim Trail** along the **Rio Grande Gorge**—it's fairly level, so you shouldn't have too much trouble, despite the elevation. Be dazzled by dinner at **El Meze.**

- **Day 3:** Drop by **San Francisco de Asis Church** in the morning, then prepare for the drive back south with breakfast at **Old Martina's Hall.** Head out along the **high road** to Santa Fe and then I-25 to the airport, which takes about four hours without much dawdling; a straight shot back down the low road will shave about 40 minutes off the trip.

through in 1540. By 1615, settlers had arrived. By the mid-18th century, Taos was the hub of a large trade in beaver pelts, which drew French fur trappers, Mexican traders, and local settlers to swap meets.

But in 1879 the railroad arrived in Raton, bumping Taos from its position as a trading hub. Fortunes turned only in 1898, when Bert Geer Phillips and Ernest Blumenschein, two painters on a jaunt from Denver, "discovered" Taos after their wagon wheel snapped near town. They established the Taos Society of Artists (TSA) in 1915, making names for themselves as painters of the American West and a name for Taos as a destination for creative types. In the 1960s, creativity took a turn to the communal, with groups such as the New Buffalo commune in Arroyo Hondo—an inspiration for Dennis Hopper's film *Easy Rider*. The culture clash at first was fierce, but in the decades since, hippies (and their richer relatives, ski bums) have become part of the town's most basic fabric.

Sights

TAOS PLAZA

The central **Taos Plaza,** enclosed by adobe buildings with deep portals, is easy to miss if you just cruise through on the main road—it's just west of the intersection with Kit Carson Road. Once an informal area at the center of a cluster of settlers' homes, the plaza was established around 1615 but destroyed in the Pueblo Revolt of 1680. New homes were built starting in 1710, as defense against Comanche and Jicarilla raiders. But fires repeatedly gutted the block-style buildings, so the structures that edge the plaza all date from around 1930—and unfortunately virtually all are now filled with rather cheesy souvenir shops.

On the plaza's north side, the **old Taos County courthouse** contains a series of WPA-sponsored murals painted in 1934 and 1935 by Emil Bisttram and a team of other Taos artists. The door is usually open when the farmers market is on, but not reliably at other times. Still, it's worth a try: Enter on the ground floor through the North Plaza Art Center and go upstairs, toward the back of the building. On the south side, the **Hotel La Fonda de Taos** harbors a small

early morning on the main plaza in Taos

Taos Area

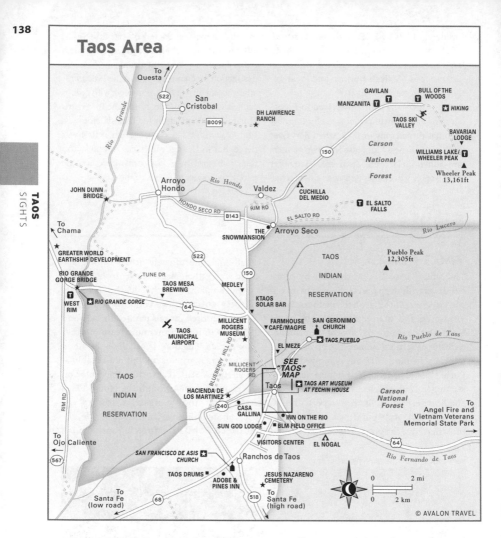

To Questa

522

San Cristobal

B009

DH LAWRENCE RANCH

GAVILAN

MANZANITA

BULL OF THE WOODS

HIKING

TAOS SKI VALLEY

BAVARIAN LODGE

Carson

WILLIAMS LAKE/ WHEELER PEAK

Rio Grande

Rio

150

National

Forest

Wheeler Peak 13,161ft

JOHN DUNN BRIDGE

Arroyo Hondo

Rio Hondo

Valdez

CUCHILLA DEL MEDIO

EL SALTO FALLS

To Chama

HONDO SECO RD

B143

RIM RD

EL SALTO RD

Rio Lucero

GREATER WORLD EARTHSHIP DEVELOPMENT

522

THE SNOWMANSION

Arroyo Seco

Pueblo Peak 12,305ft

RIO GRANDE GORGE BRIDGE

TUNE DR

150

TAOS MESA BREWING

MEDLEY

TAOS

INDIAN

WEST RIM

RIO GRANDE GORGE

64

KTAOS SOLAR BAR

RESERVATION

TAOS MUNICIPAL AIRPORT

MILLICENT ROGERS MUSEUM

FARMHOUSE CAFÉ/MAGPIE

SAN GERONIMO CHURCH

Rio Pueblo de Taos

EL MEZE

TAOS PUEBLO

BLUEBERRY HILL RD

MILLICENT ROGERS RD

SEE "TAOS" MAP

TAOS

INDIAN

HACIENDA DE LOS MARTINEZ

240

Taos

TAOS ART MUSEUM AT FECHIN HOUSE

Carson National Forest

To Angel Fire and Vietnam Veterans Memorial State Park

RIM RD

RESERVATION

CASA GALLINA

SUN GOD LODGE

INN ON THE RIO

BLM FIELD OFFICE

To Ojo Caliente

567

SAN FRANCISCO DE ASIS CHURCH

VISITORS CENTER

EL NOGAL

Ranchos de Taos

Rio Fernando de Taos

64

TAOS DRUMS

ADOBE & PINES INN

JESUS NAZARENO CEMETERY

To Santa Fe (low road)

68

518

To Santa Fe (high road)

0   2 mi
0   2 km

© AVALON TRAVEL

collection of D. H. Lawrence's "erotic" paintings (10am-6pm daily, guided $6, unguided $3, free to guests). The paintings are tame by today's standards, but they flesh out (no pun intended) the story of the writer's time in Taos, some of which is described in his book *Mornings in Mexico.*

In the center is a **monument** to New Mexicans killed in the Bataan Death March of World War II. The U.S. flag flies day and night, a tradition carried on after an incident during the Civil War when Kit Carson and a crew of his men nailed the flag to a pole and guarded it to keep Confederate sympathizers from taking it down.

In front of the historic La Fonda hotel, a large bronze **statue of Padre Antonio Martinez** gestures like a visionary. This local hero produced the area's first newspaper, *El Crepúsculo de la Libertad* (The Dawn of Freedom), which later became the *Taos News;* he also established a co-ed school, a seminary, and a law school. Bishop Lamy in Santa Fe criticized his liberal views, especially

Taos

TAOS CLAY STUDIO
ORLANDO'S

To Arroyo Seco and Taos Ski Valley

To TAOS PUEBLO

PASEO DEL PUEBLO NORTE

MILLICENT ROGERS RD

HAIL CREEK RD

Rio Pueblo de Taos

TAOS DINER

HACIENDA DEL SOL
GUTIZ
MABEL DODGE LN
THE LOVE APPLE

Lucero

UPPER RANCHITOS RD

TAOS PIZZA OUT BACK
64

Rio

RANCHITOS RD

CAMINO DE LA PLACITA

EL PUEBLO LODGE

UPPER

SEE "TAOS PLAZA" MAP

PASEO DEL PUEBLO NORTE

BROOKS ST

VALVERDE ST

Taos Plaza

TAOS ART MUSEUM AT FECHIN HOUSE

Kit Carson Park & Cemetery

LA LOMITA RD

RANCHITOS RD

SILER RD

240

To Hacienda de los Martinez

LOS CORDOBA RD

MONTOYA ST

EL MONTE SAGRADO

MANTE'S CHOW CART

PALACIO DE MARQUESA

Rio

PANDOS RD

DOLAN ST

VIGIL ST

KIT CARSON RD

LA POSTA RD

SALAZAR RD

PASEO DEL PUEBLO SUR

Fernando

de

ALBRIGHT ST

GUSDORF RD

LOS

0   0.25 mi
0   0.25 km

FRONTIER LN

Taos

PANDOS RD

64

To Inn on the Rio and Angel Fire

WIRED?

To Ranchos de Taos and
SAN FRANCISCO DE ASÍS CHURCH

© AVALON TRAVEL

Taos Plaza

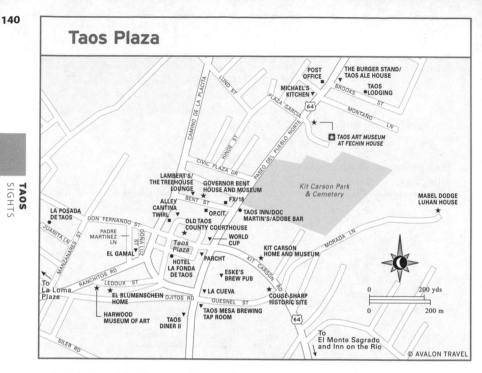

after Martinez defied Lamy's call for mandatory tithing, and Lamy later excommunicated him. Martinez continued to minister to locals at a chapel in his house until his death in 1867. The statue's enormous hands suggest his vast talent and influence in the town.

Harwood Museum of Art

The **Harwood Museum of Art** (238 Ledoux St., 575/758-9826, 10am-5pm Mon.-Sat., noon-5pm Sun., closed Mon.-Tues. Nov.-Mar., $10), set in the sprawling Pueblo Revival-style home of the Harwood patrons, tells the story of Taos's rise as an art colony, beginning with Ernest Blumenschein's fateful wagon accident, which left him and his colleague Bert Phillips stranded in the tiny town in 1898.

Modern Taos painters are represented in changing exhibit spaces upstairs and down, and it's interesting to see the same material—the mountain, the pueblo, the river, local residents—depicted in different styles over time. Also upstairs is a small but good

assortment of Hispano crafts, including some beautiful 19th-century tinwork and a couple of santos by Patrocinio Barela, the Taos wood-carver who modernized the art in the 1930s. A separate back wing is dedicated to seven ethereal abstractions by painter Agnes Martin; a local teacher offers yoga in the gallery every Wednesday. The Arthur Bell Auditorium hosts music concerts and artist talks.

E. L. Blumenschein Home

Ernest Blumenschein, one of the founding fathers of the Taos Society of Artists, moved into what is now the **E. L. Blumenschein Home** (222 Ledoux St., 575/758-0505, www.taoshistoricmuseums.org, 10am-5pm Mon.-Sat., noon-5pm Sun. Apr.-Oct., 10am-4pm Mon. and Thurs.-Sat., noon-4pm Sun. Nov.-Mar., $8) in 1919 with his wife, Mary Shepherd Greene Blumenschein, also an accomplished artist. The house's decoration largely reflects her taste, from the sturdy wood furnishings in the dining room to the light-filled studio and the cozy wood-paneled library.

The original rooms of the house feature rotating exhibits, while other rooms, including the "Green Room," are hung with works by their contemporaries, including a beautiful monotype of Taos Mountain by Oscar E. Berninghaus. The main bedroom, entered through a steep arch, is decorated with Mary's lush illustrations for *The Arabian Nights*. Throughout, you can admire the variety of ceiling styles, from rough-hewn split cedar (*rajas*) to tidy golden aspen boughs (*latillas*).

La Loma Plaza

To see what Taos Plaza looked like before the souvenir-shop economy, stroll down Lower Ranchitos Road and turn on Valdez Road to reach **La Loma Plaza.** The center of a fortified settlement created by 63 Spanish families in 1796, the ring of adobe homes around a central open space is dusty and little changed through the centuries. Exit the plaza by continuing uphill and bearing right—this takes you past La Loma's tiny old chapel and onto paved San Antonio Street, which leads downhill and back to Lower Ranchitos.

Governor Bent House and Museum

This dusty little backroom exhibit space is odd, but well worth a visit if it happens to be open (the posted hours aren't always maintained). The **Governor Bent House and Museum** (117 Bent St., 10am-5pm daily, $3) is the former residence of Charles Bent, who, following the onset of the Mexican-American War, was appointed the first governor of the territory of New Mexico in 1846, based on his extensive experience as a Western trader (he and his brother had built Bent's Fort, an important trading center in southern Colorado). But Bent died in 1847, at the hands of an angry mob dissatisfied by the new U.S. government.

Amid the slightly creepy clutter, which includes a malevolent-looking ceremonial buffalo head and photos of Penitente rituals from an old *Harper's* magazine, is the very hole in

the very wall that Bent's family quickly dug to escape while Bent tried to reason with the murderous crowd. The back room only gets stranger, with weird taxidermy (including an eight-legged lamb), sinister early 1900s doctor's instruments, and lots of old guns. The place may feel like an antiques store where nothing's for sale, but it still gives a surprisingly good overview of the period.

★ Taos Art Museum at Fechin House

This sunny space, the former home of artist and wood-carver Nicolai Fechin, is a showcase not only for a great collection of paintings, but also for Fechin's lovely woodwork. When the Russian native moved to Taos in 1927, hoping to cure his tuberculosis, he purchased seven acres of land, including the small, two-story **Taos Art Museum at Fechin House** (227 Paseo del Pueblo Norte, 575/758-2690, 10am-5pm Tues.-Sun. May-Oct., till 4pm Nov.-Apr., $10). He proceeded to hand-carve the lintels, staircases, bedsteads, and more, in a combination of Russian Tartar and local styles. His blending of traditions is flawless and natural—a small altar, also in the dining room, is set with Orthodox icons but could just as easily hold local santos.

The permanent collection rotates through three times a year, so the collection varies at any given time. One thing you can count on is that all will be eclectic: Victor Higgins's 1936 *Indian Nude* recalls Gauguin, while Dorothy Brett's *Rainbow and Indians* from 1942 is more enamored of the powerful landscape. One room is dedicated to Fechin's own portrait work, characterized by broad, dynamic brushstrokes and a canny eye for distinctive facial features. After all the work Fechin did on the house, he stayed in Taos only six years, when his wife divorced him. He moved on to Los Angeles with his daughter, Eya (her sunny study, on the ground floor, contains the child-scale furniture that her father made for her). After her father died in 1955, Eya, by then practicing psychodrama and dance therapy, returned to live in the studio (the back

Mabel Dodge Luhan's home is open as an inn and retreat center.

building that also houses the gift shop) and helped establish the main house as a museum.

Mabel Dodge Luhan House

Now used as a conference center and B&B, the **Mabel Dodge Luhan House** (240 Morada Ln., 575/751-9686, 9am-7pm daily, free) is open to curious visitors as well as overnight guests. Knock at the main building first; the caretaker will give you a history brochure for a self-guided tour around the public areas of the house.

Mabel Dodge, a well-off, freethinking woman who had fostered art salons in New York City and Florence, decamped to Taos in 1916, following her third husband. Eventually she got married again, to Taos Pueblo member Tony Luhan, and her name became inextricably linked with Taos's 20th-century history, thanks to all the budding artists and writers she encouraged to visit. D. H. Lawrence dubbed Taos "Mabeltown," and figures as grand and varied as Greta Garbo, Willa Cather, Ansel Adams, Georgia O'Keeffe, Robinson Jeffers, and Carl Jung made the long trek to her home.

Bordering the Taos reservation, the house was built to Luhan's specifications starting in 1918. Unsurprisingly, given her artistic taste, she exercised a firm hand in its design. Alongside a small original structure—a low row of adobe rooms that were already a century old at that point—she added a three-story main building, topped with a huge sunroom open on three sides. This, and the similarly glass-enclosed bathroom on the 2nd floor, scandalized her neighbors, the pueblo residents.

One of them, however, didn't seem to mind: Tony Luhan, the foreman of the construction project, became her next husband. But Mabel's custom love nest brought out some latent prurience even in D. H. Lawrence, who objected to the curtainless bathroom windows; to soothe his sensibilities, if not Mabel's, he painted colorful swirls directly on the glass.

Kit Carson Park and Cemetery

After seeing where Mabel Dodge Luhan lived, you can also visit her grave, in Taos's oldest cemetery. A shady sprawl of gravestones in a corner of **Kit Carson Park** (on Paseo del Pueblo Norte north of the Taos Inn), the cemetery was established in 1847 to bury the dead from the Taos Rebellion, a melee incited by wealthy Spanish landowners and Catholic priests anxious about their loss of influence under the Americans. Mobs killed New

Mexico's first American governor, the veteran merchant Charles Bent, as well as scores of other Anglo landowners in the area. The cemetery earned its current name when the bodies of Carson and his wife were moved here in 1869, according to his will.

Many of Taos's oldest families, particularly the merchants of the late 1800s, are buried here. Mabel had been a very close friend of the trader Ralph Meyers, and they often joked about being buried together. When Mabel died in 1962, a few years after Ralph, writer Frank Waters recalled their wishes and suggested that Meyers's grave be scooted over to make room for Mabel. She was the last person to be buried in the cemetery, in 1962, and her grave is squeezed into the far southwest corner. Other local luminaries at rest here include Padre Antonio Martinez, who stood up to Catholic bishop Lamy, and an Englishman named Arthur Manby, whose grave actually stands outside of the cemetery proper, due to his lifetime of shady business deals, land grabs, and outright swindles perpetrated in town. Manby was found beheaded in his mansion in 1929, and the unsympathetic populace was happy to attribute the death to natural causes.

Couse-Sharp Historic Site

Tours of the **Couse-Sharp Historic Site** (146 Kit Carson Rd., 575/751-0369, www. couse-sharp.org, May-Oct., donation) are by appointment and during open houses (3pm-5pm, first Saturday of the month June-Oct.), but it is well worth arranging to see the interior of the painter Eanger Irving Couse's home and studio. Couse, a friend of E. L. Blumenschein's, came to Taos in 1902 with his wife, Virginia, and spent the summers here, working as a figurative painter, until he died in 1936.

Not only has the Couse home and garden been meticulously kept up, as has adjacent property owned by friend and fellow painter Joseph Henry Sharp, but the tours are led by Couse's granddaughter and her husband, who have a wealth of stories to share. And not only artists will be intrigued; Couse's son, a mechanical engineer who developed mobile repair vehicles, built a vast machine shop here.

Kit Carson Home and Museum

Old photographs, memorabilia, and assorted trinkets from the frontier era conjure the spirit of the legendary scout at the **Kit Carson Home and Museum** (113 Kit Carson Rd.,

a chapel converted to an art studio at the Couse-Sharp Historic Site

575/758-4945, www.kitcarsonhomeand-museum.com, 10am-5pm daily in summer, 10am-4pm daily in winter, $7), where he lived with his third wife, Josefa Jaramillo, from 1843 until they both died in 1868.

The definitive mountain man, Carson was one of many solitary scouts, trackers, and trappers who explored the American West. He was an intrepid adventurer who, after a childhood on the barely settled edge of Missouri, joined a wagon train headed down the Santa Fe Trail; he arrived in Taos in 1826. His talent for tracking, hunting, and translating from Spanish and various Indian languages soon put him in high demand. Whether he was scouting for John C. Frémont as the explorer mapped the trails west to Los Angeles or serving as an officer in the Civil War or, less heroically, forcing the Navajos on the Long Walk to Fort Sumner, he called Taos home.

Taos Inn

Distinguished by its large glowing thunderbird sign, the oldest neon sign in town, the **Taos Inn** (125 Paseo del Pueblo Norte, 575/758-2233, www.taosinn.com) was as central to previous generations of Taoseños' lives as it is now. Granted, today it's the hotel bar that everyone goes to, but starting in the 1890s, it was the home of Dr. T. P. Martin, Taos's first and only county doctor, who had a good reputation for accepting chickens or venison from his poorer patients in lieu of cash. His home looked out on a small plaza and a well—which has since been covered over and made into the hotel lobby.

HACIENDA DE LOS MARTINEZ

The word *hacienda* conjures a sprawling complex and fields, but the reality in 19th-century Taos was quite different, as seen at the carefully restored 1804 **Hacienda de los Martinez** (708 Hacienda Rd., off Lower Ranchitos Rd., 575/758-1000, www.taoshistoricmuseums.org, 10am-5pm Mon.-Sat., noon-5pm Sun. Apr.-Oct., 10am-4pm Mon. and Thurs.-Sat., noon–4pm Sun. Nov.-Mar., $8), one of the last remaining homes of its kind in the Southwest. Its builder and owner, Don Antonio Severino Martinez, was a prominent merchant who hosted the Taos trade

Hacienda de los Martinez

fairs at the hacienda and eventually became the mayor of Taos in the 1820s. His oldest son was Padre Antonio Martinez, the valley leader who clashed with the French bishop Jean-Baptiste Lamy.

Despite the family's high social standing, life was fairly rugged, cramped, and dangerous. The 21 simple rooms arranged around two courtyards allowed room for sleeping, cooking, and protection against raids. Some of the spaces have been furnished to reflect their original use; others are dedicated to exhibits, such as a very interesting display on slavery in the area, and a wood carving of Doña Sebastiana, Lady Death, with her glittering mica eyes, in the collection of Penitente paraphernalia. During the spring and summer, local craftspeople are on hand to demonstrate weaving, blacksmithing, and the like in the house's workshops; in the fall, the trade fair is reenacted over a weekend.

★ SAN FRANCISCO DE ASIS CHURCH

Just as photographs of the Great Pyramid of Cheops seldom show the sprawl of modern Cairo crowding up to its base, **San Francisco de Asis Church** (east side of U.S. 68 in Ranchos de Taos, 575/758-2754, 9am-4pm daily, Mass 7am, 9:30am, and 11:30am Sun., donation) as depicted in, say, Georgia O'Keeffe's paintings and Ansel Adams's photographs, is a shadow-draped fortress isolated on a hilltop. In fact, the iconic church, completed in the early 19th century as a Franciscan mission, is at the center of a plaza, ringed with buildings.

It's easy to see what has fascinated so many artists: the clean lines, the shadows created by the hulking buttresses, the rich glow of the adobe in the sun. The church is living architecture, as much a part of the earth as something raised above it. As with every traditional adobe structure, it must be refinished every year with a mix of clay, sand, and straw; it is then coated with a fine layer of water and sand, and buffed with sheepskin. This happens over two weeks in June, during which the church is open only at lunchtime and on Sunday.

Inside, the whitewashed walls are covered with the stations of the cross; two Spanish Colonial reredos decorate the altars. In the

The San Francisco de Asis Church receives a fresh coat of mud every year.

parish hall (9am-3:30pm Mon.-Fri., $3) is the 1896 painting *The Shadow of the Cross,* an eight-foot-high canvas in which the figure of Christ can be seen to luminesce—allegedly miraculously.

★ TAOS PUEBLO

Even if you've been in New Mexico for a while and think you're inured to adobe, **Taos Pueblo** (575/758-1028, www.taospueblo. com, 8am-4:30pm Mon.-Sat., 8:30am-4:30pm Sun., 8:30am-4pm daily in winter, closed for 10 weeks Feb.-Mar., $16) is an amazing sight. Two clusters of multistory mud-brick buildings make up the core of this village, which claims, along with Acoma Pueblo, to be the oldest continually inhabited community in the United States. The current buildings, annually repaired and recoated with mud, are from the 1200s, though it's possible that all their constituent parts have been fully replaced several times since then.

About 150 people (out of the 1,200 or so total Taos reservation residents) live here year-round. These people, along with the town's designation as a UNESCO World Heritage Site, have kept the place remarkably as it was in the pre-Columbian era, save for the use of adobe bricks (as opposed to clay and stone), which were introduced by the Spanish, as the main structural material. The apartment-like homes, stacked up at various levels and reached by wood ladders, have no electricity or running water, though some use propane gas for heat and light.

As you explore, be careful not to intrude on private space: Enter only buildings that are clearly marked as shops, and stay clear of the ceremonial kiva areas on the east side of each complex. These round structures form the ritual heart of the pueblo, a secret space within an already private culture.

You're welcome to wander around and enter any of the craft shops and galleries that are open—a good opportunity to see inside the earthen structures and to buy some of the distinctive Taos pottery, which is only very lightly decorated but glimmers with mica from the clay of this area. These pots are also renowned for cooking beans.

Ceremonial Dances at Taos Pueblo

In addition to the Feast of San Geronimo, ceremonial dances are open to visitors. This is only an approximate schedule—dates can vary from year to year, as can the particular dances. Contact the **pueblo** (505/758-1028, www.taospueblo.com) for times, or check the listings in the *Tempo* section of the paper for that week.

Every night May-October, there are demonstration dances at the **Kachina Lodge** (413 Paseo del Pueblo Norte)—a little touristy, but nice if your trip doesn't coincide with a dance at the pueblo itself.

- **January 1** - Turtle dance
- **January 6** - Deer or buffalo dance
- **Easter** - Various dances
- **May 3** - Feast of Santa Cruz: corn dance
- **June 13** - Feast of San Antonio: various dances
- **June 24** - Feast of San Juan: corn dance
- **July 25-26** - Feast of Santiago and Santa Ana: corn dances and footraces
- **September 29-30** - Feast of San Geronimo
- **December 24** - Sundown procession and bonfire
- **December 25** - various dances

San Geronimo Church

The path from the Taos Pueblo admission gate leads directly to the central plaza, a broad expanse between Red Willow Creek (source of the community's drinking water, flowing from sacred Blue Lake higher in the mountains) and **San Geronimo Church.** The latter, built in 1850, is perhaps the newest structure in the village, a replacement for the first mission the Spanish built, in 1619, using forced Indian labor. The Virgin Mary presides over the room roofed with heavy wood beams; her clothes change with every season, a nod to her dual role as the Earth Mother. (Taking photos is strictly forbidden inside the church at all times and, as at all pueblos, at dances as well.)

The older church, to the north behind the houses, is now a cemetery—fitting, given its tragic destruction. It was first torn down during the Pueblo Revolt of 1680; the Spanish rebuilt it about 20 years later. In 1847 it was again attacked, this time by U.S. troops sent in to quell the rebellion against the new government, in retaliation for the murder of Governor Charles Bent. The counterattack brutally outweighed what had sparked it. More than 100 pueblo residents, including women and children, had taken refuge inside the church when the soldiers bombarded and set fire to it, killing everyone inside and gutting the building. Since then, the bell tower has been restored, but the graves have simply intermingled with the ruined walls and piles of dissolved adobe mud. All of the crosses—from old carved wood to new finished stone—face sacred Taos Mountain.

EL PRADO AND WEST ON U.S. 64

Millicent Rogers Museum

A dashing, thrice-married New York City socialite and designer, Millicent Rogers visited Taos in 1947 after breaking things off with Clark Gable. After moving to Taos, she brought Southwestern style to national attention, as she modeled Navajo-style velvet broomstick skirts, concha belts, and pounds of silver-and-turquoise jewelry for photo spreads in *Vogue* and *Harper's Bazaar.* Though she died just six years after she moved to Taos, at the age of 51, she managed to accumulate a fantastic amount of local art. The **Millicent Rogers Museum** (1504 Millicent Rogers Rd., 575/758-2462, www.millicentrogers.org, 10am-5pm daily Apr.-Oct., 10am-5pm Tues.-Sun. Nov.-Mar., $10) was established by her son, Paul Peralta-Ramos, and is set in the warren of adobe rooms that make up her former home.

Her belongings form the core collection, with flawless pieces of pottery, rugs, and jewelry—both local works and her own designs. Peralta-Ramos also contributed his own collection, including beautiful pieces of Navajo rugs and Hispano devotional art. An entire gallery is devoted to the work of San Ildefonso potter Maria Martinez. Aside from the works' individual beauty, they make an excellent broad introduction to the crafts of the area, from ancient times to modern. But it's not all rooted in local culture: Rogers's goofy illustrations of a fairy tale for her children fill the last room. The gift shop here is particularly thorough and includes beautiful vintage jewelry and circa-1900 rugs.

★ Rio Grande Gorge

Heading west on U.S. 64 from the "old blinking light," you pass the Taos airstrip on the left; then, after a few more miles, the ground simply drops away. This is the **Rio Grande Gorge** (also called the Taos Gorge), plunging at its most alarming point 800 feet down into malevolent-looking basalt. The river courses below, but it's not just millions of years of rushing water that have carved out the canyon—seismic activity also caused a rift in the earth's surface. The crack extends north to just beyond the Colorado state line and south almost to Española.

The elegant, unnervingly delicate-looking bridge that spans it was built in 1965 to supplement entrepreneur John Dunn's rickety old toll crossing eight miles north. Critics mocked the newer structure as "the bridge to nowhere" because the highway on the western bank had yet to be built, but the American Institute of Steel Construction granted it the Most Beautiful Steel Bridge award in 1966. At 650 feet above the river, the cantilever truss was a stunning engineering feat; it is still the seventh-highest bridge in the United States. On either side of the bridge is the stretch of white water called the Taos Box, two words that inspire wild tales in any seasoned river-runner. The Class III and IV rapids are considered the best place for rafting in New Mexico.

On the west side of the gorge is a rest area, and the start of the **West Rim Trail,** running south from the parking lot and yielding great views of the bridge to the north.

Greater World Earthship Development

If you brave the slender gorge bridge and continue a mile or so west on U.S. 64, you soon see some whimsically curved and creatively stuccoed houses along the right side of the road. These are Earthships: modular, low-priced homes that function entirely on collected rainwater and wind and solar power.

Rio Grande Gorge west of Taos

Although they look like fanciful Hobbit homes or Mars colony pods, Earthships are made of rather common stuff: The walls, built into hillsides for efficient heating and cooling, are stacks of used tires packed with rammed

New Mexico's Communes

Something about New Mexico's vast empty spaces inspires utopian thinking, as if the landscape were a blank slate, a way to start from scratch and do things right. Spanish settlers felt it in the 16th century. Gold miners banked on it in the 1800s. And in the 1960s, freethinkers, free-lovers, and back-to-the-landers fled crowded cities and boring suburbs to start communities such as the Hog Farm and the New Buffalo commune, both near Taos. For a while, New Mexico was the place to be: Dennis Hopper immortalized New Buffalo in his film *Easy Rider,* Janis Joplin chilled out in Truchas, and Ken Kesey drove his bus, *Further,* through the state. At the end of the decade, some 25 communes had been established.

In most of the rest of the United States, these experimental communities and their ideals were just a brief moment of zaniness—their legacy appears to be Hog Farm leader Wavy Gravy's consecration on a Ben & Jerry's label. But in New Mexico, many of the ideals set down by naked organic gardeners and tripping visionaries took root and sprouted in unexpected ways. Yogi Bhajan, a Sikh who taught mass kundalini yoga sessions in New Mexico in 1969, later became a major contributor to the state economy through all the businesses he established. Buddhist stupas dot the Rio Grande Valley, the product of Anglo spiritual seekers working with Tibetan refugees brought to New Mexico by Project Tibet, cofounded by John Allen, who also ran the commune Synergia Ranch near Santa Fe. Allen was also instrumental in building Biosphere 2, the experimental glass dome in the Arizona desert—probably the most utopian vision yet to have sprouted in New Mexico.

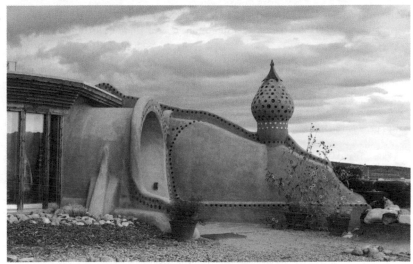

Greater World Earthship Development proves ecofriendly homes don't have to be dull.

earth, while bottles stacked with cement and crushed aluminum cans form front walls and colorful peepholes.

Greater World is the largest of three local all-Earthship subdivisions, and headquarters of the architecture office that developed the design. The **Greater World Earthship Development visitors center** (575/613-4409, www.earthship.com, 9am-5pm daily in summer, 10am-4pm daily in winter, $7) is the most unconventional model home and sales office you'll ever visit. You can take the self-guided tour of a basic Earthship and watch a video about the building process and the rationale behind the design. If you're hooked, you can of course get details on buying a lot in the development or purchasing the plans to build your own place elsewhere. Or try before you buy: You can stay the night in an Earthship here, starting at $130. Look for the green building on the right 1.8 miles past the bridge.

TAOS SKI VALLEY

North on Highway 150 takes you to the village of **Arroyo Seco,** a small cluster of galleries and stores at a bend in the road. The highway then winds relentlessly up through Hondo Canyon, the steep mountain slopes crowded with tall, dense pines that in winter disappear into a wreath of clouds. The road dead-ends at the village of **Taos Ski Valley.** When you get out of the car and take in the vertiginous view up to Kachina Peak (elevation 12,481 feet and often white-capped even in July), you'll see why it inspires legions of reverential skiers every winter, when an

bustling downtown Arroyo Seco

average of 305 inches of snow falls on the mountain—almost 10 times the amount they get down in town.

For decades, it was *only* skiers here. Snowboarders were banned, allegedly because the slopes were too steep—more than half the trails are rated expert level, and many of them are left ungroomed. But the mountain was finally opened to all in 2008.

In the summer, there's occasional live music, and Hondo Canyon's many trails make for very good hiking or picnicking. The road is dotted on either side with picnic areas and campgrounds—Cuchilla del Medio is a particularly nice area for a picnic. The **visitors center** (575/776-1413, www.taosskivalley.com) in the ski area parking lot stocks trail descriptions and maps.

Entertainment and Events

Taos is a small town: no glitzy dance clubs, no bars where you're expected to dress up. Nighttime fun is concentrated in places where, even after just a couple of visits, you'll get to know the regulars. The various townwide celebrations—including music and dancing on the plaza on summer Thursdays—draw a good cross section of the population.

NIGHTLIFE
Classic Bars

Starting around 5pm, the **Adobe Bar** (125 Paseo del Pueblo Norte, 575/758-2233), in the lobby of the Taos Inn (look for the neon thunderbird sign), is where you'll run into everyone you've seen over the course of the day, sipping a Cowboy Buddha ($12) or some other specialty margarita—the best in town. Mellow jazz or acoustic guitar sets the mood from 7pm. To give hotel residents a break, the bar closes at 10pm.

Wood-paneled **Eske's Brew Pub** (106 Des Georges Ln., 575/758-1517) is across from the plaza, tucked back from the southeast corner of the intersection of Paseo del Pueblo Sur and Kit Carson Road. With live music on Friday and Saturday, it serves its house-made beer to a chummy après-ski crowd. You're in New Mexico—you should at least *try* the green-chile ale.

Everyone's default late-night spot is **The Alley Cantina** (121 Teresina Ln., 575/758-2121). This warren of interconnected rooms (one of which is supposedly the oldest in

Taos . . . but don't they all say that?) can be potentially baffling after a few drinks. There's shuffleboard for entertainment if you're not into the ensemble onstage—its name usually ends in "Blues Band"; a cover of $5-10 applies on weekends. The kitchen is open until 11pm.

Wine and Cocktails

A more upscale member of Taos's bar scene is **The Treehouse Lounge** (123 Bent St.,

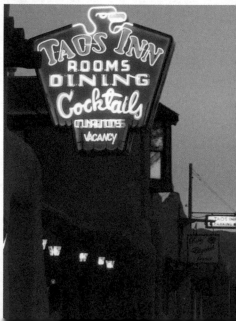

time for a margarita at the Adobe Bar in the Taos Inn

KTAOS Solar Bar

575/758-1009, 2:30pm-close daily), the upper floor of an adobe house downtown. With a full bar and the creative minds running it, the range of cocktails ($10) is highly stimulating. Happy hour ($6) is 2:30pm-6pm.

On the plaza, the wine shop **Parcht** (103 E. Plaza, 575/758-1194, 2pm-9pm Tues.-Sat) pops the cork on a dozen bottles a night, offering glasses and tastings along with vino-friendly small bites, such as burrata with kale pesto on toast. It's popular with both the après-work and après-ski sets.

Live Music

Is your drinking unsustainable? Fix that at the **KTAOS Solar Bar** (9 Hwy. 150, 575/758-5826 ext. 206, www.ktao.com, 3pm-9pm daily), the social wing of the KTAO radio station, which happens to be entirely solar-powered. You can peek into the radio studios, or dance on the lawn out back, in front of the large stage that hosts major shows. Happy hour (4pm-6pm) sees drinks as low as $2, and kids are usually welcome, with plenty of room to play.

If your style is cramped by old adobes, head out to **Taos Mesa Brewing** (20 ABC Mesa Rd., 575/758-1900, www.taosmesabrewing. com, noon-late daily), on U.S. 64 opposite the airport, where there's plenty of room to groove. The metal Quonset hut looms like a far-flung Burning Man camp. The entertainment roster is eclectic, with everyone fom theremin masters to major global artists performing outside (cover from $5 some nights). The crowd is all of Taos's younger hippies,

Taos Mesa Brewing has plenty of space for live bands and dancing.

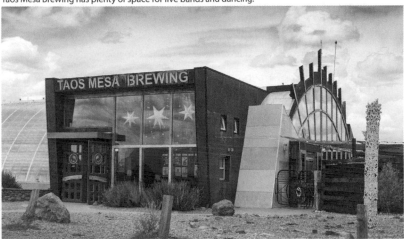

plus hops aficionados of all stripes. The food ($10) is veg- and beer-friendly. More centrally, the company's "in town" **tap room** (201 Paseo del Pueblo Sur, 575/758-1900, 11am-11pm daily) also hosts bands and fuels the crowd with pizza.

Finally, check the schedule at **Old Martina's Hall** (4140 Hwy. 68, 575/758-3003, www.oldmartinashall.com) for special events in this renovated old adobe theater. It may not get as wild as back in the days when Dennis Hopper owned the joint, but the new wood dance floor is a treat.

FESTIVALS AND EVENTS

July is chockablock: the loopy creativity of the **Arroyo Seco Fourth of July parade,** then, in the second week, the **Taos Pueblo Powwow** (www.taospueblo.com), a major get-together of Pueblo Indians and tribal members from around the country. Try to be there for the Grand Entry, the massive opening procession. The event takes place at the powwow grounds in El Prado near the Overland Sheepskin store. The next

weekend, the town turns out for the **Fiestas de Taos** (www.fiestasdetaos.com), a three-day celebration of Santiago de Compostela and Santa Ana, with a parade, food and crafts booths on the plaza, and the crowning of the Fiestas Queen.

Taos galleries put out their finest at the **Taos Fall Arts Festival** (www.taosfallarts.com), a two-week-long exhibition in late September and early October that shows the works of more than 150 Taos County artists.

Taos's biggest annual festivity (for which many local businesses close) is the **Feast of San Geronimo,** the patron saint assigned to Taos Pueblo by the Spanish when they built their first mission there in 1619. The holiday starts the evening of September 29 with vespers in the pueblo church and continues the next day with footraces and a pole-climbing ritual. Hacienda de los Martinez usually reenacts a 19th-century Taos trade fair, with mountain men, music, and artisans' demonstrations.

On the first weekend in October, the **Taos Wool Festival** (www.taoswoolfestival.org)

What to Expect at Pueblo Dances

Visiting a pueblo for a ceremonial dance or feast-day celebration is one of the most memorable parts of a trip to New Mexico. But it's important to remember that a pueblo dance is not at all for the benefit of tourists. It is a ceremony and a religious ritual, not a performance—you are a guest, not an audience.

Keep this in mind as a guide to your own behavior. Applause is not appropriate, nor is conversation during the dance. Queries about the meaning of the dances are generally not appreciated. Never walk in the dance area, and try not to block the view of pueblo residents. The kivas, as holy spaces, are always off-limits to outsiders. During feast days, some pueblo residents may open their doors to visitors, perhaps for a snack or drink—but be considerate of others who may also want to visit and don't stay too long. Photography is strictly forbidden at dances (sometimes with the exception of Los Matachines, which is not a religious ritual). Don't even think about trying to sneak a shot with your camera phone, as tribal police will be more than happy to confiscate it.

On a practical level, be prepared for a lot of waiting around. Start times are always approximate, and everything depends on when the dancers are done with their kiva rituals. There will usually be a main, seasonal dance—such as the corn dance at the summer solstice—followed by several others. If you go in the winter, dress very warmly, but in layers. Ceremonies often start inside the close-packed, overheated church, and then dances often proceed outside in the cold.

has drawn textile artists as well as breeders since 1983. Admire the traditional Churro sheep or an Angora goat and then pick up a scarf made from its wool.

In winter, the glow of luminarias and torchlight on snow produces a magical effect. On the first weekend in December, the **tree-lighting ceremony** on the plaza draws the whole town, and the rest of the season sees numerous celebrations, such as the reenactments of the Virgin's search for shelter, called Las Posadas, which take place at Our Lady of Guadalupe Church west of the plaza on the third weekend in December. At the pueblo, vespers is said at San Geronimo Church on Christmas Eve, typically followed by a children's dance. On Christmas Day, the pueblo hosts either a deer dance or the Spanish Matachines dance.

Come spring, the town hosts the Sundance of short film gatherings, the **Taos Shortz Film Fest** (www.taosshortz.com), which screens 150 films from around the globe over one weekend in April.

Shopping

ARTS AND CRAFTS

In the Overland Ranch complex, **Magpie** (1405 Paseo del Pueblo Norte, 781/248-0166, 11am-5:30pm Tues.-Sat., 10am-4pm Sun.) promises "wonderful things for your nest." The owner, a Taos native returned from living on the East Coast, has selected a colorful array of handcrafted furniture, pottery, handmade jewelry, and more, nearly all produced by Taos residents.

Taos Drums (3956 Hwy. 68, 800/424-3786, 9am-5pm Mon.-Fri., 10am-5pm, Sat., 11am-5pm Sun.) is a giant shop and factory dedicated to making Taos Pueblo-style percussion instruments, from thin hand drums to great booming ones out of hollow logs. Trying out the wares is encouraged. The shop is located on the west side of the highway five miles south of the plaza.

Taos Clay Studio (1208 Paseo del Pueblo Norte, 307/272-8388, 10am-5pm daily), in El Prado, is a homegrown affair. Local artists turn the ceramics at the on-site studio; classes are available too.

GIFT AND HOME

FX/18 (103-C Bent St., 575/758-8590, 11am-6pm Mon.-Sat., noon-5pm Sun.) has a great selection of goodies: groovy housewares, lively kids' stuff, nifty stationery. The selection of contemporary Southwest-style jewelry is particularly good.

Tap into Taos's environmental ethic at **Seconds Eco Store** (120 Bent St., 575/751-4500, 10am-6pm Mon.-Sat., 11am-6pm Sun.), with nifty upcycled and green goods, such as earrings made of skis and circuit boards turned key chains.

Up Highway 150, **Arroyo Seco Mercantile** (488 Hwy. 150, 575/776-8806, 10am-5:30pm Mon.-Sat., 11am-5pm Sun.) is the town's former general store, now a highly evolved junk shop that has maintained the beautiful old wood-and-glass display cases. Its stock ranges from the practical (books on passive-solar engineering and raising llamas) to the frivolous, with lots of the beautiful, like antique wool blankets.

TOYS

Taos is also home to an exceptionally magical toy store, **Twirl** (225 Camino de la Placita, 575/751-1402, www.twirlhouse.com, 10am-6pm daily). Tucked in a series of low-ceilinged adobe rooms, it's crammed with everything from science experiments to wooden trains to fairy costumes. Even the kiva fireplace gets a fantastical 1,001 Nights treatment, and it has the best play structure in town out back.

Sports and Recreation

The wild setting presses in all around Taos, and the mountains loom up behind every town view. Downhill skiing is the main draw in the winter, but you can also try more solitary snowshoeing and Nordic skiing. In summer, peak-baggers will want to strike out for Wheeler, the state's highest, while rafters, rock climbers, and mountain bikers can head the other direction, to the dramatic Rio Grande Gorge cliffs. In the water, river-runners challenge the churning rapids of the legendary Taos Box (late May and early June, with winter runoff, are the most intense season for this).

Information

Stop in at the **Carson National Forest Supervisor's Office** (208 Cruz Alta Rd., 575/758-6200, 8am-4:30pm Mon.-Fri.) for booklets on recommended trails and maps. Just down the street, the **Bureau of Land Management Taos Field Office** (226 Cruz Alta Rd., 575/758-8851, 8am-4:30pm Mon.-Fri.) can help with rafting or camping trip prep, with plenty of maps and brochures.

The **Taos Youth and Family Center** (407 Paseo del Cañon, 575/758-4160, 9am-8pm Mon.-Thurs., 9am-7pm Fri.-Sun.) has a big indoor pool, as well as an ice-skating rink. Hours are more limited in fall and winter.

Sudden thunderstorms are common in summer, as are flash floods and even freak blizzards. Well into May, snow can blanket higher passes, so wherever you go, always carry more warm clothing than you think you'll need. And don't skimp on the sunscreen, even when it's below freezing.

★ HIKING

With Taos Mountain and Wheeler Peak in the backyard, you can ramble along winding rivers or haul up 2,000 feet in less than four miles. Be prepared for a cold snap or storm at any time, and don't plan on anything before May—it takes that long for the snow to thaw, though even in high summer, you can still hit white stuff in the alpine meadows. If you prefer some animal companionship (and something to carry your pack), contact **Wild Earth Llama Adventures** (800/758-5262, www.llamaadventures.com), which runs day hikes with lunch ($125), as well as multiday treks (from $425). These are just a few suggestions for spots to hike.

Dennis Hopper in Taos

In 1968, a Taos Pueblo elder told Dennis Hopper, "The mountain is smiling on you!" No wonder the *Easy Rider* actor and real-life renegade claimed the town as what he called his "heart home." His early years here were wild: He's notorious for having ridden his motorcycle across the roof of the Mabel Dodge Luhan House, which he bought in 1969. Over the decades, he mellowed just a bit, and Taos locals came to think of him as one of their own. In 2009, as part of a 40th-anniversary celebration of the Summer of Love, the Harwood Museum mounted an exhibit of his photography and paintings, along with works by some of his compatriots from that era.

Hopper died not long after, in 2010. His funeral was held at the San Francisco de Asis Church, and attended by fellow 1960s veterans Peter Fonda and Jack Nicholson. Following pueblo tradition, Hopper was buried in a pine box under a dirt mound, in the nearby **Jesus Nazareno Cemetery.** Fans can pay their respects there. To find it, take Highway 518 south; about a quarter mile along, turn left (east) on Espinoza Road. The cemetery is a short way along, off the left side of the road. From the main gate Hopper's grave is near the back, on the right-hand side.

Taos Ski Valley

Varied trails lead off Highway 150 en route to Taos Ski Valley. Just before the parking lot for the ski area, **Gavilan Trail** (no. 60) leads off the north side of the road. It's plenty steep but leads to a high mountain meadow. The route is five miles round-trip, or you can connect with other trails once you're up on the rim.

Purists will want to head for **Wheeler Peak Summit Trail** (no. 67), which scales New Mexico's highest mountain in about four miles (one-way). The first two miles of the route are on the relatively easy and popular **Williams Lake Trail** (no. 62), which starts near the end of Twining Road, a narrow dirt road that leads out of the top of the Taos Ski Valley parking lot. (Before starting up Twining Road, stop first at the visitors center for trail descriptions.) Williams Lake is a nice destination and, after you get past the early rocky stretch, the trail is pleasant hiking. In summer, on the night of the full moon, there's a free guided **moonlight hike** to Williams Lake, starting at 7:30pm; check the schedule at www.taosskivalley.com.

If all that sounds too strenuous, you can take the **chairlift** (10am-4pm Thurs.-Mon. June-Aug., $15) up to the top of the mountain, then wander down any of several wide, well-marked trails, all with stunning views.

El Salto Falls

Some theorize that the mysterious "Taos Hum"—the faint, low drone that many in the area claim to hear—emanates from the caves at **El Salto Falls** (575/776-2371, $4), a scenic spot on a patch of private land in Arroyo Seco. Whether or not you solve this sonic mystery, the falls are a great Taos natural landmark, and an easy hike or a challenging one, depending on just how much you'd like to see. Save this hike for dry weather, unless you have a four-wheel drive—the road is rough when muddy or snowy.

In Arroyo Seco, take El Salto Road east (go straight where Highway 150 makes a hard right); after about a mile is a sign on the left asking visitors to pay. Leave cash in the honor box on the porch of the green house just off the road, and fill out a waiver and a permit to place on your dashboard. Continue driving another 0.7 mile and bear left; from here, it's 0.9 mile up to a green gate and small parking area. Walk in, following the road as it curves left, then bearing right. This leads in just a few minutes to the lowest, largest cave and the

El Salto Falls is a short hike up in the foothills.

first waterfall—though most of the year, it is often just a trickle. Intrepid hikers can climb up to the right of the cave, to ever smaller falls and notches in the cliff face.

BIKING

Taos has several great trails for mountain biking. A popular ride close to town is **West Rim Trail** along the Rio Grande Gorge, either from the gorge bridge up to John Dunn Bridge, about 15 miles round-trip, or from the gorge bridge south to the Taos Junction Bridge near Pilar, about 18 miles out and back. Either way, you'll have great views and fairly level but rugged terrain. For some downhill action, **Taos Ski Valley** offers mountain biking in summer; the 3.6-mile Berminator route is good for intermediate cyclists.

For road touring, you can make a pleasant 25-mile loop from Taos through Arroyo Hondo and Arroyo Seco. With no steep grades, it's a good way to get adjusted to the altitude. Head north up Paseo del Pueblo Norte, straight through the intersection with Highway 150, then, in Arroyo Hondo, turn right onto County Road B-143. Cross Highway 230, and you arrive in Arroyo Seco, behind The Snowmansion. Turn right on Highway 150 to loop back to Taos.

For a longer road challenge, take on the 84-mile Enchanted Circle. Each September, more than a thousand riders participate in the **Enchanted Circle Century Tour** (800/348-6444, www.redriverenchantedcirclecenturytour.com), sponsored by the Red River Chamber of Commerce.

Gearing Up (129 Paseo del Pueblo Sur, 575/751-0365) rents mountain and hybrid bicycles for $50 per day. If you're bringing your bicycle with you, consider having it shipped here, and they'll reassemble it and have it waiting when you arrive.

RAFTING AND TUBING

The **Taos Box,** the 16-mile stretch of the Rio Grande between the John Dunn Bridge and Pilar, provides perhaps the best rafting in New Mexico, with Class III rapids with ominous names like Boat Reamer and Screaming Left-Hand Turn. The river mellows out south of the Taos Box, then leads into a shorter Class III section called the Racecourse—the most popular run, usually done as a half-day trip. Beyond this, in the Orilla Verde Recreation Area around Pilar, the water is wide and flat, a place for a relaxing float with kids or other water newbies; you can flop in an inner tube if you really want to chill. North of the John Dunn Bridge, there's another intermediate run called La Junta that's a half-day trip.

Los Rios River Runners (800/544-1181, www.losriosriverrunners.com) leads trips to all these spots as half-day outings ($54), day trips (from $105), and overnight trips. Another outfitter, **Far-Flung Adventures** (575/758-2628, www.farflung.com), can add on rock climbing and horseback riding. With both organizations, you can choose whether you want a paddle boat—where you're actively (and sometimes strenuously) paddling—or an oar boat, where guides row, and you can sit back. The best season is late May and early June, when the water is high from mountain runoff.

ROCK CLIMBING

From popular sport-climbing spots such as the basalt Dead Cholla Wall in the Rio Grande Gorge to the more traditional routes at Tres Piedras, Taos is a climber's dream. One of the most impressive pitches is at Questa Dome, north of Taos on Highway 378, where the flawless granite on the Questa Direct route is graded 5.10 and 5.11. And you're not limited to the summer, as winter sees some terrific ice climbs at higher elevations. **Taos Mountain Outfitters** (113 N. Plaza, 575/758-9292, www.taosmountainoutfitters.com, 9am-6pm Mon.-Wed., 9am-8pm Thurs.-Fri., 8am-8pm Sat., 10am-6pm Sun.) can provide maps, ropes, and more details. For climbing lessons or guided tours, contact **Mountain Skills** (575/776-2222, www.climbtaos.com) in Arroyo Seco.

WINTER SPORTS

Taos Ski Valley (866/968-7386, www.ski-taos.org, $86 full-day lift ticket) is a mecca for downhill skiing. The resort is open late November-first weekend in April, with 110 trails served by 14 lifts, and snowmaking capacity on all beginner and intermediate areas in dry spells. In early 2015, TSV opened a lift to just shy of the 12,481-foot Kachina Peak, making it some of the highest lift-served terrain in North America. Devotees of hike-to terrain still have areas dedicated to them, including a 35-acre tree-skiing area. The highly regarded Ernie Blake Snowsports School is one of the best places to learn the basics or polish your skills. Novice "yellowbirds" can take one ($120) or two ($190) days of intensive instruction specially geared to new skiers.

For cross-country skiing and snowshoeing, **Enchanted Forest** (575/754-6112, www.enchantedforestxc.com, $18 full-day pass), between Elizabethtown and Red River on the Enchanted Circle loop, offers miles of groomed trails. There are also easy ski access points in the Carson National Forest—at Capulin Campground on U.S. 64, for instance, five miles east of Taos, and along **Manzanita Trail** in Hondo Canyon on the road to the ski valley.

Don't have your own gear? **Cottam's Ski & Outdoor** (207-A Paseo del Pueblo Sur, 575/758-2822, 7am-7pm Mon.-Fri., 7am-8pm Sat.-Sun.) has the biggest stock of rental skis, snowboards, and snowshoes. The shop also sells everything else you'll need to get out and enjoy the snow; there's another location at the ski valley (575/776-8719) and one at the Angel Fire ski resort (575/377-3700).

Food

For a town of its size, Taos has a broad selection of quality restaurants. But most close relatively early, and many smaller places don't take plastic—so load up on cash and get seated by 8pm. You'll need reservations for fine-dining restaurants on the weekends, but the whole scene is relatively casual. At one of the New Mexican places, be sure to try some posole—it's more common here than in Albuquerque or Santa Fe, often substituted for rice as a side dish alongside pinto beans. Also, the breakfast burrito—a combo of scrambled eggs, green chile, hash browns, and bacon or sausage in a flour tortilla—is commonly wrapped in foil and served to go, perfect if you want an early start hiking or skiing.

CENTRAL TAOS

New Mexican

A small, festively painted place on the north side of town, the family-run **Orlando's** (1114 Don Juan Valdez Ln., 575/751-1450, 10:30am-2:30pm and 5pm-8:30pm Mon.-Thurs. and Sun., 10:30am-2:30pm and 5pm-9pm Fri.-Sat., $10) is invariably the first restaurant named by anyone, local or visitor, when the question of the best chile comes up. That said, there are occasional whisperings about inconsistency (heresy!). But Orlando's still generally serves very satisfying, freshly made New Mexican standards, such as green-chile chicken enchiladas. The posole is quite good too—perfectly firm, earthy, and flecked with oregano. It's always busy, but a fire pit outdoors makes the wait more pleasant on cold nights.

Mexican

Tiny ★ **La Cueva** (135 Paseo del Pueblo Sur, 575/758-7001, 10am-3pm daily, $8) looks like a New Mexican restaurant at first glance, as it has all the usual green-chile-smothered dishes. But its owners are from south of the border and round out the menu with fantastically fresh and homemade-tasting dishes like chicken mole enchiladas and an omelet with house-made chorizo, as well as exceptionally savory beans. No alcohol, though.

Cafés

The location of **World Cup** (102-A Paseo del Pueblo Norte, 575/737-5299, 7am-7pm daily, $3) on the corner of the plaza makes it a popular pit stop for both tourists and locals—the latter typically of the drumming, dreadlocked variety, lounging on the stoop.

Breakfast and Lunch

Michael's Kitchen (304-C Paseo del Pueblo Norte, 575/758-4178, 7am-2:30pm Mon.-Thurs., 7am-8pm Fri.-Sun., $8) is famous for New Mexican breakfast items like huevos rancheros and blue-corn pancakes with pine nuts, served all day, but everyone will find something they like on the extensive menu at this down-home, wood-paneled family restaurant filled with chatter and the clatter of dishes. "Health Food," for instance, is a double order of chile cheese fries. The front room is devoted to gooey doughnuts, cinnamon rolls, and pie.

Taos Diner (908 Paseo del Pueblo Norte, 575/758-2374, 7am-3pm daily, $10) is as straight-ahead as its name. The pleasant surprise: Much of the enchiladas, egg plates, pancakes, and other typical diner fare is prepared with organic ingredients. Plus, the largely local scene provides good background theater to your meal—the servers seem to know everyone. There's a second outpost, **Taos Diner II** (216-B Paseo del Pueblo Sur, 575/751-1989, 7am-3pm daily), just south of the plaza.

Euro-Latino might be the best catchall term for the menu at ★ **Gutiz** (812-B Paseo del Pueblo Norte, 575/758-1226, 8am-3pm Tues.-Sun., $10), which borrows from France and Spain and adds a dash of green chile. Start your day with a chocolate croissant or an impressive tower of scrambled eggs and spinach. Lunch sees traditional croques monsieurs or cumin-spiced chicken sandwiches.

Set in bucolic gardens with a view of Taos Mountain, **Farmhouse Café** (1405 Paseo del Pueblo Norte, 575/758-5683, 7am-9pm Mon.-Sat., 6am-3pm Sun., $12) is a beautiful spot to revive over a hearty salad, a bison burger, or a homemade pastry, including killer gluten-free options like a chocolate-peanut-butter

crispy-rice bar. Service can be a little spotty, but the meals are worth the wait. Look for it behind the Overland Sheepskin store.

Just west of the plaza, **El Gamal** (112 Doña Luz St., 575/613-0311, 9am-5pm Mon.-Wed., 9am-9pm Thurs.-Sat., 11am-3pm Sun., $7) brings the best of Israeli street snacks to Taos, with *shakshuka* (spicy scrambled eggs) and bagels for breakfast and falafel and *sabich* (eggplant and egg) sandwiches at lunch, washed down with a fizzy yogurt soda. There's also more standard hippie fare on the menu: homemade granola and the like.

In the Taos Inn, elegant **Doc Martin's** (125 Paseo del Pueblo Norte, 575/758-1977, 11am-3pm and 5pm-9pm Mon.-Fri., 7:30am-2:30pm and 5pm-9:30pm Sat.-Sun., $10) is fine at dinner, but weekend brunch is when the kitchen really shines—especially on dishes like the Kit Carson (poached eggs on yam biscuits topped with red chile) or blue-corn pancakes with blueberries. The lunch menu is also tasty and doesn't reach the stratospheric prices of dinner.

Burgers

★ **The Burger Stand** (401 Paseo del Pueblo Norte, 575/758-5522, 11am-11pm daily, $9) is an outpost of a Kansas restaurant—but it fits right in in Taos, in large part because it makes not one but two killer veggie burgers. We recommend the one topped with feta cheese, pickled green beans, and rich romesco sauce. (The beef and lamb burgers are great too, and decked out in similarly creative ways.) It doesn't hurt that it's set inside the Taos Ale House, where there's great beer and music—and, best of all, it's open relatively late.

Fresh and Local

★ **The Love Apple** (803 Paseo del Pueblo Norte, 575/751-0050, 5pm-9pm Tues.-Sun., $20) wears its local, organic credentials on its sleeve, and the food delivers in simple but powerful flavor combinations in seasonal menus with dishes such as a quesadilla made sweet with apple and squash, and posole enriched with local lamb and caramelized

The Burger Stand doesn't cut corners on veggie burgers.

onions. The atmosphere is like early-days Chez Panisse filtered through a northern New Mexican lens: a thick-walled adobe chapel, with candles glimmering against wine bottles along the walls. It's one place in town where reservations are useful, and in an old-school move, it only accepts cash and checks.

Mid-May-October, the **Taos Farmers Market** (www.taosfarmersmarket.org, 8am-12:30pm Sat.) takes place on the plaza. Vendors sell some prepared food and good gifts like local honey, so you won't be left out even if you don't have a kitchen.

Italian

Taos Pizza Out Back (712 Paseo del Pueblo Norte, 575/758-3112, 11am-10pm daily, $8) serves up the best pie in town, using mostly local and organic ingredients. A glance at the menu—with items like green chile and barbecue sauce, and the popular portobello-gorgonzola combo—often makes first-timers blanch, but after a bite or two they're converts, like everyone else in town.

Fine Dining

★ **El Meze** (1017 Paseo del Pueblo Norte, 575/751-3337, 5:30pm-9:30pm Mon.-Sat., $24) just might be Taos's best restaurant, thanks to both its exceptional food and tiny touches such as complimentary mineral water and plush blankets for cool evenings outside. Chef Frederick Muller shows the link between New Mexico, Spain, North Africa, and the Middle East in dishes that are both brainy and deep-down satisfying. Delectable mountain trout is seasoned with Spanish paprika and served with a lavish herb salad, while fried green olives stuffed with blue cheese are the bar snack to beat in all of New Mexico. The setting is cozy in winter, inside a thick-walled hacienda, and expansive in summer, with a large patio with a view of Taos Mountain.

Open since 1988 but relatively new to this cozy adobe house, **Lambert's** (123 Bent St., 575/758-1009, 11:30am-2:30pm and 5:30pm-9pm Mon.-Fri., 5:30pm-9pm Sat.-Sun., $32) is a Taos favorite, where everyone goes for anniversaries and other special nights. Its New American menu is a bit staid, but everything is executed perfectly. Get one of the game-meat specials if you can; otherwise, the braised lamb shank is fantastic. A full liquor license means good classic cocktails, which you can also enjoy upstairs at **The Treehouse Lounge** (2:30pm-close daily).

RANCHOS DE TAOS

Just off the plaza near the church, **Ranchos Plaza Grill** (6 St. Francis Plaza, 575/758-5788, 11am-3pm and 5pm-8:30pm Tues.-Sat., 11am-3pm Sun., $11) is a casual spot, known for its red *chile caribe*, made from crushed, rather than ground, chiles, for a really rustic effect.

Across the road, the chile at **Old Martina's Hall** (4140 Hwy. 68, 575/758-3003, www.old-martinashall.com, 7am-9:30pm Mon. and Wed.-Sat., 9am-3pm Sun., $20) may be dialed down for out-of-state palates, but this somewhat upscale place has other redeeming qualities. The once-derelict adobe theater with a soaring ceiling has been lovingly redone, now hosting special events, and serves the likes of goat-cheese salads, farro risotto, and truffle fries. It's more casual for breakfast and lunch ($10 for sandwiches). Check out all the rooms and levels. The building is across the road from the turn to the church.

ARROYO SECO

A creaky old all-purpose general store/diner/saloon, ★ **Abe's Cantina y Cocina** (489 Hwy. 150, 575/776-8516, 7am-5pm Mon.-Fri., 7am-1:30pm Sat., $4) has earned fans from all over for its satisfying and cheap breakfast burritos. There's a full menu of tacos and green-chile cheeseburgers, if you care to eat in, and a nice back patio. And don't miss the sweet, flaky empanadas next to the cash register in the store.

For coffee, though, you'll want to go next door to **Taos Cow** (485 Hwy. 150, 575/776-5640, 7am-7pm daily), a chilled-out coffee bar par excellence, with writers scribbling in one corner and flute players jamming in another. But it's the ice cream that has made the Taos Cow name (you'll see it distributed all around town, and elsewhere in New Mexico and Colorado). The most popular flavors are tailored to local tastes: Café Olé contains cinnamon and Mexican chocolate chunks, while Cherry Ristra is vanilla with piñon nuts, dark

chocolate, and cherries. Sandwiches ($9) are an option too, if you want real sustenance.

The husband-wife chef team at the restaurant, bar, and wine shop **Medley** (100 N.M. 150, 575/776-8787, 3pm-9pm Mon.-Fri., 10am-2pm and 3pm-9:30pm Sat.-Sun., $20) have cooked all over the world. The menu mixes eclectic global flavors (chimichurri, saffron) with New American staples such as roasted brussels sprouts. The food is great, if not flawless, and the atmosphere is casual.

TAOS SKI VALLEY

For nourishment by the ski area, fortify yourself with a green-chile cheeseburger or bowl of smoky-hot green-chile stew at the **Stray Dog Cantina** (105 Sutton Pl., 575/776-2894, 8am-9pm daily in winter, $12), which gets busy after 3pm, when tired skiers come down from a day on the slopes. In the summer, it doesn't open till 11am on weekdays, but it's a nice destination for a drive, as you can sit on the deck and listen to the river flow by.

Stray Dog Cantina serves hot chile in the ski valley year-round.

More adventurous drivers can head for **Bavarian Lodge** (100 Kachina Rd., 575/776-8020, 11:30am-9pm daily in ski season, $15), way up Twining Road near the southeast edge of the ski area and Kachina Lift 4. You'll need four-wheel drive in winter; in summer, the huge front deck is a lovely place to have a beer (served by actual German speakers) in the pines, though note that it's open only around the weekend (11:30am-close Thurs.-Sun.). The menu is typical Wiener schnitzel and spaetzle.

Accommodations

Taos hotels can be overpriced, especially at the lower end, where there are few reliable bargains. But because Taos is awash in centuries-old houses, bed-and-breakfasts have thrived. For those skeptical of B&Bs, don't despair: The majority have private bathrooms, separate entrances, and not too much country-cute decor. Certainly, just as in Santa Fe, the Southwestern gewgaws can be applied with a heavy hand, but wood-burning fireplaces, well-stocked libraries, hot tubs, and big gardens make up for that.

For better deals, consider staying outside of Taos proper. Arroyo Seco is about a half-hour drive from the plaza, and rates here and in Ranchos de Taos can be a little lower. In the summer, the lodges near the ski valley cut prices by almost half—a great deal if you want to spend time hiking and don't mind driving for food and entertainment. If you're in town without a car, Taos's Chile Line bus serves a few good budget choices; the line caters to skiers in the winter, with pickups from down on the southern end of town all the way up to the ski valley.

CENTRAL TAOS
Under $100
Of the various motels on the south side, none are excellent, but **Sun God Lodge** (919 Paseo del Pueblo Sur, 575/758-3162, www.sungodlodge.com, $69 d) is better than most. Maintenance can be spotty, but rooms are set around a big, grassy, tree-shaded courtyard and, in back, a small hot tub. But note that this can foster a somewhat rowdy atmosphere, especially in ski season or after big summer events.

Not a hotel at all, but simply a clutch of well-maintained one- and two-bedroom private casitas, **Taos Lodging** (109 Brooks St., 575/751-1771, www.taoslodging.com, $75 studio) is in a quiet, convenient block about a 10-minute walk north from the plaza. Here, eight cottages, arranged around a central courtyard, have assorted floor plans, but all have porches, full kitchens, and living rooms, as well as access to a shared outdoor hot tub. The smallest, a 350-square-foot studio, sleeps two comfortably; the largest ($140 for two) sleep up to six. Plus, the same group manages two additional properties nearby, for those who want a larger condo.

$100-150
In addition to being a tourist attraction, the ★ **Mabel Dodge Luhan House** (240 Morada Ln., 575/751-9686, www.mabeldodgeluhan.com, $116 d) also functions as a homey bed-and-breakfast. Even the least expensive rooms, in a 1970s outbuilding, feel authentically old and cozy, with wood floors and antique furniture. In the main house, Mabel's original bedroom ($220) is the grandest (you can even sleep in her bed). But for those who don't mind waking at the crack of dawn, the upstairs solarium ($145) is gloriously sunny, with gorgeous views of the mountain. Either way, you'll feel a little like you're bunking in a museum (which means those who want modern amenities like air-conditioning should look elsewhere). Breakfast is a cut above standard B&B fare.

Of the two landmark hotels in town, **Hotel La Fonda de Taos** (108 S. Plaza,

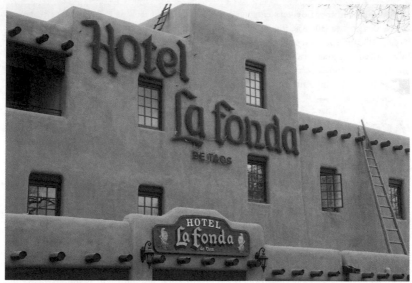

Hotel La Fonda de Taos overlooks the main plaza.

575/758-2211, www.lafondataos.com, $119 d) has a few more modern perks, such as gas fireplaces in some rooms and mostly reliable Internet. Plus, you can feel quite grand opening your balcony doors over the plaza (though you may also be subjected to predawn street-cleaning noise).

Walking distance from the plaza, **El Pueblo Lodge** (412 Paseo del Pueblo Norte, 575/758-8700, www.elpueblolodge.com, $120 d) is a budget operation with nice perks such as free laundry and a full breakfast. Rooms vary from a snug nook in the oldest adobe section to new, slick motel rooms complete with gas fireplaces. Those in the 1960s motel strip are a good combo of atmosphere and amenities. The grounds are pleasant, with a hot tub and a heated pool in the summertime.

$150-200

Inn on the Rio (910 E. Kit Carson Rd., 575/758-7199, www.innontherio.com, $160 d) might be more accurately called Motel on the Creek. But what a motel: Each of the 12 thick-walled rooms has been decorated with rich colors and retro Western details. The vintage wall heaters, still cranking from the old motor-court days, keep the rooms as toasty as a fireplace would. A hot tub between the two wings, plus luxe sheets and locally made bath gels, are nice upgrades. Pair this with long-time resident owners and a great morning meal, and you have all the benefits of a bed-and-breakfast without the feeling that you have to tiptoe in late at night. Rates are lower on weekdays in summer.

Everything at **Hacienda del Sol** (109 Mabel Dodge Ln., 575/758-0287, www.taoshaciendadelsol.com, $160 d) is built in relation to Taos Mountain. With this view, even the smallest of the 11 rooms in the adobe complex feel expansive. The style is cozy without being too oppressively Southwestern. Once owned by Mabel Dodge Luhan, the house was where she often put up guests; modern perks like robes and bathtubs make it feel homey.

La Posada de Taos (309 Juanita Ln., 575/758-8164, www.laposadadetaos.com, $169 d) hits the sweet spot between luxury comforts and casual charm. All the amenities are here, such as wood fireplaces (in five of the six rooms) and whirlpool tubs (in three), but the overall atmosphere is homey and informal, and the decor is distinctly Taos without being heavy-handed, with sparing country touches. The price is right too, coming in on the lower end compared to other places with the same perks. El Solecito, in the older adobe section with its own back terrace, is a particularly nice room.

The **Historic Taos Inn** (125 Paseo del Pueblo Norte, 575/758-2233, www.taosinn. com, $189 d), established in 1936 in the former home of the town doctor, is the other historic hotel, with a cozier feeling than La Fonda, even if it is slightly overpriced. Rooms in the main building are more historic feeling and cheaper (about $120 in high season); in the courtyard section or other outbuildings, you may get a kiva fireplace.

Decorated with an artist's eye, the five guest cottages at **Casa Gallina** (613 Callejon, 575/758-2306, www.casagallina.net, $195 d) showcase beautiful handicrafts from Taos and around the globe. Kitchens can be stocked with occasional goodies from the garden and eggs from resident hens (they're also pressed into service for the fresh and delicious breakfasts).

$200-250

A somewhat storied and star-crossed luxury hotel, **El Monte Sagrado** (317 Kit Carson Rd., 575/758-3502, www.elmontesagrado. com, $219) is now owned by the excellent New Mexico company Heritage Hotels and Resorts, which, at press time in 2016, was giving all of its details a fresh look and restoring some of its eco-friendly infrastructure. The hotel has eclectic style in the Global Suites ($450 and up), but entry-level Taos Mountain rooms, while a little generic with their white-linens-and-dark-wood, are reasonably priced. The grounds are well kept, and there's a lovely spa.

Over $250

Fully renovated in 2013, **Palacio de Marquesa** (405 Cordoba Rd., 575/758-4777, www.marquesataos.com, $275 d) is an exquisite eight-room inn, also run by Heritage Hotels and Resorts. The rooms have an air of what might be called pueblo minimalism: dark viga ceilings, with white walls, white leather chairs, and marble baths. What might feel too austere is warmed up with pops of color, silver cow skulls, and kiva fireplaces. Rooms are dedicated to Taos women of influence, such as Mabel Dodge Luhan and Agnes Martin. Spa services and the option of a made-to-order breakfast delivered to your room add to the cocoon-like feel.

ARROYO SECO
Under $100

The best lodging bargain in the area is **The Snowmansion** (Hwy. 150, Arroyo Seco, 575/776-8298, www.snowmansion.com). Conveniently set midway to the Taos Ski Valley in bustling "downtown" Arroyo Seco, this cheerful place offers bunks in dorm rooms ($30) and private rooms (from $74). In the summer, you can also camp (from $25) or sleep in a tepee ($60), and nosh on veggies from the hostel garden. But as the name suggests, winter sports fanatics are the main clientele, and if you don't want to be woken by skiers racing for the Chile Line bus outside, opt for an individual cabin with shared bath ($60).

RANCHOS DE TAOS
$150-200

At the south edge of Ranchos de Taos, **Adobe & Pines Inn** (4107 Hwy. 68, 575/751-0947, www.adobepines.com) is built around an 1830s hacienda, shaded by old trees and overlooking a lush garden. Of the eight rooms, six are quite large (from $179), with especially lavish bathrooms. But even the two smallest rooms ($109 and $119) have fireplaces—and everyone gets the exceptionally good breakfasts, with fresh eggs from the on-site chickens and veggies from the garden. The hotel was under new ownership as this guide went to press, so check current reviews to ensure it's kept its high standards.

NORTH AND EAST OF TAOS
Under $100

Nestle into a snug sheepherder's cabin at **Taos Goji Eco Lodge** (Old State Rd. 3, 575/776-3971, www.taosgoji.com, $85 d), in the village of San Cristobal, 11 miles north of Taos. The 10 cabins have wood stoves and kitchens, and the surrounding 40-acre farm is lively with sheep, goats, and chickens.

$150-200

For an only-in-Taos experience, stay the night in an **Earthship** (U.S. 64, 575/751-0462, www.earthship.com, $190 d). Four of the curvy, off-the-grid homes are available, with room for up to six people in the largest one. Not only does an Earthship feel like a Hobbit house with banana trees (in the south-facing greenhouse areas), but you're out in the larger, all-Earthship subdivision, with great views of the mountain. And yes, you'll have running water, a refrigerator, and all the other comforts. It's a bit of a drive from town (west of the Rio Grande), but it's well worth it.

West on U.S. 64

Coming through the mountains on U.S. 64 gives you a dramatic descent into the Chama Valley, where U.S. 84 is one of the more spectacular drives in northern New Mexico. (It starts getting good down south in Abiquiu.)

TRES PIEDRAS

This settlement about 30 miles west of Taos is only a handful of houses scattered around the crossroads of U.S. 64 and U.S. 285, but the **Chili Line Depot Café** (38429 U.S. 285, 575/758-1701, 8am-7pm daily, $7), just north of the intersection, is a bright spot for food in the wilderness, with friendly staff and hearty burritos. Call ahead to check hours; the restaurant may close early if business is slow.

TIERRA AMARILLA AND LOS OJOS

U.S. 64 climbs up and over the Brazos Mountains, the view from the pass taking in the sheer limestone of 3,000-foot-high cliffs

dramatic weather near Tierra Amarilla

King Tiger and the *Mercedes*

The pastoral village of **Tierra Amarilla** gives little indication that it was once a battleground in the Chicano rights movement and the local Hispano fight for land-grant restitution. The Tierra Amarilla *merced* (land grant) was established in the 19th century, and when Nuevo México became a U.S. territory in 1848, the Treaty of Guadalupe Hidalgo specified it would be preserved. But cattle ranchers and the national forest system gradually appropriated it, so that, by the 1960s, many families in largely Hispano Rio Arriba County found themselves landless and subsisting on less than $1,500 per year.

Around this time, Reies López Tijerina, a charismatic activist in the growing Chicano movement, took up the land-grant cause. In 1967, he and more than 150 local men stormed the Tierra Amarilla courthouse, calling themselves the Political Confederation of Free City States and bearing a banner proclaiming "Give Us Our Land Back." Their plan was to make a citizen's arrest of the district attorney. But the DA was nowhere around, the activists wound up taking everyone in the courthouse hostage, and 300 National Guard troops were called in. The incident made headlines across the country, and Tijerina was an overnight legend. The press dubbed him King Tiger, and he was praised in the ballad "El Corrido de Rio Arriba," penned within weeks by the band Los Reyes de Albuquerque.

Trials the next year were equally gripping: Tijerina wept on the witness stand, a lawman present at the raid turned up murdered, and even New Mexico's governor gave heartfelt testimony. Tijerina came away with a minimal sentence for second-degree kidnapping. He went on to lead the Chicano faction as part of Martin Luther King Jr.'s Poor People's Campaign.

In Tierra Amarilla, meanwhile, the battle lines became hopelessly tangled. With seed money from a generous donor, the Sierra Club announced in 1970 that it would donate a new "land grant" to the area, but it failed to materialize—perhaps because environmentalists soon were battling the local sheepherders over the effects of grazing. In 1995, a local shepherd successfully sued the Sierra Club for the never-applied donation, and the economic situation in the valley has somewhat improved. But many people must lease land on which to graze their sheep, resentments run deep, and the heroism of King Tiger is still recalled with feeling.

to the north. Descending into the golden valley along the Rio Chama, you soon reach the junction with U.S. 84 and the village of Tierra Amarilla, off the east side of the highway. Next door to the courthouse is the cool little **Three Ravens Coffeehouse** (15 Hwy. 531, 575/588-9086, 7am-4pm Mon.-Fri., also Sat. May-Sept.), a labor of love and the active community center; ask the owner about how he renovated the ancient adobe building.

Just a few miles north of Tierra Amarilla and west of the highway, Los Ojos is a two-block-long main street of adobe and Victorian wood-frame buildings, most connected in some way with **Ganados del Valle,** a cooperative established in 1983 to preserve the economy in the region, which for hundreds of years had been based on raising sheep and selling their products. But young people could no longer earn a living from this, and many of the most traditional weaving and spinning techniques had already been lost. The cooperative was gradually able to provide employment for dozens of artists, administrators, and sheepherders, and in 1990, one of its founders, Maria Varela, who got her start as a Chicana activist in the Student Nonviolent Coordinating Committee in the 1960s, earned a MacArthur "genius grant" for her efforts.

Once a Ganados project though now a consignment shop, **Tierra Wools** (91 Main St., 575/588-7231, www.handweavers.com, 9am-6pm Mon.-Sat., 11am-4pm Sun. Apr.-Oct., 10am-5pm Mon.-Sat. Nov.-May) has become a pilgrimage site for anyone engaged in fiber arts. The shop showcases the work of local weavers—rugs, pillows, ruanas—as well as brilliantly dyed skeins of handwoven wool

Tierra Wools sells local weaving products.

yarn from the hardy, four-horned Churro sheep, a breed the conquistadors introduced to New Mexico. If you're interested in the process, you can join a weeklong class. The last weekend in April, the **Spring Harvest Festival** involves demonstrations of sheep-shearing, hand-spinning, and more, along with music and other entertainment. The shop also offers two lodgings in a sweet rental *casita* (from $95), for those who'd like a taste of village life.

EL VADO LAKE AND HERON LAKE STATE PARKS

These two reservoirs west of Tierra Amarilla are nearly linked. Of the two, **El Vado Lake State Park** (575/588-7247, www.nmparks. com, $5/car day use) is smaller but busier, as motorboats are permitted here, and it's a popular recreation spot, with large **campgrounds** at its south end (accessible via Hwy. 112, 17 miles southwest of Tierra Amarilla).

A 5.5-mile one-way hiking trail leads from Shale Point, north of all the campgrounds, up along the Rio Chama, across a bridge, up past Heron Dam, and into the south end of **Heron Lake State Park** (575/588-7470), which is also accessible via U.S. 64/84 and Highway 95.

This lake is much quieter, as boats can only operate at no-wake speeds, which also makes it popular for kayakers. During the week, free ranger-led hikes are available on request—ideally, call ahead to the park office to let the staff know you're coming. There are scores of attractive campsites all along the banks here.

Both lakes offer excellent fishing, though you'll need to arrange for a boat at **Stone House Lodge** (Hwy. 95, 575/588-7274, www. stonehouselodge.com, from $175/four hours), as there are no rentals at the lake itself. The stretch of the Chama River from El Vado Dam to Abiquiu Lake is a good rafting run, one of the best places in the state for a multiday trip. **Kokopelli Rafting Adventures** (505/983-3734, www.kokopelliraft.com) in Santa Fe and **Los Rios River Runners** (575/776-8854, www.losriosriverrunners.com) in Taos both run trips through these remote canyons; expect to pay about $115 for a one-day outing and $495 for a multiday trip.

CHAMA

A tiny high-mountain town, Chama is a perfect getaway for people who find Durango or Silverton, Colorado, too crowded. With just 1,000 residents, the place was and still is focused on the railroad that begins here and

El Vado Lake State Park

threads its way between the mountains to Antonito, just over the state line. Even if the train isn't your thing, you can drive north on Highway 17 for the views, though note that when the train isn't running, neither is much of the town; check for winter closures.

Chama is small because it's bordered on both sides by land belonging to the Jicarilla Apache. The tribe operates an elite hunting ranch, The Lodge at Chama, that's a favorite politico getaway. But the natural attractions here are accessible to all—with the Rio Chama running right through town, you could theoretically walk out the front door of your (very affordable) rental cabin, snag a trout, and cook it for dinner. On a day visit, the star of the show is the great steam train. If you stay a little longer, you'll have a chance to appreciate the remarkable vistas—particularly in the fall, when the mountains are blanketed with a thick patchwork of color.

★ Cumbres & Toltec Scenic Railroad

The biggest attraction in Chama is the historic steam-driven **Cumbres & Toltec Scenic Railroad** (575/756-2151, www.cumbrestoltec. com), which has been running 64 miles from Chama up to Antonito, Colorado, since 1880.

It is now jointly owned by the two neighboring states and maintained as a sort of museum.

You can travel the route in several ways, depending on how much of a train ride you want. The shortest ride is the four-hour Sunday Express, running only that day in summer. The year-round standard outing is from Chama to the midpoint, the ghost town of Osier, just over the state border—you hop off there, have lunch, stroll around, and get back on the train for the ride back down the pass (from $95 adults, $45 kids). The whole trip takes a little more than six hours. Hard-core rail fans can go the whole way to Antonito—stopping in Osier for lunch—and return to Chama by bus, which takes eight hours ($95 adults, $49 kids); this way, you'll get to see the dramatic Toltec Gorge, just north of Osier.

Trains run most frequently in June, July, and early August, then again late September-mid-October, for autumn leaf season. Reservations are advised, and you can choose from three classes of service (windows open in tourist class, which is fun, but soot from the steam engine can make things a little gritty). The hot lunch included in the ticket price is pretty generous, with turkey and all the standard vegetables, plus pie to finish.

The Cumbres & Toltec steam train descends to Chama.

You can also prowl around the depot and rail yards. Pick up a flyer at the station that identifies all the structures, as well as distinguishes between drop-bottom gondolas, flangers, and other specialized train cars.

Recreation

Elk are prevalent throughout the mountains around Chama, and in the fall, the elk's distinctive mating call, or bugle, can be heard. North of town, the **Edward Sargent Wildlife Management Area** (575/476-8000, www.wildlife.state.nm.us) has a viewing spot just inside the borders of the reserve, overlooking a big basin where the animals often graze. You can also hike into the center of the 20,000 acres, along the Rio Chama (for excellent fishing)—ask at the Chama visitors center for more information and other area hiking spots. If you want to hike or explore further, you'll need a GAIN permit, which you can pick up at the Chama Valley Supermarket.

Food

For an honest steak and potato, plus not-so-carnivorous items like grilled trout and cold beer, head to the **High Country Restaurant & Saloon** (2289 S. Hwy. 17, 575/756-2384, 11am-10pm daily, $10-20), a big wood-paneled operation that's popular with through-bikers as well as locals. It serves a massive breakfast buffet on Sunday 8am-noon.

Across the street from the train yard, **Box Car Cafe** (425 Terrace Ave., 575/756-2706, 7am-10pm daily Apr.-Nov., $8) serves hearty breakfast burritos smothered in piquant chile and good burgers for lunch. The menu is fairly limited, but the food is good and priced well.

The Brew House (587 Terrace Ave., 575/756-1259, 1pm-10pm Wed.–Sun.) serves local beer, wine, hard cider, and mead made with wild honey. Stop in for a drink and occasional live music.

Accommodations

Chama has a reasonable selection of places to stay. The south side of town is largely devoted to rustic riverside cottage operations. **Chama River Bend** (2625 Hwy. 64, 575/756-2264, www.chamariverbendlodge.com) offers clean, basic rooms in a motel-like strip (from $89 d), as well as cabins closer to the water (from $119). Neighboring **Vista del Rio Lodge** (2595 Hwy. 64, 575/756-2138, www.vistadelriolodge.com) is one of the nicest in town. Spacious, newly renovated rooms are furnished in a contemporary Southwest style and have modern bathrooms.

Up near the depot, the lodging is a bit less rustic. The pretty ★ **Chama Station Inn** (423 Terrace Ave., 575/756-2315, www. chamastationinn.com, May-mid-Oct., $90 d) is just across from the train. Most of the nine rooms have wood floors, and all are decorated sparingly with country touches; the extra $10 for a deluxe room is well worth it, as it gets you a fireplace, a graceful high ceiling, and a little more space.

One of the least expensive beds can be found at **The Hotel** (501 S. Terrace Ave., 575/756-2416, www.thehotel.org, $64 d), a 1930s building with small rooms that are nonetheless very clean, and a pleasant throwback. At press time the business was for sale—check that a change in owners hasn't changed the quality.

Campers will do well at the **Rio Chama RV Park** (U.S. 64, 575/756-2303, May-mid-Oct.), on the north edge of town, where tent sites ($16) are nestled amid tall trees and the river flows right by.

Information and Services

Chama's **visitors center** (575/756-2235, 8am-6pm daily) is located at the junction of U.S. 64/84 and Highway 17, on the southern edge of town. In addition to maps and other info (for the whole state), it also provides free Internet access and coffee. In the winter, the office closes one hour earlier.

JICARILLA APACHE NATION

The village of **Dulce** is the main town of the 750,000-acre **Jicarilla Apache Nation** (575/759-3242), which stretches north to the state line and south almost to the town of Cuba. The area is not the ancestral homeland of this band of Apache—originally, they had lived around the Platte and Arkansas Rivers in what is now central Colorado. But they were pushed south by white settlers in the 19th century, eventually scattering to live with other tribes as far south and east as Tucumcari. The current reservation wasn't designated until

1887, when the band's numbers had dwindled to just 330 and the group had split into two factions. Although the land was hard-won, it proved very fortunate when oil and gas were discovered on it in the 1930s. Profit from these resources, as well as a casino in Dulce and the luxurious Lodge at Chama, has made this a relatively prosperous reservation.

The tribe now numbers about 3,400 members, with 2,500 or so based in Dulce. The village is set in a high, grassy valley that feels hidden away from the rest of the world, with bison, cattle, and sheep grazing beneath the snowcapped Rockies. The **Jicarilla Cultural Center** (U.S. 64, 575/759-1343, 8am-5pm Mon.-Fri., free) has a small museum that describes the role of buffalo, medicinal herbs, and other heritage. In a trailer south of the tribal headquarters, the **Arts and Crafts Museum** (U.S. 64, 575/759-3242, 8am-5pm Mon.-Fri., free) is more of a shop, where you can also see people making the intricate baskets for which the tribe is known.

Festivals and Events

On the third week in July, the **Little Beaver Roundup** is a well-attended powwow and rodeo in Dulce that's open to visitors, and photography is permitted. Similar events, plus traditional footraces, mark **Go-Jii-Ya,** the tribe's feast day on September 15; it takes place at Stone Lake.

Recreation

Most visitors come here to hunt mule deer and elk on the reservation lands, or to fish in one of the many lakes; contact **Jicarilla Game and Fish** (575/759-3255, www.jicarillahunt. com) for rules and permits. **Stone Lake** ($5, or free with fishing and hunting licenses), 18 miles south of Dulce, has pretty campsites around its three miles of shoreline.

Getting There

Dulce is 25 miles west of Chama on U.S. 64, about 30 minutes away.

The Enchanted Circle

The loop formed by U.S. 64, Highway 38, and Highway 522 is named for its breathtaking views of the Sangre de Cristo Mountains, including Wheeler Peak. The area is a cultural shift from Taos, much of it settled by Anglo ranchers and prospectors in the late 1800s and currently populated by transplanted flatlander Texans enamored of the massive peaks. The main towns on the route—Angel Fire and Red River—are ski resorts. As the scenery is really the thing, you can drive the 84-mile route in a short day, with time out for a short hike around Red River or a detour along the Wild Rivers scenic byway. If you like country music, you might want to plan on being in Red River for the evening.

Driving counterclockwise around the loop, as described below, gives you the breathtaking descent into the Taos Valley from Questa—but note that your eating options dwindle near the end of the route. Avoid driving the circle on a Sunday, as significantly more attractions and businesses are closed.

To start, head east on Kit Carson Road, which turns into U.S. 64, winding along next to the Taos River and past numerous campgrounds and hiking trails. At Palo Flechado Pass, the road descends into the high Moreno Valley, a gorgeous expanse of green in early spring and a vast tundra in winter.

ANGEL FIRE

A right turn up Highway 434 leads to this tiny ski village, a cluster of timber condos at the base of a 10,600-foot mountain. In comparison with Taos Ski Valley, **Angel Fire Resort** (800/633-7463, www.angelfireresort.com, $71 full-day lift ticket) looks like a molehill, with a vertical drop of 2,077 feet. But it's friendly to families, has two freestyle terrain parks, and is the only place in the state for night skiing. For those with no snow skills at all, the 1,000-foot-long tubing hill provides an adrenaline rush.

In summer, the resort transforms itself with activities like fishing at **Monte Verde Lake** ($25/person) and an elaborate zipline course ($119), one of two in New Mexico. Off the slopes, **Roadrunner Tours** (Hwy. 434 in town, 575/377-6416, www.rtours.com) offers trail rides on horseback into the mountains.

But the main warm-weather diversion is mountain biking, on the mountain itself at **Angel Fire Bike Park,** the largest bike park in the Rocky Mountains, and on the storied **South Boundary Trail** (no. 164), which runs from a trailhead off Forest Road 76 south of Angel Fire. The route to Taos is about 5 vertical-seeming miles over the pass, then another 22 or so back to El Nogal trailhead on U.S. 64, a couple of miles east of Taos. **Gearing Up** (129 Paseo del Pueblo Sur, 575/751-0365) offers shuttle service ($55), so you can bike one-way.

Food

Café Espresso (3375 Mountain View Blvd., 575/377-6669, 7am-2pm daily, $8) serves breakfast burritos—including to-go versions so you can hit the slopes earlier.

For lunch, **Hail's Holy Smoked BBQ** (3400 Hwy. 434, 575/377-9938, 11am-7pm Tues.-Thurs., 11am-8pm Fri.-Sat., $12) represents Texan cuisine, with smoked brisket, cowboy beans, and house-made desserts.

If you happen to be around for dinner, check **The Pub 'n Grub** (52 N. Angel Fire Rd., 575/377-2335, 3pm-8pm daily in winter, 5pm-9pm daily in summer) for fresh, hearty bar food like buffalo burgers and gargantuan steaks; it's closed October and November.

Information

The Angel Fire CVB maintains a **visitors center** (3365 Hwy. 434, 575/377-6555, www.angelfirefun.com, 9am-5pm daily) just south of the T intersection with Angel Fire Road.

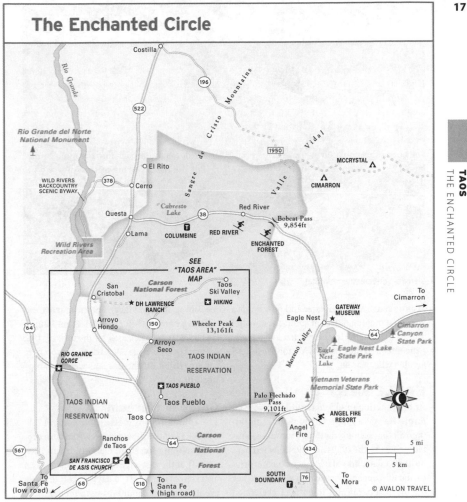

The Enchanted Circle

The **Angel Fire Chamber of Commerce** (3407 Hwy. 434, 575/377-6353, www.angel-firechamber.org, 9am-5pm Mon.-Fri.) has its own office where the lobby is open 24 hours, so you can pick up brochures and maps anytime.

VIETNAM VETERANS MEMORIAL STATE PARK

Back on U.S. 64, a little more than a mile past the turn for Angel Fire, a swooping white structure rises on the hill to your left. This is the **Vietnam Veterans Memorial State Park** (575/377-2293, www.nmparks.com, 9am-5pm daily Apr.-Oct., 9am-5pm Thurs.-Mon. Nov.-Mar., chapel open 24 hours), built by Victor "Doc" Westphall as a remembrance for his son David, who was killed in the war. When Westphall commissioned Santa Fe architect Ted Luna to design the graceful white chapel in 1968, it was the first such memorial for the casualties of Vietnam. An adjacent

Vietnam Veterans Memorial State Park

visitors center was built later and now holds a small but moving museum about the conflict and its aftermath. In the garden are a Huey helicopter and the graves of Victor Westphall and his wife, Jeanne.

EAGLE NEST

At the junction of U.S. 64 and Highway 38, **Eagle Nest** is a small strip of wooden buildings, all that's left of what was a jumping gambling town in the 1920s and 1930s, when bars hosted roulette and blackjack, and enterprising businesspeople would roll slot machines out on the boardwalks to entice travelers en route to Raton and the train. The small lake here is the main focus of fun, but there's also good hiking just east in Cimarron Canyon State Park.

Eagle Nest Lake State Park

East of U.S. 64, south of town, **Eagle Nest Lake** was created in 1918 with the construction of a privately financed dam on the Cimarron River. Today it's a state park, stocked with trout, and a popular recreation spot (the Fourth of July fireworks display and

ice fishing are legendary). For the marina and **visitors center** (575/377-1594, 8am-4:30pm daily, $5/car day use), look for the turn off U.S. 64 marked by a large RV park sign. Stop here for an exhibit on the dam, as well as camping ($10).

Gateway Museum

The community **Gateway Museum** (U.S. 64, 575/377-5978, www.gatewaymuseum.org, 9:30am-4pm Mon.-Sat., 11am-4pm Sun., donation), at the east edge of Eagle Nest, gives an overview of the good old days and often hosts events, such as a mountain-man rendezvous.

Food and Accommodations

In the town's oldest hotel, built out of old railroad ties, **Calamity Jane's** (51 Therma Dr., 575/377-9530, 11am-9pm daily, $10) is the town's main restaurant and bar hangout, though the steakhouse food is inconsistent.

Retro **Kaw-Lija's** (Therma Dr., 575/377-3424, 8am-8pm daily May-Sept., $6) is the most reliable place to eat here, with burgers and the like. Opening hours can be erratic, and it closes in the winter.

Eagle Nest Lake

Laguna Vista Lodge (575/377-6522, www.lagunavistalodge.com, $85-125 d) has standard motel rooms connected by a screened porch, as well as cabins and apartments with a view of the lake.

Information

The **Eagle Nest Chamber of Commerce** (51 Therma Dr., 575/377-2420, www.eaglenestchamber.org, 8am-4pm Mon.-Fri. mid-May-mid-Oct.) has an enthusiastic staff.

ELIZABETHTOWN

Blink and you'll miss it: A small sign on the right side of the road 4.8 miles past Eagle Nest points to a left turn to the former gold-rush site of Elizabethtown, the first incorporated village in New Mexico. When gold was discovered in 1866, it grew to more than 7,000 people, then faded to nothing after a dredge-mining project failed in 1903. It's now a barely discernible ghost town, with the paltry stone ruins of the Mutz Hotel, the former center of social activity. The only signs of life are, ironically, in the **cemetery,** which is still used by residents of Colfax County and contains graves dating as far back as 1880.

RED RIVER

The ski village of Red River is a cluster of tidy rows of wooden buildings, all done up in Old West facades, complete with boardwalks and swinging saloon doors. Like Elizabethtown, this was once a community of wild prospectors, but when mining went bust, the town salvaged itself by renting out abandoned houses to vacationers escaping the summer heat. Just when air-conditioning started to become widespread in the 1950s, the ski area opened, saving the town from a major slump. Red River still thrives, with a year-round population of only about 485. The town hosts a rowdy Memorial Day Motorcycle Rally, as well as a large Fourth of July parade and a Mardi Gras street party; contact the **Red River Chamber of Commerce** (575/754-2366, www. redriverchamber.org) for more details.

Hiking

This is the back side of Wheeler Peak, so the ascents are much more gradual, while

Wild West meets alpine ski style in Red River.

still yielding dramatic views. Stop in at the **visitors center** (101 W. River St., 575/754-3030, www.redriver.org, 8am-5pm daily), in the town hall, for area maps and trail guides. The easy **Red River Nature Trail** starts in town at Brandenburg Park and runs two miles one-way, with signs identifying plants and geological formations.

West of town, the road leads past a number of trailheads that make for a good amble. **Columbine Trail,** on the left (south) seven miles out (or about four miles east of Questa), starts out easy, crossing Deer Creek, but soon climbs switchbacks that lead through a large aspen grove, then above the tree line to the ridge, a total of about five miles. As an incentive, wild berry bushes flourish alongside the trail in late summer. The right side of the road, however, is a little less scenic because a molybdenum mine has stripped a good chunk of the mountain.

Skiing

Compared with Taos Ski Valley, **Red River Ski & Snowboard Area** (575/754-2223, www.redriverskiarea.com, $67 full-day lift

ticket) may be a baby hill, but it's nothing if not convenient: The trails run into town, so it's walking distance from anywhere to the chairlift. (In summer, the ski slopes are converted into a dry-tubing area, from $18/three runs. A seated zip-pull line glides 70 feet above Pioneer Road, $10/flight.)

Cross-country skiers should follow Highway 38 east of town, to the **Enchanted Forest** cross-country ski area (575/754-6112, www.enchantedforestxc.com, $18 full-day pass), which has more than 20 miles of groomed trails through the trees and up the mountainside. Nonskiers can rent snowshoes. And, for a special overnight experience, you can trek in to a **yurt** ($50-150, depending on season), nicely appointed with a woodstove. It's available year-round, and snowmobile delivery of your gear is an option in winter. (At research time in 2016, the business was for sale, so check ahead regarding changes.)

Entertainment

Red River has a lively country music scene, heavily influenced by the Texans who have long come here for vacation. "Outlaw country" singer and songwriter Michael Martin Murphey, whose song "The Land of Enchantment" is the official state ballad, has long been an active participant here, and he performs regularly July-first week of September at **Rocking 3M Chuckwagon Amphitheater** (178 Bitter Creek Rd., 575/754-6280). **Bobcat Pass** (1670 Hwy. 38, 575/754-2769, www.bobcatpass.com, 5:30pm Tues., Thurs., and Sat. mid-June-Aug.), which offers horseback riding by day, hosts "cowboy evenings," which include a home-style steak dinner along with a night of singing and picking and a bit of poetry. And in town, you can pretty much always count on music at the aptly named **Lost Love Saloon** (400 E. Main St., 575/754-2922), the bar at Texas Reds, and the adjoining **Motherlode Saloon** (406 E. Main St., 575/754-6280)—because you can't have too many.

Food

Red River has the largest selection of lunch options on the Enchanted Circle, but none of them are particularly remarkable. Business turnover can be high here, but at least **Texas Reds** (400 E. Main St., 575/754-2922, 4:30pm-9pm Mon.-Thurs., 11:30am-3pm and 4:30pm-9pm Fri.-Sun., $17) is consistent; it has relocated twice and still packs 'em in for big steaks in a wood-paneled Western-look room, the floors scattered with peanut shells. For Tex-Mex, **Sundance** (401 High St., 575/754-2971, 5pm-9pm Thurs.-Tues., $13) is equally reliable—it's on the street uphill and parallel to the main drag. For smaller meals, **Dairy Bar** (417 E. Main St., 575/754-9969, 11am-9pm daily in summer, 11am-7pm Thurs.-Mon. in winter, $5) does burgers, chile, quesadillas, and, of course, soft-serve ice cream.

Information

The chamber of commerce staffs a **visitors center** (101 W. River St., 575/754-3030, 8am-5pm daily) inside the town hall, off the north side of the main drag.

QUESTA

Arriving in Questa, at the junction of Highway 38 and Highway 522, you're back in Spanish New Mexico. The town, which now has a population of about 1,700, was established in 1842 and is still primarily a Hispano farming village, though a few Anglo newcomers have set up art spaces here. **Ocho** (8 Hwy. 38, www.ochozone.org) is one; it hosts community music jams and other events.

Across the road is the **visitors center** (Hwy. 38, 575/613-2852, www.questa-nm.com/visitor-center, 9:30am-5pm Thurs.-Sun. June-Aug.), though it has little to share. The heart of town, a few blocks back, is the 1841 **San Antonio Church,** recently restored by volunteers over about eight years of nights-and-weekends work.

Unfortunately, the few eating options here can't be recommended with enthusiasm; **Bronson's Burgers** (Hwy. 522, 575/586-1445, 11am-4:30pm Mon.-Sat., $6), in the B&R gas station on the south edge of town, will do. The better strategy is to head north a bit to **My Tia's Café** (Hwy. 378, 575/586-2203, 11am-6pm Mon. and Thurs.-Fri., 8am-7pm Sat.-Sun., $7), which does New Mexican home cooking.

Wild Rivers Recreation Area

In 2014, the **Río Grande del Norte National Monument** (575/758-8851, www.blm.gov) was established, protecting the river from the Colorado state line to Pilar, south of Taos. Perhaps the wildest section of the land is found north of Questa, in the **Wild Rivers Recreation Area,** where the Red River meets the Rio Grande. Red-tailed hawks circle over gnarled, centuries-old piñon and juniper trees, and river otters thrive here, after their reintroduction in 2008. White-water **rafting** is very popular in the Class III rapids of the Red River Confluence run; contact an outfitter in Taos.

The access road to the recreation area is three miles north on Highway 522 from the main Questa intersection, then west on

Highway 378, which leads through the town of Cerro and to the area's **visitors center** (575/586-1150, 10am-4pm daily June-Aug., $3/car day use).

Steep **hiking** trails lead down into the gorge and along the river, so you can make a full loop, starting down from **La Junta Overlook,** then taking Little Arsenic Trail back up (about 4.5 miles total), or **Big Arsenic Trail** for a longer hike (6 miles). If you'd prefer not to descend (and, necessarily, ascend) the canyon, follow the more level 1.7-mile **Pescado Trail** along the Red River rim and gently down to the Red River Fish Hatchery.

Five developed **campgrounds** (but no RV hookups; $7/car) on the rim can be reached by car, or you can hike in to campsites by the river ($5).

D. H. LAWRENCE RANCH

After Questa, the view opens up as you descend into the valley, with mesas stretching far to the west. Five miles east on a rutted road is the 160-acre **D. H. Lawrence Ranch** (10am-2pm Thurs.-Fri. June-Oct.), also known as the Kiowa Ranch, where English writer and provocateur D. H. Lawrence lived in 1924 and 1925 with his wife, Frieda, and the painter Dorothy Brett. The ranch was closed to visitors for several years, but reopened in 2014, with a docent on-site to answer questions. Though there's not much to see, it is as good a reason as any to drive up a back road and into the fragrant pine forests. (Don't bother driving up on a closed day—the property is fully fenced and locked up.)

The 160-acre spread was a gift from Mabel Dodge Luhan—generous, but nonetheless a bare-bones existence, as you can see in the cabins the artists occupied. Lawrence soon returned to Europe, but Frieda stayed on. Years after the writer died of tuberculosis

"that outhouse of a shrine" for D. H. Lawrence

in France in 1930, Frieda exhumed and cremated his body and brought the ashes to New Mexico. This plan sparked anger among Lawrence's friends, including Mabel, who characterized Frieda's planned site for the ashes as "that outhouse of a shrine." Tales abound about how the ashes never made the trip. Some of the earliest visitors to pay their respects at the ranch include Tennessee Williams and Georgia O'Keeffe, whose painting *The Lawrence Tree* was inspired by the view from the base of a gnarled pine in front of the Lawrences' cabin.

Coming from the north, turn left at the *second* sign for County Road B-009 (the first is in the town of San Cristobal). Coming up from Taos, look for the historical marker on the right side of the road, immediately before the turn.

Information and Services

TOURIST INFORMATION

A few miles south of the plaza, the **Taos Visitors Center** (1139 Paseo del Pueblo Sur, 575/758-3873, www.taos.org, 9am-5pm daily) is helpful, as long as you don't show up right before closing time. Stop here for flyers and maps galore, free coffee, and the very thorough weekly news and events bulletin (also posted online), which includes gallery listings, music, and more.

Books and Maps

Op.cit. (124-A Bent St., No. 6 Dunn House, 575/751-1999, 10am-6pm daily), formerly Moby Dickens, stocks new and used books, local titles, and maps.

Local Media

The *Taos News* comes out every Thursday; its *Tempo* entertainment section covers music, theater, and film listings. Many hotels offer free copies of *Tempo* to their guests. The *Albuquerque Journal* publishes a special northern edition daily, focused on local issues.

Radio

While you're in town, don't miss tuning in to **KTAO** (101.9 FM), a local radio station that's all solar-powered. The musical programming is broad, and you're sure to learn interesting tidbits about the community as well.

SERVICES

Banks

US Bank (120 W. Plaza, 575/737-3540, 9am-5pm Mon.-Fri.), just off the southwest corner of the plaza, is the most convenient bank and ATM while on foot. The drive-through service at **Centinel Bank of Taos** (512 Paseo del Pueblo Sur, 575/758-6700, 9am-5pm Mon.-Fri.) is easily accessible from the main drag.

Post Offices

The Taos **post office** (710 Paseo del Pueblo Sur, 575/751-1801, 9am-1pm and 2pm-4:30pm Mon.-Fri.) is on the south side; there's another on the north side (318 Paseo del Pueblo Norte, 575/758-2081, 8:30am-5pm Mon.-Fri.).

Internet

Wired? (705 Felicidad Ln., 575/751-9473, www.wiredcoffeeshop.com, 8am-5pm daily), behind Albertson's off La Posta Road, is a laid-back Internet café and business center with a big garden, good veggie and raw-food meals, and free wireless access for laptops; computer use is $2 for 15 minutes.

Getting There and Around

CAR

From Santa Fe, the drive to Taos takes about 1.5 hours (70 miles) along the direct "low road" through the river valley (via Española, U.S. 84/285 to Hwy. 68). If taking the high road (via Chimayó and Truchas, mostly on Hwy. 76), plan on at least 2 hours for the 80-mile drive.

From Albuquerque, add at least an hour's travel time for the 60-mile drive up I-25 (the most direct route).

Once in Taos, you will need a car to get to outlying sights, but will also have to bear the daily traffic jam on Paseo del Pueblo. There are paid parking lots close to the plaza, and a free one less than a quarter mile down Kit

Carson Road. For rental cars, **Enterprise** (1350 Paseo del Pueblo Sur, 575/758-5333, www.enterprise.com, 8am-5pm Mon.-Fri., 9am-noon Sat.) has a convenient office.

BUS AND SHUTTLE

For pickup at the Albuquerque airport, **Twin Hearts Express** (575/751-1201, www.twinheartsexpress.com, $50 one-way) runs a shuttle four times a day (11:30am, 1:30pm, 3:30pm, and 5:30pm), with drop-offs at most hotels. Allow at least 2.5 hours for travel time; reservations are required.

From Santa Fe, there's great weekend service from city-sponsored **Taos Express** (575/751-4459, www.taosexpress.com, $10 round-trip), which runs from Taos and back once on Saturday and Sunday, completing a loop in the morning and another in the afternoon. The one-way trip takes 1 hour and 50 minutes.

In Santa Fe, the bus picks up passengers near the Rail Runner main depot (Montezuma at Guadalupe) and at the South Capitol station (Sunday). In Taos, it drops off at Our Lady of Guadalupe parking lot, one block west of the plaza; going back south, it also picks up passengers at the Sagebrush Inn (1508 Paseo del Pueblo Sur). The schedule syncs with the Rail Runner's arrival in Santa Fe (and it can carry bicycles), making it a potentially seamless three-hour trip all the way from Albuquerque.

Within Taos, the **Chile Line bus** runs north-south from the Ranchos de Taos post office to the Taos Pueblo, approximately every 40 minutes 7:30am-5:30pm Monday-Friday. In town, it's free. Mid-December-April, a **ski shuttle** ($1 one-way) runs to Taos Ski Valley, with five buses daily making stops at key motels en route to the mountain; not all buses stop at all hotels. Contact the city (575/751-4459, www.taosgov.com) for maps and schedules.

Las Vegas and the Northeast

Pecos and Villanueva 184
Las Vegas. 186
Mora Valley. 194

The Northern Plains 195
The Rockies. 204

Look for ★ to find recommended
sights, activities, dining, and lodging.

Highlights

COLORADO

Johnson Mesa

Raton ★

Capulin ○

Capulin Volcano National Monument

Cimarron ★

St. James Hotel

Clayton Lake ★ State Park

Clayton ○

OK

Taos ○

Los Alamos ○

Montezuma Castle ★

TEXAS

Santa Fe ◉

Montezuma ★ Las Vegas

Las Vegas Plaza

San Ysidro ○

0   25 mi
0   25 km

© AVALON TRAVEL

★ **Las Vegas Plaza:** The heart of "Meadow City" is this grassy spread surrounded by grand territorial and old adobe buildings. It's so well preserved, it has been used frequently as a movie set—but it's blessedly free of souvenir shops (page 188).

★ **Montezuma Castle:** The glamour of the early railroad era is captured in this Queen Anne-style confection built as a resort hotel, now used as a college student center. Schedule a tour of the interior if possible, and don't miss the nearby hot springs (page 189).

★ **Clayton Lake State Park:** Stop by this oasis in the prairie to stand in—or at least near—the footsteps of giants. Dinosaurs left their immense tracks in the prehistoric mud here 100 million years ago (page 198).

★ **Capulin Volcano National Monument:** To get a great view across the plains, wind your way along the unnervingly narrow road that spirals up this perfectly round peak. You can also hike down into the crater (page 202).

★ **Johnson Mesa:** Outside of Taos, this is probably the most striking scenery in northern New Mexico—the Rockies rise up to the north, and the plains slip away far below the edge of this empty pastoral expanse (page 203).

★ **St. James Hotel:** The history of Cimarron, and its present social life, is intrinsically caught up with this old inn, the state's best 19th-century hotel (page 209).

The northeast section of the state bridges central New Mexico and the great American plains. The alpine Pecos Wilderness forms a natural barrier east of Santa Fe, then the land levels out into a grassy vista stretching to the horizon.

This was the northern border for the Spanish, and only after Mexico gained its independence in 1821 were traders' wagon trains welcome to enter the area from Kansas. For the three decades when the Santa Fe Trail was at its peak of activity, then with the subsequent prosperity brought in by the railroad, northeastern New Mexico was a lively place.

Now, though, especially since the Dust Bowl ate away at the eastern edge, it's a relatively silent swath of territory, traversed only by cattle and motorists. The latter usually stick to the interstate that runs north to Colorado. A few people stop to visit the town of Raton, at the base of a precipitous pass over the Rockies, or Cimarron, deeper in the mountains and that much more untouched by time. Just off I-25 in the lowlands, Las Vegas is the region's biggest center of activity. No bright lights and high rolling here: This Vegas is a college town with a population of about 13,600, a sedate place extending from a tree-shaded plaza edged with colonial and Victorian buildings that manage to be well preserved without feeling like a theme park. This can be refreshing after Santa Fe's enforced historicism.

The other major landmark on the plains is Capulin Volcano, which was active 60,000 years ago. Its cinder cone rises a thousand feet above the surrounding land, and from its rim you can see the earth fall away to the edge of the Sangre de Cristo Mountains. This area may not exude the barren drama of New Mexico's western desert or the thrill of the rugged mountains, but these placid flatlands, interrupted by only a few roads and small towns, offer a sense of space and tranquility unmatched elsewhere in the state.

HISTORY

Dinosaurs traipsed through in the Early Cretaceous (most notably leaving footprints north of Clayton), and Comanche and other

---

Previous: the empty northeastern corner of New Mexico; happy cows graze on the New Mexico's grassy northern plains. **Above:** a remnant of Las Vegas's film-set history

Plains Indians crisscrossed the area for hundreds of years before the Spanish arrived. But northeast New Mexico is even more indelibly marked by the Santa Fe Trail. The trade route proved to be the thin end of the wedge that opened up the West to American domination. First came goods from Missouri to the hungry market in Santa Fe (previously restricted to trading only with Spain), then came military supplies during the Mexican-American War, followed by homesteaders, prospectors, and entrepreneurs.

It was these prospectors who caused substantial trouble in the Rocky Mountains when, in 1866, gold was discovered not far from the northern branch of the Santa Fe Trail. Scores of hopeful miners flooded in—never mind the strike was on the Maxwell Land Grant, 1.7 million acres of private property. By the 1870s, a battle was brewing between the land-grant owners and the squatting miners. The resulting Colfax County War involved assassinations, lynchings, and Republican conspiracies in Santa Fe. Finally, an 1887 Supreme Court ruling gave squatters the boot, along with Spanish families who had been settled for generations. But by then, the railroad was bringing surer money than gold anyway—as well as another point of conflict. Anglo businessmen piled off the train in Raton and East Las Vegas, buying up land and earning the wrath of the Hispano shepherds who had been living in a much simpler economy for centuries.

Meanwhile, homesteaders on the plains northeast of Las Vegas had set the stage for another drama. Beginning in 1862, when the Homestead Act doled out 160-acre parcels to any family with enough nerve to take them, the would-be farmers struggled to work the thin topsoil that lay over limestone bedrock.

They were able to displace the native Plains Indian tribes in many areas, but they had no defense against the drought that struck in the 1920s. Soon, this was the western edge of the Dust Bowl, where the sky turned black for days at a time and children died from inhaling the grit. It was an unrivaled economic and environmental disaster that emptied the region of all but the ranchers who had initially settled the area for the United States.

After many decades, the northern plains' fortunes finally turned again, with the discovery of carbon-dioxide fields and the expansion of cattle ranching. But the area remains sparsely populated, just as much of the former Maxwell Land Grant is still relative wilderness.

PLANNING YOUR TIME

On the surface, Clayton, Las Vegas, Raton, and Cimarron are all one-night towns, as there are few formal sights and little to do in the evenings. But you could easily settle down somewhere for a few days (Cimarron or Las Vegas are the strongest candidates) while you investigate the spaces in between, hiking, fishing, or just driving the pretty back roads. The drive to Las Vegas on I-25 is a fairly dull one just for a day trip from Santa Fe, but the town is a great diversion if you're staying awhile or heading farther into the plains. Few tourists make it all the way to Clayton, in the farthest corner. But if you think of it as a point of contrast with central, mountainous New Mexico, it can be a worthwhile journey. Winter can be harsh here: Tourist services in Raton and Cimarron are severely curtailed beginning in September and lasting through the end of April, and a cold snap in early fall is not uncommon.

Las Vegas and the Northeast

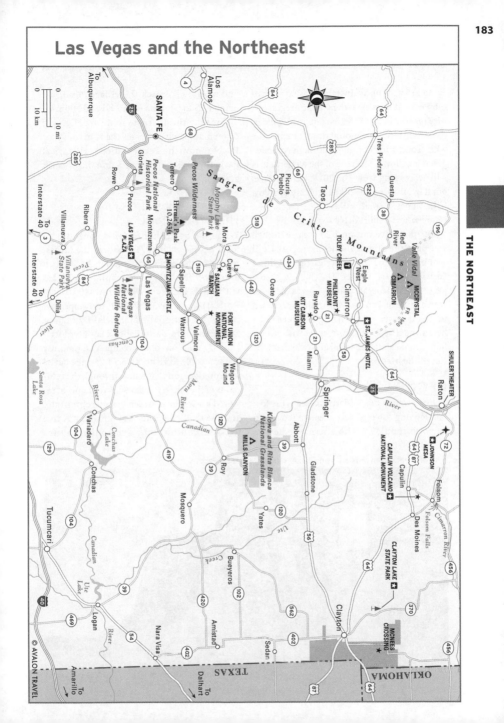

© AVALON TRAVEL

Pecos and Villanueva

Santa Fe backs up against the 223,000 acres of the Pecos Wilderness, the second-largest nature reserve in New Mexico (after the Gila, in the southwest). The mountain streams seethe with trout, and elk ramble through emerald-green meadows. The core of the wilderness is still recovering from the 2011 Pacheco Fire, but day visitors will still find plenty to enjoy. Villanueva, a small village near a gem of a state park, is a short drive southeast.

On the drive out on I-25, near exit 295, you pass the site of the westernmost Civil War battle in the United States, the **Battle of Glorieta Pass**. It raged March 26-28, 1862, part of a Confederate plan to invade the West with a force of Texans—a plan that was foiled in this decisive rout. The fight is reenacted here annually, and the property owner maintains a makeshift memorial and exhibit on the side of the highway.

PECOS

The gateway to the wilderness area is the former logging town of Pecos, where mountain men rub shoulders with alternative healers and monks. To reach the village, head east along I-25 to Glorieta (exit 299) and Highway 50; or take the alternate route via Highway 63 (exit 307), which passes the ruins of Pecos Pueblo, now the Pecos National Historical Park, the regional power before the Spanish arrived.

Pecos National Historical Park

When the Spanish made first contact with local people in 1540, Pecos was the largest pueblo in the region, population 2,000, with four- and five-story stone buildings sealed with mud. In **Pecos National Historical Park** (Hwy. 63, 505/757-7241, www.nps.gov/peco, 8am-6pm daily Memorial Day-Labor Day, 8am-4pm daily Labor Day-Memorial Day, $7), the ruins of this complex community are accessible to visitors via a 1.25-mile paved interpretive trail that winds through the remnants of the Pecos Pueblo walls, a couple of restored kivas, one of which you can climb into, and the shell of a Franciscan mission. A free **guided walking tour** around the site runs

ruins of a Franciscan mission inside Pecos National Historical Park daily at 10am in summer. Additional **van tours** ($2) cover different aspects of local history; check the website for schedules.

On a ridge looking out on the plains to the northeast and the mountains behind, the park provides a beautiful view today; around 1100, when the area was being settled with the first villages, it also provided a livelihood. The ridge was part of a natural trade path between the Rio Grande farmers and the buffalo hunters of the Great Plains. Both groups met in Pecos, itself an agricultural community, to barter. What began as a series of small villages consolidated in the 14th century into a city, with a layout so orderly it appears to have been centrally planned, and by 1450, the fortress of Pecos was the major economic power in the area.

Perhaps it was the city's trading culture and relative worldliness that made the Pecos Indians welcome Francisco Vásquez de Coronado and his men in 1540 with music and dancing rather than bows and arrows. Nearly 60 years later, Don Juan de Oñate visited the area and ordered a mission church built—a giant structure with six bell towers and buttresses 22 feet thick in some spots. The building was destroyed during the Pueblo Revolt, however, and the Pecos people dug a kiva smack in the middle of the ruined convent area—symbolic architecture, to say the least.

But the Spanish returned, and they were even welcomed and aided at Pecos. When they built a new church over the ruins in the early 1700s, it was noticeably smaller, maybe as a form of compromise. But even as a hybrid Pueblo-Spanish culture developed, the Indian population was falling victim to disease and drought. When the Santa Fe Trail opened up in 1821, Pecos was all but empty, and in 1838, the last handful of dwellers marched to live with fellow Towa speakers at Jemez Pueblo, 80 miles west; their descendants still live there today.

Pecos Wilderness
Stop in at the **Pecos Wilderness ranger**

station (Hwy. 63, 505/757-6121, 8am-12pm and 12:30pm-4:30pm Mon.-Fri.) on the south end of Pecos town to get maps and information on trail conditions, as well as the eight developed campgrounds. At this high elevation, summer temperatures are rarely above 75°F and can dip below freezing at night, so pack accordingly.

Highway 63 is the main access route into the wilderness, running north out of town along the Pecos River. If you've forgotten anything, including a fishing license, you can probably get it at the **Terrero General Store** (1911 Hwy. 63, 505/431-1132, 8am-5pm daily June-Aug.), about 13 miles along the two-lane road. The road then narrows and steadily rises, passing fishing access points and campgrounds.

About a mile after Mora Campground is the turn for Forest Road 223, a very rough road (ideally, for high-clearance cars only, or proceed very slowly) that leads 4.5 miles up to Iron Gate Campground and **Hamilton Mesa Trail** (no. 249), a fairly level 3.8-mile hike to a wide open meadow—look for strawberries among the wildflowers.

At Cowles Ponds, a developed fishing area where a mining camp once stood, you can turn left on Windsor Road to follow a paved one-lane road 1.5 miles to Panchuela Campground, the start of **Cave Creek Trail** (no. 288). It's an easy 3.6-mile out-and-back that follows a small waterway up to three caves that have been carved out of the white limestone by the stream's flow. If you go past the caves, up a steep hillside, you reach an area burned in the 2013 Jaroso Fire; this is not recommended, however, due to the danger of falling trees.

Continuing straight past Cowles on Highway 63 brings you in about three more miles to Jack's Creek Campground and **Jack's Creek Trail** (no. 257), a short out-and-back. Turn back at the junction with Dockweiler Trail (no. 259), about four miles in, to avoid the burned area. All trails in this area require a $2 trailhead parking fee; additional fees apply for camping or picnicking, depending on the spot. Check for seasonal closures January-April.

Food and Accommodations

At the main crossroads in Pecos, where Highway 50 meets Highway 63, **Frankie's at the Casanova** (12 Main St., 505/757-3322, 8am-2pm daily, 5:30pm-8:30pm Fri.-Sat., $9) is the town social center, set in an old adobe dance hall. The food isn't always a hit, but it's worth a stop just to see the murals over the bar.

For staying the night, the **Our Lady of Guadalupe Abbey** (Hwy. 63, 505/757-6600, www.pecosmonastery.org, $85 pp) maintains simple rooms with beautiful views; the rate is a suggested donation and includes meals. Guests are invited, though not required, to participate in prayer.

Several mountain lodges deeper in the forest, such as **Los Pinos Ranch** (505/757-6213, www.lospinosranch.com, $145 pp, two-night minimum), are typically open summers only and offer multiday packages with all meals and a variety of outdoor activities.

SOUTH TO VILLANUEVA

From exit 323 off I-25, 14 miles past Pecos, Highway 3 is a beautiful drive south. The two-lane road runs through a narrow valley with rich red earth cut into small farm plots.

Villages such as Ribera and El Pueblo were founded in the late 18th century, after the establishment of the San Miguel del Vado Land Grant in this valley. Named for a ford (*vado*) on the Pecos River, this area later became the official customs point for caravans entering Mexican territory via the Santa Fe Trail.

Villanueva, centered on its own historic church, is the largest settlement along the road; it has a small general store, handy if you're staying at the nearby campground.

Villanueva State Park

The small but beautiful **Villanueva State Park** (135 Dodge Rd., 575/421-2957, www.nmparks.com, $5/car) occupies a bend in the Pecos River against 400-foot-tall sandstone cliffs. Because the parkland is small, it doesn't draw big crowds—even in the summer, it's busy only on the weekends. Otherwise, you'll probably have the 2.5-mile Viewpoint Loop Trail to yourself and the choice of **camping** ($8) on the cottonwood-shaded river bottom (near flush toilets and shower), or up on the canyon rim amid juniper and piñon. The river is stocked with trout and can be deep enough for canoeing. Spring comes early, filling trails with wildflowers by late April; fall is a burst of red scrub oak and yellow cottonwood leaves, in sharp contrast to the evergreens.

Las Vegas

The city in New Mexico that suffers most from misplaced expectations, Las Vegas is a quiet community about 50 miles northeast of Santa Fe. Its centerpiece is a tree-shaded plaza, and nearly a thousand registered historic buildings stand in the surrounding blocks.

Set near Starvation Peak—a landmark butte on the Santa Fe Trail—the city was a Spanish settlement well before it was a stop on the trade route. In the middle of town, the Gallinas River still marks the historic division between the 1835 settlement of Nuestra Señora de los Dolores de las Vegas (Our Lady of Sorrows of the Meadows) and the railroad boom town of East Las Vegas, begun in 1879. The old Hispano plaza-centered town and the new, largely Anglo community didn't merge until 1970—probably because for decades, East Las Vegas was huge, anarchic, and populated with cattle rustlers, scam artists, and outlaws like Doc Holliday, who owned a saloon here for a year. Poor relations between the two towns were exacerbated by fights over land use. A band of Hispano vigilantes called

Las Vegas

To Fort Union Drive-In, Storrie Lake, and Mora

To Interstate 25, Fort Union National Monument, and Raton

518

85

25

Gallinas River

To MONTEZUMA CASTLE and Hermit's Peak Trail

HOT SPRINGS BLVD

65

MILLS AVE

8TH ST

7TH ST

4TH ST

UNIVERSITY

FRIEDMAN AVE

5TH ST

6TH ST

BACA AVE

GRAND AVE

RAILROAD AVE

HILLCREST RESTAURANT

COLONIAS ST

SANTA FE TRAIL INTERPRETIVE CENTER

RANGER OFFICE

CARNEGIE LIBRARY

CITY OF LAS VEGAS MUSEUM

To Montefiore Cemetery

329

INDIGO THEATER

TOME ON THE RANGE

NEW MEXICO HIGHLANDS UNIVERSITY

EL FIDEL HOTEL/ RESTAURANT

To Las Vegas Wildlife Refuge

UNIVERSITY AVE

104

TRAVELERS CAFE

PLAZA HOTEL AND SALOON/ GILDED AGE

NATIONAL AVE

CASTANEDA HOTEL

CHARLIE'S SPIC & SPAN

S GONZALES ST

DOUGLAS AVE

12TH ST

LINCOLN ST

Lincoln Park

VISITORS CENTER/ AMTRAK DEPOT

GALLERY 140

JACKSON ST

LAS VEGAS PLAZA

ABRAHAM'S TIENDITA

85

S PACIFIC ST

NEW MEXICO AVE

25

0   0.25 mi
0   0.25 km

To Interstate 25, Villanueva, and Santa Fe

© AVALON TRAVEL

the Gorras Blancas (White Caps) went around snipping through Anglo fencing in the night, so that their sheep could continue to graze.

But the changes wrought by the railroad were irrevocable, and along with Anglo economic supremacy came telephones, an electric streetcar, an opera house, and other trappings of modern life. For a period in the late 19th century, "Meadow City" was the biggest metropolis between Missouri and San Francisco, with an opera theater and a huge Harvey

House hotel, the Castañeda. Times changed again, and the Harvey House went derelict (though it's been slated for renovation).The New Mexico Normal School, established during this early boom period to train teachers, is now Highlands University, and philanthropist Armand Hammer established a branch of the United World College system outside of town in the 1980s. Together, the two institutions cater to several thousand students, who give the town a lot of its life.

SIGHTS

The best way to explore Las Vegas and appreciate its historic architecture is on foot. Start on the old plaza and notice how the building styles and the street layouts change as you head east across Bridge Street, which leads toward the New Mexico Highlands University campus. Douglas Avenue, two blocks south, is the main shopping district on the east side; still farther east are the rail yards, now relatively derelict but at one time the liveliest part of town.

If Las Vegas looks vaguely familiar, maybe it's because you watched the Cold War scare flick *Red Dawn* too many times, or you're a fan of Tom Mix Westerns such as *The Tenderfoot's Triumph*. The city was the setting for scores of silent films shot in the early 20th century, as well as later productions such as *Easy Rider, All the Pretty Horses,* and *No Country for Old Men. Red Dawn* used the area most thoroughly; the "Calumet Says Howdy" mural just off Grand Avenue is a relic of the shoot.

You can pick up a thorough walking-tour guide from the visitors center or from the **Citizens' Committee for Historic Preservation** (116 Bridge St., 505/425-8803, www.lvcchp.org, 10am-3pm Mon.-Sat.). The pamphlet covers the plaza and outlying historic districts, each with a distinctive building style; some structures date back as far as 1846. The group also occasionally organizes tours inside many of the private homes.

★ Las Vegas Plaza

The large, tree-edged **Las Vegas Plaza** on the west side of town shows only a few remnants of the original Spanish settlement, which had been built entirely of adobe, in a defensive ring meant to be sealed off against Apache raids. Many buildings later got spruced up with territorial details when the railroad brought in bricks, tin cornices, and other modern details. **Desmarais House/Our Lady of Sorrows Parish Hall** (1810 E. Plaza) is one of the few older adobe structures (built before 1883), though the curvy roofline is a bit of 1930s whimsy. The old *acequia madre* (main

irrigation ditch) runs along South Pacific Street, one block south of the plaza.

On the corner with Bridge Street, **Plaza Drugs** (178 Bridge St., 505/425-5221, 8am-6pm Mon.-Sat.) is a great old-school soda fountain and pharmacy. Sip a cherry-lime soda and check out the Lego model and the house-brand medicinal herbs, harvested nearby.

Bridge Street

Bridge Street, which leads toward the Gallinas River, was built up in the mid-19th century and now mixes old and new: A tattoo parlor and galleries have filled the empty spaces near Popular Dry Goods, which deals in rodeo wear. **Gallery 140** (140 Bridge St., 505/425/1085, 1pm-4pm Tues.-Thurs. and Sat., 1pm-7pm Fri.), home of the Las Vegas Arts Council, features monthly themed exhibitions of local art, some crafty and some fine. The exhibits at the **Santa Fe Trail Interpretive Center** (116 Bridge St., 10am-3pm Mon.-Sat.) are heavy on historic photos and low on artifacts. But entrance is free, and the place is run by the local historic preservation group, members of which are happy to answer questions of all kinds.

East Las Vegas

New Mexico Highlands University occupies either side of the street once you cross the river. Up the hill and past the campus, you enter some of the finer residential districts, with many examples of beaux arts and Queen Anne architecture—the best is around **Carnegie Park** (4th St. and National Ave.). The park's green lawn surrounds the elegant domed **Carnegie Library** (500 National Ave., 505/426-3304, 8am-5pm Mon.-Fri., 8am-2pm Sat.), a mini-Monticello. Of the more than 2,500 libraries around the world funded by steel magnate and philanthropist Andrew Carnegie, it's one of the few that still houses the public library, and the only one of three in the state to have survived.

About five blocks south is Douglas Avenue, where the commercial buildings range from sleek 1940s storefronts to the enormous Romanesque **Masonic Temple** (514 Douglas Ave.) of 1895. Farther south still, **Lincoln Park** (Lincoln and 7th Sts.) is another square surrounded by gracious large homes.

Castañeda Hotel

The owner of the Plaza Hotel is also overseeing renovations to this 1898 hotel, a onetime Harvey House adjacent to the train station. Kathy Hendrickson of **Southwest Detours** (505/459-6987, www.southwestdetours.com) offers guided tours by appointment of the railroad-era monolith and of Montezuma Castle ($30 pp for both).

City of Las Vegas Museum and Rough Riders Memorial Collection

It takes almost more time to say the name of the **City of Las Vegas Museum and Rough Riders Memorial Collection** (727 Grand Ave., 505/426-3205, www.lasvegasmuseum. org, 10am-4pm Tues.-Sat., $2 donation) than it does to tour it, but the exhibits are informative and based on well-chosen artifacts. It starts with a glass case of pots and baskets from the pre-Columbian era, but quickly gets to Vegas's glam years in the late 19th century, when the town supported two opera houses and had all the trappings of high society and general civilization, including the first telephone line in the state, installed in 1879.

One room is dedicated to souvenirs from Teddy Roosevelt's Rough Riders, the spirited regiment he led in the Spanish-American War of 1898. The soldiers, chosen for their skills with horses and guns, were volunteers from all over the West, with the majority from New Mexico; they chose Las Vegas as the site of their first reunion and continued to gather over the years, until the last soldier died in 1975.

Montefiore Cemetery

On the west edge of town, at the end of Colonias Street (you'll probably want to drive), the rambling **Montefiore Cemetery** is an interesting place to visit, especially the back corner, dedicated to the sizable Jewish population that settled here in the mid-1800s and set up stores and other trade operations. After walking around downtown, you'll recognize many of the names: Charles Ilfeld, for instance, and Samuel Nahm of the Stern & Nahm building on Bridge Street. Although this community established the first synagogue in the state, Congregation Montefiore, in 1881, only about 50 Jewish families are left in Las Vegas today.

★ Montezuma Castle

About six miles north of town (head north off the plaza on Hot Springs Blvd.), **Montezuma Castle** is a 90,000-square-foot architectural confection perched on the mountainside. The turreted Queen Anne-style building stands as a reminder of more glamorous travel days, when the Atchison, Topeka & Santa Fe Railroad envisioned an elite resort here, connected to the main line with a spur track. The firm of Burnham & Root (one of whose principals went on to make his name

Montezuma Castle

with the Chicago World's Fair complex of 1893) created the spectacular building, which opened to guests in 1885. But despite the patronage of Billy the Kid as well as American presidents, the place closed after less than 20 years. It later became the Montezuma Baptist College, then a Jesuit seminary for Mexican priests until 1972.

It was nearly in ruins when the **Armand Hammer United World College of the American West** (505/454-4221, www.uwc-usa.org) acquired it in 1981 and invested more than $10 million in its restoration. Historically accurate, but with modern touches such as vivid Dale Chihuly chandeliers, the interior is as lavish as the exterior—it's well worth seeing if your schedule allows. It is open to visitors only during free, student-led tours, on Saturday afternoons—call or check the website for the schedule.

Also on the college grounds is **Dwan Light Sanctuary** (505/454-4200), which *is* open to the public between 6am and 8pm daily. The serene meditation space is at its most

Take in the full spectrum at Dwan Light Sanctuary.

remarkable during daylight, when it dazzles with prism installations by Charles Ross, an artist who is building an earthwork sculpture nearby called *Star Axis* (www.staraxis.org). Register first at the visitors booth.

What makes the drive up more worthwhile are the **Montezuma Hot Springs** (5am-midnight, free), the waters that first inspired the construction of the castle resort. The set of three pools is alongside Highway 65—just drive half a mile past the main school entrance and look for signs and breaks in the guardrail on the right side. Those farthest along are the most appealing, terraced round concrete pools, screened from the road with a basic fence.

In the winter, Montezuma Pond, just west of the campus, may be frozen solid enough for **ice skating** (call 505/454-4200 for info). The pond was originally built by the hotel for ice harvesting.

ENTERTAINMENT AND EVENTS

Even though it's a college town, Las Vegas isn't particularly rambunctious, and it rolls up its sidewalks entirely on Sunday.

Nightlife

In July and August, the plaza hosts live music on Friday afternoons (5:30pm-7:30pm), after which you could check out the **Fort Union Drive-In** (3300 7th St., 505/425-9934, Fri.-Sun. May-Sept.), a great little relic of cinematic history for $20 per carload. Downtown, **Indigo Theater** (146 Bridge St., 505/434-4444, www.indigotheater.rocks) is the town's first-run movie theater, a cheery, 51-seat space.

After the nightly movie, you could head to **Plaza Saloon** (230 N. Plaza, noon-midnight daily), the bar at the Plaza Hotel, which has big show windows overlooking the square and a great mix of local drinkers, craft beers, vintage cocktails, and live music.

Festivals and Events

On the second Saturday evening of each month,

Bridge Street gets lively with the town **Artwalk,** when galleries and shops are open late.

If you're in town over Fourth of July weekend, you'll see the **Fiestas de las Vegas,** when vendors of traditional foods (as well as fair staples like caramel apples) set up all around the plaza and down Bridge Street, and bands perform in the gazebo. Festivities last for five days, beginning with Mass at Our Lady of Sorrows Church, one block west of the plaza, and ending with the crowning of the Reina de las Fiestas.

In August, Plaza Park and an indoor venue—it shifts each year—resound with toe-tapping tunes from local and regional acts during the **Meadow City Music Festival** (www.meadowcitymusicfest.com). Outdoor daytime concerts at Plaza Park are free, but reserve your tickets for the indoor, evening concerts.

SPORTS AND RECREATION

For maps and current conditions in the mountains, visit the **Pecos/Las Vegas Ranger District office** (1926 N. 7th St., 505/425-3534, 8am-5pm Mon.-Fri.).

Santa Fe National Forest

North of town, Highway 65 winds up an ever-narrowing valley to the borders of Santa Fe National Forest and **El Porvenir Campground,** in a pretty patch of pine forest, with campsites ($8) near a stream shaded by ponderosas at the base of Hermit's Peak. **Hermit's Peak Trail** (no. 223) leads 9.5 miles to the 10,260-foot summit. The peak's name refers to wandering mendicant Giovanni Maria Agostini, who was born in Italy and traveled all over the Americas on foot. He walked from Kansas to Las Vegas with a wagon train in the 1860s and took up residence in a cave ministering to the sick; he eventually wound up in the Organ Mountains near Las Cruces, where he was mysteriously killed.

Storrie Lake State Park

Just a few miles north of town, **Storrie Lake**

State Park (Hwy. 518, 505/425-7278, www.nmparks.com, $5/car day use, $8/night camping) is heavily used for waterskiing and windsurfing. But as a place to camp, you can do much better, as it's rather barren, and campsites are so close to the highway that you hear the rush of traffic. As long as you're not hauling an RV, head instead toward Mora to **Morphy Lake State Park** (575/387-2328, www.nmparks.com, $5/car day use, $8/night camping), which is much more scenic and secluded.

Las Vegas National Wildlife Refuge

Southeast of town via Highway 104, the remarkably lush **Las Vegas National Wildlife Refuge** is part of a chain of wetlands cultivated to accommodate migratory birds. A number of bald eagles winter here, and Swainson's hawks and more than 10 other species of raptors pass through every fall. A rectangular eight-mile driving route cuts through the 8,672-acre area, passing **McAllister Lake.** The second half of the circuit is unpaved and can get quite muddy, and is closed entirely November-February.

Stop in first at the **visitors center** (Hwy. 281, 505/425-3581, 8am-4pm Mon.-Fri.) to get an idea what birds are visiting; ask, too, if the secondary driving route is open, as it occasionally is in the late fall. To stretch your legs, take the short **Meadowlark Trail,** a nature trail at refuge headquarters, or the 1.75-mile **Gallinas Nature Trail,** in the southwest corner of the refuge. The latter hike descends into a small canyon, where you can usually spot prairie falcons and swallows; register first (weekdays only) at the visitors center.

FOOD

Aside from the chains on Grand Avenue, dining choices are limited in Las Vegas, but there are a few gems.

New Mexican

Get goodies to eat in the park from **Abraham's Tiendita** (151 Bridge St.,

505/425-0930, 9am-4pm Mon.-Fri., $5), a tiny storefront that doles out empanadas, tamales, and other handheld treats. Its ATM burrito packs a punch.

Cafés

Charlie's Spic & Span Bakery and Café (715 Douglas Ave., 505/426-1921, 6:30am-6pm Mon.-Sat., 7am-3pm Sun., $8) is a roomy restaurant where the glass cases burst with monster-size éclairs, jelly doughnuts, and cinnamon buns. But the real specialty is the flour tortilla—be sure to get one with whatever you order, whether it's chile-smothered eggs (breakfast is served all day) or spicy green-chile stew, or just a green-chile cheeseburger. After tasting the delectably fluffy things, you'll be ruined for the supermarket variety, so pick up a to-go bag at the door.

On the plaza, the all-purpose **Travelers Café** (1814 S. Plaza, 505/426-8638, 7:30am-7pm Mon.-Sat., $5) is the place for a coffee, Wi-Fi, and veggie-sandwich fix.

Hillcrest is a classic American family restaurant.

Diner

Up on the north side, not far from the freeway, the family-run diner **Hillcrest Restaurant** (1106 N. Grand Ave., 505/425-7211, 6am-8:30pm daily, $9) is a wonderful time capsule, and its food will satisfy anyone, as it smoothly switches between Americana (hot turkey sandwiches) and great New Mexican classics—the same way all the local customers chat in Spanish and English. It's open a bit later in the summer.

Fine Dining

For dinner, the Plaza Hotel's **Gilded Age** (230 N. Plaza, 505/425-3591, 7am-2pm and 5pm-9pm daily, $14) is popular with local politicians and the like for its steak and enchiladas served in a gold Venetian-plastered dining room. The new chef emphasizes local and seasonal ingredients. Breakfast and lunch are also both quite good—a fine option if you're not staying at the hotel but want to enjoy its atmosphere.

★ **El Fidel Restaurant** (510 Douglas Ave., 505/425-6659, 10am-3pm and 5pm-10pm Mon.-Fri., 5pm-10pm Sat., 10am-2pm and 5pm-10pm Sun., $16-24) feels like it was beamed in from a much bigger city, with a crisp black-and-white interior and jazz playing softly. This could seem pretentious, but the semi-organic and local menu is both creative and satisfying, with great flavor combos such as lamb meatballs with walnut-mint pesto. If you're coming from Santa Fe, you might not be stunned, but if you're coming in from the country, it's like an oasis of urbanity.

ACCOMMODATIONS

Just about all of Las Vegas's hotels and motels are on North Grand Avenue. The newest chain operations are on the far end, at exit 347.

Las Vegas has two historic hotels. **El Fidel Hotel** (500 Douglas Ave., 505/425-6761, $45 s, $63 d) gets less press than its rival on the plaza, but you can't beat the

Las Vegas's Plaza Hotel was built with early railroad money.

price. Hotel rooms will appeal to those with basic tastes—who don't mind mismatched furniture and styles—but the small rooms are clean and the vast tile-floor lobby relaxing. You're also right next to an excellent restaurant, and there's pretty much always a vacancy.

But if budget allows, the ★ **Plaza Hotel** (230 N. Plaza, 505/425-3591, www.plazahotell-vnm.com) is beautiful, the grandest building on the main square. Under new ownership in June 2014, the hotel has received a major overhaul. The standard rooms ($89) are perfectly nice, but the deluxe rooms and suites ($129-149), in the original building, have the most atmosphere, with towering ceilings, velvet drapes, and stately antiques. Grab a seat on a colorful hand-painted chair—originals from La Fonda in Santa Fe—for coffee in the morning; full breakfast is served at an additional fee in the dining room.

Check to see if the **Castañeda Hotel,** adjacent to the train station, has reopened—though renovations are not expected to be complete in the lifetime of this book.

INFORMATION

The Las Vegas **visitors center** (500 Railroad Ave., 505/425-3707, www.visitlasvegasnm. com, 9am-5pm daily), run by the City of Las Vegas, occupies a tiny office in the former rail depot where Lincoln Street dead-ends at the tracks.

Tome on the Range (158 Bridge St., 505/454-9944, 10am-6pm daily) is an excellent bookstore, with a fine selection of local history and other Western lore, along with all the best sellers.

GETTING THERE

By car, Las Vegas is 65 miles (about 1 hour) east of Santa Fe via I-25, and 107 miles (1.5 hours) south of Raton. From Taos over the pass through Mora is 75 miles (nearly 2 hours).

Amtrak (800/872-7245, www.amtrak.com) stops at the nicely remodeled old train depot, with service once daily each way from Chicago and Los Angeles. As a weekend trip, you could take the train up from Albuquerque—it takes about three hours and costs $28. There is no Greyhound service.

Mora Valley

Highway 518 heads north from Las Vegas, along the Sangre de Cristo foothills. It eventually turns west to begin the ascent over the mountains—here you'll find the communities of La Cueva and Mora, which are culturally and historically linked with the Hispano towns on the other side of the range, such as Peñasco. A drive through here will take only a few hours (or the better part of a day, if you come during raspberry season), but several mountain retreats might entice you to stay awhile.

MORPHY LAKE STATE PARK

Gem-like **Morphy Lake State Park** (575/387-2328, www.nmparks.com, $5/car) used to be one of the most difficult-to-reach parks in New Mexico. The narrow road up to the lake, off Highway 94 (turn in Sapello), has finally been paved, but it's still not navigable by RVs. Once you get there, the lake is open only to rowboats or electric-engine craft, so the quiet isn't disturbed. The deep-blue water is stocked with trout and ringed with tall ponderosa pines, which provide shade for the primitive **campsites** ($8).

LA CUEVA

At the junction of Highways 518 and 442, **La Cueva** is no longer a town, but a national historic site. It was settled as part of the Mora Land Grant in the early 19th century, and the old mill, built in the 1870s, still creaks and clanks as the *acequia* streams over the waterwheel, which generated electricity for nearby homes until 1949. To the northeast, the small adobe **San Rafael Mission Church** displays the French Gothic windows in vogue in 1862, when it was built. **Salman Ranch** (575/387-2900, www.salmanraspberryranch.com) occupies some of the La Cueva outbuildings, and it has built beautiful rambling gardens inside the mill complex's old adobe walls. These are a

wonderful place to stretch or enjoy a picnic in the summertime. The **you-pick raspberry farm** is open early August-mid-October, depending on the weather, as is a basic café to feed hungry pickers. Year-round, the **farm store** (9am-5pm daily July-Dec., 9am-4pm Thurs.-Mon. Jan.-June) sells raspberry jam and vinegar, fresh berries (in season), and other local foodstuffs.

MORA AND CLEVELAND

The center of the 1835 land grant and of the lush valley, the town of Mora is also the county seat—though it's no bustling metropolis. Visitors often come for **Tapetes de Lana** (Hwy. 518, 575/387-2247, www.moravalleys-pinningmill.com, 7:30am-5pm Mon.-Fri., 8am-4pm Sat., 9am-2pm Sun.), at the main intersection in Mora. Inside, locally spun yarn from the nearby mill, and handwoven rugs are for sale. The group works with Churro sheep and locally raised alpaca wool.

About a mile down the road in the neighboring village, the **Cleveland Roller Mill Museum** (Hwy. 518, 575/387-2645, www.clevelandrollermillmuseum.org, 10am-3pm Sat.-Sun. Memorial Day-Labor Day, free) is a two-story adobe structure built around 1900 and kept in use until the mid-1950s. It doesn't look too impressive from the outside, but the building houses a complex system of heavy-duty machinery, from the massive steel rollers that crushed the wheat to the "sock dusters" that absorbed the potentially explosive flour dust. Everything's intact and put into use every Labor Day for the annual Millfest, when there's also live music and arts and crafts booths.

Food and Accommodations

At the south end of Mora, **Hatcha's Café** (Hwy. 518 at Hwy. 434, 575/387-9299, 10:30am-7pm Mon.-Fri., 9:30am-2pm Sun., $8) does a mean green-chile stew.

Across from the Cleveland Roller Mill Museum, **Mora Inn & RV Park** (Hwy. 518, 575/387-5230, www.morainn.com) is a quiet spot to bunk for the night, with motel rooms ($65 d) as well as campsites for RVs ($25) and tents ($10). It also has a good café, **Krystal's Korner Kafe** (7am-6:30pm Mon.-Fri., 7:30am-6:30pm Sat., 7:30am-3pm Sun., $7), where the pinto beans are especially good.

The Northern Plains

New Mexico's plains are a subtly shifting blanket of gold, brown, or green, depending on the season. This requires a certain mindset to appreciate. The trick is to stop craving switchbacks, vertigo-inducing views, and all the other adrenaline-fueled drama of the mountains. Then you'll find this area incredibly relaxing, as the low-hanging, puffy clouds scud out to the horizon. After a bit of driving, you'll begin to discern the smallest changes: a shimmer of silver where a certain grass flourishes, or the brief contrast afforded by a dark rock outcropping.

Granted, there's very little to do. The major public lands, the Kiowa and Rita Blanca National Grasslands, are virtually indistinguishable from the surrounding private ranches and offer little in the way of recreation. The whole area is home to herds of pronghorn, some elk, and thousands and thousands of cows, the lifeblood of the economy. It's modern cowboy country, but it's also scarred by the traumatic Dust Bowl years, when dirt lay in drifts up to the fence posts. Some of the older locals still recall those hard times. In the unreconstructed small towns, there are few galleries or other signs of modern gentrification. If you're interested in prehistoric goings-on, though, the place is fascinating. Dinosaurs roamed through the mud, and then so-called Folsom Man hunted bison during the last ice age; you can see the lingering evidence in several places.

FORT UNION NATIONAL MONUMENT

On a barren plain 80 miles from Santa Fe, **Fort Union National Monument** (Hwy.

old adobe walls at Fort Union, once the largest military depot in the Southwest

161, 505/425-8025, www.nps.gov/foun, 8am-5pm daily June-Aug., 8am-4pm daily Sept.-May, free) was the largest military depot in the Southwest, located strategically where the two branches of the Santa Fe Trail joined. Built largely of adobe, the fort has melted away, leaving not much more than the outlines of the buildings; however, you can still get an idea just how vast the complex was, and the experience is heightened by audio clips that play in front of buildings like the jail and the latrine.

It took three tries to build the fort. The first, made of logs, was built in 1851 as a base for campaigns against Apache raiders, but it soon rotted away. A second was a star-shaped earthen fortification built in a hurry to defend against a rumored Confederate attack in 1861; fortunately, the Union triumphed in the Battle of Glorieta Pass, just a year later, and the troops could abandon the muddy hovel.

The third structure, the stone and adobe outlines of which are preserved today, had relatively luxurious officers' quarters and plenty of room for both a military post and a very busy supply depot for items on the trade route. But like so many settlements in New Mexico, Fort Union became obsolete when the railroad was laid through the state, and by 1891, after less than three decades of use, the massive installation was decommissioned.

Walk out northeast from the ruins to see the ghostly imprints of wagon ruts from the Santa Fe Trail—they're most visible early or late in the day.

Along the Santa Fe Trail

Whether Bing Crosby is crooning about it, Ronald Reagan is riding along it, or a modern traveler is retracing it, the Santa Fe Trail has earned a certain golden glow in American popular culture. The route, which cut across the frontier from Missouri to the middle of New Mexico, was used for less than 60 years, but it has become one of the great symbols of American westward expansion, all bundled up with the era when the cowboy and his horse were the masters of the new land.

The trail holds up well under the pressure of symbolism, especially when you consider the effort it took to traverse its 900 miles. A certain entrepreneur named William Becknell is credited with making the first trading trip, in 1821, without even knowing yet that the Mexican government, newly independent from Spain, had opened the borders of Nuevo México to outsiders. When Becknell was welcomed in Santa Fe, rather than imprisoned, and made a profit of 2,000 percent on his first load of calico cloth, it wasn't long before wagons loaded with more than three tons of goods were groaning across the plains.

Not that it was easy money. On this highway, wagons took close to three months to make the trip. At the far edge of Kansas, traders had to make a choice: the slow-going Mountain Route through frigid Colorado and the brutal Raton Pass, or the level and easy Cimarron Cut-off, where wagon trains faced scarce water and attacks by Comanche and Apache raiders. The biggest wagon trains, bursting with everything from basic cotton cloth to fripperies like parasols and playing cards, had no choice but to take the latter. Despite the dangers, the traders forged on, driven by dreams of profit. In the process, they also carried the dreams of the expansionist United States—an abstract concept until the U.S. Army used the Santa Fe Trail for supply caravans when it went to war with Mexico in 1846.

So many tons of trade goods and, later, settlers to the new American territory were hauled along the plains that in places, the earth is still scored by wagon ruts. But even such an influential, profitable trail was not a permanent one. First the trail shortened as America's frontier border moved west, then the railroad displaced it entirely. But perhaps the very fact that the Santa Fe Trail was outmoded so quickly by more modern technology is what has fixed it so well in the American imagination.

EAST FROM WAGON MOUND

Named for a rock outcropping that faintly resembles a Conestoga wagon, the small town at exit 387 on I-25 is the turning point for Roy—a pretty route to Clayton, preferable to U.S. 56 from Springer. There's not much here but a couple of gas stations, though on Labor Day weekend, Wagon Mound hosts **Bean Day** (http://beanday100.com), a harvest celebration more than a century old, with rodeos, a free barbecue, and a big parade—bigger than the tiny downtown can hold, so it runs through twice.

Highway 120 to Roy

You're really getting off here for Highway 120, which heads east across flatlands that are often surprisingly green. Another surprise: the dip down into Canadian River Canyon, striated with red and white. The road then heads to **Roy**—home to not quite 250 people, giving it the dubious title of the largest town in Harding County. Its last claim to fame was that Western-swing bandleader Bob Wills penned "San Antonio Rose" here in 1927, as he worked as a barber by day. At the time, Roy was a shipping point for coal to Tucumcari and a major dry-ice manufacturing site, thanks to its location on top of the Bravo Dome carbon-dioxide field.

La Frontera del Llano Scenic Byway

Although the drive from Wagon Mound is arguably more awe-inspiring, Highway 39, which runs north and south from Roy, is an *official* scenic route, a section of La Frontera del Llano Scenic Byway. To the south and east, the "Edge of the Plains" route goes to the cattle-ranching centers of **Mosquero** and **Bueyeros,** passing pink-striped buttes, a string of beautiful old churches, and dilapidated little bars. Mosquero, population 93, has become a colorful destination as high school students, overseen by artist Doug Quarles,

have painted murals depicting Harding County history on several downtown storefronts. At Bueyeros, you can turn south to follow the byway to its end at Logan (near Ute Lake State Park and I-40), or head north to make a roundabout route up to Clayton.

Back at Roy, the byway follows the northern stretch of Highway 39 through the **Kiowa and Rita Blanca National Grasslands.** The 230,000 acres of short-grass prairie are federally managed to maintain the natural flora, so as to avoid a repeat of the 1930s devastation. The land is home to quail, bobcats, and lots of pronghorn, but don't expect pristine wilderness—cattle are still allowed to graze here. You can camp at **Mills Canyon,** 10 miles north of Roy on Highway 39, then about 10 miles west, where a narrow, rocky road leads 800 feet down into the canyon. A former commercial farm, the sheltered river bottom still harbors a few fruit trees, as well as wildlife such as mule deer and Barbary sheep, introduced in 1950. During dry summers, the campground can be closed due to fire danger—call the grasslands headquarters in Clayton (575/374-9652) to check the status before heading out.

Highway 39, and the scenic byway, ends at Abbott (describing it as a "town" is generous), at the junction with U.S. 56—from here, it's virtually a straight shot east to Clayton.

SPRINGER

At the I-25 exit for U.S. 56, which runs directly to Clayton, the tiny town of Springer was formerly named Maxwell, for Lucien B. Maxwell, whose land grant covered all of Colfax County. It was also the county seat between 1882 and 1898 (Raton now holds the title). When political power moved away, so did most of the action. Now there's not much here except a handful of antiques stores, the largest and most obsessively organized of which is **Jespersen's Cache** (403 Maxwell Ave., 575/483-2349, by appointment only).

CLAYTON

Only 12 miles from Texas, Clayton is a place where most of the 2,900 people in town spend their days on horseback or otherwise engaged in the large cattle operations on the surrounding ranches and feedlots. (If the wind blows the wrong way, the smell is hard to ignore, though on a crisp autumn evening, there's a positive spin: You definitely get a sense of place.) By night, attention focuses on the gem of a vintage movie theater or the high school football stadium. The big annual event is the rodeo on Fourth of July weekend, and there are easily more churches than restaurants in town. In short, you're a long way from Santa Fe.

Clayton was established relatively late by New Mexican standards—in 1888, well after the railroad cut through. But it soon rocketed to notoriety as the place where outlaw Thomas "Black Jack" Ketchum met his end, two years after he was picked up for attempting to rob a train near Folsom.

Sights

Bone up on local history at the interesting **Herzstein Memorial Museum** (S. 2nd St. at Walnut St., 575/374-2977, 10am-5pm Tues.-Sat., free), a collection of local ephemera bequeathed to the town by a prominent shopkeeper. Spread over two floors of a stately 1919 Methodist church, the displays are kept sparkling and dust-free, with period furniture, clothing, and medical equipment alongside vitrines dedicated to local luminaries such as Cowgirl Hall of Famer and single mom Bernice McLaughlin. There's also a small but fascinating display on the Dust Bowl. Tucked away in a small hall are photographs of Black Jack Ketchum being hanged on the courthouse square in 1901, a grisly event that ended in his accidental beheading. Ketchum (both parts) is buried in the **cemetery** (Princeton Ave.), in the southeast corner of town. During winter, call ahead to make sure it's open during posted hours.

The thorough sightseer can also cruise the **Baca House** (320 Oak St.), where the fence and gate are the work of Dionicio Rodríguez, a folk artist known for his elaborate faux-bois cement creations, particularly in Brackenridge Park in San Antonio, Texas, as well as in Little Rock and Memphis. The Oak Street work dates from the early 1940s, commissioned by a well-traveled land speculator who'd seen Rodríguez's work in Texas.

★ Clayton Lake State Park

Fifteen miles north of Clayton, sunk down just below the level of the surrounding

Trains rumble through in the background of Clayton.

Clayton

THE NORTHEAST
THE NORTHERN PLAINS

plain, **Clayton Lake State Park** (Hwy. 370, 575/374-8808, www.nmparks.com, $5/car, $8 camping) is a lovely haven for day use or camping and a prime spot for stargazing, with viewing parties at its Star Point Observatory. But the real attraction is the **dinosaur footprints** preserved in stone at the east end of the lake, one of the few places such trackways are open to the public in the Southwest. Made some 100 million years ago in what was then mud, they are part of a long series of tracks that stretches to Fort Collins, Colorado, a route that ran along the edge of an ancient sea. They're accessible via a quarter-mile-long recreational trail—look for signs to the right as you enter the park. Try to go early in the morning or in late afternoon, when the longer shadows make the prints stand out more clearly. The **visitors center** (8am-4:30pm daily) also has a small display about dinosaur life in this area.

Dinosaur tracks dot Clayton Lake State Park.

Sports and Recreation

McNees Crossing gets frequent mention in tourist literature, but even true Santa Fe Trail enthusiasts will find the trail ford a bit underwhelming; look for the marker on Highway 406, east and north of Clayton. Better to head for another point in the **Kiowa National Grasslands** where a short walk leads to some better-preserved wagon ruts, as well as a ruined homestead. Getting to the unofficial trailhead requires zigzagging along dirt ranch-access roads. Head east on U.S. 64/56, then 13 miles north on Highway 406; turn left (west) on Campbell Road and go 3 miles, then north 1 mile to a small pullout for parking. On your way out of Clayton, you might want to stop at the grasslands' **ranger station** (714 Main St., 575/374-9652, 8am-12pm and 12:30pm-4:30pm) for a map.

Should you need to cool off, the **municipal swimming pool** (Water St., 575/374-8014, 1pm-6pm daily summer) is a good-sized outdoor facility with a kiddie slide. It's on the east side of town—go through the gate to the armory and the airport. A nine-hole **municipal golf course** (Princeton Ave., 575/374-9253) works on the honor system, so stop by any time to tee off.

Entertainment

If you're a vintage cinema buff, don't miss the **Luna Theater** (4 Main St., 575/374-2712), under the neon winking moon. Built in 1916, it was redone in 1935, complete with a ballroom in the basement. Pay the $7 admission regardless of what's showing, just to see the glowing interior, set with art deco sconces and the beautiful original embroidered velvet curtain. You can also try knocking during the day—if someone's there, they'll show you around. Shows are Friday-Sunday only.

Food

The **Hotel Eklund** (15 Main St., 575/446-1939, 10:30am-2pm and 4pm-9pm Mon.-Fri., 10:30am-9pm Sat.-Sun., $10) is a major hub for lunch and dinner, and a great excuse to sit in the front saloon (though now, sadly, the 1850s wood bar can only serve beer and wine, even in margaritas). The menu has the usual mix of steaks ($15-18), New Mexican standards, and burgers, but a lot is made from scratch, including dangerously sweet desserts.

The other popular spot—which doesn't mean it's great—open for breakfast too, is the **Rabbit Ear Café** (1201 S. 1st St., 575/374-3277, 7am-8pm Tues.-Sat., 7am-2pm Sun., $9). The chef reaches to American cheese and white bread often. But the chile is hot and the burritos are stuffed. Either way, it's a good slice of life in Clayton.

The other option is **Crossroads Coffee** (2 S. Front St., 575/374-5282, 7am-3pm Mon.-Fri., 8am-11am Sat., $7), a funky wood-paneled place in the old feed store that also happens to be an unlikely outpost of espresso with house-roasted beans. It serves a different sandwich, soup, and salad every day; breakfast burritos and biscuits and gravy are on offer in the morning.

Accommodations

Clayton has a remarkable number of fine places to sleep. Locally owned independent **Holiday Motel** (U.S. 87, 575/374-2558, $64 s, $74 d) is a gem, well kept and scrupulously clean. The owners are so enthusiastic, they fold the towels into elephants. It's on the northwest edge of town, about a quarter mile out from the big bridge.

Downtown at the main crossroads, **Hotel Eklund** (15 Main St., 575/446-1939, www.hoteleklund.com, $90 d) is a three-story trove of history, with a cool saloon. Rooms are spare, with metal bedsteads, lace curtains, and nice new bathrooms that only look old, with their honeycomb tiles and pedestal sinks. Rooms on the front (east) side are preferable to those on the west, to dampen freight-train noise.

Rates include a hot breakfast, often with made-there quiche.

If you want a pool, head to **Best Western Kokopelli Lodge** (702 S. 1st St., 575/374-2589, www.bestwestern.com, $115 d). It's a million times nicer than it has to be, considering the feeble competition from the other chain hotels: big outdoor swimming area, wireless Internet, a free hot breakfast buffet, and plush, spacious rooms.

Information

The **Clayton-Union County Tourist Information Center** (1103 S. 1st St., 575/374-9253, www.claytonnewmexico.net, 8am-5pm Mon.-Fri. Sept.-May, 9am-4pm daily June-Aug.) has a few brochures, plus souvenir Dust Bowl postcards and free wireless Internet.

Getting There

By car, Clayton is 84 miles (1.5 hours) east along U.S. 56/412 from Springer at I-25, and about the same distance from Raton via U.S. 64/87. From Santa Fe, it's about 220 miles (3.5 hours).

Greyhound (800/231-2222, www.greyhound.com) runs through once a day, but only via Amarillo, Texas, dropping you off at

Hotel Eklund is Clayton's main meeting spot.

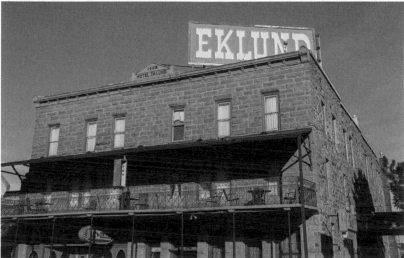

the station (113 E. Walnut St., 575/374-6207, 8am-5pm Mon.-Fri.).

WEST TO RATON

U.S. 64/87 heads roughly northwest out of Clayton, another hypnotizing drive through golden prairie. The terrain changes a bit halfway along, as defunct volcanoes punctuate the horizon. The most distinctive is the perfectly conical peak of Capulin; a drive up to the top (an adventure in itself) gives you a break from all the flatness, as well as a stunning view.

From Capulin, you can detour north to the ghost town of Folsom, a starting point for two smaller, more scenic roads. Backtrack east along a rough byway through the washes and ridges strung along the border with Colorado, or keep heading west on Highway 72, which takes you across a dramatic high mesa, the perfect way to meet the mountains at Raton.

★ Capulin Volcano National Monument

Unmissable on the skyline, the soft dome of **Capulin Volcano National Monument** (575/278-2201, www.nps.gov/cavo, 8am-5pm daily June-Aug., 8am-4:30pm daily Sept.-May, $7/car) reaches 8,182 feet above sea level and stands approximately as tall as the Empire State Building. About 60,000 years ago, Capulin spewed hot ash and rock into the air, which settled into an almost perfect cone—its top edge looks like a carefully opened soft-boiled egg. At the summit, you can walk a quarter-mile trail down into this crater, where steam vents are noticeable in the winter, as the surrounding patches are covered with greenery. Or hike up the one-mile trail around the rim: From this vantage point you can see more clearly how this whole region was shaped by volcanic activity, from the lava-topped mesas to the hulking Sierra Grande. The latter formation is another dormant volcano, about a million years old, that's also the largest lone mountain in the United States, covering 50 square miles and rising 2,200 feet above the surrounding plain. Ranger talks at the crater in summer at 11am and 1pm (free) can point out more details.

But to reach the top of Capulin, you have to negotiate a two-mile road that spirals up the side of the volcano. It's narrow and doesn't have as many guardrails as you might expect; put your steeliest driver in charge, and take it slow. It's much easier coming down, as you're on the inside lane. Keep an eye out for bald eagles at the top, and watch out for mule deer in the road around the base. The area at the top has limited parking, so if you're visiting in the busy months of July and August, go very early or late in the day, or you'll have to wait to drive up.

the view from Capulin Volcano

Folsom

Hard by the railroad tracks, late 19th-century Folsom drew cattle-traders and outlaws—most notably "Black Jack" Ketchum, whose gang held up trains three times here. In 1908, a flood demolished a good part of the town, and even claimed the life of the village telephone operator, who stayed at her post to warn residents of danger. Around the same time, floods also uncovered a collection of bison skeletons embedded with spear points in a wash west of town. When the site was excavated in 1927, the spear points were determined to be at least 10,000 years old—a shock to archaeologists, who'd previously thought American Indians had arrived on the continent only around 2000 BC.

In an old general store at the intersection of Highways 325 and 456, **Folsom Museum** (575/278-2122, www.folsomvillage.com, 10am-5pm daily June-Sept., 10am-5pm Sat.-Sun. May, other times by appointment, $1.50) tells these stories in more detail, if not always in the most illuminating way. Some collections (carefully labeled river rocks) are surreal and cryptic; others, such as the one on slave-turned-cowboy-and-accidental-archaeologist George McJunkin, are genuinely illuminating. Perhaps the best item is the odd diorama of the Ketchum hanging.

Dry Cimarron Byway

A network of rural highways stretching into Colorado and Oklahoma, this route roughly follows the path of the Dry Cimarron River, with Highway 456 as the backbone; it eventually winds up back in Clayton.

About 3.5 miles northeast of Folsom on Highway 456, on the right (southeast) side of the road, look for a pullout and a sign warning against swimming. A small trail leads a short way to **Folsom Falls,** where water pours directly out of the rock face. It's visible from the edge of the shallow canyon, but you'll need to clamber down the rocks to get to the water's edge.

From here, Highway 456 zigzags across the river bottom as it heads east. At the junction with Highway 370, you can drive south to Clayton Lake State Park, but if you continue east, you'll pass towering buttes dubbed Battleship and Wedding Cake. You then loop back to Clayton via Highway 406.

★ Johnson Mesa

If time (and weather—the road is often closed in winter due to snow) permits, don't skip the drive along Highway 72 out of Folsom, one of the most beautiful in New Mexico. The narrow paved byway dips and rises, roller-coaster-like, as it gradually climbs the

a lone church on the top of Johnson Mesa

foothills, and then you're deposited on the top of **Johnson Mesa**, a bucolic expanse of grazing land studded with smaller hills, including the perfectly round Red Mountain. At one point, the road passes close to the mesa edge, and you can see the land plunge away. About the only evidence of human habitation up here is a small stone church, **St. John's Methodist**, built in 1897. No one lives on the mesa regularly now, though a few hardy souls come up for the summer along with the livestock. If you drive this way at dusk, watch out for deer on the road, even on the outskirts of Raton.

The Rockies

Where the laden caravans of traders struggled through Raton Pass on the Santa Fe Trail's mountain route, drivers now zip up with ease. Raton is still a watering hole, but it sates visitors with fast-food restaurants and travel centers; go beyond the off-ramp economy to see the town's century-old core, laid out along the railroad depot. South and west of Raton, smaller Cimarron was another stopping point on the mountain route, and one that wears its history well.

RATON
The glowing red RATON sign on the hilltop on the northwest side of town suggests a bit more glitz than this mountain burg currently has. But traces of past glamour remain in the sturdy downtown, in the art deco fire station on North 2nd Street, for instance, the quirky castle facade of the El Raton Theatre, and the elegant Colfax County Building on North 3rd Street.

Raton is defined entirely by the mountain behind it. In 1866, an entrepreneur by the name of Richens Wootton took it upon himself to blast out a proper road through the mountains over Raton Pass, wide enough to accommodate wagon trains—then he set up a toll gate and charged Santa Fe Trail traders to come through. "Uncle Dick," as he was known, sold his road to the AT&SF Railroad for $1 and a lifetime grocery stipend. The railroad helped keep the town of Raton in money too, and some wealth came from coal mining in the surrounding mountains, though nothing like the giddy get-rich-quick silver and gold mines in the south. All of this was enough to bring big theaters and the first public school in the state—though, like everywhere in the late 19th-century West, Raton had its fair share of lynchings, mob violence, and more.

Now it's more peaceful, overlooking the plains to the east, but with its heart in the Rockies. If you are just passing through, note that nearly everything shuts on Sunday—you'll be hard-pressed to find somewhere to eat outside of the usual chains.

Sights
The gem of 2nd Street is the rococo **Shuler Theater** auditorium (131 N. 2nd St., 575/445-4746, www.shulertheater.com), beautifully restored by the town and used for live performances. Visitors can tour the theater weekdays 9am-5pm when there's someone available—definitely worth a stop to see the 1930s lobby murals and the beautiful cloud-studded "sky" above the proscenium. Three of the original drop curtains survive as well—they're painted with scenes depicting a Roman villa, the palisade cliffs near Cimarron, and Raton's Ripley Park. Building the theater was a bit of a battle, as the city council used money that had been earmarked for a new city hall. Later, the municipal auditorium was named in honor of the mayor who'd perpetrated the boondoggle, in a council resolution that was

Raton

worded to effectively tell Raton residents, "See, we told you you'd love it."

The main thoroughfare for cars is 2nd Street, where the **Raton Museum** (108 S. 2nd St., 575/445-8979, 9am-5pm Tues.-Sat. in summer, 10am-4pm Wed.-Sat. in winter, free) occupies two large tin-ceilinged shop fronts. Displays about the coal camps and other facets of local life are nicely presented, along with vintage dolls, works by Taos painters, and some good *santero* carvings in the front upstairs area.

Pick up a walking-tour brochure here or at the visitors center to guide you along 1st Street, Raton's **historic downtown** where the handsome old storefronts are trimmed in cast-iron garlands, graceful figureheads, and jutting cornices. Business isn't exactly booming, but there are a few antiques shops and the **Old Pass Gallery** (145 S. 1st St., 575/445-2052, www.ratonarts.org, 10am-4:30pm Tues.-Sat.), run by the local arts council. It occupies a renovated Wells Fargo office, and next door is the train depot, the only surviving building of a huge complex that used to manage the comings and goings of more than 60 trains a day.

You could also seek out the **Arthur Johnson Memorial Library** (244 Cook Ave., 575/445-9711, 1pm-6pm Mon., 10am-6pm Tues.-Wed. and Fri.-Sat., 10am-9pm Thurs.), between 2nd and 3rd Streets, a neo-classical structure built as a post office in 1917, then converted to a library under the Carnegie program. It houses a good collection of Southwest-themed art, including some of the early Taos artists.

By car, you can head up **Goat Hill,** where the RATON sign is perched; take Moulton Avenue west to Hill Street. This hill is geologically famous, as it has a visible stripe of iridium running through it—the stripe of detritus that marks the meteorite crash that ended the dinosaurs. Just before the top of the hill, bear right rather than left at the fork—this dirt road will carry you around the ridgeline a few miles to a marked spot and a scenic overlook.

Raton's stately Shuler Theater and El Raton Theatre

Entertainment

A quirky castle facade marks **El Raton Theatre** (115 N. 2nd St., 575/445-7008, www.elratontheatre.com, 7pm Thurs.-Sat., 4pm and 7pm Sun.), a movie palace built in 1929, now souped up with a digital projector for first-run films. If you want a peek inside during the day, just knock—if someone's free, they're happy to let you in and show you around.

nighttime at Goat Hill above Raton

Sports and Recreation

An eight-mile drive from Raton, **Sugarite Canyon State Park** (211 Hwy. 526, 575/445-5607, www.nmparks.com, $5/car) encompasses 3,600 acres along either side of Chicorica Creek. In 2011, the Track Fire burned much of the large trees on the hillsides, making the campgrounds and trails here less scenic, but Lake Maloya is still a charming destination for trout fishing and casual boating. From behind the visitors center, two miles up Highway 526, the **Coal Camp Trail** runs through the ruins of a mining settlement and up to two old mine shafts; a few longer trails lead up to the bluffs that line the road—ask at the visitors center for maps.

Hunting is a very big deal in the high mountains around Raton. **Whittington Center** (Hwy. 64, 575/445-3615, www.nrawc. org), a 52-square-mile complex established in 1973 by the National Rifle Association, is a starting point for many hunters. It's the largest gun club in the United States, offering classes for beginners and experts (from $300), target and skeet shooting at the range (from $20/ day), plus real-life hunting for deer, antelope, and even mountain lions. There's also space for tent and RV camping (from $12) or simple cabins (from $44 d).

Food

Raton's restaurants have limited opening hours, and if you don't plan well, you'll be relegated to the fast-food joints on Clayton Boulevard. For morning coffee, **Enchanted Grounds Espresso Bar** (111 Park Ave., 575/445-2129, 7am-2pm Mon., 7am-4:30pm Tues.-Fri., 7:30am-4:30pm Sat.) is the place to go; it also serves French toast, egg sandwiches, and light lunches.

Pappas' Sweet Shop (1201 S. 2nd St., 575/445-9811, 10am-2pm and 5pm-8pm Mon.-Fri., 5pm-7:30pm Sat., $10) bears mention just because it's the longest-running restaurant in town. In fact, the atmosphere can be a bit geriatric, but fair enough, since it's been going since 1923. It has a (freshly revived) vintage soda fountain and classics like chicken salad on the menu.

Locally owned **Bruno's Pizza and Wings** (244 S. 1st St., 575/445-9512, 11am-8pm Mon. and Wed.-Thurs., 11am-9pm Fri.-Sat., $12) serves just what you'd expect from the name, with solid takes on both in a sports-bar environment.

Alfonso's (412 Clayton Rd., 575/445-8022, 7am-9pm Mon.-Sat., 8am-8pm Sun., $8) is open a little bit later than other places—though you'll be dining in one end of a Conoco gas station. The setup is fast-food-y, but the food is good, authentic Mexican.

Accommodations

Most chain motels are on Clayton Boulevard, which runs from exit 451 off I-25—but some of the old-time independent options here, at the north and south ends of town, will restore your faith in American roadside hospitality. On the north side, **Raton Pass Inn** (308 Canyon Dr., 575/445-3641, www.ratonpassinn.com, $60 d) is an excellent choice. The 1950s exterior sports jazzy green-and-salmon paint; inside, the 14 large rooms are decorated with a special touch and include Wi-Fi, mini-fridges, and microwaves. The hotel came under new ownership in April 2016; check reviews to see if the high standards are being maintained.

Just to the south, the ★ **Budget Host Melody Lane Motel** (136 Canyon Dr., 575/445-3655, www.budgethost.com, $55 d) is remarkable for its nifty slant-ceiling rooms, eight of which have a vintage steam sauna built into the tub, a real treat after a long drive. Rooms are meticulously clean and come with a continental breakfast.

On the south side of town, **Robin Hood Motel** (1354 S. 2nd St., 575/445-5577, www. robinhoodmotelusa.com, $72 d, open May-Sept. only) is yet another fine old-style inn, though a touch more up-to-date than others. Behind butter-yellow doors are fairly standard modern motel trappings, though the groovy original orange linoleum shows in some bathrooms. There's also a small outdoor pool.

At the southernmost edge, just by the I-25 on-ramp, the **Maverick Motel** (1510 S. 2nd St., 575/445-3792, $45 s, $62 d) is the greatest throwback of all, a block of 10 snug rooms straight from the 1940s, maintained by a man who seems stuck in that decade himself. Pale-blue chenille bedspreads, screen doors, and even an old soda machine will make you feel like you're sleeping in a museum, in the best way. Fair warning: That means no Wi-Fi, not even a website (and hence no TripAdvisor reviews). But connoisseurs of Americana ought to pick up the phone and reserve, before the owner decides to retire.

If you prefer motels of a slightly more

recent vintage, **Casa Lemus Inn** (350 Clayton Rd., 575/448-5538, www.casalemus.com, $59 d) is another decent option, with spacious and clean rooms. There's also a small outdoor pool in summer. Rates include a continental breakfast, and the Casa Lemus Restaurant, which serves passable steaks and diner fare, is in the parking lot.

Information

The **New Mexico Visitor Information Center** (100 Clayton Blvd., 575/445-2761, www.raton.info, 8am-5pm daily) is maintained by both the Raton Chamber of Commerce and the state tourism board.

Getting There

By car, Raton is 83 miles (1.5 hours) from Clayton (about 20 minutes longer if you go via Johnson Mesa). From Santa Fe, it's 175 miles (2.5 hours) via I-25, and 220 miles (3.25 hours) from Denver. Cimarron is 40 miles (45 minutes) away, and Taos is 95 miles (2 hours).

Amtrak (800/872-7245, www.amtrak.com) trains pull in to the historic depot on 1st Street once each day on the eastbound and westbound routes. The trip from Albuquerque takes about 4.5 hours and costs $46. The only direct **Greyhound** (800/231-2222, www.greyhound.com) buses come in from Denver and Amarillo, Texas, and drop you off at the station (144 S. 1st St., 575/445-9071, 8am-9am and 11am-1pm daily).

VALLE VIDAL

South of Raton, U.S. 64 bears west, away from I-25 and deeper into the mountains. About 35 miles along (5 miles east of Cimarron) is the turn for Forest Road 1950. This dirt road is the only access route (and a circuitous one) to Valle Vidal, a 102,000-acre chunk of the Carson National Forest that straddles some of the highest peaks in the Sangre de Cristo range. For anyone seeking pristine wilderness, Valle Vidal is perhaps the last, best place to get a sense of what New Mexico was like before mining and ranching took off in the 19th century. The area is home to the state's largest

Warm up with the Melody Lane Motel's in-room saunas.

elk herd, and its watershed is essential for the now-rare Rio Grande cutthroat trout.

Though little visited, it is probably one of the best-known public lands in New Mexico, as the area was the topic of strenuous debate from 1982, when Pennzoil traded the land to the National Forest Service in exchange for tax breaks, until 2006, when a long grassroots campaign finally got a law passed to prohibit mining and drilling for natural gas.

There are no services in the wilderness, very few trails, and only two formal camping areas with no services but toilets. Coming from U.S. 64, the first one you reach is **McCrystal Campground** ($8), set on a flat plain with a few ponderosas providing shade; this is where people exploring on horseback often camp. If you want more privacy, head eight more miles to the 35 sites at the higher-elevation **Cimarron Campground** ($10), which are tucked amid trees; many trout-fishing creeks are right nearby. For current conditions and advisories (parts of the valley are closed seasonally to protect the elk), contact the **Questa Ranger District office** (575/586-0520), on the west side, which manages the whole area.

VERMEJO PARK RANCH

Formerly part of the Maxwell Land Grant, the 200,000 acres of **Vermejo Park Ranch** (575/445-3097, www.vermejoparkranch.com) belong to media mogul and conservationist Ted Turner. Guided hunting and fishing trips go from the swanky Costilla Lodge (from $950) or Casa Minor (from $525); other guesthouses, as well as Turner's former home, Casa Grande, are also available to rent. The land climbs from short-grass plains to 13,000-foot peaks, and wildlife includes Rocky Mountain elk, pronghorn, and black bear—as well as the North American bison Turner raises here.

CIMARRON

This community of less than a thousand people still feels like a 19th-century mountain town. A few times a year, the streets are filled with horses being driven to various pastures on the vast Philmont ranch that adjoins the community, and the assorted rivalries of the Colfax County War are spoken of as though they happened yesterday—perhaps because so much of the town's social life takes place at the old St. James Hotel, where the ceiling is pocked with bullet holes.

But more than this violent history, the wilderness is what defines Cimarron. Established in 1861 by Lucien Maxwell, the town was the most substantial settlement on the giant land grant that Maxwell would later own outright. The surrounding mountains (and all the wildlife they harbor) still press in close; when the sun starts to set and the stars glimmer overhead, you're reminded just how small the town is. Amid so much empty land, you have to wonder what all the fighting was about . . . and was that a bear rustling in the trees?

By day, you can visit a handful of galleries on 9th Street, one block north of U.S. 64 and the old *acequia,* or watch the fish jump in the Cimarron River. You can hike between granite cliffs or tour the mansion of the oilman who ran Philmont ranch and dedicated it to the Boy Scouts of America. But at the end of the day, you'll likely be back at the St. James, drinking a beer and talking about the past.

Sights
★ ST. JAMES HOTEL

The center of Cimarron's social life, past and present, is the **St. James Hotel** (Hwy. 21, 575/376-2664), a beautifully maintained building that's as packed with legends, lore, and (perhaps) ghosts as it is with beautiful antiques and stuffed buffalo heads. Opened first as a saloon by a French chef named Henri Lambert (former employer: Abraham Lincoln) in 1872, the St. James became a Wild West playground bar none, with just about every famed outlaw passing through its swinging doors. Buffalo Bill Cody met Annie Oakley in the saloon, Jesse James always requested the same room, and Billy the Kid, "Black Jack" Ketchum, and Wyatt Earp all signed the guest register. Cimarron was considered calm and quiet when three days passed without the sound of gunfire in the St. James; bullets are still embedded in walls and ceilings, particularly in the main dining room.

Specifically, one act of the **Colfax County War** played out here, when in 1875 the ranch hand and freelance gunman Clay Allison killed Francisco Griego in alleged self-defense as Griego was seeking vengeance for the murder of his nephew, the constable Cruz Vega, whom Allison had lynched, in retaliation for his alleged participation in the murder of Franklin Tolby, a young minister who supported the rights of the local settlers. Sound complicated? It was, and it only got more so, as some 200 people were killed trying to settle the debate over who got to live on the Maxwell Land Grant.

All that history still feels very present in the chandelier-lit hallways lined with peeling wallpaper. Visitors are welcome to poke around on the ground floor, where some of the guestroom doors are left open. You can also pick up a **walking-tour guide** to other, far less preserved monuments in the "old town" part of Cimarron.

OLD AZTEC MILL MUSEUM
Round out the local history with a visit to the **Old Aztec Mill Museum** (220 W. 17th St., 575/376-2417, 10am-5pm daily June-Aug., free), four floors of fun just across the street from the hotel. Built by Lucien Maxwell in 1864, the structure now houses Boy Scouts memorabilia, relics of the Colfax County War, and a two-headed calf.

You can also visit the **cemetery,** a short walk south on Highway 21, where the grave of settler-rights supporter Reverend Franklin Tolby sits alongside more recent (and longer-lived) Cimarron residents.

Sports and Recreation
West of town about 12 miles, straddling U.S. 64 and stretching nearly to Eagle Nest, **Cimarron Canyon State Park** (575/377-6271, www.nmparks.com, $5/car) is known for its excellent trout fishing in the Cimarron River and its tributaries, as well as the dramatic granite palisades that form the canyon walls. Backcountry camping is not permitted, and the only established campgrounds are several spots fairly close to the road.

Hiking, however, is excellent, especially on **Clear Creek Trail,** a 7-mile out-and-back you can do in about three hours. The route runs along a creek and passes several small waterfalls while gaining about a thousand feet; it's particularly nice in the fall when the aspens turn yellow. Look for a signed pullout on the south side of the road, around mile marker 292. Running about 6 miles one-way, **Tolby Creek Trail** makes a longer outing, but most of the trek is pleasantly shaded and damp, ending in beautiful high meadows. This trail is not so clearly marked—you should double-check the route at the **park office,** across the highway from the trailhead at the western park boundary, just before you reach the town of Eagle Nest.

the Old Aztec Mill Museum in Cimarron

Food
Cimarron has few dining options. As usual, the main action, especially at night, when it's the only game in town, is at the **St. James Hotel** (Hwy. 21, 575/376-2664, 7am-10:30am and 11am-9pm daily, $8-20). Unfortunately the food—burgers, steaks, and burritos—is pretty standard. The bar here is the only one in town; it's open 11am-midnight, or "whenever the bartender gets tired of looking at people."

The only other dinner option, and even then it's an early one, is eight miles up the road toward Raton, at the **Colfax Tavern** (32230 U.S. 64, 575/376-2229, 11am-8pm Mon.-Sat., 1pm-8pm Sun., $9), better known as Cold Beer, due to these very words painted in extremely large letters on the front of the building. Monday is spaghetti night, its pizza gets praise, and bands play on weekends.

★ **The Porch** (636 E. 9th St., 575/376-2228, 5pm-9pm Thurs.-Sat., 10am-2pm Sun.

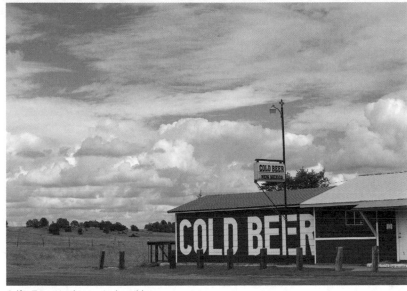

Colfax Tavern is a beacon in the wilderness.

June-Aug., $6) is the locavore's choice, with a chalkboard menu based on what's fresh. Sunday brunch sets you up right with strong coffee and pastries. The porch in question faces U.S. 64, but the entrance is on the street one block north.

Accommodations

The **St. James Hotel** (Hwy. 21, 575/376-2664, www.exstjames.com) is the obvious pick here, even if the 12 rooms in the main building have been very gently remodeled in recent years. In most cases the floors still creak atmospherically, but the bathrooms, with small tubs, are new and shiny. Most have private baths ($120-155), and a few share a more deluxe facility in the hall ($85-100). If you can't live without a TV, phone, and air-conditioning, opt for one of the 10 modern rooms in the annex ($95-105).

Just up the road, the excellent-value **Cimarron Inn & RV Park** (U.S. 64, 575/376-2268, www.cimarroninn.com) offers a different taste of history: Its main building is a converted old motel with snug, thick-walled rooms, each one in a different Western theme. Four small rooms ($49) are a steal for solo travelers or couples, while the eight larger rooms ($75 d) are divvied up like tiny apartments, so there's a wall separating beds. Families or groups might like the Cowboy Cabin ($140), which sleeps up to six people, or the Casita ($240), with room for a baker's dozen.

Information

Cimarron's **visitors center** (104 N. Lincoln Ave., 575/376-2417, www.cimarronnm.com, 10am-5pm Mon.-Sat., 1pm-5pm Sun. May-Aug., 10am-1pm Wed.-Sat. Sept.-Apr.) occupies a small house just off U.S. 64. You can pick up a walking-tour brochure here, along with other background info. To really get into the history of the place, you could take the **Legends by Lantern Light tour** (575/445-8373, www.legendsbylantern.com, 7:30pm Sat. in summer, $8) to hear the tales of local outlaws.

Getting There

From Raton, Cimarron is 40 miles southwest, about a 45-minute drive on U.S. 64. Taos is

55 miles away to the west, also on U.S. 64; the drive takes about 1.5 hours.

PHILMONT SCOUT RANCH

South out of Cimarron, Highway 21 takes the roundabout way back to Springer at I-25. The first leg roughly follows the old Santa Fe Trail route, passing the headquarters of **Philmont Scout Ranch** (575/376-2281, www.philmontscoutranch.org), the 137,000-acre spread that's now the property of Boy Scouts of America. More than a million scouts and leaders have ventured here since 1939. Practically an independent village, the place has its own post office, fire brigade, and hospital.

Visitors are welcome at **Philmont Museum & Seton Memorial Library** (575/376-1136, 8am-5:30pm daily June-Aug., 8am-5pm Mon.-Fri. Sept.-May, free), which displays a history of the ranch, photos of the Santa Fe Trail, and the art collection of Ernest Thompson Seton, a cofounder of the Boy Scouts. Fans of lavish manors will want to make reservations with the Philmont Museum to see **Villa Philmonte** (call for tour schedule, free), the vacation home of Oklahoma oilman Waite Phillips, the Boy Scouts' benefactor. His Spanish Mediterranean manse was completed in 1927, and it's still chockablock with European antiques, as well as Waite's collection of Western paraphernalia.

Philmont Scout Ranch also manages the **Kit Carson Museum** (Hwy. 21, 8am-5pm daily June-Aug., free), about seven miles farther down Highway 21. The adobe building is near where Lucien Maxwell and his friend Kit Carson set up a camp in the late 1840s to deal with Santa Fe Trail traders (ruts are still visible where the trail crosses the Rayado River), and the museum re-creates life in that period, with costumed "mountain men" demonstrating how to fire a blackpowder rifle, forge a horseshoe, and cook up a meal on a campfire.

Navajo Nation and the Northwest

Route 66: Albuquerque
  Toward Gallup 218

Zuni Pueblo 227

Gallup 229

Navajo Nation 237

Farmington.................... 240

Aztec.......................... 247

Bloomfield 250

Chaco Culture
  National Historical Park....... 252

U.S. 550 South to Bernalillo 259

Highlights

★ **Acoma Pueblo:** This windswept village atop a mesa west of Albuquerque is one of the oldest communities in the United States. Visit for the views as well as for the delicate black-on-white pottery made only here (page 219).

★ **Crownpoint Rug Auction:** Pick up a beautiful piece of handmade craftsmanship, and a good story while you're at it. This monthly auction in a Navajo village is a shopping event like no other (page 223).

★ **Nuestra Señora de Guadalupe Church:** Stunning murals decorate the white-washed walls of Zuni Pueblo's oldest adobe church. Colorful and intricately detailed, the kachinas look vividly real (page 228).

★ **Bisti/De-Na-Zin Wilderness:** Hiking this windswept landscape of dusty gray, red, and black stones is like taking a trip to another planet. There are no marked trails, but the weird mushroom-shaped rocks make good landmarks (page 243).

★ **Pueblo Bonito:** The largest set of ruins at **Chaco Culture National Historical Park,** this 12th-century complex was also the largest building in North America in pre-Columbian times, marking the center of a vast, complex network of trade and culture (page 255).

American Indian culture is often relegated to museums, its crafts and relics preserved behind glass or mounted on walls. But in New Mexico, especially in the northwestern part of the state, native traditions are lived every day.

The Navajo Nation, the largest reservation in the United States, occupies much of the northwest and stretches across 27,000 square miles into Arizona and Utah, while the Acoma, Laguna, and Zuni reservations are three outlying Puebloan communities. Visitors can appreciate a remarkable continuity of culture, from ancient ruins to contemporary powwows. The backdrop is slablike mesas, jagged canyons, spired red-rock buttes—the sort of classic Southwestern scenery that has photographers, mountain bikers, and hikers all reaching for their gear.

The most common route around the area begins on I-40 west out of Albuquerque, toward Acoma Pueblo. A thousand-year-old settlement atop a natural fortress of stone, "Sky City" is one of the most striking spots in New Mexico, rivaling Taos for the title of oldest inhabited town in the United States. Farther on, Gallup is the self-proclaimed Indian capital of the world, a major business hub for more than a hundred years. Along with its old-fashioned trading posts, it's emerging as a great outdoor destination, thanks to some excellent trails and rock-climbing sites nearby.

Heading due north brings you into the heart of Diné Bikéyah (Navajo land) and past Shiprock, a great plume of volcanic stone sticking straight out of the plain that, like so many natural features in this area, is the subject of scores of legends and tales.

Just beyond the eastern border of the reservation, Farmington and neighboring Aztec are towns built by the petroleum industry. They're also one common base (Cuba, to the south, is the other) for exploring the biggest draw in the region: Chaco Canyon. This site is where, between AD 850 and 1250, the Ancestral Puebloans (Anasazi) built a nine-mile-long city, a metropolis that served as the ceremonial and religious capital for this influential culture.

Previous: landscape in the Four Corners region; a dog tries to visit four states at once at Four Corners Monument. **Above:** Pyramid Rock Trail, east of Gallup.

Navajo Nation and the Northwest

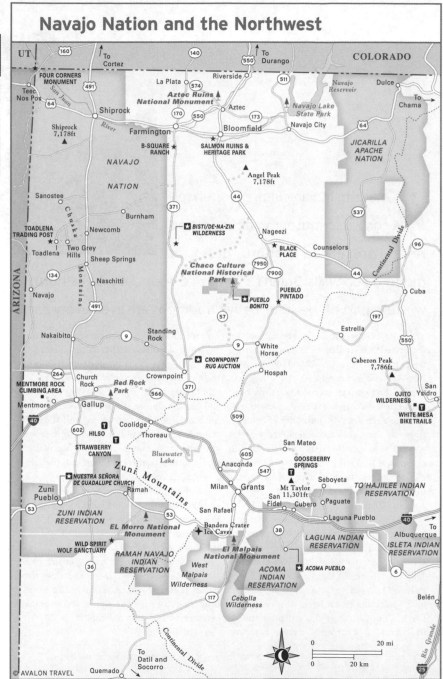

HISTORY

Northwestern New Mexico shows evidence of human occupation as early as 8000 BC, but it was not until the middle of the 9th century AD that people really began to flourish here. At this point, the residents of Chaco Canyon started building homes above ground that grew into multistory blocks. Chaco was part of a network of communities as far north as Mesa Verde and as far south as Zuni, all displaying a similar architectural style and connected by skillfully engineered roads. For unknown reasons, though, people eventually left these towns and dispersed, some toward the Rio Grande, some to Zuni, and some onto the Hopi lands in what is now Arizona.

Meanwhile, bands of Navajo had migrated from northern climes into the desert a bit west of Chaco. No one has been able to pinpoint the date of their arrival here; the tribe's oral tradition says that Chaco was still inhabited, but archaeological evidence suggests the Navajo were not in their current territory until after Chaco was empty, around 1300, and perhaps not even until shortly before the Spanish made their first *entrada*, in 1540. In any case, the Navajo settled in quickly, and when the Spanish brought livestock, they added sheepherding—as well as raiding on horseback—to their already highly developed agricultural lifestyle.

Because the region was farther away from Santa Fe and the main trade routes, it avoided some of the worst suffering brought by early Spanish rule. Trouble began when the United States took control of the New Mexico territory in 1846, and optimistic homesteaders began flooding in. American expansionists also discovered rich mineral deposits in the Navajo homeland. The worst confrontations came in the 1860s, the era when federal Indian agent Kit Carson embarked on a scorched-earth campaign, burning crops, slaughtering sheep, and chopping down orchards. On the brink of starvation, the Navajo began to surrender in 1863, and Carson promptly marched them all, in the dead of winter, 400 miles southeast to Fort Sumner. Thousands died during "the Long Walk" and in the following years of captivity. They returned to a federally granted reservation in 1868. Much of modern Navajo history has involved wrangling with the federal government, private energy interests, and the neighboring Hopi people (in Arizona) over the use of coal and other natural resources.

PLANNING YOUR TIME

The driving distances are not so great here, so you could cover this territory in as little as three days, staying one night in Zuni or Gallup and the next in Farmington. But this would leave you time to see only, say, Acoma Pueblo the first day, a long scenic drive including Four Corners the next, and the ruins at Chaco Canyon on the third. If you really want to appreciate how this part of New Mexico is culturally different from the rest of the state, four days will give you a little more time, also allowing for a hike or two. For anyone with more than a passing interest in ancient archaeological sites, Chaco can take a whole day, or even three. Mountain bikers and hikers could concentrate on the trails around Gallup—a great mix of mountains and rugged rock, and a couple of good places to hang out in town at night.

As there are few mountain ranges, a lot of the terrain in this region is devoid of shade. For outdoor activities, try to avoid the peak of summer. The lower elevations relative to the rest of the state mean that most of this area does not get heavy snow in the winter, but the road to Chaco may be muddy and difficult.

Route 66: Albuquerque Toward Gallup

I-40 climbs west out of Albuquerque and heads straight across a plateau lined with flat mesas—archetypal Southwest scenery. Ancient Acoma Pueblo dominates one of these mesas, a veritable rock tower and an amazing place to visit and meet the people whose ancestors have lived here for nearly a thousand years. At the small town of Grants, you can turn south from the highway to enter the volcanic badlands of El Malpais; nearby is El Morro National Monument, a natural pool amid cliffs adorned with centuries-old graffiti. If you're on this loop on Highway 53, you'll next reach Zuni Pueblo, and Gallup (and I-40) is straight north from there.

Dedicated drivers can hop off the interstate and cruise a remote, sometimes winding two-lane stretch of old Route 66, resurfacing at Laguna and then cruising parallel to I-40 almost to Gallup. Outside Albuquerque, take exit 126, heading south on Highway 6. Then turn right (southwest) on old Route 66, by the Major Land Company billboard. This road eventually meets, then crosses I-40, winding a bit, and eventually settling in as the frontage road up to exit 47, west of Thoreau.

LAGUNA PUEBLO

About 18 miles west of Albuquerque, I-40 crosses the border onto the 45 square miles of **Laguna Pueblo** (505/552-6654, www.lagunapueblo.org), on which 7,000 Keresan-speaking Ka-waikah (Lake People) live in six villages.

From the highway, the only impression you get of Laguna is its Dancing Eagle Casino, but if you have time, get off at exit 114 to visit the **San José Mission Church.** Established in 1699 when the Laguna people requested a priest (unlike any other pueblo), it stands out for its stark white stucco coating, but this is a relatively recent addition, following a 19th-century renovation. It was mudded and white-washed every year until the 1950s, when the boom in uranium mining in the area left no time for this maintenance; it's now sealed with stucco.

Inside, between a packed-earth floor and a finely wrought wood ceiling, the late

a rugged stretch of old Route 66 west of Albuquerque

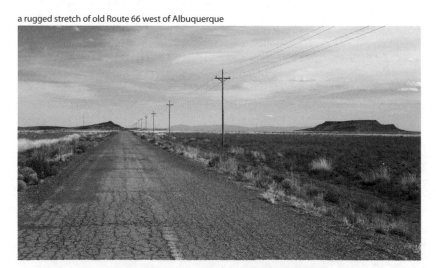

18th-century altar screen commands the room. It's the work of the so-called Laguna Santero, an unidentified painter who made the innovation of placing icons inside a crowded field of decorative borders and carved and painted columns, creating a work of explosively colorful folk art that was copied elsewhere in the region in subsequent decades.

If you're lucky, **Alfred Pino,** a local artist and informal guide, will be around the church and offer you a personal tour and explanation of the symbols on the altar and the painted elk hides on the walls, in exchange for a tip and donation to the church. The doors are usually open 9am-3pm weekdays (after a 7am morning Mass), but the church can be open later and on weekends if Alfred's around.

Each of the six villages of Laguna celebrates its own feast day, and then the whole pueblo turns out at the church September 17-19 for the Feast of San José, one of the bigger pueblo events in the Albuquerque area.

Food

One of New Mexico's most acclaimed green-chile cheeseburgers is served at ★ **Laguna Burger** (Old Rte. 66, 505/552-1022, 10:30am-10pm daily, $5), at the 66 Pit Stop gas station at exit 114. The ragged patties are made of fresh, never frozen beef, the buns are toasted on the griddle, and the fries are hand-cut, with skins on. Still, the cheery staff's T-shirts wonder, "Is it the beef, or is it the love?"

There are also branches of Laguna Burger at other major pueblo exits: at the Dancing Eagle Marketplace in Paraje (exit 108), and, closest to Albuquerque, exit 140, at the 66 Pit Stop north of the highway.

★ ACOMA PUEBLO

At exit 102 off I-40, visitors to Acoma turn south. On the road to Acoma, you may feel as though you've crossed through a pass into a Southwestern Shangri-la, for none of this great basin is visible from the highway. Down in the valley, the route runs directly toward a flat-topped rock that juts up like a tooth.

Atop the rock is the original **Acoma Pueblo,** the village known as **Sky City.** The community covers about 70 acres and is built largely of adobe, as it has been since at least 1100. Only a hundred or so people live on the mesa top year-round, given the hardships of no running water or electricity. But many families maintain homes here, and the place is thronged on September 2, when the pueblo members gather for the **Feast of San Esteban,** and the day after Christmas, for

view from Acoma's Sky City

Ceremonial Dances

Feast days typically involve carnivals and markets in addition to dances. Dates can vary from year to year. Confirm details and start times—usually afternoon, but sometimes following an evening or midnight Mass—with the **Indian Pueblo Cultural Center** (505/843-7270, www.indian-pueblo.org) before setting out. For the Navajo dances in Shiprock, check with the organizers of the **Northern Navajo Nation Fair** (505/368-4305, www.northernnavajonationfair.org).

- **February, first or second weekend** – Acoma (Sky City): governor's feast, various dances
- **February 19** - Laguna (Old Laguna): Feast of San José
- **Easter** - Most pueblos: various dances
- **May 7** - Acoma: Feast of Santa María
- **July 26** - Laguna (Seama): Feast of Santa Ana
- **August 10** - Acoma (Acomita): Feast of San Lorenzo
- **August 15** - Laguna (Mesita): Feast of the Assumption
- **September 2** - Acoma (Sky City): Feast of San Esteban
- **September 8** - Laguna (Encinal): Feast of the Nativity of the Blessed Virgin Mary
- **September 19** - Laguna (Old Laguna): Feast of San José
- **September 25** - Laguna (Paguate): Feast of Saint Elizabeth
- **Early October** - Shiprock: Yei Bichei dances
- **October 17** - Laguna (Paraje): Feast of Saint Margaret Mary
- **Thanksgiving** - Zuni: Christmas light parade; Acoma (Sky City): craft show
- **Late November/early December** - Zuni: Shalako
- **December 24** - Acoma (Sky City): luminaria display; Laguna (Old Laguna): dances after evening Mass
- **December 25-28** - Acoma (Sky City) and Laguna (Old Laguna): Christmas dances

holiday dances. The rest of the 2,800 Acoma (People of the White Rock, in their native Keresan) live on the valley floor, which is used primarily as ranchland.

Visiting Sky City

All visits start at the **Sky City Cultural Center and Haak'u Museum** (Indian Rte. 23, 800/747-0181, www.acomaskycity.org, 8am-5pm daily Apr.-Oct., 9am-4pm Sat.-Sun. Nov.-Mar.) on the main road, which houses a café and shop stocked with local crafts, along with beautiful rotating exhibits on Acoma art and tradition. From here, you must join a guided tour ($23), which transports groups by bus to the village. The road to the top is the one concession to modernity;

previously, all goods had to be hauled up the near-vertical cliff faces. The tour lasts about an hour and a half, after which visitors may return by bus or hike down one of the old trails, using hand- and footholds dug into the rock centuries ago. In summer, tours start at 9:30am and depart every 45 minutes or so, with the last one going at 3:30pm. In the winter, the first tour begins at 10:15am, and they go about hourly until 3pm. Definitely call ahead to check that the tours are running and verify times, as the pueblo closes to visitors periodically.

The centerpiece of the village is the **Church of San Esteban del Rey,** one of the most iconic of the Spanish missions in New Mexico. Built between 1629 and 1640, the graceful, simple structure has been inspiring New Mexican architects ever since. Its interior is, like many New Mexican pueblo churches, spare and simple, the white walls painted with rainbows and corn. (Unfortunately, tours do not enter the church; visitors are welcome for dances and feast days, though.)

As much as it represents the pinnacle of Hispano-Indian architecture in the 17th century, the church is also a symbol of the brutality of Spanish colonialism, as it rose in the typical way: forced labor. The men of Acoma felled and carried the tree trunks for the ceiling beams from the forest on Mount Taylor, more than 25 miles across the valley, and up the cliff face to the village.

Acoma is well known for its pottery, distinguished by the fine black lines that sweep around the curves of the creamy-white vessels. On the best works, the lines are so fine and densely painted, they shimmer almost like a moiré. The clay particular to this area can be worked so thin that the finest pots will hum or ring when tapped. Throughout the village, you have opportunities to buy pieces. Given the constraints of the tour, this can feel slightly pressured, but in many cases, you have the privilege of buying work directly from the artisan who created it.

Food and Accommodations

The cultural center contains the **Y'aak'a Café** (8am-5pm daily Apr.-Oct., 9am-4pm

Acoma vs. Oñate: Grudge Match

The early history of the conquistadors at Acoma was one of brutal back-and-forth attacks, each escalating in violence after the initial Spanish incursion. In a 1599 attack following many previous skirmishes, Don Juan de Oñate, the first governor of Spain's newest province, killed 800 people, leaving only 80 men alive in the hilltop village.

But Oñate was not content. He then brought his enemies into a makeshift court and tried them for the murder of 11 Spaniard soldiers. The sentence for the inevitable guilty verdict was that every male in Acoma over the age of 25 would have one foot cut off; everyone between the ages of 12 and 25 was pressed into slavery; and the children were sent to convents in Mexico.

Oñate was eventually recalled from his post and chastised for his actions. But in 1640, as if to add insult to injury, the Spanish friars presented the Church of San Esteban del Rey—built by Acoma slaves over more than a decade—to the maimed pueblo population as "restitution" for Oñate's cruelties. As a further gift of salvation, the friars publicly purged and hanged the village's spiritual leaders in the churchyard.

Don Juan de Oñate

Variations on this treatment happened up and down the Rio Grande, eventually inspiring the Pueblo Revolt of 1680. But Oñate's particular brand of viciousness is probably the most remembered. Shortly after a monument to the conquistador was erected north of Española in 1998, the right foot of the bronze statue turned up missing—someone had snuck in at night and sawed it clean off. An anonymous letter to newspapers stated that the act was "on behalf of our brothers and sisters at Acoma Pueblo." Rumor adds that the prankster vandals also left behind at the statue two miniature feet made of clay, attached to a shield inscribed with the words "The Agony of Defeat."

Sat.-Sun. Nov.-Mar., $8), which serves earthy local dishes like lamb stew, tamales, and corn roasted in a traditional *horno* oven—as well as Starbucks coffee.

Acoma Pueblo operates the small-scale **Sky City Casino & Hotel** (888/759-2489, www.skycity.com, $89 d), also at exit 102. Its rooms are perfectly clean and functional, and there's a little pool.

GRANTS

This town of 8,000 has gone through several career changes since its start in the 1880s. It began as a railroad camp, but it soon grew into a lumber town, based on the rich forests of the Zuni Mountains to the south. In the 1940s, logging restrictions kicked in, and locals turned to farming, mustering the questionable boast of "carrot capital of the world."

But just a decade later, Grants reinvented itself as the much more au courant "uranium capital of the world," after a local sheepherder happened across some of that valuable ore on the edge of town. It turned out to be one of the largest uranium fields in the world. With the best ore depleted in the 1980s and the last mine closed in 1999, Grants is now retired, so to speak, but it welcomes guests for a meal and a story or two about its past before they carry on to Gallup or Albuquerque. Just to the north, Mount Taylor (elevation 11,305 feet) is a destination for hikers.

Sights

Make time for the surprisingly good **New Mexico Mining Museum** (100 N. Iron Ave., 505/287-4802, 9am-4pm Mon.-Sat., $3), where you descend below the earth into a mock mine shaft. The narration from former miners gets pretty technical, but the narrow tunnels and clanking machinery give you a very real appreciation for the physical labor and risk involved in mining. The museum is on the west side of town, at the corner of Santa Fe Avenue, the main east-west drag.

On the west side of town, the **Cibola Arts Council** (1001 W. Santa Fe Ave., 505/287-7311, 1pm-5pm Tues.-Sat., free) shows local

work and houses the Route 66 Vintage Museum, with postcards and other trinkets from Grants' motoring heyday. And flying geeks can check out the **Aviation History Museum** (505/287-4700, 9am-1pm Sat., free), built around a restored beacon for Midcontinental Airway, established by Charles Lindbergh in the 1920s. It's at the airport near Milan, west of I-40 between exits 81 and 79.

Recreation

Heading north out of town, 1st Street (Hwy. 547) turns into Roosevelt Avenue then Lobo Canyon Road, headed toward **Mount Taylor,** aka Tsoodzil (Turquoise Bead) to the Navajo, who count it as one of their nation's four sacred mountains (although it is not technically on the reservation). Just past mile marker 10 on Highway 547, **Coal Mine Campground** (505/287-8833, www.recreation.gov, May-Sept., $5) is thick with pines and has some nice shady sites, with a stream running nearby.

Just as the pavement on Highway 547 ends, a right turn onto gravel Forest Road 193 takes you five miles to the head of **Gooseberry Springs Trail** (no. 77). From here, you can hike 3.5 miles to the mountain's summit, at 11,301 feet. Although the elevation gain is 2,400 feet, it's not a very strenuous climb, and it delivers an incredibly rewarding view—on a clear day, you can see as far as the Arizona border. Allow about three hours for the round-trip.

Food and Accommodations

Few people stay the night here, as Grants is so close to Albuquerque, but it can be handy after the Crownpoint rug auction. And oldmotel aficionados will appreciate the Route 66 gem that is **Southwest Motel** (1000 E. Santa Fe Ave., 505/287-2935, $35 s, $45 d), greeting visitors with a vivid neon sign and tidy little rooms with mini-fridges and desks. A couple of blocks west, **El Cafecito** (820 E. Santa Fe Ave., 505/285-6229, 7am-9pm Mon.-Fri., 7am-8pm Sat., $8) is a family-run restaurant with excellent red and green chile, as well as some

Look for Nimitz Drive on the east side, next to El Cafecito; turn north and follow the road as it curves and crosses a small bridge.

For a good, quick stop right off the interstate, the classic gleaming stainless-steel **Wow Diner** (1300 Motel Dr., 505/287-3801, 6am-midnight Tues.-Sun., $8) beckons from exit 79 (really Milan, just west of Grants). The menu has something for everyone, from pork *carnitas* to spinach salad to old-fashioned ice cream shakes.

Information

Definitely stop in at the helpful and attractive **El Malpais Visitor Center** (1900 E. Santa Fe Ave., 505/876-2783, 8am-5pm daily), just south of I-40 at exit 85. Pick up maps, brochures, and suggested driving routes and hiking tours for this corner of the state.

Don't be fooled by the bland exterior: El Cafecito's food is spicy.

non-spicy American standards to round out the menu.

For coffee, **Coco Bean Café** (333 Nimitz Dr., 505/285-4143, 7am-5:30pm Mon.-Fri., 8am-4pm Sat., 9am-2pm Sun., $4) is a good excuse to get off the main road through town.

★ CROWNPOINT RUG AUCTION

The curiously named town of **Thoreau** (pronounced thu-ROO) at exit 53 inspires no Walden-style reveries, but it is the turnoff for one of the best shopping experiences in northwestern New Mexico. Twenty-five miles north is a small Navajo community, home of the

inspecting the wares at the Crownpoint Rug Auction

Crownpoint Rug Auction (505/736-2130, www.crownpointrugauction.com), which has been connecting buyers and sellers from all around the region since 1968. Even if you have no interest in buying, it's a great cultural experience, and an opportunity to see some beautiful work up close.

The sales, in the elementary-school gym on the second Friday of the month (usually; check the website), draw casual shoppers as well as big gallery owners from Santa Fe. Jewelers and potters set up tables in the hall, and food is available in the school cafeteria. It's easy to find the school in the tiny town—turn left from Highway 371 and look for lots of parked cars. Rugs are on view 4pm-6:30pm; bidding starts at 7pm and usually lasts till around 10pm. Often with more rugs on offer than customers, there's a good chance you'll find something you like for a reasonable price—a good 4- by 6-foot rug can go for $300 or so, and small sampler rugs can go for $30. Cash, credit cards, and checks are accepted as payment.

There's nowhere to stay in Crownpoint; Grants and Gallup are both about an hour's drive, and Farmington is due north on Highway 371, about an hour and a half away.

EL MALPAIS NATIONAL MONUMENT

The product of three volcanic events, the lava-strewn landscape of the **El Malpais National Monument** (505/783-4774, www.nps.gov/elma, free) is not exactly the barren terrain that *el malpaís* (el-mal-pie-EES, literally, "the badlands") suggests. A surprising amount of greenery has taken root in the millennia since the last eruption, between 2,000 and 3,000 years ago, and in the spring, wildflowers stand out against the jagged black rock. The lava fields are riven with deep, cave-like tubes that formed as the hot rock cooled. Some of the most scenic areas are along the monument's eastern border, where the lava meets red sandstone cliffs, as well as New Mexico's largest natural arch. Stay around at dusk to see bats fly out around El Calderon; there is a ranger-led talk twice a week in summer.

a section of lava tube at El Malpais National Monument

For those who just want a quick look, the easiest access point is **Sandstone Bluffs Overlook,** where, on a short walk along the edge of the eastern cliffs, you can admire the lava fields and see north to Mount Taylor. It's about 11 miles south from I-40 on Highway 117. Drive another 7 miles to reach **La Ventana Arch,** a great sandstone arc; a short trail leads to a scenic viewing spot.

If you'd like a longer hike or drive into the park, stop first at the **El Malpais Visitors Center** (1900 E. Santa Fe Ave., 505/876-2783, 8am-5pm daily), near I-40 at exit 85, midway between the two highways that access different parts of the badlands. National Park Service employees can give you detailed maps and current conditions, and from there you can decide whether to take Highway 53 or Highway 117 south into the monument area. The monument **information center** (505/783-4774, 8am-4:30pm daily Mar.-Sept.) is less conveniently located on Highway 53, 23 miles south of I-40.

In addition to the hikes detailed below,

there are more demanding but worthwhile places to explore outside the borders of the national park, in the BLM land designated **Cebolla Wilderness** (off the southeast border of the park) and **West Malpais Wilderness** (to the south and west)—ask at the visitors center for details on these areas as well.

Zuni-Acoma Trail

By far the most strenuous hike, the shadeless 7.5-mile **Zuni-Acoma Trail** cuts across the lava beds roughly along the path used for centuries by the Puebloans in this region. It's rough going because the ground is uneven and you have to keep your eye out for cairns, but if you're interested in the plants and animals that thrive in El Malpais, this can be a rewarding trek. The eastern trailhead is on Highway 117, before you reach La Ventana Arch; the western one is on Highway 53.

Lava Falls Area

For the best up-close look at the lava, head farther south on Highway 117 to the **Lava Falls Area.** Here you can still make out the swirls and eddies of the molten stuff as if it had cooled yesterday; the variety of shapes and textures is fascinating, as are the odd pockets of stunted trees that manage to flourish here. The three-mile route (a mile-long loop with a one-mile spur) is marked only by rock cairns, so bring a compass, as it's easy to get disoriented.

El Calderon Area

At **El Calderon Area** on Highway 53, a 3.8-mile loop trail heads up to the Continental Divide, then around the edge of **El Calderon Cinder Cone,** a former lava vent. Calderon Crater, the oldest of the three lava flows that make up the area, dates back some 115,000 years—as a result, the rock is more weathered, and not the stark black found around younger McCartys Crater on the south side of the park. This is also the area where lava tubes are closest to the road—a short walk from the car reveals the entrance to **Junction Cave,** a

tube that partially collapsed—you see a sliver of daylight on the other end. Farther up the trail is **Xenolith Cave,** a similar lava tube with odd rocks jumbled in with the lava; the famous **Bat Cave** (closed to hikers), less than a mile from the parking area, has a circling cloud of the nocturnal critters at sunset.

Big Tubes Area

The **Big Tubes Area,** a network of 17 miles of lava caves on the west side of the monument, has by far the weirdest terrain. Two caves are open here, Big Skylight and Giant Ice Cave. You'll need a high-clearance truck, as the road is often very rough, as well as headlamps (with extra batteries), sturdy boots, and heavy work gloves to protect your hands from the jagged rocks.

Bandera Crater Ice Caves

A family-run tourist attraction that was grandfathered in when El Malpais was made a national monument, the **Bandera Crater Ice Caves** (Hwy. 53, 888/423-2283, www.icecaves. com, 9am-5pm daily Mar.-Oct., $12) are an impressive natural sight, especially during the heat of summer, when you can descend from 90°F outside to 31°F underground, the chill emanating from a permanent layer of greenish ice at least 20 feet thick. Although the same phenomenon is visible elsewhere in El Malpais (for much less money), this is the most accessible spot, and generally more impressive. The other half of the attraction, Bandera Crater, 750 feet deep, is actually not much to look at—literally, just a big hole in the ground.

EL MORRO NATIONAL MONUMENT

This area may seem like relative wilderness today, but in fact, it has always been a fairly well-traveled route. The proof is at the **El Morro National Monument** (Hwy. 53, 505/783-4226, www.nps.gov/elmo, 9am-5pm daily, free), where Don Juan de Oñate carved his name in the bluff *(morro)* and darkened the inscription with lamp soot, as a way of passing the time while his men rested and horses drank at the natural pool formed by snow-melt. It's also a vivid image of the early Spanish power in the Southwest—Oñate made his mark in 1605, seven years after his first official colonizing mission, and two years before the English even set foot in the New World. In the centuries since, seemingly every celebrity of the American West, major and minor, has left a graffiti autograph: Don Diego de Vargas was here in 1692, early in his campaign to reclaim Nuevo México following the Pueblo Revolt of 1680. P. Gilmer Breckenridge, who led an experimental caravan of 25 camels from Texas to California, visited in 1857, and his compatriot, E. Pen Long, left a curlicue signature that gets the prize for best penmanship.

The half-mile **Inscription Loop Trail** is paved and leads first to the year-round pool at the base of the rocks, then along the cliff face. The longer you stare at the rocks, the more names—as well as figures, carved by the Zuni centuries earlier—pop out. The natural ground level has sunk over the centuries too, so the graffiti crawls up the cliffs well above your head. For a view, continue on up to the top of the bluffs on the **Headland Trail.** The loop, which takes another hour, passes Atsinna, the ruins of a small pueblo occupied by the Zuni in the 13th and 14th centuries.

Food and Accommodations

Just west of the national monument, **El Morro RV Park & Cabins** (Hwy. 53, 505/783-4612, www.elmorro-nm.com) is a great place to stay in the wilderness. Tent campsites are $15 per night, while tidy little cabins with queen and double beds start at $84; RV sites are $30. The on-site **Ancient Way Café** (9am-5pm Sun.-Tues. and Thurs., 9am-8pm Fri.-Sat., $8) has tasty brisket and beans, and good veggie options; weekend dinners are one set entrée (jerk chicken, for instance), and you should call to reserve.

Just east on the highway a few miles is **La Tinaja Café** (Hwy. 53, 505/783-4126, 10am-6:30pm Thurs.-Sun., $10), which serves everything from "Navajo fajitas" to German sausage specials to home-baked zucchini bread. Look for the big barn on the south side of the road, and call ahead, as it can close earlier than posted hours.

RAMAH

Twelve miles west of El Morro, Ramah (pronounced RAY-muh) was originally settled by Mormons, though it is now part of the Navajo reservation. The local Ramah Navajo Weavers Association, like the collective in Tierra Amarilla in northern New Mexico, has helped

historic American graffiti at El Morro National Monument

revive an economy based on sheep, particularly the old Churro breed. The settlement's history is told in the tiny **Ramah Museum** (505/783-4392, 10am-2pm Sat. June-Aug., donation); at the curve in town, turn north.

Wild Spirit Wolf Sanctuary

Just before you reach Ramah, you pass the turn for the **Wild Spirit Wolf Sanctuary** (505/775-3304, www.wildspiritwolfsanctuary.org, 10am-5pm Tues.-Sun., $10), where you can hang out with some 50 captive-bred wolves and wolf-dogs that would otherwise go homeless. **Guided tours** (required) run at 11am, 12:30pm, 2pm, and 3:30pm. You can also **camp** ($15 for tents or RVs) or stay the night in a cabin or house ($125-$250)—then you're here in the morning to help feed the animals (reserve ahead; $25 pp). Signs off Highway 53 point to Mountainview and Pine Hill; it's another 12 miles on Indian Route 125 and 120.

Zuni Pueblo

Covering more than 600 square miles and with a population of more than 10,000, Zuni is the largest of the pueblos. For centuries, the Zuni people were spread over a wide area in several settlements. The pueblo Halona:wa (Anthill), around which the modern town of Zuni is based, was established long ago, but did not become the center of population until 1692, after the people made a peace agreement with Don Juan de Oñate and gathered here. There is a splendid church to visit, and this is the only pueblo where you can stay overnight, giving a much better appreciation for the community.

Isolation from the Rio Grande-area pueblos has helped keep Zuni culture more distinct—its *"olla* maidens," for instance, perform a traditional dance with pots balanced on their heads. Zuni is also famous for its delicate inlay jewelry, called "needlepoint," in which the tiniest bits of turquoise, coral, and other stones are set in intricate patterns on a silver field; the texture almost resembles beadwork. Collectors also hold Zuni kachinas (figurines of spirit beings) and fetishes (tiny carved animals) in high esteem. If you're coming here to shop, avoid late June and late December,

roadside scenery near Zuni Pueblo

when a period of fasting called Deshkwi bans buying or selling.

SIGHTS

Register first at the **visitors center** (Hwy. 53, 505/782-7238, www.zunitourism.com, 8:30am-5:30pm Mon.-Fri., 10am-4pm Sat., noon-4pm Sun.), midway through town on the north side of the road. Here you can get information on artists' studios as well as arrange a number of tours, including the highly recommended **walking tour** around Old Zuni (Middle Village).

All tours require advance notice, but if you have a particular interest, they are a wonderful way of seeing a different side of Zuni. The visitors center can arrange a 2.5-hour **artist workshop tour** ($75 for up to four people), based on your preferred medium (silver, stone, etc.). Archaeological site visits are also available, to **Hawikku,** where ancestral Zuni lived and where Coronado thought one of the "Cities of Gold" might be, and to the **Village of the Great Kivas,** inhabited in the 11th century. Both are $75 for two people and require a week's notice.

★ Nuestra Señora de Guadalupe Church

The core of the historic area called the Middle Village is the **Nuestra Señora de Guadalupe Church,** where the walls, first erected in 1629 and rebuilt in 1692, are painted with larger-than-life Shalako figures and other elements of the Zuni tradition as they function in the four seasons. The brilliantly colored murals, created over more than 20 years beginning in 1970, are the work of one esteemed pueblo artist, Alex Seowtewa, and his sons. Together with the blankets and buffalo heads, this is one of the most syncretic churches in the state—a beautiful, fervent expression of faith over millennia.

The church is accessible only by **guided tour** (10am, 1pm, and 3pm Mon.-Sat., 1pm and 3pm Sun.), which departs from the Zuni visitors center. Theoretically, two separate tours are offered: one around the old town and one to the church, each for $10. But in practice, all visitors are usually lumped into a single tour of everything for $15. The whole combined tour takes a little over an hour.

A:shíwi A:wan Museum and Heritage Center

Zuni's small **A:shíwi A:wan Museum and Heritage Center** (2 E. Ojo Caliente Rd., 505/782-4403, www.ashiwi-museum.org, 9am-6pm Mon.-Fri., free) is fascinating. It tells the story of the Zuni people, from creation myths through more contemporary issues with archaeologists and other researchers, such as Frank Cushing, who brought the pueblo to broader attention in the 19th century and became a local hero for a time. Cushing's endeavors are portrayed in a few hilarious cartoons by a Zuni artist. Also on display are artifacts from the ancestral settlement of Hawikku, excavated in 1916. They had been whisked away to a basement in a branch of the Smithsonian; Zuni leaders negotiated for this selection to be returned, leaving the remainder to be better preserved at the Smithsonian.

The museum is just south of Highway 53: Turn at the major stop sign on the west end of town; the museum is at the next big intersection, on the northwest corner, across from Halona Plaza.

FESTIVALS AND EVENTS

The largest event of the year, the ritual of **Shalako** (also spelled Sha'la'ko) marks the end of the agricultural season and the beginning of winter in late November or early December. Although many of the prayers and dances take place in areas closed to visitors, it is still a remarkable time to visit the pueblo.

The Shalako, part of the extensive pantheon of kachinas, act as messengers between man and gods; when they depart the village, they are bearing the Zuni prayer for rain in the spring. For this ceremony, they are men who are elected each year to impersonate these godlike forces, and they spend the entire year preparing. The 24-hour ritual begins around noon, but the real excitement comes at dusk, when the figures descend from the sacred mesa south of town. With giant eagle-feather masks with goggle eyes and wooden beaks, they are frightening, noisy, 10-foot-tall creatures, an awesome sight as they swoop through the crowds and the bonfires, their beaks clacking and the drums pounding behind them.

Shortly after Shalako, the whole community gathers for the **Give-Away,** to thank the clans involved in the ritual, for which preparation is a massive expense. People bring specific gifts as well as all manner of unused items, from deer meat to refrigerators, which are redistributed according to need. Again, it's a ceremony that outsiders may not entirely get, but it's a festive time to be in town.

Other secular events throughout the year include the **Zuni Cultural Arts Expo,** in late July or early August; the **McKinley County Fair,** also in August; the **Ancient Way Fall Festival,** an arts and harvest festival all along Highway 53 in early October; and the **Holiday Arts Market,** in early December. The visitors center can confirm dates.

FOOD AND ACCOMMODATIONS

The main place to eat is the adjacent general store, **Halona Plaza,** where the deli counter serves up excellent fried chicken ($6) with smoky-hot red-chile sauce on the side—New Mexican fusion at its finest. There's a bit more of a social scene at night down at **Chu-Chu's** (1344 Hwy. 53, 505/782-2100, 11am-10pm, Mon.-Sat., $8), on the east end of the town, where there's pizza, subs, and a nice little patio. The seriously food-curious should also stop in to **Paywa's Bakery** (noon-5pm Wed.-Fri.), down a dirt road opposite Chu-Chu's. The operation bakes sourdough and sweet pies in a giant adobe *horno.*

Unlike most pueblos, where visitors are welcome for the day or as casino customers, Zuni offers a unique opportunity to stay overnight and just soak up the atmosphere of the place: wood smoke, red dirt, and sparkling stars. The supremely comfortable ★ **Inn at Halona** (23-B Pia Mesa Rd., 505/782-4547, www.halona.com, $75 d) is run by a family with century-old roots on the reservation. The older main house has five rooms (no. 4 upstairs is beautifully sunny, while the basement no. 5 is big yet cozy-feeling), but you might prefer the side house if you like to sleep late, because the scene in the main house's breakfast room can get pretty animated. Guests dig in to what seems like an endless array of breads, eggs, meats, and the signature blue-corn pancakes. Book well ahead if you plan to be in town during any special events.

Gallup

Initially just a wide spot along the railroad, Gallup took its name from the man who doled out cash in exchange for the coal that companies hauled in from the surrounding mines in the 1880s. By the 1920s, Gallup was known for its exceptionally pure coal, which meant higher wages for workers, who flooded in from Britain, China, Italy, Greece, and scores of other places, making the town a polyglot community from early on. The mining business has slowed, but at least a hundred trains still rumble through every day—it's a near-constant background noise, and as the freight loads cruise right through the center of town, you often have the disconcerting sensation of looking down a street and seeing the background in motion.

Gallup's other disconcerting effect is the sense you've stepped onto a movie set. The place was a popular Hollywood location from the 1930s on through the Route 66 heyday, and it's not hard to see why, what with

Gallup

© AVALON TRAVEL

the glowing neon, the red sandstone cliffs, and the jagged Hogback Mountains, which inspire visions of Wild West adventure. Less glamorously, in the 1970s and 1980s, Gallup struggled with high unemployment and astronomical rates of drunk driving and alcoholism. But one get-tough mayor started a turnaround, and now downtown is clean and lively, and the civic pride is palpable.

SIGHTS

The railroad and I-40 divide Gallup in two, and most of what visitors want is on the south side. The historic downtown area is on Highway 66 and Coal Avenue, lined with the most notable buildings and shops. The far east and west ends of town cater to through travelers on the interstate, with all the chain hotels and restaurants.

You can cover most of Gallup's attractions on foot after parking downtown. Some of the best art is outdoors, in the many murals around town, some painted by the WPA in the 1930s and others put up in the 21st century. There's one dedicated to the Navajo code talkers on South 2nd Street just south of Highway 66, as well as a great modern one on the side of the city hall (Aztec Avenue at South 2nd Street) that evokes modern life in Gallup: kids in pickup trucks, road construction, and rodeo events.

McKinley County Courthouse

Downtown is anchored by the Pueblo Revival **McKinley County Courthouse** (207 W. Hill St.), one block south of Coal Avenue. If you ask nicely and it's a slow day, you can walk around inside the courthouse and admire the tile work, the punched-tin light fixtures, and the 2,000-square-foot WPA mural in the main courtroom. Painted by Lloyd Moylan, it's the largest surviving work from that period in the state.

WWII Navajo Code Talkers Museum

Adjoining the chamber of commerce, the **WWII Navajo Code Talkers Museum** (103 W. Hwy. 66, 505/722-2228, 8am-5pm Mon.-Fri., free) is a large collection of memorabilia arranged in fluorescent-lit glass cases—ask the chamber employees to turn the lights on. No frills here: The room is mostly used for business meetings, but the collected papers, photographs, and clippings trace the use of the Navajo language as code through the fight. Given the importance of the code to the success of the U.S. campaign, it's a little depressing to realize this is one of the largest permanent exhibits on the subject (there's another inside the Burger King in Kayenta, Arizona).

Gallup Cultural Center

The old Santa Fe Railway station has been converted into a well-used community arts center. Visitors will enjoy the upstairs **museum** (201 E. Hwy. 66, 505/863-4131, 9am-4pm Mon.-Fri., free). The nifty collection of dioramas—scenes involving model trains, a replica trading post—are accompanied by headphones to listen to a local's explanation of the scene. You'll also find a café, a visitors info desk, a music and gift shop, and the **Ceremonial Gallery,** which exhibits local student art.

Between Memorial Day and Labor Day, free guided **walking tours** of downtown depart from here, usually at 10am daily.

Rex Museum

Like many small-town collections, the **Rex Museum** (300 W. Hwy. 66, 505/863-1363, 8am-3.30pm Mon.-Fri., $2 donation) is a hodgepodge, from roller skates to programs from the Inter-Tribal Indian Ceremonial. But perhaps it's most interesting to see the traces of the various immigrant groups that have settled in Gallup, from Chinese to Greeks.

Red Rock Park & Museum

East of town about six miles, **Red Rock Park** is Gallup's public party spot, with rodeo grounds and an outdoor amphitheater. It also has the surprisingly large **Red Rock Museum** (505/722-3839, 8am-noon

Sandstone rocks around Gallup entice hikers, bikers, and climbers.

The Navajo Code Talkers

Navajo code talkers and victims of the Bataan Death March are memorialized in downtown Gallup.

The ingenuity and heroism of the Navajo code talkers of World War II has only come to full light in recent decades, after the system was declassified. As a result, this team of more than 300 men (and one Anglo fighter fluent in Navajo) have become a novel footnote in the history of the war, rather than a crucial element in the U.S. military's victory. In fact, the never-broken code, based on Navajo vocabulary, was an essential part of the Battle of Iwo Jima, and the code talkers were involved in every Marine battle in the Pacific.

Twenty-nine recruits formed the first team of code talkers, who also developed the code. At its core, the system used Navajo words to represent letters of the alphabet—these could be used to spell, or combined to form larger words and concepts. For instance, *w* was represented by the Navajo word for weasel, *gloe-ih*. To say "when," the code talker said "weasel" and "hen": *gloe-ih-na-ah-wo-hai;* "will" was *gloe-ih-dot-sahi,* or "sick weasel." Military terms required more creativity: a *bish-lo,* or "iron fish," was a submarine.

The advantage of Navajo was that it was a highly complex yet completely oral language, with only a handful of nonnative speakers. Moreover, it was extremely fast to transmit, because unlike previous systems, it didn't require a machine at either end. The code talkers have long been a point of pride for the Navajo, especially as symbols of the power of speaking the ancestral language. A mural by Be Sargent on South 2nd Street in Gallup depicts the code in visual form, showing the original 29 code talkers, now all deceased, along with the various animals and objects used as keys in the code.

and 1pm-5pm Mon.-Fri., $2 donation), which feels as though it was set up in the 1970s, then left to its own devices. The display cases, filled with information on the Zuni, Hopi, and Navajo, are a little dusty; you'll probably have to turn the lights on yourself. It houses one of the most elaborate displays of Zuni kachinas anywhere—all the figurines labeled and their roles explained. There's also a model hogan (the traditional Navajo home) and a selection of local jewelry styles. Access the park via the frontage road (E. Hwy. 66), from exit 33 or exit 26 off I-40, then turn north on Highway 566.

ENTERTAINMENT AND EVENTS

On an average day, the streets of Gallup are not exactly hopping. You will notice a significant rush on weekends, though, as people from surrounding communities come into town to do business. And expect crowds during the two big annual events, a powwow and a balloon rally. The landmark **El Morro Theatre** (207 W. Coal Ave., 505/863-1250, www.elmorrotheatre.com) is downtown, built in 1926 in the Spanish colonial revival style. It's huge, recently renovated, and a bargain for movies ($5). It also hosts local theater and music.

Nightlife

Gallup's past alcohol problems mean a somewhat subdued night scene. Still, one lively outpost is **Sammy C's Rock N Sports Pub & Grille** (107 W. Coal Ave., 505/863-2220, 11am-11pm Mon.-Thurs., 11am-1am Fri.-Sat., 10am-9pm Sun.), run by New Mexico sports-broadcasting legend Sammy Chioda. He's a charming host who will win over even the sports-bar averse (the walls are solid with memorabilia and TVs).

Another option is **Coal Street Pub** (303 W. Coal Ave., 505/722-0117, 11am-10pm Sun.-Wed., 11am-11pm Thurs.-Sat.), which serves only beer and wine. There's often some kind of live music on the weekends.

The **49er Lounge** (1000 E. Hwy. 66, 5pm-1am daily) in the El Rancho Hotel does serve booze, but you might not need it because the setting is dizzying enough—like the rest of the hotel, this place exudes an almost overwhelming aura of decaying Western glamour. Go early, as it tends to close before the posted time if business is slow.

Festivals and Events

Every night at 7pm between Memorial Day and Labor Day, Navajo, Hopi, and other **dance groups** perform in the plaza in front of the courthouse, for free.

For four days in late July or early August, Gallup hosts the **Inter-Tribal Indian Ceremonial** (www.theceremonial.com), which draws more than 20,000 participants from various tribes in Canada and Mexico, as well as from all over the United States. Also on the schedule are a beauty pageant, a fashion show, and lots of music.

The other big annual event is the **Red Rock Balloon Rally** (www.redrockballoonrally.com), on the first weekend in December. With about 200 participating hot-air balloons, it has been going strong since 1981, probably because the setting, against the vibrant sandstone at Red Rock Park, is unbeatable. The balloonists often need extra volunteers, so it's a good chance to get a free ride or join a chase crew—show up early and ask around.

SHOPPING

With a historic trading post or overstocked pawnshop seemingly every 10 feet, Gallup can be an exciting place to shop, or an overwhelming one, depending on your point of view. But even if you don't feel up to sifting through treasure troves of Navajo turquoise, the **trading posts,** some in business for the better part of a century and still doing business primarily with the local Indian population, are worth a visit simply as another town attraction. They're stocked with everything from hand-spun skeins of wool to crisp new blue jeans, and of course, heaps and heaps of jewelry.

One of the oldest, most respected trading posts downtown is **Richardson's Trading Co. & Cash Pawn** (222 W. Hwy. 66, 505/722-4762, 9am-6pm Mon.-Sat.), where the warren of storefronts is permeated with the smell of old leather.

Another shopping hot spot is **City Electric Shoe Shop** (230 W. Coal Ave., 505/863-5252, 10am-6pm Mon.-Sat.), where you can pick up a pair of street-ready moccasins in butter-soft suede or an embossed leather belt—both are made in a workshop in the basement.

On the south side, **Ellis Tanner Trading Co.** (1980 Hwy. 602, 505/863-4434, 8am-7pm Mon.-Sat.) has deep roots in Gallup; check inside for a huge mural by local artist Chester Kahn, honoring locals who have been good role models. You can pick up roasted piñon nuts, Diné-English children's books, vintage dance regalia, and more.

But perhaps the best shopping experience in town is at the **Gallup Flea Market** (505/722-7328) every Saturday on the north side of town. It's a great swap meet where you can pick up anything from a beaded necklace to a wolf-mix puppy to a bale of hay—not to mention all kinds of traditional foods. Vendors get rolling around 10am and wind things up in the mid-afternoon. To get there, head north on U.S. 491, then cut east to North 9th Street on West Jefferson Avenue.

SPORTS AND RECREATION

The city of Gallup has developed great trails on the nearby sandstone bluffs and in the ponderosa-covered Zuni Mountains. There's a lot to do in a relatively small area, and it's all still crowd-free. For additional details to what follows, see the **Adventure Gallup website** (www.adventuregallup.org), or pick up a comprehensive map from the chamber of commerce.

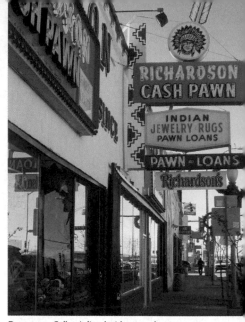
Downtown Gallup is lined with pawn shops.

Hiking

Hikers are also welcome on the High Desert and Zuni Mountain Trails, though two-wheelers have the right-of-way. In the latter area, **Strawberry Canyon Trail** is a shady, easy 1.5-mile hike up to a lookout tower, and it runs along a rough forest road, so there's room for both bikers and hikers. Follow Highway 400 past Hilso Trailhead, up to mile marker 0; just past the entrance to McGaffey Campground is a parking area on the right.

At two accessible trails close to town, you get the whole place to yourself. They both start in Red Rock Park: **Pyramid Rock Trail** is a 1.7-mile hike up to 7,487 feet, atop an aptly named butte. **Church Rock Trail** is 2.2 miles round-trip (a stem with a loop at the end)—it's less of a climb, working around the base of some dramatic rocks. An optional connector trail (1.3 miles) links the two routes, making a full hike of 3-4 hours.

Biking

The main mountain biking network is the **High Desert Trail System.** The three interconnecting loops, each rated for a different skill level, run along the mesas northwest of town. In addition to great views over cliff edges and some tricky constructed switchbacks, the trails are marked by occasional public art—so just when you think the weird rock formations are sculpture enough, you might look up to see a black steel bobcat peering down at you. The east trailhead, called Gamerco, is two miles north on U.S. 491, then left on Chino Loop; the gravel parking lot is on the left side of the road. The westside trailhead is accessible via County Road 1, just west of exit 16 from I-40.

For shady forest biking, head to the **Zuni Mountain Trail System,** a patch of national forest southeast of Gallup. From exit 33 on I-40, Highway 400 runs south about six miles to Hilso Trailhead, the beginning of several climbs up through ponderosa forests and aspens; nearly all intersect up on the ridgeline, so you can come back a different way.

In town, **Brickyard Park** (700 E. Aztec Ave.) is a mountain-bike terrain park in Gallup's old clay quarry. Come here to practice your skills on dirt tracks and jumps.

Rock Climbing

A well-maintained public park east of town, **Mentmore Rock Climbing Area** has cliff faces between 40 and 70 feet high, with scores of routes spread over six different walls, along with quite a few bouldering options. At least some of the rocks get sun all the time, so it's climbable in the winter, but check the weather before heading out. The sandstone is fragile when wet, so local policy is to stay off the rocks for a couple of days after heavy rain. To get there, take exit 16 from I-40 and head west on Highway 66 for half a mile; turn north on County Road 1, then turn west after the bridge, on Mentmore Road, and follow the road straight as it turns to dirt; this ends in the parking area.

Swimming

Gallup Aquatic Center (620 S. Boardman Ave., 505/726-5460, $4) is a kid's dream, with curvy slides galore, cactus-shaped sprinklers,

and even a "lazy river" setup; adults get a separate competition-size pool for laps. It's all indoors, but still a lot of fun.

FOOD

As with the hotels, all the chain places (and a couple of vintage diners) are near the freeway exits. You definitely get more local flavor, in every sense, if you venture into the center of town.

New Mexican

Family-owned, with a battered neon sign, ★ **Jerry's Café** (406 W. Coal Ave., 505/722-6775, 8am-9pm Mon.-Sat., $8) has a crowd of dedicated followers (read: addicts) who drive miles for the stuffed sopaipilla, drenched in superhot red-chile sauce. The place is tiny and often packed with courthouse employees during lunchtime, so go late or early.

It may not have the absolute best food in town, but **Earl's** (1400 E. Hwy. 66, 505/863-4201, 6am-8:30pm Mon.-Sat., 7:30am-6:30pm

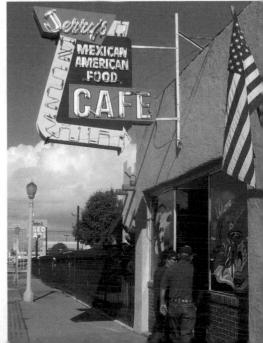

Jerry's Café is a beloved Gallup institution.

Sun., $8) has a timeless atmosphere that can't be beat. Since 1947, it has been serving biscuits and gravy, Navajo tacos, and enchiladas. It's conveniently close to the east-side freeway exit, and gets packed after the Saturday flea market. You'll either love or hate the fact that local artisans go table to table selling their wares.

If you're not staying at El Rancho, you could pop in for a perfectly good meal at the **El Rancho Restaurant** (1000 E. Hwy. 66, 505/863-9311, 6:30am-10pm daily, $11), where all the dishes are named after Hollywood stars. New Mexican food is your best bet, including *atole* (cornmeal mush) for breakfast; the margaritas ($7 for "top shelf" with fresh lime juice) are dangerously strong.

Cafés

The **Gallup Coffee Company** (203 W. Coal Ave., 505/410-2505, 7am-7pm Mon.-Thurs, 7am-8pm Fri., 8am-8pm Sat., $7) has an old tin ceiling, contemporary photography on the walls, and a mellow atmosphere where Navajo artists and fleece-clad mountain bikers mingle. Evenings often see some local singer-songwriter. The menu ranges from fresh salads and big sandwiches to a full breakfast.

With a nice small-town diner vibe, **Angela's Café** (201 E. Hwy. 66, 505/722-7526, 9am-3pm and 6pm-9pm Mon.-Fri., $9), in the cultural center in the former train station, serves burgers, big sandwiches on locally baked bread, and a good selection of craft beers to locals. Breakfasts include scones, crepes, and assorted egg dishes. In the evenings, there's occasionally acoustic music.

★ **Glenn's Bakery** (901 W. Hwy. 66, 505/722-4104, 6am-8pm Mon.-Fri., 6am-6pm Sat., $3-10) is impressive for its dazzling doughnut case, which includes wonderfully flaky cinnamon rolls. If you need more than a sugar fix, settle in alongside locals reading the morning papers for breakfast burritos, pizza, or one of the daily specials, such as lamb stew.

Aside from the fact that all burgers are served well-done, **The 505 Burgers & Wings** (1981 Hwy. 602, 505/722-9311, 11am-8pm Mon.-Fri., 11am-5pm Sat., $9) is pretty good,

with hand-cut fries, pretzel-bread buns, and nice fresh sides. And, with an almost entirely local clientele, it's a good glimpse of regular life in Gallup. Look for it in a small strip mall on the south side of town.

Middle Eastern

Anyone needing a fresher take on road food will appreciate **Aladdin Express** (1512 E. Hwy. 66, 505/863-8187, 9am-8pm Mon.-Sat., 10am-6pm Sun., $7), a Mediterranean-and-beyond restaurant tucked in the Duke City Fueling gas station. Falafel and fresh salads provide a good respite for vegetarians.

ACCOMMODATIONS

Look no further than ★ **El Rancho Hotel** (1000 E. Hwy. 66, 505/863-9311, www.elranchohotel.com, $113 d), one of the best places in New Mexico to get a taste of what tourism must've been like back when this was still the wild frontier. The lobby alone—worth a stop even if you're not planning to spend the night—is a Western fantasia of rustic wood paneling, furniture made of bull horns, a giant stone fireplace, and glossy photos of all the Hollywood actors who passed through the doors back in Gallup's heyday as a movie backdrop. (It helped that the man who built the place in 1937 was D. W. Griffith's brother.) Rooms named after Kirk Douglas, Ronald Reagan, and others are kitted out with wagon-wheel headboards and vintage bathroom tile; some even have back porches.

A separate motel wing has significantly less character but perfectly clean and functional rooms—rates here start at $60. Guests at both have access to a decent swimming pool, and there's wireless Internet access everywhere. The online booking engine doesn't show the motel rooms—just call to reserve.

INFORMATION

Conveniently located right downtown, the staff at Gallup's **chamber of commerce** (106 W. Hwy. 66, 505/722-2228, www.thegallupchamber.com, 8:30am-5pm Mon.-Fri.) can answer just about any question. Memorial

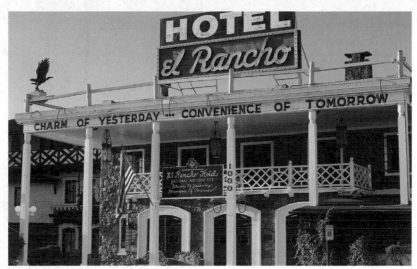

El Rancho Hotel

Day-Labor Day, it's also open 8:30am-5pm Saturday.

GETTING THERE

By car, Gallup is two hours (140 miles) west of Albuquerque on I-40, and nearly three hours (187 miles) east of Flagstaff, Arizona. From Farmington, it's a two-hour drive west, then south (120 miles).

Trains stop at Gallup's station on Highway 66 once a day, eastbound and westbound. From Albuquerque, the trip takes about 2.5 hours and costs $20, making it a pleasant option for a car-free outing. The station, which is used as the Multi-Cultural Center, is not staffed; you'll have to contact **Amtrak** (800/872-7245, www.amtrak.com) for tickets and train status.

Greyhound (800/231-2222, www.greyhound.com) serves Gallup from Albuquerque, with departures from a truck stop on the west side (3405 W. Hwy. 66, 505/863-9078) three times daily.

The truly adventurous traveler can hop a **Navajo Transit System** (928-729-4002, www.navajotransit.com) bus to head out across the whole Navajo Nation; fare is a very reasonable $2 (note that the entire system operates on Mountain Standard Time). **Gallup Express** (505/722-0777, www.gallupexpress.com) runs around town and down to Zuni Pueblo.

Navajo Nation

Covering some 27,000 square miles in New Mexico, Arizona, and Utah, the Navajo Nation is the largest reservation in the United States, and with nearly 300,000 people claiming Navajo ancestry (about 175,000 of whom live on the reservation), the Navajo are the largest tribe in the country. They call themselves Diné (The People); the term Navajo came from Tewa via the Spanish, translating as "cultivated field," for which these settled people were already well known when the conquistadors met them.

Although the reservation was granted in 1868, the Navajo Nation didn't take on its current shape until decades later, when the eastern border was expanded through a series of complex land swaps with the U.S. government—the ruins at Chaco Canyon, for instance, are on federal land but surrounded by Navajo territory. This fringy edge, where reservation land alternates with private land in carefully delineated squares, is often referred to as the Checkerboard. Some portions of the reservation, such as Ramah, near Zuni, are completely separate from the rest of the "Big Rez."

The main route through New Mexico's Navajo land is U.S. 491 north from Gallup. Until 2003, the highway was known as U.S. 666, but the Department of Transportation reportedly got sick of the chronic sign theft and changed the number. It still hasn't completely shaken its nickname, the Devil's Highway, due to regular car crashes and tales of people being attacked by "skinwalkers" (Navajo shapeshifters) along its most remote stretches.

The drive north to Shiprock is beautiful but solitary, passing only a few chapter houses (reservation administrative centers) and the occasional hogan, the traditional Navajo ceremonial building. With their straight, faceted sides, hogans resemble the cliffs that often tower above them, and their doors always face east, toward the rising sun.

The terrain shifts to a sandy pink as you head north, punctuated by the Chuska Mountains, to the west on the border with Arizona, then the occasional mesa. Finally, there is Shiprock, a dramatic spike that does look like a prow gliding through the sandy sea—or, as the Navajo see it, a "rock with wings" (Tsé Bit'a'í).

TOADLENA TRADING POST

The community of Two Grey Hills is widely considered the source of some of the finest rugs in the Navajo tradition, made of undyed wool carefully selected for its natural gray, brown, cream, and black, then woven into intricate geometric patterns rich with symbolic meaning. Some can be so thin and tightly woven, they resemble paper. The creaky old **Toadlena Trading Post** (505/789-3267, 9am-6pm Mon.-Sat., free) near Newcomb is one of the main places where Two Grey Hills

Toadlena Trading Post

rugs are sold, and in addition to exquisite work for sale, it has a museum dedicated to skilled artisans of New Mexico. The exhibit changes every two years. It's a nice excuse to drive off the highway and into the foothills of the Chuskas.

On U.S. 491, look for the Shell station around mile marker 60; head west on the paved road, about 10 miles, and follow it as it turns south through the village of Toadlena. The trading post is on a small hill, a few curves after the road turns to dirt. From there, if you have a sturdy car, you can continue on the dirt road as it heads back southeast, passing through Two Grey Hills proper, where its own **trading post** (505/789-3270, 8am-6pm Mon.-Sat.) is less artfully arranged but also holds some treasures. Look for it just past the intersection with a paved road leading north. This northbound road drops you back on the paved Toadlena road, to connect to U.S. 491.

SHIPROCK

Not to be confused with Window Rock (the Navajo Nation capital in Arizona), the town of Shiprock is the largest community in the Navajo Nation, home to a little over 8,000 people. Diné College is also here, as well as a regional hospital and a major Bureau of Indian Affairs office. Visitors won't find a lot going on, though, unless they're in town for the **flea market,** in the parking lot at the intersection of U.S. 491 and U.S. 64—it's appealing not just for the random assortment of merchandise (CDs from Navajo rock bands, as well as crafts and jewelry) but also for the seriously traditional Navajo food, such as blue-corn mush and stewed sumac. If you're staying in Farmington, the flea market is definitely worth the short drive over. There are usually a few vendors there every day (8am to 5pm), but it's biggest and most interesting on Saturday.

The big annual event is **Northern Navajo Nation Fair** (505/368-4305, www.northern-navajonationfair.org), celebrated for more than a century. It happens the first weekend in October, when there's a major powwow, the Miss Northern Navajo pageant, a free barbecue, and a fry bread cook-off, as well as the nine-day Yei Bichei dance ritual.

The rest of the time, Shiprock is as good a place as any to fill up on gas and admire the view across the San Juan River and desert plateau. In the strip mall at the intersection with U.S. 64, look for **Navajo Arts & Crafts Enterprise** (505/488-0101, 9am-8pm Mon.-Sat., noon-6pm Sun.). It may not have the charm of an old trading post, but as a project of the Navajo Nation government, it's very well priced and shows some excellent work, along with books, music, and Western wear.

Food

If you miss the **flea market,** you can get green-chile stew and fry bread tacos at **Mannings Thatsaburger** (U.S. 491, 505/368-4019, 10am-8pm daily, $7) and at **KFC** (U.S. 491, 505/368-4805, 10am-9pm Sun.-Wed., 10am-10pm Thurs.-Sat., $4). Honestly, everything is better at Mannings, but there is novelty value in subverting the fast-food establishment by marching up to the plastic KFC counter and ordering the local goods.

In the summer, keep an eye out for roadside vendors of fresh produce and "kneel down bread," fresh corn pudding steamed in corn husks.

FOUR CORNERS MONUMENT

In 2009, the **Four Corners Monument** (U.S. 160, 928/871-6647, 8am-7pm daily May-Sept., 8am-5pm daily Oct.-Apr., $5) where the state

Visit four states at once at Four Corners Monument.

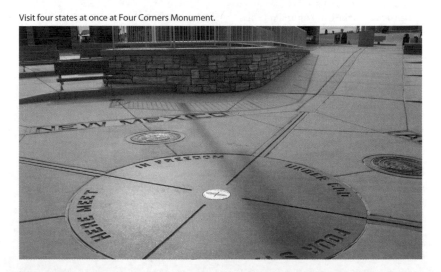

boundaries of New Mexico, Arizona, Utah, and Colorado all meet came under scrutiny, as analysis of old surveying techniques suggested that the point might be a good 2.5 miles off. But rebuttal from the National Geodetic Survey settled the matter, and the monument rests easy again. It's not much to see, though: Even after a renovation, it's recommended only for aficionados of roadside Americana, fans of Twister, and land surveyors.

It does at least provide an excuse to tour around the barren, butte-spiked lands up here, and you'll be wanting to get out and stretch your legs just about the time you pass by the entrance on U.S. 160. And what a stretch you'll get, as you put one limb in each state and pose for your travel companion's camera. There's also a gift shop, some fry bread vendors, and a short hiking trail for a view around the surrounding canyons. (And farther north on U.S. 160, just past the San Juan River, be sure to stop at the scenic overlook for another awesome view across the flatlands to Shiprock.)

Farmington

The most common base for visiting the ruins at Chaco Canyon to the south, Farmington is a pleasant enough city in its own right, tidy and filled with parks. Even though (or perhaps in part because) it's set right against the border of the Navajo Nation, Farmington has a different feel from Shiprock, at least on the surface. The largely Anglo population of 45,000 prospers from coal, oil, and natural-gas deposits, and the nearby Four Corners Power Plant is a major employer. Still, keep your radio tuned to 89.7 FM (KUUT) for Native news and music, and stop off at a good Navajo diner— you get a taste of the true cultural mix here.

Farmington's first settlers, from England, were attracted by the fertile land around the confluence of the San Juan, La Plata, and Animas Rivers (the Navajo name for the area is Tótah, "the place where the waters meet"). The first well was drilled in the 1890s—but the investor was dismayed to hit gas rather than the water he'd been looking for. The Farmington Oil & Gas Co. was established in 1906, but it wasn't until 1922 that the industry got any attention, with a wildcat well in Hogback producing crude so pure that cars could run on the stuff, no refining necessary. In the meantime, though, Farmington's growth was based on the prosperous farms and orchards in the surrounding river valley. The 1950s marked the first true oil boom, and many of the orchards were plowed under to make room for new houses; another came in the 1970s, thanks to the limited supply from overseas.

SIGHTS

The town proper has only a handful of typical attractions; pick up the *Footloose in Farmington* brochure for a walking tour of some of the nicer historic buildings downtown. The town of Aztec and the ruins there are just 30 minutes by car, so it's easy to hit the highlights in one day.

Farmington Museum

In the same building as the convention and visitors bureau, the **Farmington Museum** (3041 E. Main St., 505/599-1174, www.farmingtonmuseum.org, 8am-5pm Mon.-Sat., free) has some pretty slick exhibits, including a gee-whiz display, complete with video holograms, about the oil and gas industry—underwritten by major corporations, naturally. Once you get away from the hissing steam and chattering touch-screen games, you'll find more on Farmington's general history, as well as an interesting replica trading post and information on just how the posts' complex, usually cashless economies functioned.

B-Square Ranch

A 12,000-acre spread, **B-Square Ranch** (3901

Farmington

© AVALON TRAVEL

To
Shiprock

64

SILVER RIVER
ADOBE INN

To
BISTI/DE-NA-ZIN
WILDERNESS

371

BISTI HWY

TWIN PEAKS BLVD

LA PLATA HWY

170

La Plata River

FOUR CORNERS
REGIONAL AIRPORT

APACHE   ST

W MAIN ST

AIRPORT   DR

MUNICIPAL   DR

PIÑON HILLS BLVD

KOKOPELLI'S
CAVE

San Juan   River

MURRAY   DR

PIÑON ST

ASH-KII'S
NAVAJO GRILL

W BROADWAY   ST

ANIMAS   ST

THREE RIVERS
BREWERY

ORCHARD AVE

N COURT ST

N DUSTIN ST

BROOKSIDE
POOL

30TH   ST

CRESTRIDGE   DR

GLADE RD

TU'S
DOWNTOWN
DINER

K8
DILLON'S

312 MAIN

LA PLATA ST

CASA
BLANCA
INN

BUTLER   AVE

FARMINGTON
AQUATIC CENTER

SPARE RIB
BBQ

20TH   ST

BUTLER   AVE

REGION
INN

SCOTT   AVE

E BROADWAY   ST

San Juan Blvd

SULLIVAN AVE

PUBLIC
LIBRARY

FARMINGTON AVE

MURRAY   DR

Berg Park

Animas   River Park

HOMETOWN
HAMBURGERS

E MAIN   ST

HABANERO
GRILL

HUTTON   AVE

GLADE RUN   T

BLM OFFICE

B-SQUARE
RANCH

516

RIVERSIDE NATURE
CENTER

FARMINGTON MUSEUM/
VISITORS CENTER

COLLEGE   BLVD

30TH   ST

PIÑON HILLS BLVD

E MAIN   ST

Lions Wilderness Park

BROWNING   PKWY

64

To
Salmon Ruins
and Bloomfield

Animas   River

516

To
Aztec

FOOTHILLS DR

0   0.5 mi

0   0.5 km

Bloomfield Hwy./U.S. 64, www.bolackmuseums.com, 505/325-4275, tours by appointment only, 9am-3pm Mon.-Sat., free) is home to two of the weirdest (in a great way) museums in New Mexico. It's not the hunting trophies and electrical gizmos on display that are odd—it's the glimpse you get into the obsessive minds of the men behind them.

At the main ranch house, the **Bolack Museum of Fish & Wildlife** is the work of Tom Bolack, oilman and erstwhile lieutenant governor of New Mexico, who until his death was an outspoken environmentalist—and a passionate hunter. One-hour tours begin with Bolack's "big five" hunting trophies from Africa and carry on through a veritable menagerie of taxidermy, with thousands of specimens from all over the globe, as well as tiger-skin rugs, elephant-foot spittoons, and specimen trays of Indonesian flying lizards. And then there's the whole display of marine life, including a stuffed shark.

On the other side of the property, Tom Bolack's son, Tommy, is steadily adding to the **Bolack Electromechanical Museum,** a jumbled but awesome array of obsolete or near-obsolete technology: electric meters, radio antennae, TV cameras, a vintage DC-3, and one of Elvis's Cadillacs. The walk through the collection takes two hours and is peppered with odd information about the family and Tommy's interests, which include country music and pyrotechnics (he sets off a massive display every Fourth of July).

The ranch driveway is immediately west of Browning Parkway, running south, marked by a small sign. Make reservations for tours at least a day ahead, and at least four days ahead for a Saturday tour.

Salmon Ruins & Heritage Park

Ten miles east of Farmington, the **Salmon Ruins & Heritage Park** (6131 U.S. 64, 505/632-2013, www.salmonruins.com, 8am-5pm Mon.-Fri., 9am-5pm Sat.-Sun., $3) is not exactly the best place to contemplate the mysteries of the ancients, what with the traffic drone from the highway and the dilapidated mobile homes that clutter the view behind the 11th-century semicircular complex.

The Bolack Electromechanical Museum walks the fine line between collecting and hoarding.

But the site is intriguing for this very reason: Here, the layers of accumulated culture include the present day, as well as homesteaders' cabins and a gnarled apple orchard planted in the 19th century. And even though the area feels crowded now, you can see why the spot, next to the San Juan River and towering cottonwoods, must have appealed to each wave of settlers. The buildings from the earliest period, between 1088 and 1263 (when the place was abandoned following a major fire), were probably built by colonists from Chaco, as they use the same masonry style and a similar layout. There are more than 300 rooms in a single large block.

The "heritage park" includes the rough timber home of George Salmon, whose family helped preserve the ruins, as well as facsimile hogans, tepees, and other examples of local architecture over the millennia. The small **museum** here is also quite good, with its emphasis on tools and daily life. In the winter (Nov.-Apr.), the ruins don't open till noon on Sunday.

The **San Juan County Archaeological Research Center and Library,** based at Salmon Ruins, runs small-group tours around Chaco Canyon as well as some of the more obscure sites on Navajo land. Rates for an eight-hour outing, including a sandwich lunch, start at $350 for one or two people.

ENTERTAINMENT AND EVENTS

Farmington turns in early—if you can't find fun at the places mentioned here, there's always the mall and multiplex cinema on East Main Street, on the north side of town.

Nightlife

Your best bet for a relaxed bar scene is **Three Rivers Brewery & Tap Room** (101 E. Main St., 505/325-6605, noon-midnight daily), where most people play pool while savoring pints of the house-made Chaco Nut Brown Ale and other brews. Also downtown, **K. B. Dillon's** (101 W. Broadway, 505/325-0222, 11am-9pm Mon.-Sat.) is a bit rowdier; there's

a steakhouse attached, if you need something to soak up the beer.

Every Friday and Saturday afternoon in the summer, there's **live music** on the small square at the corner of Main Street and Orchard Avenue.

For a very mellow evening, chill out at board-game parlor **Game Changers** (217 W. Main St., 505/330-8479, 2pm-9pm Tues.-Sat., $5), which stocks some 450 games to play.

Festivals and Events

Farmington's main get-together is the **Totah Festival** (505/599-1174, www.farmingtonnm.org), a Navajo art market on Labor Day weekend. The city also hosts the **Connie Mack World Series** in August, the final contest of the youth baseball teams that aren't in the Little League.

SPORTS AND RECREATION

With three rivers and dramatic sandstone formations nearby, as well as a few in-town parks, the Farmington area is good for getting out and about. For maps, permits, fishing licenses, and more information on these and other activities, stop in at the **BLM Farmington field office** (6251 College Blvd., 505/564-7600, 8am-5pm Mon.-Fri.).

★ Bisti/De-Na-Zin Wilderness

Some 41,000 acres of barren shale hills and weird rock formations, this wilderness area is about 30 miles south of Farmington, most directly accessible by Highway 371. You have to be self-sufficient to enjoy this place—there are no marked trails, no bicycles allowed, nor groups of more than eight people. You'll find no services, water, or information at the access points. But if you can commit a few hours to a hike (or better, camp on a moonlit night), you will find it one of the more fascinating terrains in the state. It's also relatively easy to navigate, as the ravines and washes form natural paths, and the larger formations and hills are good landmarks (though definitely bring a compass).

The BLM-managed patch of land has two

access points. The **Bisti** side (36.5 miles south on Hwy. 371, then 2 miles east on gravel Road 7297, then left at the T intersection) is less than stunning when you get out of your car—you probably passed more intriguing hoodoos (wind-eroded pillars of sandstone) on the drive down. The land in front of the small parking area looks like poorly maintained pavement, and the low hills resemble mud-caked elephants. Farther off, deep-red hills are a by-product of intensely hot coal fires millions of years ago.

Walk roughly southeast about 30 minutes (two miles), and you're surrounded by precarious-looking towers of rock and undulating walls of ravines; another 1.5 hours due east from here, and you pass all of the best formations. Keep an eye out for fossils in the rocks and chunks of petrified wood on the ground.

The other access point, the **De-Na-Zin** side, is on County Road 7500, 13 miles east from Highway 371 and a little over 11 miles west of U.S. 550. The pull-off on the north side of the dirt road is marked only by a small sign that's easy to miss. Here, there's a marked trail for about three-quarters of a mile, through low scrub, to De-Na-Zin Wash.

Hiking

The relatively wild-feeling **Animas River Park** runs along the riverbank on the east side of town, with trails winding through the trees. It's a pretty place for a morning run or a sunset stroll, and the paved waterside path, dotted with picnic tables, runs a full five miles. The easiest access to this walk is at **Berg Park**, on the west bank of the river, off Scott Avenue; on the east bank, the **Riverside Nature Center** (505/599-1422, 10am-6pm Tues.-Sat., free) opens onto more trails, as well as a village of fat prairie dogs. It's also open 1pm-5pm Sunday in summer.

Mountain Biking

Local mountain bikers developed the BLM-managed **Glade Run Trail System** through the sandstone cliffs north of the city. It's the site of the venerable **Road Apple Rally** (505/599-1184, www.roadapplerally.com), which has run every October since 1981 (back then, competitors rode single-speed, fat-tire

hoodoo in Bisti Wilderness

cruisers). You can do the rally route on your own, or one of several other loops through the foothills.

It's easy to get lost in the network of single-track and dirt roads—download a map from www.4corners.info. An expert at **Cottonwood Cycles** (4370 E. Main St., 505/326-0429, 10am-6pm Mon.-Fri., 10am-5pm Sat.) should be able to get you oriented better. The Glade Run trails are also open to hikers, though bicyclists get the right-of-way.

FOOD

Meals in Farmington are rarely anything to write home about, but there are a few reliable options among the scores of fast-food outlets.

New Mexican

A rare opportunity to eat Navajo food, made by and for Navajo, the very popular **AshKii's Navajo Grill** (123 W. Broadway, 505/326-3804, 10:30am-5pm Mon.-Fri., $7) is a cheerful diner run by a family that used to sell food at flea markets. All the favorites are here, with squash stew, Navajo tacos, and mutton sandwiches. But there are a few novelties too, like the Ace pizza, topped with bits of lamb. Wash it down with Navajo tea (an herb called *cota*).

Tucked in the back of a Chevron station, **Habanero Grill** (2834 E. Main St., 505/324-9876, 6am-6pm Mon.-Sat, 8am-2pm Sun., $6) gets high marks for its made-to-order burritos.

Breakfast

For your morning macchiato, stop by **302 Main Espresso** (302 E. Main St., 505/327-2907, 7:30am-3:30pm Mon.-Fri., 8am-2pm Sat., $3), which shares a vast old lumber warehouse with an arts-and-crafts gallery. It also has a few select pastries.

For a bigger meal, head down the block to **TJ's Downtown Diner** (119 E. Main St., 505/327-5027, 5:30am-2:30pm Mon.-Fri., 6am-12:30pm Sat., $9), where specialties include the One Car Pile Up, a towering concoction of biscuits and gravy plus green chile and eggs.

Burgers and Barbecue

Farmington's favorite burgers are made in

an aptly named "pile-up" at TJ's Downtown Diner

the tiny white building that is **Hometown Hamburgers** (2133 E. Main St., 505/326-5580, 10am-10pm Mon.-Sat., 11am-6pm Sun., $5). With hand-cut fries and the option of a one-pound patty, it beats McDonald's in quality *and* quantity.

It's a little disorienting to walk into **Spare Rib BBQ** (1700 E. Main St., 505/325-4800, 11am-8pm Tues.-Sat., $9), which looks exactly like a roadside joint somewhere in the South—except the picnic tables are indoors, on carpeting. Hush puppies, sweet tea, and collard greens are all on the menu next to succulent pulled pork.

Brewhouse

In a stately old downtown block that once housed a drugstore and the daily *Times-Hustler,* the sprawling ★ **Three Rivers Brewery** (E. Main St.) takes up the better part of a block, with a bar, brewery, sit-down restaurant, and pizzeria—all with separate menus and entrances along Main Street. The main **restaurant** (101 E. Main St., 505/324-2187, 11am-9pm Mon.-Sat., noon-9pm Sun., $22), on the corner with North Orchard Street, is a lovely old tin-ceilinged room, with an original soda fountain, serving housemade root beer for kids and real beer for grownups. The menu shows a love of drink with items like the super-marinated Drunken Steak. Sandwiches are fresh-tasting items like herbed chicken salad.

Next door is the bargain **pizzeria** (107 E. Main St., 505/325-0308, 11am-10pm Sun.-Thurs., 11am-11pm Fri.-Sat., $8), where you can build your own pie with a stupendous array of toppings, from garlic-pistachio cream to homemade meatballs. From a brick oven, they're nice and crispy, and very reasonably priced. And if *that* doesn't satisfy, it also has a whole menu of New Mexican items, plus pinball and old arcade games to distract the kids.

Finally, you can toddle down to the **tap room** (113 E. Main St., 505/325-6605, noon-midnight daily) for a game of pool, or just a beer in the backyard.

Three Rivers Brewery restaurant

ACCOMMODATIONS

Many of Farmington's visitors are here for work, which creates a market for decent hotels in all price brackets—though none are particularly cheap. You will find better deals in nearby Aztec. All the chain hotels are represented, on the east and north fringes of town.

$100-150

Independent **Region Inn** (601 E. Broadway, 505/325-1191, www.theregioninn.com, $105 d) matches all the chain hotels in amenities but charges a bit less; there's free wireless Internet, and even an outdoor pool. Not far from downtown and the river walk along the Animas, the location is very convenient, and the on-site Mexican restaurant, **Tequila's,** is not bad.

If you can find it, down a precipitous little gravel road just off U.S. 64 on the west side of town, **Silver River Adobe Inn** (3151 W. Main St., 505/325-8219, www.silveradobe.

com, $115 d) makes a wonderful, natural oasis. The breakfast room, packed floor to ceiling with plants, overlooks the river, and the whole place has a pleasant, hand-built-in-the-1970s feel, complete with solar panels, as well as exposed adobe-brick walls in the two rooms and one suite.

In a quiet residential neighborhood, ★ **Casa Blanca Inn** (505 E. La Plata St., 800/550-6503, www.4cornersbandb.com, $149 d) encompasses three separate properties—humdrum split-level ranch homes on the outside, but completely transporting inside, with a tasteful and uncluttered mix of hand-carved furniture, brick and wood floors, and decorative treasures like Guatemalan bedspreads, Indian headboards, and Chinese vases. The main "hacienda" has two separate garden areas and includes the Vista Grande suite, with a wraparound sun porch. Across the street are two smaller properties, with two rooms each. Main Street is easy walking distance down the hill.

Over $150

For sheer novelty value, you can't beat **Kokopelli's Cave** (3204 Crestridge Dr., 505/860-3812, www.kokoscave.com, $280 d), a "luxury cave dwelling" in the cliffs on the north side of town. To get to your fully appointed, 1,650-square-foot home, you have to edge along a sandstone path down the side of a cliff face—so once you're in, you'll probably stay in for a night or two. But with a full kitchen, a barbecue grill, a hot tub, and a deck with a great view, you're pretty well set. Note that it's closed December-February.

INFORMATION

The **Gateway Park Visitors Center** (3041 E. Main St., 505/326-7602, www.farmingtonnm.org, 8am-5pm Mon.-Sat.), in the same building as the Farmington Museum, is the place to pick up flyers and maps, including a very detailed one published by the chamber of commerce.

GETTING THERE AND AROUND

By car, Farmington is three hours (180 miles) northwest from Albuquerque on U.S. 550 and two hours (120 miles) northeast from Gallup via U.S. 491 and Highway 371. It's a little over one hour (55 miles) south from Durango, Colorado, on U.S. 550, and just over 30 minutes east from Shiprock on U.S. 64.

Thanks to the oil and gas industry, **Four Corners Airport** (FMN), on the west side of town, receives flights from Denver and Alamosa on Great Lakes Airlines (800/554-5111, www.flygreatlakes.com). National car-rental chains have branches at the airport.

Aztec

A half-hour drive northeast from Farmington, Aztec nearly counts as a suburb. But this town of 7,000 has its own character. Its pretty restored main street is lined with brick-front shops, including a giant historical museum. Aztec became the first town in the state to use natural gas to heat homes in 1921.

SIGHTS

The scenery around here is a study in dusty tones, with white and beige rocks studded only with sagebrush and the occasional piñon tree—a stark backdrop for the Ancestral Puebloan ruins on the north side of town that are worth the visit for the great kiva alone.

Aztec Ruins National Monument

The "place by flowing waters" was misnamed Aztec by American settlers in the 19th century, who assumed people from central Mexico had established this place. **Aztec Ruins National Monument** (84 County Rd. 2900, 505/334-6174, www.nps.gov/azru,

8am-6pm daily in summer, 8am-5pm daily in winter, $5) doesn't have the dramatic setting of Chaco Canyon or Mesa Verde, but it's the best place to see Ancestral Puebloan (Anasazi) architecture if you can't make it to those more remote spots.

The main excavated area is only a portion of a larger city. When you're up on a high point looking over the surrounding ground, you'll see that the other "hills" are really unexcavated rubble. The cleaned-up **West Ruin** contains some 400 rooms, as well as a few nice details that show off the Ancestral Puebloans' knack for building. As you walk out of the visitors center and along the side wall of the great house, for instance, notice the band of green stone embedded in the wall, apparently an intentional bit of decoration. This is also a rather neat place to explore because you can go inside many of the rooms, some of which have their original ceilings: 800-year-old timber, insulated with mud-daubed twigs. The interior walls would have been plastered; some were painted as well.

But the really fascinating detail here is the fully reconstructed **great kiva,** a submerged room 40 feet across, the roof of which originally weighed 95 tons. Descending the stairs into the gloom, stepping onto the packed earth of the floor, you can easily imagine the whole community (or at least the men) gathered together for meetings and ceremonies.

Culturally, Aztec appears to have been first affiliated with Chaco Canyon; later, its construction style imitated that used at Mesa Verde in Colorado. It was occupied only for about two centuries and abandoned before 1300.

A number of burials found in the lower rooms led archaeologists to reexamine the long-held assumption that these buildings—and similar complexes at other Ancestral Puebloan sites—functioned like apartment blocks. According to that theory, lower rooms were most often used for storage. But here at Aztec, the ritually prepared bodies suggest that the rooms had a more specialized use, and that perhaps these stone buildings were

an excavated kiva at Aztec Ruins National Monument

dedicated to ceremonies and city administration, while people lived in outlying structures made of perishable materials that haven't stood the test of time.

The small **museum** addresses this issue, just one in the ever-changing field of archaeology, with a small item in one corner noting that the exhibits have yet to be updated to reflect the new ideas about the use of great houses. No matter, as the items on display are particularly interesting regardless of what theory they prop up. There's a shred of a woven reed mat, a portion of a blanket made of turkey feathers and rabbit fur, and an original ladder (rare, because they were so heavily used and usually left out in the elements), among other small comforts of life eight centuries ago.

Aztec Museum & Pioneer Village

The ultimate in small-town historical collections, the **Aztec Museum & Pioneer Village** (125 N. Main Ave., 505/334-9829, www.aztecmuseum.org, 10am-5pm Tues.-Sat. May-Sept., $5) certainly has the usual array of old telephone switchboards, vintage eyeglasses, and farming implements—but it has an enormous number of them, all obsessively laid out in what seems like an endless series of rooms. Then there's a beautiful "cyclorama," a huge, meticulously carved rotating diorama of Wild West scenery, as well as an annex devoted to gas-drilling history, including an unnerving exhibit on a nuclear fracking program in the late 1960s.

And finally, when you thought you were done browsing through the complete interior of an old barbershop and the large gun room, you go outside to find . . . an entire town. Set in orderly rows, all the usual Old West establishments are there, built at a slightly smaller scale: the sheriff's office, the one-room schoolhouse, the general store, the village doctor, even the church, which in this case was a real building from a nearby community that was moved here and scaled down to fit with the others. And of course, each building is kitted out with period-specific knickknacks.

SPORTS AND RECREATION

The mountain biking and hiking trail called **Alien Run** traces a route up Hart Canyon, past the site of an alleged UFO crash. It's a scenic bit of single-track, with a few patches of slick sandstone. There are 5-, 9-, and 16-mile routes, and about four miles in, a plaque marks the site where in 1948 the remnants of a 100-foot-wide disc were spotted, along with dead creatures resembling small humans. According to locals, the crash was swiftly followed by heavy-breathing military reps who whisked all the evidence away—though apparently the site does register a slightly abnormal amount of radiation. To reach the trailhead, take U.S. 550 north four miles, then turn right on County Road 2770. Follow this three miles to a left turn, then it's half a mile up a hill and a right turn; the parking area is on the left. There's an annual **bike race** (www.alienrun.com) on the trail in early May, and **Cottonwood Cycles** (200 S. Main Ave., 505/334-2703, 10am-6pm Mon.-Fri., noon-5pm Sat.) can provide advice and gear.

FOOD AND ACCOMMODATIONS

The Bistro (122 N. Main Ave., 505/334-0109, 7am-2:30pm Mon.-Fri., 8am-noon Sat., $8) is across the street from the Aztec Museum. It offers good strong coffee, homemade pastries, and quiche. Much beloved local Thai restaurant **ThanThip** (104 S. Main Ave., 505/334-1234, 11am-9pm daily, $10) does good curries and other standards.

At the **Step Back Inn** (103 W. Aztec Blvd., 505/334-1200, www.stepbackinn.com, $98 d), the rooms nod to the past with Victorian-style armoires and reproduction wallpaper; you get homemade cinnamon rolls at breakfast. For those on a budget, the motel-style

Enchantment Inn (1800 W. Aztec Blvd., 505/334-6143, $58 s, $65 d) is an exceptionally great deal. It looks a little bare-bones outside, but the rooms are modern, solidly built, and clean, and there's even a pool.

INFORMATION

The **Aztec Welcome Center** (110 N. Ash St., www.aztecchamber.com, 505/334-9551, 8am-5pm Mon.-Fri.), run by the chamber of commerce, can answer all pressing questions.

GETTING THERE

Aztec is 16 miles (30 minutes) northeast of Farmington via Highway 516, and 9 miles (15 minutes) north of Bloomfield on U.S. 550.

Bloomfield

The town of Bloomfield, at the intersection of U.S. 64 and U.S. 550, is about the same size as Aztec but doesn't really present any strong reason for visitors to stop. It's the gateway to the best state park in the region, though.

ANGEL PEAK SCENIC AREA

Think of **Angel Peak Scenic Area** (free) as the cheater's version of Bisti/De-Na-Zin—a great place to take in northwestern New Mexico's unique geology, from the comfort of your car. The area gives you the big picture, down into a dramatic expanse of striated sandstone, rather than the ground-level view you get at Bisti. The landscape of peaks and pinnacles, carved by ancient rivers and millennia of wind, is a short drive south of Bloomfield, accessible by a road winding along the canyon edge for about six miles. Each turn yields new photo-worthy vistas; you'll also find several sets of picnic shelters. At the end of the road is a tidy primitive **campground** (no water) with nine sites. From U.S. 550, 15 miles south of Bloomfield, turn east on County Road 7175.

NAVAJO LAKE STATE PARK

Approaching **Navajo Lake State Park** (36 Road 4110, 505/632-2278, www.nmparks.com,

$5/car), Highway 539 crosses the dam itself in an unnerving, guardrail-free swoop. The lake is the second largest in the state (after Elephant Butte), its 15,500 acres of water stretching like fingers up into Colorado. The glassy surface reflects the sky and year-round snow on the Rocky Mountains to the north. The main access point (of three) is **Pine Site,** just across the dam on Highway 511, with a visitors center and a large developed **campground** ($10, $14 with electric) that has great views over the lake, although it's somewhat removed from the water's edge. This entrance also leads to the main **marina,** offering houseboat rentals and a snack bar. This area can get pretty packed in the summertime, but the shoulder seasons can be beautifully empty. The alternate access to the lake is at **Sims Mesa Site,** on the east side via Highway 527, which has a significantly smaller camping area and can be a little quieter in high season.

Fishing

The park encompasses a portion of the San Juan River that's renowned for its fishing: rainbow, cutthroat, and brown trout, as well as kokanee salmon and largemouth bass. The San Juan's "quality waters," as they're called, have special regulations: The first quarter mile after the dam is catch-and-release only, and in the next 3.5 miles, you may use only the view into the canyon at Angel Peak Scenic Area

flies with a single barbless hook, and keep only one fish of 20 inches or more. There are pull-offs for riverbank access all along Highway 511. On the opposite bank (reached via Road 4280 off Highway 173) is pretty, tree-shaded **Cottonwood Campground,** with nearly 50 sites. You can pick up a fishing license at any of the lodges and guide shops in the community of Navajo Dam, at the junction of Highways 173 and 511.

SIMON CANYON

Technically not part of Navajo Lake State Park but accessible by the same road as Cottonwood Campground, **Simon Canyon** is BLM land that has been labeled an "area of critical environmental concern," due to the presence of golden eagles, prairie falcons, and other treasured species. Use is restricted to hikers and anglers, and the trails are not

frequently used. The main route, up through the canyon that runs due north where Road 4280 dead-ends, also passes a Navajo defensive fort, built in the 18th century on a pillar of rock.

ACCOMMODATIONS

The very well-kept **Best Western Territorial Inn & Suites** (415 S. Bloomfield Blvd., 505/632-9100, www.bestwestern.com, $105 d) is the closest you can stay to Chaco Canyon without camping.

Just east of the last turn to Navajo Lake from U.S. 64, **The Monastery of Our Lady of the Desert** (10258 U.S. 64, 505/419-2938, www.ourladyofthedesert.org, $50 pp) has four spare, newly built retreat rooms. Guests are also given meals. The price is a suggested donation, and guests are encouraged to do some light chores.

Chaco Culture National Historical Park

State politicians make periodic threats to pave the two rutted access roads to **Chaco Culture National Historical Park** (505/786-7014, www.nps.gov/chcu, 7am-sunset, $20/car, good for seven days), but fortunately this has not yet come to pass. Much of the appeal of Chaco is its location in a valley that has remained relatively untouched since the Ancestral Puebloans (Anasazi) departed sometime in the 13th century. The long, bumpy ride to this hidden valley gives you time to get into the right frame of mind—you're turning back the calendar 800 years as you drive.

Arriving via the northern route, you first see Chaco through a small pass in the reddish rocks, with the striking Fajada Butte directly in front of you. The long valley, bordered with sheer cliff faces, was once home to more than 6,000 people, and now just you and the other visitors who made the drive are there to appreciate the ruins.

HISTORY

The first people to settle in Chaco Canyon arrived sometime between 5,000 and 10,000 years ago, but a distinctive Chacoan culture (also called Anasazi and Ancestral Puebloan) only developed around AD 850. In an arid valley with a harsh climate and very little water, the people of Chaco worked extremely hard to build a society that supported thousands of residents and spread its influence all over the region.

Aerial surveys done in the 1980s revealed a network of roads connecting the settlements here with some 150 outlying communities, farms, and forests where timber was gathered. The roads were perfectly straight (even going up and over cliffs and mesas, rather than around) and up to 30 feet wide—a great deal of effort for a culture that did not have wheels or beasts of burden. Chaco was at the center of a sophisticated trade network, as shown by the tropical bird feathers, baby macaw skeletons, copper bells, and seashells, all from Mexico, that have been uncovered here. It is also likely that the people who lived here were from many different tribes and bands, rather than a single distinct culture—this would explain how today's Pueblo people, who all claim ancestry from here, speak a number of languages.

Far more impressive is the Chacoans' knack for large-scale construction, often taking into account solar and lunar alignments. They developed the **"core and veneer"** style of building, in which walls consisted of an inner mass of rubble faced with thin panels of sandstone, which had been chipped from the surrounding cliffs. With this sturdy technique,

Chaco Canyon

Chaco Culture National Historical Park

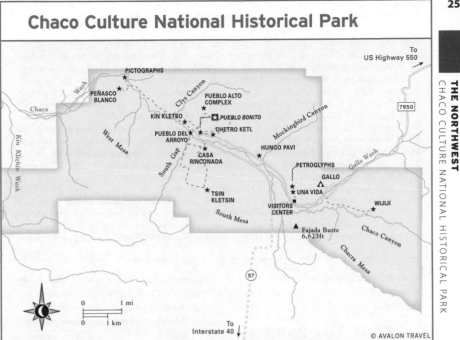

To
US Highway 550

PICTOGRAPHS

PEÑASCO
BLANCO

Chaco

Wash

Clys Canyon

PUEBLO ALTO
COMPLEX

7950

KIN KLETSO

⊞ PUEBLO BONITO

Mockingbird Canyon

West Mesa

PUEBLO DEL
ARROYO

CHETRO KETL

Kin Klizhin Wash

CASA
RINCONADA

HUNGO PAVI

South Gap

PETROGLYPHS

Gallo Wash

GALLO
∧

TSIN
KLETSIN

UNA VIDA

WIJIJI

VISITORS
CENTER

South Mesa

▲ Fajada Butte
6,623ft

Chaco Canyon

Chacra Mesa

0   1 mi

0   1 km

To
Interstate 40

57

© AVALON TRAVEL

they raised the ceremonial complexes we now call **great houses,** which could be up to five stories tall. That the walls are thickest on the first floors, then taper at each subsequent level, suggests that the Chacoans had planned the construction before setting out, even though the growth of the largest great houses, such as Pueblo Bonito, took place over a couple of centuries.

Chacoan ceilings were another durable innovation. They were made of layers of wood stacked at right angles: First, whole tree trunks (which were dried before use, to reduce their weight), then thinner, stripped poles, then twigs, then scraps of juniper bark, all smoothed over with a layer of plaster. Many of these roofs survive, nearly a thousand years later—even more impressive when you consider that most wood had to be carried in from the Chuska Mountains, 50 miles west.

The Chacoans' sophistication is also evident in the **"sun daggers"** discovered at the top of Fajada Butte. There, three rocks are positioned to allow light to fall in a particular pattern on a spiral drawn on a boulder behind. The sun falls on it differently according to the time of year. On the summer solstice, a dagger of light shone through the rocks directly across the center of the spiral; on the winter solstice, two daggers framed the spiral; and on the equinoxes, a smaller dagger of light marked a smaller spiral off to one side. The cycles of the moon are also reflected in shadows. Unfortunately, the rocks shifted in recent years, in part due to visitors wearing away the dirt at their base, and the daggers are no longer aligned; the butte is now closed off.

The pace of construction slowed in the 12th century, and by 1300 or so, the canyon seems to have been empty, and the Chacoans dispersed, some to what is now Hopi territory in Arizona, some south to Zuni, others to the Rio Grande pueblos. No one has determined for certain whether the migration was due to environmental degradation, attacks from outside, or some other factor, and every new

The Anasazi and the Cannibalism Debate

The popular conception of the Ancestral Puebloans (previously known as the Anasazi) has been of a peaceful, egalitarian society based on agriculture. But a theory advanced by physical anthropologist Christy Turner suggests the Pueblo Indians might be better off disavowing their ancestors. In his 1999 book *Man Corn: Cannibalism and Violence in the Prehistoric American Southwest*, Turner proposed that the Anasazi culture was a violent one obsessed with ritual consumption of human flesh. Granted, the cannibalism could have been introduced by a Mexican culture, perhaps the Toltecs, and used against the Anasazi as a means of terrorizing them. In any case, his theory proposed an answer to a nagging question: What about all those piles of mangled human bones and fire-blackened skulls found at Chaco Canyon, Mesa Verde, and other Anasazi sites?

Many of Turner's colleagues were skeptical, if not downright shocked, and Pueblo Indians were, and still are, outraged at the accusations about their people. Turner and other archaeologists were banned from excavations in Mesa Verde. In the years since Turner published *Man Corn*, however, evidence to support his theory seems to have grown. For instance, other researchers found coprolites (preserved human feces) that tested positive for human proteins. Turner died in 2013, with the cannibalism issue still unanswered. Regardless, the evidence he uncovered does create a bleak and violent picture of life in what today appear to be peaceful valleys and canyons.

archaeological discovery seems to open up more possibilities, rather than confirm any one theory.

VISITING THE PARK

This is one of New Mexico's greatest treasures, as well as a UNESCO World Heritage Site. Even if you're not a big fan of ruins, the remote setting makes the place well worth the drive for an afternoon visit. If you're intrigued by ancient culture or wildlife, then you may want to allot several days, pitching a tent at the campground near the entrance to the valley. And regardless of how long you stay, don't burn yourself out following trail guides or hitting all the spots on a map. Better to spend time in one quiet spot, listening to the rush of ravens' wings, the whisper of the breeze, and the other subtle sounds of this now-empty place.

Visitors Center

Stop first at the **visitors center** (505/786-7014, 8am-5pm daily) to pay the entrance fee, pick up a map, find out what birds and animals have been spotted recently, and get a free backcountry permit if you think you'll be hiking. You can also join a ranger-led tour of Pueblo Bonito (free). If your schedule allows,

time your visit with a **Chaco Night Sky Program,** a stargazing event three nights a week April-October that takes advantage of Chaco's location, more than 75 miles from any population center. Visitors can peer through a number of high-powered telescopes, and the sky positively glitters at night.

Una Vida

The small **Una Vida** ruins, accessible via a 1.6-mile trail behind the visitors center, represent the earlier phase of great-house building in Chaco, begun around 850. They're worth a quick look, if only to see how an unexcavated (yet well-preserved) site differs from one where all the debris has been cleared. Blowing sand has gradually accumulated, just as the walls have slowly crumbled. You can see evidence of later occupation, probably by shepherds in the 19th century—the slabs of stone have been freshly piled up, in a different style from the original building. If you follow the trail behind the ruins, you'll see a few petroglyphs chiseled into the rock.

Camping

Before you reach the visitors center, **Gallo Campground** offers 49 sites (877-444-6777, www.recreation.gov, $15), water, restrooms, and a dump station for RVs. The closest hotels, all about a two-hour drive, are in Bloomfield and Farmington north on U.S. 550; Cuba, southeast on U.S. 550; and in Grants on I-40 to the south.

Note that **no food is available in the park**—no café, restaurant, or shop. You must stock up in Cuba, Farmington, or Grants.

CANYON LOOP DRIVE

A nine-mile one-way loop runs up to the northwest end of the canyon and back, with parking areas near each great house.

Hungo Pavi

Like Una Vida, **Hungo Pavi** is one of the earlier complexes in the valley, built between 940 and 1040; also like the other ruins, it's largely unexcavated. If you're short on time, you can easily skip this, though the gentle curve of the back wall and the numerous tiny windows in it are rather striking.

Chetro Ketl

The defining element of **Chetro Ketl**, built over a century beginning around 1010, is its huge raised plaza. The elevated platform, some 12 feet high, required tons of packed earth and stone in its construction. With more than 500 rooms, it's the second-largest great house in Chaco. It also displays a long colonnaded wall—a very rare style in this region, and perhaps an idea borrowed from Paquimé, in northern Mexico, a city with which the Chacoans are known to have traded. You can also walk from Chetro Ketl to Pueblo Bonito (the next stop on the ruins road), along a flat, quarter-mile trail that passes clusters of petroglyphs on the canyon wall.

★ Pueblo Bonito

The largest complex in the canyon and the pinnacle of Chacoan engineering, **Pueblo Bonito** is thought to be the ceremonial heart of the ancient community. It began in the mid-800s as a sliver of an arc, a few rooms deep, and by the 12th century grew into a compound with more than 600 rooms, at least 30 kivas, and walls up to five stories tall in some sections. Roads lead straight to it from every smaller settlement in the area. The various masonry styles used in construction make

Pueblo Bonito at the Chaco Culture National Historical Park

it clear where the various phases begin and end, and where, for instance, an old wall and a new one converge to enlarge the arc. In some sections, the masonry is as regular as brick; in others, you can see where worn stone has been reused.

The 0.6-mile trail leads first through an alarming array of sandstone boulders that seem to have just yesterday tumbled down from the cliff above. (In fact, they fell in 1941, crushing part of the compound.) The route then continues through the Pueblo Bonito complex, including some of the enclosed rooms, but it is hard to get a true sense of the scale of the place from the ground. If you have time and energy, hike to the mesa top via the Pueblo Alto trail.

Wetherill Cemetery

One of the few relics in this valley from a more recent era, the tiny **Wetherill Cemetery** near the end of the ruins road (look for a trail from Pueblo Bonito) is easily overlooked. It is the final resting place of Richard Wetherill, a Colorado rancher turned profiteering archaeologist. He was the first to bring Cliff Palace at Mesa Verde to national attention, and in 1896, the American Museum of Natural History hired him to dig up relics at Chaco Canyon. Wetherill is also credited with being the first to apply the name Anasazi to the people who inhabited the Four Corners area between the 9th and 12th centuries.

At that time, archaeology was only just developing as a science, and many academics in the field saw Wetherill—who worked on his own, removing pots and other valuable items as he pleased—as a threat to the accurate study of these ancient places. It was irrelevant that Wetherill was often far more knowledgeable about the area and the culture than they were. Wetherill was disparaged as a "pot-hunter," and the Antiquities Act of 1906 was devised to designate national monuments and keep people like him out—Wetherill had actually staked a homestead claim on the land around Pueblo Bonito. He was operating a trading post there when he was shot and killed by a Navajo man in 1910. His wife, Marietta, is also buried here, along with several unnamed Navajo.

Pueblo del Arroyo

This is a beautiful spot in spring or summer during the rains, when the tall cottonwoods are thick from the water in the wash that gives **Pueblo del Arroyo** its name. The large, rounded stones used in many of the rooms indicate a slightly later construction than Pueblo Bonito and Chetro Ketl, which are built of the thin, regular, sharp-edged slabs that were easily collected from the mesa top. This stone was eventually used up, forcing a switch to the rounder, more irregular stone found here. For the most part erected in the early 12th century, the complex also displays some of the "tri-wall" construction that is more common in Mesa Verde.

Kin Kletso

If you've been noting the different styles of masonry throughout the various great houses, then you should also stop at **Kin Kletso**, at the far north end of the road, and a short walk from the parking lot. It displays the clearest example of what's dubbed the McElmo style of masonry (after the McElmo Valley in Colorado), associated with Mesa Verde. Its presence in Chaco Canyon is taken as an indication that the two communities were in regular contact (although now archaeologists debate who influenced whom). Whereas the best Chacoan stone walls incorporate thick rubble cores and exceptionally regular facing stones, McElmo masonry is characterized by a relatively thin rubble core and the use of large, rounded pieces of sandstone on the surface, chinked with tiny, irregular bits of rock. It was first used at Chaco in the early 1100s.

Casa Rinconada

Relatively isolated from the other great

the ruins of Kin Kletso at Chaco Culture National Historical Park

houses, **Casa Rinconada** is an enormous great kiva, meant to hold hundreds of people. Unlike other kivas, it stands alone, rather than as part of a larger complex, and it is aligned on a north-south axis with the great house of New Alto, on the opposite mesa top. It displays all the signature elements, from the wall niches to the two raised floor vaults, which may have been topped with wood to create large drums.

To visit just the kiva, bear right at the fork in the trail shortly after it begins. The trail then loops south, past a number of small villages, similar to the great houses, but on a much more limited scale. The oral histories of the contemporary Pueblo people—Zuni, Acoma, Hopi, etc.—all refer to Chaco Canyon as their ancestors' home; however, the Puebloans represent such a variety of languages and traditions that Chaco must have been home to a mix of peoples even then. Some archaeologists have proposed that these distinct villages near Casa Rinconada were inhabited by one of the different peoples.

HIKING

For all the longer hikes, you must have a permit, available from the visitors center, or, if you're indecisive, at the trailhead. There's no additional fee for the permit, and no limit on numbers—this is just a way for rangers to keep track of who's out in the wilderness.

Pueblo Alto

This 4.4-mile loop hike, which runs off the north end of the valley from behind Kin Kletso (park at Pueblo del Arroyo), is definitely the most worthwhile of the day hikes, as long as you can handle the first clamber up the cliff face to the canyon rim. From here, it's a level walk back along the mesa top to a point where you can peer down on Pueblo Bonito—the geometry of the buildings and the successive layers of development all pop into focus from this perspective. You can backtrack from the Pueblo Bonito overlook, which makes for a 2-mile hike, or carry on to the **Pueblo Alto Complex site.** The trail then passes by stairs and ramps the Anasazi carved in the cliffs, through a slot canyon, and back up to the mesa edge for a view over Chetro Ketl. You finish by climbing back down the same route to Kin Kletso. Allow between three and four hours for the full hike.

Peñasco Blanco

From the Pueblo de Arroyo parking lot at the north end of the ruins road, this longer out-and-back leads to seldom-visited Chacoan and Navajo petroglyphs (rock carvings) and pictographs (paintings on the rock), and the unexcavated ruins of **Peñasco Blanco,** the third-largest great house in the canyon, with a unique oval layout. It's a bit of a drab hike just for this, but mostly level. The first batch of pictographs is 1.8 miles in. The whole hike, 7.4 miles round-trip, will take between four and six hours; it can be especially tiring due to the sandy ground along most of the route.

South Mesa

Parts of this 3.6-mile loop follow some old Chacoan roads, from near Casa Rinconada on the west side of the canyon to the unexcavated great house **Tsin Kletsin,** which appears to have been used as a lookout and signal post, as the view from its main kiva has sightlines to six other great houses. The trail first rises to the mesa top, about 450 feet, then descends through South Gap via one of the ancient roads. The full trip can take up to four hours, or you can just hike up to Tsin Kletsin and back in about two.

Wijiji

A perfectly flat hike (also accessible to bicyclists), this trail leads 1.5 miles through a natural wash to a **great house** from AD 1100. It's a piece of wholly planned architecture, apparently built in a single phase, unlike the other great houses in the area. Though relatively small, it is exceptional for its symmetry. Allow 2-3 hours.

PUEBLO PINTADO

A separate, unexcavated great house about 20 miles southeast of Chaco and technically part of the same park, **Pueblo Pintado** is recommended for completists only. If you come here after an extensive visit to Chaco, you will almost certainly wonder why you made the drive; however, if you happen to be going to nearby Crownpoint for the rug auction, then you might want to stop in.

GETTING THERE

The only way to reach Chaco is by car, and you should allow ample time for the drive—at least two hours from Farmington, Cuba, or Grants. There are two approaches: the better-used northern route from U.S. 550 and the often bumpier southern route, up from I-40. Some maps and GPS devices suggest that Highway 57 provides access to Chaco Canyon on the north side. It does not.

The **northern** route is from U.S. 550 near Nageezi, onto County Road 7900, which is paved. After eight miles you turn onto the smaller County Road 7950 (well signed), and the paving gives out. The full drive is 21 miles and takes no more than 45 minutes when conditions are good.

From the **south,** the approach is via paved Highway 371 from Thoreau and Highway 9, then 20 miles on dirt Highway 57. But you'll want a high-clearance vehicle, and patience—the top practical speed on this bumpy road is 35 miles per hour at best. Call ahead (505/786-7014) to check conditions before taking this route.

U.S. 550 South to Bernalillo

The drive back south to the Albuquerque area is a scenic one, with a couple of possible stops in some lesser-visited wilderness areas.

THE BLACK PLACE

Fans of Georgia O'Keeffe may recognize the **gray-black hills** hills along U.S. 550, about two miles south of the junction with County Road 7900 (the turn to Chaco). Off either side of the road around mile marker 111 are shadowy arroyos, hollowed-out cliffs, and silvery buttes, just ripe for abstract painting.

CUBA

Forty-eight miles south of the turn to Chaco Canyon (County Road 7900), Cuba is a very small settlement, founded in the late 18th century, where you can get a good meal and a good deal on a bed.

Food

Cuba's Hispano roots have yielded the exemplary ★ **El Bruno's** (6449 Main St., 575/289-9429, 11am-10pm daily, $12), where every fall a team of women hand-preps all the green chile the restaurant will use for the rest of the year. In this season, you can order a bowl of "Hazel's green chile," which is really just a bowl of the stuff, barely seasoned with pork and tomato. The rest of the year, the chile works its way into stuffed sopaipillas, tamales, and a Cubita sandwich (a play on the classic ham-and-Swiss-cheese *cubano*). There are occasional reports of bad meals, but when it's good, it's great—and you can't really argue, as it's one of the few restaurants for miles around.

For a great to-go meal, **Chaco Grill** (6454 Main St., 575/289-0338, 8am-10pm daily, $4), at the gas station where the road curves northwest, does excellent tamales, fry bread, and burritos—its basic bean-and-chicharron is a great amalgam of creamy, spicy, and crunchy.

You may recognize the Black Place from Georgia O'Keeffe's paintings.

Accommodations

Cuba is a handy place to sleep before or after visiting Chaco Canyon. On the north side of town, the **Frontier Motel** (6474 Main St., 575/289-3474, $63 s, $74 d) is a bargain, and its 33 rooms (in two complexes, across the road from each other) were last renovated in 2013. Families will like the two-bedroom suite with a kitchen. If the Frontier is full, the next best option is **Cuban Lodge** (6332 U.S. 550, 575/289-3269, $65 d), on the south edge of town. It shows its age, but it is clean and has very nice management; discounts are available for Continental Divide Trail hikers.

If you don't mind a bit more winding driving, then the B&B **Sueños Encantados** (off County Rd. 11, 575/289-3327, www.suenos-encantados.com, $80 d) makes a lovely rural retreat, out on an old adobe homestead about 6.5 miles off U.S. 550, just south of Cuba. To-go lunches are an option, nice if you're headed to Chaco.

Another neat remote option, especially good for groups or families, is **Chaco Lodge Hacienda** (200 Nacimiento Rd., 505/252-7488, www.chacolodgehacienda.com, $140 d), a private two-bedroom home about 30 minutes' drive southeast of Cuba.

CABEZON PEAK

West of U.S. 550, this 2,000-foot-tall "big head" butte is popular for **rock climbing,** or you can **hike** up to the peak for a view as far as Mount Taylor. According to Navajo legend, Mount Taylor represents a slaughtered giant whose head rolled to form Cabezon, while his blood settled into El Malpais. To reach the trailhead, turn west off U.S. 550 at County Road 279, about 20 miles north of San Ysidro. Then go 12 miles southwest to BLM Road 1114, which leads to the parking area in 3 miles.

OJITO WILDERNESS

These badlands were designated the **Ojito Wilderness** in late 2005. Two trails now loop through the terrain of stark, striped red hills, scored by rivulets of glittering white gypsum—not quite as dramatic as Bisti/De-Na-Zin, but also not as remote. The partial skeleton of the herbivore *Seismosaurus* was discovered here in 1979, and one trail leads to that canyon, where you may spot other fossils in the walls. A second trail leads into the most picturesque section of hoodoos. From U.S. 550, turn onto Cabezon Road (County Road 26), south of San Ysidro, then bear left at the fork—the trailhead for Seismosaurus Trail is 10 miles in, on the left; Hoodoo Trail starts 11 miles on, also on the left.

On the way to Ojito (about 4 miles down Cabezon Road), you pass gray gypsum hills that are traced by **White Ridge Bike Trails,** 15 miles of single- and double-track. The system runs in two concentric loops. About a third of it, the "Dragon's Back" section, is exceptionally challenging, while the rest is fairly accessible to all riders. Although the trails were laid out for two-wheelers (and a stretch for horses), they're also open to hikers.

Both Ojito and Cabezon are managed by the **BLM Rio Puerco field office** in Albuquerque (100 Sun Ave. NE, 505/761-8700).

Las Cruces and the Southwest

South from Albuquerque 266

Socorro and the
  Plains of San Agustín 267

El Camino Real 272

Truth or Consequences 274

The Geronimo Trail 281

Mesilla Valley 285

Las Cruces 287

West to the Bootheel 298

Silver City 307

Trail of the Mountain Spirits.... 312

Gila National Forest 316

Look for ★ to find recommended
sights, activities, dining, and lodging.

Highlights

★ **The Very Large Array:** Studding the plains west of Socorro, 27 giant radio telescopes look into deep space. You can see them up close for free at the operation's visitors center (page 270).

★*The Lightning Field:* An equally innovative, yet completely different, use of these central plains, Walter de Maria's mesmerizing sculpture requires a long drive and a 24-hour time commitment (page 272).

★ **Bosque del Apache National Wildlife Refuge:** Some of the best birdwatching in the state happens on these wetlands near the Rio Grande. Time your visit with the arrival of the sandhill cranes in October (page 272).

★ **New Mexico Farm & Ranch Heritage Museum:** Ancient tractors, actual livestock, and crafts demonstrations are among the attractions at this vast museum that tells the history of New Mexico in a practical yet fascinating way (page 290).

★ **Gila Cliff Dwellings National Monument:** The cliffside ruins are not too striking, but they're a good starting destination within the immense Gila Wilderness, the state's largest (page 313).

South from Albuquerque along I-25, the New Mexican landscape is dramatically split between the stark, scrubby Chihuahuan Desert and the lush green of the Rio Grande valley.

At the wildlife sanctuary in the Bosque del Apache, the river nurtures migratory birds, such as sandhill cranes. Elsewhere it feeds alfalfa fields, pecan orchards, and acre upon acre of green chile. The town of Hatch, which lends its name to the state's favorite chile variety, turns out tons of the stuff every year. And, appropriately, in the city of Las Cruces, New Mexico State University is known for its agriculture program.

But beyond the reach of irrigation, the Chihuahuan Desert is the largest in North America, beginning around Socorro and stretching south all the way to Zacatecas in Mexico. From a car window, the view can be monotonous and dreary—no wonder Spaniards along the Camino Real trade route called this waterless stretch the Jornada del Muerto (Dead Man's Trail). Up close, though, the terrain is studded with a surprising variety of yucca and cactus, as well as roadrunners, jackrabbits, and coyotes. And

when the scenery does shift, as in the Florida Mountains near Deming or at the strange outcroppings called the City of Rocks, it is all the more striking in this barren expanse.

Farther west rise the mountain ranges of the Continental Divide, where the ancient Mogollon people made their home—you can see their living spaces at the Gila Cliff Dwellings. Elsewhere in the Gila Wilderness, the largest reserve in the state, are remnants of the phenomenal, if short-lived, mining boom of the late 19th century. Silver City, on the southern edge of the Gila, has held up quite well, and now harbors a laid-back creative community that holds "Carpe mañana" as its unofficial motto.

Along the north side of the Gila Wilderness, the mountains level onto the Plains of San Agustín, a great empty bowl dotted with herds of pronghorn—as well as the giant white radio telescopes that make up the Very Large Array, a major space research center. This is ranch land, with an independent ethos held over

Previous: ocotillo bloom in front of the Florida Mountains near Deming; Gila Cliff Dwellings National Monument. **Above:** church in Palomas, on the Mexico side of the border.

Las Cruces and the Southwest

from the rough-and-tumble mining days and range wars. Landowners in Catron County are required by law to carry a gun, and it's not uncommon to see folks swaggering around with full hip holsters. But even the most weather-beaten Westerner will sweeten up in Pie Town, where, just as you'd hope, you can get a fresh slice of America's favorite dessert.

HISTORY

This corner of New Mexico saw the first extensive human habitation in the American Southwest, with the Mogollon (moh-gui-YONE) and Mimbres cultures (named for the places in which relics of their culture were first discovered) settling here around AD 700. With the exception of the late-era Gila Cliff Dwellings and the remnants of a few pit houses, however, these ancient people left few traces. Around 1300, about the same time that the Ancestral Puebloans (Anasazi) left Chaco and Bandelier, the Mogollon abandoned their territory, for reasons that are still not clear. Presumably they moved east to the Rio Grande to meld with and expand the Pueblo culture that had just started there.

They were replaced (or perhaps edged out) by the Apache, a nomadic people spread across what's now Arizona, New Mexico, and northern Mexico. The Chiricahua and the Mimbres bands ranged over what's now the Gila Wilderness. Geronimo, the best-known Apache, said he was born on the Gila River in 1829. Their raiding culture put them at odds with the Mexican government, then the American one, which was keen to protect the gold miners who'd arrived in the new territory in the 1850s.

The U.S. Army was soon engaged in a small-scale war with the most tenacious Apache leaders, such as Cochise, Victorio, the woman fighter Lozen, and Mangas Coloradas (Red Sleeves). Instrumental in the fight was the African American cavalry, better known as the Buffalo Soldiers; they also helped build many of the forts in southern New Mexico. In the meantime, Apache women and children were being forced onto trains and resettled as far away as Florida and Alabama; the Chiricahua were the only American Indians who were not granted a reservation.

Geronimo finally surrendered in 1886, but violence continued. The mining boomtowns (now focused on silver) that sprang up were brutal, lawless places. The towns faded rapidly when silver currency was replaced with the gold standard in 1893. Meanwhile, south of the mountains, the growing cattle-ranching industry had its own share of vicious infighting, which consumed big businessmen, mercenary cattle rustlers, hit men, and every politician in the southern flatlands; assassinations were not uncommon. And the small town of Columbus, on the border with Mexico, was all but demolished by Pancho Villa in a 1916 raid.

These early battles have moved to the courtroom, where preservationists face off against cattle ranchers. Citing the long-term damage caused by overgrazing, environmentalists have successfully sued to take more wilderness acreage out of ranchers' control. Long-standing debates—over reintroduction of the Mexican gray wolf, for instance—have yet to be resolved, making the contrast all the more stark between deep-rooted families who've lived on and worked the land for generations and transplants who've moved here for the natural beauty.

PLANNING YOUR TIME

Given the driving distances, it's difficult to visit New Mexico's southwest if you're also interested in Santa Fe or other northern destinations. You're better off focusing on this area exclusively, perhaps even flying in to El Paso and working your way north, rather than driving down from Albuquerque. You can lounge around Truth or Consequences for a couple of days, and Las Cruces and Silver City both merit a long weekend, though you could get the spirit of each place in a day. What will interest most visitors is the Gila Wilderness, where hiking and relaxing in hot springs can occupy a day or a week.

Relatively speaking, the plains west of

Socorro hold less appeal, but it's nice to at least cruise through this ranching area if you can (and it does complete a logical driving loop), as it's a sharp contrast to the hippie-holdover outlook in Silver City. Likewise, Deming and points west could be left off an arts- or hiking-focused itinerary. As largely empty land, studded by occasional crags, the bootheel south and west of Lordsburg appeals largely to naturalists.

South from Albuquerque

The desert terrain beyond Albuquerque on I-25 doesn't look immediately promising, and there's no escaping to a more scenic frontage road in this stretch. Los Lunas and Belén have their own heritage, in farming and railroads, but in recent years they have become bedroom communities for Albuquerque. By exit 152, though, you can strike out into truly remote New Mexico along the scenic Quebradas Backcountry Byway.

ISLETA PUEBLO

Tiwa-speaking **Isleta Pueblo** (505/869-3111, www.isletapueblo.com) had a good deal of interaction with the first Spanish settlers and was the only community that didn't participate in the Pueblo Revolt of 1680, during which many of its people fled to Hopi lands and intermarried. Notably, Isleta was home to civil rights hero Miguel Trujillo, who in 1948 successfully sued the New Mexico government for American Indians' right to vote, ending 24 years of the state's disregard for federal law.

Visitors can see the whitewashed **St. Augustine Church,** a beautiful example of early mission architecture. Established in 1612, it was rebuilt in 1716, and it now glows with whitewashed walls and a sky-blue back wall. Take exit 215, heading south on Highway 47, then west on Highway 147, to the village. The pueblo celebrates the **Feast of St. Augustine** (Aug. 28-Sept. 4), with the biggest dances on the first and last days.

LOS LUNAS AND BELÉN

The Rail Runner train has made these towns an easy outing from Albuquerque. Of the two, Belén is the more interesting destination, and more accessible by train (as the Los Lunas Rail Runner station is in a residential neighborhood). In Belén, the **Harvey House Museum** (104 N. 1st St., 505/861-0581, 9am-4pm Tues., 12:30pm-4pm Wed.-Sat., donation) is over the bridge from the station, across Reinken Avenue. It tells the story of the town's past as a major rail hub. Just across the street, **Pete's Café** (105 N. 1st St., 505/864-4811, 11am-8pm Mon.-Thurs., 11am-8:30pm Fri.-Sat., $9) has been open since 1949. Chile con queso—a melty, Velveeta-heavy mess—starts every meal, and everything else is similarly basic and popular, up to the homemade pies for dessert.

Walk south one block to reach Becker Avenue, Belén's historic main drag. Not much is hopping here, though feminist artist Judy Chicago lives in the old Belen Hotel building and runs the nonprofit arts organization **Through the Flower** (107 Becker Ave., 505/864-4080) across the street; its archive is open by appointment. A few more blocks east is the **Art League Gallery** (509 Becker Ave., 505/861-0217, noon-4pm Wed.-Sat.), and one block north is **Buckland Pharmacy** (600 Dalies Ave., 505/864-7434, 8:30am-6:30pm Mon.-Fri., 8:30am-3pm Sat.), which runs a nice old-fashioned soda fountain.

Tomé Hill

Midway between Los Lunas and Belén, east of I-25 and the Rio Grande, **Tomé Hill** is an important Catholic pilgrimage site, especially on Good Friday; it is topped with three 16-foot-high crosses. A natural lookout point, the hill was a landmark on the Camino Real, and that

QUEBRADAS BACKCOUNTRY BYWAY

This 24-mile dirt road, which runs in a jagged arc down to U.S. 380, just south of Socorro, more than makes up for the previous miles of dreary highway driving. The rounded hills here are striped with rainbow hues, and the scrub desert teems with hawks, mule deer, and foxes. Requiring two to three hours, the route makes a good slow way to or from the Bosque del Apache. Don't attempt the drive if it has rained recently—the route is named for the deep "breaks," or drainage channels it crosses, and the mud in the bottoms can be impossible to pass. Look out for sandy patches at all times, as well as the occasional hardy mountain biker.

Leave I-25 at Escondida (exit 152), then go north for 1.3 miles on the east-side frontage road; turn east at Escondida Lake and continue for 0.8 mile, crossing the river, to Pueblito, where you turn right at a T intersection. After about a mile, you see a sign for the byway beginning on your left (west); the road ends on U.S. 380 about 10 miles east of San Antonio and the road to the *bosque*. Coming north, the start is easier to find: From the intersection of the *bosque* road (Highway 1) in San Antonio, in front of the Owl Café, head east on U.S. 380 for just over 10 miles; then turn north on County Road A-129, the beginning of the byway.

Pilgrims leave mementos on Tomé Hill.

history is commemorated with a sculpture at the base of the trail. A 20-minute climb gives a good view down the Rio Grande; keep an eye out for petroglyphs on the rocks near the top. Take exit 203 from I-25, head east, then south about three miles on Highway 47 and turn east. Tomé's old town church is across Highway 47 to the west.

Socorro and the Plains of San Agustín

The small town of Socorro is the gateway to the Plains of San Agustín, a prehistoric lake bed transformed into a vast bowl of grazing land that is, in one spot, punctuated by a field of enormous radio telescopes, known as the Very Large Array. U.S. 60 used to be a well-used cross-country route. Now this part of the state is seldom visited, except by hunters and ranchers. It is beautiful, expansive landscape, especially after a wet winter or a good summer rainy season, when the plains turn into lush fields of wildflowers. And the same dark skies that aid the VLA's research are also great for amateurs—this is probably the easiest outing from a city for a night or two of stargazing. The tiny communities that mark the west edge of the plains—Datil, Pie Town, and Quemado—are, not coincidentally, a day's horseback ride apart.

SOCORRO

Once a pueblo that offered food to conquistador Don Juan de Oñate, Socorro (Succor, or Relief) now shelters people en route to the Bosque del Apache (about 20 miles south), as well as the students of the **New Mexico Institute of Mining & Technology** (aka New Mexico Tech, 575/835-5011, www.nmt. edu), which has been training engineers since 1889. The town has a small time-warp historic plaza, but the mission-style campus is scenic as well. To reach it, turn west from the main north-south route, California Street, onto Bullock Street and follow it toward the hills.

Entertainment

Wet your whistle at the **Capitol Bar** (575/835-1193, noon-2am Mon.-Sat., noon-midnight Sun.), on the plaza, which doesn't seem to have changed much in more than 120 years of doing business—this is one of those creaky-wood-floor saloons that you thought existed only on movie sets. But with friendly bartenders, pool tables, and live bands, it also has what every modern bar-goer needs.

Food

For your caffeine fix, ★ **Mountain Coffeehouse** (110 Manzanares St., 575/838-0809, 7am-8pm daily), just off the plaza, has the necessary espresso, as well as house-made gelato, sandwiches, full breakfasts, and occasional Indian dinner specials. The vibe is distinctly nerdy-intellectual.

La Pasadita (230 Garfield St., 575/835-3696, 10am-2pm Mon.-Fri., $7) has Socorro's best homey New Mexican, with solidly good red and green chile—but note the limited opening hours. Garfield Street is off the southwest corner of the plaza; the restaurant is easy to miss among the other houses on the block.

Out on the main drag, **Yo Mama's Grill** (400 N. California St., 575/838-3962, 11am-9pm Mon.-Sat., noon-8pm Sun., $9) has a great range of fresh diner standards, from juicy burgers to succulent Reubens, with house-made potato chips. And vintage Americana fans—or anyone hungry after 9pm—should head for **El Camino** (707 N. California St., 575/835-1180, 24 hours, $6), an

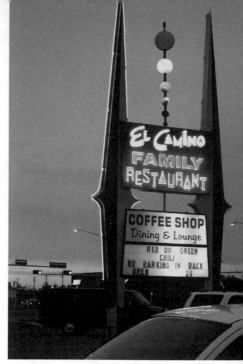

El Camino restaurant is a 24-hour beacon for weary road-trippers.

all-night diner that's plucked straight from the early faux-wood-paneling era.

Accommodations

Socorro has two B&Bs, both small, and both quite nice. **Socorro Old Town B&B** (114 Baca St., 575/418-9454, www.socorrobandb.qwestoffice.net, $125 d), in a renovated 1800s adobe with a nice back patio, has just two rooms and gets high marks for its blueberry muffins. **Dos Casitas en Socorro** (317 Eaton Ave., 575/835-2858, www.doscasitasensocorro.com, $110 d) has two stand-alone cottages, done in bright colors, with gas fireplaces; it is open only in birding season, September-mid-May. Both are an easy walk to the central plaza.

As for the numerous motels, you can choose from the various chain options, and on the low end, **America's Best Value Inn** (1009 N. California St., 575/835-0276, $68 d) is especially nice for the price, with a few chips in its furniture but otherwise very well kept up.

Getting There

Socorro is 80 miles south of Albuquerque on I-25, a bit more than an hour's drive. If you're heading west from here on U.S. 60, through Magdalena and on to the Very Large Array, be sure to fill up your gas tank, as there's only one station farther west, in Datil, and it's very expensive.

MAGDALENA

An escape for those who find Socorro too bustling, Magdalena sits on the edge of the plains, a small clutch of houses under a great sky. Established in 1884, the town was a commercial hub: Ranchers drove cattle here, and miners shipped ore, to be loaded on a rail spur from the main line at Socorro. But the last cattle drive happened in 1970, and the rails were torn out in 1981, and now the place feels a bit windswept. Still, it's the largest town along U.S. 60.

For orientation: U.S. 60 becomes 1st Street in town; Main Street runs north-south in the center.

Sights

Follow signs south from U.S. 60 to the **Box Car Museum** (Main St., 575/854-2261, 10am-6pm Tues. and Thurs.-Fri., 10am-8pm Wed., 10am-4pm Sat., donation), a small collection of historic artifacts, including some items from the remote Alamo Navajo reservation (29 miles north), set next to the former train depot.

Sports and Recreation

The little-visited mountains south of town provide a great chance to hike or mountain bike in solitude. The main trail access point is **Water Canyon Campground,** reached via Forest Road 235 (Water Canyon Rd.), which runs south from U.S. 60, 11 miles east of Magdalena. Southwest of Magdalena in the San Mateo Mountains, the remote

Withington Wilderness is 19,000 acres on the north flank of the San Mateo Mountains; it's almost always devoid of people. For info on trails here and closer to town, visit the **Magdalena Ranger District office** (575/854-2281, 8am-4:30pm Mon.-Fri.), on the east side.

Food and Accommodations

The **Western Motel & RV Park** (404 1st St., 575/412-7278, www.thewesternmotel.com, $56 s, $60 d) has flower boxes and lace curtains in the windows, plus lavish pine paneling for a, yes, Western feel.

One block off the main street, creaky two-story **Magdalena Hall Hotel** (404 2nd St., 575/517-5290, www.magdalenahallhotels. com, $65 d) is a reasonably well-kept blast from the past, and its lobby café, **M&M Café** (noon-5pm Wed.-Sun., $8), is a nice local hangout with good burgers, fruit smoothies, and tortilla soup.

A fine old relic, the **Golden Spur Saloon** (1st St., 575/854-2558, 10am-10pm Mon.-Sat., noon-10pm Sun.) is worth a stop even if you're not drinking the hard stuff. On summer weekends, it's a popular stop for bikers, but it's really the locals who prop up the bar all week. Look for it just east of Main Street.

To really enjoy Magdalena's light-free solitude, a good option is three miles west of town, at **Rancho Magdalena** (U.S. 60, 575/517-0644, www.ranchomagdalena.com, $115 d). This B&B has three cozy rooms with corner fireplaces, all in a recently built house set on a small rise, overlooking rolling ranch land. The same owners also offer a rental house in Magdalena proper ($175), and two other cabins ($175) farther out. For the B&B, turn south off U.S. 60 near mile marker 109.

Also of note, outside town, is **Concho Hills Guest Ranch** (1522 Remuda Tr., 575/772-5757, www.conchohillsranch.com, $300 pp), a low-key and very pleasant dude ranch where you can ride horses and target-shoot to your heart's content. Rates include all activities and meals.

★ THE VERY LARGE ARRAY

A little more than 20 miles west of Magdalena, strange structures jut out of the plains. These are the 27 radio telescopes—which look like enormous satellite dishes—that compose the Very Large Array, a research center devoted to the study of deep space. Reach the **visitors center** (575/835-7243, www.vla.nrao.edu, 8:30am-sunset daily, $6) by turning south onto Highway 52 and following signs to the VLA access road. The center explains, first of all, just what radio astronomy is, as well as how the telescopes are focused to see deep into the Milky Way and show images as precise as the shading on Mercury's poles that may be ice. Then you can walk up close to one of the telescopes, as large as a baseball diamond and weighing 230 tons; with any luck, the array will be refocusing, and you'll get to see the massive structure slowly, grindingly turn, eerily in synch with all the others stretching up to 20 miles away. The first Saturday of the month, there are guided tours at 11am, 1pm, and 3pm.

For a long back-road drive, continue south on Highway 52, passing through a 600-acre private elk reserve and the town of Winston (with a possible detour to the ghost town of Chloride), to eventually connect with I-25 just north of Truth or Consequences.

DATIL

For visitors and Datil's 50 or so locals, life centers on the **Eagle Guest Ranch** (U.S. 60, 575/772-5612, 7am-9pm Mon.-Sat.), an all-purpose motel, gas station, taxidermy shop, saloon, and steakhouse. Radio techies from the VLA rub shoulders with hunting parties over thick slabs of meat and a salad bar. The motel rooms ($55 d) will do in a pinch. It's a chummy, frontier-feeling place, but most people blow right through on their way to . . .

PIE TOWN

Aside from Truth or Consequences, no other town name in New Mexico looks as intriguing on a map as Pie Town. In fact, "town" is overstating it, as it has a population of about 45, though its cafés cater to some of Catron County's crustiest ranchers; keep your cool

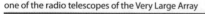

one of the radio telescopes of the Very Large Array

when folks swagger in with guns strapped to their hips. The second weekend in September is the annual **Pie Festival.**

The place got its name in the 1920s, when an entrepreneur began dishing out a sweet pick-me-up to famished homesteaders and, later, intrepid cross-country motorists. But after the federal interstate diverted traffic, the pie market dried up, and the place went pie-less for decades. In 1995, a disappointed visitor to Pie Town took matters into her own hands and opened the ★ **Pie-O-Neer Café** (U.S. 60, 575/772-2711, 11am-4pm Thurs.-Sun. Mar.-Nov., $5), still by far the best of the four pie vendors now in operation. The daily roster of pies is dazzling—apple-cranberry, double cherry, pecan-oat, to name just a few—and each one is encased in perfectly flaky crust. So you might want a slice to eat in, and another to go. Call ahead to confirm hours—and note that it's totally closed for several months in winter. It typically opens for the season on, of course, Pi Day (Mar. 14).

In winter (or perhaps as a second stop), your next best bet is **The Pie Source** (U.S. 60, 575/772-2919, 9am-6pm Sun.-Wed., $5), which specializes in caramel pecan, and is set in a neat 1920s homesteader's wood cabin. Look for it behind the windmills on the east edge of town.

For more nourishing food, **Pie Town Café** (U.S. 60, 575/772-2700, 10am-5pm Mon.-Thurs., 3pm-8pm Fri. Mar.-Nov., $7) is another option, with a selection of New Mexican and diner standards along with the sweets; consult the "pie chart" to see what varieties are available that day. With the most generous opening hours, **The Gatherin' Place** (U.S. 60, 575/772-2909, 7:30am-6pm daily, $9) is more of an all-purpose hangout, with breakfast burritos and lunch specials like veggie curry; pie is a slight afterthought.

QUEMADO

Quemado is little more than a wide spot along the highway, but it does provide some basic services for travelers. The **Largo Motel** (U.S. 60, 575/773-4686, $65 d), on the west edge of town, has very comfortable beds. Its **café** (6am-9pm Mon.-Wed., 6am-11pm Thurs.-Sat., 7am-9pm Sun., $10) is quite good—its "Mexican cheeseburger" is the stuff of legend,

Who wouldn't stop in Pie Town?

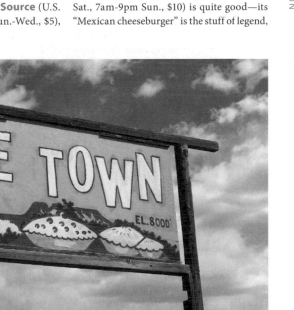

a patty wrapped in a flour tortilla and smothered in green chile and cheese.

★ The Lightning Field

Quemado is also the unlikely starting point for a visit to an elaborate work of land art called **The Lightning Field** (505/898-3335, www.lightningfield.org, May–Oct.). In 1977, sculptor Walter de Maria installed 400 stainless-steel poles in a grid measuring one mile by one kilometer. The light glints off the poles, and summer storms create a field of crackling, brilliant electricity across their pointed tips. De Maria envisioned an immersive experience, in which the viewer, in pure isolation, watches the light shift over the course of the day. To this end, casual visitors are not allowed, and the road to the site is unmarked; you must make reservations for an overnight stay and leave your car in Quemado. At $150 per person ($250 during the prime storm months of July and August), the basic accommodations may seem a bit steep, but this ranks as one of the state's most remarkable places to spend the night, not to mention one of the great places to meditate on New Mexico's phenomenal landscape.

El Camino Real

As I-25 continues south from Socorro, the highway passes alongside Bosque del Apache, one of the largest nature reserves in the United States. Then the Chihuahuan Desert scenery takes over, with dusty grasses occasionally punctuated by yucca trees. Highway 1, the interstate frontage road now designated **El Camino Real National Scenic Byway,** grants a quieter perspective and leads directly to the two major sights in this area: the remains of a Civil War-era fort and a monument to El Camino Real de Tierra Adentro (the Royal Road of the Interior), forged between central Mexico and Santa Fe during the Spanish colonial period. Just one of a network of trade routes through Spanish territory in the Americas, this north-south trail brought fur and silver into the heart of Mexico, from where it was shipped out to seaports.

★ BOSQUE DEL APACHE NATIONAL WILDLIFE REFUGE

Occupying more than 57,000 acres on either side of the Rio Grande, the **Bosque del Apache National Wildlife Refuge** is in a sense a manufactured habitat: Controlled flooding creates the marshes that draw the birds, which find food on farm plots dedicated to tasty grains. But this is really restoring a process that happened naturally before the Rio Grande was dammed. The birds certainly have no objection. Arctic geese, sandhill cranes, bald eagles, and a whole variety of ducks happily settle in for the winter. In the spring, migratory warblers and pelicans stop off on their way back to points north, while great blue herons make their spring nests here. Summer is relatively quiet, as only the year-round species remain: hummingbirds, swallows, flycatchers, and the like.

Access to the *bosque* is via Highway 1, south from U.S. 380, where the small town of **San Antonio,** just a blip on the map, provides a couple of lunch spots for hungry birders. Five miles inside the north border of the reserve, you pass the **visitors center** (575/835-1828, www.friendsofthebosque.org, 8am-4pm daily), where you can pick up maps and find out which birds have been spotted that day.

A bit farther south on Highway 1, a 12-mile paved car loop passes through all the marshlands and the grain fields; at certain points along the drive, you can get out and hike set trails, such as a quarter-mile boardwalk across a lagoon or a trail to the river. Some areas are open to mountain bikers. The **loop drive** ($5/car) opens when birdlife is at its best, one hour before sunrise; cars need to be out by an hour after dark. With all its marshland, the *bosque* could just as well be called a mosquito sanctuary—slather on plenty of repellent before you start your drive.

The biggest event of the year is the arrival of the sandhill cranes—they were the inspiration for the refuge, as their population had dwindled to fewer than 20 in 1941. But now more than 15,000 of these graceful birds with six-foot wingspans winter over in the *bosque*. They're celebrated annually at the five-day **Festival of the Cranes** (www.festivalofthecranes.com) in November, when birders gather to witness the mass morning liftoffs and evening fly-ins.

Food

San Antonio manages to support two legendary green-chile cheeseburger joints: the **Owl Bar & Café** (U.S. 380, 575/835-9946, 8am-8pm Mon.-Sat., $7) and **Buckhorn Burgers** (U.S. 380, 575/835-4423, 11am-7:50pm Mon.-Fri., 11am-2:45pm Sat., $7), just across the street. Both have been open since the 1940s, both serve beer and burgers, both have chummy local staff and plenty of lore—so how to choose? Go to the Owl if you like your burgers thin, to Buckhorn if you like them a little fatter.

Actually, the Owl gets extra points for historic details: It kept atomic-bomb engineers such as Robert Oppenheimer supplied with cheeseburgers and booze while they worked at Trinity Site, about twenty miles away. And the Owl's wooden bar is salvaged from the world's first Hilton hotel, started here in San Antonio by the father of modern hospitality, magnate Conrad Hilton.

If, for some reason, you're not in the mood for a burger, follow the signs for **San Antonio Crane** (17 Pino St., 575/835-2208, 10am-4pm Tues.-Sat., noon-3pm Sun., $8), one block south off U.S. 380, for homemade New Mexican food (including especially good tamales) served in a tiny dining room. In the winter, during birding season, it opens for breakfast too.

Accommodations

If you want to wake up and get straight to the birds, **Casa Blanca B&B** (13 Montoya St., 575/835-3027, www.casablancabedandbreakfast.com, $90 d), in San Antonio, can put you up for the night in one of three cozy rooms in an 1880 Victorian farmhouse. It caters to birders only, so is closed in the low migration season, May-September, but rambling, Western bonanza **Fite Ranch** (Fite Ranch Rd., 575/838-0958, www.fiteranchbedandbreakfast.com, $110 d), about seven miles east of San Antonio, is open year-round. It has a two-night minimum.

For camping, **Bosque Birdwatchers** RV **Park** (575/835-1366, $25) is just 100 yards north of the reserve border on Highway 1.

FORT CRAIG NATIONAL HISTORIC SITE

One of the largest forts in the Southwest and the staging point for the crucial Battle of Valverde during the Civil War, **Fort Craig National Historic Site** (dawn-dusk daily, free) is a long way to drive for precious little to see. Only true military buffs will have the imagination to bring the few building outlines and crumbling earthworks to life.

As a place to stretch your legs, though, you could do worse: The site is near the Rio Grande (a bit of a walk over level ground), in view of Black Mesa to the north. In the days of the Camino Real, this striking landmass was known as the Mesa del Contadero, as its position next to the river formed a natural chute for counting livestock herds. In February 1862, the north side of the mesa saw the Battle of Valverde, in which the fort's forces managed to damage a Confederate supply train, setting the stage for a more decisive Union victory in the Battle of Glorieta about a month later.

EL CAMINO REAL HISTORIC SITE

Hidden from view about 2.5 miles east of I-25 (exit 115), **El Camino Real Historic Site** (575/854-3600, www.caminorealheritage.org,

El Camino Real Historic Site

8:30am-5pm Wed.-Sun., $5) is well worth a detour. The stark modern museum stands on a windswept bluff with no sign of human population in sight—a fitting locale for this tribute to the often-difficult Spanish trade route that for centuries linked Zacatecas, Mexico, with the frontier town of Santa Fe. Inside the heritage center, the information-packed exhibits describe the major points along the royal road. Outside are traditional gardens, a dramatic vista on the Chihuahuan Desert, and a six-mile trail north to Fort Craig.

Truth or Consequences

For decades, the town of Hot Springs was just a dot on the map 150 miles south of Albuquerque. In the early 20th century, its bathhouses had been packed with health-seekers enjoying the underground reservoir of mineral-rich water, but by the 1940s, the place had slumped into obscurity. Around this time, popular radio show *Truth or Consequences* was offering national publicity to any town willing to change its name to match the show's, and the Hot Springs council took the bait. The stunt was completed in the spring of 1950, with host Ralph Edwards and a convoy of press and celebrities on hand. National notoriety faded, but T or C (as it's commonly known) has managed to hang on, acting as a diversion from the interstate for through travelers and a bargain retirement spot for people fleeing frigid Minnesota and Dakota winters.

In the 21st century, the town has received a boost from younger artists who have relocated here from the coasts, helping revive the small downtown area with galleries and hot-springs operations. Equally influential: Richard Branson, whose Virgin Galactic commercial space-flight company is the anchor tenant at the Spaceport America east of town. While wealthy space tourists have put their money up and await the eventual first launch into low-Earth orbit for just a few minutes, T or C remains a pleasant, if slightly ramshackle, place to spend a night or two. Ideally stop here on a weekend, as many businesses close at least Monday and Tuesday.

ORIENTATION

Drivers enter T or C either at its farthest north end (exit 79), where Highway 181 turns into the long commercial strip known as North Date Street, or on the south side (exit 76), where Highway 187 runs through an adjunct town called Williamsburg. Both routes lead downtown, bounded by Main Street and Broadway. Most of the bathhouses and hotels with springs are on or south of Main Street. Of the more than 15 galleries downtown, **RioBravoFineArt** (110 N. Broadway, noon-5pm Wed.-Sun.) is the oldest, representing, among others, the town's best-known painter, Delmas Howe, who made his name with lush murals and homoerotic cowboy portraits. Howe painted the **Civic Center** (W. 4th Ave. between Grape St. and N. Foch St.) in lush flowers.

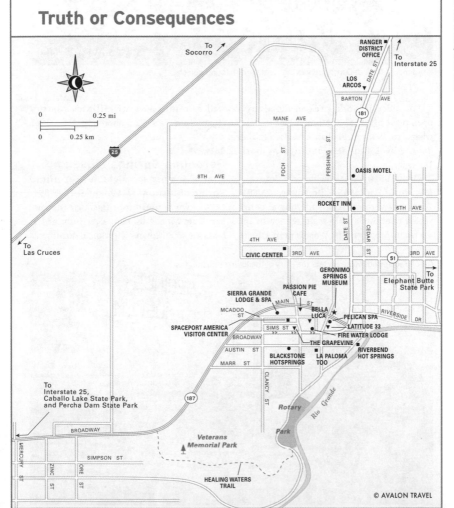

Truth or Consequences

To Socorro

RANGER DISTRICT OFFICE
To Interstate 25

LOS ARCOS

DATE ST

BARTON   AVE

181

0   0.25 mi

0   0.25 km

25

MANE   AVE

FOCH ST

PERSHING ST

8TH   AVE

OASIS MOTEL

ROCKET INN

6TH   AVE

DATE ST

CEDAR ST

4TH   AVE

To Las Cruces

CIVIC CENTER   3RD   AVE

51

3RD   AVE

To Elephant Butte State Park

GERONIMO SPRINGS MUSEUM

PASSION PIE CAFE

SIERRA GRANDE LODGE & SPA

MAIN   ST

MCADOO ST

BELLA LUCA

PELICAN SPA

RIVERSIDE   DR

SPACEPORT AMERICA VISITOR CENTER

SIMS ST

LATITUDE 33

FIRE WATER LODGE

BROADWAY

THE GRAPEVINE

AUSTIN   ST

RIVERBEND HOT SPRINGS

MARR   ST

BLACKSTONE HOTSPRINGS

LA PALOMA TOO

CLANCY ST

To Interstate 25, Caballo Lake State Park, and Percha Dam State Park

187

Rotary

Rio Grande

Park

BROADWAY

MERCURY ST

ZINC ST

ORE ST

SIMPSON ST

Veterans Memorial Park

HEALING WATERS TRAIL

© AVALON TRAVEL

Residents of Truth or Consequences get creative with found objects.

For older artwork, peek in the always-open **post office** (300 Main St.) for a somewhat eerie 1938 mural of an American Indian dance, by Lithuanian immigrant Boris Deutsch.

On the hill south of downtown is **Veterans Memorial Park** (996 S. Broadway, 575-894-7640, www.torcveteransmemorial.com), which contains a half-scale replica of the Vietnam Memorial in Washington DC, as well as a **museum of military history** (10am-4pm Tues.-Sat., noon-4pm Sun., free).

SIGHTS

Geronimo Springs Museum

T or C's must-see sight is **Geronimo Springs Museum** (211 Main St., 575-894-6600, www.geronimospringsmuseum.com, 9am-5pm Mon.-Sat., noon-5pm Sun., $6). A fantastic small-town collection, it documents

Geronimo Springs Museum tells the story of the town's renaming.

both the monumental and the mundane in T or C since its founding. Seven rooms display everything from mammoth skulls to portraits of local bankers to an authentic log cabin. Local rebel Geronimo gets a lot of attention, as does town-maker and radio and TV host Ralph Edwards.

Spaceport America

For sheer potential, **Spaceport America** is thrilling. This is the first commercial spaceflight hub in the world. The setting—here in southern New Mexico, with its empty space, history of rocket research, and alleged alien spacecraft activity—is appropriate. Yet the Norman Foster-designed facility, tucked into the desert about 30 miles southeast of Truth or Consequences, still awaits Virgin Galactic passengers, so there is relatively little activity. **Tours** (844/727-7223, www.spaceportamerica.com, 9am Thurs.-Mon. year-round, also 1:30pm Fri.-Sun. May-Sept., $45) visit only a small wing of the main Spaceport building and a second building where specialized fire trucks wait for occasional rocket launches by other Spaceport clients.

Still, as activity develops here, the tours too may be a better window on this desert industry. Even if you don't take a tour, it's worth stopping by the downtown **visitors center** (301 S. Foch St., 8:30am-4:30pm, free) to see displays about the facility.

ENTERTAINMENT AND EVENTS

T or C's version of nightlife is the outdoor group pool at **Riverbend Hot Springs** (100 Austin St., 575/894-7625, www.nmhotsprings.com, 8am-10pm daily). The most festive night out is the downtown **Second Saturday Art Hop** (Main St. and Broadway, 6pm-9pm), every month, year-round. Doors stay open late, and residents toddle from spot to spot, sharing gossip and free refreshments.

The biggest annual event is the **T or C Fiesta** (www.sierracountynewmexico.info), celebrated with style on the first weekend in May every year since 1950. Ralph Edwards himself attended until 1999, often with assorted TV and movie personalities in tow. Even without him (he died in 2005), the festivities are pretty grand for such a small town, pulling together what feels like all of T or C's disparate population of 8,000, with the Old Time Fiddlers Association marching alongside youngsters dressed as aliens. Expect lots of goofy floats, art cars, Spam-craft contests, and more.

waiting for commercial space flights to take off at Spaceport America

SPORTS AND RECREATION

Truth or Consequences caters largely to the layabout, what with all the warm baths, although sports aficionados enjoy the artificial lakes just minutes from town.

If you'll be heading west into the Gila National Forest from here, stop by the **Black Range Ranger District office** (1804 N. Date St., 575/894-6677, 8am-4pm Mon.-Fri.), in the Lakeway Shopping Center, to pick up maps and other info.

Hot Springs

Of the dozen or so spots to take the waters, **Riverbend** (100 Austin St., 575/894-7625, www.nmhotsprings.com, 8am-10pm daily) is the best if you prefer the open air. Perched at the water's edge, the cascading communal pools ($10/hour) offer a range of water temperatures. If you're feeling less social, opt for one of three private tubs, similarly open-air and facing the river ($15/hour).

For a more historic vibe, head for **La Paloma Too** (300 Austin St., 575/894-2228, www.lapalomahotspringsandspa.com, 7am-noon and 5pm-11pm Mon.-Thurs., 10am-8pm Sat.-Sun.), also known as Hay-Yo-Kay. This restored bathhouse from the 1920s has small but clean indoor pools for one or two people; rates start at $6 for half an hour. Out back, the "longhouse" is one very large tub in a semi-open shelter, shielded from the weather.

Healing Waters Trail

This three-mile walking route around and a bit out of town is half history, half nature. Downtown, the route passes many of the iconic hot springs and historic buildings, with markers at crucial points. Across the river, southeast of downtown, a dirt trail winds through wetlands and into the scrub-covered hills, giving a good view over the old part of town. Signs along the way tell the story of how the favorite Apache bathing spot became the town of Hot Springs. Pick up a map at the museum or the visitors center on Broadway.

Elephant Butte Lake State Park

Named for a distinctive rock formation in the center of the water, 40-mile-long Elephant Butte Lake is the largest body of water in New Mexico. So long as there's no drought, it maintains a steady buzz of activity in summertime, with the party spilling over to the small town of Elephant Butte, immediately north of Truth or Consequences on Highway 181.

Elephant Butte Lake State Park (575/744-5923, www.nmparks.com, $5/car) contains a huge number of **campsites** ($10-14). Follow the frontage road along the west edge of the lake to quieter campsites such as North and South Monticello Point.

Campers and day-trippers alike should stop first at the **visitors center** (575/744-5421, 7:30am-4:30pm daily) near the south end, to pay fees and check on current conditions. Major services are here too, at the marinas or in town. **Marina del Sur** (101 S. Hwy. 195, 575/744-5567, www.marinadelsur.info) rents pontoons, houseboats, and kayaks.

Caballo Lake State Park

Smaller **Caballo Lake** (Hwy. 187, 575/743-3942, www.nmparks.com, $5/car), 16 miles south of Truth or Consequences, is quieter than Elephant Butte, frequented mainly by anglers out for white bass and walleye. The **Lakeside Recreation Area** has boat access and a few easy hiking trails. The developed sites at **Stallion Campground** ($8 for tents, $14 for RVs), overlooking the lake, are preferable to those at Appaloosa, and the primitive camping area is fairly private; you can also park your car about a mile north of the park entrance and hike in to camp at **Eagle Point.**

South of Caballo Dam, the **Riverside Recreation Area** has fairly attractive developed camping spots right on the water, though the spaces are not particularly private-feeling. The best ones are at the far south end of the recreation area.

Percha Dam State Park

Five miles south of Caballo Lake, this small

recreational area is a **birding** hot spot for vermilion flycatchers, among other rare migratory birds. Otherwise, the area is not particularly lush and can feel a little dusty despite the big old cottonwood trees that line the river.

Armendaris and Ladder Ranches

Media magnate and conservationist Ted Turner owns more than half a million acres in southern New Mexico, land that was strictly private property for centuries. As of 2015, it is finally open for tours with **Ted Turner Expeditions** (877/277-7637, www.tedturnerexpeditions.com), based at Sierra Grande Lodge (which Turner also owns). Tours (from $150 pp for a five-hour outing) are not cheap, but if you have a hankering to see land that most others have only glimpsed from the interstate, this is an exciting option. One tour visits an active paleontology site; another visits a bat cave at dusk.

FOOD

Start your day right with an "Elvis waffle" (banana slices and peanut butter sauce), or perhaps even more brilliantly, a waffle with bacon in the batter and real maple syrup on the side. ★ **Passion Pie Café** (406 Main St., 575/894-0008, 7am-3pm daily, $6) is where this magic happens, plus plenty more (Greek salads, cupcakes, etc.), all fresh and homemade.

Another good breakfast-lunch option is **The Grapevine Bistro** (413 Broadway, 575/894-0404, 8am-3pm Mon.-Fri., 7am-3pm Sat.-Sun., $8), a cheery one-man operation that serves fresh breakfast burritos, creative salads, and killer peanut-butter pie.

To call **Latitude 33** (304 S. Pershing St., 575/740-7804, 11am-2pm and 5pm-8pm Tues.-Thurs., 11am-8pm Fri.-Sun., $11) an "Asian fusion" restaurant conjures up something too grand. This is creative, home-style food that happens to have ingredients like coconut milk and ginger. The cabbage salad is packed with flavor; so is the Thai-style iced tea.

BellaLuca (303 Jones St., 575/894-9866, 3pm-9pm Mon. and Wed.-Thurs., 3pm-10pm Fri.-Sat., 3pm-8pm Sun., $16-25) serves crispy-crust pizzas, inventive pastas, and more, in a very sleek setting with floor-to-ceiling windows and art on the walls. Not everything hits the mark, but the food is always fresh (organic eggs and more) and appealing.

In the mood for a hefty dry-aged steak, shrimp cocktail, and deep-fried zucchini strips? Seek out the time-warp steakhouse

BellaLuca does fresh Italian in downtown T or C.

★ **Los Arcos** (1400 N. Date St., 575/894-6200, 5pm-9:30pm Sun.-Thurs., 5pm-10:30pm Fri.-Sat., $17), where the calendar seems never to have changed from opening day in 1970. Nonetheless, the food and wine has kept up with the times just enough to be fresh and satisfying, without turning trendy.

ACCOMMODATIONS

Places with in-room hot springs are all downtown, cheaper options are on North Date Street, and a few chain hotels are very close to the interstate. Rates go up slightly on the weekend.

Under $75

Just out of the downtown loop, the ★ **Rocket Inn** (605 N. Date St., 575/894-2964, www. rocketinn.net, $61 d) is a very well-tended old motor court from 1948, with all-new insides. Sparkling bathrooms, ceiling fans, and fantastic beds are all a steal at this price—and the owners are efficient and friendly. You can walk to hot springs downtown (guests get a discount at Riverbend).

Two blocks north, **Oasis Motel** (819 N. Date St., 575/894-6629, $56 d) is also worth noting in the same price bracket, and in fact a couple other lower-end motels in this stretch are in excellent shape as well.

$75-100

However, the lure of the hot springs is hard to resist, and for not too much more per night, **Riverbend Hot Springs** (100 Austin St., 575/894-7625, www.riverbendhotsprings. com) gives you a more efficient commute to its nice outdoor soaking facilities. The "artist rooms" ($79) are their cheapest option, built in mobile homes but with all new furnishings; casitas and suites (from $116) with kitchenettes are also available. Note that kids younger than 12 are not welcome.

The truly luxurious—if less sociable, and with less of a view—option is to have hot-spring water pour directly into your bathroom tub. Of these operations,

Rocket Inn is very down to earth.

★ **Blackstone Hotsprings** (410 Austin St., 575/894-0894, www.blackstonehotsprings. com) is probably the best. Its ten rooms are decorated (tastefully) in retro-TV themes, from the black-and-white Twilight Zone studio ($75) to the 1950s space-age Jetsons suite ($135). Some setups have patios and/or kitchenettes, and every room has a large soaking tub.

In a similar motor-court setting, **Fire Water Lodge** (311 Broadway, 575/740-0315, www.firewaterlodge.com, $95 d) has eight rooms painted in jewel tones, with handcarved furniture and mosaic spring-fed tubs. Two have outdoor pools, and some have kitchens. The decor can be a bit haphazard, but it's a good backup option.

Over $100

By far the ritziest choice in T or C, **Sierra Grande Lodge & Spa** (501 McAdoo St., 575/894-6976, www.sierragrandelodge.com, $155 d, $285 suite) occupies a historic hotel building, with 16 wood-floor rooms decorated in a spare Southwest style, plus a separate casita. Rooms on the front upstairs have balconies with a view of the mountains. Hotel rates include a one-hour soak in the spa, which has indoor and outdoor baths.

INFORMATION AND SERVICES

Stop in at the helpful **visitors center** (301 S. Foch St., 575/894-1968, www.sierracountynewmexico.info, 9am-4:30pm Mon.-Sat., noon-4pm Sun.) for a map of the town and scads of brochures to surrounding attractions, including the Geronimo Trail.

For local reads and more, **Black Cat Books and Coffee** (128 Broadway, 575/894-7070, 8am-5pm Fri.-Mon.) stocks new and used titles.

GETTING THERE

Truth or Consequences is a little over two hours' drive south of Albuquerque (150 miles), and one hour (75 miles) from Socorro. From Las Cruces, it's 75 miles north on I-25, about an hour and 15 minutes in a car.

The Geronimo Trail

Named for the Apache leader who held out against American forces until 1866, longer than any other Native fighter, this **scenic route** (www.geronimotrail.com) winds through the former territory of his tribe, the Black Range. This is the longest and most rugged stretch of mountains in the state, where many of the battles between U.S. troops and the Apaches were waged. That period lives on only in such place names as Massacre Canyon. More prevalent are the relics of the short-lived silver boom of the late 19th century. Some of the saloons, general stores, and banks from that era still stand, empty and listing dangerously or propped up and turned into museums.

The route is technically a loop, but the west side of the circuit (Forest Road 150) is 46 miles of rudimentary dirt that's recommended only for those with four-wheel drive, in dry weather. Instead, most people will drive either the northern section to Chloride, Winston, and Monticello or, more commonly, the southern section, through Hillsboro and Kingston, and winding over the pass to Silver City. Many of the more interesting sights are short side trips off the main trail. Before you head out, fill your tank—there are no gas stations between the interstate and Silver City.

THE NORTHERN ROUTE

Head north out of T or C along the I-25 frontage road, then turn west into the Cuchillo Mountains on Highway 52.

Winston to Beaverhead

The road passes through what was once **Cuchillo,** founded in the 1850s and, off the east side of the road, the home of the Cuchillo Creek Café, which was closed at the time of research but considering reopening; if it does, expect excellent red chile and sopaipillas.

The road then winds up and over the mountains to **Winston,** a clutch of wood buildings set on a wide plain. All the action is at the general store with a gas pump (8am-6pm daily)— fitting, considering Winston took its name from a generous shop-owner who gave credit to residents suffering through the crash of 1893, when silver was devalued and prospectors lost everything. Now Winston is a hub for hunters, who head farther into the wilderness via Highway 52. The last leg of the Geronimo Trail (few people get this far) is Highway 59, a narrow road across the northern reaches of the Gila National Forest, paved all the way to **Beaverhead.** The route then turns south, onto gravel, and heads about 10 more miles into the wilderness.

Chloride

In Winston, most drivers turn left at the T junction (off Highway 52), which takes you to **Chloride,** a highly picturesque little ghost town, maintained as a sort of outdoor museum. Established in 1879, Chloride went bust less than 20 years later. The "hanging tree" still stands in the middle of Wall Street, and, most interesting, the **Pioneer Store Museum** (575/743-2736, www.pioneerstoremuseum.com, 10am-4pm daily, donation) is a fine time capsule. It is stocked almost precisely as it was when it closed in 1923, thanks to an owner who closed for business by simply locking the door and sealing the windows. The current owners have restored the place with tender care, and they also run a gallery and gift shop next door. They can tell you the story behind the few other buildings in town, and advise on nearby trails up to abandoned mines.

The bank building is now the excellent **Chloride Bank Café** (575/743-0414, 11am-6pm Thurs.-Sat., 11am-4pm Sun., $7), with fresh, homemade, and creative food—including new pies and cakes every day. In summer, it is open on Wednesday as well, and usually until 7pm. There is also an RV park in town, with five spots.

Monticello

Backtrack on Highway 52 about halfway, then cut east on dirt Tortilla Flats Road (County Rd. 16, but unsigned) to Las Placitas and, farther northwest on Highway 142, **Monticello.** This is a pretty, tiny farming community that was an early Spanish settlement; it is still centered on the traditional plaza established in the 1850s. One farm (www.organicbalsamic.com) specializes in organic lavender, desert-hardy fruit trees, and balsamic vinegar, and one artist in town has the astonishing **PharrWest Gallery** (575/743-0868, by appointment).

You can then return to T or C via Highway 142.

THE SOUTHERN ROUTE

Twelve miles south of Truth or Consequences, Highway 152 heads west into the Black Range,

vestiges of mining history in Chloride

passing a couple of old mining towns. The road is serpentine and best driven in the daytime.

Hillsboro

Seventeen miles along the road, Hillsboro has an Old West feel. It became the seat of Sierra County in 1884, then managed to weather the silver devaluation and a bitter murder trial in 1899, as cattlemen's feuds and other range rivalries split the whole region. But in the early 20th century, it suffered floods and the flu epidemic, and after a long legal struggle, lost its county-seat status to Hot Springs (later T or C) in 1936, along with most of its remaining population. Just to be certain there was no going back, the courthouse was dismantled; you can still see its ruins along the "high road" through town.

On the east edge of town, the exceedingly dusty **Black Range Museum** (Hwy. 152, 575/895-5233, 11am-4pm Thurs.-Sat., 1pm-5pm Sun., $2 donation) merits a poke around if you happen to arrive during its open hours.

the Hillsboro General Store Café

The haphazard collection includes fittings from "The Chinaman's Café" that occupied this building after legendary madam-made-good Sadie Orchard sold the property to Tom Ying. The **Hillsboro Historical Society**

(Hwy. 152, 575/895-3321, 11am-4pm Fri.-Sun.) also has a small museum, largely of old photos of the town. There's a farm market here at 10am on Saturday.

The **Hillsboro General Store Café** (10697 Hwy. 152, 575/895-5306, 8am-3pm Fri.-Wed., $7), a homey place in an 1879 building (that still works as a store as well), is good for a snack. Road-food standards like burritos and grilled cheese with green chile are on the menu.

Lake Valley Historic Site

From the main junction in Hillsboro, Highway 27 detours south, out of the mountains and into the rolling hills around **Lake Valley Historic Site** (9am-4pm Thurs.-Mon.), an especially well-kept relic. The slumping buildings with rusted tin roofs are all the evidence that remains of the richest single silver mine ever discovered, in 1881: a glittering cavern lined with solid ore that prospectors dubbed The Bridal Chamber. The find was marred by typical tragedy for that period, as George Daly, the man who'd led the exploration, was killed by Apaches the same day the trove was unearthed. The strike prompted all the usual expansion, with saloons, stagecoach and railroad service,

Lake Valley Historic Site is an old mining town.

and plenty of gunfights. Although the silver crash and a catastrophic fire in 1895 ruined this town, Lake Valley was inhabited by a few hardy old-timers until as recently as 1994. As a result, some of the buildings are in recognizable shape, and the schoolhouse is still used for special events.

Stewards should be on-site to give you a walking-tour map and answer questions. Even when the site isn't open, you can drive a dirt road alongside it, with signs explaining the full history of the area.

Highway 27 ends at the intersection with Highway 26 and the **Nutt Corner Bar** (19160 Hatch Hwy., 575/267-4567, 10am-8pm Wed.-Sat., noon-6pm Sun.). It used to be called the Middle of Nowhere Bar, but the land to the west is now much busier since a solar and wind farm has been installed, so it's not as remote-feeling as it once was. Head east to Hatch (18 miles) or southwest to Deming (28 miles).

Kingston

Back in Hillsboro, continue nine miles west on Highway 152 to where a Dead End sign points to Kingston. A population of more than 7,000 made this the largest town in New Mexico in 1890, when the surrounding mountains were being stripped of their silver in mines called Ready Pay and Opportunity. Butch Cassidy, Mark Twain, and Billy the Kid all passed through, and Lillian Russell performed in the opera house, but the market panic in 1893 inspired a mass exodus. All that's left now is a community even smaller than Hillsboro, a clutch of buildings along a narrow road. The only one that looks just as it did during the boom years is the faithfully restored 1884 **Percha Bank** (575/895-5652, 11am-3pm Fri.-Sun. June-Aug., free), complete with all the woodwork and fittings, as well as an enormous working vault. A gallery space exhibits local art.

The **Black Range Lodge** (119 Main St., 575/895-5652, www.blackrangelodge.com, $95 d) is an atmospheric mountain outpost where you'll get a real sense of the outdoors. The main building, with its heavy stone walls and wood ceiling beams, may inspire memories of summer camp. The bedrooms upstairs are far better than bunks, however, with sensible, not-too-frilly antiques, old quilts, and cozy radiant heat in the floors. A separate building showcases the owners' expertise in straw-bale construction; the upstairs guesthouse has a full kitchen and a deck, while the downstairs studio has a kitchenette. A larger property across the street can sleep up to 14. Kids will appreciate the foosball in the game room. Full breakfast (with eggs from the resident chickens) is provided; for dinner, you're welcome to cook your own food in the kitchen.

West to Silver City

After Kingston, Highway 152 snakes up to Emory Pass (elev. 8,228 feet), which was hard hit by the Silver Fire in 2013. The route can be tedious and tiring in even the best of weather. If heavy rain is forecast, better to take the southern route to Silver City; snow often closes the pass entirely.

Continuing to Silver City through the Mimbres Valley, you will pass Chino Mine (see "Trail of the Mountain Spirits" later in this chapter).

Mesilla Valley

Heading due south from T or C on I-25 (or, more scenically, on Highway 187 and Highway 185), you're in the fertile river valley and the heartland of New Mexico's distinctive cuisine. This is chile country, where the bulk of the state's crop is grown and processed. In the summer, the fields are hot and still and solidly green. By the fall harvest, the air is almost noticeably spicy (those with allergies, beware!).

HATCH

This community has earned a much bigger name than its population of 2,000 would suggest. Every Labor Day weekend, the **Hatch Chile Festival** celebrates the town's most famous crop. As you'd imagine, food vendors are plentiful, and you can shop for chile-themed crafts and wave to the Chile Festival Queen. The tiny **Hatch Museum** (149 W. Hall St., 575/267-3638, 9am-3pm Mon.-Fri., donation) should document this a bit more, but instead features locally made doilies and a whole wall full of rocks and minerals.

If your visit doesn't coincide with the fiesta, head to **Sparky's** (115 Franklin St., 575/267-4222, 10:30am-7pm Thurs.-Sun.), which is its own kind of festive attraction—just look for the mass of colorful kitsch at the main town intersection. Its specialties are green-chile cheeseburgers and barbecue.

For more home-style New Mexican, visit **Valley Café** (335 W. Hall St., 575/267-4798, 8am-3pm Mon.-Fri., 7:30am-3pm Sat., $6), which does chiles rellenos and other green-chile standards hot and fast. It has only five tables, though, so if it's full, or you want takeout anyway, opt for **B&E Burritos** (303 N. Franklin St., 575/267-5191, 7am-4:30pm Mon.-Fri., 7am-3pm Sat., $6), another one of the more esteemed places to eat the hot stuff in Hatch. Its rellenos are dangerously greasy, but the chile-meat burrito is good, and if you like the salsa, you can buy whole jars of it. It's on the right when coming in from I-25, set back a bit at the corner of West Hill Street.

You can buy chile year-round in Hatch,

Sparky's restaurant in Hatch is impossible to miss.

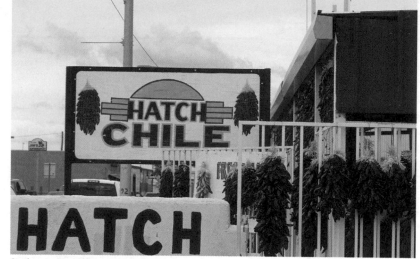

Stock up on New Mexican chile in Hatch.

whether freshly roasted in late August and early September, or frozen or dried and ground. One well-stocked shop is **Hatch Chile Sales** (265 W. Hall St.), which also sells pint jars of great homemade salsa.

FORT SELDEN STATE MONUMENT

Established in 1865, **Fort Selden State Monument** (1280 Ft. Selden Rd., 575/526-8911, 8:30am-5pm Wed.-Mon., $3), 22 miles south of Hatch and 16 miles north of Las Cruces, was never the site of a dramatic battle—but that doesn't mean a visit here is dull. On the contrary, because the small museum isn't bogged down in troop maneuvers, it has space to dedicate to the humdrum details of life on the 19th-century frontier. Here you learn, for instance, that women often accompanied their husbands to forts, and that a soldier's diet consisted of not much more than flour, bacon grease, and the occasional apple. Recipes, building fixtures, and remnants of letters flesh out the portrait of the soldiers stationed here to escort trading caravans. The adobe fort itself has melted to the outlines of a few walls surrounding a central parade ground; a monument to the Buffalo Soldiers, many of whom were stationed here, sits adjacent.

DOÑA ANA

South of Fort Selden, Highway 185 cuts just west of the village of Doña Ana. West of the highway, Shalem Colony Trail leads into the foothills, then via dirt road to **Prehistoric Trackways National Monument** (575/525-4300), an area in which the keen-eyed hiker can spot ancient dinosaur tracks preserved in the red sandstone here.

East of the highway, via Highway 320, Doña Ana, established in 1842 as a way station along the Camino Real, claims to be the oldest settlement in southern New Mexico. It is home to the lovely old **Church of Nuestra Señora de la Candelaria** (5525 Cristo Rey St., 575/526-2114, 9am-noon and 1pm-5pm Mon.-Fri.), which resembles a Mexican village church more than it does anything in the northern part of the state. The whitewashed adobe building was carefully restored in 2001; ask at the church office to be let inside to see the beautiful *latilla* wooden ceiling, and the new but compelling wood carvings. The bells are from the old Shalam Colony nearby.

Utopia on the Rio Grande

Even before the Hog Farm and other communes were established in the 1960s, New Mexico was a destination for visionaries. In 1882, a New York City dentist named John Newbrough claimed angels had channeled his hands to type almost a thousand pages of revelation in a manuscript he called *Oahspe*. The text lays out an elaborate cosmology in which, among other things, the earth moves along with the sun through different regions of space, each having a spiritual effect on the human race. It also details a plan for dealing with the world's orphans, through the building of a model village called the Shalam Colony that would be dedicated to children's education.

Oahspe's text inspired followers, who called themselves Faithists, and with 20 of these people Newbrough set about realizing Shalam Colony on the banks of the Rio Grande, about a mile from the village of Doña Ana, north of Las Cruces. A wealthy Bostonian put up the money for 1,500 acres of rich farmland, and the Faithists built some 35 buildings, plus innovations such as heated chicken pens, and a grand residence for the children. But farming proved difficult for the inexperienced colonists, and they were able to relocate only about 50 orphans. When Newbrough died of the flu in 1891, Shalam was already suffering. His wife and the Boston investor (who married in 1893) struggled to keep the place afloat, but the group dispersed in 1901, and the few remaining children were shipped to orphanages in Texas and Colorado.

A few Faithists carried on and settled in other parts of the West, but the only remnant of the Shalam Colony's social experiment is a historical marker on Highway 185.

Las Cruces

Built along the Rio Grande, with mountains jutting up to the east, Las Cruces resembles a miniature Albuquerque in its geography. But this city of 97,000 is distinct in several respects. As the home of New Mexico State University, which has a dedicated Chile Pepper Institute, this is a farm town and proud of it. And while Las Cruces may not literally abut Mexico (El Paso, Texas, 42 miles south, gets in the way), the neighboring country's influence is strongly felt here, in a cross-border culture that's distinct from the Hispano communities in the northern part of the state.

SIGHTS

Las Cruces was founded in 1849. The most notable landmarks are its mural-adorned water towers—you'll see a few coming in from the north on I-25. The largest historic area is the adobe enclave of Mesilla on the city's east side, technically a separate town, though functionally just a particularly scenic neighborhood. Another small section of old Las Cruces, a clutch of old adobe homes, can be found in the scenic **Mesquite Historic District:** Mesquite, Tornilla, San Pedro, and Campo Streets, between Chestnut and Colorado Avenues. There is also one outlying pueblo, **Tortugas,** wedged on a patch of land next to I-10; on an average day, there's not much to see, but it does host a great event for the Virgin of Guadalupe at the beginning of December.

Mesilla

For the most scenic approach to Mesilla, drive via University Avenue in the south. Fields line the road, and you'll feel as if you have indeed arrived in a different town when you turn north on Calle de El Paso. The historic village, which has largely preserved its original adobe architecture, centers on a trim plaza that's more sedate than Albuquerque's or Santa Fe's, but also less plagued with tourist tackiness. The twin-spired **Basilica of**

Las Cruces

To
Church of Nuestra
Señora de la Candelaria

To
Truth or Consequences

To
Dreamcatcher Inn,
Aguirre Springs Recreation Area,
and White Sands National Monument

To
Prehistoric Trackways National Monument,
Leasburg Dam State Park,
and Fort Selden

MYLES RD

DONA ANA RD

VALLEY DR

25

70

ROADRUNNER PKWY

0   0.5 mi

0   0.5 km

N MAIN ST

LAS CRUCES
COUNTRY CLUB

Apodaca
Park and
Pool

MADRID AVE

TELSHOR BLVD

85

185

ALAMEDA BLVD

70

SOLANO DR

SPRUCE AVE

ROADRUNNER LN

HADLEY   AVE

WALNUT   AVE

To
Las Cruces KOA

Lions
Park

A BITE OF
BELGIUM

HOTEL ENCANTO
DE LAS CRUCES

PICACHO   AVE

70

80

HADLEY

LAABS
POOL

S MESILLA

RAILROAD
MUSEUM

DOWNTOWN
MUSEUMS

LA NUEVA
CASITA

MESQUITE ST

MESQUITE
DISTRICT

LOHMAN   AVE

TELSHOR BLVD

MOTEL BLVD

AMERICA'S BEST
VALUE INN

HIGH DESERT
BREWING CO

AVE

ZEFFIRO
NAPOLETANA

342

AMADOR

CALICHE'S

Burn Lake
Park

LUNDEEN INN
OF THE ARTS

VALLEY DR

80

EL PASEO

HABANEROS
FRESH MEX

IDAHO AVE

To
NEW MEXICO FARM
& RANCH HERITAGE MUSEUM
and Dripping Springs Natural Area

10

292

CALLE DE EL PASO

LA QUINTA INN
LAS CRUCES ORGAN
MOUNTAINS

28

INTERNATIONAL
DELIGHTS

RD

SOLANO   DR

MEMORIAL
GENERAL HOSPITAL

To
Deming

188

BEST
WESTERN
MISSION INN

FARNEY LN

PARK DR

STATE
POLICE

AV DE MESILLA

THE BEAN

ZEFFIRO
NEW YORK

VISITORS CENTER/
ZUHL MUSEUM

COLLEGE DR

UNIVERSITY AVE

UNIVERSITY
ART GALLERY

PAN-AMERICAN
CENTER

¡ANDELE!'S
DOG HOUSE

MESILLA
VISITORS
CENTER

101

UNIVERSITY AVE

NEW MEXICO

Central
Plaza

LA POSTA

FOUNTAIN
THEATRE

373

STATE UNIVERSITY

10

25

LAS ALTURAS DR

CALLE DEL NORTE

LA MESILLA

UNION AVE

MAIN ST

359

TORTUGAS

To
Mesilla Valley Bosque State Park

CALLE DE EL PASO

478

28

To
Chope's
and Vineyards

To
El Paso, TX

© AVALON TRAVEL

ALLE de SANTIAGO

old-style street sign in Mesilla

young son, a victim of the range wars; his presumed murder prompted a contentious 1899 trial of cattleman Oliver Lee in the town of Hillsboro.

After you've toured around the plaza, walk west, to the residential section, where you'll get an idea of what the all-adobe village looked like 150 years back. (Be respectful when taking photos, though.)

Downtown Museums

The heart of old Las Cruces has been through a lot. It once looked just like Mesilla and the Mesquite District, all old adobes and "modern" mercantiles. But a 1960s urban renewal scheme razed all that and installed a covered pedestrian mall that made the whole area dark and hard to reach. Starting in 2005, this was gradually reversed, and Main Street has emerged into a slightly livelier place, with a few anchor theaters and a farmers market on Saturday mornings.

The city runs four **museums** (10am-4:30pm Tues.-Wed. and Fri., 10am-8pm Thurs., 9am-4:30pm Sat., free) in the downtown area. Individually, no one place is notable, but together, they give a good outlook on the area. Three are adjacent downtown. The **Branigan Cultural Center** (501 N. Main St., 575/541-2154) hosts special events and houses a concise history of the city. Next door to the south, the **Las Cruces Museum of Art** (491 N. Main St., 575/541-2137) shows off local talent, and next door to that (doors on both Main Street and Water Street, in the back) is the **Las Cruces Museum of Nature and Science** (411 N. Main St., 575/522-3120), which gives a good overview of the ecosystems in this part of New Mexico, illustrated with terrariums showcasing native reptiles.

A few blocks west is the old Santa Fe depot, now the **Las Cruces Railroad Museum** (351 N. Mesilla St., 575/647-4480), with some nice period details in the furniture. But of course the real fun is in the model-train room, which re-creates the AT&SF line around Las Cruces.

San Albino (575/526-9349, 1pm-3pm Mon.-Sat.), which dates from 1906, stands on the north side of the plaza. It replaced an earlier adobe built in the mid-19th century, when the settlement of Mesilla had finally attained, after seven years, some security from Apache raids, as well as legal surety when the Gadsden Purchase settled the dispute over the land on which Mesilla sat.

For more on Mesilla's historic buildings, stop in at the **visitors center** (2231 Avenida de Mesilla, 575/524-3262 ext. 117, www.old-mesilla.org, 9:30am-4:30pm Mon.-Thurs., 10am-2pm Fri.-Sat.), inside the town hall, for an annotated map. It will point out such venerable spots as the Fountain Theatre, off the southeast corner of the plaza. It was established by Albert Jennings Fountain, the powerful political leader who lived in Mesilla with his Mexican wife; his family performed melodramas on its stage. Fountain later disappeared, along with his

New Mexico State University

Founded in 1888, **New Mexico State University** (NMSU, www.nmsu.edu), home of the Aggies, is on the south side of town in the triangle formed by the intersection of I-10 and I-25, on a modern campus with a few Spanish and Southwestern touches. On the northwest corner, next to the visitors center (where it's easiest to park), look in at the **Zuhl Museum** (775 College Dr., 575/646-3616, 8am-5pm Mon.-Fri., free), a collection of geological items; particularly beautiful are the slabs of petrified wood. In Williams Hall, on University Avenue just east of Solano Drive, the **University Art Gallery** (575/646-5423, 10am-4pm Tues.-Sat., free) has a beautiful collection of painted wood *retablos* (saint portraits) from the 19th century. Just opposite to the west, in Kent Hall, the **University Museum** (575/646-3739, noon-4pm Tues.-Sat., free) displays recent archaeological finds.

★ New Mexico Farm & Ranch Heritage Museum

Even avowed city slickers will find something intriguing at the **New Mexico Farm & Ranch Heritage Museum** (4100 Dripping Springs Rd., 575/522-4100, www.frhm.org, 9am-5pm Mon.-Sat., noon-5pm Sun., $5), on the east edge of town near the Organ Mountain foothills. Indoors, trace the history of agriculture in New Mexico by peeking inside a traditional Mogollon pit house, then hearing the personal histories of homesteaders who replaced the Spanish in the 1860s. Space is given to Blackdom, the African American farmers' settlement begun in the Pecos Valley and relocated to Las Cruces in 1921, as well as the travails of other immigrant groups. Ag geeks can admire giant cotton pickers and learn more about the Spanish *acequia* system of irrigation. Outside, the museum sprawls for acres, encompassing a dairy barn and goats and longhorn cattle. Look out for demonstrations of sheep shearing, blacksmithing, home canning, and the like. Throughout, the volunteer docents have the zeal of missionaries—you too may have a real appreciation for vintage tractors by the time you leave.

Get to know your livestock at the New Mexico Farm & Ranch Heritage Museum.

ENTERTAINMENT AND EVENTS

With a student body of more than 16,000, NMSU is a strong influence on local nightlife, so casual bars with free-flowing beer are the norm. Special events highlight the city's ties to Mexican culture.

Nightlife

"None of our beers suck," boasts **High Desert Brewing Co.** (1201 W. Hadley Ave., 575/525-6752, 11am-midnight Mon.-Sat., noon-10pm Sun.), but they needn't set standards so low. This brewpub's products are all quite savory, and they wash down good basic bar grub. There's live music on Tuesday, Thursday, and Saturday, though you'd never guess it from the outside of the place, which looks like an office.

On the plaza in Mesilla, **El Patio Cantina** (2171 Calle de Parian, 575/526-9943, 5pm-11pm Mon., 4pm-11pm Tues., 2pm-2am Wed.-Sat., noon-midnight Sun.) is a good old-fashioned bar. Wednesday night is jazz night, and weekends are usually booked with classic-rock cover bands that draw a cross section of Las Cruces. A few blocks away, **Palacio Bar** (2600 Avenida de Mesilla, 575/525-2910, noon-11pm Sun.-Wed., noon-midnight Fri.-Sat.) is another local legend, tacitly men-only until only a quarter century ago, but now more welcoming and run by the previous owner's daughter. Multiple generations drink here, especially during the day.

Performing Arts

Downtown on Main Street is a fine movie palace of yore, the Italianate **Rio Grande Theatre** (211 N. Main St., 575/523-6403, www.riograndetheatre.com). It now hosts live performances. Nearby too is the **Las Cruces Community Theatre** (313 N. Main St., 575/523-1200, www.lcctnm.org), set in the historic State Theater.

Cinema

In Mesilla, the **Fountain Theatre** (2469 Calle de Guadalupe, 575/524-8287, www.

the Rio Grande Theatre

mesillavalleyfilm.org, $7) has been open since 1870 and operating as a cinema since 1905. It's a tiny, anonymous adobe building, the anti-movie palace, but a cool place to see a film, as you settle in between walls painted with murals of the Rio Grande. The place is entirely run by volunteers, with all kinds of interesting international films shown nightly at 7:30pm, plus weekend matinees.

Festivals and Events

The city's annual party, a fund-raiser for a cancer charity, used to be called the Whole Enchilada, devoted to cooking the world's largest enchilada, but the chef hung up his apron. Starting in 2016 the party (minus the large-scale food) became known as simply **The Big Event** (www.carelascruces.org), held over three days in late September. The festival of *lucha libre* (Mexican wrestling), motorcycle shows, and food vendors takes place downtown.

In December, residents of Tortugas Pueblo host the three-day **Our Lady of Guadalupe Fiesta** (575/526-8171), well worth attending if your schedule allows. On December 10 after sundown and continuing all night, there are Matachines and other dances in front of the Our Lady of Guadalupe Shrine and Parish at the pueblo. On the morning of December 11, a procession climbs nearby Tortugas Mountain (also known as "A" Mountain). On the last day are more dances and a big free community lunch. There are feasts and dances in front of Our Lady of Guadalupe Shrine and Parish, in the pueblo. Like so much culture in southern New Mexico, the event follows Mexican styles more closely than anything in the northern half of the state.

Other city parties reflect the city's Mexican history. Mesilla's plaza celebrates Mexico's victory in the 1862 Battle of Puebla on **Cinco de Mayo,** with fireworks, music, piñatas, and folk-dancing performances on the weekend closest to May 5. Likewise, the **Diez y Seis de Septiembre Fiesta** commemorates Mexico's independence movement with all the usual fun on the weekend nearest September 16. At the end of October, the colorful fun of **Dia de los Muertos,** the Day of the Dead, gives kids a chance to see a different sort of Halloween.

NMSU's Pan-American Center fills with the blare of trumpets for four days in June, for the **Las Cruces International Mariachi Conference & Festival** (www.lascrucesmariachi.org), which draws a long roster of musicians from northern Mexico, California, and across the Southwest. The daytime shows in Young Park are convivial.

SPORTS AND RECREATION

Las Cruces' proximity to the Organ Mountains—now a designated national monument—as well as Doña Ana and Robledo Peaks, both north of the city, makes it an outdoorsy town. The **Southwest Environmental Center** (275 N. Main St., 575/522-5552, www.wildmesquite.org, 9am-6pm Mon.-Fri.) is a great resource for anyone interested in the wild areas around the city. Ask here for trail recommendations, and learn what the latest efforts to protect the desert have yielded.

Hiking

The most accessible day hikes are in the foothills of the Organs, directly east of Las Cruces. **Dripping Springs Natural Area** (575/522-1219, 8am-7pm Apr.-Sept., 8am-5pm Oct.-Mar., $5/car) is 10 miles east of the city. The visitors center (8am-5pm daily) is also the head of the 1.5-mile Dripping Springs Trail, which winds through the ruined buildings of the 19th-century resort that gives the area its name. Just before you reach the visitors center, **La Cueva Picnic Area** is high enough that it affords a fine view across the basin. A trail from here leads past a cave that was the home of an Italian hermit for a few years in the 1860s, until he was found dead with a knife in his back; his murder was never solved.

Running six miles up and over the mountains to the east side, **Baylor Pass Trail** is a bit more challenging. It begins in the foothills

Mesilla's Fountain Theatre is run by volunteers.

east of Baylor Canyon Road—look for the turn 1.9 miles south of U.S. 70. After ascending about 1,600 feet to the pass, you have a view of both the Mesilla Valley to the west and White Sands to the east, then the trail descends over two miles to end in **Aguirre Springs Recreation Area** (575/525-4300, $5/car), a campground on the east side of the mountains. It takes about four hours to traverse; alternatively, you could make a shorter—but steeper—hike by starting on the east (city) side and going only up to the pass and back, about 2.5 hours. From the same campground, you have access to **Pine Tree Trail,** a 4.5-mile loop that's a little shadier, without much altitude gain—it takes only about three hours to do the circuit.

Biking

Las Cruces is flat and relatively slow-paced, making it easy to get around on two wheels; empty roads and rugged trails nearby cater to any recreational style. **Ride On Sports** (525 S. Telshor Blvd., 575/521-1686, www.

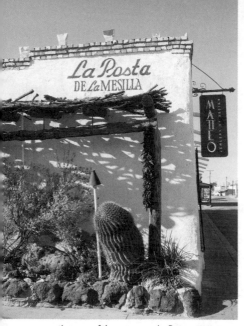

one tiny part of the enormous La Posta restaurant

Bird-Watching

Encompassing three miles of wetlands on the west side of the Rio Grande, **Mesilla Valley Bosque State Park** (5000 Calle del Norte, 575/523-4398, 7:30am-4:30pm daily, $5/car) is a solid birding spot close to the city. Entrance is via the visitors center on the northern side, where **guided hikes** go out at 2:30pm on weekends, and birding tours run at 7:30am on Saturday. Take Calle del Norte (Hwy. 359) west from central Mesilla, then drive south 1.2 miles within the park.

Rock Climbing

With the near-vertical Organ Mountains nearby and Hueco Tanks closer to El Paso, this is one of the best areas for bouldering and climbing in the United States. The options are too many to detail here, so your best bet is to contact **Outdoor Adventures** (1424 Missouri Ave., 575/521-1922, www.outdooradventures-lc.com, 10am-6pm Mon.-Fri., 10am-5pm Sat.) for guidance and maps.

Swimming

Las Cruces has several public pools. **Laabs** (750 W. Picacho Ave., 575/524-3168) is a modern outdoor pool with slides, open only during the summer. Admission is $4 for adults, $2 for children. The **Las Cruces Regional Aquatic Center** (1401 E. Hadley St., 575/541-2782) is a year-round indoor facility with slides and multiple pools.

rideonsports.com, 10am-8pm Mon.-Fri., 9am-8pm Sat., 11am-6pm Sun.) is the best local shop, with all kinds of gear and plenty of tips on where to ride.

One of the best-loved mountain biking trails is **Robledo Trail** (also known as SST Trail, 575/525-4300, www.blm.gov), 6.5 miles of single-track (13 miles round-trip) with lots of technical challenges—definitely for experienced riders. It's north of the city, just off Highway 185 west of the Rio Grande, in the same area as Prehistoric Trackways National Monument and a noncontiguous patch of land included in the Organ Mountains National Monument designation.

A more accessible circuit, **"A" Mountain Trail** (also signed as Tortugas Mountain Trails) starts just 10 minutes east of the NMSU campus and loops around the cone-shaped hill bedecked with a big red capital "A." The counterclockwise route around the low peak is the easier option, though beginning riders might still have to walk in a couple of spots.

FOOD
Mesilla

A couple of landmark spots cluster around the plaza, and there are some casual options that are good to know about if you're just out strolling around.

LANDMARK RESTAURANTS

One deservedly famous place is ★ **La Posta** (2410 Calle de San Albino, 575/524-3524, 11am-9pm Mon.-Thurs., 11am-9:30pm Fri., 9am-9:30pm Sat., 9am-9pm Sun., $11), one of those epically large and much beloved old restaurants where families go to celebrate special occasions. From the colorful parrots and macaws in the lobby to the waitstaff in billowing Mexican skirts to the two-page-long margarita menu, it's a party. It occupies an old adobe that was a stop on the Butterfield Overland Mail & Stage route, as well as room upon room in adjacent buildings—unspool a string to find your way back from the bathroom. Considering the scale of the place, the food is unexpectedly good and reliable.

The other big special-night-out place is **Double Eagle** (2355 Calle de Guadalupe, 575/523-6700, 11am-10pm Mon.-Sat., noon-9pm Sun., $24), with a grand old atmosphere of fogged mirrors and chandeliers. But it's best for a drink at the bar and an appetizer, to admire the scenery, rather than a full meal from its fancy-steakhouse menu.

If you're up for a drive, consider landmark roadhouse **Chope's** (Hwy. 28, 575/233-3420, 11:30am-1:30pm and 5:30pm-8:30pm Tues.-Fri., 5:30pm-8pm Sat., $8), in the village of La Mesa, about 20 minutes south of Mesilla. It's famous for its chiles rellenos.

NEW MEXICAN

By day, **Double Eagle** is the more casual New Mexican café **Peppers** (575/523-4999, 11am-3pm Mon.-Sat., $12), inside two smaller front rooms.

Emilia's on the Plaza (2290 Calle de Parian, 575/652-3007, 11am-9pm Thurs.-Sun., $10) is a casual place with a nice patio. The menu features chiles rellenos and other New Mexican goodies, as well as BLTs and Cuban sandwiches.

¡Andele!'s Dog House (1983 Calle del Norte, 575/526-1271, 11am-9pm daily, $10) is good for *tacos al carbon* (with meat fresh off the grill), great salsas, and Mexican-style hot dogs (wrapped in bacon and doused in jalapeños and other goodies). And, true to its name, it's canine-friendly and has a nice patio where pooches are welcome. (If you prefer no pets, head to the main restaurant, in the strip mall across the street, another epic room-upon-room family place.)

Chope's, a road-food icon south of Las Cruces

CAFÉS

For both coffee and community, ★ **The Bean** (2011 Avenida de Mesilla, 575/527-5155, 7am-5pm daily, $3) is the most popular place to chill out with a cup of joe. Set in an old gas station, the coffeehouse hosts an array of quirky regulars, while serving up pastries, omelets, and grilled sandwiches.

Las Cruces

Dining options skew a bit more global in Las Cruces proper.

NEW MEXICAN

Chef Alfredo does just about everything at ★ **Habaneros Fresh Mex** (600 E. Amador Ave., 575/524-1829, 8am-8pm Sun.-Thurs., 8am-9pm Fri.-Sat., $6), whipping up gorditas, house-made mole, carne asada fries, and more in this casual order-at-the-counter place. It's all hot and fresh, and a fantastic bargain—you even get free "welcome soup."

There's nothing new about **La Nueva Casita** (195 N. Mesquite St., 575/523-5434, run from typical pepperoni to lemon slices and asparagus; there's pasta too. The same team runs the student-friendly **Zeffiro New York Pizzeria** (901 University Ave., 575/525-6770, 11am-9pm Mon.-Sat., noon-7pm Sun.), where you can get a greasier pizza by the slice.

INTERNATIONAL

Las Cruces is short on global cuisine, but **International Delights** (1245 El Paseo Rd., 575/647-5956, 7am-11pm Mon.-Thurs., 7am-midnight Fri.-Sat., 8am-11pm Sun., $8) satisfies a lot of cravings. The menu includes Middle Eastern standards like falafel along with familiar deli combos and a good selection of coffee, tea, and pastries, including baklava with local flair: date pecan, vanilla piñon, and more. Look for it in the back corner of a strip mall next to Albertson's supermarket.

For a break from chile, head to **A Bite of Belgium** (741 N. Alameda Blvd., 575/527-2483, 7am-2pm daily, $8), where the food is European and the service American-friendly, with bottomless cups of coffee to go with your Liège-style waffles or fluffy-custardy French toast. Lunch is soups and sandwiches (try the lamb with caramelized onions).

DESSERTS

On a hot summer night, there's no better place to be than **Caliche's** (590 S. Valley Dr., 575/647-5066, noon-9pm Sun.-Thurs., 11am-10pm Fri.-Sat., $4), which serves frozen custard under pink and blue neon. A caliche (Spanish for hard clay) is the local equivalent of a St. Louis-style concrete, a shake so thick you have to eat with a spoon. Of course there are New Mexican mix-ins such as pine nuts and red chile.

ACCOMMODATIONS

Las Cruces is short on distinctive lodging. Of the numerous chain operations, the most conveniently located ones are on Avenida de Mesilla where it passes under the interstate, before you reach Mesilla proper.

La Nueva Casita

8am-3pm Sun.-Mon., 8am-7:30pm Tues.-Thurs., 8am-8:30pm Fri.-Sat., $9), an old-school place with tile-topped tables, mariachi horns, and plenty of neighbors as customers. The food is homey, with the welcome variation of *fideos* (soupy, spicy thin noodles) as a side instead of rice. Bonus: It's in the pretty Mesquite Historic District.

FRESH AND LOCAL

The **farmers market** on Main Street downtown usually has a number of good snack vendors—tamales and more. It sets up on Wednesday and Saturday (8:30am-1pm), with more activity on the latter day.

ITALIAN

As pizza purists demand, it's all about the crust at ★ **Zeffiro Pizzeria Napoletana** (136 N. Water St., 575/525-6757, 11am-2pm and 5pm-8pm Mon.-Thurs., 11am-2pm and 5pm-9pm Fri.-Sat., $9). Pies come out of the wood oven with almost comically blistered and bubbling edges. Toppings

Under $100

Campers can set up at the **Las Cruces KOA** (814 Weinrich Rd., 575/526-6555, www.koa.com), west of the city just south of U.S. 70, with fantastic views of the mountains, a heated swimming pool, and wireless Internet. Cabins ($58) and tent sites (from $29) are available. You can also camp at **Leasburg Dam State Park** (Hwy. 157, 575/524-4068, www.nmparks.com), 15 miles north of town adjacent to Fort Selden. The park runs along a series of irrigation canals and is favored by kayakers and bird-watchers; it has 31 developed campsites ($8 for tents, $14 for RVs).

The hospitable owners of ★ **America's Best Value Inn** (2160 W. Picacho Ave., 575/524-8627, www.abvi.com, $55 s, $60 d), also known as the Big Chile Inn, deserve commendation for giving a distinctly homey feel to a generic 50-plus-room motel complex. The grounds have a swimming pool and a big koi pond, and the rooms are quite large and very clean. You can't miss it—there is a giant (world's largest, in fact) red-chile sculpture out front.

Near Mesilla, **La Quinta Inn & Suites Las Cruces Organ Mountains** (1500 Hickory Dr., 575/523-0100, www.lq.com, $79 d) is in excellent shape and has a small pool. The **Best Western Mission Inn** (1765 S. Main St., 575/524-8591, www.bwmissioninn.com, $85 d) is well kept, and its large rooms have nice little Southwestern details like tile mirror frames. Rates include a full breakfast, and you can often get very good online discounts.

$100-150

Walking distance from downtown, the rambling, Spanish-style **Lundeen Inn of the Arts** (618 S. Alameda St., 575/526-3326, www.innofthearts.com, $89 s, $125 d) has been open for decades, and the walls crowded with paintings reflect that age. The place feels a bit dim and dusty, but the owner, an architect, is interesting, and the history is palpable. Some rooms have fireplaces.

The newly built **Dreamcatcher Inn** (10201 Starfly Rd., 575/522-3035, www.dreamcatcherinn.com, $120 d) is just northeast of the city, with three spacious rooms looking out on the

America's Best Value Inn is easy to find: Look for the giant chile.

South of Las Cruces

Drive south out of Mesilla on Calle de El Paso (Highway 28), and you're almost immediately in lush agricultural land: Pecan orchards, vineyards, and cotton fields sprawl almost all the way to the Texas border. The two-lane road winds by you-pick farms, corn mazes, and other seasonal entertainment. Year-round, you can break up the drive with stops at wineries, such as **Rio Grande Vineyards** (5321 Hwy. 28, 575/524-3985, noon-5:30pm Fri.-Sun.), closest to Mesilla, or **La Viña** (4201 Hwy. 28, 575/882-7632, noon-5pm Thurs.-Tues.), the oldest vineyard in New Mexico, in La Union. Both stock other local products, such as honey and chiles, in addition to wine.

Loop through the little village of La Union (west off Highway 28), then head back north and conclude with a meal at **Chope's** (Hwy. 28, 575/233-3420, 11:30am-1:30pm and 5:30pm-8:30pm Tues.-Fri., 5:30pm-8pm Sat., $8), back close to Las Cruces, in the village of La Mesa. It's a down-at-the-heels roadhouse and restaurant, famous for its heavily egg-battered chiles rellenos, red chile beans, and rural New Mexican ambience. The restaurant is in the house to the south of the parking area. You can also eat in the bar, and even if you don't, you should have a beer there just to people-watch.

desert. They're prettily furnished with country-Southwest style, and all have an extra single sofa bed, convenient for traveling friends. Also notable: All three rooms have separate entrances and are wheelchair-accessible.

The city's plushest hotel, **Hotel Encanto de Las Cruces** (705 S. Telshor Blvd., 575/522-4300, www.hotelencanto.com, $129 d) perches on a hill, affording great views across the valley. Inside, the decor is a rich palette of tan and wine, with a hint of Spanish colonial style, and the beds are particularly comfortable. Request either a west-facing top-floor room for a great sunset view or something on the pool level, where patios open onto the swimming area. The only drawback is that its location on the east side is a bit isolated, and the only place in walking distance is the Mesilla Valley Mall.

INFORMATION AND SERVICES

Las Cruces Convention & Visitors Bureau (211 N. Water St., 575/541-2444, www.lascrucescvb.org, 8am-5pm Mon.-Fri.) has free high-speed Internet service, along with a helpful staff and piles of brochures.

On the old plaza, the excellent **Mesilla Book Center** (2360 Calle Principal, 575/526-6220, 11am-5:30pm Tues.-Sat., 1pm-5pm Sun.) has perhaps every book you'd ever want to read about the American West and the Mexican border, plus current and classic fiction, guides to horse care and bike repair, and plenty more. Downtown, **Coas Books** (317 N. Main St., 575/524-8471, 9am-6pm Mon.-Sat., 11am-5pm Sun.) is crammed with secondhand titles of every kind.

GETTING THERE AND AROUND

By car, Las Cruces is 225 miles (3 hours) south of Albuquerque on I-25 and U.S. 85, and 45 miles (about 45 minutes) north of El Paso, Texas. From Alamogordo, it's 68 miles (1 hour) west on U.S. 70; from Deming, it's 60 miles (1 hour) east on I-10; and from Truth or Consequences, 75 miles (1.25 hours) south on I-25.

Rather than making the drive from the Albuquerque airport, many visitors to Las Cruces fly into El Paso (ELP) **Las Cruces Shuttle** (575/525-1784, www.lascrucesshuttle.com) runs an airport transport service at least eight times daily. Rates are $47 one-way, or $79 round-trip. Las Cruces International Airport (LRU, 575/541-2471) is only for private aviation—but it does have a large collection of scale-model planes.

The **Greyhound bus** (800/231-2222, www.

greyhound.com) stops at the Chucky's convenience store (800 E. Thorpe Rd., 575/524-8518, 7am-11pm daily). Two buses run daily from Albuquerque; five run from El Paso.

RoadRunner Transit (575/541-2500, www.las-cruces.org) is the city bus system,

though buses run infrequently, and only until 7pm Monday-Friday, till 6pm on Saturday, and not at all on Sunday. Fare is $1 (exact change, bills accepted), and buses are equipped with front bike racks. Route No. 40 runs to Mesilla from downtown.

West to the Bootheel

From Las Cruces, I-10 runs west through the flatlands up to the Chiricahua Mountains on the Arizona border. Most of the area is unrelenting desert punctuated by spikes of mountains, such as the Floridas, rising 2,800 feet above the surrounding plain. The area is known for dust storms and shimmering heat, but in the southwestern corner of the state, a little stub of virtually untouched wilderness juts farther south. Jaguars have been spotted here on very rare occasions, and critters like coatimundi, tarantulas, rattlesnakes, and particularly enormous locusts thrive. By late August, when the summer rains are strong enough, the desert turns a lush green; avoid May and June, however, before the rains have started, as this is the hottest, driest period.

DEMING

"Pure water and fast ducks" boasts Deming of its charms, and surely no other town in the United States can make such a claim to fame. The water comes from a large aquifer under the city of 15,000; as for the speedy birds, they're part of the Great American Duck Race, the city's biggest annual event. The business leaders who came up with the scheme in 1980 (to rival Ruidoso's horse-racing industry) admitted the initial brainstorming session did involve liquor.

Deming is popular with retirees from the upper Midwest, and its greater cityscape is one of RV and trailer parks, as well as truck stops. But its old downtown, south of the intersection of Pine and Gold, is a few blocks of surprising elegance, and it's a great place to pull

off the highway for authentic Mexican food or a slice of pie. Street addresses with directionals (SW, NE, etc.) are outside of town, not in central Deming.

Sights

Most visitors start with the **Deming-Luna Mimbres Museum** (301 S. Silver Ave., 575/546-2382, 9am-4pm Mon.-Sat., donation), one block south of Pine Street. Set in a 1917 armory, the museum is the county's vast repository of historic flotsam, lovingly curated and carefully arranged. Novelty whiskey bottles, nutcrackers, geodes, beautiful Mimbres pottery—it's all here, in incredible detail and profusion.

At the end of South Silver Avenue, the redbrick **Luna County Courthouse,** restored in 2006, looks like it would be more at home in Iowa. It was built in 1910, then in 1916 saw the trial of many of Pancho Villa's alleged accomplices in the rebel leader's raid on Columbus, New Mexico; four of the "Villistas" were subsequently hanged on the green lawn in front of the building.

The **Deming Arts Center** (100 S. Gold Ave., 575/546-3663, 10am-4pm Tues.-Sat.) occupies a grand old building at the main crossroads, showing local artists with a selection that changes monthly.

Entertainment and Events

The **St. Clair Winery** (1325 De Baca Rd. SE, 575/546-2408, 9am-6pm Mon.-Sat., noon-6pm Sun.), established by a French family in 1984, occupies 15 acres a few miles outside of

Deming

town (head east on Pine Street) and is an easy hop off the interstate. This is just part of some 120 acres the group owns, to produce most of the grapes for winemakers all over the state. You can taste a wide range of wines; the better ones are under the D. H. Lescombes label—especially the syrah, which does well in the sun here. The winery also has a wine festival in early October.

Deming's annual hoedown is the last weekend in August, when the **Great American Duck Race** (www.demingchamber.com) takes over. In addition to the headline duck sprint, festivities include a cash-prize tortilla toss, outhouse races, a parade with more fake foam beaks than you can count, and a balloon rally.

Sports and Recreation

Beat the summer heat at **Sam Baca Aquatic Center** (815 W. Buckeye St., 575/546-7958, $2), which has three big outdoor pools and a waterslide, with frolicking kids segregated from the lap swimmers. It's open summers mid-May-end of September; call for hours.

For a more outdoorsy experience, head southeast to the Florida (Flowering) Mountains, so named for the colorful wildflowers that blanket their steep slopes in springtime. In summer, though, they can feel a bit barren and hot, and nowhere more so than at **Rockhound State Park** (9880 Stirrup Rd. SE, 575/546-6182, www.nmparks.com, $5/car). Its setting in the foothills is picturesque, especially around sunset, but a day poking around with a pickax (you're allowed to carry out 15 pounds of finds) is rewarding only for the truly geologically minded. Everyone else will probably be satisfied with the exhibits of geodes and other mineral miracles in the visitors center.

For more scenic hiking and good bird-watching, head to **Spring Canyon Recreational Area** (8am-4pm Wed.-Sun.), immediately adjacent to Rockhound. While you're out, you have a slim chance of spotting an ibex, a variety of goat with large curving horns. The Department of Game and Fish imported them from Iran and released them here in 1970, as part of a now-discontinued program to create an exotic game-hunting industry; about 400 of the animals live in the mountains now.

Food

Deming doesn't look like a promising gourmet stop, but it is a good place to sample some Mexican (as opposed to *New* Mexican) food. **Tacos Mirasol** (309 E. Pine St., 575/544-0646, 9am-9pm daily, $5) is a tiny but sparkling-clean roadside hut that does tacos, of course, but also Mexican-style sandwiches (*tortas*), which consist of a choice of meat on a soft fluffy roll, usually slathered with avocado, mayonnaise, and a thin layer of refried beans. Both come with a tangy-hot tomatillo salsa; cut the heat with a banana milkshake or fresh limeade.

Don't miss Elisa's House of Pies & Restaurant.

For a heartier meal, head for ★ **Las Cazuelas** (108 N. Platinum St., 575/544-8432, 11am-7pm Tues.-Sat., 11am-4pm Sun., $8), a cheery Mexican restaurant hidden in the back of a butcher and grocery. Of course you can get a big *churrasco* platter of grilled meats, but you can go smaller, with a burger or a spicy soup, as well as burritos and other goodies. Everything's fresh and homemade-tasting.

For New Mexican, the time-warp **Si Señor** (200 E. Pine St., 575/546-3938, 9:30am-8pm Mon.-Sat., 10am-2pm Sun., $7) shouldn't be discounted for its walls tiled like a 1970s bathroom. On the plus side: low prices, huge portions, and an ingenious platter of chicken-fried steak slathered with green chile and cheese (the "milanesa"). Regulars also recommend the carne adovada-stuffed sopaipilla.

In a side alley by the Wells Fargo parking lot, ★ **Elisa's House of Pies & Restaurant** (208 S. Silver Ave., 575/494-4639, 7am-7pm Tues.-Fri., 9:30am-7pm Sat., 9am-4pm Sun., $10) is not messing around: pecan, lemon meringue, millionaire (cream pie with pecans and pineapple), French silk (creamy chocolate), and more make up the daily pie list. Elisa and her husband also dish out a full soul-food menu that includes barbecue ribs, collard greens, and red beans and rice. The sides are good for vegetarians—a nice break from cheese enchiladas.

Finally, if you've got a car full of kids (and/or you just can't face another enchilada), **Forghedaboudit Pizza** (115 Silver Ave., 575/275-3881, 11am-2pm and 4pm-9pm Mon. and Wed.-Fri., 3pm-9pm Sat., $10) is worth a detour. Solo diners can ask for a 12-inch pizza (not on the menu), and the homemade meatballs and tomato sauce are good. There are also hot sandwiches and salads.

Accommodations

Travelers seldom plan to spend the night in Deming, but if you're deciding between here and Lordsburg for the night, Deming has a slightly larger selection of upper-end chain hotels (with more chance of a vacancy), and also better options for dinner. For better, non-chain value, though, consider driving south to Columbus—or to the one vintage motel in Lordsburg. Ordinarily, you should have no trouble rolling into Deming without a reservation, but book ahead when the duck races are on at the end of August.

On the east side of town, **Grand Motor Inn** (1721 E. Pine St., 575/546-2632, www.grandmotorinndeming.com, $52 d) delivers good value for the money—though, oddly, it charges $1 for toiletries, and breakfast is an extra $4. You get a nice big room, with a minifridge, and even a swimming pool.

Information

Make your first stop in town the **Deming Visitor Center** (800 E. Pine St., 575/567-1962, 9am-5pm Mon.-Fri., 9am-11am Sat.), where you'll find chatty staff and answers to all your area questions. **Readers Cove Books** (200 S. Copper St., 575/544-2512, 10am-5pm Tues.-Sat.) is cozy shop with an eclectic selection.

Getting There

By car, Deming is 60 miles (one hour) west of Las Cruces via I-10; it's another 60 miles west to Lordsburg. Silver City is 53 miles (one hour) north via U.S. 180. The **Greyhound bus** (800/231-2222, www.greyhound.com) comes in twice a day from Las Cruces and drops you at the Shell station (420 E. Cedar St., 7am-10pm daily).

CITY OF ROCKS STATE PARK

Bristling out of the flat basin north of Deming, **City of Rocks State Park** (327 Hwy. 61, 575/536-2800, www.nmparks.com, $5/car) does indeed resemble a metropolis, as imagined by Dr. Seuss. Hardened lava, eroded over 35 million years, has formed a skyline of towering pinnacles and bulbous growths. With expansive views across the flatlands and all sorts of birds and other wildlife to check out up close, this is a great spot for a picnic and short hike, or an overnight in one of the 52 campsites (10 have water and electrical hookups). The visitors center is well equipped, with showers for overnighters. The park is 24 miles from Deming (28 miles from Silver City) on U.S. 180, then 4 miles northeast on Highway 61.

City of Rocks State Park

Faywood Hot Springs

On the road to City of Rocks is **Faywood Hot Springs** (Hwy. 61, 575/536-9663, www. faywood.com); the springs are much easier to reach than those on the Gila River, as the route here from surrounding towns is a straight highway. Once the site of a posh resort, which was later razed, the pools have been redeveloped in a more natural way. All outdoors, shaded with small trees, they're sealed inside and cleaned regularly. They're perched around a small rise, and surrounded by campsites and cabins.

The public pools (10am-10pm daily, $13/day) are split between clothing-optional and swimsuits-required; private pools ($26/hour) are also available. The very nice **tent sites** ($31 d) and **cabins** ($110) include access to the pools. The visitors center stocks water, snacks, and towels, in case you don't have your own.

COLUMBUS

Devastated in a raid by Pancho Villa in 1916, the border town of Columbus is still not exactly jumping. It's centered on a park and a WPA-built town hall, with most of its commerce and community linked with Mexico in some way. As you drive south from Deming on Highway 11, the terrain grows sandier, more dotted with cactus and yucca, and generally more like what people imagine Mexico to look like. You may see a giant white blimp in the sky—it's an aerostat, a balloon-borne radar system used by the U.S. Border Patrol.

Sights
PANCHO VILLA STATE PARK
The southeast corner of the main crossroads (Highways 9 and 11) in Columbus, formerly a U.S. Army encampment, has been transformed into small **Pancho Villa State Park** (400 W. Hwy. 9, 575/531-2711, www. nmparks.com, $5/car). It includes an excellent **museum** (8am-5pm daily, free) dedicated to Villa's 1916 attack, in which 90 of Columbus's 400 residents were killed. The subsequent

Faywood Hot Springs

manhunt for the Mexican rebel leader, led by General John J. Pershing, involved some 2,000 troops traveling by car and airplane—the first mechanized military campaign in history. The museum does a great job of portraying both the personal tragedy felt in Columbus and the impressive scale of Pershing's military operation, which was a crucial training ground for World War I.

South of the museum and a large cactus garden are 79 **campsites** ($8 car, $14 RV) with good facilities but in somewhat spartan surroundings.

COLUMBUS HISTORICAL SOCIETY MUSEUM
The **Columbus Historical Society Museum** (575/531-2620, 10am-4pm daily Sept.-Apr., 10am-1pm daily May-Aug., donation) is across the intersection from the state park. Housed in the old depot, it has nifty train paraphernalia, as well as some morbidly

Get a little taste of Mexico in Palomas.

interesting items, such as a replica death mask of Pancho Villa and a diorama showing the wreckage of the town in 1916.

PALOMAS

While you're in Columbus, you may as well see a bit of Mexico. Immediately past the customs gates and the dead-straight border fence is a five-block strip of dentist offices, pharmacies, fruit-pop vendors, and taco shops, with the central plaza a couple of blocks to the west. One mega-mart, the impossible-to-miss **Pink Store** (575/531-7243, 9am-6pm daily), sells crafts from all over Mexico, plus the obligatory margaritas at the in-house restaurant.

Crossing the border is usually as easy as being waved through; coming back to American soil, however, you'll need to show your passport, and your car may be subject to X-ray. It's a lot easier to walk over (do take your passport). Free parking is available just before the border, and the Pink Store can arrange a golf-cart escort if you buy too much to carry yourself.

Food and Accommodations

For breakfast and lunch, **Irma's Kitchen** (Hwy. 11, 7am-7pm Wed.-Mon., $7), at the main crossroads, is a major gathering spot with excellent red chile and other very homey New Mexican food. The **Patio Café** (211 Broadway, 575/531-2495, 9am-3pm Mon.-Sat., $7) has good burgers and green-chile stew. For dinner, it's practical—and preferable—just to walk to Mexico and have great *barbacoa* and more at the various street carts and restaurants.

In this relative middle of nowhere, there are two good places to sleep. Formerly known as Martha's Place, **Los Milagros** (204 Lima Rd., 575/531-2467, www.marthas-placehotel.com, $59 d) is a great surprise—in fact, you might want to make the detour from Deming if you prefer B&Bs. Each of the five sunny, freshly renovated rooms has a balcony. Across Highway 11, **Hacienda de Villa** (220 S. Hwy. 11, 575/531-1000, $55 d) is a nicely kept little motel that's a real bargain. The main building used to be the town's museum.

Hacienda de Villa motel in Columbus

LORDSBURG

Aesthetically, Lordsburg is lacking—a quick cruise around town suggests this is where the chain-link-fence salesman made his first million. It's also a bit tragic economically, as the freight train industry that drove the place has all but died, leaving a desolate strip of 1st Street (now Motel Drive) running parallel to the tracks. Why stop? Well . . .

Sights

LORDSBURG-HIDALGO COUNTY MUSEUM

The **Lordsburg-Hidalgo County Museum** (710 E. 2nd St., 575/542-9086, 1pm-5pm Mon.-Fri., free) has a fascinating exhibit on the history of POW camps in New Mexico during World War II. One was located near Lordsburg, and German and Italian prisoners were put to work farming. The rest of the museum is a bit of a jumble, though there are some relics from local mines (another defunct Lordsburg industry).

SHAKESPEARE

Two and a half miles south of Lordsburg on Highway 494, the ghost town of **Shakespeare** (575/542-9034, www.shakespeareghosttown.com, $4) is in perhaps the

ideal state of repair—just enough to spark the imagination, but not so polished as to seem museum-like.

What's even more interesting is how the typical Old West buildings such as the saloon, the assay office, and the blacksmith's shop are overlaid with the history of the family that has owned and maintained the place since 1935. There's also a dance studio, where a generation of Lordsburg girls took classes, and a shack that the family matriarch squatted in to protest the expansion of I-10. The result is a more poignant monument to the fading American West than you find in most ghost towns.

The place is open only one weekend a month—check the schedule online. If you go on a reenactment day ($5, four weekends a year), you'll also get to see shootouts and maybe a mock hanging.

Food and Accommodations

For New Mexican food, head into town to ★ **Ramona's** (904 E. Motel Dr., 575/542-3030, 8am-8pm Tues.-Fri., 8am-2pm Sun., $7), a tiny café with pretty curtains in the windows. On Sunday, they serve a fantastic *menudo*. Another fine option is **El Charro** (209 Southern Pacific Blvd., 575/542-3400,

Special tours at the ghost town of Shakespeare end with shootouts.

8am-10pm daily, $7), where you can watch the trains rumble right through downtown while you eat. The food is hit or miss, but its neon sign and general vintage style is splendid.

Thanks to the U.S. Border Patrol setting up headquarters here, Lordsburg's accommodation options are a little better than the town might suggest. Independent, old-style **Holiday Motel** (600 E. Motel Dr., 575/542-3535, $48 d) and the recently renovated **Motel 6** (1303 S. Main St., 575/542-8807, www.motel6, $60 d) are both good-value options; the latter has a pool.

RODEO

The gateway town, such as it is, to New Mexico's "bootheel" is a string of barely a dozen buildings along Highway 80, fronting now-vanished railroad tracks and the Arizona state line. Rodeo sits in a dramatic bowl between small but spiking mountain ranges; coming over the low pass into the valley affords one of the more awe-inspiring views in southern New Mexico, especially in late afternoon when the sun glints off the crags. This flat terrain, which develops temporary shallow lakes (called playas) in the wet season, is hospitable to a huge range of birds. Nine miles away is Portal, Arizona, world-famous as a birding destination.

Sights

Two miles north of Rodeo proper, the **Chiricahua Desert Museum** (4 Rattlesnake Canyon Rd., 575/557-5757, 9am-5pm daily, $5) is a herper's dream—dedicated to all things reptilian. The entry fee allows access to two rooms full of live, rare rattlesnakes and lizards, as well as a profusion of slithery tchotchkes, from Steve Irwin memorabilia to vintage snake-bite kits. Also on display are beautifully detailed paintings and prints of snakes by noted wildlife illustrator Tell Hicks. For those who get nervous just reading about snakes, there's a large gift shop to browse (plenty of local guides and more) and a garden with rare cacti (free).

Ten miles over the border in Arizona, alongside Highway 80, the **Geronimo Surrender Memorial** is the final chapter to the Apache leader's story, lived so vividly around New Mexico. For nearly 30 years, Geronimo fought against the incursions into Apache lands after Mexicans killed his family; he finally submitted to American terms in 1886, effectively ending the Indian Wars. After his surrender, he was taken prisoner and toured as an exotic attraction, including at the 1904 World's Fair in St. Louis. Just as Geronimo's birth monument is not at the "headwaters of the Gila," but in an accessible parking lot, the stone memorial pillar is placed for convenience by the highway. The actual surrender site is in privately owned **Skeleton Canyon,** in the Peloncillo Mountains, unfortunately now gated off.

Sports and Recreation

The wilderness areas around here are almost completely devoid of trails; if you fancy adventure (and carrying plenty of water), the **Big Hatchet** and **Animas** ranges to the south await.

If you prefer a bit more structure, make the short drive past Portal and on to **Cave Creek Canyon** in Arizona's Coronado National Forest, strikingly lush, teeming with birds, and lined on either side with sheer cliffs pocked with caves. To get there, take Highway 533 (Portal Rd.) west from Highway 80, directly across from the Chiricahua Desert Museum.

You can't miss the Chiricahua Desert Museum, home to the world's largest rattlesnake tail.

Stop first at the **visitor information center** (Forest Rd. 42, 8am-4pm Fri.-Sun.) for maps and a bird checklist. (Note that Arizona does not observe Daylight Saving Time; in summer, the closing time is really 5pm New Mexico time.)

Up the road a couple of miles is the turn for **South Fork Trail** (no. 243), a birding pilgrimage site because the rare elegant trogon is often in residence along the creek here. Even if you're not interested in our feathered friends, it's hard not to love the elegant trogon, which lives up to its name with its scarlet breast and long chestnut-brown tail. The area is also lovely in the fall, when the maple leaves turn. The full trail is nearly seven miles, with an elevation gain of 2,500 feet, but the first mile or so is level.

For more local information and books, stop off at the **Southwestern Research Station,** an ecologists' camp maintained by the American Museum of Natural History. Its **Chiricahua Nature Shop** (520/558-2396,

8:30-noon and 1pm-4:30pm Wed.-Sat.) is a good place to find out what interesting critters have been spotted here. Farther up the road from here is another good walk, the **Herb Martyr Trail** (no. 247); at 2.8 miles it's much shorter than the South Fork route, but more strenuous.

Food and Accommodations

For meals and a bit of social contact, head to the **Rodeo Grocery & Café** (Hwy. 80, 575/557-2295, 7:30am-3pm Mon.-Sat., $7), which posts its food specials for the month—school-cafeteria-style, but so much tastier. (The grocery is open until 5:30pm, for basic DIY provisions.) For dinner, the **Rodeo Tavern** (Hwy. 80, 575/557-2229, 4pm-10pm Wed.-Sat., $12) makes excellent fried chicken, and also has a pool table and a varied crew of regulars. In summer, it serves lunch on Friday and Saturday as well.

Reason alone to drive all this way, the lovely ★ **Casa Adobe** (Hwy. 80, 575/557-7777, www.casaadobe.net, $160 d) fulfills every get-away-from-it-all fantasy. Rodeo has no cell phone coverage, and there's no Internet in this beautiful casita, leaving you free to sit and admire the dramatic mountains on either side. The whole house is yours, impeccably decorated with rustic furniture and stocked with goodies like eggs from the hosts' chickens. Similar digs on better-trod paths in the state would cost at least twice as much. There's a two-night minimum.

The **Mountain Valley Lodge RV Park** (223 Hwy. 80, 575/520-3731, www.mountainvalleylodgesite.com) has two rooms ($75) to rent, and two larger cabins with kitchens ($95 and $125).

With 24 hours' notice, you can also eat at the cafeteria at the **Southwestern Research Station** (520-558-2396, www.amnh.org) or stay in the lodge rooms ($90 pp, including meals), if they're not booked by researchers.

Silver City

Called just "Silver" by the locals, this casual mountain burg ranks high on quality-of-life lists. It has lured a portion of its 11,000 population from out of state with a near-utopian combination of outdoor activities, an educated populace (Western New Mexico University is here), and beautiful housing stock that dates from the city's boom in the late 19th and early 20th centuries. Unlike more slapdash towns, Silver was built to last, and its stone and cast-iron structures have helped the town maintain its grandeur. Over the decades, it has been home to Billy the Kid, who came here in 1873 at about age 13 and got into trouble from the start, then many wealthy tuberculosis patients in the 1890s.

For decades, the primary industry fueling the town was mining, but as that has diminished, creative transplants have remade the center of Silver. Contemporary hippies have set the mellow pace downtown and drive the local food co-op and other local institutions, while rat-race dropouts, young artists, and a small gay and lesbian community have bought up the territorial-style bungalows and downtown storefronts, repainted them in candy colors, and created a distinctive, unpretentious cultural scene.

Navigating Silver is not immediately intuitive because the main downtown drag is Bullard Street, though Hudson Street, a couple of blocks east, is larger and runs directly south from U.S. 180. The original Main Street, which ran parallel to and between Bullard and Hudson, was washed away in a series of floods between 1895 and 1903, leaving what's evocatively called the Big Ditch. A greenery-filled chasm some 50 feet below the street level, it's an unorthodox park for

creatively painted shopfronts in Silver City

Silver City

an unorthodox populace. Most of the rest of Silver's attractions are on the west side of it.

SIGHTS

The first stop in learning about the town, the **Silver City Museum** (312 W. Broadway, 575/538-5921, www.silvercitymuseum.org, 9am-4:30pm Tues.-Fri., 10am-4pm Sat.-Sun., $3 donation) is an intriguing, polished collection in an old Victorian home. You'll see photos of Main Street before and after it became

the Big Ditch, a fascinating exhibit on the culture and economy of tuberculosis treatment in New Mexico, and more than you thought you wanted to know about mining history and science. Be sure to climb up to the cupola to take in the view of the whole town.

Just up the hill at the end of Broadway, the **Grant County Courthouse** is a small but elegant building. The highlight is 1934 murals depicting the local ranching and mining industries.

A bit farther afield, the **WNMU Museum** (1000 W. College Ave., 575/538-6386, www. wnmumuseum.org, 9am-4:30pm Mon.-Fri., 10am-4pm Sat.-Sun., free) has an excellent collection of Mimbres pottery, on which critters such as coatis, turkeys, and pronghorns dance, not to mention a grand antique urinal in the basement men's room. The museum is in Fleming Hall. Head west on 10th Street; on campus, look for the building near the top of the hill on the right.

ENTERTAINMENT AND EVENTS

Although it's a college town, Silver City isn't rowdy at night. A few bars along Bullard give some evening options. Of these, **Little Toad Creek Brewery & Distillery** (200 N. Bullard St., 575/956-6144, 11am-11pm daily, later on weekends) is probably the most consistently busy, with live music, trivia nights, and housemade booze. People also make the drive to Pinos Altos for music at the saloon there.

Silver's excellent new-old downtown cinema is the **Silco Theatre** (311 N. Bullard St., 575/956-6090, www.thesilco.com, $8), first opened in 1923 and was renovated and reopened in 2016. It shows first-run films. For second-run films and occasional live shows, **Light Hall Theater** (1000 W. College Ave., 575/538-6300, http://movies.wnmu.edu, $2), on the WNMU campus, is another good venue.

As for events, Silver is internationally known for the bike race **Tour of the Gila** (www.tourofthegila.com), which, thanks to its winding routes through the surrounding mountains, is known as a warm-up for the Tour de France. If you're a cycling fan, this is a great time to see teams sweat up close. Plan well ahead: All hotels are packed for the event, and surrounding highways are restricted on certain days.

Later in May, Silver's biggest cultural event is the **Silver City Blues Festival** (www.mimbresarts.org), over Memorial Day weekend. Since 1995, it has gained a strong reputation, and the likes of Odetta and the Dirty Dozen

Brass Band have graced the stage (usually at Gough Park; some years also at bars around town).

In mid-September, the **Gila River Festival** (575/538-8078, www.gilaconservation.org) rallies an excellent roster of musicians and artists for an environment-friendly party. While the center of the action is Silver City, activities such as guided hikes, bird-watching, and archaeological tours take place in the forest to the north. It's a great opportunity to explore less-visited spots in the company of experts. The same organization hosts the **Wild & Scenic Film Festival** in January as well.

SPORTS AND RECREATION

Surrounded on almost every side by the Gila National Forest, Silver is an outdoorsy town. The **Silver City Ranger District office** (3005 Camino del Bosque, 575/388-8201, 8am-4pm Mon.-Fri.) is just north of U.S. 180 off the 32nd Street Bypass on the east side of town.

Hiking and Horseback Riding

In town, you can stroll up **Boston Hill**, a network of trails around the abandoned mines that started Silver. The view from the top of the hill is fine. The trailhead nearest to downtown is at the end of Spring Street, just off Cooper Street.

For more in-depth or complex excursions, Chiricahua Apache guide Joe Saenz runs **Wolf Horse Outfitters** (Arenas Valley Rd., 575/534-1379, www.wolfhorseoutfitters.com), specializing in low-impact, educational trips into the wilderness. His excellent services range from a half-day hike or horseback ride ($95) to custom packhorse adventures (from $230/day).

Biking

The staff at **Gila Hike & Bike** (103 E. College Ave., 575/388-3222, 9am-5:30pm Mon.-Fri., 9am-5pm Sat., plus 10am-4pm Sun. Mar.-Dec.) are veterans, with lots of tips on where to ride in the area. Ambitious road cyclists can trace some of the routes of the Tour de Gila, while mountain bikers can head to **Little Walnut Picnic Area,** north of town via Little Walnut Road from near the intersection of U.S. 180 and Highway 90. This is the starting point for a couple of short, relatively easy outings, as well as one seven-mile loop that's more challenging. You can get detailed trail guides from Gila Hike & Bike.

FOOD

Silver has a large number of amazing places to eat, all in the downtown area—so many, it's hard to designate just one as a top pick. Note that most restaurants close early, and some of the best are open only a few days a week.

New Mexican and Mexican

Occupying a string of old storefronts on the south end of downtown, **Jalisco Café** (103 S. Bullard St., 575/388-2060, 11am-8pm Mon.-Sat., $12) is the most popular New Mexican joint in town. Along with a small selection of seafood dishes, you'll get all the green- and red-chile-smothered classics, though they're not nearly as hot as the menu warns, and the green chile is typical of southern New Mexico, all mellow and creamy—a relief for some diners, a travesty for others. Everyone can agree on the sopaipillas, though, which are huge and perfectly pillowy.

Cafés

Get your java at **Javalina** (117 W. Market St., 575/388-1350, 6am-7pm Mon.-Sat., 6am-6pm Sun., $3), a rambling, old-style coffeehouse with lots of thrift-store sofas and people sitting for hours over a game of chess or the daily paper.

Set in the former Elks Lodge, **Vicki's Eatery** (315 N. Texas St., 575/388-5430, 11am-2:30pm Mon.-Thurs., 11am-2:30pm and 5pm-8pm Fri., 7am-2:30pm and 5pm-8pm Sat., 8am-2pm Sun., $9) is a prime spot for lunch, with big sandwiches that range from familiar and hearty (green-chile turkey melt) to the more exotic (chutney and turkey).

For the icebox pie of your dreams, **Millie's Bake House** (602 N. Bullard St., 575/597-2253, 7am-3pm Tues.-Sat., $4) is a fantastically home-style operation, with nice sandwiches and salads to balance out the myriad sugar-fix options.

Silver's lively food co-op runs the **Market Café** (614 N. Bullard St., 575/956-6487, 8:30am-7pm Mon. and Wed.-Sat., 8:30am-5pm Sun., $9), a good place to get picnic items if you're going hiking.

International and Eclectic

★ **Burgers & Brownies & Beers, Oh My!** (609 N. Bullard St., 575/597-6469, 11am-9pm Sun.-Wed., 11am-10pm Fri. and Sat.) may have a slightly corny name and a fast-food layout, but it is some of the tastiest and freshest food in town. (Owner Shevek long ran a creative fine-dining restaurant across the street.) Burgers use excellent-quality meat, the salads are packed with flavor, and the brownies are blissfully intense.

Silver residents love long-established **Diane's** (510 N. Bullard St., 575/538-8722, 11am-2pm and 5pm-9pm Tues.-Fri., 9am-2pm and 5pm-9pm Sat., 9am-2pm Sun., $17). It's the go-to spot for familiar flavors like meatloaf and lasagna, in a pleasant atmosphere, and is very popular for brunch. The adjacent "parlor" (from 2pm daily) hosts live music some evenings.

Another busy spot is **Tre Rosat** (304 N. Bullard St., 575/654-4919, 11am-3pm and 5pm-9pm Thurs.-Mon.), which does upscale bar food, such a green-chile poppers, big burgers, and a "bulgogi hoagie," for lunch (all around $11). The dinner menu aims a bit higher with dishes like elk osso buco and sous-vide Moroccan chicken stew ($15-20).

Decked out with Bollywood art and Mexican crafts, ★ **1zero6** (106 N. Texas St., 575/313-4418, www.1zero6.com, 5pm-8:30pm Fri.-Sun., $18) is small and thoroughly personal. Each night's menu has just a few options, but they could be anything from tortellini Bolognese to Indonesian chicken in a banana leaf, all cooked from scratch and

1zero6 restaurant is colorful inside and out.

with such a reverence for flavor you'd think there's a grandmother in the kitchen. Check the menu on the website on Wednesday, and call to put dibs on the dishes you want.

ACCOMMODATIONS

Downtown Silver has a couple of excellent lodging options. Most chain hotels and motels are on U.S. 180 on the east side of town (also called Silver Heights Boulevard), which is not walkable to downtown.

Under $100

The **Palace Hotel** (106 W. Broadway, 575/388-1811, www.silvercitypalacehotel. com, $58 s, $78 d) embodies the phrase "faded charm," but it is moderately priced and full of historic ambience—even if the beds can be a bit saggy. Street noise can be a problem; the quietest of the 22 rooms are no. 61 ($58), a cozy hideaway with one double bed in the back of the building, and no. 59 ($94), a two-room suite. A basic continental breakfast is included in the rate.

$100-150

Silver's "newer" historic hotel is the ★ **Murray Hotel** (200 W. Broadway, 575/956-9400, www.murray-hotel.com, $109 d), a glamorous slab of a building erected in the late 1930s. It reopened in 2012, after major renovation, and its rooms are both comfortable and fabulously located. Room 426 has beautiful glass bricks in the bathroom.

As for B&Bs, the 1883 **Inn on Broadway** (411 W. Broadway, 575/388-5485, www.innonbroadwayweb.com) is in a fine location, across from the Silver City Museum. Three sunny rooms upstairs ($120-150) are spacious, with especially nice bathrooms (although some might find the old-fashioned hand shower in the Hummingbird Room a bit of a nuisance). The cozier downstairs room ($150) has a marble fireplace. Decorating styles range from subdued Victorian to subdued Western.

If you'll be in town for a few nights, or just want the full comforts of home, consider **West Street Inn** (1303 West St., 575/534-2302, www.weststreetinn-nm.com), which contains three well-kept apartments with full kitchens. Casa Bonita ($125) is good for groups or families, with two bedrooms and a yard; the other two apartments ($105) are one-bedrooms with king beds.

Over $150

Set on 178 acres up against the national forest, **Bear Mountain Lodge** (60 Bear Mountain Ranch Rd., 575/538-2538, www.bearmountainlodge.com, $160 d) is a homey retreat where you can get a taste of the Gila in comfort—trails crisscross the land out back. The beautiful adobe main building was built in the mid-1920s. The creative, unpretentious café here is open to non-guests with prior reservations.

INFORMATION

The **Silver City Visitors Center** (201 N. Hudson St., 575/538-5555, www.silvercitytourism.org, 9am-5pm Mon.-Sat. 10am-2pm Sun.) is just east of Big Ditch Park at

Broadway. There's info available out front all the time, and its website is very thorough.

GETTING THERE

By car, Silver City is closest to Deming, about 60 miles (1 hour) south via U.S. 180. From Truth or Consequences, the closest town on I-25, it's 88 miles west, but the drive takes more than 2 hours on the winding road over Emory Pass; count on 4.5 hours from Albuquerque via I-25. Tucson, Arizona, is 200 miles (3 hours) west, and El Paso is 2.5 hours southeast.

Grant County Airport (SVC), about 10 miles southeast of Silver City, receives flights two or three times daily from Albuquerque and one daily from Phoenix on Boutique Air (855/268-8478, www.boutiqueair.com).

Trail of the Mountain Spirits

A romantic name for the usual driving circuit out of Silver City, the **Trail of the Mountain Spirits** runs north on Highway 15 through the little town of Pinos Altos, then up to Gila Cliff Dwellings National Monument and many hiking trails into the wilderness. After backtracking from the cliff dwellings, the route continues through the pine forest east on Highway 35, past Lake Roberts, over the Continental Divide to Bear Canyon Lake, and through the village of Mimbres. Highway 152 then leads back west to Silver City via the region's modern mining center around Bayard.

PINOS ALTOS

About seven miles north on Highway 15, a sign points to the optimistically named Pinos Altos Business Loop. In fact, this tiny community offers just a couple of commercial attractions, and that's the way folks like it. "P.A.," as the village is known, is the retreat for those who think Silver is too big and busy.

In terms of sights, you can stop in at the obligatory **Pinos Altos Museum & Curio Shop** (33 Main St., 575/388-1882, 10am-5pm daily, $2), an 1860s log cabin packed with cast-iron gewgaws; it sets the tone for the rest of the buildings in the area, which are functional if not always accurate replicas of what used to stand here in the 19th century.

Across the street, the ★ **Buckhorn Saloon** (32 Main St., 575/538-9911, www. buckhornsaloonandoperahouse.com,

5pm-10pm Mon.-Sat.) serves burgers ($13) and steaks ($33) in a wood-paneled, Wild West setting. The kitchen can be hit or miss, but the excellent old bar is recommended without reservations. The place is open for drinks starting at 3pm and continuing past the dinner hour, with very well attended live music starting around 7pm.

Also look for **Hearst Church** (Golden Ave., 10am-5pm Fri.-Sun. May-Oct.), an odd pitched-roof adobe structure built in 1898 by William Randolph Hearst's mother, Phoebe, who had gained her family fortune from a gold mine in the area. It's now home to the **Grant County Art Guild** (575/538-8216, www.gcag.org). It's west of the main street—follow Historic Route signs as you come into town.

GILA HOT SPRINGS

A small collection of services for wilderness visitors, the village of Gila Hot Springs is the last chance to stock up before heading farther north. **Doc Campbell's Post** (575/536-9551, 10am-4pm daily) sells basic provisions, books, fishing and hunting licenses, and homemade ice cream.

Just south of here are two semi-developed hot springs. Look for a turn labeled Access Road and signs to **Gila Hot Springs Campground** (gilahotsprings@gmail.com). The three riverside pools ($5 pp for day use only), kept at different temperatures, are lightly developed, and there are a few tent

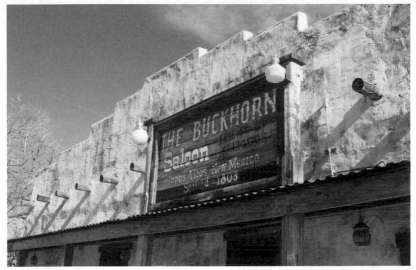

Buckhorn Saloon in Pinos Altos

campsites here ($6 pp), which should be reserved ahead. The whole place is quiet and tightly run, with a ban on booze and loud music at the pools.

An earlier right turn, at the four-way intersection down the hill from Highway 15, leads to **Wildwood Retreat & Hot Springs** (575/536-3600, www.wildwoodhotspringsretreat.com), which is closed in the winter. The springs are channeled into paved pools ($5/day). You can camp here ($15 pp), or stay in a snug cabin ($60 d) or larger straw-bale hogan ($80).

One safety note: The hot springs water in this area harbors an amoeba that can cause a fatal brain infection—but don't panic! The amoeba can only enter your system through your nose—so as long as you keep your head above water, you'll be fine.

★ GILA CLIFF DWELLINGS NATIONAL MONUMENT

The big destination on the byway is the **Gila Cliff Dwellings National Monument** (575/536-9461, www.nps.gov/gicl, 8:30am-5pm daily June-Aug., 9am-4pm daily Sept.-May, $5 pp or $10/family), just past Gila Hot Springs and 44 miles north of Silver City. Compared with the ruins at Bandelier National Monument or Chaco Canyon, these are relatively small and in a less spectacular setting, but if these are the only cliff settlements you'll be near on your trip, don't miss

Gila Cliff Dwellings National Monument

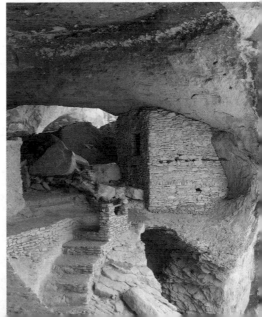

them. The drive up from Silver, along a narrow road often with no center stripe, takes up to three hours.

Stop in first at the **visitors center** (8am-4:30pm daily), which gives a basic overview of the environment as well as the Mogollon culture that inhabited the cliff dwellings for only a generation near the end of the 13th century, through excavated relics of daily life such as reed mats and mosaic work. The rock cairn in the parking lot is a discreet monument to the Apache chief Geronimo, born far up the canyon ("at the headwaters of the Gila," as he said) in 1829.

A two-mile drive gets you to the pay station at the **trailhead** and a basic nature center, where enthusiastic rangers will let you know what kind of animals are out and about. You reach the **caves** via a mile-long loop trail that takes about an hour to walk. The route is level for the first half, then increasingly steep as it winds up and through the dwellings. The trail passes three of the five caves, which once housed up to 60 people in about 40 rooms; the central one is a large, bilevel arrangement that included the central ceremonial chambers. Much of the wood you see in the rooms is original, preserved perfectly in the dry air; the Mogollon, who did not have steel, shaped it by burning it and hacking it with stone tools.

Recreation

This is the most easily accessible part of the Gila Wilderness, with some very scenic hiking along canyon bottoms. Check the status of trails and hot springs at the visitors center—as of fall 2013, fire and flooding had done yet-to-be-determined damage to some routes.

HIKING

The three forks of the Gila River converge near the cliff dwellings, and the canyons formed by the water are usually a nice place to walk, though there was massive flooding in 2013, which may have shifted routes and changed scenery. In any case, be prepared for wet and muddy stream crossings, and in summer, plan

to hike in the morning, so you're not caught in canyons during afternoon rainstorms.

At 34 miles, the **West Fork Trail** (no. 151) is the longest in the Gila wilderness. The first three miles provide a pleasantly varied, fairly easy day hike. The trail begins at Scorpion Campground, across from the Gila Cliff Dwellings. Just off the trail to the south after the first river crossing, a small ruined cabin sits next to the grave of one William Grudging, murdered in 1893—eerie evidence of the violent past of this otherwise peaceful setting. Further traces of past inhabitants can be seen at a small cliff dwelling on the west side, which marks the turnaround point for most day hikers. Others do the full length as a multiday backpacking trek.

Given the complex network of trails in this area, it's easy to make a number of loop hikes through varied terrain. Ask for suggestions in the visitors center, where you can also pick up a topographical map and check which areas might still show flood damage.

HOT SPRINGS

A refreshing warm bath in the great outdoors is a fine motivator for a hike, and there are several natural springs in the vicinity of the cliff dwellings' visitors center—although they too were washed out in the 2013 floods and may or may not be accessible. The closest ones to the visitors center are **Lightfeather Hot Spring,** just half a mile up the Middle Fork Trail; however, the water here is scalding hot, and you may have to reroute the river water to dilute it to a usable temperature. The deep pools of **Jordan Hot Springs** are worth the longer hike (about eight miles) up the same trail; you can shorten the trip by starting at the trail behind TJ Corral, farther up the road to the cliff dwellings, but get precise directions from the visitors center.

LAKE ROBERTS

Heading east from the intersection with Highway 35, you reach **Lake Roberts,** a pristine 69 acres stocked with trout. Shaded heavily by tall pine trees, it's a popular getaway during the summer months; you can **camp** at the lake, in developed sites ($7) or undeveloped ones (free), which have no water. There are also several lodges in the area.

MIMBRES VALLEY

The wide, green valley surrounding the village of Mimbres is the epicenter of the ancient culture of the same name, best known for its elegant black-on-white pottery designs, done about a thousand years ago. One of the sites where these were unearthed is the **Mimbres Valley Cultural Site** (14 Sage Dr., no phone, 11am-3pm daily, free). There's virtually nothing to see in terms of ancient settlement, but you can also visit the museum set in two more recent (19th-century) homesteads. Look for the turn off the north side of the road.

A Mennonite family runs ★ **Three Questions Coffee House** (Hwy. 35, 575/536-3267, 7am-2pm Tues.-Sat., $6.50), serving a generous all-you-can-eat breakfast and lunch buffet of simple but wholesome food, plus giant cinnamon rolls and other great baked goods.

Mimbres also has a gas station, and the **Gila Wilderness Ranger District office** (Hwy. 35, 575/536-2250, 8am-4:30pm Mon.-Fri.) is here. Just after the turnoff to the old Spanish settlement of **San Lorenzo,** Highway

35 dead-ends at Highway 152, which runs west to Silver City.

CHINO MINE

Off the east side of Highway 152, you can't help but notice the monumentally altered landscape around the **Chino Mine,** the pit of which measures more than a mile across. The oldest continuously mined claim in the United States, it was first known by Apaches, who took copper from the area. In 1799, the Spanish, with the help of convict labor, began extracting copper and sending it to Mexico. Production was so great that the majority of the early 19th-century copper coins from Mexico and Spain can be traced back to Santa Rita del Cobre, as the mine was known then. Open-pit mining began in 1910, eventually swallowing up the town of Santa Rita, which had grown adjacent to the mine.

The hole now reaches 1,600 feet into the ground, dwarfing the trucks and shovels that toil on its terraces, and a good portion of Grant County's population is employed here in some capacity. You can't miss Chino from the road, but if you want an up-close look, stop at the observation point maintained by current owners Freeport-McMoRan, just south of mile marker 6. If you're able to ignore

Chino Mine, east of Silver City, is one of the world's largest.

the obvious environmental ravages, you could call it an impressive piece of land art.

FORT BAYARD

Located just after the junction of Highway 152 with U.S. 180, **Fort Bayard** (575/956-3294, www.fortbayard.org) was built in 1866 by the Ninth Cavalry, some of the Buffalo Soldiers who earned renown fighting the Apaches. During the 1920s, it was a center of tuberculosis treatment for the military, and the tidy rows of white barracks are a product of that period. For decades, it was a veterans hospital, but now it has a ghostly feel, as it has been deemed too costly to maintain, and left to ruin—except for a **museum** (tours 9:30am and noon Sat. June-Sept., second and fourth Sat. only Oct.-May) in the old officers' quarters. **Fort Bayard Days** reenactments are in mid-September.

Gila National Forest

From Silver City, U.S. 180 runs north about 45 miles to the junction with Highway 12 and the town of Reserve. For much of the drive, the road is surrounded by the **Gila National Forest,** the larger region surrounding the more tightly controlled Gila Wilderness. Its 2.7 million acres stretch west to Arizona and north as far as Quemado. Passing through rolling grassy plains and between mountain peaks, this is a beautiful—and often empty—drive.

GILA

Not to be confused with Gila Hot Springs, the village of Gila is often a jumping-off point for trips into the wilderness area or down the Gila

Exploring the Gila Wilderness

Covering 558,000 acres, the Gila Wilderness is the largest such protected area in any state but Alaska, and it's also the first. With the adjacent 200,000 acres of the Aldo Leopold Wilderness, plus the Gila National Forest to the south and north, it's an almost overwhelming place to explore. The terrain ranges from piñon forests dotted with spring wildflowers to the flat beds of the three forks of the Gila River. Fires and massive flooding in 2013 burned trails and changed watercourses—so any exploration should start with a check with the visitors center at the Gila Cliff Dwellings, or one of the national forest district offices.

The most common access point to the wilderness is on the south side, via Highway 15 north of Silver City. This serpentine road makes its way up through pine trees to the Gila Cliff Dwellings National Monument and several well-used trailheads.

While you're driving or hiking around, keep your eyes open for the area's rich wildlife. At lower elevations, javelinas (small wild pigs) are plentiful, as are packs of coatimundis. Nimble, raccoon-like animals with long snouts, coatis usually live in more tropical climates; southern New Mexico is the only area they're found in the United States. You might see one scampering across the road or napping in a tree. Less exotic, skunks are plentiful (four different species, in fact), and you'll surely encounter at least the traces of one at some point on your trip. In the higher mountains, you may see herds of mule deer and elk. The eponymous Gila monster, a venomous lizard that can grow up to two feet in length, makes its home here, as do lots of rattlesnakes. Be alert in the springtime, when the snakes have just come out of hibernation and are on the prowl for mates. Wear boots that come above your ankles, and don't place your feet between rocks or in crevices when hiking.

River to the southwest. And as it's less than 30 miles from Silver City, it counts as a sort of suburb.

Set on 90 acres with a stream running through, ★ **Casitas de Gila** (50 Casita Flats, 575/535-4455, www.casitasdegila.com) is a great way to enjoy the area in comfort. Nightly rates go down the longer you stay—and once you get a glimpse of the night sky from the hot tub, you'll probably want to settle in. The apartments, furnished with custom Mexican woodwork, have kiva fireplaces, kitchens stocked with breakfast food, and private patios. Foldout couches in the living rooms make the standard casitas ($165) family-friendly, while a larger two-bedroom option ($225) can sleep six.

SAN FRANCISCO HOT SPRINGS

The **San Francisco Hot Springs** are some of the most beautiful in the area, with a large warm pool tucked in a canyon about 1.5 miles from the trailhead. The hot water bubbles out of the river plain, and the specific pool locations may change from year to year, but the general spot is easy to reach. Look for the turn west off U.S. 180, about five miles south of Glenwood, around mile marker 58. A dirt road leads to a well-marked trail. Avoid the area during summer rainstorms—not only is there a risk of flash flooding, but the trail is heavy clay that's a slog when wet. If you happen to miss the turn, you can always stop in the Glenwood ranger office and ask directions—and check the status.

GLENWOOD

The road north from Gila skirts the mountains and races through grasslands, reaching the small town of Glenwood after about 30 miles. It's a nice quiet spot to stay the night on this loop.

For info on local trails, stop in at or call the **Glenwood Ranger District office** (Mineral Creek Rd., 575/539-2481, 8am-4:30pm Mon.-Fri.).

Catwalk Trail

Closed due to flood damage in 2013, this easy hiking area is expected to finally reopen in fall 2016, after this book went to press. A Civilian Conservation Corps project in the 1930s, the **Catwalk Trail** is a hanging walkway over a stream for the first half of its 1.1 miles, sometimes suspended more than 20 feet above the water and pink canyon walls pressing in close on either side. The catwalk follows the route of a water pipeline built in the 1890s as part of a mining operation. The first, easiest part is also wheelchair-accessible. Normally, the entrance fee is $3 per car, and the turnoff for the trail is in the middle of Glenwood, well marked as Highway 174 (Catwalk Road). For details, confirm with the Glenwood ranger office.

Food

There are limited options: For breakfast, **Golden Girls Café** (U.S. 180, 575/539-2457, 7am-10am daily, $5) is cozy and very, very inexpensive. Homemade jelly is a highlight, and coffee is $1, like it ought to be—but you pay extra for milk. At dinnertime, **Mario's Pizza** (U.S. 180, 575/539-2316, 4pm-8pm Thurs. and

the upper part of the Catwalk Trail

Fri., 2pm-8pm Sat., 2pm-6pm Sun., $8) is the only option, but decent.

Accommodations

The **Whitewater Motel** (U.S. 180, 575/539-2581, www.whitewatermotel.com), next to the post office near the south entrance to the town, is a simple place where the owners clearly care about details. Beds are a bit springy, but the 10 rooms are tidy, comfortable, and trimmed with lace curtains, with back porches overlooking a shady garden and stream. Configurations range from one double bed ($58) to three twin beds and a double ($74), great for families or groups.

Actually a few miles south in Pleasanton, **D and D's Organic Haven** (13 Blue Heron Ln., 575/539-2483, http://d-and-d-organic-haven.homestead.com, $65 s, $85 d) is a pretty straw-bale hideaway with three rooms, lush gardens, and great food. It's open only March-mid-November.

If you're traveling as a family, you'll appreciate the cute stone cabins at **Los Olmos Lodge** (U.S. 180, 575/539-2224, www.losolmoslodge.com, $80 d), with plenty of beds for everyone. There's also an outdoor pool, a creek, a fishing pond, and other activities.

MOGOLLON

Unlike many old mining towns, Mogollon bursts with color and cheer—at least on weekends between May and October, when the businesses up here are open. Its old buildings, including the **Silver Creek Inn** (www.silvercreekinn.com, $110 d), the **Purple Onion Café** (575/539-2710, 9am-5pm Fri.-Sun., $8), and the village archives, are painted in vibrant shades. It's a great place to get away for a night or two, as it feels quite cut off from the world.

In fact it *is* quite cut off from the world, nine miles up Highway 159, which locals call the **Bursum Road.** The road washed out due to floods in 2013, and it is very often closed with snow in the winter. From a turn east, about three miles north of Glenwood, it starts off easily enough, crossing rolling scrub, but then it ascends steeply into the mountains.

Mogollon's main street

About halfway into the climb, the road reduces to a harrowing single lane with steep switchbacks and no guardrails.

But the view across the rolling grasslands below is stunning. Hardier drivers can carry on past Mogollon, where the road grows increasingly rough and enters aspen glades that glow gold in the fall. Wind your way very, very carefully back down the way you came in. Avoid doing this at sundown, however, as the glare just adds to the risk.

ALMA

Once a hideout for Butch Cassidy, this wide spot in the road is the turnoff for a good hiking trail into the Gila, the **Mineral Creek Trail.** The first 1.5 miles are an easy family hike, and the scenery beyond gets even better. To reach the trail (no. 201), turn east in Alma onto Mineral Creek Road, a dirt track; this turns into Forest Road 701 and dead-ends at the trailhead after 5.5 miles. Just before mile 5, look for **"Cooney's tomb,"** a giant boulder made into the gravesite for miner James

James Cooney, unfortunate miner, lies in a tomb in Alma.

Cooney and a few of his men, who were killed here by Apaches in 1880.

On the east side of the road, **Alma Grill** (U.S. 180, 575/539-2233, 6am-3pm Fri.-Wed., $6) serves all the necessary food for a good road trip: enchiladas, biscuits, and more.

RESERVE

Hunting is big business in **Reserve,** the Catron County seat, with expeditions leaving from here and plenty of taxidermy shops in town. First settled by Mexican homesteaders in the early 1800s, the town is notorious for an 1884 shootout between 80-odd Texan cowboys and the local deputy sheriff, Elfego Baca, who held off the gang for 36 hours, until they ran out of ammunition. In what many saw as a blatantly racist move, Baca was later brought to trial for murdering one of the cowboys; he was finally acquitted when he displayed the bullet-riddled door he'd hidden behind. Look for a memorial to Baca at the main crossroads.

The **Reserve Ranger District office** (575/523-6232, 8am-4:30pm Mon.-Fri.), on Highway 12 just west of town, has information on the Gila National Forest, as well as the wilderness area.

For food, ★ **Adobe Does BBQ** (16-B N. Main St., 575/533-6145, 7am-8pm Mon., 7am-3pm Tues.-Wed. and Fri., $8) serves espresso and excellent homemade baked goods in the morning and barbecue for lunch. The same owners run **Adobe Café and Bakery** (U.S. 180., 575/533-6146, 7am-8pm Sun.-Mon., 7am-3pm Thurs.-Fri., $8), southwest of Reserve, about a quarter-mile from the junction with Highway 12 (you'll pass this first if you're coming from the south). It also has a fresh, varied menu of breakfast goodies, as well as salads and creative sandwiches. Service can be a bit slow, though, and it usually closes February-mid-April. And the same team has the adjacent **Hidden Springs Inn** (www.the-hiddenspringsinn.com, $69 d), a very good deal, and nicely kept.

For dinner other nights, **Ella's** (96 Main St., 575/533-6111, 7am-8pm Tues.-Sat., 7am-2pm Sun.-Mon., $8), in Reserve proper, will do just fine—locals in Carhartts and hats dig in to chicken-fried steak and enchiladas.

Carlsbad Caverns and the Southeast

East on the Interstate
and Route 66. 324

The Llano. 331

Roswell. 338

Carlsbad. 346

Carlsbad Caverns National Park 352

Cloudcroft. 355

Alamogordo. 358

White Sands National Monument . . 362

Ruidoso 364

Billy the Kid Trail. 370

Northern Tularosa Basin 372

Barren land stretches between the atypical tourist sights in southeastern New Mexico: the vast, bat-filled spaces of Carlsbad Caverns, the ghostly gypsum dunes at White Sands, and a museum dedicated to UFOs in Roswell.

You'll find surprising things if you make the drive—and what a long drive it is. The blank expanse the Spanish dubbed the Llano Estacado starts in Fort Sumner (where sharpshooter Billy the Kid finally met his end in 1881) and stretches east and south into Texas. The roads are straight, the horizon unbroken, and soon you can't tell if you've been driving for 20 minutes or two hours. The occasional oil derrick, wind turbine, or herd of cattle breaks up the monotony, and tiny towns loom up suddenly and disappear in the rear-view mirror just as fast. Portales, center of the "peanut basin of the Southwest," is a rare green spot, thanks to a deep aquifer. Roswell is the area's largest settlement, and perhaps its strangest, as many people are still obsessed with an alleged crash-landing of an alien spacecraft here in 1947.

Southwest of Roswell, the Sacramento Mountains spike along the edge of the plains.

Here, the resort towns of Cloudcroft and Ruidoso cater to Texans who've fled the flatlands. The steep trails at Ski Apache, with a base elevation of 9,600 feet, provide winter entertainment. At the base of the mountains, orderly Alamogordo is home to the International Space Hall of Fame and is the closest town to White Sands, a 275-square-mile landscape that's fascinating as a natural attraction, but also inextricably linked with the world's first atomic bomb test, which took place in this desert in 1945.

Carlsbad Caverns, another natural wonder, fortunately has no such legacy. Getting there requires the longest drive of all, nearly to the Texas state line in the south. But when you see the so-called Big Room, the vast main cave that drips with stalactites and takes more than an hour to explore, you'll know there's nothing else like it in New Mexico, nor in the whole country.

Previous: White Sands National Monument; Dalley Windmill Museum. **Above:** roadside attraction in Tucumcari.

Look for ★ to find recommended
sights, activities, dining, and lodging.

Highlights

★ **International UFO Museum & Research Center:** Mysteries of deep space revealed! Government conspiracies uncovered! Plush alien dolls for sale! Roswell's most popular museum may seem campy, but it takes its mission very seriously (page 340).

★ **Anderson Museum of Contemporary Art:** Roswell is also home to this excellent collection of artwork in every media, which rivals the galleries in Santa Fe in quality and wins for sheer gutsy enthusiasm (page 342).

★ **The Big Room:** Some 600,000 visitors a year tour the main cave at **Carlsbad Caverns National Park**—for good reason. It's amazing in both its vast scale and its smallest details, such as clusters of tiny stalactites as delicate as lace. Silence is requested on the tour—not hard, as you'll be too awed to speak (page 352).

★ **Heart of the Sands:** Visiting the eerie landscape at the center of **White Sands National Monument** is like going to the beach and the North Pole both at once. It's certainly unlike any place you've ever seen (page 364).

★ **Lincoln State Monument:** The late 19th century's "most dangerous town in America" is now a quiet place, half of its main-street buildings preserved as museums that conjure life in Billy the Kid's era, without all the usual Wild West kitsch (page 370).

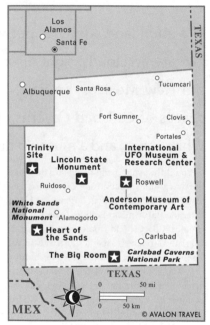

★ **Trinity Site:** You can visit the site of the first atomic bomb blast (fittingly set in a stretch of the stark Jornada del Muerto desert) only two days a year, but it's an essential stop if your schedule allows (page 374).

Carlsbad Caverns and the Southeast

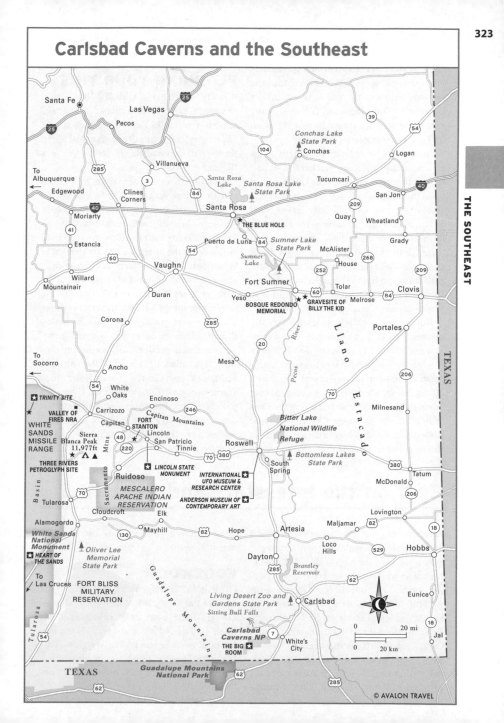

© AVALON TRAVEL

HISTORY

Hundreds of millions of years ago, southeastern New Mexico's modern history was already set in stone: The dinosaurs that roamed the swampy banks of the sea were eventually transformed into the fossil fuel that many a contemporary Lovingtonian or Artesian makes a living extracting today.

In between, New Mexico's southern plains and mountain ranges saw much the same patterns as the rest of the state. The U.S. Army set upon the resident Indian tribes, and General James Carleton ordered Kit Carson, "All Indian men of that [Mescalero] tribe are to be killed whenever and wherever you can find them." Billy the Kid got up to no good and eventually died here, at the age of 21. And railroad lines and highways (especially the legendary Route 66) brought modern thrills to previously untouched patches of plain.

But a single cataclysmic event really marked the area. Just before sunrise one summer morning in 1945, White Sands was lit brighter than high noon by a towering mushroom cloud—the successful test of the first atomic bomb, which was then deployed over Japan to win World War II. During the Cold War, White Sands was the proving ground for some essential technology in the space race. In this respect, the region is an odd juxtaposition of humankind's most current obsessions against a timeless landscape.

PLANNING YOUR TIME

If you're focusing on Carlsbad, White Sands, and even Cloudcroft or Ruidoso, it can make sense to fly in to El Paso (ELP), then stay in Las Cruces (one hour's drive) your first night; the town of Carlsbad also receives commuter flights from Albuquerque.

Driving from Albuquerque, you could take the leisurely route via the Salinas Pueblo Missions and Carrizozo, reaching Ruidoso or Alamogordo by dinnertime, then carrying on to White Sands the next day—or you could cruise down the interstate and get straight to White Sands by the afternoon. In any case, allow about three hours for a basic visit to the park, or more if you plan to do any hiking or photography. Carlsbad Caverns calls for the better part of a day to see just the basics, though the more adventurous small-group tours are well worth allotting a second day. Both these places get busy in the summer, and the caverns can feel crowded; the sands absorb crowds better. At any rate, if you can push your visit till mid-August, you may miss some crowds (as kids head back to school), and also see the landscape a bit greened by summer rains.

East on the Interstate and Route 66

After crossing the pass between the Sandia and Manzano Mountains east of Albuquerque, I-40 heads into the high plains. Get used to the scenery, because it won't change until well into Texas. The wind blows constantly across gold tufts of grass, and the barbed-wire fences are clotted with tumbleweeds. The most excitement along this stretch is counting down the billboards to truck stops like the Flyin' C, where you can stock up on everything from moccasins to fireworks. It's not quite the glamour of Route 66 of old, but the combination of tacky signage, big sky, and a whole lot of nothing says "American road trip" like nothing else.

EDGEWOOD

Off exit 187 in Edgewood, **Wildlife West Nature Park** (505/281-7655, www.wildlifewest.org, 10am-6pm daily mid-Mar.-Oct., noon-4pm daily Nov.-mid-Mar., $9) is a better-than-average roadside attraction. This "enhanced zoo" is a 122-acre wildlife sanctuary for wolves, cougars, elk, and other native animals.

For solid road food at the same exit,

Katrinah's East Mountain Grill (150 Hwy. 344, 505/281-9111, 7am-8pm Tues.-Sat., 8am-2pm Sun., $8) has a menu of standard diner goodies, from enchiladas to veggie wraps, all made from fresh ingredients. Look for it three miles north of I-40, just past Walmart.

SANTA ROSA

This town of 2,500 is easy to cruise past on I-40. But for a refreshing swim, take time out for the "City of Natural Lakes," where cool springs well up alongside the Pecos River. From 1901, Santa Rosa was a stop on the Chicago, Rock Island & Pacific freight line, and in the 1930s, the place began to grow as Route 66 travelers passed through. John Steinbeck set a scene of *The Grapes of Wrath* here, which was then re-created for film in the town in 1940. Its stretch of the historic highway, which runs parallel to I-40 to the south, is lined with stately old warehouses and lurid neon.

Sights

THE BLUE HOLE

Most people come to Santa Rosa for an unexpected natural attraction: **The Blue Hole** (575/472-3763, dawn-dusk daily), an 81-foot-deep pool of water that's a constant 64°F year-round. Only about 80 feet across, it doesn't look like much from the surface, but it's more impressive when you consider that water is gushing from the spring at the bottom at 3,000 gallons per minute (check the overflow channel on the south side to get an idea just what that number means). The steady temperature and perfect clarity of the water makes it a popular place for scuba divers—who create an incongruous image with the tumbleweeds blowing by. And the place is popular with local kids, who can spend a whole summer day doing cannonballs off the high rocks on one side. (There are less adventurous ways of getting into the water, including cement stairs.)

Admission is free, but to dive you'll need a **permit** ($20 weekly), available from the visitors center or the dive shop, both adjacent to the Blue Hole. To reach the area, get off at exit 278 or 275 and follow signs to Blue Hole Road (also a section of Historic Route 66).

If you want more room to play, backtrack on Blue Hole Road to **Park Lake,** an adjacent natural spring that's the town's biggest recreation spot. Zip down the free waterslide, rent a pedal boat, or just jump into the cool, clear water. (Compared with these natural springs, **Santa Rosa Lake State Park,** the product of a dam on the Pecos River north of town, is quite dull.)

ROUTE 66 AUTO MUSEUM

For car buffs, the **Route 66 Auto Museum** (2866 Historic Rte. 66, 575/472-1966, www.route66automuseum.com, 7:30am-6pm daily Apr.-Oct., 7:30am-5pm daily Nov.-Mar., $5), on the east side of town, is a showroom of Mother Road paraphernalia and a couple dozen curvaceous machines from the heyday of American road-tripping; most are for sale.

Food

Santa Rosa boasts of its PDL chile, a special strain grown just to the south in the village of Puerto de Luna; it's usually eaten in its green form. Unfortunately, there's nowhere reliable to eat it. **Comet II** (217 Historic Rte. 66, 575/472-3663, 11am-9pm Tues.-Sun., $8), bathed in neon, has potential for simple, diner-style New Mexican, but doesn't always deliver; and the landmark **Joseph's Bar & Grill** (865 Historic Rte. 66, 575/472-3361, 8am-10pm daily, $7), is better for its kitschy decor (including its "Fat Man" logo, salvaged from a Depression-era restaurant) than its food. Still, if you're headed east on I-40, this is about your last chance for chile before blander Texan-style fare takes over.

Accommodations

Santa Rosa has the normal chain places, with a couple, such as **Comfort Inn** (2524 Historic Rte. 66, 575/472-5412, www.comfortinn.com, $109 d), in better condition than their counterparts in Tucumcari. If you want a vintage Route 66 motel, the recently renovated **La Mesa Inn** (2415 Historic Rte. 66,

575/472-3021, $45 s, $54 d) is your best bet; it's been in the same family since 1962, though the carpet, bathrooms, and flat-screen TVs are brand new. Still, if your taste runs to vintage, there are better places in Tucumcari.

Information

Next to the Blue Hole, the **Santa Rosa Visitors Center** (1085 Blue Hole Rd., 575/472-3763, www.santarosanm.org, 8am-5pm Mon.-Fri., 9am-noon Sat.) sells dive permits, in addition to stocking all the usual brochures.

PUERTO DE LUNA

Santa Rosa's historic roots are in this tidy collection of tin-roofed adobe buildings in a protected valley 10 miles south of I-40 on Highway 91. There's nothing precisely to see here, but, as part of the larger **Mesalands Scenic Byway,** which zigzags across I-40 between Santa Rosa and Tucumcari, it's a pretty way to head south to Fort Sumner, through red-striped rocky hills and chile fields. (The next legs of the byway are U.S. 84 back north to I-40, then Highway 156 from Santa Rosa and Highway 209 north to Tucumcari.)

Founded in 1842, Puerto de Luna was the county seat in the 1880s and later the childhood home of writer Rudolfo Anaya, who described the place in detail in his seminal novel *Bless Me, Ultima*. It's also alleged to be the place Billy the Kid enjoyed his last Christmas dinner, while Pat Garrett was taking him to jail in Lincoln.

SUMNER LAKE STATE PARK

A welcome bit of lushness amid the dry grasses, **Sumner Lake State Park** (Hwy. 203, 575/355-2541, www.nmparks.com, $5/car) is an excellent birding spot, as it's on a major migration route (check the canyon below the dam in summer). The **camping** spots ($8-14), spread out in four areas amid cottonwoods and junipers, are very pretty. The state park is midway between Santa Rosa and Fort Sumner, six miles west of U.S. 84 via Highway 203.

FORT SUMNER

A small town bedecked in Old West style, **Fort Sumner** is 42 miles south of I-40 and Santa Rosa via U.S. 84. It's best known as the final resting place of Henry McCarty, aka Henry Antrim, aka William H. Bonney, aka Billy the Kid. It was here in 1881 that Lincoln County sheriff Pat Garrett finally tracked down the gunfighter and shot him (in ambush, in the dark, the Kid's fans will point out), to mete out justice for the 21 men Billy had allegedly killed in his short life—he was only 21, in fact, when he died in a farmhouse kitchen.

For more than a century, this legend of a Wild West antihero had all but obliterated the memory of what Fort Sumner had first been: a failed reservation-turned-concentration-camp for about 9,000 Navajo and 500 Mescalero Apache for five years during the Civil War. In 2005, a state monument finally gave more public recognition to this tragic period in the settling of the American West.

Sights

In town proper, seek out the **WPA murals** in the De Baca County Courthouse (514 Ave. C, 575/355-2601, 8am-4:30pm Mon.-Fri.), just northeast of the main intersection in town. Inside the redbrick building, head upstairs to see vivid images of the taming of the Western frontier. On the main street is the **Billy the Kid Museum** (1435 E. Sumner Ave., 575/355-2380, www.billythekidmuseumfortsumner.com, 8:30am-5pm daily mid-May-Sept., 8:30am-5pm Mon.-Sat. Oct.-mid-May, $5), a tourist outpost of the highest order: room upon room of gewgaws, a gift shop, and a replica of Billy's grave.

The real deal is down the road: Head 3 miles east of town on U.S. 84, then 3.5 miles south on Billy the Kid Road, and you reach the *real* **gravesite of Billy the Kid** (free), in a desolate little cemetery behind the so-so **Old Fort Sumner Museum** (575/355-2942, 8:30am-4pm daily, $3.50). Fitting, due to his repeated jailbreaks in life, William Bonney is now penned in by a wrought-iron fence as well as cemented over, along with a couple of his "pals." (Really, the fencing is to deter grave robbers.) Also buried nearby is Lucien B. Maxwell, owner of the enormous Maxwell Land Grant in northern New Mexico, as well as this property, after the fort was decommissioned. It was in Maxwell's son's home, less than a mile away, that Billy the Kid was fatally shot. The museum offers yet another collection of Old West relics and plenty more detail about the young star of the Lincoln County War.

BOSQUE REDONDO MEMORIAL

Immediately south on the road from here, the **Bosque Redondo Memorial** (3647 Billy the Kid Rd., 575/355-2573, www.nmmonuments.org, 8:30am-4:30pm Wed.-Sun., $3) is a long-overdue museum and monument to the exceptional misery endured by most of the Navajo and a handful of Mescalero Apache, beginning in 1863. Force-marched in to this reservation at Fort Sumner from the northern corners of the state, the people endured what the Navajo came to call the Long Walk, a midwinter trek of hundreds of miles, during which the weakest were shot for holding up the group and many women and children were sold into slavery.

The two bands, which had little in common culturally and shared only a history of raiding each other, were penned in here and told to make a life together. But the allotted stretch of river basin was not enough land to support so many, so crops failed and disease tore through the overcrowded communities. The Mescalero Apache defied the U.S. military and left as a group two years into the terrible experiment. Nearly 3,000 Navajo—almost a third of the tribe—died in what they named H'weeldi (Place of Suffering) before they were allowed to return to their homelands.

The museum is a conceptual modern building—Navajo hogan meets Apache tepee—with a detailed exhibit on the camp, plus extra room for rotating displays on other low points in human rights history. Opt for the audio tour to explore the path out back, leading past the site where the Navajo leaders finally signed the treaty that released them (and established the Navajo Nation) in 1868, and into the greenery alongside the river, where the fort itself used to stand. It's a deceptively pretty setting.

Food

Rodeo Grill (451 W. Sumner Ave., 575/355-8000, 7:30am-2pm Mon.-Fri., $9), a few blocks east of the main intersection, serves burgers and hand-cut fries, as well as nice breakfast burritos, heated on the grill till the tortilla gets crispy, in a casual room hung with lariats and saddles.

If you're visiting on a Saturday, your best bet is **Fred's** (1408 Sumner Ave., 575/355-7500, 11am-8pm Tues.-Sat., $7), a cinder-block building that, despite its unwelcoming facade, draws raves for its chile, guacamole, and chicken-fried steak; check out the neat old wood bar in the back.

On Sunday, you're left with **Sadie's** (257 Sumner Ave., 575/355-1461, 11am-2pm and 5pm-8pm Mon. and Thurs.-Fri., 8am-2pm and 5pm-8pm Sat.-Sun., $7), which is not a bad deal at all—it's good for New Mexican food. But note that awkward closure between lunch and dinner—in short, if you're hungry in Fort Sumner on a Sunday afternoon, you're out of luck.

Information

Visit the **De Baca Chamber of Commerce** (707 N. 4th St., 575/355-7705, www.fortsumnerchamber.com, 9am-4pm Mon.-Thurs.) for all the basic tourist details.

TUCUMCARI

For the California-bound on Route 66, Tucumcari was the first real stop on New Mexico's stretch of the Mother Road. "Tucumcari Tonite!" urged the billboards leading up to the town strip—and they still do today. The neon glow is not as bright as it once was, but Americana buffs should get off the highway here, to see the Tepee Curios shop and other architectural oddities, and bunk down in one of the well-preserved old motor courts. Dinosaur freaks will find a great museum.

Tucumcari's existence predates Route 66: Main Street is oriented with the old railroad depot, north of the highway. When the tracks were being laid, this spot on the plains was dubbed Six-Shooter Siding, but the gunplay quieted down once regular trade got going, and the place took the name of nearby Tucumcari Mountain. The railroad provided steady employment until it closed operations here in 1999. But the residents of the sturdy, low bungalows that line the wide side streets have kept the town from being blown away in the wind—they are stubborn and dedicated to keeping the place alive.

Sights

After you've cruised the neon signs on Historic Route 66 (aka Tucumcari Boulevard), stop in the **New Mexico Route 66 Museum** (1500 W. Rte. 66 Blvd., 575/461-3064, www.nmrt66museum.org, 9am-1pm Sun.-Tues., 9am-4pm Sat., free), in a back room of the Tucumcari Convention Center. The museum displays vintage photos, a juke box, gas

pumps, and a few honeys, including a couple Studebakers and a classic Model A. If your cruise isn't complete, check out the *other* main drag: Turn north on 1st Street and drive about eight blocks up to **Main Street** and the train depot; along the way, elaborate photo-realistic **murals,** most by a husband-and-wife team, adorn many buildings.

The surprisingly spiffy **Mesalands Dinosaur Museum** (222 E. Laughlin St., 575/461-3466, www.mesalands.edu, 10am-6pm Tues.-Sat. Mar.-Aug., noon-5pm Tues.-Sat. Sept.-Feb., $6.50) is in this area too, just east of 1st Street and two blocks north of Tucumcari Boulevard. The exhibit hall contains a huge number of beautiful bronze casts of dinosaur skeletons (neat, because you're allowed to touch them), as well as some dinosaur eggs and lots of other fossils. It also owns a rare, nearly complete 30-foot-long skeleton of the giant carnivore *Torvosaurus,* and has an interactive, augmented reality sandbox where kids can manipulate the topography.

Two blocks farther north (look for the windmill), the **Tucumcari Historical Museum** (416 S. Adams St., 575/461-4201,

Tucumcari's architecture is vintage Route 66.

the Odeon Theater in Tucumcari

its coastline weaving along many inlets, sandy beaches, and canyons. The setting is rather austere, however, and there's very little shade—it's nicer to visit in the cooler spring or fall, when crowds are lighter as well.

In town, the **public pool** (415 W. Hines St., 575/461-4582) is open summers only, and closes as soon as school is in session, by the third week in August.

Food
Look for the big fiberglass steer above the sign at **Del's** (1202 E. Route 66 Blvd., 575/461-1740, 11am-9pm Mon.-Sat., $10), where you'll find a mighty fine chicken-fried steak (lovely crunchy batter, with rich mashed potatoes on the side), as well as a nicely appointed soup-and-salad bar. It's been serving locals since 1956, and feels like a chummy living room because of it.

Because it's open late and has a full bar, **Pow Wow Restaurant & Lizard Lounge** (801 W. Route 66 Blvd., 575/461-2587, 7am-10pm Sun.-Thurs., 7am-midnight Fri.-Sat., $9) is a major town hangout—there are portraits of locals, such as the magistrate judge, on the walls to prove it. The restaurant serves sandwiches and New Mexican dishes, and is a perfectly serviceable place to have lunch or dinner.

For lunch, **Cornerstone Deli** (711 E. Route 66 Blvd., 575/461-3326, 11am-8pm Mon.-Sat., $6) serves sandwiches with ingredients from the local small-scale **Tucumcari Mountain Cheese Factory** (foodies, check out the factory store at 823 E. Main St.), as well as homemade potato chips and super-creamy frozen custard.

For breakfast, it's hard to beat **Kix on 66** (1102 E. Route 66 Blvd., 575/461-1966, 6am-2pm daily, $6), where you can smell the bacon from the parking lot. The old-style diner slings hash browns, biscuits, and other morning standards to regulars in teal vinyl booths or at the long Formica counter. It has the same owners as Del's—you'll recognize the white gravy.

If your love of the past doesn't stretch to good old-fashioned American coffee, head to **Circa Espresso** (1620 E. Route 66 Blvd.,

9am-3pm Tues.-Sat. Sept.-May, 9am-5pm Tues.-Sat. June-Aug., $5) takes up an entire two-story redbrick house with old saddles, slot machines, and Indian relics, then spills over into a yard full of vintage boxcars, Route 66 paraphernalia, and more.

Entertainment
Built in 1936, the elegant deco-style **Odeon Theater** (123 S. 2nd St., 575/461-0100, $5.50) is a small-town treasure, with a modest but cool pink neon sign, offset with yellow zia symbols. Shows are Thursday-Sunday at 7pm, and also at 3pm on Sunday. The concession stand includes hot dogs, in case you want to make a dinner of it (only the Pow Wow Restaurant is open after the movie lets out).

Sports and Recreation
In the summer, locals decamp to one of New Mexico's bigger reservoirs, **Conchas Lake State Park** (575/868-2270, www.nmparks.com, $5/car), northwest of town 34 miles on Highway 104. It stretches for about 25 miles,

575/461-6099, 7am-11:30am daily, $3), at the Historic Route 66 Motel, for your morning blast of steam-powered caffeine. It serves no real food, though.

Accommodations

Tucumcari has a handful of excellent-value retro motels—worth a stop just to enjoy a taste of the past. A relic of the Route 66 days, the pink-and-turquoise ★ **Blue Swallow Motel** (815 E. Route 66 Blvd., 575/461-9849, www.blueswallowmotel.com, $75 s, $85 d), on the east side of town, dates from 1939, making it perhaps the oldest standing motel on Route 66. The 12 rooms are cozy, with honeycomb-tiled bathrooms and chenille bedspreads; rotary phones heavy enough to be weapons round out the historic feel. Several rooms have adjacent garages, and the Lilly Redmond Suite ($135), named after the longtime owner of the motel, has a claw-foot tub for soaking. If you stop just for a photo op, it's polite to ask for permission.

If you prefer your retro style in the form of midcentury groovy, head to the jaunty cinderblock court of the **Motel Safari** (722 E. Route 66 Blvd., 575/461-1048, www.themotelsafari.com, $55 d), with firm beds and flat-panel TVs, plus mod, spindly legged furniture

that conjures 1959. One suite nods to Wanda Jackson, the queen of rockabilly ($95).

Just a tiny bit later in the timeline of motel architecture, the **Historic Route 66 Motel** (1620 E. Route 66 Blvd., 575/461-1212, www.rte66motel.com, $50 d) conjures Palm Springs in Tucumcari, and its owners have maintained the minimalist style. It might not have a fabulous neon sign, but all rooms have floor-to-ceiling windows, and most have very cool turquoise vinyl ranch chairs original to the 1963 motel.

Information

The **Tucumcari-Quay County Chamber of Commerce** (404 W. Route 66 Blvd., 575/461-1694, 8:30am-5pm Mon.-Fri.) has the usual assortment of information.

Getting There

By car, Tucumcari is 59 miles (less than one hour) east along I-40 from Santa Rosa, 176 miles (three hours) east from Albuquerque, and 113 miles (two hours) west from Amarillo, Texas. By bus, **Greyhound** (800/231-2222, www.greyhound.com) stops in Tucumcari three times a day, at the McDonald's (2608 S. 1st St., 575/461-1350, 5am-8pm daily).

The Blue Swallow Motel is one of several excellent old motels on the Mother Road.

The Llano

Texans refer to these barren plains as the Llano, and much of this area could be mistaken for the neighboring state, from the fields of cattle (for both beef and dairy) to the oil derricks that dot the horizon. "West West Texas" rarely sees tourists, but some of this land is exceptionally pretty: South on Highway 209 from Tucumcari, for instance, takes you closer to the mesas and leaves the visual clutter of billboards and semitrucks behind. Scored by deep channels, the red earth is studded with cholla cactus and yucca, as well as black, brushy mesquite. The occasional farmhouse—often built only feet away from a ruined homestead from 50 years ago—shows the optimism required to live in this windy, harshly beautiful landscape. (If you jog west toward Fort Sumner, you'll see the state actually profiting from the rough climate here, through a field of wind turbines that feed the electricity grid.)

CLOVIS

Like many other chronically windy spots on the plains, Clovis has a problem keeping its signboards straight, so WELCOMET OCLOVIS will have to do. Busy as it is with rail freight, cattle auctions, and the adjacent Cannon Air Force Base, Clovis doesn't really court tourists anyway. It had its big moment in the national spotlight in 1957, when Buddy Holly recorded "That'll Be the Day" in a music studio here. And even though its population is nearly 40,000 and growing, it feels like a fairly small town, especially along its wide, brick-paved Main Street, which dead-ends at the rail yard. The downtown area sports some stylish art deco buildings, including the glamorous Hotel Clovis, once the tallest building between Dallas and Albuquerque, recently converted to lofts, but now overshadowed by grain silos.

Sights

No one talks about it much today, but in the late 1950s, the "Clovis Sound" was an unmistakable, and deeply influential, musical phenomenon. It was the product of a single recording studio here on the edge of the Texas

the Clovis skyline

plains, and it's commemorated in the small but thorough **Norman & Vi Petty Rock & Roll Museum** (105 E. Grand Ave., 575/763-3435, 8am-noon and 1pm-5pm Mon.-Fri., $5). The displays of ephemera tell the story of how local boy Norm Petty and his wife, Vi, scored a hit with their smooth version of "Mood Indigo," then returned here to build a recording studio. Norm was an acoustic obsessive, and his attention to detail came through when he helped an aspiring country star named Buddy Holly, from Lubbock, Texas, revamp his tunes into pop hits. After Holly shot to stardom, other hopeful artists beat a path to Clovis to work with the Pettys.

The Beatles, who saw Holly in concert in 1958, were indelibly marked by the big, clean Clovis Sound, and the young Rolling Stones covered "Rave On." Norman Petty helped launched the careers of Roy Orbison and

Waylon Jennings, and kept producing through the 1960s (as rockabilly bands morphed into psychedelia) and the 1970s, and died in 1984.

The museum also contains a re-creation of the studios that made the Clovis Sound. But if your schedule allows, call ahead to arrange a tour of the actual **Norman Petty Recording Studios** (1313 W. 7th St., 575/356-6422, donation). You get to hold the mic Buddy Holly used and see where he and the Crickets lived, in a small apartment at the back of the studio. If you're lucky, an old-timer who sang backup tracks at the studio will be there to serenade you.

Otherwise, Clovis's attractions are just the regular business activities: You can watch the action every Wednesday morning at the **Clovis Livestock Auction** (504 S. Hull St., 575/762-4422), south of the tracks at the corner of Brady. Or follow the freight trains' comings and goings from the bridge over Hull Street.

The *Llano Estacado*

The early explorers on Francisco Vásquez de Coronado's first excursion through the West, in 1541, referred to the stretch east from the Sacramento Mountains as the *llano estacado,* describing the place as an endless sea of green, with grass as high as their horses' bellies. It's an evocative image, but it doesn't explain exactly what the conquistadors may have meant by the word *estacado.*

The common translation is "stockaded" or "staked" plains, which hardly clarifies the issue. Some academics have reasoned that the great green expanse was as disorienting as being at sea, so the Spanish horsemen pounded stakes in the ground to mark their way. Meanwhile, those in the "stockaded" camp reason that the Spanish thought the mesas that punctuated the flatlands—particularly the 300-foot-high Caprock Escarpment near Tucumcari—stood up, straight-walled, like defensive stockades. A third, far less common interpretation proposes that in 16th-century Spanish, *estacado* also had the meaning of "covered in spikes." That is, these were the "stickered plains," due to the spiny yucca plants and thorn-covered mesquite bushes that flourish here. Whatever the case, although the "sea of green" that Coronado traversed is not so green today, the mesas remain as stark and straight.

Entertainment and Events

Local country acts play at **Kelley's Bar** (2208 N. Prince St., 575/762-0044), the only real bar in town. The annual Petty-inspired jam, the **Clovis Music Festival** (575/763-3435, www.clovisnm.org), happens every September and draws a roster of throwback rockabilly and roots acts. The Norman Petty studio is also open during that weekend.

Learn the history of the "Clovis Sound" at the Norman & Vi Petty Rock & Roll Museum.

Food

For Mexican, head to **Taqueria Jalisco** (217 W. 7th St., 575/763-1865, 6:30am-9:30pm Sun.-Thurs., 6:30am-10pm Fri.-Sat., $8), where you can get a huge slab of steak and homemade flour tortillas, as well as deep-fried gorditas, stuffed *tortas,* and creamy, cinnamon-spiked *horchata* to drink—far more food than you can eat, served with style (the trompe l'oeil mural takes you right to Mexico's Pacific coast), at astonishingly low prices.

Downtown, a popular spot for the noon meal is **Eddie's Subs & More** (517 N. Main St., 575/762-6911, 10:30am-4pm Mon.-Fri., $7), good for hamburgers and green-chile stew—in addition to the aforementioned heroes, served on fresh-baked bread.

Then there's the category of 1950s-style drive-in restaurants, the likes of which are seldom seen these days—especially not of this caliber. ★ **Foxy** (720 W. 7th St., 575/763-7995, 7am-10pm daily, $5) excels at crispy taquitos and steak fingers. Buddy Holly and the Crickets would eat lunch here when recording just down the street at Norman Petty Recording Studios. **Twin Cronnie** (709 Commerce Way, 575/763-5463, 7am-9pm Mon.-Thurs., 7am-10pm Fri.-Sat., $5) is the home of a tasty combination involving two hot dogs, chili, and a round bun, among a million other menu items.

If you're staying on the north side of town,

Fat Boys BBQ (901 E. Llano Estacado Blvd., 575/763-9543, 11am-8pm Mon., 11am-9pm Tues.-Sat., 11am-3pm Sun., $12) is a handy dinner spot, with a broader menu than just smoked meat (you can even get a salad!). But it's not quite so stupendous that it's worth a drive north for its own sake.

Accommodations

Most of the cheaper motels in Clovis are on Mabry Drive, parallel to the very busy railroad tracks through town—which can make for a bad night's sleep if you're sensitive to noise. If you can afford it, go for the town's branch of **La Quinta** (4521 N. Prince St., 575/763-8777, www.lq.com, $139 d), one of a few options on the north side of town, with a nice indoor pool and well-kept, suite-layout rooms.

Information

The Clovis **chamber of commerce** (105 E. Grand Ave., 575/763-3435, www.clovisnm.org, 8am-5pm Mon.-Fri.) has its offices downtown, in the same building as the Petty Museum.

Getting There

By car, Clovis is 85 miles (1.5 hours) south from Tucumcari zigzagging on Highway 209, 110 miles (2 hours) northeast from Roswell on U.S. 70, 3.5 hours from Albuquerque, and 2 hours from Lubbock, Texas. Fort Sumner is 60 miles (1 hour) west on U.S. 84.

Clovis Municipal Airport (CVN), six miles east of town, receives three flights daily from Dallas on **Boutique Air** (855/268-8478, www.boutiqueair.com). **Greyhound** (800/231-2222, www.greyhound.com) stops at Cortez Gas (2207 S. Prince St., 575/762-4584, 9am-5pm Mon.-Sat.); buses come from Las Cruces once a day.

PORTALES

Anchored by Eastern New Mexico University, Portales is also home to some prairie chickens and a whole lot of peanut farmers. The farmland surrounding Portales may produce a mere 24 million pounds of legumes a year— less than 1 percent of the nation's peanut

Portales

crop—but that accounts for 90 percent of the exceptionally tasty red-skinned Valencia variety. Its downtown, fanning out from a deco-goes-West courthouse (look for the cowboy friezes above the windows), is slowly being revitalized, and the most attractive area of town is the campus of brick buildings and green lawns in the southwest corner of town. On the 21-mile drive down from Clovis, you might see the biggest tumbleweeds of your trip—just slow down and let 'em roll on by.

Sights

Three collections on the ENMU campus merit a quick look, depending on your interests. Another is impossible to miss from the road.

BLACKWATER DRAW MUSEUM

The **Blackwater Draw Museum** (Lea Hall, 575/562-2202, 10am-5pm Mon.-Sat., noon-5pm Sun. June-Aug., closed Mon. Sept.-May, $3) tells the story of a major discovery in ancient history that happened nearby. In the

1940s and 1950s, archaeologists discovered fluted spearheads embedded in a mammoth carcass, effectively proving the existence of humans in North America at the end of the last ice age, in roughly 11,300 BCE. Clovis Man, as this "type site" was dubbed, is still the oldest known culture in the New World—or at least the oldest one that researchers can agree on. The museum displays the site findings, which also include later layers of occupation: Remnants of the later Folsom Man culture were stacked atop the Clovis points, with early agricultural efforts on top of that. (Your museum admission also gives you access to the site—ask for directions.)

ROOSEVELT COUNTY MUSEUM

Featuring an interesting assortment, **Roosevelt County Museum** (575/562-2592, 8am-noon and 1pm-5pm Mon.-Fri., call for weekend hours, free) is a very manageable size, with some great paintings (see the cowboy's ode to the mountain lion in the main hall) and cool dioramas, along with items from Japan and Peru, donated by well-traveled locals. The museum is at West 2nd Street and University Place. Weekend hours in summer may vary—call ahead.

JACK WILLIAMSON SCIENCE FICTION COLLECTION

Upstairs at Golden Library is the voluminous **Jack Williamson Science Fiction Collection** (8am-5pm Mon.-Fri.), more than a dozen long shelves of sci-fi and fantasy work collected by Williamson, both a fan and author (his lifetime achievement Nebula Award is on display) who happened to live in Portales. Fittingly, the library's style is a bit midcentury space-age—it's a nice place to settle into a low-slung lounge chair and flip through a 1963 *Science Fiction* back issue.

DALLEY WINDMILL MUSEUM

Equally obscure and similarly impressive, the **Dalley Windmill Museum** (Lime St. at U.S. 70) is a collection of 85 windmills, amassed as a private collection and donated to the city.

Look for the machines clustered at the fairgrounds west of the highway. And while you're there, you can buy fresh Valencia peanuts at **Borden's** (620 E. Lime St., 575/356-6691, 9am-5pm Mon.-Fri.), which has a lot of other locally made snacks as well.

Festivals and Events

Near the end of October, ENMU and the chamber of commerce sponsor the annual **Peanut Valley Festival** (575/356-8541). It's not *completely* peanut-obsessed, what with distractions like a big craft fair, funnel-cake booths, and the like, but it is a lively time to be in town.

Food and Accommodations

Sample Portales's produce in a deliciously creamy peanut-butter shake at ★ **Pat's Twin Cronnie** (100 N. Chicago Ave., 575/356-5841, 10am-9pm Mon.-Fri., 10am-10pm Fri.-Sat., noon-8pm Sun., $5), where you can also fill up on taquitos, burgers, and chili dogs.

On the plaza, the **Do Drop Inn** (123 S. Main St., 575/226-5282, 7am-7pm Mon.-Thurs., 7am-8pm Fri., 7am-6pm Sat., $6) is a chummy little café that serves supremely gooey homemade baked goods and assorted sandwiches.

Just across the street, ★ **Roosevelt Brewing Co.** (201 S. Main Ave., 575/226-2739, 11am-9pm Sun. and Tues.-Thurs., 11am-10pm Fri.-Sat., $10) serves a more substantial meal, using local farm products in the timeless combo of wood-oven pizza, house-brewed beer, and killer craft-brew-inspired cupcakes.

Along with a couple of chain hotels, there's **Almost Home Bed and Breakfast** (8168 Hwy. 206, 575/356-0011, www.almosthomebedandbreakfast.com, $89 d), a ranch-style home on the outskirts of town. The rooms are simple but clean, with private entrances. Be prepared to chat with the owners over breakfast.

Information

The **Roosevelt County Chamber of Commerce** (100 S. Avenue A, 575/356-8541,

Dalley Windmill Museum

www.portales.com, 8am-5pm Mon.-Fri.) can help you out with maps and brochures.

Getting There

By car, Portales is 21 miles (20 minutes) southwest of Clovis on U.S. 70; it's about 90 miles (1.5 hours) northeast of Roswell, and 228 miles (3.5 hours) southeast from Albuquerque. **Greyhound** (800/231-2222, www.greyhound.com) drops passengers at McDonald's (1020 W. 1st St.); buses come from Las Cruces once a day.

LOVINGTON

The seat of Lea County, Lovington has a handsome art deco courthouse and tidy streets. The town-operated **Lea County Museum** (103 S. Love St., 575/396-4805, www.leacountymuseum.org, 9am-5pm Tues.-Sat., free), across from the courthouse, contains all the usual pioneer-era items. In addition, one room is dedicated to Western writer Max Evans, who lived until the age of 12 in nearby Humble City, now all but vanished (Evans rechristened the place Starvation, Texas, in one of his novels).

If you're hungry in Lovington, hit the **Lazy 6** (102 S. 1st St., 575/396-5066, 10am-2pm Mon.-Fri., $6), where the knickknack-to-customer ratio is 10 to 1, even when the place is packed for lunch. Don't let it distract you from the good home cooking, though. It's one block west of Main Street.

HOBBS

Yet another oil town with the smell of, shall we say, "money" in the air, Hobbs is just five miles from the Texas border and the largest settlement in Lea County, with more than 37,000 residents. It's a destination only for people working in the industry, students at New Mexico Preparatory College and the College of the Southwest, and fans of gliding—the flat land and empty skies are ideal for delicate sailplanes.

Wild West fanatics will want to pay their respects at the **Western Heritage Museum and Lea County Cowboy Hall of Fame** (5317 Lovington Hwy., 575/392-6730, www.nmjc.edu/museum, 10am-5pm Tues.-Sat., 1pm-5pm Sun., $5), a sleek bit of architecture that renders an oil derrick in green glass. The complex on the north edge of town honors rodeo champions (of which Lea County has a disproportionately high number) and all-around good local citizens. It also gives an interesting overview of the region's history, from dinosaur stomping ground to homesteaded territory to modern source of black gold, first tapped in 1927.

ARTESIA

To quote the travel cliché, Artesia is a town of contrasts. One of the most discordant views of New Mexico can be had at the junction of U.S. 285 and U.S. 82 in Artesia. Look west and you'll see an attractive, modernized Main Street that boasts a concert hall, a revamped movie palace, shops, and sturdy old buildings. Look east and you'll see the state's largest oil refinery, all concrete towers, blinking lights, and plumes of steam and smoke. More practically, Artesia is less than an hour's drive from Carlsbad, and it has two decent hotels—so you could conceivably sleep here, for slightly better value, before or after visiting the caverns. But don't stay here if you're up to no good—Artesia is all about law-abiding behavior, thanks to the presence of a federal law-enforcement training center.

Sights

If you keep your back to the refinery, you can spend a pleasant hour or two (or more, if you go to a movie) checking out the **Artesia Historical Museum & Art Center** (505 W. Richardson Ave., 575/748-2390, www.artesia-museum.com, 9am-noon and 1pm-5pm Tues.-Fri., 1pm-5pm Sat., free), in a pretty area two blocks south of Main Street.

Larger-than-life bronze statues dot the main drag, including a very cool series of life-size figures in the midst of a cattle-rustling operation, arranged across three intersections. Stroll by the **Artesia Public Library** (205 W. Quay St., 575/746-4252, 9:30am-6pm Mon.-Sat.) to see a 46-foot-long fresco by New Mexico painter Peter Hurd, installed here in late 2015 after being saved from demolition in its original home in Houston. The lush farm scene is the focal point of the new building; it's visible from the street through floor-to-ceiling windows.

If your schedule allows, attend a show at the **Ocotillo Performing Arts Center** (310 W. Main St., 575/746-4212, www.artesiaartscouncil.com), a classy refurbished theater that draws touring musicians.

oil derricks at work in Artesia

Food

For caffeine, a slab of German chocolate cake, or a hearty sandwich, head to **The Jahva House** (105 N. 5th St., 575/746-9494, 7am-8pm Mon.-Thurs., 7am-9pm Fri., 10am-4pm Sun., $8), where it's hard to say what is worshiped more: espresso drinks or Jesus. There's a Bible open on the counter, but also an impressively detailed menu of Italian terminology. The groovy marbleized pink sinks in the bathrooms (labeled ADAM and EVE) are so yummy-looking, you'll want an ice-cream sundae as well.

For dinner, pickings are slim. **Piccolino** (201 N. 1st St., 575/748-1100, 10:30am-9pm Mon.-Sat., $11) does passable red-sauce Italian (stick to the pastas), though service can be glacial. Or head to **The Wellhead** brewpub (332 W. Main St., 575/746-0640, 11am-9pm Mon.-Sat., $11) for livelier atmosphere; the menu is pretty standard bar food, though.

Accommodations

Heritage Inn (209 W. Main St., 575/748-2552, www.artesiaheritageinn.com, $119 d) is a historic hotel that has been smartly renovated on the points that matter: modern bathrooms and comfy beds. The glitzier **Hotel Artesia** (203 N. 2nd St., 888/746-2066, www.hotelartesia.com, $123 d) looks like it has been beamed in from Miami. The 52 spacious rooms are done in a somewhat generic sleek modern style, with every

The Ocotillo brings culture to downtown Artesia.

convenience for business travelers. The lobby lounge is popular after work.

Information

Stop in at the **Artesia Chamber of Commerce** (107 N. 1st St., 575/746-2744, www.artesiachamber.com, 9am-5pm Mon.-Fri.), in the old train depot, for additional info.

Roswell

Launched into national notoriety in 1947 by an alleged UFO crash (and subsequent government cover-up) on a ranch northwest of town, Roswell has been marked indelibly by the odd events. Popular fascination was renewed with "truth-seeking" exposés in the 1980s, and the town has become a pilgrimage site for true believers and kitsch seekers alike. The city seal sports an alien, the green streetlamps have eyes, and the McDonald's resembles a spaceship about to lift off.

But there's a lot more to this city of 48,000, the largest metro area in this region. Founded in 1870, it has its roots in ranching, then agriculture, after an artesian well was discovered in 1890; Chaves County is the largest dairy producer in the state. The 1910 courthouse has a tall, green-tiled dome, built by Isaac

Roswell

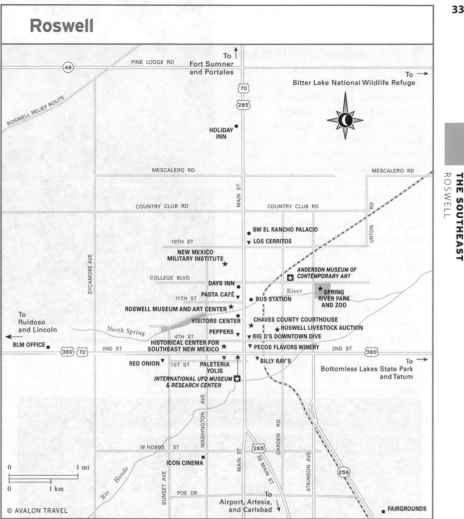

Hamilton Rapp, who was also instrumental in designing Santa Fe's zoning codes to create a homogenous downtown.

Over the long term, Roswell has probably been more influenced by the Rapp-designed New Mexico Military Institute, established in 1891. There's a conservative streak, to the point it's hard to find a bar at night. As if to balance the scales, Roswell has hosted a small clan of contemporary artists every year since

the mid-1960s, which has fostered strong arts appreciation and two excellent museums. These disparate elements can keep a visitor entertained for a day or two.

SIGHTS

The central intersection is at North Main Street (U.S. 285) and West 2nd Street (U.S. 70/380), also the location of the UFO museum. Like debris around a crash site, space-themed gift shops and other attractions dot the surrounding blocks.

★ International UFO Museum & Research Center

Most visitors to Roswell make a beeline to the **International UFO Museum & Research Center** (114 N. Main St., 800/822-3545, www.roswellufomuseum.com, 9am-5pm daily, $5), a converted movie theater where the events of July 1947 are dissected with obsessive care. The museum founders are two men peripherally involved in the incident, and they're occasionally at the front desk, ready to talk shop with anyone who asks. The mass of data—newspaper clippings, affidavits, faded photos—is a little overwhelming and presented with a minimum of gloss; an audio tour only heaps on more detail. Related issues such as ancient alien cults, Area 51, abductions, and crop circles get the same thorough documentary treatment.

The mood lightens a bit with a section about Roswell in the movies and an "alien autopsy." And be sure to press the button for special effects on the central installation of four gawky aliens below a silver disc.

Roswell's courthouse

Watch out for aliens at the International UFO Museum & Research Center.

New Mexico's Alien Obsession

New Mexico's extreme weather may account for some UFO sightings.

In 1947, strange objects were spotted in American skies. First an incident was reported in Washington State, then another in Idaho. When the next one happened, less than a month later, in Roswell, it was all over the press, with stories of a "flying disc," complete with alien crew, crashing on a ranch outside of town. No sooner did journalists descend than stories were revised, the military got involved, and a haze of confusion swirled up around the event.

The military's denial of the event did not squash the story, and soon enough, the United States seemed to be in the grip of a UFO frenzy, as scores of sightings were reported. A 1950 book titled *Behind the Flying Saucers,* by a reporter for *Variety,* Frank Scully, described yet another strange encounter in New Mexico: In March 1948, just nine months after the Roswell incident, the residents of Aztec, near Farmington, apparently had a similar occurrence in their own backyard—although no one actually saw the disc in the sky or at the crash site, as all but a scrap had been whisked away by the military. In fact, Scully was the first to investigate the crash, when he was in the area looking into the "Farmington Armada" spotted earlier in the year.

Two years later, it came out that the spaceship wreckage Scully had seen was actually the work of Silas Newton and Leo Gebauer, who had been seeking investors in their device for finding oil. The crash had been their backstory for the alien technology that allegedly drove their gadget, and they hoped to secure investors in their scheme. The two con men were convicted of fraud in 1953.

That didn't stop UFO enthusiasts from reviving the Aztec story in the 1980s, along with the Roswell incident, which became the subject of fresh fascination. Now both towns have a respectable alien-inspired tourism industry. The general perception in New Mexico toward these and other events (such as the creepy cattle mutilations in the 1970s, and not-uncommon tales of alien abductions) is not one of feverish conviction, nor of outright dismissal. It's more an attitude of resigned acceptance—as if the UFOs are just one more weird happening in a very weird state.

Roswell Museum and Art Center

The wide-ranging **Roswell Museum and Art Center** (100 W. 11th St., 575/624-6744, www.roswellmuseum.org, 9am-5pm Tues.-Sat., 1pm-5pm Sun., free) is a real treasure. The original gallery space, built in 1937 as a WPA project, is an attraction in itself, with high viga ceilings and tin chandeliers; it contains work by local luminaries like Peter Hurd and Henriette Wyeth, as well as a beautiful collection of Western paraphernalia, such as finely wrought spurs.

The place celebrates science too, with an exhibit on space-flight visionary Robert Goddard, who moved from Massachusetts to Roswell in the 1930s to continue his work on liquid-fueled rockets in a less populated area—his workshop has been re-created, piece by piece, in one room. Adjacent to the main museum, the **Robert H. Goddard Planetarium** (912 N. Main St.), the second-largest in the state, has several public shows a month; call the museum for the schedule.

★ Anderson Museum of Contemporary Art

As good as the Roswell Museum is, it's no match for the 17,000-square-foot **Anderson Museum of Contemporary Art** (409 E. College Blvd., 575/623-5600, www.roswellamoca.org, 9am-4pm Mon.-Fri., 1pm-5pm Sat.-Sun., free), an invigorating collection from the past four decades, in media ranging from oil paintings to wood inlay. The works on view are representative samples from an artist-in-residence program established in 1967 by oilman Donald Anderson, whose work is also displayed. Since then it has hosted luminaries like abstract expressionist Milton Resnick and sculptor Luís Jiménez (best known for his *Blue Mustang* outside the Denver airport), along with scores of others still working and developing their reputations.

In the museum, more than 400 products of the "gift of time" (as the foundation calls the residency) fill the walls alongside photos of the artists. They're posed in the compound they're granted on the fringes of town—a sort of yearbook photo, which also pegs the art to a certain period. It's an unorthodox approach to contemporary art, and it lends an exuberance to the place that's hard to resist, even if you generally prefer older, less experimental artwork.

General Douglas L. McBride Military Museum

A visit to the array of military paraphernalia at the **General Douglas L. McBride Military Museum** (800/421-5376, www.nmmi.edu/museum, 8am-4pm Mon.-Fri., free) is an excuse to get inside the giant fortress that is the New Mexico Military Institute, on North Main Street at College Boulevard. The institution has about 1,000 high school students from all over the country, and alumni include newscaster Sam Donaldson, hotelier Conrad Hilton, historian Paul Horgan, painter Peter Hurd, actor Owen Wilson, and even Miss New Mexico 2001. The museum entrance is in the back of the main building; head west on College, then turn right on Kentucky, then through the gates at Duty Street.

Historical Center for Southeast New Mexico

The trials of pioneer living are detailed at the **Historical Center for Southeast New Mexico** (200 N. Lea Ave., 575/622-8333, www.roswellnmhistory.org, 1pm-4pm daily, free), a 1910 Prairie-style brick bungalow filled with period furniture and mannequins. You can pick up a brochure for a walking tour around Roswell's other historic houses, in a variety of styles.

ENTERTAINMENT AND EVENTS

You're lucky to find even a restaurant open past 8pm in Roswell, much less a bar. The city lets loose for a couple of annual parties, though. **Icon Cinema** (900 W. Hobbs St., 575/208-2810, www.iconcinemas.com) is a four-screen theater on the south side of town. Given the limited nightlife in Roswell, it's usually pretty packed. For a glimpse of local business, visit the **Roswell Livestock Auction** (900 N. Garden St., 575/622-1279, 9am Mon.); feel free to walk in and take a seat in the bleachers.

Nightlife

Roswell is pretty tame at night, and almost completely dry. **Stellar Coffee** (315 N. Main St., 575/623-3711, 7am-9pm Mon.-Fri., 8am-9pm Sat., 8am-7pm Sun.) is one of the livelier places, with a small stage for acoustic acts. If you want just a little bit rowdier, **Billy Ray's** (118 E. 3rd St., 575/627-0997, 11am-midnight Tues.-Sat.) has a decent scene, with popular karaoke, and live music on the weekends.

It's not strictly nightlife, as the tasting bar shuts at 5pm, but **Pecos Flavors Winery** (113 E. Third St., 575/627-6265, 10am-7pm Mon.-Thurs., 10am-8pm Sat.-Sun.) does give you a chance to sample local vino. Thanks to a handsome antique wood bar and a convivial atmosphere, this feels more like a town hangout than a formal tasting room, and it's a nice place to put your feet up after walking around downtown. It also stocks other local bounty, such as salsas and pistachios, and occasionally hosts live music in the evenings.

Festivals and Events

The town dedicates Fourth of July weekend to visitors from space, as well as around the world, for the **Roswell UFO Festival** (www.ufofestivalroswell.com), which melds serious science with all the geekiness of a *Star Trek* convention. More than 50,000 space fans gather for an alien costume contest, screenings of vintage sci-fi films, a nighttime disc-golf tourney, and lectures by scientists and assorted actors. By contrast, the **Eastern New Mexico State Fair & Parade** (575/623-9411, www.enmsf.com), at the fairgrounds on the southeast side of town in early October, seems pretty mundane.

SPORTS AND RECREATION

A big park in town caters to kids, while a state park to the east offers a few opportunities for swimming and mountain biking. Overall, though, the flat terrain around Roswell doesn't lend itself to exciting outdoor activities. The **BLM Roswell field office** (2909 W. 2nd St., 575/627-0272, 8am-4:30pm Mon.-Fri.), on the far west edge of town, is the contact point for questions about nearby public lands.

Spring River Park and Zoo

Like many small-town zoos, the animal component of **Spring River Park and Zoo** (1306 E. College Blvd., 575/624-6760, 10am-8pm Wed.-Mon. in summer, 10am-5:30pm Wed.-Mon. in winter, free) might be a little distressing—although the massive prairie dog village (allegedly the largest in the state) is always a crowd-pleaser, and there's a fishing hole just for kids. And the 1926 carousel costs just a quarter, as does the miniature train that loops around the grounds. The park is the head of the **Spring River Trail**, a five-mile paved route to the town golf course.

Bottomless Lakes State Park

The pools at **Bottomless Lakes State Park** (575/624-6058, www.nmparks.com, $5/car), just east of Roswell, are a rare phenomenon in New Mexico. Like the Blue Hole in Santa Rosa, they began as water-filled caverns, then the ceilings collapsed. Lea Lake, the deepest and largest of the pools here, plunges 90 feet. It's also the only lake open for swimming and diving, but it's a pretty small patch of water for the crowds that descend on it in the summertime.

There's tent **camping** at Cottonwood Lake, adjacent to the park office. (If you're interested in archaeology, ask here for directions to **Garnsey Arroyo,** a barely excavated bison "kill site" from about 500 years ago.) You'll find RV camping farther down the access road at Lea Lake.

Skidmarks Trail, good for biking or hiking, runs for a little more than three miles over some of the limestone bluffs on the north edge of the park area. Wildflowers bloom here in the spring, and you'll see lots of waterbirds. Look for the trailhead just as you turn onto the loop road around the park (if you get to Lazy Lagoon, you've gone too far).

To reach the park, head east of Roswell 12 miles on U.S. 380, then turn south on Bottomless Lakes Road, which loops around the lakes after about 3 miles.

Bitter Lake National Wildlife Refuge

Established in 1937, the **Bitter Lake National Wildlife Refuge** (4067 Bitter Lakes Rd., 575/622-6755) encompasses nearly 25,000 acres of grasslands, dunes, and wetlands around the Pecos River. As at Bottomless Lakes, there are a number of freshwater sinkholes. The area is great for birding, as well as for spotting more than 90 species of colorful dragonflies and damselflies, best viewed in late summer. There's even a **Dragonfly Festival** in early September. To reach the refuge headquarters, from North Main Street (U.S. 70/285), turn east onto East Pine Lodge Road and follow it until it turns into Bitter Lakes Road and runs into the park. The visitors center is open weekdays only.

FOOD

New Mexican

Peppers (500 N. Main St., 575/623-1700, 11am-10pm Mon.-Sat., $10) is one of the most popular restaurants in town. It feels a bit like a family-owned Chili's, with an all-over-the-place menu. It's strongest on meat, from fajitas to baby-back ribs, but there's also a good vegetarian burrito and some other solid New Mexican dishes. Get a seat on the patio if you can, and wash it all down with a microbrew.

Mexican

A nice dose of Mexico can be had at the **Red Onion** (1400 W. 2nd St., 575/622-3232, 7am-8pm Tues.-Sat., 7am-3pm Sun.-Mon., $7), which transports you to Mexico for breakfast or lunch, with big platters of *migas* (scrambled eggs with tortilla bits mixed in) and other standards, with Jarritos sodas to wash it down. It

also has a surprisingly appetizing lunch buffet 11am-1pm. Look for it in a half-empty strip mall a bit out of the center on the west side.

Los Cerritos (2103 N. Main St., 575/622-4919, 7am-9pm Mon.-Sat., 7am-5pm Sun., $9) is more mainstream mash-up Mexican. The place has all the interior charm of a Denny's, but it does great fresh table-side guacamole and giant refreshing *micheladas* (beer, spicy tomato juice, and lime). On Tuesday evenings, crispy tacos are $0.79 each.

Cafés

Stellar Coffee (315 N. Main St., 575/623-3711, 7am-9pm Mon.-Fri., 8am-9pm Sat., 8am-7pm Sun.) supplies both caffeine and sociability, with plenty of room to lounge.

Diner

The one tragedy of ★ **Big D's Downtown Dive** (505 N. Main St., 575/627-0776, 11am-9pm Mon.-Fri., $7) is that it's open only on weekdays. Don't be fooled by the name, the casual order-at-the-counter setup, and the walls covered with New Mexico license plates. This is no dive at all, but a gourmet operation in fast-food disguise. "Bergs" (burgers) have toppings like sautéed mushrooms and sherry mayonnaise, salads burst with goodies like toasted pine nuts, the waffle fries are sprinkled with garlic, and even the water is laced with cucumber and lime.

Italian

As one of the few places serving on a Sunday night, **Pasta Café** (1208 N. Main St., 575/624-1111, 11am-9:30pm Sun.-Thurs., 11am-10:30pm Fri.-Sat., $13) does solid Italian. Despite the name, the place is a bit more formal than a café, and the menu's not just pasta—it also has well-executed favorites like a delectably light eggplant Parmesan.

Desserts

For afternoon refreshment, head to ★ **Paleteria Yolis** (510 W. 2nd St., 11am-9pm daily, $2) for a fresh-fruit ice pop or

Big D's Downtown Dive

other cold treat. The place feels straight out of Mexico in the best possible way, from the sparkling pink-and-white decor to the case full of flavors like tamarind and *fresas con crema* (strawberries and cream). The *mangoneada,* mango sorbet doused in sweet-tart-hot sauce and chile, is a taste sensation. Everything's made fresh (and translated into English).

ACCOMMODATIONS

Most of the motels are along the northern section of Main Street (U.S. 70/285); unfortunately, the only respectable options are national chains.

Under $100

Of the chains, the **Best Western El Rancho Palacio** (2205 N. Main St., 575/622-2721, www.bestwestern.com, $76 d) almost always can be booked for under $100. "Palace" may be stretching it, but the rooms, which open onto exterior hallways, are in good shape and fairly modern feeling; those upstairs have nice higher ceilings. Breakfast is included, and there's an outdoor pool.

For about the same price, the **Days Inn** (1310 N. Main St., 575/623-4021, www.daysinn.com, $76 d) is admittedly not quite as sturdy-feeling; walls and ceilings are a bit thin, breakfast is skimpier, and the pool is smaller. But it is well kept, and it's located a bit closer to the center of town, so is a good option if you prefer to walk around, rather than drive.

$100-150

In this price bracket, the **Holiday Inn** (3620 N. Main St., 575/623-3216, www. holidayinn. com, $120 d) is functional and modern. The lobby has a full restaurant—a fine option if you want to stay in. Guests get discounts on breakfast there too.

INFORMATION AND SERVICES

The **Roswell Convention & Visitors Bureau** (912 N. Main St., 575/624-7704, www.seeroswell.com, 8:30am-5pm Mon.-Fri., 8:30am-4pm Sat., 9am-3pm Sun.) has info on all parts of the state and free wireless Internet access.

GETTING THERE AND AROUND

By car, Roswell is 40 miles (40 minutes) north of Artesia on U.S. 285, 185 miles (3.25 hours) northeast of Las Cruces via U.S. 54 and U.S. 70, and 200 miles (3 hours) southeast of Albuquerque. **American Airlines** (800/443-7300, www.aa.com) operates two flights daily, sometimes more, from Dallas and Phoenix to Roswell (ROW). The airport is five miles south of town. **Greyhound** (800/231-2222, www.greyhound.com) runs one bus a day from Las Cruces to the station (1100 N. Virginia Ave., 575/622-2510, 8am-4pm Mon.-Fri., 11:30am-3:30pm Sat.).

In town, Roswell has a surprisingly good bus system, **Pecos Trails Transit** (575/624-6766, www.roswell-nm.gov). The most useful bus for visitors is no. 1, which runs up and down Main Street roughly every half hour; the no. 2 bus runs west along 2nd Street. Fare is $0.75.

Carlsbad

Tourists rarely hear the word Carlsbad without "caverns" tacked on the end, which means that few people come to see the town itself (the national park is 30 miles farther south on U.S. 62/180). But the place is pleasant, thanks to an orderly plan laid out in 1888 and the broad ribbon of the Pecos River. Shaded with old trees, the river makes a great place to swim. You'll be excused if you make a beeline for the caves, though.

SIGHTS

Canal Street is the big north-south route now, but the historic main drag was Canyon Street, which still has a few cute shops, galleries, and antiques stores, as well as a Pueblo Revival-style courthouse, its front door bordered with cattle brands. The Pecos River glides along the east side. On the north edge of town, the **Pecos River Flume**, erected in wood in 1890 then rebuilt more permanently in 1903, brings irrigation water to farm plots; it was the largest concrete structure in the world at the time.

Carlsbad Museum & Art Center

The town's **Carlsbad Museum & Art Center** (418 W. Fox St., 575/887-0276, 10am-5pm Mon.-Sat., free) holds a small trove of excellent Southwestern art, including some beautiful pieces by Ernest Blumenschein and other early Taos painters, and rotating exhibits by local artists. There are also a few early photographs of the caverns, a real stagecoach, and lots of local arrow points and pottery, as well as a whole array of Peruvian crafts and textiles, donated by a local collector.

Cruisin' Through Time Auto Museum

Though it doesn't overflow with artifacts, the **Cruisin' Through Time Auto Museum** (223 W. Fox St., 575/361-1078, 10am-5pm Tues. and Sat., $7) has enough classic cars to get your motor running. Items such as license plates and Coca-Cola signage fill out the vintage exhibits.

Living Desert Zoo and Gardens State Park

Immediately north of Carlsbad, off U.S. 285, the zoo and gardens at **Living Desert Zoo and Gardens State Park** (1504 Miehls Dr. N., 575/887-5516, www.nmparks.com, 8am-5pm daily June-Aug., 9am-5pm daily Sept.-May, $5) is a great place to familiarize yourself with the area habitat. Planted with endemic cactus, grasses, and yucca, the place also keeps a few rescued native animals in cages, so you can get an up-close look at elk, peccary, and even bobcats and a black bear with a penchant for painting. Last entrance is 3:30pm.

Carlsbad

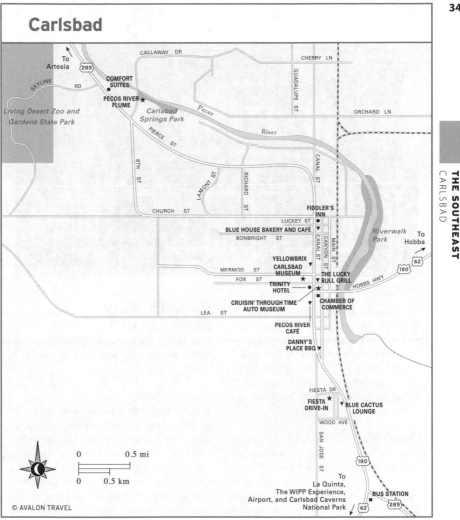

© AVALON TRAVEL

ENTERTAINMENT AND EVENTS

In the summer, hit the drive-in; in the winter, cruise the Pecos.

Nightlife

The three-screen **Fiesta Drive-In** (401 W. Fiesta Dr., 575/885-4126, Fri.-Mon., www. fiestadrivein.com) still draws crowds to first-run movies year-round. Fully renovated in 2004, it's high-tech for an outdoor cinema, and the concessions stand includes burgers and fries, in addition to the usual popcorn and candy.

As for evening drinks, **Trinity Hotel & Suites** (201 S. Canal St., 575/234-9891, 5pm-10pm Mon.-Sat.) is a popular place, with a long wood bar in a high-ceilinged room. Only beer, wine (from around New Mexico,

Trinity Hotel & Suites in Carlsbad

including the hotel owner's own label), and faux cocktails are served, but there's a good selection of snacks. For a rowdier night out, the **Blue Cactus Lounge** (1829 S. Canal St., 575/887-2851), in the Best Western Stevens Inn, is the place to go for occasional live music, and an illuminating cross section of Carlsbadians.

Festivals and Events

If you're in Carlsbad in the winter, don't miss **Christmas on the Pecos** (575/887-6516, www.christmasonthepecos.com, $15 Sun.-Thurs., $20 Fri.-Sat.), an extravaganza of twinkling lights, leaping reindeer, and even glowing margarita glasses strung across more than a hundred homes along the river. View the spectacle from a pontoon boat gliding along the water; the whole ride takes an hour. The city has obligingly extended the "Christmas" season from Thanksgiving to New Year's Eve, and you should book tickets in advance, especially on weekends.

SPORTS AND RECREATION

Essential when the temperature climbs above 90°F in the summer, Carlsbad offers a number of ways to cool off.

Pecos River

The great **Beach Recreation Area,** at the end of Church Street, is essentially the city's public pool, with protected swimming areas, a little island for diving, and even a few palm trees and seagulls (migrants from the Gulf of Mexico), which lend a beachfront feel. With **Carlsbad Cruise Lines** (800/976-3021, www.carlsbad-cruises.com), you can rent pedal boats ($10/30 minutes) and kayaks ($12/hour) or take an hour-long cruise on a pontoon boat ($8). A **river walk** runs 4.5 miles along the water on both banks.

Sitting Bull Falls

West of town, the 130-foot cascade of **Sitting Bull Falls** (9am-5 pm daily Oct.-Mar., 8:30am-6pm daily Apr.-Sept., gate closes to incoming traffic an hour before close, $5/car) is a nice

Hot Rocks in Carlsbad

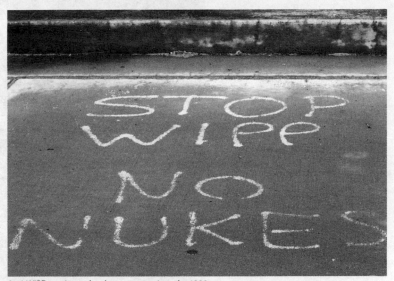

Anti-WIPP sentiment has been strong since the 1990s.

When many New Mexicans think of Carlsbad, they think of an entirely different sort of cave from the ones preserved in the national park here. More than 2,000 feet below ground is a vast, deep salt bed into which 16 square miles of storage halls have been carved. This is the Waste Isolation Pilot Plant (WIPP), a dump for low-level nuclear waste that sits just east of town, south of the highway to Hobbs.

Bitterly fought from the day it was proposed in 1979 until after it opened in 1999, the site became a symbol of a sort of New Mexican fatalism. Judging from decades of prior oafishness, corner-cutting, and corruption, most people believed New Mexican leaders were just too incompetent to pull off such a tricky, potentially dangerous operation.

For years, the site operated smoothly, and expansion was even considered, thanks to the jobs the project offered. But critics' fears were realized in February 2014, when a barrel in the repository burst. (The barrel was full of wheat-based kitty litter used to absorb plutonium-contaminated salts, typical of the kinds of radioactive waste products trucked here from Los Alamos National Labs.) The room was sealed to prevent further damage, and engineers have since improved the poor ventilation in the rest of the site (thought to be one factor in the accident). WIPP was set to resume operations and receive additional nuclear materials by the end of 2016, though this time amid even further concern.

While this debate rages, the Department of Energy office hosts a chipper little exhibit in its lobby about the current operation, **The WIPP Experience** (4021 National Parks Hwy., 800/336-9477, 8am-4:30pm daily, free).

spot for an easy hike on a paved path, a picnic, and a dip in the small, icy pool. Sixteen miles of dirt trails also wind through the area (though fire damage from 2011 is still visible). Look for the turn 12 miles north of town, onto Highway 137. The drive takes about 50 minutes.

FOOD

Carlsbad isn't bursting with choices, and the best options are open only for lunch. Most places are on or very near Canal Street.

Breakfast and Lunch

Good for a quick coffee and morning pastry, or for a more leisurely meal in the yard, the ★ **Blue House Bakery & Café** (609 N. Canyon St., 575/628-0555, 6am-noon Mon.-Sat., $7) is relaxing and comfortable, tucked away in a residential area. The menu ranges from homemade granola to daily soups and sandwiches.

Pecos River Café (409 S. Canal St., 575/887-8882, 6:30am-2pm Mon.-Fri., $8) is better than its architecture (a former Pizza Hut) might suggest. Thanks to its spicy green-chile enchiladas and other New Mexican platters, and its killer cinnamon rolls, it gets packed; try to avoid the noon lunch rush.

Barbecue

The eponymous owner of ★ **Danny's Place BBQ** (902 S. Canal St., 575/885-8739, 11am-9pm Wed.-Mon., $10) is obsessive, in a good way. He earned a reputation for quality 'cue while operating a pit off the side of the Dairy Queen he managed. Now on his own, he keeps not much more on the menu than smoked meat in a sweet-hot sauce (though the meat's so succulent, it's fine plain). There are the usual sides, including some great bacon-y pinto beans.

Fine Dining

For a slightly dressed-up dinner scene, the **Trinity Hotel Restaurant** (201 S. Canal St., 575/234-9891, 7am-1:30pm and 5pm-8:30pm

Sitting Bull Falls

Mon.-Sat., $16) has a familiar menu of pastas and steaks at dinner, and a mix of sandwiches for lunch. It doesn't break any new ground, but it's better than a chain restaurant and consistently good. The split-level, high-ceilinged dining room buzzes with conversation while chandeliers add to the elegant ambience. At breakfast, there are fresh pastries and sun shining in through the big front windows. There's a free New Mexico wine tasting daily (3pm-7pm).

The Lucky Bull Grill (220 W. Fox St., 575/725-5444, 11am-9pm Tues.-Sat., $18) is a laid-back steakhouse with a sports-bar vibe. Locals rave about the burger topped with pepper jack, bacon, green chile, and a fried egg.

Set in a butter-yellow craftsman bungalow, **Yellowbrix** (201 N. Canal St., 575/941-2749, 11am-2:30pm and 5pm-9pm Sun.-Thurs.,

5pm-10pm Fri.-Sat., $9) is Carlsbad's toniest lunch spot, with dishes like French onion soup and poached-pear salad. At night, it aspires to fine dining, which isn't particularly inspired or worth the money ($23 or so for mains)—but there's a good $13 green-chile cheeseburger on the menu, which is a fine excuse to sit out on the front patio, which often has live music.

ACCOMMODATIONS

The lodging situation in Carlsbad is lackluster. Hotels have a captive clientele in the half-million visitors to the caverns every year, and prices reflect that—there is no decent room here under $100, and many hideous rooms go for $150. A few of the chains have spiffy new places, but the independent scene hasn't caught up. Almost all hotels are on Canal Street and its continuation, National Parks Highway (U.S. 62/180), for an easy start on the drive to the caverns. You might consider staying up the highway in Artesia—although you'll have to allot an extra hour's driving time.

On the north end of town, **Comfort Suites** (2600 W. Pierce St., 575/689-8222, www.choicehotels.com, $129 d) is a perfectly good modern hotel with spacious rooms. Connecting doors are a convenience for groups traveling together, but a bit of a noise sieve for those who aren't. On the south end of town, **La Quinta** (4020 National Parks Hwy., 575/236-1010, www. laquintacarlsbadnm.com, $129 d) offers similar amenities in a location closer to the caverns. Both were built in 2014.

There are two bright spots in Carlsbad's dreary hotel scene; they're both pricier than anywhere else in town, though not by much, and both vastly nicer. **Trinity Hotel & Suites** (201 S. Canal St., 575/234-9891, www.thetrinityhotel.com, $169 s) occupies a stately old bank building downtown. Within the historic setting, rooms are thoroughly modern, with sleek black furniture and all the tech trimmings, set under high ceilings. Opt for an upstairs room, as those on the ground floor have large windows facing the street, so you need to keep the drapes shut for privacy. Also note that only two of the nine rooms have more than one bed.

The one B&B in town, **Fiddler's Inn** (705 N. Canyon St., 575/725-8665, www.fiddlersinnbb.com, $169 d) opened in 2015 and takes a pleasant modern approach. The four rooms are airy and lace-free, and you don't have to worry about pressure to chat over breakfast—it's served two doors down, at the excellent Blue House Bakery & Café. One suite ($196) has a full kitchen; another, two bedrooms ($209).

INFORMATION AND SERVICES

Stop in at the **Carlsbad Chamber of Commerce** (302 S. Canal St., 575/887-6516, www.carlsbadchamber.com, 8am-5pm Mon.-Fri.) for a visitors guide and a detailed map.

GETTING THERE

By car, Carlsbad is 37 miles (40 minutes) south of Artesia on U.S. 285, and 207 miles (3.5 hours) east of Las Cruces by the fastest route, I-10 south to U.S. 62/180 east via El Paso, Texas (165 miles; 3 hours). From Albuquerque, it's 275 miles (4.25 hours). **Greyhound** (800/231-2222, www.greyhound.com) buses come through from Albuquerque and El Paso, Texas, once a day, stopping at Food Jet (3102 National Parks Hwy., 575/628-0768, 5am-midnight daily).

Boutique Air (855/268-8478, www.boutiqueair.com) flies in to Carlsbad airport (CNM) from Albuquerque and Dallas. The airport is south of town on U.S. 62/180.

Carlsbad Caverns National Park

One of the country's most awesome natural wonders, Carlsbad Caverns is mesmerizing, even in a two-hour stroll around the biggest cavern. But you could easily spend days here (your entrance ticket is good for three days) visiting ever more obscure underground worlds. Aboveground, the Chihuahuan Desert is especially scenic here, studded with spiky plants; you may also want to make time for a bit of a drive through the terrain.

VISITING THE PARK

The park is 23 miles south of the town of Carlsbad and 7 miles in on a winding access road. In prime conditions, it takes about 45 minutes to get to the **visitors center** (727 Carlsbad Caverns Hwy., 575/785-3137, www.nps.gov/cave, 8am-7pm daily June-Aug., 8am-5pm daily Sept.-May, $10). In the summer months, allow an extra hour's waiting time at the visitors center. Probably the best time to go is in December, before the holidays, or in January and February, because you'll have the whole place to yourself, in near ghostly silence. One summer treat: Hundreds of thousands of bats fly out every evening, and the 56°F temperature underground is a relief.

Always pack a sweater, no matter how hot it is outside, and wear sturdy shoes, even if you're only going on the main self-guided tours. You might want to pack a lunch too, as the cafeteria at the caverns is pretty institutional. Fill your gas tank in Carlsbad, as once you head south you're at the mercy of one pricey station in White's City.

★ The Big Room

The basic entrance ticket gives you access to two major parts of the cave: the **Natural Entrance Trail** (last entrance 3:30pm daily June-Aug., 2pm daily Sept.-May), which descends about 800 feet in the course of a mile, on a paved trail dense with switchbacks, and **The Big Room** (last entrance 5pm daily June-Aug., 3:30pm daily Sept.-May), the largest cave in the Carlsbad complex. If you don't want to hike down, an elevator will whisk you 754 feet down to the cavern floor. Instead of floors, the display panel shows 50-foot increments. The 1.5-hour walk down is preferable,

Go deep via the natural entrance to Carlsbad Caverns.

Guided Tours in Carlsbad Caverns

The tour schedule varies by season. Times given here are typical for low season; additional tours are offered in summer. Please confirm at www.nps.gov/cave or www.recreation.gov.

TOUR	Cost	Duration	Length	Age Limit	Schedule
King's Palace	$8	1.5 hours	1 mile	4 and up	9:30am, 11:30am, 1pm daily
Left Hand Tunnel	$7	2 hours	0.5 mile	6 and up	10:30am daily
Lower Cave	$20	3 hours	1 mile, plus 60-foot descent on rope ladders	12 and up	8:30am Mon., Thurs., Fri.
Slaughter Canyon Cave	$15	5.5 hours, including driving time	1.75 miles, including steep 0.5-mile hike to entrance	8 and up	8:30am Tues., Sat.
Hall of the White Giant	$20	4 hours	1 mile, very strenuous	12 and up	8:30am Wed.
Spider Cave	$20	4 hours	1 mile, very strenuous	12 and up	8:30am Sun.

as it gives you a better sense of what it must have been like for cowboy Jim White to first explore this place in the early 20th century. It also gives an idea of the scale you'll be dealing with once you get underground—at one point, you have to hike for about 30 minutes around Iceberg Rock, a 200,000-ton boulder.

The Big Room is lit in tasteful white lights and glows like a natural cathedral: The ceiling soars up into the dark, and the space is 1.25 miles long. If you think of caves as claustrophobia-inducing, this one will change your mind. (But it's not all natural—there's still a snack bar down on the cave floor, as well as restrooms, discreetly hidden behind rock formations.)

Scientists theorize that The Big Room—and many of the other caverns in this network—began to form more than 20 million years ago, as the petroleum deposits under the Guadalupe Mountains reacted with groundwater to create sulfuric acid, which ate through the stone to form vast hollow spots under the ground. These spaces started to fill with stalagmites and stalactites about 500,000 years ago, and now the intricate formations—still growing in some spots—range from hulking towers that ripple like clay to delicate needles that look more like icicles than stone.

For both routes, you can rent an **audio tour** for $5—it includes some interesting information, but don't get too caught up in listening to every entry. It's just as rewarding to let your imagination roam.

Ranger-Led Tours

These small-group side tours are an alternative to the crowds in The Big Room. You get a little more quiet and, of course, see a lot more of the caverns. During peak season, reservations are practically required (877/444-6777, www.recreation.gov). Be sure to ask what time to arrive; some tours require hour-long hikes in to the departure point. Note that if you'd like to see more once you're down in The Big Room, you have to come back up to the surface to buy the extra ticket.

The easiest addition to your itinerary,

King's Palace is the deepest part of the caves open to the public. Limited to 75 participants, the tour passes giant formations as well as tiny details such as a bat's skeleton grown into a stalagmite. Best of all, it includes a few minutes with the lights turned off, when you get to stand in the cool, smothering black. Unlike all the other ranger-led tours, the trail is paved and not particularly steep except at the entrance.

Left Hand Tunnel is best for a sheer sense of discovery. On the trek, limited to 15 people, you carry just a flickering lantern through fantastic rock formations—made all the more bizarre as they loom up out of the darkness. **Lower Cave** requires a bit more exertion, starting with a clamber down 50 feet of rope and narrow ladders. The formations here include toothpick-like stalactites and the perfectly round and white formations called "cave pearls."

Slaughter Canyon Cave is the only spot not accessible through the visitors center. Instead, you have to drive five miles south of White's City, then turn west onto a well-signed county road; there's also a steep hike to the entrance. Once in the cave, though, the walk isn't too difficult, and it goes past formations like the glittering, crystal-covered column dubbed the Christmas Tree.

Finally, for people who aren't afraid of tight spaces, **Hall of the White Giant** and **Spider Cave** are strenuous but rewarding trips. Each one takes about four hours, and you have to bring batteries and gloves (the rangers provide headlamps and helmets). Expect to wiggle through some very narrow tunnels and get muddy in the process.

Special Events

Late May-mid-October, hundreds of thousands of bats rush out from the depths of the caverns and into the bug-filled twilight. Half an hour before sunset at an amphitheater at the top of the Natural Entrance Trail, rangers give a short talk about the bats (ask at the visitors center or call 575/785-3012 for times). When the **Bat Flight** begins, you hear the soft flapping of their wings and feel the rush of air as they pass overhead.

Most are of the Brazilian free-tail variety, which migrate to Mexico in the winter. Another group of larger cave *Myotis* live in the Lake of the Clouds, the deepest point in the cave system; they too come out every night, and if you're at the underground cafeteria near closing time, you might feel them whir through. Whether you're underground or at the amphitheater, keep your camera stowed—the flash and auto-focus devices disorient the animals.

Throughout the summer, the park also hosts monthly **Star Party** (www.nps.gov/cave) events, with rangers on hand with telescopes.

WHITE'S CITY

This so-called town at the junction of U.S. 62/180 and Highway 7 is an unreconstructed tourist trap—there's a bad restaurant, two hopelessly dumpy hotels, a wildly overpriced gas station, and a junk-filled gift shop. Blindfold your kids as you drive past the giant waterslide (for hotel guests only), or you'll never hear the end of it. The **Greyhound** bus can be prevailed upon to pull up here, though it's not a regularly scheduled stop.

GUADALUPE MOUNTAINS NATIONAL PARK

Adjacent to the caverns land and just over the border in Texas, **Guadalupe Mountains National Park** (915/828-3251, www.nps.gov/gumo, $5) is mentioned here because it's where people usually camp ($8) when visiting Carlsbad Caverns. The largest area, with both tent and RV sites (but no hookups), is **Pine Springs Campground,** near the visitors center, about 35 miles south of White's City on U.S. 62/180.

You can also hike the exceptionally scenic **McKittrick Canyon,** where a 6.8-mile out-and-back trail leads through a narrow limestone canyon thick with deciduous trees—truly stunning in late October when the leaves turn, though often crowded. The park also encompasses **Salt Basin Dunes,** a glittering landscape similar to White Sands National Monument, but more isolated.

Cloudcroft

The closest mountains to the Texas flatlands, the Sacramentos have drawn vacationers with a drawl since 1899, when a local railroad man built a resort at Cloudcroft, now accessible by U.S. 82, due west of Artesia. The village is still barely more than a cluster of rustic cabins and a few gift shops—but the view, looking down as far as White Sands, is majestic, especially when the clouds are gathering below you. The view straight up is great too—hence the location of a major solar observatory nearby.

SIGHTS

The main street in town is Burro Avenue, just north of U.S. 82—here's where you'll find a row of Old West-style false-front buildings along a wooden boardwalk.

Sacramento Mountains Historical Museum

Across the street from the chamber of commerce, the local **Sacramento Mountains Historical Museum** (U.S. 82, 575/682-2932, www.cloudcroftmuseum.com, 10am-4pm Mon.-Tues. and Fri.-Sat., 1pm-4pm Sun. in summer, 10am-4pm Fri.-Sat. in winter, $5) has the usual assortment of memorabilia from the past, plus a "pioneer village" made up of several old log cabins, furnished with antique tools and furniture.

Sunspot

Sixteen miles south of Cloudcroft on Highway 6563 (named for the wavelength of the orange-red light we associate with images of the sun; most people call it Sunspot Highway), **Sunspot National Solar Observatory** and privately owned Apache Point Observatory take advantage of the high altitude and clear skies to spy on deep space. The Sunspot **visitors center** (575/434-7190, 9am-5pm daily Mar.-Jan.) explains how the telescopes work, but ideally, join the guided tour ($3) at 2pm on Saturday and Sunday in summer.

Even if you're not interested in the science side, the highway is a pretty drive, with dramatic vistas down to White Sands, and you'll pass **Karr Canyon,** another nice place for a picnic. Look for signs en route labeled with the names of planets—they're placed along the road according to their relative distance to one another, at a scale of 1:250 million.

SPORTS AND RECREATION

Cloudcroft has a lot to do year-round. As long as you're adjusted to the altitude, the hiking trails are not too strenuous. Check current conditions with the **Sacramento Ranger District office** (4 Lost Lodge Rd., 575/682-2551, 8am-4pm Mon.-Fri., plus 9am-2:30pm Sat. in summer), one mile up Highway 130 toward the Sunspot Highway.

Hiking

The old railroad that used to zigzag up the mountain is gone, but the rail bed makes for excellent hiking on the well-maintained 11-mile **Cloud-Climbing Rail Trail.** The **Mexican Canyon Loop** is probably the best introduction—it's just 2.5 miles and leads to the picturesque (and vertigo-inducing) Mexican Canyon trestle, built in 1899. The trail starts on the west edge of town, off the south side of the road, by a replica of the original train depot. For a map on the rest of the rails-to-trails network, stop in at the chamber of commerce.

Another popular route is **Osha Trail** (no. 10), maintained by the National Forest Service. It runs three miles through relatively level, shaded forest that's especially pretty when the leaves change in the fall. The trailhead is on the opposite side of the road from the Mexican Canyon trestle.

Mountain Biking

The 28-mile **Rim Trail** is legendary for its

Cloudcroft's old railroad is now a walking trail.

amazing views as it winds along the spine of the mountains, roughly parallel to Sunspot Highway (Hwy. 6563). It climbs about a thousand feet over the course of the whole ride, though it has some zippy downhill sections, as well as some jarring rocky terrain. Only the first 13 or so miles are official Forest Service trail (no. 105), but it runs all the way to Sunspot, then down to Forest Road 90 to the southeast. You can cut in at the observatory and take the paved road back downhill. The trailhead is just off Highway 6563—look for parking on the right side almost immediately after you make the turn from Highway 130.

A handful of other loop trails start in town and nearby. Stop in at the chamber of commerce or the exceptionally helpful **High Altitude Outfitters** (310 Burro Ave., 575/682-1229, 10am-5:30pm Mon.-Thurs., 10am-6pm Fri.-Sat.), a shop that also organizes a race, the High Altitude Classic, every April, for maps and other guidance.

Winter Sports

Two miles east of town on U.S. 82, **Ski Cloudcroft** (575/682-2333, www.skicloudcroft.net, $45 full-day lift ticket) has modest ski runs as well as a tubing area. With no snowmaking abilities, the ski area is highly weather dependent. There's more reliable fun

in town, at **Cloudcroft Ice Rink** (575/682-4585, 3:30pm-9:30pm Tues.-Fri., 10am-9pm Sat.-Mon.) at the west end of Zenith Park, and tubing all over the hills. Many of the town's rail trails are good for **cross-country skiing.**

FOOD

Cloudcroft's unofficial social center, the **Western Bar & Café** (304 Burro Ave., 575/682-9910, 6am-9pm daily, $7) satisfies just about every social need, whether you want a breakfast omelet, a cold beer, or a crazy night of karaoke (the bar is open till 11pm during the week and 1am Fri.-Sat.). The vibe is friendly and the crowd is eclectic.

Up the hill at The Lodge, **Rebecca's** (575/682-2566, 7am-10:30am, 11:30am-2:30pm, and 5:30pm-9pm Mon.-Sat., 8am-2pm Sun.) has historic ambience, though the prices for only average sandwiches and steaks are high ($12 at lunch, $24 and up at dinner). But it's a good spot for a drink and a snack.

ACCOMMODATIONS

The main type of accommodation in town is the guest cabin. Location isn't too essential, considering how small the town is.

Under $100

Halfway down the mountain on the way

to Tularosa, the excellent ★ **Cloudcroft Mountain Park Hostel** (1049 U.S. 82, 575/682-0555, www.cloudcrofthostel.com) has three rooms with eight bunks each ($19 pp), as well as two basic private rooms ($35) and one big family room ($60), all with access to shared baths and a big common area and kitchen. Everything's clean and colorfully painted, with a casual but orderly atmosphere.

Summit Inn (Chipmunk Ave. at Curlew Pl., 575/682-2814, www.summitinn-nm.com, $62.50 s, $86 d) has clean and tidy, if dated, rooms, with tiny kitchenettes, vintage TVs, and showers (no tubs). Don't bother with the cabins, though—they're relatively expensive and short on charm.

At the east end of town, **Spruce Cabins** (100 Lynx Ave., 575/682-2381, www.sprucecabins.com, $75 d) are pleasant enough stand-alone apartments with a faintly rustic feel. The wood paneling has a certain 1970s mobile home vibe, but that's offset by attractive quilts on the beds and cozy wood-burning fireplaces.

Burro Street Boardinghouse (608 Burro Ave., 575/682-3601, $89) has just three rooms, but each one is very nicely done, with choice antiques and details like vanity sinks. The

building is a big, airy, pine-paneled A-frame, and the owner is an old Cloudcroft hand.

$100-150

Smack in the center of town, ★ **Cloudcroft Hotel** (306 Burro Ave., 575/682-3414, www.cloudcrofthotel.com, $99 s, $104 d) is affordable and very well kept. Each of the eight rooms is carefully decorated and fastidiously clean; all have claw-foot tubs and lots of pine paneling. There are a couple of odd rooms that don't have windows to the outside—potentially dreary, but a bargain and a bit quieter than those on the front of the building (though room no. 1, for $139, with access to the front balcony, is a gem).

At the top of the hill—and the price range—**The Lodge** (601 Corona Pl., 800/395-6343, www.thelodgeresort.com, $125 d) is a fairly well-restored relic from the early railroad era. The current structure, with its vaguely Tyrolean look, was built in 1911 by the Alamogordo & Sacramento Railway. With lots of chintz, brocade, and dark wood, the style may be historically accurate, but some of the 58 rooms can feel cramped, especially the standard queens. Rooms in the Retreat wing (from $315) are newer construction and have fireplaces and whirlpool tubs. Down the hill, the Pavilion is the oldest section, a large wood

the Western Bar & Café on Burro Avenue

THE SOUTHEAST
CLOUDCROFT

cabin with a wraparound porch—the rooms here are a bit more rustic, and rates (from $145) include breakfast at Rebecca's, the resort's main restaurant.

INFORMATION

Cloudcroft's **chamber of commerce** (U.S. 82, 575/682-2733, www.coolcloudcroft.com, 10am-5pm Mon.-Sat.) occupies a tiny cabin on the east side of town and has just about any info on the town you could need.

GETTING THERE

Cloudcroft is 20 miles (30 minutes) by car east from Alamogordo via U.S. 82 and 90 miles (1.5 hours) west from Artesia.

Alamogordo

For most visitors, Alamogordo functions as the gateway to the stunning White Sands National Monument, the largest field of pure gypsum in the world. It also has a couple of interesting sights of its own. Founded in 1899 as a railroad stop, the town has been shaped more by the early space industry and Holloman Air Force Base, which also trains German pilots. It fits between the railroad tracks and the foothills of the Sacramento Mountains, with some 41,000 residents in a low-rise sprawl—though it feels much smaller.

SIGHTS

Navigating Alamogordo is straightforward: Almost everything is located on or very near White Sands Boulevard (U.S. 54/70), which runs roughly north-south through town. On New York Avenue, one block east, is Alamogordo's historic downtown, along a couple of blocks south of 10th Street. The space museum is far up in the foothills, but it's visible from a long way off.

New Mexico Museum of Space History

The state-run **New Mexico Museum of Space History** (Hwy. 2001, 575/437-2840, www.nmspacemuseum.org, 9am-5pm daily, $6) began in 1976 as a hall of fame for astronauts, including the first chimpanzee in space, who's buried here. Then it expanded

The New Mexico Museum of Space History showcases space-race technology.

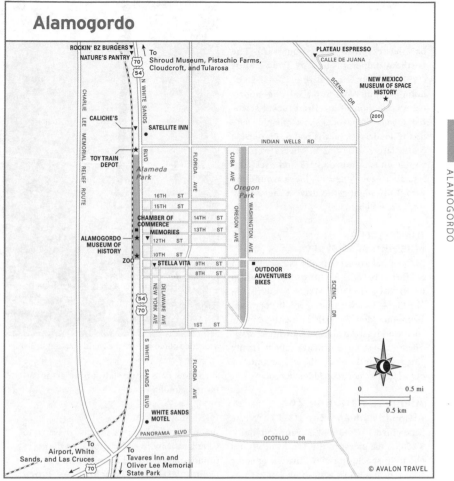

Alamogordo

ROCKIN' BZ BURGERS

NATURE'S PANTRY

70
54

To
Shroud Museum, Pistachio Farms,
Cloudcroft, and Tularosa

PLATEAU ESPRESSO

CALLE DE JUANA

NEW MEXICO
MUSEUM OF SPACE
HISTORY

SCENIC DR

2001

CHARLIE LEE MEMORIAL RELIEF ROUTE

N WHITE SANDS

CALICHE'S

SATELLITE INN

INDIAN WELLS RD

BLVD

TOY TRAIN
DEPOT

Alameda
Park

FLORIDA AVE

CUBA AVE

Oregon
Park

16TH ST

15TH ST

CHAMBER OF
COMMERCE

14TH ST

OREGON AVE

WASHINGTON AVE

ALAMOGORDO
MUSEUM OF
HISTORY

MEMORIES

13TH ST

12TH ST

10TH ST

ZOO

STELLA VITA

9TH ST

8TH ST

OUTDOOR
ADVENTURES
BIKES

SCENIC DR

54
70

NEW YORK AVE

DELAWARE AVE

1ST ST

S WHITE SANDS BLVD

FLORIDA AVE

0   0.5 mi

0   0.5 km

WHITE SANDS
MOTEL

PANORAMA BLVD

OCOTILLO DR

To
Airport, White
Sands, and Las Cruces

70

To
Tavares Inn and
Oliver Lee Memorial
State Park

© AVALON TRAVEL

into this comprehensive look at space exploration—which in many ways got its start in rocket tests in the Tularosa Basin below. Working your way down through four floors, you pass assorted relics from the space race, a chunk of moon rock, and more. But perhaps the most interesting items are those that hint at what everyday life in zero gravity is like, such as the space station interior model and a space-shuttle food system. It's a surprisingly un-high-tech museum. The cobbled-together rockets and patched-up spacesuits serve as a reminder of just how mechanical and hardware-driven space exploration has been—not a sleek, digital process at all.

The current state of space exploration looks a little slicker: The bottom floor of the museum is devoted to the X Prize, which encourages commercial space flights, and a hangar outside contains a model of the first winner: glossy, bulbous SpaceShipOne, covered in corporate-sponsor logos. Next to it, a 1940s accelerator for testing G-forces looks brutally primitive.

Toy Train Depot

You can't miss Alamogordo's nifty miniature train: It runs straight through town, parallel to White Sands Boulevard. The northern endpoint is the **Toy Train Depot** (1991 N. White Sands Blvd., 575/437-2855, noon-4:30pm Wed.-Sun., $6), the model-train collection of a retired rocket scientist. One of the layouts shows the old route up to Cloudcroft. But the real fun is outside on the larger-scale tracks, where two trains run down to Alameda Park and back, and a smaller-gauge one runs loops around the yard. Kids might get to drive it themselves, if they're well behaved.

Alamogordo Museum of History

In the usual assortment of pioneer gear and old furniture is the **Alamogordo Museum of History** (1301 N. White Sands Blvd., 575/434-4438, www.alamogordohistory.com, 10am-4pm Mon.-Sat, $3); the highlight of the collection is an American flag with 47 stars. There's also some information about Trinity Site, as well as the older Hispano community of La Luz, just north of Alamogordo.

Alameda Park and Zoo

Alameda Park and Zoo (1321 N. White Sands Blvd., 575/439-4290, 9am-5pm daily, $2.50) is the oldest in the Southwest. It has about 90 species on view, including some frisky otters and even some kangaroos, which don't look too out of place in this desert. There's also a nice shaded picnic area inside. The entrance is on 10th Street just west of White Sands Boulevard.

Shroud Exhibit and Museum

Tucked inside the White Sands Mall is Alamogordo's most surprising attraction, the **Shroud Exhibit and Museum** (3199 N. White Sands Blvd., 575/415-5206, 1pm-5pm Mon.-Tues. and Fri.-Sat., 2pm-4pm Sun., free), devoted to a photo-replica of the Shroud of Turin, the work of a group of researchers based in New Mexico, who examined the

a roadside photo op with the world's biggest pistachio at McGinn's

shroud in 1978 using state-of-the-art imagining technology.

Pistachios

Just north of Alamagordo, past the turn to Cloudcroft, are two places focus on the area's proudest agricultural accomplishment: pistachios. **McGinn's Pistachio Tree Ranch & Arena Blanca Winery** (7320 Hwy. 54/70, 575/437-0602, 10am-5pm daily) is home to the world's largest pistachio, making it a necessary stop for roadside attraction devotees. Just next door is **Heart of the Desert Pistachios and Wine at Eagle Ranch** (7288 Hwy. 54/70, 575/434-0035, 8am-6pm Mon.-Sat., 9am-6pm Sun.), known for its green-chile pistachios.

SPORTS AND RECREATION

For general info on trails and other recreation, stop in at the **Lincoln National**

Forest supervisor's office (3463 Las Palomas Rd., 575/434-7200, 8am-4:30pm Mon.-Fri.) or **Outdoor Adventures Bikes & Sports** (1516 10th St., 575/434-1920, 10am-6pm Mon.-Fri., 10am-5pm Sat.), where you can also rent bikes.

Hiking

The one big rec area nearby is **Oliver Lee Memorial State Park** (409 Dog Canyon Rd., 575/437-8284, www.nmparks.com, $5/car), 12 miles south of Alamogordo. The 5.5-mile **Dog Canyon Recreational Trail** begins at the visitors center and leads through a surprisingly lush canyon where you'll see everything from moss to orchids growing, if you look closely. It then heads up to a ridge with great views of the desert basin—a strenuous climb, with an elevation gain of 3,100 feet. Many hikers just go about 2.5 miles in to a stone cowboy cabin, then turn around. There are also more than 40 developed **campsites** ($8-14)—the closest camping to White Sands National Monument.

FOOD

It's slim pickings for distinctive dining in Alamogordo—and no surprise most people wind up eating at the chain restaurants on White Sands Boulevard.

For a pick-me-up after the space museum, **Plateau Espresso** (2724 N. Scenic Dr., 575/434-4466, 6am-9pm daily) will do the trick, while providing awesome views over the city from its patio.

Diners with text anxiety might not like the ordering system at **Rockin' BZ Burgers** (3005 N. White Sands Blvd., 575/434-2375, 11am-8pm Tues.-Sat., 11am-3pm Sun., $7), which involves filling out a form to select burger toppings and sides. If in doubt, go for the signature Champ burger, which has made an excellent showing in the state fair green-chile cheeseburger cook-off in recent years; it adds grilled onions to the mix. Another nice touch: buttered buns.

For a healthy lunch, the deli counter at the back of **Nature's Pantry** (2909 N. White

Sands Blvd., 575/437-3037, 10am-3pm Mon.-Sat., $7) makes vegetarian-friendly wraps and sprout-stuffed sandwiches, which you can wash down with a shot of wheatgrass juice or a smoothie—a great antidote to standard road food.

Caliche's (2251 N. White Sands Blvd., 575/439-1000, noon-9pm Sun.-Thurs., 11am-10pm Fri.-Sat., $4) is an outpost of the frozen-custard specialist in Las Cruces. It's no balanced meal, but given the options in Alamogordo, you're excused if you have a thick shake for dinner.

All matte gray and faux stone, **Stella Vita** (902 New York Ave., 575/434-4444, 11am-2pm Mon.-Wed., 11am-2pm and 5pm-9pm Thurs.-Fri., 5pm-9pm Sat., $10) is by far the most stylish place in Alamogordo. The menu is slightly fancy Americana, heavy on salads at lunch. At dinner (three nights a week), you can get steaks and pork chops (about $25 per entrée). Service is very attentive.

Set in a homey bungalow, **Memories** (1223 New York Ave., 575/437-0077, 11am-9pm Mon.-Sat., $12) is a bit of a time-warp restaurant, with a menu of baked-potato soup and prime rib, and, at lunch, hot turkey sandwiches.

It requires a 20-minute drive to the south edge of Tularosa, but ★ **Casa de Sueños** (35 St. Francis Dr., 575/585-3494, 11am-8pm Mon.-Thurs., 11am-8:30pm Fri.-Sat., 10:30am-8pm Sun., $12) is a big step up from Alamogordo dining. Red-chile-rubbed pork chops are just one of several tasty (and very meaty) dishes on the menu. You can also get the usual enchiladas and rellenos, as well as burritos to go. The ambience is warmly lit, with a pretty patio out back.

ACCOMMODATIONS

A rare case in which an eye-catching neon sign actually points to quality lodging, ★ **White Sands Motel** (1101 S. White Sands Blvd., 575/437-2922, www.white-sandsmotel.biz, $55 s, $69 d) is a tidy little shell of an old motel court, nicely updated inside. The rooms are snug, but they're kept clean, and many are well back from the main road, for slightly less traffic noise. Rooms all have mini-fridges, microwaves, and wireless Internet.

On the south edge of town, **Tavares Inn** (153 San Pedro Dr., 575/437-8779, www.tavaresinn.com, $105 d) puts the "breakfast" back in bed-and-breakfast, with a massive morning spread. The three rooms are in a rambling white ranch house, with an indoor pool and horses and more out back.

INFORMATION

The **Alamogordo Chamber of Commerce** (1301 N. White Sands Blvd., 575/437-6120, www.alamogordo.com, 8am-5pm Mon.-Fri.) dispenses a very detailed free map. The associated visitors center is open daily.

GETTING THERE AND AROUND

By car, Alamogordo is 68 miles (1.25 hours) northeast from Las Cruces via U.S. 70, and 215 miles (3.25 hours) from Albuquerque via I-25, then U.S. 380 and U.S. 54. Cloudcroft is about 20 miles (30 minutes) due east up the mountains, and Ruidoso is 50 miles (1 hour) northeast. **Greyhound** (800/231-2222, www.greyhound.com) connects Alamogordo to Las Cruces once a day,

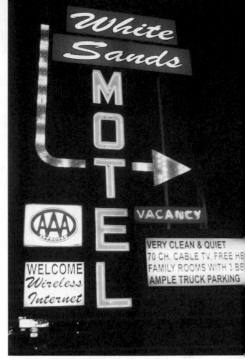

Turn right for a fine night's sleep.

stopping at the station on the north side (3500 N. White Sands Blvd., 575/437-3050, 7am-11am and 4pm-8pm Mon.-Fri., 7am-9am and 5pm-8pm Sat.-Sun.).

White Sands National Monument

White Sands, 275 square miles of blinding, shimmery gypsum, is a surreal and magnificent place. At every turn, you have to remind yourself what you're really looking at. In the summer, temperatures exceed 100°F, but the sand looks like no desert you've ever seen. On a cool winter day, especially after rainwater has pooled along the road, your brain can't stop thinking snow and ice. For the best photography, as well as a break from the heat, you'll probably want to visit either early or late in the day—but there is also something appropriately overwhelming

about this featureless landscape at high noon.

Although the barren dunes at the core of the park are the most popular image of the place, there's a surprising amount of life here, from tiny kangaroo mice to the beleaguered tufts of skunkbush sumac that are the last holdouts as the sand shifts around them. A number of nature trails lead off the eight-mile-long Dunes Drive, and if you have time, you should definitely join one of the ranger-led walks—usually near sunset. There are periodic—and sometimes short-notice—closures due to testing at the nearby White Sands Missile Range, so check ahead.

VISITORS CENTER

Stop in at the pleasantly old-fashioned **visitors center** (575/479-6124, www.nps.gov/whsa, $5) at the main gate to check the schedule of ranger tours and maybe pick up a plastic sled, for sliding down the dunes, at the gift shop. Among the ranger outings is a car trip to **Lake Lucero** ($8, reserve ahead), the crystal-filled lake bed that's the source of the sands, as well as occasional full-moon **hikes** and **bicycle tours** ($8) and outings for **sunrise photography** ($8). If you plan to do any backcountry hiking, you'll need to get a permit at the center ($3)—there's only one designated hike-in camping area, about a mile from the road, so check for a vacancy.

Hours for the visitors center and the park vary substantially month to month. You can count on at least 9am-5pm year-round, but it's also open from 8am during the holidays in December and early January. In the shoulder seasons (mid-Mar.-mid-May and mid-Sept.-Nov.), it's open 9am-6pm. Mid-May-mid-September, it's open 8am-7pm.

DUNES DRIVE

The road into the park leads from the shaggy, brush-covered hills at the edge of the white desert into the pure dunes at the center. In between is the transition area, where hills are being carved away by wind, and yuccas teeter on lone sand pedestals. As long as you park in one of the designated pullouts, you're welcome to walk wherever you like, but make careful note of landmarks; even in the areas with lots of vegetation, it's easy to wind up walking in circles.

The first stop on the drive, **Playa Trail** runs 500 yards along the border where the gypsum meets the regular desert terrain, ending up at a playa, the term for a depression that forms a temporary lake after rainfall. These playas are all over White Sands, as well as in the desert areas of the rest of New Mexico. Of all the trails, this may be the least remarkable—skip it if you're not planning to spend all day here.

The one-mile-long **Dune Life Nature Trail** does a quick loop up to the top of a dune and past the most typical types of vegetation. At least stop to pick up one of the trail guides, which can help you identify animal tracks.

in the Heart of the Sands

The **Interdune Boardwalk** is another quick trail– a very easy way to check out some of the more common plants, without trudging through sand.

★ HEART OF THE SANDS

This is the main destination inside the park. You can set up camp in one of the mod metal picnic shelters (which include grills), then go out to clamber, slip, and slide down the pristine white hills. (There are also restrooms out here, but no water.) From the end of the parking area, the **Alkali Flat Trail** is a 4.6-mile loop into the most austere part of the dunes. This can be extremely disorienting—heed the stern warnings to turn back if you can't see the orange trail markers, which periodically get covered with sand. Allow about three hours for the whole hike, and be sure to register at the trailhead before you proceed.

Ruidoso

North of Alamogordo and east on U.S. 70, Ruidoso (Spanish for "noisy") is named for the audible stream that flows through a canyon in the center. Like Cloudcroft, it's a patch of Texas in the high mountains—but it's quite a bit bigger and, at least in spots, substantially more upscale. It's very much a resort town, dedicated to golf (at five courses in the immediate area), horse racing, and skiing on southern New Mexico's highest mountain. Don't go for culture, but for cool air and a cabin in the woods.

And brace yourself for cutesy kitsch—the number of tree-trunk bear sculptures is higher per capita than anywhere else in the state.

On the drive up on U.S. 70, you pass through the Mescalero Apache reservation, established in 1883 on some 463,000 acres. The tribe (which got its name from the Spanish, who remarked on its ritual use of peyote, or mescal) operates the ski area as well as a resort and casino about a 20-minute drive south of town.

Ruidoso, unofficial state capital of tree-trunk art

Ruidoso

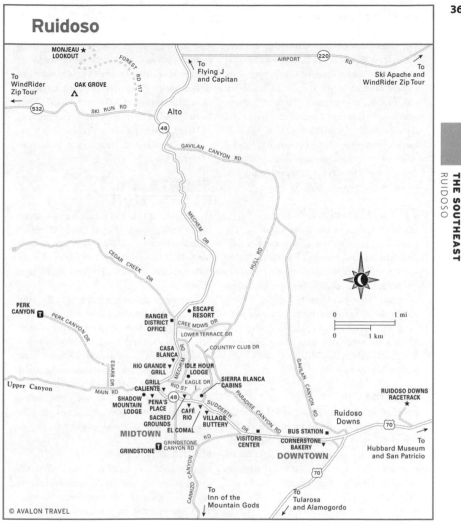

© AVALON TRAVEL

SIGHTS

Ruidoso's main drags are Sudderth Drive (east-west) and Mechem Drive, running north from the west end of Sudderth, to form a big L. The town is divided into districts by the major intersections. Uptown is lower Mechem and the west end of Sudderth (higher address numbers); Midtown, the densest business area, refers to the stretch of Sudderth from up near Mechem to Carrizo Canyon Road. Finally, Downtown is the east end of Sudderth (the lowest street numbers), and "the Y" is the junction of Sudderth and U.S. 70, where most of the chain businesses are. Farther east along U.S. 70, Ruidoso Downs is technically a separate town, but there is no physical gap between it and its neighbor.

Hubbard Museum of the American West

The small **Hubbard Museum of the American West** (26301 U.S. 70 W, 575/378-4142, www.hubbardmuseum.org, 9am-5pm Thurs.-Mon., $7), the only real "sight" in Ruidoso, is the collection of a local woman who loved all things equine, and had good taste in Native American crafts. Her assortment of horse-drawn carriages, from a sulky to a chuckwagon to a hearse, fills the downstairs. Upstairs is space for temporary, Western-themed exhibitions.

ENTERTAINMENT

Midtown is the place to be at night, but the track is where the action is on weekend afternoons. In Alto, **Flying J Ranch** (575/336-4330, www.flyingjranch.com, June-Aug.) is unapologetically cheesy, but it may be just the thing if you have kids to delight. Expect pony rides, staged gunfights, and gold panning, followed by a whole lotta grub and a wholesome, Opry-style stage show. The price is actually relatively old-timey too: $27 for adults, $15 for kids.

Nightlife

For margaritas, **Casa Blanca** (501 Mechem Dr., 575/257-2495, 11am-9pm daily) is the top spot, enhanced by a great patio surrounded by tall pines. After the first round of drinks and dinner, action usually moves to the two dueling mega-bars in Midtown: **The Quarters** (2535 Sudderth Dr., 575/257-9535) and **Win, Place and Show** (2516 Sudderth Dr., 575/257-9982), which play both kinds of music (that'd be country *and* western) to inspire some speedy two-stepping around the dance floors. The Quarters also has pool tables.

Spencer Theater for the Performing Arts

Just up the road from Ruidoso in the satellite community of Alto, the 514-seat **Spencer Theater for the Performing Arts** (108 Spencer Rd., 575/336-4800, www.

spencertheater.com) hosts touring musical productions as well as local performers. The building alone, a white wedge jutting from the plain, is an attraction; the architect is New Mexican Antoine Predock, who designed buildings as diverse as the UNM architecture school and the Hotel Santa Fe at Euro Disney. The interior features a number of Dale Chihuly glass sculptures. Free tours run on Tuesday and Thursday at 10am (call to reserve).

SPORTS AND RECREATION

For details on national forest areas, contact the **Smokey Bear Ranger District office** (901 Mechem Dr., 575/257-4095, 8am-4pm Mon.-Fri.). Birders should keep an eye out for hummingbirds, which summer here in great numbers.

Sure, there are *real* golf courses in the area, but **Funtrackers** (101 Carrizo Canyon Rd., 575/257-3275, 10am-9pm daily in summer, Sat.-Sun. in winter) has 18 miniature holes, as well as go-carts, an arcade, a human-scale maze, and more. Even Ruidoso's **public swimming pool** (515 Sudderth Dr., 575/257-5030, noon-4:45pm, $3) is pretty fun, with a giant loop-de-loop slide; but it closes when the school year starts, in mid-August.

Hiking and Biking

Intense wildfires in 2012 closed off much of the forest around Ruidoso, so recreation is limited while the area recovers. In town, **Two Rivers Park,** right behind the **visitors center** (720 Sudderth Dr.), is a little walking trail along the river all the way into Upper Canyon, sometimes so far below the main road level that you forget you're in the middle of town.

Handy **Perk Canyon Trail** begins basically in people's backyards and runs about three miles up to some open meadows. To get to the trailhead, follow Main Road to Ebarb Drive (next to Story Book Cabins); turn right, go about 0.3 mile to Perk Canyon Road, and turn left. The paved road dead-ends at the trail.

Quarter horses put Ruidoso on the map.

Winter Sports

Head 18 miles north to **Ski Apache** (575/464-3600, www.skiapache.com, $68 full-day lift ticket), which can get more than 15 feet of snow a year. Of the 55 trails, 40 percent are advanced, with a vertical drop of 1,900 feet across the mountain. Snowboarders have the run of the trails, as well as the Boneyard, a special park with all kinds of rails and jumps. Don't go driving up here just on a lark, though—Ski Run Road is dangerously narrow, so uphill traffic is banned 3pm-6pm during ski season.

Opened in 2014, the **Apache Wind Rider ZipTour** ($75) gives thrill seekers a way to enjoy the mountain year-round. Three ziplines stretch a total of 8,900 feet, making the system one of the longest in the world, and riders can get going up to 65 miles per hour. The whole excursion, starting with a gondola ride up the mountain, takes about 1.5 hours.

The International Mountain Biking Association designed the 17-mile **Grindstone Trail System** (575/257-4905) with cyclists in mind, but the path is good for running and walking too. Take Grindstone Canyon Road to park at Grindstone Lake; the trail climbs up to a mesa from there.

Horse Racing

Memorial Day-Labor Day, **Ruidoso Downs** (26225 U.S. 70, 575/378-4431, www. raceruidoso.com) hosts races Friday-Monday, starting at 1pm. There are a few thoroughbred meets, but historically Ruidoso has been a quarter-horse track. The All-American Futurity, which draws nearly 20,000 people to town over Labor Day weekend, has been dubbed the World's Richest Quarter Horse Race, thanks to its purse of more than one million—not bad money for 21 seconds of running. (As in any futurity, owners start the gambling early—they buy into the race as soon as a horse is born, with incremental payments over the next two years.)

FOOD

Ruidoso's best dining is at the casual end. Many places cater to more delicate Texan palates—you'll see green chile on the menu, but it's the mildest possible form.

Mexican

For enchiladas and tamales in a more convenient location, **El Comal** (2117 Sudderth Dr., 575/258-1397, 10am-6pm Mon.-Sat., 11am-3pm Sun., $9) is known for its tamales and its *enmoladas,* tortillas doused in rich mole sauce. Look for it in the Gazebo shopping center, and enjoy a seat on the back porch.

For a slightly lighter, fancier take on Mexican food, visit **Grill Caliente** (2800 Sudderth Dr., 575/630-0224, 11am-2:30pm and 5pm-9pm. Tues.-Sat., $14) for dishes like stuffed poblano peppers and mushroom tacos. Like much food in Ruidoso, it can veer toward bland, but at least it's veggie-friendly and has nice outdoor seating.

Brewhouse

The menu at **Rio Grande Grill and Taproom** (441 Mechem Dr., 575/808-8456,

11am-9pm Sun.-Thurs., 11am-10pm Fri.-Sat., $16) has a little bit of everything—steaks, burgers, and sandwiches—but the craft brews are the real stars here. Sierra Blanca Brewery owns the place, offering its own beers and others from around New Mexico. Try one of the seasonal sours, which Sierra Blanca is perfecting.

Cafés

Hidden away at the small traffic circle where Sudderth Drive turns into Main Road, tiny **Peña's Place** (2963 Sudderth Dr., 575/257-4135, 7:30am-2pm Thurs.-Sat.,7:30am-1pm Sun., $8) is a homey operation, a labor of love where the owner made the wood-slab tables himself. Like everywhere in Ruidoso, the chile on the huevos rancheros packs exactly zero punch, but it's balanced out by stupendous blueberry-pecan whole-wheat pancakes. It's small, so go early or be prepared to wait.

Cornerstone Bakery & Café (359 Sudderth Dr., 575/257-1842, 7am-2pm Mon.-Fri., 7am-3pm Sat.-Sun., $8) helps you start the day right—with French toast, for instance, a BEST sandwich (bacon, eggs, spinach, and tomatoes), or a super-sticky sweet roll. This is many residents' and regular visitors' morning favorite, so the atmosphere is chummy, and you see a good slice of the town.

Sacred Grounds Coffee and Tea House (2704 Sudderth Dr., 575/257-2273, 7am-6pm Sun.-Thurs., 7:30am-10pm Fri.-Sat., $8) is an all-around crowd pleaser on the main drag. It's a go-to for healthy soups, wraps, and salads, plus a huge selection of baked goods and gelato. If you're up early, you can help yourself to coffee service on an honor system before official opening time, and it stays open later than most places for dessert and coffee.

Good thing **Village Buttery** (2107 Sudderth Dr., 575/257-9251, 10:30am-2:30pm Mon.-Sat., $8) doesn't open too early, or you might be tempted to start your day with pie. For lunch, you can get hearty soups, quiches, and sandwiches with a Texan twist (pimento cheese, say) before you embark on a pie-case tour. Despite the café's name, the crusts aren't bursting with butter—pies with crumb crusts are preferable.

Italian

For pizza, head to super-casual **Café Rio** (2547 Sudderth Dr., 575/257-7746, 11:30am-8pm daily, $8), which earns the local vote for best pie. All the usual toppings are on offer, along with rarer treats like artichoke hearts and capers, and the rest of the menu reflects the owners' quirky outlook, with items like shrimp jambalaya and Portuguese kale soup. You can wash it all down with a milkshake—it does not serve beer. It often closes Wednesday in spring and fall. Cash only.

ACCOMMODATIONS

The signature lodging of Ruidoso is the cozy wood cabin, with kitchen and fireplace, and most of these are in what's called Upper Canyon, on Main Road, which follows the river up a narrowing route. If country-cute is not to your taste, you might prefer the guesthouses at the Hurd La Rinconada Gallery in San Patricio, 20 miles east of town. The majority of the chain hotels are at the east end of town, around the Y, but it's hard to find anything decent for less than $100.

Under $100

The cheapest lodging in Ruidoso is camping. Head five miles up Ski Run Road to **Oak Grove** ($6), with 30 sites, including a few walk-in spots that are wonderfully secluded under oak trees; you'll have to bring your own water. It's closed during winter.

$100-150

Set on the river in the Midtown area, **Sierra Blanca Cabins** (215 Country Club Rd., 575/257-2103, www.ruidoso.net/sbcabins, $139 d) are nicely outfitted one- and two-bedroom cabins that have lovely views, and a prime location not too far from Sudderth. The cabins were overhauled by new owners in 2013, with brand-new beds and other fresh details.

A key feature of **Idle Hour Lodge** (112 Lower Terrace Dr., 575/808-8484, www.

Sierra Blanca Cabins are typical of Ruidoso's riverside lodging.

$150-250

There's only one true alternative to mountain-cabin style in town: **Escape Resort** (1016 Mechem Dr., 575/258-1234, www.theescaperesort.com, $229 d), a cluster of five minimalist-Southwest-style casitas. Each one is enormous, with a full living room, a small kitchen, and a patio, in addition to a lavish bedroom (or two) and bath with separate tub and steam shower. Yes, it's definitely Ruidoso's upper end—but a bargain compared with what you'd pay for such digs in Santa Fe.

The other alternative is **Inn of the Mountain Gods** (287 Carrizo Canyon Rd., 800/545-9011, www.innofthemountaingods.com, $149 d, $299 suite), run by the Mescalero Apache. In 2014, the hotel received a complete remodel, with sleek new guest rooms with dark-wood furniture and modern art. In-house dining also has a new bent, with a bistro featuring an impressive 100-beer tap list. The resort's casino and theater are also popular entertainment spots that can draw national acts.

INFORMATION

The Ruidoso chamber of commerce operates a very cheery **visitors center** (720 Sudderth Dr., 575/257-7395, www.discoverruidoso.com), positively bursting with information and helpful staff. The lobby section is even open 24 hours.

GETTING THERE

By car, Ruidoso is 74 miles (1.25 hours) west from Roswell on U.S. 70, 170 miles (3 hours) from Albuquerque via I-25 south and east on U.S. 380, and 115 miles (2 hours) northeast from Las Cruces via U.S. 70. **Greyhound** (800/231-2222, www.greyhound.com) stops at Apache Motel (344 Sudderth Dr., 575/257-2660) once a day from Las Cruces.

idlehourlodge.com, $139 d) is its location, tucked away from the main roads yet still easy walking distance to a grocery store and restaurants in Uptown. The 14 cabins come in one- and two-bedroom configurations, in typical Ruidoso style, with wood paneling, quilts on the beds, and little porches out front.

Of the cabins in Upper Canyon, **Shadow Mountain Lodge** (107 Main Rd., 575/257-4886, www.smlruidoso.com, $129-149) is conveniently located at the near end, so you can easily walk into town, if you're so inclined. You have a choice of 19 rooms in the central lodge or in four standalone cabins. All are geared to couples, with king beds in the pine-paneled lodge and queens in the cabins, which are more modern but still rustic enough. There are fireplaces and kitchenettes in all the rooms.

Billy the Kid Trail

This scenic driving route forms a triangle with Ruidoso, Tinnie, and Capitan at the points. The loop is an easy day's drive, meandering through orchards, horse farms, and deep forest. If you're feeling thorough, you can stop first at the **Billy the Kid Interpretive Center** (U.S. 70, 575/378-5318, 10am-5pm Thurs.-Tues.) in Ruidoso Downs, next to the Hubbard Museum. November-April, it closes at 4:30pm.

SAN PATRICIO

This bucolic village in a valley 20 miles east of Ruidoso glows with the sort of light painters praise—no surprise, then, that it was the home of artists Peter Hurd and Henriette Wyeth, daughter of N. C. Wyeth. Their son owns the family ranch and operates ★ **Hurd La Rinconada Gallery** (100 Rinconada Ln., 800/658-6912, www.wyethartists.com), which displays the family's work. It also rents some beautiful guest homes, scattered over the Wyeth land. These are an excellent alternative to staying in Ruidoso—the smallest ones ($140) cost little more than you'd pay at the high end in town, and they're much larger and more attractive overall, furnished with original art and

antiques. The original Wyeth House ($250) has an especially lovely sunroom for breakfast (but note you'll have to bring your own groceries, as breakfast is not provided, and there are no restaurants nearby).

HONDO

The **Hondo Iris Farm** (575/635-4062, 8am-5pm Tues.-Fri, 8am-2pm Sat., 10am-2pm Sun.) is a lovely garden oasis, dedicated in part to growing iris bulbs. But just as important is the owner's gallery of dramatic handmade jewelry, all of pewter. It's a pretty place to shop and enjoy the greenery. The farm is also open on Monday during May for the iris bloom.

★ LINCOLN STATE MONUMENT

More of an open-air museum than a town, **Lincoln State Monument** is an artfully preserved Old West village where many of the buildings have been turned into public monuments. A stroll up and down the road is a chance to meditate on history without the distraction of souvenir vendors.

During the Lincoln County War (1878-1881),

Billy the Kid escaped from this Lincoln courthouse.

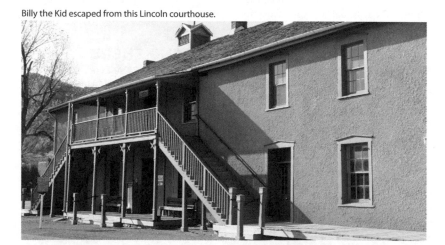

when the area was wracked by retaliatory killings triggered by a struggle to control the town dry-goods business, the national press dubbed this "the most dangerous town in America." The local feud also put Billy the Kid, who'd been causing low-grade trouble around New Mexico, in the spotlight. He burnished his outlaw reputation when he took sides with the upstart Tunstall faction and the band of "Regulators" who later sought vengeance for Tunstall's murder. Near the end of the war, Billy made a daring escape from the town jail, killing two guards in the process.

Anderson-Freeman Visitors Center & Museum

You can learn all about the Kid's exploits—as well as the Mexican families who first settled the town in 1846, and the Buffalo Soldiers who bunked at nearby Fort Sumner—at the **Anderson-Freeman Visitors Center & Museum** (U.S. 380, 8:30am-4:30pm daily, $5). Then tour the other buildings in town, which have been filled with period furnishings and small historical displays. (A couple of them are open only Apr.-Oct.) The Tunstall Store—which started the whole fracas—is kitted out with 19th-century stock, and you can see the holes in the courthouse wall where Billy the Kid fired bullets as he made his getaway.

Food and Accommodations

"No guests gunned down in over 100 years," boasts the **Wortley Hotel** (U.S. 380, 575/653-4300, www.wortleyhotel.com, $110 d), which was formerly owned by Sheriff Pat Garrett. The historic building is smack in the middle of town, so after visiting the museums, you can toddle over here and settle into a rocking chair on the porch, and feel like you're part of the exhibit. The five whitewashed rooms, all with corner fireplaces, are simply furnished with appropriate antiques. New owners as of 2016 gave the place a fresh coat of paint and serve a great breakfast; at research time, they were also at work on a farm-to-table restaurant, using their own chickens and goats, a welcome addition in Lincoln.

The beautiful **Dolan House** (U.S. 380, 575/653-4670, 9am-3:30pm Fri.-Tues., $10), a restored adobe in the center of the village, also serves a good breakfast and lunch with a salad buffet in the summer. It also has a single room for rent ($100).

In a stone house with blue trim, **Annie's Little Sure Shot** (U.S. 380, 575/653-4045, 10am-5pm Tues.-Sat., $4), is a funky coffeehouse and art gallery. Stop in for a pick-me-up latte, Italian soda, or lavender lemonade to sip while strolling.

FORT STANTON

A well-signed detour off U.S. 380, **Fort Stanton** is one of the largest historic military outposts in the West. Its buildings were made of stone, rather than adobe, so the complex looks remarkably intact, and the tree-shaded grounds are pleasant for a picnic. A small but interesting **museum** (10am-4pm Mon.-Sat., noon-4pm Sun. Mar.-Dec., 11am-3pm Mon.-Thurs., 10am-4pm Fri.-Sat., noon-4pm Sun. Jan.-Feb., free) details the fort's myriad uses, from staging ground for the Indian Wars to a tent hospital for tuberculosis patients to internment camp for hundreds of German sailors in World War II (alas, the swimming pool these industrious men built is in ruins). It stops short of more recent uses—as a women's prison and drug-rehab center—before it was made a state monument in 2007.

Past the fort is a wilderness reserve most remarkable for being set over the state's third-largest cave system, though it's currently closed to protect bat life. More accessibly, the area is cut through with numerous horse and hiking trails—you can pick up a map at the fort museum.

CAPITAN

Capitan is all about Smokey Bear, the tiny cub discovered clinging to a tree after a fire raged across 17,000 acres in the Capitan Mountains in 1950. Badly burned, the cub was nursed back to health, dubbed "Smokey," and eventually shipped off to the National Zoo in Washington DC, where a generation of schoolkids got to visit the living symbol of fire prevention. (The image of Smokey Bear was invented in 1944—but the campaign didn't catch on until the real, adorable bear took over the mantle.) Smokey died in 1976, but, like Elvis, his spirit lives on, especially here in Capitan, where he's buried, and where nearly every business name is some ursine pun. The place really goes crazy for **Smokey Bear Days,** on the first weekend in May.

The state forestry office operates **Smokey Bear Historical Park** (118 W. Smokey Bear Blvd., 575/354-2748, www.smokeybearpark.com, 9am-5pm daily, $2). It's a bit dry, in a 1970s-education way, though kids will probably be impressed by the displays of forest-fighting gear, and adults might be interested to see how the fire-prevention ads have changed over the years. There's also a short walking trail to Smokey's grave.

Smokey Bear was born and laid to rest in Capitan.

Food

A lovely surprise in this tiny town, **Renee's Real Food** (435 Smokey Bear Blvd., 575/973-0351, 10am-3pm Tues.-Sat., $7) is just that—an eclectic, unpretentious menu cooked from scratch. Depending on the chef's whim, you may encounter shrimp po'boys, meatball sandwiches, and, at weekend brunch, crème brûlée French toast. One constant is handmade bagels, hot and fresh at opening time, and pizza on Thursday.

Northern Tularosa Basin

Both U.S. 70 and U.S. 380 descend to meet U.S. 54, which runs north through a broad, dry valley between the Sacramento and San Andres Mountains. Much of it is part of the White Sands Missile Range, which does industrial and military testing.

THREE RIVERS PETROGLYPH SITE

Five miles off U.S. 54, in an unremarkable stretch between Tularosa and Carrizozo, the BLM-managed **Three Rivers Petroglyph Site** (8am-7pm daily Apr.-Oct., 8am-5pm Nov.-Mar., $5/car) is easy enough to drive right past. A trail leads up to a series of low hills, marked by volcanic rock that appears to cover the ridgeline like scabs. Look carefully, and you'll soon see why these 50 acres are protected: The dark rocks are scored with thousands of intricate designs—lizards, mountain goats, snakes, checkerboards, spirals. Because it's so far from any modern settlement, the area has barely been marred by more recent carving (as the West Mesa in Albuquerque has). Archaeologists estimate that the inscriptions here date from between 900 and 1400, when the Mogollon people had a settlement nearby (a separate short trail leads to its remnants), and the farther off the trail you go, the more carvings you'll see.

Farther down County Road B-30 about eight miles, just at the base of massive Sierra Blanca,

Three Rivers Campground ($7-18) is a very pretty place with tent and RV sites, a creek running nearby, and trails up into the hills. Unlike high-elevation campgrounds, this one is open year-round, and it's rarely crowded.

CARRIZOZO

The seat of Lincoln County, Carrizozo was a booming railroad town until the early 1950s, but now is perhaps most notable for its gallery scene. **Gallery 408** (408 12th St., 575/648-2598, 10am-5pm Mon. and Fri.-Sat., noon-5pm Sun.) exhibits fine abstract and modern art, and is responsible for the painted burros around town. **Tularosa Basin Gallery of Photography** (401 12th St., 575/937-1489, 10am-5pm Mon. and Thurs.-Sat., noon-5pm Sun.) is the largest photography gallery in the state. All works are by New Mexico photographers and of the Land of Enchantment. **Carrizozo Heritage Museum** (103 12th St., 575/648-1105, 10am-2pm Thurs.-Sun. Mar.-Nov.) has a small collection devoted to local history, some model trains, and a very large collection of barbed wire.

At the corner of Central Avenue and Airport Road, one block south of the intersection of U.S. 54 and U.S. 380, the **chamber of commerce** (575/648-2732, www.carrizozochamber.org, 10am-2pm Fri.-Sun.) has its office in a vintage caboose. If it's not open, you can grab brochures from the display outside—one is a very detailed walking/driving tour of all the old buildings in town.

VALLEY OF FIRES NATIONAL RECREATION AREA

Four miles west of Carrizozo on U.S. 380, the little-visited **Valley of Fires National Recreation Area** (575/648-2241, $3 pp or $5/car) is far smaller than the more commonly visited El Malpais National Monument, west of Albuquerque. But the geology is striking because it's the product of a more recent explosion, just 1,500 years ago; the rocks here are still shiny, craggy, and often a very dramatic black, unlike the duller, almost purple hue of older volcanic stone. Up close, you'll be surprised at how much scrubby greenery has managed to grow—a short **nature trail** leads around part of the site.

The **campground** ($7-18) has 19 sites, most with electricity hookups, as well as showers and restrooms. The tent sites are in a very nice secluded gully.

on Carrizozo's colorful 12th Street

the lava beds at Valley of Fires

★ TRINITY SITE

This portion of **White Sands Missile Range,** where the first atomic bomb was detonated on July 16, 1945, is open to the public only on the first Saturday in April and October. The gate is open 8am-2pm; the site closes at 3:30pm. If this happens to coincide with your schedule, do try to go. At first, it doesn't seem there's much to see beyond the ranch house where the bomb was assembled and the small depression left by the explosion, but then small details, such as shards of the green glassy substance that the heat of the bomb created on the desert floor, pop out as you look around. Perhaps the most disturbing thing about the place is just how normal it looks.

Access is via the Stallion Gate to the missile range, off U.S. 380, at a turn south 53 miles west of Carrizozo or 12 miles east of San Antonio. Contact the missile range **public affairs office** (575/678-1134, www.wsmr. army.mil) to confirm dates and directions. A car convoy makes the 72-mile drive from Alamogordo, starting in the Tularosa High School parking lot; contact Alamogordo's **chamber of commerce** (575/437-6120) for details.

WHITE OAKS

It's worth the nine-mile detour to White Oaks for a lesson in impermanence: Unbelievably, this used to be the second-largest city in New Mexico, after Las Vegas, and now it's a rough settlement of a couple dozen hardy creative types. Its social heart is the **No Scum Allowed Saloon** (575/648-5583, 11am-8pm Wed.-Thurs., noon-late Fri.-Sat., noon-8pm Sun.), cheerier than its name suggests and also well worth the drive—you might stumble on amazing fiddle playing or a biker bash.

The bar is open year-round, but the rest of this former mining settlement is near-silent in the off-season. At the end of April, it opens with its annual **artist studio tour** (www.villageofcapitan.com/whiteoaks.html). The most intriguing buildings—such as spooky, fenced-off Hoyle's Castle to the south, and the equally looming Gumm House, on the north side—are closed to visitors, but the brick schoolhouse and a little miner's home both contain small museums open weekends in the summer. In June, **Gold Rush Days** offers a parade, vendors, and exhibitions.

Look for the turn for White Oaks off U.S. 54 three miles north of Carrizozo; head east on Highway 349.

Background

The Landscape 376

Plants and Animals 378

History 382

Government and Economy 386

Local Culture 388

The Arts 391

The Landscape

Sharp peaks, deep gorges, harsh desert, sweeping plains—everything about New Mexico's landscape is dramatic. The light glints off surfaces at surprising angles, and the scenery can change at any bend in the road. The altitude ranges from around 2,800 feet down by the Texas border to more than 13,000 at Wheeler Peak north of Taos, but the average is about 5,700 feet, more than a mile high. So even if the scenery doesn't make you gasp for breath, the thin air might.

GEOGRAPHY AND GEOLOGY

Much of New Mexico's landscape is the product of volcanic activity that ceased (at least for now) around the year AD 500. The main mountain ranges, which form part of the **Continental Divide,** are relatively young, pushed up in the Eocene era between 55 million and 34 million years ago, when shock waves from the collision of the North American plate and the Farallon plate caused the continent to heave.

Just a few million years later, the **Rio Grande Rift**—one of the biggest rift valleys in the world—formed, as eras' and eras' worth of accumulated rock was pulled apart by shifting faults, leaving the perfect path for the Rio Grande when it began to flow about three million years ago. The water carved deep canyons, such as the 800-foot-deep gorge west of Taos. These canyons are perfect slices of geologic time, layers of limestone, sandstone, clay, and lava neatly stacked up.

A million years ago, a volcano's violent eruption and subsequent collapse created the huge **Valles Caldera,** and the jagged edges of the crater have barely softened in the intervening time. Only 1,500 years ago,

in the Tularosa basin, molten lava hardened into black badlands. One tangible benefit of the state's volcanic activity is the numerous hot springs, especially in the young Jemez Mountains (15 million years old).

Beneath all this is evidence of a stabler time. For some four billion years, the land was completely underwater, then spent hundreds of millions of years supporting prehistoric sealife—hence the marine fossils found at the top of the Sandia Mountains, 10,000 feet above the current sea level. Dinosaurs, too, flourished for a time. One of the first, the nimble meat-eater *Coelophysis,* lived during the Triassic period around Abiquiu, but all of them were apparently killed at once, perhaps by a flash flood. Another product of the dinosaur age (specifically, the Jurassic) was the lurid red, pink, and orange sandstone. It began as a vast desert, then petrified into the very symbol of the American Southwest, and is visible around Abiquiu as well as Jemez Pueblo.

CLIMATE

For the most part, altitude determines the climate in New Mexico, where central Albuquerque, in the river valley, can be crisp and cloudless while Sandia Peak, 20 miles away and almost 5,000 feet up, is caught in a blinding snowstorm. (Yes, it snows plenty in New Mexico.) Nowhere, though, is it a particularly gentle climate; expect sudden changes in weather and temperature extremes.

At the lower elevations, winter is cold—days usually between 40°F and 55°F—but rarely cloudy, with a few snowstorms that never add up to as much moisture as people hope. Come spring, which starts in late April or May, the number of wildflowers that dot the hills is a direct reflection of the previous

---

Previous: rock formations at Plaza Blanca in Abiquiu; a Catholic pilgrimage site south of Albuquerque.

snowfall at Santuario de Chimayó in Santa Fe

winter's precipitation. The higher the elevation, the later the spring: At 8,500 feet, snow could still be on the ground in May. Little rain falls in May and June, typically the hottest and windiest months of the year, with temperatures climbing into the 90s—though it can still drop to the 50s at night.

By early or mid-July, the so-called monsoon season brings heavy, refreshing downpours and thunderstorms every afternoon for a couple of months. If you're out hiking in this season, steer clear of narrow canyons and arroyos during and after rains, as they can fill with powerful, deadly flash floods in a matter of minutes. Summer nights are rarely too warm.

September, October, and November are again dry, with the temperature dipping lower each month. Snow can often start falling in late October or November, although in recent years, overall winter precipitation has been quite low, so it takes months for a good base layer to build up at the ski areas.

ENVIRONMENTAL ISSUES

For thousands of years, New Mexicans have faced a water shortage. In prehistoric times,

farming in the river valley was relatively easy, if subject to flooding. But at higher elevations, mountain streams had to be channeled into irrigation ditches. This system was perfected by Spanish settlers, who called their ditches acequias, a word they'd learned from the Arabs (as-saqiya), who used the system to cultivate the Iberian Peninsula.

Today, as an ever-growing population demands more amenities, traditional ways of managing water have given way to more complex legal wranglings and outright hostility (*No chingen con nuestra agua*—don't f—k with our water—reads a bumper sticker on some trucks in northern New Mexico). Some 49 billion gallons are pumped out of the middle Rio Grande aquifer every year, and only a portion of that is replenished through mountain runoff. Albuquerque started using filtered river water in late 2008. "Smart growth" gets lip service in city council meetings, although construction continues apace on Albuquerque's arid West Mesa. Neo-homesteaders install cisterns to catch rain, as well as systems to reuse gray water, but these features are still far from standard.

Years of relative drought can make

tinderboxes of the forests. In a few weeks in the summer of 2012, for instance, the Whitewater-Baldy fire in the Gila National Forest burned almost 300,000 acres, the largest recorded fire in New Mexico history (almost double the scale of the previous record-setter, near Los Alamos the year before).

Visitors to New Mexico can help by following local environmental policies: Take scrupulous care with fire in the wilderness (no campfires, of course), and follow drought measures such as keeping showers short. Golfers may want to consider curtailing their play here. New courses, improbably, have been installed at every new casino resort and high-end residential development, despite the fact that they're intense draws on the water table.

Plants and Animals

Just as humans have managed to eke a life out of New Mexico, so have plants and animals—and a rather large variety of them. The state supports the fourth most diverse array of wildlife in the country.

PLANTS

Although much of the plant growth in New Mexico is nominally evergreen, the landscape skews toward brown, until you get up to the wetter alpine elevations.

Vegetation Zones

Below 4,500 feet, New Mexico's **Lower Sonoran** zone, in the river valleys in the southern part of the state, is dotted with cactus, yucca, and scrubby creosote bushes. The **Upper Sonoran** zone, covering the areas between 4,500 and 7,000 feet, is the largest vegetation zone in the state and includes the high plains in the northeast and most of Albuquerque and Santa Fe, where the Sandia and Sangre de Cristo foothills are covered with juniper and piñon trees. The **Transition** zone, 7,000-8,500 feet, sees a few more stately trees, such as ponderosa pine, and the state's more colorful wildflowers: orange Indian paintbrush, bright red penstemon, purple lupine. Above 8,500 feet, the **Mixed Conifer** zone harbors that sort of tree, along with clusters of aspens. The **Subalpine** zone, starting at 9,500 feet, is home to Engelmann spruce and bristlecone pine, while 11,500 feet marks the tree line in most places and the beginning

of the **Alpine** zone, where almost no greenery survives. At 11,973 feet, the top of Sierra Blanca, near Ruidoso, is the southernmost example of this zone in the United States.

Trees and Grasses

Trees are the clearest marker of elevation. In low areas—such as the Chihuahuan Desert outside of Las Cruces—you'll see almost no trees, only assorted cacti, such as the common **cane cholla;** the spiky **yucca** plant, which produces towering stalks of blooms in May; and the humble **tumbleweed.** Along the Rio Grande and the Pecos River, thirsty **cottonwoods** provide dense shade; the biggest trees, with their gnarled, branching trunks, are centuries old. In spring, their cotton fills the air—hell for the allergic, but the source of a distinctive spicy fragrance—and in fall, their leaves turn pure yellow. Willow and olive are also common.

Everywhere in the foothills grows **piñon** (also spelled "pinyon"), the scrubby state tree that's slow-growing and drought-resistant, evolved to endure the New Mexican climate. When burned, its wood produces the scent of a New Mexico winter night, and its cones yield tasty nuts. Alongside piñon is **shaggy-bark juniper,** identifiable by its loose strips of bark, sprays of soft needles, and branches that look twisted by the wind. In season, it's studded with purple-gray berries—another treat for foraging humans and animals alike. At ground level in the foothills, also look for

Leave No Trace

So as not to upset the rather precarious environmental balance in much of New Mexico, you should internalize the ethic of "leave no trace"—even on a short stroll. Let the phrase first guide your trip in the **planning** stages, when you equip yourself with good maps and GPS tools or a compass, to avoid relying on rock cairns or blazes. Backpackers should repackage food and other items to minimize the waste to pack out. And everyone should try to keep group size under six people; pets should not go in wild areas.

On the trail, resist the urge to cut across switchbacks. Stick to the center of the trail, even if it has been widened by others trying to avoid mud. Be quiet, to avoid disturbing wildlife and other hikers. Leave what you find, whether plants, rocks, or potsherds.

Camp only where others have, in durable areas, at least 200 feet from water sources; dig cat holes 200 feet away too. Pack out your toilet paper and other personal waste, and scatter dishwater and toothpaste. Safeguard food in "bear bags" hung at least 15 feet off the ground. Campfires are typically banned in New Mexico—please honor this policy, and keep a close eye on camp stoves. Pack out all cigarette butts.

Day hikers should also maintain a strict policy regarding litter. Tossing an orange peel, apple core, or other biodegradable item along the trail may not cause an environmental disaster, but it reminds other hikers that humans have been there and intrudes on the natural solitude of New Mexico's wilderness.

For more information, contact **Leave No Trace** (http://lnt.org).

clumps of sagebrush and bear grass, which blooms in huge, creamy tufts at the ends of stalks up to six feet tall.

Up in the mountains, the trees are a bit taller. Here you'll find the towering **ponderosa pine,** with its thick, almost crusty chunks of reddish-black bark; the crevices smell distinctly of vanilla. At slightly higher elevations, dense stands of **aspens** provide a rare spot of fall color in the evergreen forests. The combination of their golden leaves and white bark creates a particularly magical glow, especially in the mountains near Santa Fe. The highest mountain areas are home to a number of dense-needled hardy pines, such as blue-green **Engelmann spruce, corkbark fir, bristlecone pines,** and **subalpine fir,** with its sleek, rounded pinecones. Hike your way up to stands of these, which are tall but with sparse branches, and you'll know you're close to the peak.

ANIMALS

As with plants, what you see depends on whether you're down in the desert or up on the mountain slopes. And you'll have to look carefully, because a lot of the animals that have survived here this long are the sort that blend in with their surroundings—which means there are a lot of brown critters.

Mammals

In the open, low-elevation areas on Albuquerque's fringes (and sometimes in the occasional vacant urban lot), look for **prairie dogs,** which live in huge underground warrens. When you're camping, the first creatures you'll meet are **squirrels** and **chipmunks**—at higher elevations, look out for Abert's squirrel, with its tufted ears and extra-fluffy tail. Long-haunched, clever, and highly adaptable, **coyotes** roam the lower elevations and are not shy about nosing around backyards; they make a barking yelp at night.

On the plains, you may see **pronghorns** (often called pronghorn antelope, though they are not related to true antelope) springing through the grasses, while long-eared **mule deer** flourish in mountain forests, such as the Pecos Wilderness. Herds of **elk** live in the high valleys; Rocky Mountain elk are common, thanks to an aggressive reintroduction effort in the early 20th century to make up for overhunting. A group of the largest variety, Roosevelt elk, whose fanlike antlers are the stuff of dreams for trophy hunters, roams in Valles Caldera. **Bighorn sheep** live in the mountains around Taos and in the Gila Wilderness.

Taos is also a hot spot for **North American river otters,** which were reintroduced in the rivers in Taos Pueblo starting in 2008—after their absence from the whole state for some 55 years. The small aquatic mammals seem to be flourishing and can now be spotted in the Rio Grande and tributaries, from the Colorado border to Cochiti Dam.

Black bears crash around the forests, though their name is misleading—at any given time, they can be brown, cinnamon-red, or even nearly blond. (Smokey Bear, the mascot of the National Forest Service, was from New Mexico, a cub rescued from a forest fire in the southern town of Capitan.) Drought often drives the omnivorous beasts into suburban trash cans to forage, with tragic results for both people and the animals. Campers are strongly urged to pack food in bear-proof canisters.

And then there's the elusive **jackalope,** a jackrabbit sporting elaborate antlers. Alas, it seems now to appear only on postcards, although you may occasionally see a taxidermied head in a curio shop.

Birds

New Mexico's state bird is the impressive **roadrunner:** It grows up to two feet long, nests in the ground, feeds on insects and even rattlesnakes, and has feet specially adapted to racing on sandy ground. It can be spotted at lower desert elevations. Blue-and-black **Steller's jays** and raucous all-blue **piñon jays** are common in the foothills and farther up in the mountains, where you can also see **bluebirds, black-masked mountain chickadees,** and **Clark's nutcrackers,** which hoard great stashes of piñon nuts for winter. Also look around for **woodpeckers,** including the three-toed variety, which lives

lush yucca blooms

at higher elevations. On the highest peaks are **white-tailed ptarmigans,** which blend in with their snowy environment. But you can't miss the yellow-and-red **western tanager,** a vivid shot of tropical delight in the Transition zone forests.

In late summer, keep an eye out for tiny, red-throated **rufous hummingbirds** on their way to Mexico for the winter, along with hundreds of other birds that use the center of the state as a migratory corridor. The Sandia Mountains and the Las Vegas National Wildlife Refuge, among other spots, are on the flight path for **red-tailed hawks, eagles,** and other raptors, especially numerous in the springtime.

With more than 450 species spotted in New Mexico, this list is only scraping the surface. If you're a dedicated birder, first contact the **Randall Davey Audubon Center** in Santa Fe, which leads bird walks, or the **Rio Grande Nature Center** in Albuquerque. **Bosque del Apache National Wildlife Refuge,** south of Albuquerque, is a must in the winter when thousands of **sandhill cranes**—and even the occasional rare **whooping crane**—rest in the wetlands. Jim West of **WingsWest Birding** (800/583-6928, www.wingswestnm.com) is a reputable guide who has been leading groups around New Mexico since 1996.

Fish

Trout is the major endemic fish, found in the cold waters of the Rio Grande as well as the San Juan, Chama, and Pecos Rivers. The cutthroat is particularly beloved in New Mexico—the only variety of trout originally found on the eastern side of the Continental Divide. (The more aggressive rainbow and brown trout are interlopers.) The Rio Grande cutthroat, the official state fish, is now quite uncommon. Another local fish in jeopardy is the **Rio Grande silvery minnow,** listed as endangered since 1994. The last of the Rio Grande's five native fish, it's in such a dire state that biologists have scooped them out of the water individually during dry spells and taken them to the Albuquerque aquarium for safekeeping.

Reptiles

One can't step foot in the desert without thinking of **rattlesnakes,** and New Mexico has plenty of them, usually hidden away under rocks and brush, but very occasionally sunning themselves in full view. The predominant species in the Rio Grande Valley, the **Western diamondback,** can grow to be seven feet long. Although its venom is relatively weak, it has an impressive striking distance of almost three feet. Around Taos and Santa Fe, the main species is the **prairie rattlesnake,** which is only four feet long at most; the threatened **New Mexico ridgenose** is only about two feet long.

More benign cold-blooded critters include **lizards,** such as the **short-horned lizard** (aka horny toad), a miniature dinosaur, in effect, about as big as your palm. Look for it in the desert and the scrubby foothills.

Insects and Arachnids

Because it's so dry, New Mexico isn't teeming with bugs. The ones that are there, however, can be off-putting, particularly if you chance upon the springtime **tarantula migration,** usually in May around Albuquerque. It's not a true seasonal relocation, just the time when males come out of their dens to prowl for mates. The fist-size spiders move hundreds at a time, and occasionally back roads are closed to let them pass. If you'll be camping in the desert in the spring, ask the ranger's office about the status. Though they're big and hairy, they're not venomous.

Scorpions, though, can be more dangerous, if very rarely deadly. In the southern desert areas, the most common variety is the bark scorpion, which nestles in rock crevices and woodpiles and can find its way into your shoes or the bottom of your sleeping bag. Its sting can cause anything from severe pain to difficulty breathing and should be treated with antivenin as soon as possible. Hard-shelled, segmented **desert centipedes** are another local creepy-crawly; they're often out at night and can grow up to nine inches long.

tarantulas: the teddy bears of the spider world

History

The historical and cultural continuity in New Mexico is remarkable. The state has been transformed from ice-age hunting ground to home of the atom bomb, but many people claim roots that stretch back hundreds, even thousands, of years.

ANCIENT AND ARCHAIC CIVILIZATION

New Mexico was one of the first places to harbor humans after the end of the last **ice age.** Archaeological findings indicate that some 12,000 years ago, people were hunting mastodons and other big game across the state. Mammoth bones, arrowheads, and the remains of campfires have been found in the Sandia Mountains east of Albuquerque; Folsom, in northeastern New Mexico; and Clovis, in the south. Sometime between 8000 and 5000 BC, these bands of hunters formed a small temporary settlement just north of Albuquerque, but it was not enough to stave off the decline of that ancient culture, as climatic shifts caused the big game to die off. Nomadic hunter-gatherers, seeking out smaller animals as well as seeds and nuts, did better in the new land, and by 1000 BC, they had established communities built around clusters of pit houses—sunken, log-covered rooms dug into the earth.

Along with this new form of shelter came an equally important advance in food: Mexican people gave corn kernels (maize) and lessons in agriculture to their neighbors, the **Mogollon,** who occupied southern New Mexico and Arizona. By AD 400, the Mogollon had begun growing squash and beans as well and had established concentrated communities all around the southern Rio Grande basin. This culture, dubbed the Basketmakers by archaeologists, also developed its own pottery, another skill learned from the indigenous people of Mexico. So when the Mogollon made contact with the Ancestral Puebloans (also known as the Anasazi) in the northern part of the state, they had plenty to share.

THE PUEBLOS

The year 700 marks the beginning of what archaeologists call the **Pueblo I** phase, when disparate groups began to form larger communities in the upland areas on either side of the northern Rio Grande. Pit houses were still in use, but aboveground buildings of clay and sticks were erected alongside them. Increasingly, the pit houses were sacred spaces, chambers in which religious ceremonies were carried out; these are now known as kivas and are still an integral part of pueblo life.

The **Pueblo II** era began in 850 and is distinguished by the rise of Pueblo Bonito in Chaco Canyon, northwest of Santa Fe, into a full-scale city and perhaps capital of a small state. It was home to an estimated 1,500 people ruled by a religious elite. But Chaco abruptly began to crumble around 1150, perhaps due to drought, famine, or warfare. This shift marked the **Pueblo III** period, when the people who were to become today's Puebloans began building their easily defended cliff dwellings—most famously in the Four Corners area, at Mesa Verde in present-day Colorado, but also farther south, on the Pajarito Plateau in what's now Bandelier National Monument, and in Puyé, on Santa Clara Pueblo land. A drought at the end of the 13th century cleared out the Four Corners at the start of the **Pueblo IV** era, provoking the population to consolidate along the Rio Grande in clusters of sometimes more than a thousand interconnected rooms. These communities dotted the riverbank, drawing their sustenance both from the river water and from the mountains behind them.

THE SPANISH ARRIVE

These settlements were what the Spanish explorer **Francisco Vásquez de Coronado** and his crew saw when they first ventured into the area in 1540. Their Spanish word for the villages, *pueblos*, stuck and is still the name for both the places and the people who live in them. Coronado wasn't impressed, however, because the pueblos were made out of mud, not gold as he had been hoping. So after two years and a couple of skirmishes with the natives, the team turned around and headed back to Mexico City.

It took another 50 years for the Spanish to muster more interest in the area. This time, in 1598, **Don Juan de Oñate** led a small group of Spanish families to settle on the banks of the Rio Grande, at a place they called San Gabriel, near Ohkay Owingeh (which they called San Juan Pueblo). About a decade later, the settlers moved away from their American Indian neighbors, to the new village of Santa Fe. The territory's third governor, Don Pedro de Peralta, made it the official capital of the territory of Nuevo México, which in those days stretched far into what is now Colorado and Arizona.

This time the colonists, mostly farmers, were motivated not so much by hopes of striking it rich but simply of making a living. Moreover, they were inspired by Catholic zeal, and Franciscan missionaries accompanied them to promote the faith among the Puebloans. It was partly these missionaries and their ruthless oppression of the native religion that drove the Indians to organize the **Pueblo Revolt** of 1680. The Franciscans' "conversion" strategy involved public executions of the pueblos' medicine men, among other violent assaults on local traditions. But the Spanish colonists were no help either. In their desperation to squeeze wealth out of the hard land, they exploited the only resource they had, the slave labor of the Indians, who were either conscripts or stolen from their families. (The Indians did some poaching from Spanish families too, creating a violent sort of cultural exchange program.)

The leader of the Pueblo Revolt was a man

New Mexican history can be told from two sides.

named Popé (also spelled Po'pay), from San Juan Pueblo. Using Taos Pueblo as his base, he traveled to the other communities, secretly meeting with leaders to plan a united insurrection. Historians theorize he may have used Spanish to communicate with other Puebloans who did not speak his native Tewa, and he distributed among the conspirators lengths of knotted rope with which to count down the days to the insurrection. Although the Spanish captured a few of the rope-bearing messengers (Isleta Pueblo may never have gotten the message, which could explain its being the only pueblo not to participate), they could not avert the bloodshed. The Puebloan warriors killed families and missionaries, burned crops, and toppled churches. Santa Fe was besieged, and its population of more than 1,000 finally evacuated in a pitiful retreat.

The Spanish stayed away for 12 years, but a new governor, **Diego de Vargas,** took it upon himself to reclaim the area. He managed to talk many pueblos into peaceful surrender, meeting resistance only in Taos and Santa Fe, where a two-day fight was required to oust the Indians from the Palace of the Governors; in Taos, violence ground on for an additional four years. The Spanish strategy in the post-revolt era was softer, with more compromise between the Franciscans and their intended flock, and a fair amount of cultural and economic exchange. The threat of raiding Comanche, Apache, and Navajo also forced both sides to cooperate. Banding together for defense, they were finally able to drive the Comanche away, culminating in a 1778 battle with Chief Cuerno Verde (Green Horn). The decisive victory is celebrated in the ritual dance called Los Comanches, still performed in small villages by Hispanos and Puebloans alike.

The other bonding force was trade. The Spanish maintained the **Camino Real de Tierra Adentro** (Royal Road of the Interior), which linked Santa Fe with central Mexico— the route follows roughly the line carved by I-25 today. Caravans came through only every year or two, but the profit from furs, pottery,

textiles, and other local goods was enough to keep both cultures afloat, if utterly dependent on the Spanish government.

MEXICAN INDEPENDENCE AND THE FIRST ANGLOS

Spain carefully guarded all of its trade routes in the New World, even in a relatively unprofitable territory like Nuevo México. The only outside trade permitted was through the Comancheros, a ragtag band who traded with Comanche and other Plains Indians, working well into what would later be Oklahoma and even up to North Dakota. The Spanish governor encouraged them because their tight relationship with the Comanche helped protect New Mexico and Texas against intruders.

Interlopers were not welcome. Only a few enterprising fur trappers, lone mountain men in search of beaver pelts, slipped in. Spy-explorer **Zebulon Pike** and his crew were captured (perhaps intentionally, so Pike could get more inside information) and detained in Santa Fe for a spell in 1807. But in 1821, Mexico declared independence from Spain, liberating the territory of Nuevo México along with it. One of the first acts of the new government was to open the borders to trade. Initially just a trickle of curious traders came down the rough track from St. Louis, Missouri, but soon a flood of commerce flowed along the increasingly rutted and broad **Santa Fe Trail,** making the territory's capital city a meeting place between Mexicans and Americans swapping furs, gold, cloth, and more.

THE MEXICAN-AMERICAN WAR AND AFTER

Pike's expedition gave the U.S. government new details about the locations of Spanish forts. Just as important, Pike, who returned not long after Lewis and Clark completed their march across the Louisiana Purchase, helped fuel the country's expansionist fervor. In the next few decades, **"manifest destiny"** became the phrase on every American's lips, and the government was eyeing the Southwest. It annexed Texas in 1845, but New Mexico, with its small population and meager resources, didn't figure heavily in the short-lived war that followed. The Mexican governor surrendered peacefully to General Stephen Kearny when he arrived in Santa Fe in 1846. In Taos, the transition was not accepted so readily, as Hispano business leaders and Taos Pueblo Indians instigated a brief but violent uprising, in which the first American governor, Charles Bent, was beheaded.

During the **Civil War,** New Mexico was in the way of a Texan Confederate strategy to secure the Southwest, but the rebels were thwarted in 1862 at the Battle of Glorieta Pass. The territory stayed in the hands of the Union until the end of the war, and people were more concerned with the local, increasingly brutal skirmishes caused by the arrival in Santa Fe of Bishop Jean-Baptiste Lamy, a tyrannical—or at least very thoughtless—Frenchman who tried to impose a European vision of the Catholic Church on a populace that had been beyond centralized control for centuries.

Even more significant to New Mexico's development was the arrival of the **railroad** in 1880, as it was laid through Raton Pass, near Santa Fe, and close to Albuquerque. Virtually overnight, strange goods and even stranger people came pouring into one of the remoter frontier outposts of the United States. Anglo influence was suddenly everywhere, in the form of new architecture (red brick was an Eastern affectation) and new business. Albuquerque, almost directly on the new railway tracks, boomed, while Santa Fe's fortunes slumped and Taos all but withered away, having peaked back in the late days of the Camino Real.

But while wheeler-dealers were setting up shop in central New Mexico, some more intrepid souls were poking around in the less-connected areas farther north. These tourists were artists who valued New Mexico not for its commercial potential but for its dramatic landscapes and exotic populace who seemed untouched by American ways. From the early 20th century on, Santa Fe and Taos were cultivated as art colonies, a function they still fulfill today.

FROM STATEHOOD TO WORLD WAR II

Based on its burgeoning economy, New Mexico became the 47th state in the union in 1912, effectively marking the end of the frontier period, a phase of violence, uncertainty, and isolation that lasted about 300 years, longer here than anywhere else in the United States. In addition to the painters and writers flocking to the new state, another group of migrants arrived: tuberculosis patients. Soon the state was known as a health retreat, and countless people did stints in its dry air to treat their ailing lungs.

One of these patients was J. Robert Oppenheimer, whose mild case of TB got him packed off to a camp near Pecos for a year after high school. He loved northern New Mexico and got to know some of its more hidden pockets. So when the U.S. Army asked him if he had an idea where it should establish a secret base for the **Manhattan Project,** he knew just the place: a little camp high on a plateau above Santa Fe, named Los Alamos. This was the birthplace of the atomic bomb, a weird, close-knit community of the country's greatest scientific minds (and biggest egos), working in utter secrecy. Only after the bomb was tested at White Sands and Fat Man and Little Boy were dropped over Japan was the mysterious camp's mission revealed.

CONTEMPORARY HISTORY

The A-bomb ushered New Mexico into the modern era. Not only was it world-changing technology, but it also boosted the local economy. High-paying support staff jobs at Los Alamos and Kirtland Air Force Base in Albuquerque pulled some of the population away from subsistence farming and into a life that involved cars and electricity. But even so, the character of the state remained conservative and closed, so when the 1960s rolled around and New Mexico's empty space looked like the promised land to hippies, the culture clash was fierce. Staunch Catholic farmers took potshots at their naked, hallucinogen-ingesting neighbors who fantasized about getting back to the land but had no clue how to do it. After a decade or so, though, only the hardiest of the commune-dwellers were left, and they'd mellowed a bit, while the locals had come to appreciate at least their enthusiasm. Even if the communes didn't last, hippie culture has proven remarkably persistent in New Mexico. Even today, distinctly straight Hispanos can be heard saying things like, "I was tripping out on that band, man," and the state still welcomes Rainbow Gatherings, would-be Buddhists, and alternative healers.

The end of the 20th century saw unprecedented growth in both Albuquerque and Santa Fe. As usual, Albuquerque got the practical-minded development, such as the Intel chip-manufacturing plant and the services headquarters for Gap Inc., while Santa Fe was almost felled by its own artsiness, turned inside-out during a few frenzied years in the early 1990s when movie stars and other moneyed types bought up prime real estate. In just a matter of months, rents went up tenfold and houses started selling for more than $1 million. Santa Fe has yet to work out the imbalance between its creative forces, which did save the city from utter decline, and economic ones, though it implemented a living-wage law in 2009.

Meanwhile, Taos has grown slowly but steadily, as have the pueblos, thanks to the legalization of gambling on their lands, but all of these communities still have an air of old New Mexico, where the frontier flavor and solitude can still be felt.

Government and Economy

New Mexico doesn't look so good on paper—in national rankings of income, education, and more, it often ranks 49th or 50th. "New Mexico is a third-world country" is a common quip, at least among an older generation that has seen a lifetime of nepotism and incompetence. But these issues have also inspired a good deal of activist sentiment, and politics are lively.

GOVERNMENT

New Mexico's political scene is as diverse as its population, though the cities tend to vote Democrat. Still, Republican Susana Martinez became New Mexico's first woman governor in 2010 (her opponent was also a woman, incidentally), and was reelected in 2014. In the 2012 presidential election, counties skewed extremely red or blue; former governor and Libertarian Gary Johnson took 3.5 percent of the vote, his highest stake in the nation.

New Mexico is notable for its equitable Hispanic representation in every level of government, including the state legislature, where it consistently matches the state Hispanic population, just under 50 percent. This has helped keep the immigration debate at a relatively polite pitch—unlike in neighboring Arizona and Texas, where the Hispanic population is underrepresented in the government.

Each American Indian pueblo (as well as Navajo, Zuni, and Apache lands elsewhere in the state) acts as a sovereign nation, with its own laws, tax regulations, police forces, and government. Indians vote in U.S. and state elections, while in the pueblos, most domestic issues are decided by a tribal governor, a war chief, and a few other officials elected by a consensus of men in the kiva.

The Navajo Nation, with more than 250,000 people to manage, as well as a substantial cache of natural resources, does practice direct democracy, open to both men and women. In its system, the reservation, which reaches into Arizona and Utah,

Cattle graze nearly everywhere in New Mexico.

development. The Navajo Nation has extensive landholdings, but with an infrastructure that's more 19th than 21st century, businesses seldom invest. The same could in fact be said for many of the rural sections of the state, on Indian land or not.

The unemployment rate, however, is often lower than the national average, in part because Albuquerque continues to be a **manufacturing** center for computer chips, mattresses, specialty running shoes, and more. And the city where Microsoft was founded (Bill Gates and Paul Allen later moved back to Seattle to be close to their families) does foster **technology** development, as a range of tech specialists cater to Sandia National Labs. **Aerospace** manufacturing parks are growing outside Albuquerque and Las Cruces. At press time, private spaceflights were on the brink of departure from Spaceport America near Truth or Consequences.

Outside the cities, significant profits from coal, copper, oil, and natural gas —most in the southern part of the state, as well as in the northwest—keep the economy afloat. That's the big money, but the **agricultural** sector, from dairy cows in the south to apple orchards along the Rio Grande to beef jerky from the numerous cattle ranches, contributes a decent amount to the pot. And Santa Fe's **arts** sector shouldn't be overlooked— galleries post sales of $200 million every year, though they're criticized for sending much of that money right back to artists who live and work out of state. Thanks to tax rebates, the **film industry,** nicknamed "Tamalewood," has flourished. Albuquerque Studios is one of the largest production facilities in the country.

is divided into "chapters," and their elected representatives participate in the Navajo Council, which convenes in the capital at Window Rock, Arizona. Since a reform in 1991, the Navajo system has had three branches, like the American one. In 2006, Lynda Lovejoy was the first woman to run for nation president; she ran again in 2010, losing by a small margin. The 2014 election brought up a different issue, when one candidate was disqualified for failing to demonstrate fluency in the Navajo language, a legal requirement for holding the position.

ECONOMY

In New Mexico, roughly 21 percent of the population lives below the poverty level, compared with national averages around 15 percent. It's also near the bottom in the number of high school and college graduates per capita. Statistics in the pueblos and reservations have historically been grimmer, with up to 50 percent unemployment in some areas— but this has changed due to casino-fueled

Even if the economic situation isn't ideal, it's nothing New Mexicans aren't used to. Low income has been the norm for so long that a large segment of the population is, if not content with, at least adapted to eking out a living from very little (the median family income is only around $44,800, compared with the U.S. median of $53,600). In this respect, the state hasn't lost its frontier spirit at all.

BACKGROUND
GOVERNMENT AND ECONOMY

Local Culture

New Mexico's 1.8 million people have typically been described as a tricultural mix of Indians, Spanish, and Anglos. That self-image has begun to expand as residents have delved deeper into history and seen that the story involves a few more threads.

DEMOGRAPHY

The labels of Indian, Spanish, and Anglo are used uniquely in New Mexico. First, **Indian:** This is still a common term, as "Native American" never fully caught on. You'll see "American Indian" in formal situations, but even the "American" part is a bit laughable, considering "America" wasn't so named until Christopher Columbus made his voyage west. "Indian" refers to a number of different peoples who do not share a common culture or language: Navajo on the west side of the state, Jicarilla and Mescalero Apache, and the Puebloans of the Rio Grande and west as far as Acoma and Zuni. "Pueblo" refers not to a particular tribe, but to a larger group of people who speak four distinct languages but are banded together by a common way of living. Typically, people will identify themselves by their particular tribe: Santa Clara, for instance, or Taos. With about 10.2 percent of the population claiming American Indian ancestry (nearly 10 times the national average, and second only to Alaska), traditions are still strong.

Spanish really means that: the people, primarily in northern New Mexico, whose ancestors were Spaniards, rather than the mestizos of Mexico. For many families, it's a point of pride similar to that of *Mayflower* descendants. Over the years, particularly during the 20th century, a steady influx of Mexican immigrants blurred racial distinctions a bit, but it also reinforced the use of Spanish as a daily language and inspired pride in the culture's music and other folkways. In some circles, the word **Hispano** is used to label New Mexico's distinct culture with centuries-old Iberian roots, which includes the **Basques,** who came here both during the conquest (Don Juan de Oñate, the first Spanish governor, was Basque) and in the early 20th century as sheepherders. The discovery of families of **crypto-Jews** (Spanish Jews who nominally converted to Catholicism but fled here to avoid the Inquisition) has added another fascinating layer to the Spanish story, along with the knowledge that many of the first Spanish explorers likely had Arab blood as well.

Anglo is the most imprecise term, as it can mean anyone who's not Spanish or Indian. Originally used to talk about traders of European descent who came to hunt and sell furs and trade on the Santa Fe Trail, it still refers to people who can't trace their roots back to the conquistadors or farther. If you're a Vietnamese immigrant, a Tibetan refugee, or an African American whose family settled a farm here after the Civil War, you could be, at least in jest, Anglo. (As of 2014, about 38.9 percent of the population was non-Hispanic Caucasian; Asians were only 1.7 percent, and African Americans made up 2.5 percent.) But all Anglo culture is shot through with Spanish and Indian influence, whether among the organic garlic farmers from California who rely on their acequias for water or the New Age seekers who do sweat-lodge rituals.

Even with a liberal application of "Anglo," the tricultural arrangement is limiting, as it doesn't assign a place to contemporary immigrants from Mexico and other Latin American countries, and their numbers are growing steadily. It also doesn't acknowledge the strong Mexican American **Chicano** culture that's shared across the Southwest, from Los Angeles through Texas. The U.S. census form lumps both newer arrivals and old Spanish under "Hispanic"—a category (distinct from race) that made up 47.7 percent of the population in 2014, the highest in the country.

RELIGION

Four hundred years after the arrival of the Franciscan missionaries, New Mexico is still a heavily **Catholic** state—even KFC offers a Friday-night fish fry during Lent. But the relative isolation of the territory produced some variances that have disturbed the Vatican. In both Indian and Spanish churches, the pageantry of medieval Christianity is preserved. Las Posadas, the reenactment of Mary and Joseph's search for lodging in Bethlehem, is a festive torch-lit tradition every December, and during the annual Holy Week pilgrimage to Chimayó, devoted groups stage the stations of the cross, complete with 100-pound wood beams and lots of fake blood.

The Pueblo Indians play on church-as-theater too: During Christmas Eve Mass, for instance, the service may come to an abrupt end as the priest is hustled off the pulpit by face-painted clowns making way for the parade of ceremonial dancers down the aisle. In both cultures, the Mexican Virgin of Guadalupe is highly revered, and a number of saints are honored as intercessors for all manner of dilemmas, from failing crops to false imprisonment.

Eastern religions have a noticeable presence in New Mexico as well, and even a bit of political clout. A community of primarily American-born converts to **Sikhism** in Española, for example, is a major donor to both parties. Santa Fe is home to a substantial number of **Buddhists,** both American converts and native Tibetan refugees who have relocated to this different mountainous land. Stupas can be found up and down the Rio Grande.

LANGUAGE

English is the predominant language, but **Spanish** is very commonly used—about 30 percent of the population speaks it regularly. Spanish-speakers in northern New Mexico were for centuries only the old Hispano families, communicating in a variant of Castilian with a distinct vocabulary that developed in isolation. This "Quixotic" dialect changed little until the early 1900s, when immigrants arrived from Mexico and elsewhere in Latin America. For much of the 20th century, English was the only permissible classroom language, although many school districts required Spanish as a foreign language. Since the 1990s, education policy has shifted to include bilingual classrooms.

Additionally, you'll occasionally hear Indians speaking their respective languages. Of the four main Pueblo tongues, **Tewa, Tiwa,** and **Towa** are part of the Tanoan family of languages, which are also spoken by Plains Indians. They are related but mutually unintelligible, roughly equivalent to, say, French, Spanish, and Italian. Tewa is the most widely spoken, used in all of the pueblos just north of Santa Fe: Ohkay Owingeh, San Ildefonso, Santa Clara, Pojoaque, Tesuque, and Nambé. Four pueblos speak Tiwa—Taos and Picurís share one dialect, while Isleta and Sandia, in an odd pocket near Albuquerque, speak a different dialect. Towa is now spoken only at Jemez Pueblo. Part of the greater Athabaskan family, the **Navajo** and **Apache** languages are related to but distinct from one another.

Keresan (spoken in Laguna, Acoma, Cochiti, Kewa, San Felipe, Santa Ana, and Zia) and **Zuni** (spoken only at that pueblo) are what linguists call "isolates." Like Basque, they are not connected to neighboring languages, nor to any other language. Additionally, each Keresan-speaking pueblo has developed its own dialect, so immediately adjacent communities can understand each other, but those farthest apart cannot.

One interesting characteristic of the Pueblo languages is that they have remained relatively pure. Tewa vocabulary, for instance, is still less than 5 percent loan words, despite centuries of Spanish and English influence. This is probably due to the way speakers have long been forced to compartmentalize, using Tewa

New Mexico's Penitentes

a *morada* in Abiquiu

Most Hispano villages in northern New Mexico have a modest one-story building called a *morada*—the meeting place of **Los Hermanos Penitentes** (The Penitent Brothers), a lay Catholic fraternity with deep roots in medieval Spain and a history that has often put it at odds with the church.

The Penitentes developed in New Mexico in the early colonial era and were at the height of their influence during the so-called Secular Period (1790-1850), when the Franciscans had been pushed out by church leaders in Mexico but no new priests were sent to the territory. Members of the brotherhood cared for the ill, conducted funerals, and settled petty disputes and even elections. They maintained the spiritual and political welfare of their villages when there were no priests or central government to do so.

The Penitentes are best known for their intense religious rituals, which are rumored to still include self-flagellation, bloodletting, and mock crucifixion—activities that took place in public processions for centuries but were driven underground in the late 19th century following official church condemnation. The secrecy, along with sensational journalism by visitors from the East Coast, fueled gruesome rumors. For their crucifixion reenactments, it was said Penitentes used real nails, and the man drawn by lot to be the *Cristo* had a good chance of dying—though no eyewitness ever recorded the practice on paper. One well-documented ritual involves pulling *la carretera del muerte*, an oxcart filled with rocks and a wooden figure of Doña Sebastiana, Lady Death. Morbid imagery bred morbid curiosity: Photos in a *Harper's* magazine story from the early 1900s show Anglos looking on agog as Penitentes clad in white pants and black hoods whip themselves.

In 1947, after years of concerted lobbying (but not an official renunciation of its rituals), the Penitentes were again accepted into the fold of the Catholic Church. The *hermanos mayores* (head brothers) from all of the *moradas* convene annually in Santa Fe, and the group, which has an estimated 3,000 members, functions as a political and public-service club.

The rituals do continue, most visibly during Holy Week, when the group's devotion to the physical suffering of the human Jesus is at its keenest. The Penitentes reenact the stations of the cross and the crucifixion, and although ketchup is more prevalent than real blood and statues often stand in for the major players, the scenes are solemn and affectingly tragic. On some days during Holy Week, the *morada* is open to non-Penitentes—a rare chance for outsiders to see the meeting place of this secretive group.

for conversation at home and switching to English or Spanish for business and trade. For centuries, the Franciscan priests, then the U.S. government, attempted to stamp out Native American languages. Following the Civil War, Puebloan children were moved forcibly to boarding schools, where they were given Anglo names and permitted to speak only English, a policy that continued for decades.

Only in 1990, with the passage of the **Native American Languages Act,** were American Indian languages officially permitted in government-funded schools—indeed, they are now recognized as a unique element of this country's culture and encouraged. In Taos, where the Tiwa language is a ritual secret that outsiders are not permitted to learn, one public school has Tiwa classes for younger students, open only to tribe members and taught by approved teachers; as an added measure against the language being recorded, the classroom has no chalkboard. Less-formal instruction within the pueblos as well as on the Navajo Nation has also helped the Indian languages enjoy a renaissance.

The Arts

New Mexico is a hotbed of creativity, from Santa Fe's edgy contemporary art scene to traditional Spanish folk artists working in remote villages, using the same tools their great-grandfathers did, to whole American Indian villages, such as Zuni, devoted to the production of fine silverwork. Here's what to look for in the more traditional arenas of pottery, weaving, jewelry, and wood carving.

POTTERY

New Mexico's pottery tradition thrives, drawing on millennia of craftsmanship. About 2,000 years ago, the **Mogollon** people in the southern part of the state began making simple pots of brown coiled clay. A thousand years later, the craft had developed into the beautiful black-on-white symmetry of the **Mimbres** people. Later, each of the pueblos developed its own style.

By the 20th century, some traditions had died out, but almost all felt some kind of renaissance following the work of San Ildefonso potter **María Martinez** in the first half of the 20th century. Along with her husband, Julian, Martinez revived a long-lost style of lustrous black pottery with subtle matte decoration. The elegant pieces, which looked at once innovative and traditional, inspired Anglo collectors (who saw the couple's work at the 1934 Chicago World's Fair, among other places) as well as local potters. Today, many artists make their livings with clay.

The various tribal styles are distinguished by their base clay, the "slip" (the clay-and-water finish), and their shape. Taos and Picurís pueblos, for instance, are surrounded by beds of micaceous clay, which lends pots a subtle glitter. (It also helps them withstand heat well; they're renowned for cooking beans.) Acoma specializes in intricate black designs painted on thin white clay. Pottery from Ohkay Owingeh (formerly San Juan) is typically reddish-brown with incised symbols. And Santa Clara developed the "wedding jar," a double-neck design with a handle. If a particular style catches your eye in city galleries, then you can visit the specific pueblo, where you may be able to buy directly from the artisan and perhaps see where the piece was made.

TEXTILES

After pottery, **weaving** is probably the state's most widespread craft. Historically, Indian and Spanish weaving styles were separate, but they have merged over the centuries to create some patterns and styles unique to the Rio Grande Valley. The first Spanish explorers marveled at the Navajo cotton blankets, woven in whole panels on wide looms;

Luminarias or *Farolitos*?

luminarias in Santa Fe ... where most people would call them *farolitos*

The cultural differences between Santa Fe and Albuquerque don't apply just to the number of art galleries per square block and whether you eat posole or rice with your enchiladas. Every Christmas, a debate rears its head: What do you call a paper bag with a bit of sand in the bottom and a votive candle inside? These traditional holiday decorations, which line driveways and flat adobe rooftops in the last weeks of December, are commonly known as luminarias in Albuquerque and most towns to the south, and as *farolitos* in Santa Fe and all the villages to the north.

To complicate matters, another holiday tradition in Santa Fe and other northern towns is to light small bonfires of piñon logs in front of houses. And Santa Feans call these little stacks of wood ... luminarias. *Farolitos*, they argue, are literally "little lanterns," an accurate description of the glowing paper bags—and under this logic, use of the term *farolito* has spread a bit in Albuquerque, at least among people who weren't raised saying luminaria from birth.

But *Burqueños* have Webster's on their side; the dictionary concurs that luminarias are paperbag lanterns and notes the tradition comes from Mexico, where the bags are often colored and pricked with holes. Because this author's loyalties are to Albuquerque, the argument is settled, at least in these pages: Luminaria it is.

Spaniards had been working with narrow looms and stitching two panels together. Spanish weavers introduced the hardy Churro sheep, with its rough wool that was good for hand-spinning, as well as new dyes, such as indigo (although the blue-tinted rugs are often called **Moki** rugs, using a Navajo word).

In the early 1800s, in an attempt to make a better product for trade, the Spanish government sent Mexican artists north to work with local weavers. Out of this meeting came the distinctive **Saltillo** styles (named for the region the

Mexican teachers came from), such as the running-leaf pattern, which Rio Grande weavers alternated with solid-color stripes. In the 1880s, New Mexican artisans first saw quilts from the eastern United States, and they adapted the eight-pointed star to their wool rugs. Another popular motif from the 19th century is a zigzag pattern that resembles lightning.

One item that shows up in antiques shops is the **Chimayó blanket,** an invention of the tourist age in the early 20th century, when Anglo traders encouraged local Hispano weavers to make an affordable souvenir to sell to visitors looking for "Indian" blankets. They're handsome, single-width rugs with a strong central motif, perhaps the iconic Southwestern-look rug.

Also look for *colcha* work, a Spanish style in which a loose-weave rug is decorated with wool embroidery. It was revived in the 1930s by Mormons, and you will occasionally see beautiful examples from this period in collectors' shops. Contemporary weaving can draw on any and all of these innovations and is practiced just as often by a young Anglo as a Hispano grandmother. A strong small-batch wool industry in New Mexico helps the scene tremendously—expect to see vivid color-block contemporary pieces alongside the more traditional patterns.

JEWELRY

Despite a long native tradition, the familiar forms of jewelry seen today date only from the mid-19th century, when the Navajo of western New Mexico pioneered silversmithing (it's thought they learned it during their internment at Fort Sumner) and taught it to the Pueblo Indians. The most iconic piece of Southwestern jewelry, a signature Navajo design, is the turquoise-and-silver **squash-blossom necklace,** a large crescent pendant decorated with flowerlike silver beads. Actually derived from Spanish pomegranate decorations, rather than native plant imagery, it's seen in every Southwest jewelry store.

Look also for shell-shaped **concha belts** (also spelled "concho"), silver "shells" linked together or strung on a leather belt, and the San Felipe specialty, *heishi,* tiny disks made of shell and threaded to make a rope-like strand. The Zuni carve small animal **fetishes**—bears, birds, and more—often strung on necklaces with heishi. In addition to turquoise, opals are a popular decorative stone, along with brick-red coral, lapis lazuli, and black jet and marble. Whatever you buy, the gallery or artisan should supply you with a written receipt of its components—which stones, the grade of silver, and so forth.

Turquoise

Although New Mexico's turquoise is all mined out, the stone is still an essential part of local jewelry-making; most of it is imported from mines in China. It is available in shades from lime-green to pure sky-blue, and much of it has been subjected to various processes to make it stabler and more versatile, which affects the price.

Rare gem-grade turquoise is the top of the line—a high-quality piece with complex spiderwebbing from now-empty mines like Lander or Lone Mountain can cost $350 per carat. "Gem-grade" applies only to **natural stones** (those that have not been chemically treated in any way) and is based on the piece's luster, hardness, and matrix, the term for the web of dark veins running through it, which you should be able to feel in any natural turquoise, regardless of grade. Highest-quality stones from still-functioning mines in China or Tibet will cost significantly less ($10-20 per carat) but will be of the same quality as some premium American stones. Slightly less splendid natural stones are graded jewelry-quality, high-quality, or investment-quality—but they are not quite hard enough to guarantee they will not change color over decades. They cost $2-5 per carat. For any natural stone, the seller must provide you with a written certificate of its status.

Because good natural turquoise is increasingly difficult to come by and turquoise is such an unreliable stone, various treatments are a common and acceptable way of making a great deal of the stuff usable. **Treated turquoise** refers to any stone that has added resins, waxes, or other foreign elements. A certain proprietary treatment, **enhanced turquoise,** also called "Zachary process turquoise," is usually applied to medium-grade or higher stones.

Turquoise that has been **stabilized,** or submerged in epoxy resin to harden it and deepen the color, makes up the bulk of the market. Because it's less expensive, it allows for a little waste in the carving process, and good-quality stabilized turquoise is often found in expensive jewelry with elaborate inlay. Average-quality stabilized stone, the next grade down, is used by perhaps 70 percent of American Indian artisans—it can stand up to being carved and is very well priced. Though it ranks relatively low in the range of turquoise available, it produces an attractive piece of jewelry—perhaps not with the elaborate spiderwebbing of a rare piece, but with an overall good color and luster.

Below this are low-quality stabilized stones that have been artificially colored (often called "color shot," or, more confusing, "color stabilized"). "Synthetic" stones are actually real turquoise—small chunks mixed with a binding powder of ground turquoise or pyrite, then pressed into shapes and cut. The result is surprisingly attractive, with natural spiderwebbing, but it should be clearly labeled as synthetic. And of course there is the turquoise that isn't at all—plastic stuff that can be quite convincing.

Aside from the synthetic stuff, don't worry too much about getting "bad" or "cheap" turquoise—because each stone is different, the more important thing is to find a piece that's attractive to you and is priced to reflect its quality. Just remember that the words "genuine," "authentic," or "pure" have no real meaning—only "natural" is legally defined. Likewise, the phrase "authentic Indian handmade" is a legal one—any variation on this wording (such as "Indian crafted") is likely some kind of ruse. Shopping in New Mexico provides many opportunities to buy direct from the artisan—under the portal at the Palace of the Governors in Santa Fe, for instance. Otherwise, just avoid shopping in too-good-to-be-true stores that are perpetually "going out of business" or "in liquidation."

WOOD AND TINWORK

When Spanish colonists arrived in New Mexico, they had few resources, little money, and only the most basic tools. A group of settlers would typically include one carpenter, whose skills helped fill everyone's houses with heavy wood **furniture** (still made today). But the carpenter also helped the group to worship—for chief among the wood-carvers was (and is) the *santero* or *santera*, who carves images of saints. These so-called **santos** can be either flat (*retablos*) or three-dimensional (*bultos*) and are typically painted in lively colors, though some outstanding work has been produced in plain, unpainted wood.

Santo styles have shown remarkable continuity over the centuries. The most notable break from tradition was by Patrocinio Barela, whose WPA-sponsored work in the 1930s was almost fluid, utilizing the natural curves and grains of the wood. His sons and grandsons practice the art today. For centuries, the piousness of the *santero* was valued at least as much as his skill in carving, though many contemporary carvers do their work for a large market of avid collectors. One popular figure is San Isidro, patron saint of farmers, from 12th-century Spain.

Look also for **straw marquetry,** another product of hard times in the colonial period, in which tiny fibers of "poor man's gold" replaced precious metals as inlay to make elaborate geometric designs on dark wood. Tinwork is another ubiquitous craft, found in inexpensive votive-candle holders as well as elaborately punched and engraved mirror frames and chandeliers.

Essentials

Transportation 396
Food 400
Accommodations 403
Travel Tips 404
Health and Safety 408

Transportation

GETTING THERE

Air

Albuquerque International Sunport (ABQ; 505/244-7700, www.cabq.gov/airport) is the main access point to the region. It's served by the three major U.S. air carriers, plus Southwest Airlines, Alaska Airlines, Allegiant Air, and JetBlue. Fares fluctuate on the same schedule as the rest of the country, with higher rates in summer and over holidays; in the winter, it's wise to choose a connection through a more temperate hub, such as Dallas (American) or Salt Lake City (Delta).

Small **Santa Fe Municipal Airport** (SAF; 121 Aviation Dr.; 505/955-2900, www.santafenm.gov/airport), west of the city, receives direct flights from Dallas with American Eagle, and from Denver with United. For visiting the southern half of the state, you might find it easier to fly into **El Paso International Airport** (ELP; 915/780-4749, www.elpasointernationalairport.com), in Texas, just an hour's drive from Las Cruces.

Train

Amtrak (800/872-7245, www.amtrak.com) runs the *Southwest Chief* daily between Chicago and Los Angeles, stopping in **Raton, Las Vegas, Lamy** (18 miles from Santa Fe), **Albuquerque,** and **Gallup.**

Amtrak's *Sunset Limited* train, from Florida to Los Angeles via the southern edge of the state, is less useful—it runs every other day and requires a bus transfer from El Paso to **Las Cruces,** and makes stops in **Deming** and **Lordsburg.**

Arriving in Albuquerque, you're in the middle of downtown, in a depot shared with Greyhound. There are lockers here (occasionally full), and city buses are available just up

the block. Lamy (the stop nearest Santa Fe) is no more than a depot—though it is a dramatic and wild-feeling place to get off the train. Amtrak provides an awkwardly timed shuttle service to Santa Fe hotels (passengers arriving on eastbound trains must wait for passengers from the westbound train, an hour later). From Chicago, Amtrak pads its schedule heavily between Lamy and Albuquerque—so if the train is running behind, you'll be late arriving in Lamy but generally will still get to Albuquerque on schedule.

Bus

Greyhound (800/231-2222, www.greyhound.com) connects New Mexico with adjacent states and Mexico. Routes run roughly along I-40 and I-25, with little service to outlying areas. If you're coming from elsewhere in the Southwest, you may want to investigate **El Paso-Los Angeles Limousine Express** (915/532-4061 in El Paso, 626/442-1945 in Los Angeles, 505/247-8036 in Albuquerque, www.eplalimo.com), a long-established operator that originally served the Mexican immigrant population—its route runs east-west from El Paso to Los Angeles, stopping in Las Cruces and Deming. It also connects Denver and Albuquerque.

Car

Conveniently, New Mexico is crisscrossed by interstates: **I-40** and **I-10** run east-west, and **I-25** cuts roughly down the center, north-south. Denver, Colorado, to Santa Fe is 450 miles, about a 6-hour drive; add another hour to reach Albuquerque. El Paso, Texas, to Albuquerque is 275 miles, about 4 hours. Coming from Flagstaff, Arizona, Albuquerque is 325 miles along I-40, about 4.5

---

hours; from Amarillo, Texas, it's just slightly less distance in the other direction.

Southwest road-trippers often combine New Mexico with southwestern Colorado, in which case **U.S. 550** makes a good route south from Durango, and **U.S. 84** runs from Pagosa Springs. From Tucson, Arizona, a nice route into New Mexico is to cut north off I-10 at Lordsburg, following Highway 90 to Silver City and winding through the mountains northeast to reach I-25 to Albuquerque.

GETTING AROUND

Practically speaking, you will need a car. Traveling between towns by bus or train is feasible, but it certainly limits what you can see. Within Albuquerque and Santa Fe, you can often get around by walking, biking, or public transport, but getting to or around anywhere smaller requires your own wheels.

Regional Airlines

To cover the longer distances, flying is a possibility; **Boutique Air** (855/268-8478, www.boutiqueair.com) flies from Albuquerque to Los Alamos, Silver City (and from there to

Phoenix), and Carlsbad (connecting on to Dallas). **Great Lakes Airlines** (800/554-5111, www.flygreatlakes.com) flies into Farmington from Colorado.

Bus

Between Santa Fe and Taos (and communities around and in between, including the pueblos), the **North Central Regional Transit District** (866/206-0754, www.ncrtd.org) offers commuter bus service. It's not very frequent, but it's free, and it covers a lot of area, making it an option for the hard-core no-car traveler.

Another option for the dedicated car-avoider, the **Navajo Transit System** (928/729-4002, www.navajotransit.com) can get you around the northwest and into Arizona—with *a lot* of planning.

Greyhound (800/231-2222, www.greyhound.com) connects Albuquerque with Santa Fe and Las Cruces, as well as a few other midsize towns. Anything off the interstate in the southeast will require a transfer in Las Cruces. **El Paso-Los Angeles Limousine Express** (1611 Central Ave. SW, Albuquerque,

ESSENTIALS
TRANSPORTATION

Amtrak stops in Las Vegas.

505/247-8036, www.eplalimo.com) offers good alternative service to Las Cruces.

Train

The **Rail Runner** (866/795-7245, www.riometro.org) commuter train connects Belén, Albuquerque, and Santa Fe, with convenient downtown stations, making a car-free visit quite feasible, or even a day trip. The train passes through odd pockets of Albuquerque and stunning, untouched pueblo lands. Tickets are based on a zone system; the 90-minute ride between downtown Albuquerque and Santa Fe costs $9, or $10 for a day pass. (Kids: Listen for the "meep-meep!" warning as the doors close!)

Via **Amtrak** (800/872-7245, www.amtrak.com), Gallup, Raton, and Las Vegas are feasible destinations from Albuquerque.

Car

Driving New Mexico's scenic byways is definitely one of the pleasures of traveling here. On the other hand, parking in Santa Fe can be difficult, or at least expensive—and you can get around the center of town very easily on foot. So, ideally, you would rent a car only for the days you plan to go out of the city. Central Taos is small, but sights are spread out on the fringes, and only the most dedicated can manage without a car. In Albuquerque, you can live without a car for a few days, but it requires planning and rules out a few of the sights. All of the major car-rental chains are at Albuquerque's airport, in a single building; see the respective city chapters for other rental companies and offices.

All but a few roads are passable year-round. You won't need four-wheel drive, but be prepared in winter for ice and snow anywhere other than central Albuquerque and the southernmost section of the state. Also check your car-rental agreement for restrictions on driving on dirt roads—a rare clause in the United States, but occasionally employed by smaller companies. Needless to say, this is a liability, as it's almost impossible to go

anywhere interesting in New Mexico without winding up on a dirt road.

Get in the habit of topping off your tank. In the southern half of the state, especially along the Mexican border and anywhere away from I-10 and I-25, there are long stretches of smaller roads without gas stations, and prices can range by as much as $0.50 per gallon between convenient city locations and more remote areas. Contrary to logic, fuel is vastly more expensive in the southeastern side of the state around Hobbs and Artesia, where the terrain is dotted with oil derricks.

Bike

With beautiful vistas, often deserted roads, and a strong community of both road cyclists and mountain bikers, New Mexico can be a great place to get around on two wheels,

---

Riding the Rails

Traveling by train in New Mexico, if you have the time to do it, is a rewarding experience. You'll get a great sense of the state's emptiness—as well as what a dramatic change the railroad made when it arrived in 1880. The **Belen Main Street** organization (www.belenmainstreet.org) publishes a map with major sites of train history, along with a suggested seven-day all-train itinerary, visiting Belén, Gallup, Santa Fe, and Las Vegas. It's feasible because Amtrak departs Albuquerque midday, so you arrive at a reasonable hour.

For the corridor between Santa Fe and Belén, the **Rail Runner** commuter train (www.nmrailrunnervacations.com) offers periodic guided day tours, brochures for self-guided exploration, and package deals on hotels and other discounts, when you show your ticket.

Going by train does rule out some parts of the state, but it also opens up whole areas you would never see by car. And nothing's more relaxing than watching the scenery roll by. In the words of one Amtrak fan, "It's like having your own chauffeur!"

Driving Distances

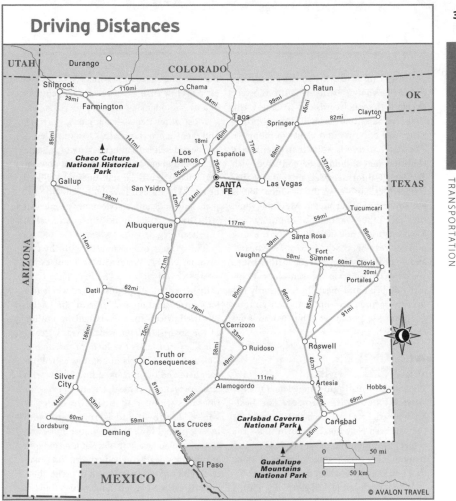

UTAH
Durango
COLORADO
Shiprock
110mi — Chama
Ratun
OK
29mi
Farmington
94mi
99mi
45mi
Clayton
Taos
82mi
Springer
141mi
18mi
46mi
77mi
68mi
Chaco Culture
National Historical
Park
Los
Alamos
Española
137mi
85mi
55mi
25mi
Gallup
SANTA
FE
Las Vegas
TEXAS
San Ysidro
138mi
42mi
64mi
Tucumcari
117mi
59mi
Albuquerque
86mi
Santa Rosa
114mi
39mi
Vaughn
58mi
Fort
Sumner
60mi Clovis
71mi
20mi
Portales
Datil
62mi
Socorro
80mi
96mi
85mi
91mi
78mi
186mi
75mi
Carrizozo
33mi
Ruidoso
Roswell
Truth or
Consequences
58mi
49mi
40mi
Silver
City
111mi
Artesia
Hobbs
Alamogordo
44mi
53mi
81mi
68mi
36mi
69mi
60mi
59mi
Lordsburg
Deming
Las Cruces
Carlsbad Caverns
National Park
Carlsbad
46mi
55mi
0   50 mi
El Paso
Guadalupe
Mountains
National Park
0   50 km
MEXICO
© AVALON TRAVEL
ARIZONA

as long as it's not your main form of transport. Whether you'll be riding your own bike or renting one here, always pack a patch kit, and consider installing tire liners. Goathead thorns and broken glass are particular scourges of the highway shoulder.

Central Albuquerque and Santa Fe are both manageable by bicycle, with separate lanes. Las Cruces is moderately accommodating. In Taos, traffic on the main road can be unpleasantly heavy and fast. But both the Rail Runner and the Taos Express bus service have space for bicycles, so it's possible to take your wheels with you from town to town.

Food

New Mexicans love their food so much, they have been known to enshrine it on lottery tickets, with scratch cards named Chile Cash, Chips and Salsa, and Sopaipilla Dough (promising "lots of honey and plenty of money"). The state cuisine is a distinctive culinary tradition that shouldn't be confused with Tex-Mex, Californian Mex, or south-of-the-border Mexican—even though most locals will say they're going out for "Mexican" when they mean they want a bowl of purely *New* Mexican green-chile stew. (But if you're eating mole or ceviche, that's "*Mexican* Mexican," and you can get more of it the farther south you drive.) New Mexican cuisine doesn't typically do bean-and-meat chili, certainly not mango-flavored anything, and only rarely guacamole—you can get it, but avocados are expensive here.

ALL CHILE, ALL THE TIME

The cuisine's distinguishing element is the **New Mexico chile pepper.** The best-known variety is the Hatch chile, named for the southern New Mexican town that's the center of the industry. In the north, Chimayó is another big chile-producing town, with its own heirloom strain, usually picked red.

When the chile is picked green, it is roasted and peeled, then used whole to make chiles rellenos (stuffed with cheese and fried in batter), or cut into chunks and cooked in sauces or used as the base of a meaty green-chile stew. In northern New Mexico, that sauce is pure chile, maybe thinned with chicken broth; in some towns in the southern part of the state, it's more like a green-chile cream gravy, often with a base of cream-of-mushroom soup.

When the New Mexico chile is left to ripen, then dried in the sun, it turns turn dark red and leathery. These dry red chiles are stored whole, in long chains called *ristras,* or ground into flakes (*chile caribe*) or finer powder to be the base of a sauce or marinade. The heartiest red-chile dish is *carne adovada,* chunks of pork shoulder stewed with pure red sauce.

Most other items—enchiladas, burritos, and eggs (huevos rancheros), to name a few—can be ordered with either variety of chile, so a standard query in restaurants (and now enshrined as the official state question) is "Red or green?" You can have both, splitting the plate half-and-half, a style many people call "Christmas," though old-timers still call it "Mexican flag."

The chile is often coupled with the traditional Native American triad of **corn, squash,** and **beans.** The beans are typically brown, meaty pintos, served whole in a stew or mashed up and "refried" (not actually fried twice—the term is a mistranslation of the Spanish *refrito,* which means "really fried"). Corn takes the form of tortillas as well as hulled kernels of hominy, called posole here and often cooked into a stew with chile, oregano, and meat. Ground corn paste (masa) is whipped with lard (or Crisco, if you're "healthy") and wrapped around a meaty filling, then tied in a corn husk and steamed to make a **tamale.** Squash comes in a common side dish called *calabacitas,* sautéed with onions and a touch of green chile. Spanish settlers brought lamb, which finds its way into tacos and stews.

American Indian cuisine isn't so distinct from what everyone else eats—its one major element is **fry bread,** a round of deep-fried dough served with honey or filled with ground meat, cheese, and lettuce to make an "Indian taco"; a "Navajo taco" often uses shredded lamb or mutton in place of ground beef. Bread baked in a traditional domed adobe *horno* oven is also popular, and the Zuni make a distinctive sourdough this way. In pueblos and on the reservations, you'll see these mud ovens in most yards. Game meat, such as deer, is also a major component of

Red-Chile Sauce

Use only freshly ground New Mexico red chile for this sauce—not the "chile powder" sold in most grocery stores. The sauce will keep in the refrigerator for a month, and you can use it to top eggs or steaks, or devote the whole batch to a tray of enchiladas. (If you're doing the latter, you'll want to keep the sauce relatively thin, so you can easily coat the tortillas with sauce before filling them.) The flavor is best if it is prepared ahead and left to sit overnight.

Yield: 2 cups
½ c. New Mexico red chile powder
½ tsp. ground cumin (optional)
1 tsp. ground coriander (optional)
2 Tbsp. all-purpose flour
2 Tbsp. lard (or vegetable oil)
2 or 3 cloves garlic, crushed or minced
2 c. chicken stock or water
1 tsp. dried oregano (optional)

Measure the chile, cumin, coriander, and flour into a heavy-bottomed saucepan and place over medium-high heat. Stir continuously until the spices are just fragrant and the flour has darkened slightly. Remove the chile-flour mix to a small bowl. Heat the lard or oil in the pan, and add the garlic and stir until fragrant. Then stir the chile-flour mix into the oil-garlic mixture—you will have a very coarse paste. Stirring constantly, slowly add half of the stock or water. Continue stirring, and the mixture will thicken and become velvety. Add the remaining stock or water and the oregano, mix well, turn heat to low, and let sauce simmer for about 20 minutes, until it is somewhat reduced and thickened to your liking. If the mixture becomes too thick, simply add more water.

ESSENTIALS
FOOD

American Indian cooking, though you'll rarely see it in restaurants.

Green chile makes its way into standard American fare as well. It's a popular pizza topping (great with pepperoni or ham), and the **green-chile cheeseburger** is a top choice everywhere. Also look out for **breakfast burritos,** big flour tortillas filled with scrambled eggs, hash browns, and some kind of meat—bacon, crumbled sausage, or sometimes Mexican chorizo, a spicy pork sausage. Some places sell them as to-go food, wrapped in foil with green chile added to the mix. At sit-down places, you get the whole construction smothered in either red or green chile.

Sopaipillas are another New Mexican specialty. They're palm-sized pillows of deep-fried dough, used to mop up chile and beans during the main meal, then slathered with honey for dessert. In a disturbing trend, some restaurants now offer a honey-flavored corn syrup, because it's cheaper and doesn't crystallize—if you encounter this, complain at top volume.

Bizcochitos, little anise-laced cookies, are the state's official sweet treat. Wash it all down with a **margarita,** which purists insist should involve only lime, tequila, and triple sec and be served on the rocks in a salt-rimmed glass. (Restaurants with only a beer-and-wine license often offer an agave-wine margarita—decent flavor, but pretty weak.)

HOW TO TAKE THE HEAT

When your server plunks down a heavy white ceramic plate covered in chile and melted cheese, the words "this plate is very hot" cover only half of the story. Every year the harvest varies a bit, and the chile can be mild or so spicy as to blister lips and produce a dizzying (and addictive) endorphin rush. Locals look back on particularly incendiary seasons with that mixture of awe, fear, and longing that junkies reserve for their best scores. In general, green chile tends to be hotter than red, but it's best to ask your server what to expect—some restaurants specialize in one or the other.

You can protect yourself against chile-heat by ordering a side of sour cream with your enchiladas or burrito—although be warned that many consider this a "Texan" affectation, and you may be derided by your fellow diners. Locals usually just reach for a **sopaipilla,** the starch from which can absorb some of the chile oils. Don't gulp down water, which only spreads the searing oils around your mouth. Beer is a marginal improvement, and margaritas are at least distracting.

FINE DINING AND WINE

While there are plenty of time-warp diners and mom-and-pop hole-in-the-wall joints in New Mexico, dining can also be very sophisticated, keeping pace with the national trend toward local and organic produce. This movement hasn't been such a huge leap here: Many small family farms didn't have to "go organic," because they were never very industrialized in the first place. At white-tablecloth places, Southwestern fusion is still common, with chile working its way into foie gras appetizers and even high-concept desserts.

The fine dining scene is enhanced by a burgeoning wine industry, initiated by Spanish settlers in the 17th century but enjoying a resurgence since the 1980s. Gruet Winery in Albuquerque is the best-known New Mexico producer, especially for its excellent sparkling wine. This makes for a nice little perk of New Mexico dining: You can get inexpensive bubbly by the glass almost everywhere. The **New Mexico Wine Growers Association** (www. nmwine.com) has information on more wineries, and you can read more about the high-end and organic food scene in *Local Flavor* (www.localflavormagazine.com), a monthly tabloid, and the bimonthly *Edible Santa Fe* (www.ediblesantafe.com).

VEGETARIAN FOOD

New Mexican food isn't meat-centric, but strict vegetarians will have to be vigilant, as many chile dishes are traditionally made with beef or chicken stock as well as lard for flavoring. The closer you get to Texas, the more likely it is that red chile sauce will contain bits of meat. Decades of hippie influence, though, have resulted in many menus stating clearly whether the chile is meatless. Some restaurants have an unreconstructed 1970s worldview, with alfalfa sprouts and squash casseroles galore.

hot fry bread at Jemez Pueblo

Accommodations

Throughout the book, distinctive choices— bed-and-breakfasts, lodges, and small, independently owned hotels and motels—are emphasized over chain options as much as possible. Just because the chains are not listed doesn't mean they're not available—and in many small towns, they're the only solid option.

The prices listed are the official high-season rack rates—that is, what you'd pay if you just walked in off the street, with no discounts; tax is not included. Most often, the numbers are the least expensive room for one person in one bed (a single, abbreviated *s*) and two people in two beds (a double, abbreviated *d*). **High season** is usually June-August. **Ski season** is January-March; prices in Taos and Santa Fe don't completely bottom out—but they are still cheaper than summer. Expect higher rates in the week following Christmas and during special events, such as Indian Market in Santa Fe and Balloon Fiesta in Albuquerque, but overall you will be able to secure lower rates than those listed simply by looking online or calling the hotel directly.

Note that while many hotels tout their swimming pools, they are often forced to leave them empty due to water restrictions imposed during droughts. If you've booked at a hotel specifically for the pool, call to check the status before your trip, so you don't wind up paying a premium for a service you can't use. Santa Fe is the strictest area in the state, and it also limits hotels to changing towels and bed linens only every four days during your visit.

Religious Retreats

Christ in the Desert Monastery

One quirk of New Mexico is that the area harbors an exceptionally high number of religious retreats of all stripes, set in some of the most scenic, quiet areas. Most of them welcome guests, with no religious strings attached. Facilities are usually basic but comfortable, and rates (suggested donations, officially) are very reasonable, especially for solo travelers, and often include meals. Look for the following properties:

- **Bodhi Manda Zen Center:** Buddhist retreat in Jemez Springs (page 67)

- **Quaker Meeting House:** A single charming guesthouse, in Santa Fe (page 105)

- **Ghost Ranch:** A large Presbyterian retreat in Abiquiu, the most secular-feeling of the bunch (page 123)

- **Christ in the Desert Monastery:** Very remote, outside Abiquiu (page 123)

- **Our Lady of Guadalupe Abbey:** In the town of Pecos (page 186)

- **The Monastery of Our Lady of the Desert:** in the northwest, east of Farmington (page 251)

Travel Tips

TOURIST INFORMATION

For pre-trip inspiration, the New Mexico Tourism Board publishes the monthly *New Mexico* magazine (www.nmmagazine.com), which does an excellent job covering both mainstream attractions and more obscure corners of the state.

Many smaller towns' chambers of commerce can also be extremely helpful.

If you plan to do a lot of hiking, you can order detailed topographical maps from the **National Forest Service** office in New Mexico (505/842-3292) or from the Bureau of Land Management's **Public Lands Information Center** (www.publiclands.org). Santa Fe's **Travel Bug** (839 Paseo de Peralta, 505/992-0418, 7:30am-5:30pm Mon.-Sat., 11am-4pm Sun.) bookstore also stocks maps.

Telephone and Internet

Albuquerque, Santa Fe, Los Alamos, Gallup, and Farmington use the area code 505, while the rest of the state's numbers start with 575.

For mobile phone reception, the corridor between Albuquerque and Santa Fe is fine, but in rural areas, phones on the GSM network (AT&T, T-Mobile) get very poor or no reception. Data service is equally spotty. If you'll be spending a lot of time outside of the cities or counting on your phone for emergencies, you might consider a CDMA phone (Verizon is best). Likewise, don't count on data service on your smartphone.

Internet access is widespread, though DSL and other high-speed service is still not necessarily the norm, and thick adobe walls can be a hindrance for wireless signals. Rural areas still rely on satellite Internet, which can be poor in bad weather. In the cities, cafés often have hotspots, and the city of Albuquerque even maintains a few free ones in public spaces, such as the Old Town plaza.

Time Zone

New Mexico is in the **mountain time** zone, one hour ahead of the West Coast of the United States and two hours behind the East Coast. It's -7 GMT (Greenwich Mean Time) during the winter and -6 GMT in summer, when Daylight Saving Time is followed statewide.

Note that neighboring Arizona does not follow Daylight Saving Time, which can lead to confusion around the border.

CONDUCT AND CUSTOMS

New Mexico is a part of the United States, but it can sometimes feel quite foreign, particularly in the high mountain Spanish villages and in the Indian pueblos. Regardless, basic courtesy rules and, in smaller communities, modest dress are appreciated, especially at the older Catholic churches.

Some Pueblo Indians, as well as Navajo, find loud voices, direct eye contact, and firm handshakes off-putting and, by the same token, may not express themselves in the forthright way a lot of visitors are used to. Similarly, a subdued reaction doesn't necessarily mean a lack of enthusiasm.

New Mexico is not a wealthy state, and the gap between rich and poor can be wide. In general, people don't appreciate conspicuous displays of wealth, and it's doubly rude to flash cash, fancy gadgets, and jewelry in tiny villages and pueblos (and public cell-phone use is still considered tacky most places). Be thoughtful when taking photos, particularly of people's homes—always ask permission, and consider that some of the more "scenic" elements of New Mexico are also the products of poverty, which some people may not be proud to have captured on film.

You can help the local economy by favoring

New Mexican-owned businesses, rather than chain operations, and buying directly from artisans wherever possible. In these situations, don't get too bent on bargaining. The item you're buying represents not just raw materials and hours of work, but a person's particular talent, skill, and heritage. Insisting on an extra-low price belittles not just the item, but the artisan as well.

Pueblo and Reservation Etiquette

When visiting pueblos and reservations, remember that you are not at a tourist attraction—you are walking around someone's neighborhood. So peeking in windows and wandering off the suggested route isn't polite. If you want to take photos, you'll usually need a camera permit, for an additional fee. Always ask permission before taking photos of people, and ask parents, rather than children, for their consent. All pueblos ban alcohol.

Some pueblos are more welcoming than others. San Ildefonso, for instance, is open year-round, whereas Jemez is completely closed except for some feast days. So it's flawed logic to seek out the less-visited places or go in the off times in order to have a less "touristy" experience. In fact, the most rewarding time to visit *is* on a big feast day—you may not be the only tourist there, but you have a better chance of being invited into a local's home.

CLASSES AND VOLUNTEERING

From afternoon cooking workshops to intensives on adobe building techniques, the opportunities to learn in northern New Mexico are broad.

General Education

Look first into the art, music, and outdoors programs at **Ghost Ranch** (877/804-4678, www.ghostranch.org), the beautiful property in Abiquiu. Santa Fe and Albuquerque are both home to renowned alternative healing,

herbal medicine, and massage schools, more than can be listed here; visit **Natural Healers** (www.naturalhealers.com) for a list.

Arts and Crafts

Taos in particular is a hotbed for art classes. **Fechin Art Workshops** (575/751-0647, www.fineartservices.info) are five-day live-in retreats that have been running for more than two decades; they are based in Taos Ski Valley. The equally long-established **Taos Art School** (575/758-0350, www.taosartschool.org) focuses on landscape techniques, in six-day painting or photo workshops that include hiking and rafting options.

For crafts, Taos is also the place to be: **Weaving Southwest** (575/758-0433, www.weavingsouthwest.com) gives three-day workshops on Navajo frame looms. **Taos School of Metalsmithing and Lapidary Design** (575/758-0207, www.taosjewelryschool.com) covers a range of jewelry-making topics, starting with half-day sessions.

In Albuquerque, **Casa Flamenca** (505/247-0622, www.casaflamenca.org) offers classes in flamenco dance and classical Spanish guitar.

Cooking

Santa Fe School of Cooking (125 N. Guadalupe St., 505/983-4511, www.santafeschoolofcooking.com) offers day classes in contemporary Southwestern cuisine, as well as traditional Native American cooking and New Mexican standards; nice farmers market trips and restaurant walking tours are offered too.

In Dixon, **Comida de Campos** (505/852-0017, www.comidadecampos.com) offers classes on cooking in a traditional outdoor *horno,* and occasionally on clay-pot cooking, all in a beautiful farm setting.

Permaculture and Alternative Construction

In Albuquerque, **The Old School** (www.

Adobe construction is a New Mexican art form.

abqoldschool.com) teaches skills such as canning, quilting, and building solar phone chargers. If you're interested in New Mexico's solar architecture movement, you can enroll in the monthlong intensive **Earthship Academy** (575/751-0462, www.earthship.org), a crash course in building the off-the-grid rammed-earth houses that have their roots in Taos. The Earthship Biotecture organization also accepts volunteers. For more on local building styles, look into the semester-long classes in adobe construction at **Northern New Mexico College** (575/581-4115, www.nnmc.edu).

FOREIGN TRAVELERS

As for any destination in the United States, check before departure whether you'll need a **visa** to enter; most European nationals do not need one.

New Mexico uses the **United States dollar,** and currency exchange is available at most banks as well as in better hotels, though the rates in the latter case will not be as good. For the best rates and convenience, withdraw cash from your home account through **automatic teller machines** (ATMs); check first, though, what fee your home bank and

the ATM's bank will charge you for the transaction, including any fee for a foreign-currency transaction.

Tipping is similar to elsewhere in the country: 15 percent to cab drivers, and 15-20 percent on restaurant bills. For larger groups, often restaurants will add 18 percent or so to the bill; this is suggested, and you may refuse it or write in a lower amount if service was poor. Add $1 or so per drink when ordered at the bar; $1 or $2 to staff who handle your luggage in hotels; and $3-5 per day to housekeeping in hotels—envelopes are often left in rooms for this purpose. **Bargaining** is acceptable only if you're dealing directly with an artisan, and even then, it is often politely deflected. But it doesn't hurt to ask, nicely, if the quoted price is the best possible one.

Electricity is 120 volts, with a two-prong, flat-head plug, the same as Canada and Mexico.

ACCESS FOR TRAVELERS WITH DISABILITIES

Wheelchair access can be frustrating in some historic properties and on the narrower sidewalks of Santa Fe and Taos, but in most other respects, travelers with disabilities should find no more problems in New Mexico than elsewhere in the United States. Public buses are wheelchair accessible, an increasing number of hotels have ADA-compliant rooms, and you can even get out in nature a bit on paved trails such as the Santa Fe Canyon Preserve loop and the Paseo del Bosque in Albuquerque.

If you'll be visiting a number of wilderness areas, consider the National Park Service's **Access Pass** (888/467-2757, www.nps.gov), a free lifetime pass that grants admission for the pass-holder and three adults to all national parks, national forests, and the like, as well as discounts on interpretive services, camping fees, fishing licenses, and more. Apply in person at any federally managed park or wilderness area; you must show medical documentation of blindness or permanent disability.

TRAVELING WITH CHILDREN

Though the specific prices are not listed in this guide, admission at major attractions is almost always lower for children than for adults. Your little ones will be welcome in most environments, the only exceptions being a few of the more formal restaurants in Santa Fe and Albuquerque. Kids are sure to be fascinated by ceremonial dances at the pueblos, but be prepared with distractions, because long waits are the norm. Prep children with information about American Indian culture, and brief them on the basic etiquette at dances, which applies to them as well. Kids will also enjoy river rafting (relaxing "floats" along placid sections of the Rio Grande and Rio Chama are good for younger ones). For skiing, Taos Ski Valley has a very strong program of classes for youngsters.

SENIOR TRAVELERS

Senior discounts are available at most museums and other attractions. If you'll be visiting a number of wilderness areas, look into a **Senior Pass** ($10), a lifetime pass for people 62 and older that grants free admission for the pass-holder and three additional adults to national parks, National Forest Service lands, and many other areas, as well as discounts on activities such as camping and boat-launching. The pass can be purchased in person at any federally managed wilderness area, or online with an additional $10 processing fee; for more information, contact the **National Park Service** (888/467-2757, www.nps.gov).

Road Scholar (800/454-5768, www.roadscholar.org) runs more than 20 reasonably priced group trips in northern New Mexico, from a five-day general introduction to Santa Fe history to more focused tours focusing on the history of crypto-Jews, for instance, or ancestral Puebloan culture.

GAY AND LESBIAN TRAVELERS

Gay marriage was legalized in New Mexico in late 2013, but Santa Fe has been one of the major gay capitals in the United States for decades, second only to San Francisco in the per-capita rates of same-sex coupledom. There are no designated "gay-borhoods" (unless you count RainbowVision Santa Fe, a retirement community) or even particular bar scenes. Instead, gay men and lesbian women are well integrated throughout town, running businesses and serving on the city council. The city's Pride parade is usually in late June, and is preceded by several big events.

Albuquerque also has a decent gay scene, especially if you want to go clubbing, which is not an option in quieter Santa Fe. As for smaller towns and pueblos, they're still significantly more conservative.

Gay culture in the state isn't all about cute shops and cabarets. One big event is the annual **Zia Regional Rodeo,** sponsored by the **New Mexico Gay Rodeo Association** (505/720-3749, www.nmgra.org). It takes place every summer (July or August), with all the standard rodeo events, plus goat dressing and a wild drag race.

Health and Safety

Visitors to New Mexico face several unique health concerns. First and foremost are the environmental hazards of **dehydration, sunburn,** and **altitude sickness.** The desert climate, glaring sun, and thinner atmosphere conspire to fry your skin and drain you of all moisture. (On the plus side, sweat evaporates immediately.) Apply SPF 30 sunscreen daily, even in winter, and try to drink at least a liter of water a day, whether you feel thirsty or not. (Request water in restaurants—it's usually brought only on demand, to cut down on waste.) By the time you start feeling thirsty, you're already seriously dehydrated and at risk of further bad effects: headaches, nausea, and dizziness, all of which can become full-blown, life-threatening **heatstroke** if left untreated. Heatstroke can happen even without serious exertion—just lack of water and very hot sun. So if you're feeling at all woozy or cranky (another common symptom), head for shade and sip a Gatorade or similar electrolyte-replacement drink.

Staying hydrated also staves off the effects of the high elevation, to which most visitors will not be acclimated. The mildest reaction to being 7,000 feet or more above sea level is lethargy or light-headedness—you will probably sleep long and soundly on your first night in New Mexico. Some people do have more severe reactions, such as a piercing headache or intense nausea, especially if they engage in strenuous physical activity. Unfortunately, there's no good way to judge how your body will react, so give yourself a few days to adjust, with a light schedule and plenty of time to sleep.

More obscure hazards include **West Nile virus** (wear a DEET-based insect repellent if you're down along the river in the summer);

hantavirus, an extremely rare pulmonary ailment transmitted by rodents; and the even rarer **bubonic plague** (aka the Black Death), the very same disease that killed millions of Europeans in the Middle Ages. Luckily, only a case or two of the plague crops up every year, and it's easily treated if diagnosed early. **Lyme disease** is almost as rare, as deer ticks do not flourish in the mountains.

If you'll be spending a lot of time hiking or camping, take precautions against **giardiasis** and other waterborne ailments by boiling your water or treating it with iodine or a SteriPen (www.steripen.com), as even the clearest mountain waterways may have been tainted by cows upstream. **Snake bites** are also a hazard in the wild, so wear boots that cover your ankles, stay on trails, and keep your hands and feet out of odd holes and cracks between rocks. Only the Western diamondback rattlesnake is aggressive when disturbed; other snakes typically will not bite if you simply back away quietly.

General **outdoor safety rules** apply: Don't hike by yourself, always register with the ranger station when heading out overnight, and let friends know where you're going and when you'll be back. Pack a good topographical map and a compass or GPS device; people manage to get lost even when hiking in the foothills, and if you're at all dehydrated or dizzy from the altitude, any disorientation can be magnified to a disastrous degree. Also pack layers of clothing, and be prepared for cold snaps and snow at higher elevations, even in the summer.

CRIME AND DRUGS

Recreational drug use is not uncommon in New Mexico—generally in a relatively benign form, with marijuana fairly widespread. (Former governor and Republican presidential candidate Gary Johnson, though no longer a user himself, has been a strenuous advocate for its legalization.) But as in much of the rural United States, crystal methamphetamine is an epidemic, and some villages in northern New Mexico have also been devastated by heroin use, with overdose deaths at a rate several hundred times higher than the national average. None of this affects travelers, except that petty theft, especially in isolated areas such as trailheads, can be an issue. Always lock your car doors, and secure any valuables in the trunk. Don't leave anything enticing in view.

Drinking and driving is unfortunately still common, especially in rural areas; be particularly alert when driving at night. A distressing number of crosses along the roadside (*descansos*) mark the sites of fatal car accidents, many of which had alcohol involved.

Resources

Glossary

abierto: Spanish for "open"

acequia: irrigation ditch, specifically one regulated by the traditional Spanish method, maintained by a *mayordomo,* or "ditch boss," who oversees how much water each shareholder receives

adobe: building material of sun-dried bricks made of a mix of mud, sand, clay, and straw

arroyo: stream or dry gully where mountain runoff occasionally flows

asado: stew (usually pork) with red-chile sauce

atrio: churchyard between the boundary wall and the church entrance, usually used as a cemetery

bizcochito: anise-laced shortbread, traditionally made with lard

bosque: Spanish for "forest," specifically the cottonwoods and trees along a river

bulto: three-dimensional wood carving, typically of a saint

caldera: basin or crater formed by a collapsed volcano

canal: water drain from a flat roof; pl. *canales*

carne adovada: pork chunks marinated in red chile, then braised; meatier and dryer than *asado*

cerrado: Spanish for "closed"

chicharrón: fried pork skin, usually with a layer of meat still attached

chile: not to be confused with Texas chili, Cincinnati chili, or any other American concoction; refers to the fruit of the chile plant itself, eaten green (picked unripe and then roasted) or red (ripened and dried)

chimichanga: deep-fried burrito; allegedly invented in Arizona

colcha: style of blanket, in which loom-woven wool is embellished with long strands of wool embroidery

concha belt: belt made of stamped, carved silver medallions; concha is Spanish for "shell"; also concho

convento: residential compound adjoining a mission church

enchilada: corn tortilla dipped in chile sauce, filled with cheese or meat, and topped with more chile; can be served either rolled or flat (stacked in layers)

farolito: in Santa Fe and Taos, a luminaria

GCCB: common abbreviation for green-chile cheeseburger

genízaro: during Spanish colonial times, a detribalized Indian (usually due to having been taken as a slave) who lived with Spaniards and followed Catholic tradition

gordita: a variation on the taco, with a thicker tortilla-like shell, sometimes deep-fried; these are a more traditionally Mexican dish (though in that case rarely fried) and are available only in the southern part of the state

heishi: fine disk-shaped beads carved from shells

horno: traditional dome-shaped adobe oven

jerga: Spanish-style wool blanket or rug, loosely woven and barely decorated, meant for daily use

kachina: ancestral spirit of the Pueblo people as well as the carved figurine representing the spirit; also spelled "katsina"

kiva: sacred ceremonial space in a pueblo, at least partially underground and entered by a hole in the ceiling *latillas:* thin saplings cut and laid across vigas to make a solid ceiling

lowrider: elaborately painted and customized car with hydraulic lifts

luminaria: in Albuquerque, lantern made of a sand-filled paper bag with a votive candle set inside; in Santa Fe and Taos, refers to small bonfires lit during the Christmas season

menudo: tripe soup, said to be good for curing a hangover

morada: meeting space of the Penitente brotherhood

nicho: small niche in an adobe wall, usually meant to hold a santo

Penitente: member of a long-established Catholic brotherhood in northern New Mexico

petroglyph: rock carving

pictograph: painting on a rock surface

piñon: any of several fragrant varieties of pine tree that grow in New Mexico

portal: the covered sidewalk area in front of a traditional adobe structure; pl. *portales*

posole: stew of hulled corn (hominy), pork, and a little chile, either green or red

pueblo: Spanish for "village," referring to the various communities of American Indians settled in the Rio Grande Valley, as well as the larger land area owned by the community (preferable to the term "reservation"); also, capitalized, the people themselves, though they speak several different languages

rajas: rough-hewn slats laid over vigas to form a ceiling; also, strips of roasted chile

ramada: simple structure built of four sapling posts and topped with additional saplings laid flat to form a shade structure and a place to hang things to dry

reredos: altar screen, usually elaborately painted or carved with various portraits of Christ and the saints

retablo: flat portrait of a saint, painted or carved in low relief, usually on wood

ristra: string of dried red chiles

santero/santera: craftsperson who produces santos

santo: portrait of a saint, either flat (a *retablo*) or three-dimensional (a *bulto*)

sipapu: hole in the floor of a kiva, signifying the passage to the spirit world

sopaipilla: square of puffed fried dough, served with the main meal for wiping up sauces and with honey for dessert

tamale: corn husk filled with masa (hominy paste) and a dab of meat, vegetables, or cheese, then steamed; usually made in large quantities for holidays

terrón: building material of bricks cut out of sod and dried in the sun, similar to adobe, but less common

Tewa: language spoken by the majority of Pueblo Indians; others in the Rio Grande Valley speak Tiwa, Towa, and Keresan

torreón: round defensive tower built in Spanish colonial times

vato: cool Chicano, usually driving a lowrider

viga: ceiling beam made of a single tree trunk

zaguán: long central hallway

Suggested Reading

ART AND CULTURE

Clark, Willard. *Remembering Santa Fe.* Layton, UT: Gibbs Smith, 2004. A small hardback edition of selections from the Boston artist who stopped off in Santa Fe in 1928. He stayed to learn printmaking and produce this series of etchings depicting city life.

Eaton, Robert. *The Lightning Field.* Boulder, CO: Johnson Books, 1995. Eaton served as a forest ranger in Chaco Canyon for five years, so his eye is for the empty and the starkly beautiful destinations around the state, including the art installation of the title (in Quemado, in western New Mexico).

His essays, each focusing on a different destination, combine history and strong description. Seek this title out if you want to get well off the usual track.

Lamadrid, Enrique. *Hermanitos Comanchitos: Indo-Hispano Rituals of Captivity and Redemption.* Albuquerque: University of New Mexico Press, 2003. Fascinating documentation, in descriptive prose and rich black-and-white photos, of the traditional Spanish dances of northern New Mexico, such as Los Comanches and Los Matachines.

Lummis, Charles F. *A Tramp Across the Continent.* Lincoln: University of Nebraska Press, 1982. In 1884, fledgling journalist Lummis decided to walk from Cincinnati to his new job in Los Angeles; this book chronicles his trip. The sections on New Mexico shine, and Lummis was so entranced that he later moved to the territory. He was the first to write stories about the Penitente brotherhood in the national press.

Myers, Joan. *Pie Town Woman: The Hard Life and Good Times of a New Mexico Homesteader.* Albuquerque: University of New Mexico Press, 2001. The biography of a woman captured in famous Farm Security Administration photos from 1940, this book also muses on the power of memory and photography.

Padilla, Carmella, and Juan Estevan Arellano. *Low 'n Slow: Lowriding in New Mexico.* Santa Fe: Museum of New Mexico Press, 2005. Lovingly lurid color photographs by Jack Parsons are the centerpiece of this book, which pays tribute to New Mexico's Latino car culture—an art form that has even landed a Chimayó lowrider in the Smithsonian.

Parhad, Elisa. *New Mexico: A Guide for the Eyes.* Los Angeles: EyeMuse Books, 2009. Informative short essays on the distinctive

things you see in New Mexico and then wonder what the backstory is: concha belts, beat-up pickup trucks, blue sky. The richly illustrated book makes good pre-trip reading or a souvenir when you return.

Price, Roberta. *Across the Great Divide: A Photo Chronicle of the Counterculture.* Albuquerque: University of New Mexico Press, 2010. Documentary photographer Price "went native" with a Colorado commune in the 1960s and visited several groups in New Mexico. She also wrote the narrative *Huerfano: A Memoir of Life in the Counterculture* (Amherst: University of Massachusetts Press, 2004).

Price, V. B. *Albuquerque: A City at the End of the World.* Albuquerque: University of New Mexico Press, 2003. Journalist and poet Price writes a travel guide to New Mexico's biggest metropolis but disguises it as a discourse on urban theory, recommending his favorite spots in the context of the city's unique position and growth processes. Black-and-white photographs by Kirk Gittings highlight the stark landscape.

Robinson, Roxana. *Georgia O'Keeffe: A Life.* Lebanon, NH: University Press of New England, 1998. A strong and intimate biography, focusing on the celebrated painter's role as a protofeminist and her difficult relationships.

FOOD

Feucht, Andrea. *Food Lovers' Guide to Santa Fe, Albuquerque & Taos.* Guilford, CT: Globe Pequot, 2012. A good companion for adventurous eaters, with especially good coverage of Albuquerque's more obscure ethnic restaurants.

Frank, Lois Ellen. *Foods of the Southwest Indian Nations.* Berkeley, CA: Ten Speed Press, 2002. Beautiful photographs are a highlight of this thorough documentation of a little-covered cuisine. They help make an ancient culinary tradition accessible and modern without subjecting it to a heavy-handed fusion treatment. For good reason, it earned a James Beard Award.

Kagel, Katharine. *Cooking with Café Pasqual's: Recipes from Santa Fe's Renowned Corner Cafe.* Berkeley, CA: Ten Speed Press, 2006. Re-create your best meals from the legendary restaurant that set the standard for Santa Fe fusion cooking. Chef Kagel is a charming contrarian too, which makes for great reading.

HISTORY

Childs, Craig. *House of Rain: Tracking a Vanished Civilization Across the American Southwest.* New York: Little, Brown, 2007. The story of the Ancestral Puebloans (Anasazi), as told by a curious naturalist, becomes less a solution to an archaeological puzzle than a meditation of why we romanticize "lost" civilizations. His more recent book, *Finders Keepers: A Tale of Archaeological Plunder and Possession* (Little, Brown, 2010), takes the drama to the academy, with tales of scholarly intrigue.

Egan, Timothy. *The Worst Hard Time: The Untold Story of Those Who Survived the Great American Dust Bowl.* New York: Mariner Books, 2006. The town of Clayton features a bit in the pages of this highly readable history that conveys the misery and environmental folly of the period.

Held, E. B. *A Spy's Guide to Santa Fe and Albuquerque.* Albuquerque: University of New Mexico Press, 2011. A former CIA agent reveals nefarious Cold War intrigue—fascinating details, if not so grippingly told.

Hordes, Stanley. *To the End of the Earth: A History of the Crypto-Jews of New Mexico.* New York: Columbia University Press, 2008. An exhaustive but intriguing account of the Jewish families who fled the Inquisition and lived in the Southwest as Catholic converts.

The communities, some still practicing distinctly Jewish rituals, came to light only a few decades ago.

Horgan, Paul. *Great River.* Middletown, CT: Wesleyan University Press, 1991. Two enormous tomes (*Vol. 1: The Indians and Spain* and *Vol. 2: Mexico and the United States*) won the Pulitzer Prize for history. They're packed with drama, on a base of meticulous analysis of primary sources.

Martinez, Esther. *My Life in San Juan Pueblo.* Champaign: University of Illinois Press, 2004. Born in 1912, Martinez has a lot of stories to tell. This free-flowing book incorporates her memories with larger pueblo folklore, and a CD with recordings of some of her stories is included.

Poling-Kempes, Lesley. *Valley of Shining Stone: The Story of Abiquiu.* Tucson: University of Arizona Press, 1997. Georgia O'Keeffe fans will like the personal stories of those in her circle in the 1930s, while historians will appreciate the detailed, linear second half of the book, about the transformation of this remote valley into an artists' haven.

Sides, Hampton. *Blood and Thunder: An Epic of the American West.* New York: Doubleday, 2006. Working from the story of Kit Carson and the campaign against the Navajo, including the Long Walk, Sides tells the gripping story of the entire American West. He's an excellent storyteller, and the 480 pages flow by in a rush of land grabs, battles on horseback, and brutality on all sides.

Simmons, Marc. *New Mexico: An Interpretive History.* Albuquerque: University of New Mexico Press, 1988. The state's historian laureate presents an easy, concise overview of the major historical events. Also look into his more specialized titles, such as *The Last Conquistador: Juan de Oñate and the*

Settling of the Far Southwest (Norman: University of Oklahoma Press, 1993).

Smith, Mike. *Towns of the Sandia Mountains*. Charleston, SC: Arcadia, 2006. This slim volume of vintage photographs and juicy stories in extended captions is about a very specific region, but it could tell the story of much of New Mexico in its shift to modernity.

Usner, Donald J. *Sabino's Map: Life in Chimayó's Old Plaza*. Santa Fe: Museum of New Mexico Press, 1995. A balanced and gracefully written history of the author's hometown, illustrated with fond photos of all the craggy-faced characters involved.

LITERATURE AND MEMOIR

Anaya, Rudolfo. *Bless Me, Ultima*. New York: Warner, 1994. Anaya's story of a young boy coming of age in New Mexico in the 1940s is beautifully told. The book, first published in 1973, launched Anaya into his role as Chicano literary hero; his later books, such as *Alburquerque* (1992), are not quite so touching, but they have a lot of historical and ethnic detail.

Blume, Judy. *Tiger Eyes*. New York: Delacorte, 2010. A young girl with family troubles relocates to Los Alamos, giving a great teen's-eye view on the landscape of New Mexico.

Connors, Philip. *Fire Season: Field Notes from a Wilderness Lookout*. New York: Ecco, 2012. In the tradition of Edward Abbey, this memoir recounts life in a remote fire tower in the Gila Wilderness.

Evans, Max. *Hi-Lo to Hollywood: A Max Evans Reader*. Lubbock, TX: Texas Tech University Press, 1998. Prolific Western author Evans coined the term "Hi-Lo Country" for the "high lonesome" eastern plains of New Mexico, and all of his works, whether essay or fiction, somehow reflect the rolling expanse and the particular dilemmas of the modern cowboys who work on them. A ranch kid himself, he has an eye for detail and a direct and affectionate tone; this reader includes many of his own favorite pieces.

Goodman, Tanya Ward. *Leaving Tinkertown*. Albuquerque: University of New Mexico Press, 2013. A poignant memoir of growing up in the wondrous folk-art assemblage outside Albuquerque. The author's father, Ross Ward, died of early-onset Alzheimer's disease, and this book logs that medical tale, unflinchingly, alongside the larger-than-life artist's own story.

Hillerman, Tony. *Skinwalkers*. New York: HarperTorch, 1990. Hillerman's breakout detective novel, set on the Navajo Nation, weaves a fascinating amount of lore into the plot—which comes in handy when Tribal Affairs police Joe Leaphorn and Jim Chee investigate homicides. Hillerman spun Leaphorn and Chee into a successful franchise, and all of the books show the same cultural depth.

Nichols, John. *The Milagro Beanfield War*. New York: Owl Books, 2005. A comic novel about water rights, set in a northern New Mexico village. Nichols's visionary environmental nonfiction in *On the Mesa* (Layton, UT: Gibbs Smith, 2005) is also stunning.

Pillsbury, Dorothy. *Roots in Adobe*. Santa Fe: Lightning Tree Press, 1983. Pillsbury's charming stories capture the strangeness and warmth of Santa Fe culture in the 1940s. The author tells hilarious stories of settling into her little home and the characters she meets.

Quade, Kirstin Valdez. *Night at the Fiestas*. New York: W. W. Norton, 2015. Quade, who grew up in New Mexico, sets many of the short stories in this collection in tiny Hispano towns, amid the most intense belief and ritual. A great mix of cultural detail and poignant characters.

Silko, Leslie Marmon. *Ceremony.* New York: Penguin, 1988. Silko's classic novel about the impact of the atomic bomb on Native Americans' worldview (and that of all Americans) is brutal, beautiful, and bleak.

NATURE AND THE ENVIRONMENT

Coltrin, Mike. *Sandia Mountain Hiking Guide.* Albuquerque: University of New Mexico Press, 2005. A print version of Coltrin's meticulously maintained website (www.sandiahiking.com), with thorough trail descriptions, GPS coordinates, and a foldout map of the east and west slopes of the mountain.

Julyan, Robert, and Mary Stuever, eds. *Field Guide to the Sandia Mountains.* Albuquerque: University of New Mexico Press, 2005. A thorough guide illustrated with color photographs, detailing birds, animals, plants, even insects of the Sandias. Most of it applies to the Santa Fe area too.

Kricher, John. *A Field Guide to Rocky Mountain and Southwest Forests.* New York: Houghton Mifflin Harcourt, 2003. A Peterson Field Guide, covering both flora and fauna: trees, birds, mammals, you name it. It's illustrated with both color photos and drawings. It's not encyclopedic, but it's a great basic reference. Peterson guides are also available for narrower categories such as reptiles and amphibians or butterflies.

McFarland, Casey, and S. David Scott. *Bird Feathers: A Guide to North American Species.* Mechanicsburg, PA: Stackpole Books, 2010. While not New Mexico-specific, it is the only guide of its kind, and its authors grew up in the state and know the birdlife well. Great for serious birders and curious hikers, with detailed photographs.

Price, V. B. *The Orphaned Land: New Mexico's Environment Since the Manhattan Project.* Albuquerque: University of New Mexico Press, 2011. Journalist Price examines New Mexico's droughts and other trials—in the same vein as Reisner's *Cadillac Desert.*

Reisner, Marc. *Cadillac Desert: The American West and Its Disappearing Water.* New York: Penguin, 1993. Not specifically about New Mexico, but an excellent analysis of the Southwest's water shortage and how the U.S. government's dam-building projects exacerbated it. Apocalyptic, sarcastic, and totally compelling.

Sibley, David Allen. *The Sibley Field Guide to Birds of Western North America.* New York: Knopf, 2003. The New Mexican birder's book of choice, with 810 species listed, about 4,600 color illustrations, and a handy compact format. Generally beats out Peterson's otherwise respectable series.

Tekiela, Stan. *Birds of New Mexico: Field Guide.* Cambridge, MN: Adventure Publications, 2003. A great book for beginning birders or curious visitors, with 140 of the state's most common species listed, many illustrated with photographs.

Internet Resources

TRAVEL INFORMATION

Albuquerque Convention and Visitors Bureau
www.visitalbuquerque.org
The official intro to the city and surrounding areas, with events listings as well as hotel-booking services.

Four Corners Geotourism
www.fourcornersgeotourism.com
A directory of sustainable tourism, sponsored by *National Geographic*.

Hiking in the Sandia Mountains
www.sandiahiking.com
Mike Coltrin hiked every trail in the Sandias over the course of a year, covering about 250 miles. He detailed each hike, complete with GPS references, here.

New Mexico Board of Tourism
www.newmexico.org
The best of the official sites, this one has thorough maps and suggested itineraries.

Public Lands Information Center
www.publiclands.org
Buy USGS, Forest Service, and other topographical maps online from the Bureau of Land Management's well-organized website. Good stock of nature guides and other travel books too.

Sangres.com
www.sangres.com
Scores of travel details about the mountain communities, culture, and history of northern New Mexico, as well as southern Colorado. Not regularly updated, however.

Santa Fe Convention and Visitors Bureau
www.santafe.org
Near-exhaustive listings of tourist attractions and services on this slickly produced site.

Southern New Mexico Travel & Tourism
www.southernnewmexico.com
Heaps of information about even the most obscure towns in the southern half of the state, though many of the articles are quite old.

Taos Vacation Guide
www.taos.org
A thorough directory and events listings.

Visit Los Alamos
www.visitlosalamos.org
Colorful and helpfully arranged with suggestions based on the time you have available.

Happy Trails!

See New Mexico through a focused lens, with these specialized guides to the state.

- **Birding Trail:** (http://wildlife.state.nm.us) A map and road signs for feathered friends

- **Clay Arts Trail:** (www.claytrail.org) A guide to the "creative economy of clay" in the southwest corner of the state

- **Fiber Arts Trails:** (www.nmfiberarts.org) Three routes around this wool-loving state

- **Green Chile Cheeseburger Trail:** (www.newmexico.org) Between this and a breakfast burrito trail, you'll never go hungry again.

- **Film Trails:** (www.newmexico.org) Filming locations for more than a dozen films, plus *Breaking Bad*

- **Space Trail:** (www.nmspacemuseum.org) Locations where rockets were launched

NEWS AND CULTURE

Albuquerque Journal
www.abqjournal.com
The state's largest newspaper is available free online after answering survey questions.

Alibi
www.alibi.com
This free weekly has been cracking wise since 1992, taking a critical look at politics and culture. Its annual "Best of Burque" guide is usually reliable.

Chasing Santa Fe
www.chasingsantafe.blogspot.com
The glamorous Santa Fe lifestyle, lovingly documented: local chefs, new shops, and fashion spotting.

Duke City Fix
www.dukecityfix.com
This Albuquerque-centric discussion forum covers everything from politics to gossip about the restaurant scene.

Las Cruces Sun-News
www.lcsun-news.com
The paper of record in Las Cruces, covering issues all across the southern half of the state, especially border debates.

New Mexico Politics with Joe Monahan
www.joemonahan.com
Analyst Monahan's obsessive, snarky blog charts the circus that is state politics.

Santa Fe New Mexican
www.santafenewmexican.com
Santa Fe's main newspaper. The gossip column *El Mitote* documents celebs in Santa Fe, and the Roundhouse Roundup does roughly the same—but with politicians.

Santa Fe Reporter
www.sfreporter.com
Santa Fe's free weekly is politically sharp and often funny. Get opinionated reviews and news analysis here.

Smithsonian Folkways
www.folkways.si.edu
Prep for your road trip at this enormous online music archive, which has a number of traditional treasures from the state, including the excellent *Music of New Mexico: Hispanic Traditions* and *New Mexico: Native American Traditions*.

Taos News
www.taosnews.com
The town paper is a weekly, but its website has daily updates and an events calendar.

RESOURCES
INTERNET RESOURCES

Index

A

A:shíwi A:wan Museum and Heritage Center: 24, 228
Abiquiu: 14, 17, 119-123
Abiquiu Lake: 121
Abó: 61
ABQ BioPark: 32-33
ABQ Trolley Co.: 31-32
Abraham's Tiendita: 17, 191-192
accommodations: 403
Acoma Pueblo: 14, 24, 219-222
Adobe Bar: 14, 150
Aguirre Springs Recreation Area: 292
air travel: 396, 397
Alameda Park and Zoo: 360
Alameda/Rio Grande Open Space: 50
Alamogordo: 358-362; map 359
Alamogordo Museum of History: 360
Albuquerque: 14, 15, 24, 25-57; maps 28, 31, 36, 38
Albuquerque International Balloon Fiesta: 45-46
Albuquerque Museum of Art and History: 33
Albuquerque Trail: 59
Alcove House Trail: 116
Alien Run: 249
Alkali Flat Trail: 22, 364
Alma: 318-319
American International Rattlesnake Museum: 33
"A" Mountain Trail: 293
Ancient Way Fall Festival: 229
Anderson Abruzzo Albuquerque International Balloon Festival: 42
Anderson-Freeman Visitors Center & Museum: 371
Anderson Museum of Contemporary Art: 15, 23, 342
Angel Fire: 170-171
Angel Peak Scenic Area: 20, 250
animals: 379-381
Animas Range: 306
Animas River Park: 244
aquarium: 32
Armand Hammer United World College of the American West: 190
Armendaris Ranch: 279
Arroyo Seco: 149
Arroyo Seco Fourth of July parade: 152
Artesia: 337-338
Artesia Historical Museum & Art Center: 337
Artesia Public Library: 337
Arthur Johnson Memorial Library: 206

Art League Gallery: 266
Artwalk: 191
AshKii's Navajo Grill: 24, 245
Aspen Vista: 97
Atalaya Mountain: 97
ATMs: 406
auto travel: 396-397, 398, 399
Aviation History Museum: 222
Aztec: 247-250
Aztec Museum & Pioneer Village: 249
Aztec Ruins National Monument: 247-249

B

Baca House: 198
ballooning: 48
Bandelier National Monument: 14, 115-117
Bandera Crater Ice Caves: 225
bargaining: 406
Basilica of San Albino: 287, 289
Bat Cave: 225
Bat Flight: 354
Battle of Glorieta Pass: 184
Baylor Pass Trail: 292
Beach Recreation Area: 348
Bean Day: 197
Beaverhead: 281
beer/breweries: Albuquerque 44; Northwest 243, 246; Santa Fe 92, 115; Southeast 335, 367-368; Southwest 290, 309; Taos 150, 151-152
Belén: 266-267
Berg Park: 244
bicycling: general discussion 398-399; Albuquerque 33, 39, 49-50, 64; Northwest 234-235, 244-245, 249, 260; Santa Fe 97-98, 119; Southeast 343, 355-356, 366-367; Southwest 269, 272, 292-293, 309-310; Taos 156, 170
Big Arsenic Trail: 176
Big D's Downtown Dive: 18, 344
Big Event, The: 291
Big Hatchet Range: 306
Big Room, The: 352-353
Big Tubes Area: 225
Billy the Kid, gravesite of: 326
Billy the Kid Interpretive Center: 370
Billy the Kid Museum: 326
Billy the Kid Trail: 370-372
birds/bird-watching: general discussion 380-381; Albuquerque 39, 41, 50; Northeast 191; Northwest 251; Southeast 343, 344; Southwest 267, 272-273, 279, 293, 299, 301

Bisti/De-Na-Zin Wilderness: 20, 243-244
Bitter Lake National Wildlife Refuge: 344
Black Place, The: 259
Black Range Museum: 282
Blackstone Hotsprings: 21, 280
Blackwater Draw Museum: 334-335
Bloomfield: 250-251
Blue Hole: 16, 325
Blue Swallow Motel: 21, 330
Bobcat Pass: 175
Boca Negra Canyon: 41
Bodhi Manda Zen Center: 67
Boese Brothers: 44
Bolack Electromechanical Museum: 242
Bolack Museum of Fish & Wildlife: 242
Bond House: 117
Bosque del Apache National Wildlife Refuge: 272-273
Bosque Redondo Memorial: 327
Boston Hill: 309
botanical gardens/arboretums: 32
Bottomless Lakes State Park: 343-344
Box Canyon: 122
Box Car Museum: 269
Bradbury Science Museum: 114
Branigan Cultural Center: 289
Breaking Bad sights: 32
Brickyard Park: 235
Bridge Street: 188
B-Square Ranch: 21, 240, 242
Budget Host Melody Lane Motel: 21, 207
Bueyeros: 197
Burning of Zozobra: 94, 95
Bursum Road: 318
bus travel: 396, 397-398

C

Caballo Lake State Park: 278
Cabezon Peak: 260
Café Pasqual's: 14, 18, 101
Camel Rock: 108
camping: Northeast 185, 186, 191, 194, 195, 197, 199, 208; Northwest 222, 227, 243, 250, 251, 254-255; Santa Fe 116, 117, 121, 123, 124, 128; Southeast 326, 343, 354, 361, 368, 373; Southwest 269, 273, 278, 296, 301, 302, 312-313, 315; Taos 166, 169, 172, 176
canoeing: *see* kayaking/canoeing
Canteen Brewhouse: 44
Canyon Loop Drive: 255-257
Canyon Road: 86-87
Capilla de Nuestra Señora de Guadalupe: 34
Capitan: 371-372
Capulin Springs Snow Play Area: 51
Capulin Volcano National Monument: 17, 202
Carlsbad: 15, 346-351; map 347

Carlsbad Caverns and the Southeast: 320-374; map 323
Carlsbad Caverns National Park: 15, 22, 352-354
Carlsbad Museum & Art Center: 346
Carnegie Library: 188
Carnegie Park: 188
Carrizozo: 373
Carrizozo Heritage Museum: 373
car travel: 396-397, 398, 399
Casa Rinconada: 256-257
Casa San Ysidro: 39
Castañeda Hotel: 189
Cathedral Basilica of St. Francis of Assisi: 83-84
Catwalk Trail: 317
Cave Creek Canyon: 22, 306
Cave Creek Trail: 185
caves/caverns: Northeast 185; Northwest 224, 225; Santa Fe 116; Southeast 352-354; Southwest 306, 314
Cebolla Wilderness: 225
cell phones: 404
ceremonial dances: general discussion 152; Albuquerque 45; Northwest 220; Santa Fe 112; Taos 146
Cerrillos: 19, 64
Cerrillos Hills State Park: 64
Chaco Culture National Historical Park: 14, 24, 252-258; map 253
Chama: 166-169
Chama River Microbar: 44
Chetro Keti: 255
Chihuahuan Desert: 22, 263, 272, 352
children, traveling with: 407
Chimayó: 14, 125-126
Chimayó Museum: 126
Chimney Rock: 121-122
Chino Mine: 315-316
Chiricahua Desert Museum: 305
Chloride: 282
Christ in the Desert Monastery: 122
Christmas on the Pecos: 348
churches/temples: Albuquerque 34-35, 39; Northeast 189, 194, 204; Northwest 218-219, 220-221, 228; Santa Fe 83-85, 127-128; Southwest 266, 286, 287, 289, 312; Taos 147, 175
Church of Nuestra Señora de la Candelaria: 286
Church of San Esteban del Rey: 220-221
Church Rock Trail: 234
Cibola Arts Council: 222
Cimarron: 14, 19, 209-212
Cimarron Canyon State Park: 210
City of Las Vegas Museum and Rough Riders Memorial Collection: 189
City of Rocks State Park: 301-302
classes: 405-406
Classical Gas Museum: 123-124

Clayton: 198-202; map 199
Clayton Lake State Park: 198-199
Clear Creek Trail: 210
Cleveland: 194-195
Cleveland Roller Mill Museum: 194
climate: 376-377
climbing: Northwest 235, 260; Southwest 293;
   Taos 156
Cloud-Climbing Rail Trail: 355
Cloudcroft: 355-358
Clovis: 331-334; map 332
Clovis Livestock Auction: 332
Clovis Music Festival: 21, 333
Coal Camp Trail: 206
Cochiti Lake: 70
Colfax County War: 209
Colfax Tavern: 19, 210
Columbine Trail: 174
Columbus: 302-303
Columbus Historical Society Museum: 302-303
communes: 148
Conchas Lake State Park: 329
Connie Mack World Series: 243
"Cooney's tomb": 318
Córdova: 127
Cordovas Handweaving Workshop: 127
Coronado Historic Site: 24, 42-43
Corrales Scenic Byway: 39
Couse-Sharp Historic Site: 143
Crest Road: 62
Crest Trail: 48
crime: 408-409
Crimson Maple Trail: 59
Crownpoint Rug Auction: 24, 223-224
Cruisin' Through Time Auto Museum: 346
Cuba: 259-260
Cuchillo: 281
Cumbres & Toltec Scenic Railroad: 167-168
currency: 406

D
Dale Ball Trails: 98
Dalley Windmill Museum: 335
Danny's Place BBQ: 15, 350
Dar al Islam: 120-121
Datil: 270
Deming: 298-301; map 299
Deming Arts Center: 298
Deming-Luna Mimbres Museum: 298
demographics: 388-389
Desmarais House/Our Lady of Sorrows Parish
   Hall: 188
D. H. Lawrence Ranch: 176
Diez y Seis de Septiembre Fiesta: 291
disabilities, travelers with: 406-407

Dixon: 123-124
Dog Canyon Recreational Trail: 361
Doña Ana: 286
Don Quixote Distillery: 108-109
Downtown Albuquerque: 35-37; map 36
Downtown Santa Fe: 79-86; map 80-81
Dragonfly Festival: 344
Dripping Springs Natural Area: 292
drugs, illegal: 408-409
Dry Cimarron Byway: 203
Dune Life Nature Trail: 363
Dunes Drive: 363-364
Dwan Light Sanctuary: 190

E
Eagle Nest: 19, 172-173
Eagle Nest Lake State Park: 172
Eagle Point: 278
Eastern New Mexico State Fair & Parade: 343
East Fork Trail: 68
East Las Vegas: 188-189
East Mountains: 62
Echo Amphitheater: 122
economy: 387
Edgewood: 324-325
Edward Sargent Wildlife Management Area: 168
E. L. Blumenschein Home: 140-141
El Bruno's: 14, 18, 259
El Caleron Area: 225
El Camino Real: 272-274
El Camino Real Historic Site: 273-274
electricity: 406
Elena Gallegos Picnic Area: 48
Elephant Butte Lake State Park: 278
El Fidel Restaurant: 14, 192
Elizabethtown: 19, 173
El Malpais National Monument: 224-225
El Morro National Monument: 225-226
El Prado: 147-149
El Pueblo Lodge: 24, 162
El Rancho Hotel & Motel: 21, 236
El Raton Theatre: 206
El Salto Falls: 155-156
El Vado Lake State Park: 166
El Zaguán: 87
Embudo: 123-124
Embudo Canyon: 50
Enchanted Circle: 14, 19, 170-176; map 171
Enchanted Circle Century Tour: 156
Enchanted Forest: 157, 174
Enchanted Grounds: 19, 207
environmental issues: 377-378, 379
Eske's Brew Pub: 150
Española: 117-118; map 117
etiquette: 404-405

F

Farmington: 24, 240-247; map 241
Farmington Museum: 240
fauna: 379-381
Faywood Hot Springs: 302
Feast of San Esteban: 219
Feast of San Geronimo: 152
Feast of St. Augustine: 266
Festival of the Cranes: 273
Fiesta de Santa Fe: 95
Fiesta Drive-In: 15, 347
Fiestas de Las Vegas: 191
Fiestas de Taos: 152
fish/fishing: Albuquerque 33; Northeast 185, 206,
    209, 210; Northwest 250-251; Southeast 343;
    Southwest 278, 314; Taos 166, 169, 170, 172
flora: 378-379
Florence Hawley Ellis Museum of Anthropology: 122
Florida Mountains: 22, 298, 299
Folsom: 17, 203
Folsom Falls: 203
food/restaurants: 18, 400-402
foreign travelers: 406
Fort Bayard: 316
Fort Craig National Historic Site: 273
Fort Selden State Monument: 286
Fort Stanton: 371
Fort Sumner: 16, 326-327
Fort Union National Monument: 17, 195-196
Four Corners Monument: 239-240
Fourth of July Canyon: 48, 59
Fourth of July Trail: 59
Frey Trail: 116
Frontier, The: 15, 16, 52-53
Fuller Lodge Art Center: 113

G

Gallery 140: 188
Gallery 408: 373
Gallinas Nature Trail: 191
Gallup: 14, 24, 229-237; map 230
Gallup Aquatic Center: 235
Gallup Cultural Center: 231
Gallup Flea Market: 18, 234
Garnsey Arroyo: 343
Gateway Museum: 172
Gathering of Nations Powwow: 46
Gavilan Trail: 155
gay and lesbian travelers: 407
General Douglas L. McBride Military Museum: 342
geography: 376
geology: 376
Georgia O'Keeffe Home: 120
Georgia O'Keeffe Museum: 86
Geronimo Springs Museum: 23, 276-277

Geronimo Surrender Memorial: 305-306
Geronimo Trail: 281-284
Ghost Ranch: 14, 121-122
Giggling Springs: 66
Gila: 316-317
Gila Cliff Dwellings National Monument: 313-314
Gila Hot Springs: 312-313
Gila National Forest: 17, 316-319
Gila River Festival: 309
Gilman Tunnels: 66
Give-Away: 229
Glade Run Trail System: 244
Glenwood: 317-318
Goat Hill: 206
Go-Jii-Ya: 169
Golden: 63
Gold Rush Days: 374
golf: 200
Gooseberry Springs Trail: 222
government: 386-387
Governor Bent House and Museum: 141
Gran Quivira: 60-61
Grant County Courthouse: 308
Grants: 222-223
gratuities: 406
Great American Duck Race: 299
Greater World Earthship Development: 23, 148-149
Grindstone Trail System: 367
Guadalupe: 87, 89
Guadalupe Mountains National Park: 354

H

Hacienda de los Martinez: 144-145
Hacienda Nicholas: 14, 106
Hall of the White Giant: 354
Hamilton Mesa Trail: 185
Harvey House Museum: 266
Harwood Museum of Art: 140
Hatch: 285-286
Hatch Chile Festival: 285
Hatch Museum: 285
Hawikku: 228
Headland Trail: 226
Healing Waters Trail: 278
health: 408-409
Hearst Church: 312
Heart of the Desert Pistachios and Wine at
    Eagle Ranch: 360
Heart of the Sands: 364
Herb Martyr Trail: 306
Hermit Peak Trail: 191
Heron Lake State Park: 166
Herzstein Memorial Museum: 198
High Desert Brewing Co.: 290
High Desert Trail System: 234-235
High Road: 125-129

Highway 120: 197
Highway 72: 17, 203
hiking: Albuquerque 41-42, 48-49, 59, 64, 66, 68, 70; Northeast 185, 186, 191, 206-207, 210; Northwest 222, 224-225, 226, 234, 243-244, 249, 251, 257-258, 260; Santa Fe 97, 114-115, 116-117, 121-122, 124; Southeast 343, 354, 355, 361, 363-364, 366-367; Southwest 269, 272, 278, 292, 299, 301, 306, 309, 314, 316, 317, 318; Taos 148, 154-156, 166, 168, 173-174, 176
Hillsboro: 282-283
Historical Center for Southeast New Mexico: 342
Historic Santa Fe Foundation: 87
Historic Taos Inn: 19, 144, 163
history: 382-386
Hobbs: 336-337
Holiday Arts Market: 229
Hondo: 370
Hopper, Dennis: 154
horseback riding: Albuquerque 64; Santa Fe 122; Southwest 309; Taos 170
horse racing: 367
hot air ballooning: 48
Hotel La Fonda de Taos: 19, 137-138, 161-162
hot springs: Albuquerque 67-68; Northeast 190; Santa Fe 118-119; Southwest 278, 302, 312-313, 314, 317
House of Eternal Return: 14, 23, 90
Hubbard Museum of the American West: 366
Hungo Pavi: 255
Hyatt Regency Tamaya: 24, 57
Hyde Memorial State Park: 99

I

Il Vicino: 44
Indian Pueblo Cultural Center: 14, 24
Indigenous Fine Art Market: 94-95
Inn at Halona: 24, 229
Inscription Loop Trail: 226
Interdune Boardwalk: 364
International Folk Art Market: 93
International UFO Museum & Research Center: 15, 23, 340
Interstate 25: 69-70; map 69
Inter-Tribal Indian Ceremonial: 233
Isla Pueblo: 266
itineraries: 14-17, 19

J

Jack's Creek Trail: 185
Jack Williamson Science Fiction Collection: 335
Jemez Historic Site: 67
Jemez Mountain Trail: 17, 65-68
Jemez Pueblo: 65-66
Jemez Springs: 66-67

Jemez Springs Bath House: 66
Jeperson's Cache: 197
Jesus Nazareno Cemetery: 154
jewelry: 393-394
Jicarilla Apache Nation: 169
Johnson Mesa: 17, 203-204
Jordan Hot Springs: 314
Joseph's: 18, 102
Junction Cave: 225

K

Karr Canyon: 355
Kasha-Katuwe Tent Rocks National Monument: 69-70
Kashina Lodge: 146
kayaking/canoeing: Southwest 278; Taos 166
Kelly's Brew Pub: 44
Kewa (Santo Domingo): 69
KiMo Theatre: 35, 37
King's Palace: 354
Kingston: 284
Kin Kletso: 256
Kiowa and Rita Blanca National Grasslands: 20, 197, 200
Kit Carson Home and Museum: 143-144
Kit Carson Park and Cemetery: 142-143
Kitchen Mesa Trail: 122

L

Laabs: 293
La Chiripada: 124
La Cueva: 194
La Cueva Picnic Area: 292
La Cumbre Brewing: 44
Ladder Ranch: 279
La Fonda: 14, 107
La Frontera del Llano Scenic Byway: 17, 197
Laguna Burger: 18, 219
Laguna Pueblo: 218-219
La Junta Overlook: 176
Lake Lucero: 22, 363
Lake Roberts: 314-315
Lakeside Recreation Area: 278
Lake Valley Historic Site: 283-284
La Loma Plaza: 141
La Luz Trail: 48-49
La Merienda: 18, 54
language: 389, 391
La Paloma Too: 278
La Rinconada Gallery: 370
Las Cruces: 15, 287-298; map 288
Las Cruces and the Southwest: 261-319; map 264
Las Cruces Cinco de Mayo celebration: 291
Las Cruces Community Theatre: 291
Las Cruces Dia de los Muertos celebration: 292

Las Cruces International Mariachi Conference & Festival: 292
Las Cruces Museum of Art: 289
Las Cruces Museum of Nature and Science: 289
Las Cruces Railroad Museum: 289
Las Cruces Regional Aquatic Center: 293
Las Lunas: 266-267
Las Trampas: 14, 127-128
Las Vegas: 14, 16, 186-193; map 187
Las Vegas and the Northeast: 179-212; map 183
Las Vegas National Wildlife Refuge: 191
Las Vegas Plaza: 188
La Tierra Trails: 98
Lava Falls: 225
La Ventana Arch: 224
La Viña: 297
Lea County Museum: 336
Left Hand Tunnel: 354
Lensic Performing Arts Center: 93
lesbian and gay travelers: 407
Lightfeather Hot Spring: 314
Light Hall Theater: 309
Lightning Field, The: 272
Lincoln: 16, 370-371
Lincoln National Forest: 360-361
Lincoln Park: 189
Lincoln State Monument: 370-371
Little Beaver Roundup: 169
Little Toad Creek Brewery & Distillery: 309
Little Walnut Picnic Area: 310
Living Desert Zoo and Gardens State Park: 346
Llano, the: 331-338
Long House: 116
Lordsburg: 304-305
Lordsburg-Hidalgo County Museum: 304
Loretto Chapel: 84-85
Los Alamos: 23, 110-111, 113-115; map 111
Los Alamos Historical Museum: 113-114
Los Alamos Nature Center: 114
Los Ojos: 164-166
Los Poblanos Historic Inn: 16, 56-57
Los Ranchos: 39
Love Apple, The: 14, 18, 158
Lovington: 336
Lower Cave: 354
Low Road: 19, 123-125
Luna County Courthouse: 298
Luna Theater: 200

M

Mabel Dodge Luhan House: 142
Madrid: 19, 23, 63-64
Magdalena: 269
Main Loop Trail: 116
Manzanita Trail: 157
Marble Pub: 44

Marigold Parade: 46
Mary & Tito's Café: 18, 53
Masonic Temple: 189
Matanza: 44
Maverick Motel: 21, 207
Maxwell Museum of Anthropology: 37
McAllister Lake: 191
McCauley Warm Springs: 67
McGinn's Pistachio Tree Ranch & Arena Blanca Winery: 360
McKinley County Courthouse: 230-231
McKinley County Fair: 229
McKittrick Canyon: 354
McNees Crossing: 200
Meadow City Music Festival: 191
Meadowlark Trail: 191
Mentmore Rock Climbing Area: 235
Mesalands Dinosaur Museum: 328
Mesalands Scenic Byway: 326
Mesa Vista Hall: 37
Mesilla: 15, 287, 289
Mesilla Valley: 285-286
Mesilla Valley Bosque State Park: 293
Mexican Canyon Loop: 355
Millicent Rogers Museum: 147
Mills Canyon: 20, 197
Mimbres Valley: 315
Mineral Creek Trail: 318
Mine Shaft Tavern: 19, 63
Misión Museum: 117
mobile phones: 404
Mogollon: 318
Montefiore Cemetery: 189
Monte Verde Lake: 170
Montezuma Castle: 189-190
Montezuma Hot Springs: 190
Monticello: 282
Mora: 194-195
Mora Valley: 194-195
Morphy Lake State Park: 191, 194
Mosquero: 197
Motel Safari: 21, 330
Mountainair: 16, 59-60
Mount Taylor: 222
Museum Hill: 89-90
Museum of Contemporary Native Arts: 84
Museum of Indian Arts & Culture: 89
Museum of International Folk Art: 89-90
Museum of Natural History and Science: 34
Museum of Spanish Colonial Art: 89

N

National Hispanic Cultural Center: 40
National Museum of Nuclear Science & History: 40-41
Native American sites: 22, 24

Navajo Arts & Crafts Enterprise: 239
Navajo code talkers: 232
Navajo Lake State Park: 250-251
Navajo Nation: 237-240
Navajo Nation and the Northwest: 213-260; map 216
New Mexico Brewers Guild: 44
New Mexico Farm & Ranch Heritage Museum: 290
New Mexico History Museum: 82-83
New Mexico Institute of Mining & Technology: 268
New Mexico, map of: 2-3
New Mexico Mining Museum: 222
New Mexico Museum of Art: 83
New Mexico Museum of Space History: 358-359
New Mexico Route 66 Museum: 328
New Mexico State Capitol: 85-86
New Mexico State Fair: 46
New Mexico State University: 290
Nob Hill: 14, 38
Norman & Vi Petty Rock & Roll Museum: 21, 332
Norski Trail: 99
Northern Navajo Nation Fair: 220, 239
Northern Plains: 195-204
Northern Tularoa Basin: 372-374
North Valley: 38-40
Nuestra Señora de Guadalupe Church: 228
Nuestra Señora del Rosario de las Truchas Church: 127

O
Ocotillo Performing Arts Center: 337
Odeon Theater: 329
Ojito Wilderness: 260
Ojo Caliente: 118-119
Old Aztec Mill Museum: 19, 210
Old Coal Town Museum: 63
Old Fort Sumner Museum: 326-327
"Old Main" State Penitentiary: 65
Old Pass Gallery: 205
Old San Ysidro Church: 39
Old Town Albuquerque: 31-35; map 31
Oliver Lee Memorial State Park: 361
Organ Mountains: 22, 292, 293
Orilla Verde Recreation Area: 124
Osha Trail: 355
Otero Canyon: 50
Our Lady of Guadalupe Fiesta: 291
Outside Albuquerque: 57-70; map 58
Owl Bar & Café: 15, 18, 273

P
Padre Antonio Martinez, statue of: 138
Pajarito Brewpub: 115
Pajarito Mountain: 115
Palace of the Governors: 82
Palomas: 303

Pancho Villa State Park: 302
Park Lake: 325
parks and gardens: Albuquerque 32-33;
    Northeast 188, 189; Northwest 231, 233; Santa
    Fe 87, 117; Southeast 366
Paseo del Bosque: 49-50
Pat's Twin Cronnie: 21, 335
Peanut Valley Festival: 335
Pecos: 184-186
Pecos Flavors Winery: 343
Pecos National Historical Park: 184-185
Pecos River: 348
Pecos River Flume: 346
Pecos Wilderness: 128, 185-186
Peñasco: 128
Peñasco Blanco: 258
Penitentes: 390
Percha Bank: 284
Percha Dam State Park: 278-279
Perk Canyon Trail: 366
Pescado Trail: 176
Petroglyph National Monument: 24, 41-42
PharrWest Gallery: 282
Philmont Scout Ranch: 212
phones: 404
Picurís Pueblo: 128
Piedras Marcadas Canyon: 41
Pie Festival: 271
Pie Town: 21, 270-271
Pilar: 124
Pine Tree Trail: 292
Pinos Altos: 312
Pioneer Store Museum: 282
Plains of San Agustín: 23, 267-277
planning tips: 10-13
plants: 378-379
Playa Trail: 363
Plaza Blanca: 121
Plaza de Española: 117
Plaza Drugs: 188
Plaza Hotel: 14, 16, 193
Poeh Museum: 108
Pojoaque: 108-109
politics: 386-387
Porch, The: 14, 210-211
Portales: 334-336; map 334
Posi Trail: 119
pottery: 391
Prehistoric Trackways National Monument: 286
Pueblo Alto: 257-258
Pueblo Bonito: 255-256
Pueblo del Arroyo: 256
Pueblo Pintado: 258
Puerto de Luna: 326
Puyé Cliff Dwellings: 110
Pyramid Rock Trail: 234

QR

Quarai: 59
Quebradas Backcountry Byway: 267
Quemado: 271-272
Questa: 175-176
rafting: Santa Fe 124; Taos 148, 156, 166, 175
rail travel: 396, 398
Railyard Park: 87
Railyard, The: 87, 89
Ramah: 226-227
Ramah Museum: 227
Rancho Bonito: 60
Rancho de las Golondrinas: 91
Ranchos Plaza Grill: 14, 160
Raton: 17, 204-208; map 205
Raton Museum: 205
Red Dot Trail: 115
Red River: 19, 173-175
Red River Nature Trail: 174
Red River Ski & Snowboard Area: 174
Red Rock Balloon Rally: 233
Red Rock Museum: 231, 233
Red Rock Park: 231, 233
religion: 389
religious retreats: 403
Reserve: 319
Rex Museum: 231
Rim Trail: 355-356
Rim Vista: 122
Rinconada Canyon: 41-42
Rio Grande del Norte National Monument: 175
Rio Grande Gorge: 147-148
Rio Grande Grill and Taproom: 367-368
Rio Grande Heritage Farm: 32
Rio Grande Nature Center: 50
Rio Grande Nature Center State Park: 39, 48
Rio Grande Theatre: 291
Rio Grande Vineyards: 297
Riverbend Hot Springs: 277, 278
Riverside Nature Center: 244
Riverside Recreation Area: 278
Road Apple Rally: 244
Robert H. Goddard Planetarium: 342
Robledo Trail: 293
Rockhound State Park: 299
Rocking 3M Chuckwagon Amphitheater: 175
Rodeo: 305-307
Roosevelt Brewing Co.: 335
Roosevelt County Museum: 335
Roswell: 15, 23, 338-346; map 339
Roswell Livestock Auction: 343
Roswell Museum and Art Center: 342
Roswell UFO Festival: 343
Route 66: 17, 21; Albuquerque to Gallup 218-227;
   Edgewood to Tucumcari 324-330
Route 66 Auto Museum: 325

Roy: 197
Ruidoso: 364-369; map 365
Ruidoso Downs: 367
Ruth Hall Museum of Paleontology: 122

S

Sacramento Mountains Historical Museum: 355
safety: 408-409
Salinas Pueblo Missions National Monument: 16,
   57, 59-61
Salinas Pueblo Missions Visitors Center: 59
Salman Ranch: 194
Salmon Ruins & Heritage Park: 242-243
Salt Basin Dunes: 354
Sam Baca Aquatic Center: 299
San Antonio: 272
San Antonio Church: 175
Sandia Peak: 15, 48-49, 50-51
Sandia Peak Tramway: 16, 41
San Diego Canyon: 66
Sandstone Bluffs Overlook: 224
San Felipe de Neri Church: 34-35
San Felipe Restaurant: 18, 70
San Francisco de Asis Church: 14, 145-146
San Francisco Hot Springs: 317
San Geronimo Church: 147
San Ildefonso: 109-110
San José de Gracia Church: 127
San José Mission Church: 218-219
San Juan County Archaeological Research Center
   and Library: 243
San Lorenzo: 315
San Lorenzo de Picurís Church: 128
San Marcos Café: 19, 65
San Miguel Mission: 85
San Patricio: 370
San Rafael Mission Church: 194
Santa Clara: 110
Santa Fe: 14, 23, 24, 74-107; maps 77, 80-81
Santa Fe architecture: 88
Santa Fe area: 108-129; map 109
Santa Fe Bite: 18, 100
Santa Fe Canyon Preserve: 97
Santa Fe Century: 98
Santa Fe Chamber Music Festival: 93
Santa Fe Indian Market: 22, 94
Santa Fe National Forest: 191
Santa Fe Opera: 93
Santa Fe Plaza: 79, 82
Santa Fe Pro Musica: 93
Santa Fe Rail Trail: 98
Santa Fe Trail: 17, 196
Santa Fe Trail Interpretive Center: 188
Santa Fe Wine and Chile Festival: 95
Santa Rosa: 325-326
Santa Rosa Lake State Park: 325

INDEX

Santo Domingo Trading Post: 69
Santuario de Chimayó: 125-126
Santuario de Guadalupe: 87
scenic drives: 17
scuba diving/snorkeling: 325, 343, 348
Second Street Brewery: 92
senior travelers: 407
Shaffer Hotel: 16, 59
Shakespeare: 304
Shalako: 24, 228-229
Shalam Colony: 287
Shiprock: 24, 238-239
Shroud Exhibit and Museum: 360
Shuler Theater: 204
Silver City: 307-312; map 308
Silver City Blues Festival: 309
Silver City Museum: 308
Silver City Wild & Scenic Film Festival: 309
Simon Canyon: 251
SITE Santa Fe: 87, 89
Sitting Bull Falls: 348, 350
Skeleton Canyon: 306
Skidmarks Trail: 343
Sky City: 219, 220-221
Sky City Cultural Center and Haak'u Museum: 220
Sky Islands: 22
Slaughter Canyon Cave: 354
Smokey Bear Days: 372
Smokey Bear Historical Park: 372
Socorro: 267-269
Soda Dam: 67
Soldiers' Monument: 79
South Boundary Trail: 170
South Fork Trail: 306
South Mesa: 258
Southwest Environmental Center: 292
Southwestern Research Station: 306
Spaceport America: 277
Spanish Market: 94
spas: 98-99
spectator sports: 367
Spence Hot Springs: 67
Spencer Theater for the Performing Arts: 366
Spider Cave: 354
Spring Canyon Recreational Area: 299-300
Springer: 197
Spring Harvest Festival: 166
Spring Loop Trail: 59
Spring River Park and Zoo: 343
Spring River Trail: 343
Star Party: 354
state parks: Albuquerque 39, 48, 64; Northeast
    186, 191, 194, 198-199, 206, 210; Northwest
    250-251; Santa Fe 99; Southeast 325, 326, 329,
    343-344, 346, 361; Southwest 278-279, 293,
    299, 301-302; Taos 166, 171-172

St. Augustine Church: 266
St. Clair Winery: 298-299
St. James Hotel: 19, 209-210, 211
St. John's Methodist Church: 204
Storrie Lake State Park: 191
Strawberry Canyon Trail: 234
Sugarite Canyon State Park: 206
Sumner Lake State Park: 326
Sunspot: 355

T
Taos: 14, 19, 23, 24, 131-164; maps 138, 139, 140
Taos and North Central New Mexico: 131-178;
    map 134-135
Taos Art Museum at Fechin House: 14, 141-142
Taos Box: 156
Taos County Courthouse: 137
Taos Fall Arts Festival: 152
Taos Inn: 19, 144, 163
Taos Mesa Brewing: 151-152
Taos Plaza: 137-138, 140-144; map 140
Taos Pueblo: 14, 24, 146-147
Taos Pueblo Powwow: 152
Taos Shortz Film Fest: 153
Taos Ski Valley: 149-150, 155, 156, 157
Taos tree-lighting ceremony: 153
Taos Wool Festival: 152-153
Tapetes de Lana: 194
telephones: 404
10K Trail: 51
Ten Thousand Waves: 23, 98
Terrero General Store: 185
Tesuque: 108-109
textiles: 391-393
Thoreau: 223-224
Three Rivers Brewery: 243, 246
Three Rivers Petroglyph Site: 372-373
Tia Sophia's: 18, 100
Tierra Amarilla: 17, 164-166
Tijeras: 57, 59
time zone: 404
Tingley Beach: 33
Tinkertown Museum: 23, 62
tinwork: 394
tipping: 406
Toadlena Trading Post: 24, 238
Tolby Creek Trail: 210
Tomé Hill: 266-267
Tortugas: 287
Totah Festival: 243
tourist information: 404
Tour of the Gila: 309
Toy Train Depot: 360
Tractor Brewing: 44
Trail of the Mountain Spirits: 312-316
train travel: 396, 398

transportation: 396-399
Tres Piedras: 164
Trinity Hotel & Suites: 15, 347, 351
Trinity Site: 23, 374
Truchas: 14, 127
Truth or Consequences: 15, 23, 274-281; map 275
Tsankawi: 116-117
Tsin Kletsin: 258
Tucumcari: 327-330
Tucumcari Historical Museum: 328-329
Tularosa Basin Gallery of Photography: 373
Turquoise Museum: 35
Turquoise Trail: 17, 19, 61-65; map 61
Two Rivers Park: 366
Tyuonyi: 116

U

UFOs: 341
Una Vida: 254
University Area of Albuquerque: 37-38; map 38
University Art Gallery: 290
University Art Museum: 37
University of New Mexico: 37-38
U.S. Highway 84: 17
U.S. Highway 550: 259-260
U.S. Highway 180: 17
U.S. Highway 64: 147-149, 164-169

V

Valles Caldera National Preserve: 20, 68
Valle Vidal: 208-209
Valley of Fires National Recreation Area: 22, 373
Vaughn: 14
Verme Park Ranch: 209
Very Large Array, The: 23, 270
Veterans Memorial Park: 276
Vietnam Veterans Memorial State Park: 171-172
Village of the Great Kivas: 228
Villanueva: 14, 186
Villa Philmonte: 212
Vinaigrette (Albuquerque): 18, 51-52
Vinaigrette (Santa Fe): 18, 102-103
visas: 406
Vista Verde Trail: 124
Vivác: 124
Volcanoes Day Use Area: 42
voltage: 406
volunteering: 405-406

WXYZ

Wagon Mound: 197
waterfalls: Northeast 203, 210; Southeast 348, 350; Taos 155

weather: 376-377
Western Heritage Museum and Lea County Cowboy Hall of Fame: 336-337
West Fork Trail: 314
West Malpais Wilderness: 225
West Rim Trail: 148, 156
Wetherill Cemetery: 256
Wheeler Peak: 20, 155
Wheelwright Museum of the American Indian: 90
White Oaks: 374
White Ridge Bike Trails: 260
White Rock Rim Trail: 114
White Sands Missile Range: 374
White Sands National Monument: 15, 22, 362-364
White's City: 354
Whittington Center: 207
Wijiji: 258
wildlife refuges: Northeast 191; Southeast 344; Southwest 272-273
Wildlife West Nature Park: 324
wildlife/wildlife-watching: general discussion 379-381; Albuquerque 41; Northeast 197, 209; Northwest 225; Southwest 267, 300, 301, 316; Taos 168, 175
Wild Rivers Recreation Area: 175-176
Wild Spirit Wolf Sanctuary: 227
Wild West sites: 16-17, 19
Williams Lake Trail: 155
wine/wineries: Santa Fe 124; Southeast 343, 360; Southwest 297, 298-299
Winsor Trail: 98
Winston: 281
winter sports: Albuquerque 50-51; Santa Fe 99; Southeast 356, 367; Taos 149-150, 157, 174
WIPP Experience: 349
Withington Wilderness: 269
WNMU Museum: 309
woodwork: 394
World Cup: 23, 158
Wortley Hotel: 16, 371
WPA murals: 326
WWII Navajo Code Talkers Museum: 24, 231
Xenolith Cave: 225
zip lining: 170
zoos and animal parks: Albuquerque 32-33, 64; Southeast 324, 343, 346, 360
Zuhl Museum: 290
Zuly's: 18, 124
Zuni-Acoma Trail: 225
Zuni Cultural Arts Expo: 229
Zuni Mountain Trail System: 235
Zuni Pueblo: 24, 227-229

INDEX

List of Maps

Front Map
New Mexico: 2–3

Discover New Mexico
Chapter Divisions Map: 10

Albuquerque
Albuquerque: 28
Old Town: 31
Downtown Albuquerque: 36
The University Area: 38
Outside Albuquerque: 58
Turquoise Trail: 61
Interstate 25 to Santa Fe: 69

Santa Fe
Santa Fe: 77
Downtown Santa Fe: 80–81
Outside Santa Fe: 109
Los Alamos: 111
Española: 117

Taos and North Central New Mexico
Taos and North Central New Mexico: 134–135
Taos Area: 138
Taos: 139
Taos Plaza: 140
The Enchanted Circle: 171

Las Vegas and the Northeast
Las Vegas and the Northeast: 183
Las Vegas: 187
Clayton: 199
Raton: 205

Navajo Nation and the Northwest
Navajo Nation and the Northwest: 216
Gallup: 230
Farmington: 241
Chaco Culture National Historical Park: 253

Las Cruces and the Southwest
Las Cruces and the Southwest: 264
Truth or Consequences: 275
Las Cruces: 288
Deming: 299
Silver City: 308

Carlsbad Caverns and the Southeast
Carlsbad and the Southeast: 323
Clovis: 332
Portales: 334
Roswell: 339
Carlsbad: 347
Alamogordo: 359
Ruidoso: 365

Essentials
Driving Distances: 399

Acknowledgments

This book is a big group effort. Thanks go first to the Moon publishing team, who tirelessly check my text, select great photos, and painstakingly draw the maps. Every edition has refinements and improvement. I'm grateful for such a lively finished product that I could never complete on my own.

Huge thanks also to Ashley M. Biggers, my research assistant on this edition. She covered Taos, the northeast, and the southeast. I was especially grateful for her fresh eyes and attention to detail.

Thanks also to Palacio de Marquesa in Taos and the Wortley Hotel in Lincoln for warm welcomes.

Thanks to Peter Moskos for keeping the home fires burning.

Extra special thanks to readers of this edition and all the previous ones, for sending suggestions, updates, and other feedback. I'm always glad to know the book is in such good hands.

Also Available

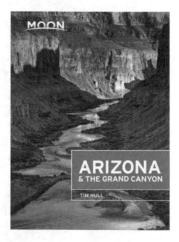

MAP SYMBOLS

≡≡≡	Expressway	○	City/Town	✈	Airport	⚲	Golf Course
—	Primary Road	◉	State Capital	✈	Airfield	🅿	Parking Area
⋯	Secondary Road	⊛	National Capital	▲	Mountain	≜	Archaeological Site
◻ ◻ ◻	Unpaved Road	★	Point of Interest	✦	Unique Natural Feature	▮	Church
———	Feature Trail					🛢	Gas Station
- - - -	Other Trail	●	Accommodation	🌿	Waterfall		
⋯⋯⋯	Ferry	▼	Restaurant/Bar	▲	Park	🗺	Glacier
≡≡≡	Pedestrian Walkway	■	Other Location	⬛	Trailhead	🗺	Mangrove
▥▥▥	Stairs	⋀	Campground	⛷	Skiing Area		Reef
							Swamp

CONVERSION TABLES

°C = (°F - 32) / 1.8
°F = (°C x 1.8) + 32
1 inch = 2.54 centimeters (cm)
1 foot = 0.304 meters (m)
1 yard = 0.914 meters
1 mile = 1.6093 kilometers (km)
1 km = 0.6214 miles
1 fathom = 1.8288 m
1 chain = 20.1168 m
1 furlong = 201.168 m
1 acre = 0.4047 hectares
1 sq km = 100 hectares
1 sq mile = 2.59 square km
1 ounce = 28.35 grams
1 pound = 0.4536 kilograms
1 short ton = 0.90718 metric ton
1 short ton = 2,000 pounds
1 long ton = 1.016 metric tons
1 long ton = 2,240 pounds
1 metric ton = 1,000 kilograms
1 quart = 0.94635 liters
1 US gallon = 3.7854 liters
1 Imperial gallon = 4.5459 liters
1 nautical mile = 1.852 km

°FAHRENHEIT / °CELSIUS

230 / 110
220 / 100 WATER BOILS
210
200 / 90
190
180 / 80
170
160 / 70
150
140 / 60
130
120 / 50
110
100 / 40
90
80 / 30
70 / 20
60
50 / 10
40
30 / 0 WATER FREEZES
20
10 / -10
0
-10 / -20
-20 / -30
-30
-40 / -40

Clock: 12 (24), 1 (13), 2 (14), 3 (15), 4 (16), 5 (17), 6 (18), 7 (19), 8 (20), 9 (21), 10 (22), 11 (23)

INCH: 0 1 2 3 4

CM: 0 1 2 3 4 5 6 7 8 9 10

MOON NEW MEXICO
Avalon Travel
An imprint of Perseus Books
A Hachette Book Group company
1700 Fourth Street
Berkeley, CA 94710, USA
www.moon.com

Editors: Kevin McLain, Kristi Mitsuda
Series Manager: Kathryn Ettinger
Copy Editor: Ann Seifert
Graphics and Production Coordinator: Elizabeth Jang
Cover Design: Faceout Studios, Charles Brock
Interior Design: Domini Dragoone
Moon Logo: Tim McGrath
Map Editor: Albert Angulo
Cartographers: Karin Dahl, Brian Shotwell
Indexer: Greg Jewett

ISBN-13: 978-1-63121-420-2
ISSN: 1543-6187

Printing History
1st Edition — 1989
10th Edition — April 2017
5 4 3 2 1

KEEPING CURRENT

If you have a favorite gem you'd like to see included in the next edition, or see anything that needs updating, clarification, or correction, please drop us a line. Send your comments via email to feedback@moon.com, or use the address above.